The Writer's Craft

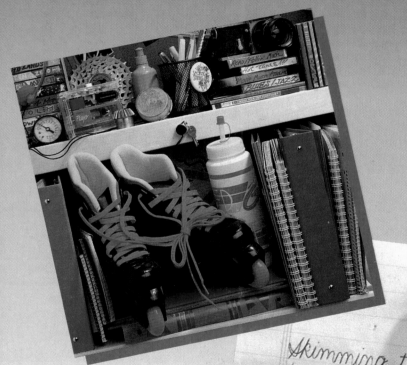

sidewalk
Skimming the cement the right
Knowing just how to move 'x
Almost falling flying
Ten-speed skates
Eleven-speed y'all!

The Writer's Craft

SENIOR AUTHOR
SHERIDAN BLAU
University of California at Santa Barbara

CONSULTING AUTHOR
PETER ELBOW
University of Massachusetts at Amherst

SPECIAL CONTRIBUTING AUTHORS
Don Killgallon
Baltimore County Public Schools

Rebekah Caplan
Oakland Unified School District

SENIOR CONSULTANTS
Arthur Applebee
State University of New York at Albany

Judith Langer
State University of New York at Albany

McDougal Littell Inc.
A Houghton Mifflin Company
Evanston, Illinois   Boston Dallas Phoenix

SENIOR AUTHOR

Sheridan Blau, Senior Lecturer in English and Education and former Director of Composition, University of California at Santa Barbara; Director, South Coast Writing Project; Director, Literature Institute for Teachers

The Senior Author, in collaboration with the Consulting Author, helped establish the theoretical framework of the program and the pedagogical design of the Workshop prototype. In addition, he guided the development of the spiral of writing assignments, served as author of the literary Workshops, and reviewed completed Writer's Workshops to ensure consistency with current research and the philosophy of the series.

CONSULTING AUTHOR

Peter Elbow, Professor of English, University of Massachusetts at Amherst; Fellow, Bard Center for Writing and Thinking

The Consulting Author, in collaboration with the Senior Author, helped establish the theoretical framework for the series and the pedagogical design of the Writer's Workshops. He also reviewed Writer's Workshops and designated Writing Handbook lessons for consistency with current research and the philosophy of the series.

SPECIAL CONTRIBUTING AUTHORS

Don Killgallon, English Chairman, Educational Consultant, Baltimore County Public Schools. Mr. Killgallon conceptualized, designed, and wrote all of the features on sentence composing.

Rebekah Caplan, Coordinator, English Language Arts K–12, Oakland Unified School District, Oakland, CA; Teacher-Consultant, Bay Area Writing Project, University of California at Berkeley. Ms. Caplan developed the strategy of "Show, Don't Tell," first introduced in the book *Writers in Training,* published by Dale Seymour Publications. She also wrote the Handbook lessons and Sketchbook features for this series that deal with that concept.

SENIOR CONSULTANTS

These consultants reviewed the completed prototype to ensure consistency with current research and continuity within the series.

Arthur N. Applebee, Professor of Education, State University of New York at Albany; Director, Center for the Learning and Teaching of Literature; Senior Fellow, Center for Writing and Literacy

Judith A. Langer, Professor of Education, State University of New York at Albany; Co-director, Center for the Learning and Teaching of Literature; Senior Fellow, Center for Writing and Literacy

MULTICULTURAL ADVISORS

The multicultural advisors reviewed the literary selections for appropriate content and made suggestions for teaching lessons in a multicultural classroom.

Andrea B. Bermúdez, Professor of Multicultural Education; Director, Research Center for Language and Culture, University of Houston—Clear Lake

Alice A. Kawazoe, Director of Curriculum and Staff Development, Oakland Unified School District, Oakland, CA

Sandra Mehojah, Project Coordinator, Office of Indian Education, Omaha Public Schools, Omaha, NE

Alexs D. Pate, Writer, Consultant, Lecturer, Macalester College and the University of Minnesota

STUDENT CONTRIBUTORS

The following students contributed student writing.

Adam Baughman, Oxnard, CA; Mousumi Behari, Aurora, CO; Regina Bly, Atco, NJ; Nathaniel Drummings, Aiken, SC; Eric Gould, Worcester, MA; Jessica Guynn, Taneytown, MD; Alissa Hamilton, Las Vegas, NV; Jazlyn Perea, Golden, CO; Penny Pobiecke, Kenosha, WI; Bret Pruehs, Lisle, IL; Sita Raiter, Santa Barbara, CA; Tonica Rickett, Charleston, IL; Paul Ryan, Mt. Prospect, IL; Jeremy Schafer, Charleston, IL; Elizabeth Smith, Aiken, SC; Kenya Lanishia Whitley, Houston, TX

The following students reviewed selections to assess their appeal.

Amanda Alberty, Evanston, IL; Bradley Jones, Barrington, IL; Lindsey Kollross, Gurnee, IL; Julie Maupin, Altamont, IL; Larry Milligan, Chicago, IL; Melissa Muchowicz, Chicago, IL; La Shara Parham, Kenosha, WI; Paul Ryan, Mt. Prospect, IL

TEACHER CONSULTANTS

The following teachers served as advisors on the development of the Workshop prototype and/or reviewed completed Workshops.

Wanda Bamberg, Aldine Independent School District, Houston, TX

Karen Bollinger, Tower Heights Middle School, Centerville, OH

Barbara Ann Boulden, Issaquah Middle School, Issaquah, WA

Sherryl D. Broyles, Language Arts Specialist, Los Angeles Unified School District, Los Angeles, CA

Christine Bustle, Elmbrook Middle School, Elm Grove, WI

Denise M. Campbell, Eaglecrest School, Cherry Creek School District, Aurora, CO

Cheryl Cherry, Haven Middle School, Evanston, IL

Gracie Garza, L.B.J. Junior High School, Pharr, TX

Patricia Fitzsimmons Hunter, John F. Kennedy Middle School, Springfield, MA

Mary F. La Lane, Driftwood Middle School, Hollywood, FL

Barbara Lang, South Junior High School, Arlington Heights, IL

Harry Laub, Newark Board of Education, Newark, NJ

Sister Loretta Josepha, S.C., Sts. Peter and Paul School, Bronx, NY

Jacqueline McWilliams, Carnegie School, Chicago, IL

Joanna Martin, Thompson Junior High School, St. Charles, IL

Karen Perry, Kennedy Junior High School, Lisle, IL

Patricia A. Richardson, Resident Teacher-Trainer, Harold A. Wilson Professional Development School, Newark, NJ

Pauline Sahakian, Clovis Unified School District, Clovis, CA

Elaine Sherman, Curriculum Director, Clark County, Las Vegas, NV

Richard Wagner, Language Arts Curriculum Coordinator, Paradise Valley School District, Phoenix, AZ

Beth Yeager, McKinley Elementary School, Santa Barbara, CA

ISBN 0–8123–8664–7

Copyright © 1995 by McDougal Littell Inc.

Box 1667, Evanston, Illinois 60204

All rights reserved. Printed in the United States of America.

2 3 4 5 6 7 8 9 10 – DCI – 99 98 97 96 95

Table of Contents

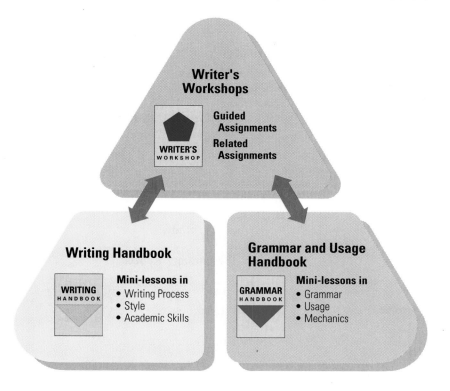

You are special. You think and act in ways that are uniquely your own. This book recognizes the fact that you are an individual. On every page you will be encouraged to discover techniques best suited to your own personal writing style. Just as important, you will learn to think your way through every writing task.

In each of the Writer's Workshops, you will experiment with ideas and approaches as you are guided through a complete piece of writing. Cross-references to the Handbooks will allow you to find additional help when you need it. Then, as you write, you will discover what you think about yourself—and about the world around you.

Starting Points

For more in-depth treatment of each stage of the writing process, see the Writing Handbook Mini-lessons on pages 214–367.

Writer's Workshops

WRITER'S WORKSHOP 1
Personal and Expressive Writing

WRITER'S WORKSHOP 2

Observation and Description

WRITER'S WORKSHOP 3

Narrative and Literary Writing

Informative Writing:
Explaining *How*

Informative Writing: Explaining *What*

WRITER'S WORKSHOP 6

Persuasion

WRITER'S WORKSHOP 7

Responding to Literature

WRITER'S WORKSHOP 8

Informative Writing: Reports

Writing Handbook

MINI-LESSONS

Grammar and Usage Handbook

MINI-LESSONS

xxi

For centuries, the Hmong people of Southeast Asia have recorded stories about their history and culture on tapestries called *pandau*, which means "cloth made beautiful like a flower." These tapestries are sewn by Hmong women without the help of patterns or sewing machines. This *pandau* tells a story about life in a Hmong village.

Starting Points

Can you imagine yourself or anyone you know saying, "I think I'll spend a few hours writing"? When was the last time you wrote something you weren't required to write?

Many people don't write unless they're forced to. Why? Perhaps because these people find writing difficult and maybe a little boring. However, writing doesn't have to be that way. Writing can also be enjoyable, exciting, and even fun.

This book can help you discover the fun and excitement in writing. In the process, you might also discover some important things about yourself.

Getting Ready

WHY SHOULD I WRITE?

Most of the writing you do is required classroom writing: lab reports for science, research reports for social studies, essays for English. Most people write only when they have to—because their jobs require it, or because they're fulfilling some social obligation.

Many people, however, write not because they *have* to but because they *want* to. They write to discover themselves and their world, to learn more about who they are and what they think and feel. They write to share their ideas and feelings with others. They write to say things they are too nervous or embarrassed to say in person. They write to express thoughts and feelings that are so personal they wouldn't dare tell a soul—except for that special person who lives in the pages of their diaries or journals.

You too can learn to write in this way. You might write to tell stories, sort out feelings, solve problems, save memories, think clearly, or argue effectively. You might write privately, just for yourself, or you might want to share your work with a wider audience. As you write, you might discover how exciting writing can be. Even when writing is hard work, it can be very satisfying.

WRITING IS DISCOVERING

WRITER TO WRITER

Writing how you feel about something helps you to understand it better yourself.

Penny Pobiecke, student, Kenosha, Wisconsin

When you begin writing something, you may not know exactly where your words will lead or even what you are writing. After you have written for a while, you may be surprised to find your writing taking you in fascinating new directions. New ideas may begin to flood your mind. A letter to a friend might become the raw material for a poem. An entry in your journal might lead to a persuasive essay. The poster you create for history class might give you an idea for a speech.

So the next time you're stuck for writing ideas, don't sit at your desk gazing idly out the window. Just start writing about whatever's on your mind. One idea will surely lead to another, and soon you'll discover what you really want to say. Remember, writers can go anywhere and do anything with their writing.

WHAT MAKES WRITING ENJOYABLE?

Almost everyone has had the experience of staring hopelessly at a blank piece of paper, wishing that brilliant ideas would appear magically. Writing can be difficult and frustrating when you try to come up with words and ideas on subjects you care nothing about. How can writing become fun?

Writing Is Caring

Some professional athletes are known as "gamers." Gamers are athletes who play their best when it matters most—in a championship game, for example. In fact, people in all walks of life usually perform best when they're working on something they feel strongly about.

So one crucial key to making writing more enjoyable is to focus on a subject that really matters to you. When you free yourself to explore whatever is on your mind, whatever seems important to you at the time, you may find that the words begin to flow faster than you can write or type them. Write about what you care about, and you might find your writing taking on an importance you haven't felt before.

Freewriting

How can you discover and explore what's on your mind? A simple and effective technique is freewriting. When you freewrite, you start writing down your thoughts and feelings and frustrations. You follow your thinking on paper. One idea leads to a second and then a third. As you write, you begin to discover what you're thinking, how you're feeling, and what's most important to you. Freewriting can reveal more ideas and more discovery.

Writing with Others

Do you sing in the shower, on your way to school, or in a choir? People often sing for the sheer joy of it. Sometimes, though, they sing for the special feeling they get from sharing their songs with an audience.

Sharing with friends can make almost any activity more fun, including writing. Although you may want to keep some of your writing private, you will probably want to show some of what you write to others. In this book, you'll be encouraged to do exactly that at many stages of the writing process.

writing with others

As you begin writing, for example, you may do prewriting activities that involve brainstorming with friends to get ideas. When you write your first draft, you may want to try it out on readers just to see how it sounds or to get their thoughts on the topic. Peer readers can give you valuable reactions and advice. Finally, you'll publish or present your writing so that you can show your ideas to a wider audience.

Writing for Yourself

Some people find writing painful because they're always worried about what others are going to think and say about their work. You can avoid this worry by doing more private writing—writing that only you will see. Private writing is a great way to work through problems and frustrations and important feelings. Because no one else need ever see what you write, you can express yourself with complete freedom. Write about whatever's on your mind. Take some risks. Be totally outrageous if that's how you're feeling. Remember, private writing is for your eyes only. Take a chance!

Sometimes, writing that you decided at first would be private may become so important to you that you'll want to share it with others. That's part of the discovery process. Share your writing when it feels right; keep it to yourself when you need to.

Getting Started

UNDERSTANDING THE WRITING PROCESS

How do you like to write? Some writers like to work in complete silence, while others enjoy music playing in the background. One writer might need to have just the right kind of paper and pens or pencils; another wouldn't think of writing without a word processor. Some writers write privately; others share their work as it takes shape.

Writers write in many different ways. Nevertheless, for most writers, writing is a way of discovering what they think. Starting from a tangled heap of unrelated ideas, a writer works toward understanding, perhaps changing direction at several points along the way.

However *you* write, you probably use some of the following activities: prewriting and exploring, drafting and discovering, sharing and getting responses, revising, proofreading, publishing and presenting, and reflecting. You may not go through these activities in the same order every time you write. Sometimes, you might repeat an activity in order to get additional ideas. You might ask others for their thinking and responses even before you begin writing, when you're still thinking about your writing. An idea that comes to you as you're revising may prompt you to change the structure of your work. You can create your own process each time you write.

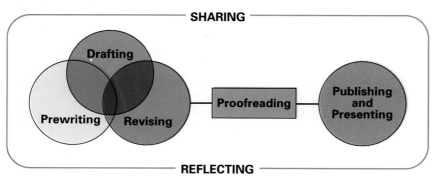

P REWRITE AND EXPLORE

PROBLEM
S O L V I N G

"How can I learn more about prewriting techniques?"

For more information about prewriting, see

- Handbooks 1-4, pages 218–234

Prewriting

W R I T E R   T O   W R I T E R

It is better to write about something that is interesting to you, something that your imagination can run wild with.
Tandy Powell, student, Clovis, California

Before beginning a painting, an artist draws many sketches, searching for one that has just the right feeling. In preparing for a concert, a pianist plays a piece of music at different tempos and volumes, listening for the sound that will thrill an audience.

As a writer, you begin by trying out a number of options too. During the **prewriting** stage, you explore writing ideas to see where they take you. You try to find a subject that is important to you, one that you care about and want to share your feelings about. You gather ideas, exploring what you already know and discovering what you still need to find out.

You may find it helpful to try a variety of activities as you begin exploring ideas. You might freewrite, talk to friends, draw some pictures, or do some reading. Whichever activities you use, the key is to let your imagination roam as far and wide as it wants to.

D RAFT AND DISCOVER

PROBLEM
S O L V I N G

"How can I learn to draft more effectively?"

For more information about drafting, see

- Handbooks 5–17, pages 235–284

W R I T E R   T O   W R I T E R

Don't try to force it; just let it flow.
Jonathan Pray, student, Golden, Colorado

When early explorers took to the high seas, they often weren't sure where the winds and the waves would take them.

Drafting is a lot like setting sail for uncharted waters. When you start writing, you usually have some idea where you want to go. But as you write, new ideas and inspirations may take hold of you, sending you off in different directions. At the end of your "voyage," you may find yourself in a place very different from the one you started for.

When you draft, don't worry about whether you're saying exactly what you want to say. Don't be concerned with getting all your ideas in the right order or using just the right words. In fact, the very process of drafting may help you discover exactly what it is you're thinking about and how you want to express your thoughts.

After you've finished your draft, you will probably want to **review** it. How does it strike you? Do you like what you read? What you've written may seem like a complete mess. That's OK; it's not done yet.

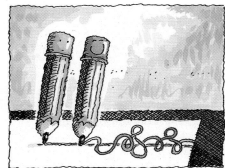

Drafting and Revising

Peer Response   You may be ready to share your writing with others. Peer response can be a big help as you consider how you want to reshape your writing. What do your readers think of your piece? How might their thoughts affect your writing?

REVISE YOUR WRITING

WRITER TO WRITER

If the finished composition is not exactly as you had planned it, don't worry—it almost never is.
Thomas James Hartnett, student, Clementon, New Jersey

Have you ever said something you wished you had said differently or maybe even never said at all? Such an experience may have started you thinking, Boy, if only I could do that over again, I'd sure do it differently.

When you write, you always have the chance to do things over again. Your early drafts are almost never what you want your finished piece of writing to be. After all, you've been exploring and discovering, starting and stopping, going off in different directions, and circling back.

Now you can rethink what you've written and start to make it read just the way you want it to. This stage of the writing process

PROBLEM
SOLVING

"How can I improve my writing?"

For more information about revising, see

• Handbook 18, pages 285–287

PROBLEM

S O L V I N G

**"What do I do when
I proofread?"**

For more information
about proofreading, see

• Handbook 19, pages
288–290

is called **revising.** Most people think revising means making small corrections—just touching things up. In fact, revising is an opportunity to rethink and rearrange what you've written.

PROOFREAD

Now it's time to read a revised draft of your writing carefully to check for errors in grammar, usage, spelling, and punctuation. **Proofreading** is an important part of getting your writing ready for a wider audience. When you've caught all the errors and solved all the problems, you can make a final copy of your work.

PUBLISH, PRESENT, AND REFLECT

PROBLEM

S O L V I N G

**"How can I get my
writing published?"**

For more information on
sharing and publishing,
see

• Handbook 20, page 291

You may have begun showing your writing to peer readers as soon as you started working on it. Now, however, it's time to decide how to present your finished piece to a larger audience. You may choose, for example, to present your work orally, to record it on videotape or audiotape, or to publish it in a class, school, or community newspaper or magazine.

After you have finished writing, you should think about what you have written, how you went about writing it, and how you have grown as a writer. You may want to ask yourself some questions like these:

• What new things did I learn about myself through writing?

• Which parts of my writing process surprised me?

• Which parts of the writing process were easiest for me? Which parts were most difficult?

• What was the biggest problem I faced? How did I solve it?

• What have I learned that I can apply to my future writing?

Jot down your answers to these questions and add both to your writing portfolio.

Using This Book

You have learned that the writing process can be like a journey that leads to the discovery of surprising new lands. *The Writer's Craft* is meant to be a guidebook for journeys in writing.

Like any good guidebook, *The Writer's Craft* does not tell you where you must go. Instead, it offers directions and suggestions so that you can choose the route that works best for you.

The Writer's Craft is divided into three sections: Writer's Workshops, a Writing Handbook, and a Grammar and Usage Handbook.

WRITER'S WORKSHOPS

Each Writer's Workshop introduces a specific form of writing. You'll explore each form in a guided assignment and a related assignment.

Guided Assignments

Each **Guided Assignment** offers detailed suggestions for exploring a type of writing. At every step of the process, you'll discover writing strategies that can help you achieve your writing goals. In addition, you'll see how another student chose to approach the same type of writing. If you need further practice with certain skills, you can turn to the Handbooks for help.

Related Assignments

A **Related Assignment** follows each Guided Assignment and helps you to build on your skills. Where the Guided Assignment offers detailed writing suggestions, the Related Assignment offers you more freedom to explore independently, make decisions, and learn to solve writing problems on your own.

Additional Writing Opportunities

Throughout *The Writer's Craft* you will find **Sketchbooks, Springboards,** and **Sentence Composing** features. These varied

Sketch Book

activities provide further opportunities for you to practice your writing.

The Sketchbooks suggest creative warm-up activities for writing. The only rule here is to let loose and have fun!

Springboards offer suggestions for applying types of writing to other school subjects.

The Sentence Composing activities spotlight sentences written by professional writers. You can study and imitate these model sentences to discover ways of improving your own style.

WRITING HANDBOOK

GRAMMAR HANDBOOK

HANDBOOKS

The Writing Handbook and the Grammar and Usage Handbook suggest strategies you can use to improve your writing. The **Writing Handbook** covers the writing process, writing style, and academic skills, such as how to write an outline and how to get better use out of a library. The **Grammar and Usage Handbook** covers the essentials of good grammar, usage, and mechanics. In the guided and related assignments you'll find **Problem Solving** notes in the margins, directing you to particular Handbook sections for more help or explanation.

USING WRITING FOLDERS
AND PORTFOLIOS

FOR YOUR **PORTFOLIO**

As you write, keep a writing folder that contains all the scraps and notes for your work in progress. Reviewing your early drafts will be helpful as you move through the various stages of the writing process.

After your work is completed, you may choose to put the finished piece in a portfolio, just as an artist does. Your portfolio will become a showcase for the work you're most proud of and a history of your progress as a writer.

Now you know how the different sections of *The Writer's Craft* work together. The Discovery Workshop that follows will show you how *The Writer's Craft* can help you explore the writing process and make it your own.

Discovery Workshop

Each Writer's Workshop in *The Writer's Craft* tells you what form you will work on—for example, a story, a persuasive essay, a poem, or an advertisement. Writers often set out knowing exactly the type of writing they will produce.

However, writers also work in another way. They start out from some feeling or incident or issue, and they work with it and wait to see what form they finally end up with. In this Discovery Workshop, you will get a chance to experience this kind of writing surprise. Instead of being told what to do, you will write to discover what you want to write about and what form your writing will take.

As you read the Discovery Workshop, notice the blue notes in the margins. These notes introduce you to the sections and special features you will find in each of the Writer's Workshops.

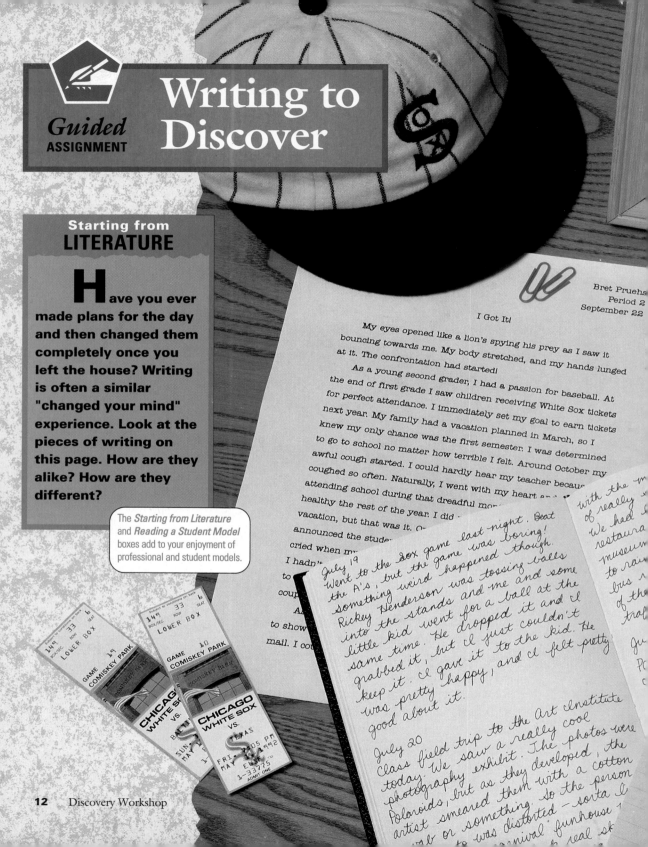

Writing to Discover

Starting from LITERATURE

Have you ever made plans for the day and then changed them completely once you left the house? Writing is often a similar "changed your mind" experience. Look at the pieces of writing on this page. How are they alike? How are they different?

The *Starting from Literature* and *Reading a Student Model* boxes add to your enjoyment of professional and student models.

Bret Pruehs
Period 2
September 22

I Got It!

My eyes opened like a lion's spying his prey as I saw it bouncing towards me. My body stretched, and my hands lunged at it. The confrontation had started!

As a young second grader, I had a passion for baseball. At the end of first grade I saw children receiving White Sox tickets for perfect attendance. I immediately set my goal to earn tickets next year. My family had a vacation planned in March, so I knew my only chance was the first semester. I was determined to go to school no matter how terrible I felt. Around October my awful cough started. I could hardly hear my teacher because I coughed so often. Naturally, I went with my heart and ___ attending school during that dreadful mon___ healthy the rest of the year. I did ___ vacation, but that was it. O___ announced the stude___ cried when m___

I hadn'___
to ___
coup___

A___
to show___
mail. I co___

July 19
Went to the Sox game last night. Beat the A's, but the game was boring! something weird happened though. Rickey Henderson was tossing balls into the stands and me and some little kid went for a ball at the same time. He dropped it and I grabbed it, but I just couldn't keep it. I gave it to the kid. He was pretty happy, and I felt pretty good about it.

July 20
Class field trip to the Art Institute today. We saw a really cool photography exhibit. The photos were Polaroids, but as they developed, the artist smeared them with a cotton swab or something. So the person ___ was distorted—sorta l___ carnival funhouse ___ real sk___

with the ___
of really ___
We had ___
restaura___
museum ___
to rai___
bus ___
of the ___
tra___

She looked at her reflection in the swimming pool. If she swam in the meet with her sprained ankle, she had no chance of winning. If she disqualified herself, then another girl could swim in her place, someone who had a chance of winning. "I've waited six years to make the finals," she thought to herself. "Why should I give it all up now just so someone else can have a chance? This is my chance, the one thing I want more than anything." Just then she saw Becky, the girl who would take her place if she disqualified herself. She felt angry and started to cry.

COMISKEY PARK II
Chicago, Illinois
The new Comiskey Park, home of the Chicago White So...

Hey Davey,
Greetings from the brand new Comiskey Park. Me and Carl were at the game last week and decided to send this card to our long-lost buddy. Game was boring, but I caught a ball Rickey Henderson tossed into the stands. Gave it to a little kid – his first souvenir, I think. Come visit us this summer.
Bret

ADDRESS
Davey Haskell
25 Broadview
Tuscaloosa, AL
35406

DO NOT WRITE BELOW THIS LINE

To a girl whose name I never knew,

Hi. You probably don't remember me, but I remember you pretty well. We sorta met 5 years ago at a baseball game in the old Comiskey Park. I never forgot what you did that night, but I never understood why.

A coach tossed a batting practice ball into the stands, remember? We both went for it at the same time. You sorta took it away from me and I was pretty mad. But then you gave me the ball. You said it was meant for me. Why?

Like I said, I was mad at you, so mad I ... to cry. That made me even madder ... not only had a girl taken a baseball ... me, but now I was crying in ... of a girl too. Did you let me have the ba... because you felt sorry for ... maybe because I was ... embarrassed...

Think & Respond

What seems to have been the starting point for these pieces of writing? Are there any other forms of writing the writer might have explored?

These *Think and Respond* questions help you to better understand professional and student writing.

INVITATION
═ TO ═
Write

This invitation is addressed
especially to you! It asks you to
share your thoughts and
feelings on subjects that really
matter to you.

The best way to learn about writing is to do it. In this special guided assignment, you will explore your personal writing process without any requirements or restrictions. You will write simply to discover what you have to say today and how you want to say it.

Explore some ideas you care about, ideas that really matter to you. Then begin writing and see where the words lead you and what form they take.

PREWRITE AND EXPLORE

Here's where you'll
discover and explore exciting
writing ideas.

1. Find an idea that matters to you. Your best writing will come from ideas that are important to you. Where do you find those ideas? They might be in the pages of your journal, the streets of your neighborhood, a conversation with a friend, or your own thoughts. Try these exploratory activities to help you find a writing idea that makes you *want* to write.

Got a writing problem? These
Problem Solving features will
direct you to the Writing
Handbook and the Grammar
and Usage Handbook for help.

Exploring Topics

- **Freewriting** Do some freewriting to see what is on your mind. What issues or emotions or incidents are important to you right now? You don't have to search for grand ideas; just write about whatever you're thinking about. What feelings nag at you? What event keeps coming back to your thoughts? These are what you need to explore.

PROBLEM
SOLVING

"How can drawing help me explore an idea?"

For more information on charts and graphs, see

- Handbook 2, "Using Graphic Devices for Writing," pages 226–230

- **Drawing out your mind** Take five or ten minutes to draw some pictures. Your subject? Perhaps it's what you see out your window or something you saw on television last night. What about that argument you had with your best friend? How would you draw that? If you don't feel like drawing pictures, try putting what's on your mind into the form of a chart, graph, or spider map.

One Student's Process

Bret Pruehs found a writing idea one day as he was writing in his journal about a baseball game he had just attended. As he wrote, his thoughts drifted back to another game, many years ago, and he began freewriting about his memories.

In One Student's Process, you'll follow the thinking, writing, and revising of student writers just like yourself.

> Thinking about what happened at last night's game . . . reminded me of that game when I was in second grade and that girl stole the ball away from me but then she gave it back. I had perfect attendance that year which is weird because I haven't done that since. How could I <u>never</u> miss school for an entire year? It was weird because it was a girl and she just grabbed the ball away from me, or maybe she kinda got there first, but I was really mad and started crying and stuff which made me even madder because I was crying in front of a girl and she was so much older and bigger than me. But then she gave it back to me. And now I wonder did she give it back to me because she thought it was the right thing to do or because she felt sorry for me because I was crying?

2. Imagine possibilities. After you have explored your ideas for a while, begin to imagine all of the possibilities for writing. You may, for example, notice the beginnings of a story, feel the urge to write in your journal or send a letter to a friend, or see in your mind a picture that you could turn into a poem or a poster.

DRAFT AND DISCOVER

1. Try it out. Drafting is a time for experimenting and discovering. Write for about ten minutes on one or two of the possibilities you imagined earlier. Which topic or approach gets your creative juices flowing and makes you want to continue writing? Trust your writing to lead you to a place you'll want to explore further.

You'll find plenty of suggestions here for putting your ideas into words.

Bret started an imaginary letter to the girl he encountered at the baseball game years ago. His freewriting had made him curious. Exactly why did she let him have the ball? What was she trying to prove? Was she embarrassed? Bret wanted to know. You can see the first part of Bret's letter on page 13.

2. Write some more.   As you continue writing, ask yourself some of the following questions. They will help you get a sense of where your writing is going.

- Am I saying what I want to say? What else do I want to say?
- Do I like the direction my writing seems to be taking? Would I rather go in a different direction?
- What part of my writing am I enjoying the most? Why?
- Does the form I've chosen suit what I'm trying to say?

Tips like these offer suggestions for using grammar, mechanics, and computers to improve your writing.

COMPUTER TIP

Try freewriting on your computer with the screen dimmed. That way you can let your mind roam freely, and you won't be influenced by what you 've already written.

One Student's Process

When Bret reread the letter he wrote, he started thinking more about what had happened at the game. He did more freewriting.

I guess she gave me the ball because she felt sorry for me because I was just a little kid. I don't think she was mad at me. I was mad at her! But I remember she said she had waited eighteen years to catch a ball at the park. How can you give up something you've waited that long for? There's a lot of things in my life I can't wait for. I wonder if I would've given that kid the ball last night if I didn't already have one? Would I have done what she did? Maybe . . . maybe not. I'm not a mean kid, but when you wait eighteen years is it mean to take what you've waited for all that time? Don't you deserve it?

Writing involves making choices, and the Writer's Choice features help you choose what's right for you.

Writer's Choice   How do you like what you've written so far? Is it turning out the way you thought it would when you started? Perhaps you need to try a different form to discover what you really have to say.

As Bret looked over his freewriting, he decided to write a short story about a girl who gives up something she's waited a long time to achieve. Here's part of Bret's story.

> She looked at her reflection in the swimming pool. If she swam in the meet with her sprained ankle, she had no chance of winning. If she disqualified herself, then another girl could swim in her place, someone who had a chance of winning. "I've waited six years to make the finals," she thought to herself. "Why should I give it all up now just so someone else can have a chance? This is my chance, the one thing I want more than anything." Just then she saw Becky, the girl who would take her place if she disqualified herself. She felt angry and started to cry.

3. Get focused. Now that you've been drafting for a while, you may begin to get a feeling about where your writing is going. Jot down some possible answers to the following questions to sharpen your focus. If you're not comfortable answering them now, you can answer some of them later. Work with your writing until it sounds just right to you.

Development

- Have I gotten to the heart of what I want to say?

Personal Goals

- What do I want this writing to do?
- Do I want to share this writing with an audience, or is it just for me? I can treat it as private for now and decide later to revise it for others.

Form and Organization

- Has my draft led me to a particular form of writing?
- What's the best way to present my ideas? What should my readers see first? next? last?

4. Keep tinkering. Continue working on your draft until you're happy with what you read. Does the beginning work for you? Have you developed each of your ideas with effective details? Do you like the ending, or does it still need some work?

5. Think about sharing. You may not feel like showing your draft to anyone. Nonetheless, it often helps to try your writing out on a friend. Are you ready now to share your draft with friends? You can try asking them questions like these:

- What parts of my writing did you find most interesting?
- What thoughts and feelings do you find in my writing?
- What do you want to know more about?
- Do you have thoughts and feelings about the topic?

One Student's Process

As Bret worked on his story, he felt frustrated. He wasn't interested in swimming, and he wasn't sure how his main character should act. Bret decided that the story he really wanted to tell was what had happened to him at the baseball game.

Here's part of Bret's draft. Notice the comments his friends made. What would you have told Bret about this part of his draft?

Peer Reader Comments

Who did the coach throw the ball to? You or her?

Comfort you? How upset were you?

Yeah, but how did you really feel?

I watched as the last coach left the field. Then he tossed a ball into the stands. I stretched and then reached for the ball. It bounced right between a teenage girl and me. I grabbed it loosely and then she wrapped her hands around it. It was at this point that my dad realized what was happening. He was too far behind me to help. After a few seconds of fighting, I lost my grip and she took the ball. My dad came down from the main aisle to comfort me. After about five minutes, the girl turned and looked at me. She then said to me, "I've waited eighteen years for a ball, but this one was meant for you." She then gave me the ball. I thanked her because I knew it was the right thing for me to say.

1. Review your responses. Think about your readers' comments, but remember that their suggestions are just that—suggestions. You can decide what changes, if any, you want to make.

Here's where you'll learn strategies for making your writing as good as it can be.

2. Look at your content. Have you said what you really want to say? Have you included enough details? Is your writing clear?

3. Examine your structure. Have you presented your ideas in the best order? Is any detail out of place?

One Student's Process

Notice the changes Bret made to part of his draft.

I watched as the last coach left the field. Then he tossed a ball into the stands. ~~into the stands~~ [looked at me and] [right at me.] I stretched and then reached for the ball. It bounced right [Unfortunately,] between a teenage girl and me. I grabbed it loosely and then she wrapped her hands around it. It was at this point that my dad realized what was happening. He was too far behind me to help. After a few seconds of fighting, I lost my grip and she took the ball. [I just stood there and felt tears running down my cheek.] My dad came down from the main aisle to comfort me. After about five minutes, the girl turned and looked at me. She then said to me, "I've waited eighteen years for a ball, but this one was meant for you." She then gave me the ball. I thanked her because I knew it was the right thing for me to say. [Inside, I resented that she didn't let me catch the ball.]

PROOFREAD

Before you prepare your final copy, you'll want to check for errors in grammar, capitalization, punctuation, and spelling. The following charts present proofreading marks that make it easy to add corrections to your draft, and a proofreading checklist to help you check your draft.

Proofreading Symbols

∧ Add letters or words.

⊙ Add a period.

≡ Capitalize a letter.

⌣ Close up space.

⌄ Add a comma.

╱ Make a capital letter lowercase.

⌐ Begin a new paragraph.

∿ Switch the positions of letters or words.

— or ℓ Take out letters or words.

Proofreading Checklist

Step 1. Check the forms of words.

Did I use the correct forms of verbs to show tense?
Did I use any adjectives where I should have used adverbs?
Did I use *-er/-est* and *more/most* correctly in comparisons?
Did I use all forms of *be* and other irregular verbs correctly?
Did I use the correct forms of pronouns?

Step 2. Check sentence structure and agreement.

Are there any run-on sentences or sentence fragments?
Do all verbs agree with their subjects?
Do all pronouns agree with their antecedents?
Did I keep all verb tenses consistent?

Step 3. Check capital letters, punctuation, and spelling.

Are all first words capitalized?
Are all proper nouns and proper adjectives capitalized?
Does each sentence have the correct end mark?
Are all words, including possessive forms, spelled correctly?
Did I use commas correctly?

PUBLISH AND PRESENT

Some writing is very personal, and you may not want to show it to anyone. That's fine. Sometimes, however, you might wish to share your writing with others—your classmates, your teacher, or even a wider audience. Here are suggestions for presenting your writing:

Want to share your writing with a wider audience? Here's how.

- **Form a writers' club.** As a class, exchange your writing with students in another class or even at another school. Meet to discuss your reactions to each other's work.

- **Publish your own book.** Put together a book of writing from your class. Some students may want to create books of their own writing.

- **Check out newspapers, magazines, and writing contests.** Send your writing to a school or community newspaper, to a magazine, or to a writing contest that accepts student writing.

REFLECT ON YOUR WRITING

Like other writers, you will probably find it useful to look back on your writing and your writing process from time to time. What can you learn about writing by actually doing it?

When it's all over, sit back, relax, and think about what you've learned about writing and about yourself as a writer.

Right now, think about the writing you just completed. Consider the following questions, which should help you better understand your own writing process. Answer the questions in the form of a letter to yourself or your teacher. Add your reflections, along with your finished piece, to your portfolio.

- What surprised me most about my subject?
- What did I discover about my subject when I wrote about it?
- Did I ever find the right subject? If so, how did I know when I had found it?
- Did I do anything differently from the way I usually write?
- What makes me happiest about my finished piece?
- What would I like to try the next time I write?

One Student's Writing

Bret Pruehs
Period 2
September 22

I Got It!

My eyes opened like a lion's spying his prey as I saw it bouncing towards me. My body stretched, and my hands lunged at it. The confrontation had started!

As a young second grader, I had a passion for baseball. At the end of first grade I saw children receiving White Sox tickets for perfect attendance. I immediately set my goal to earn tickets next year. My family had a vacation planned in March, so I knew my only chance was the first semester. I was determined to go to school no matter how terrible I felt. Around October my awful cough started. I could hardly hear my teacher because I coughed so often. Naturally, I went with my heart and continued attending school during that dreadful month! I managed to stay healthy the rest of the year. I did miss that one day due to vacation, but that was it. On the last day of school, the principal announced the students who had perfect attendance. I just about cried when my name wasn't announced. My teacher knew that I hadn't missed a day during the first semester. She told me to go down to the office and get my prize anyway. I was given a coupon to get a pair of White Sox tickets for two games.

As soon as I was dropped off at my bus stop, I ran home to show my mom the coupon for the tickets and to send it in the mail. I couldn't wait for those games!

July was fast approaching. When the day finally came, I was filled with anticipation. The ride to the games seemed longer than the semester it took to earn the tickets! When my dad and I entered Comiskey Park, we headed straight toward the White Sox dugout. I had a scorecard and pen all ready for autographs. The White Sox players were unwilling

to sign and I felt disappointment taking the place of what was once enthusiasm. I watched as the last coach left the field. Then he looked at me and tossed a ball right at me. I stretched and then reached for the ball.

Unfortunately, it bounced right between a teenage girl and me. I grabbed it loosely and then she wrapped her hands around it. It was at this point that my dad realized what was happening. He was too far behind me to help. After a few seconds of fighting, I lost my grip and she took the ball. I just stood there and felt tears running down my cheek. My dad came down from the main aisle to comfort me. After about five minutes, the girl turned and looked at me. She then said to me, "I've waited eighteen years for a ball, but this one was meant for you." She then gave me the ball. I thanked her because I knew it was the right thing for me to say. Inside I resented that she didn't let me catch the ball. I still appreciated that she thought about it and gave the ball to me.

I learned how devastating an experience of having and losing something so sentimentally valuable can be. I was able to benefit from this experience last summer when I went to a New York Yankees game. Rickey Henderson was throwing baseballs into the stands. A boy several years younger than me caught a ball and then dropped it. We both grabbed the ball at the same time. At this instant, I remembered how upset I had been when I lost my ball as a second grader. I immediately let go and let him have the ball. Looking back, I'm glad I thought about the situation before I took the thrill away from the other boy. I talk about how I let this boy have the ball with pride. I think that the experience enabled me to make the right decision when the tables were turned. I think I became a better and more considerate person because of having the first ball taken away!

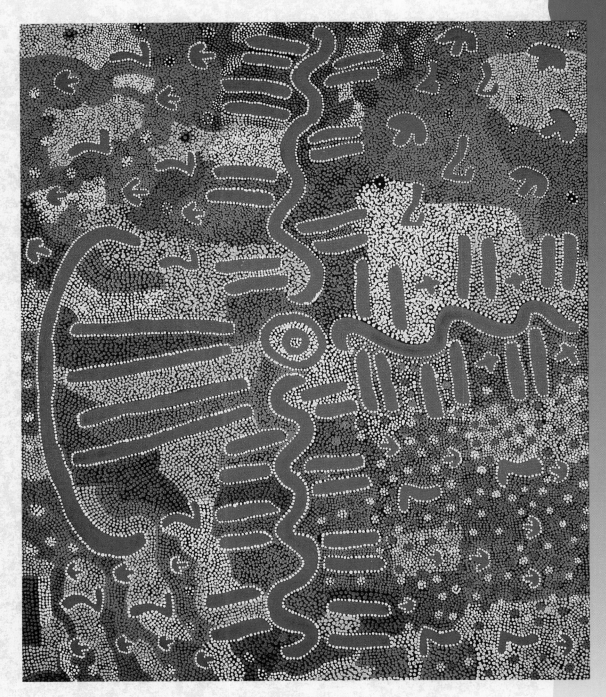

Judy Nampijinpa Granites, *Water Dreaming at Mikanji*, 1986. Among the images represented in this acrylic painting are clouds, lightning, rain, and animal tracks. The artist, an aborigine who lives in central Australia, learned about these symbols from her father and her aunts.

Writer's Workshops

At school they say my name funny as if the syllables were made out of tin and hurt the roof of your mouth. But in Spanish my name is made out of a softer something, like silver, not quite as thick as sister's name—Magdalena—which is uglier than mine. Magdalena who at least can come home and become Nanny. But I am always Esperanza.

I would like to baptize myself under a new name, a name more like the real me, the one nobody sees. Esperanza as Lisandra or Maritza or Zeze the X. Yes. Something like Zeze the X will do.

Sandra Cisneros,
THE HOUSE ON MANGO STREET

- Make a list of names that describe the many sides of you—the secret you, the funny you, the ambitious you, the angry you.

- Tell a story about how you got your name.

Show, Don't Tell

Whether you're writing for yourself or for an audience, you can show your experiences—instead of just telling about them—by using examples, anecdotes, and plenty of descriptive details. Try turning one of the *telling* sentences below into a *showing* paragraph.

- I was in a good mood.

- I was completely confused.

1

Personal and Expressive Writing

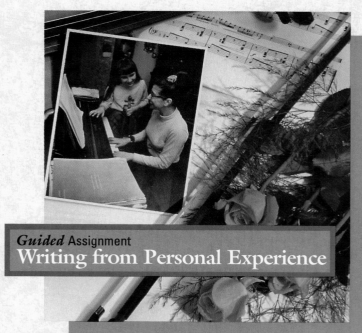

Guided Assignment
Writing from Personal Experience

Related Assignment
Collage

You are an expert about one very important person: yourself. One of the best ways you can share this special knowledge—and learn even more—is by writing.

In this workshop you are invited to write about a personal experience that was important to you. As you work your way through a guided assignment, you will learn ways to help your readers relive the experience with you. In the related assignment, you will use words, pictures, and objects to create a piece of art that shows the world just who you are.

Writing from Personal Experience

Have you ever experienced a moment when everything felt perfect—when you discovered yourself at your best? You probably will never forget that feeling or the moment itself.

Nadja Salerno-Sonnenberg, a well-known professional violinist, began studying music at an early age. As you read Nadja's account of her first performance for her family, think about how that experience may have influenced her life.

FROM

NADJA
On My Way

by
Nadja
Salerno-Sonnenberg

The kind of music teacher any beginner should have is someone who isn't too strict, who smiles and makes jokes and tells you you're good. You need someone who makes learning the instrument fun, because that's really what music is truly about.

Signore Antonio Marchetti, a violinist with the Italian Radio Symphony, was everything I could want. He wore the most fabulous cologne. I could even put up with the violin just to sit next to him and *mmmm*, inhale that Aqua di Selva.

"Nadja," Signore Marchetti said after I'd learned the basics, "elbow up! Keep the violin high, and our next lesson we'll start something special!"

What he meant by "something special" was a new piece. It was called *Czardas* by Alberto Curci, played with open strings; but it had a piano part as well.

When people came to eat at our house, they didn't just get a meal. After having the most fabulous food you can imagine, we would sit around the piano and start right in. Eric would sing, Mama would play, Papa John would play; polkas, arias, waltzes, I mean anything.

After I learned *Czardas*, Mama and I were to play a duet after one of our family dinners. I should add that I was not going to be the headliner. Who wants to hear the kid who just started to play the violin? I was going to be the evening's opening act—when everybody still had dessert and coffee to keep them happy.

I played *Czardas* for my teacher every week in our lesson for two weeks . . . three weeks . . . four weeks . . . five weeks.

Finally, he said, *"Bene! Sei pronto!"* That meant Okay, now you're ready to play it with the piano.

Signore Marchetti was wrong. I wasn't at all ready for what happened next.

Mama's part was equally easy. There was a two-bar vamp and then the violin squeaks in with an *eeh, eeh, eeh*.

So Mama played her vamp; *um-cha, um-cha, um-cha, um-cha.* Then I came in *eeh, eeh, eeh* . . .

And there was music! I was playing my part and she was playing her part and together it was harmony!

I started to cry and couldn't stop. I could only say how beautiful, what a beautiful thing we had done. It was the first time I made music, right there in the living room, rehearsing with my mama.

I pulled her back to the piano so we could play it again and again. That was the moment for me; the thrill of making music went straight into my blood.

Then came the night of our performance. We played our duet and I looked at the people and heard clapping. Relatives were smiling and saying, "Oh, isn't she cute!"

Wow, I thought, I can do this and people *appreciate* it. That went straight into my bloodstream as well.

Think & Respond

How would you have felt about performing in front of your family and friends? What senses does Salerno-Sonnenberg use to remember her experience and show it to her readers?

One Student's Writing

The Cabin
by Alissa Hamilton

My family and I have a cabin on Cedar Mountain in Utah that we visit every weekend during the summer. I love it up there because it is so peaceful and quiet. I remember one event, however, that was not so peaceful and quiet. It was a frightening yet silly incident that showed me that my mother was determined and self-reliant.

One weekend my dad had to stay in town and work, so my mom, my sister, my cousin, and I were alone on the mountain. On Sunday morning we were all upstairs. Mom was cleaning, and the rest of us were putting a puzzle together. It was windy outside, and some gusts were getting up to sixty miles per hour. Suddenly, we heard a huge crash!

"What the heck was that?" my mother exclaimed.

My cousin Anthony was the first downstairs. He looked through the glass door and called out, "Uh-oh, Aunt Rusty! Your truck!"

To my mom's horror, a sixty-foot aspen had been whipped down onto our Toyota 4 X 4, smashing it.

Determined to move the tree, Mom had no choice but to cut it up. She had to figure out how to start the chain saw, something I'm not sure she'd ever done before. As my mom cut up the tree, she shoved the pieces off the truck one at a time. While she was trying to be careful and not do even more damage to the truck, we kids were standing on the porch cheering, "She-Ra! She-Ra!" the name of our favorite female superhero. I don't think Mom was amused.

When she finished, we could see what had happened. The truck's roof was crushed, and the windshield was shattered. The driver's window was also broken, and the whole truck was kind of twisted so that the doors didn't fit right. The driver's door wouldn't even open.

We had no way to get down the mountain except that truck, so we closed up the cabin and prepared to leave. Slowly and carefully, my mom began to back out toward the road. Then, the icing on the cake. I guess the truck was twisted so badly that the right side door wouldn't close right. As we backed out, it swung open, caught on a stump, and was torn wide open. Mom really had to slam it to get it to stay closed after that.

My sister, cousin, and I were so embarrassed at how the truck looked, we made Mom make up a sign. At our first stop she got a paper bag from a clerk, wrote "A tree fell on it" on the bag, and taped it in one of the truck's windows.

About halfway home, it began to rain. With the windshield broken, the rain seemed to pour in freely, drenching my poor mother. By the time we got home, my mom was soaked, and we kids were exhausted.

Keeping the smashed truck was out of the question; it was too badly wrecked. So, we had to get a new one.

Now when the wind picks up on the mountain, my mom makes sure the truck is out in the meadow, away from any trees. As long as we have our cabin, as long as the wind blows, I'm sure Mom will never forget those words, "Uh-oh, Aunt Rusty! Your truck!"

Cedar Mountain

Think & Respond

Respond as a Reader

▶ How do you think you would have felt in Alissa's place?

▶ What do you think Alissa learned from her experience?

Respond as a Writer

▶ How does Alissa's use of dialogue help you become involved in her story?

▶ What details show rather than tell you how she feels about what is happening?

INVITATION
══ TO ══
Write

Nadja Salerno-Sonnenberg wrote about a violin recital. Alissa Hamilton described a tree falling on her family's truck. These experiences were so important to the writers that they recorded their stories to share with others.

Think about a memorable incident or event in your life. Re-create the experience for your readers by showing them what happened, how it made you feel, and why you'll always remember it.

PREWRITE AND EXPLORE

1. Find an experience to write about. Think about a time when your world seemed to be falling apart—or when everything just fell into place. When were you as happy or sad or frightened or angry as you had ever been in your life? Doing one or more of the following activities can help you recover a meaningful memory.

Exploring Topics

- **Learning a lesson** With classmates, **brainstorm** about experiences that have taught you important lessons. You might make a list or use a graphic device such as a cluster to help you remember important details.

- **Your greatest hits** List your accomplishments or things you have done that you are proud of. Choose one or two of the experiences you remember best. **Freewrite** about the feelings you had at the time and what made you feel that way.

- **Memory map** Take a real or imaginary tour in search of memories. You might tour your neighborhood or school, or visit a place from your past. Sketch a map showing where the events most important to you took place.

PROBLEM
S O L V I N G

"How else can I explore my past?"

For more sources of ideas, see

- Sketchbook, page 26
- Springboards, page 45
- Handbook 1, "Finding Writing Ideas," pages 218–224

Freewrite about the memory that you'd most like to explore, or talk about it with classmates.

2. Explore your idea. Once you have chosen a memory, you can begin to bring it to life by recalling specific details about it. Try the following activities to get your words and ideas flowing.

- **Play back the experience.** Replay the experience as if you were watching a movie in your mind. Think of what your senses tell you: what you saw, heard, touched, smelled, and tasted. If you wish, freewrite about the experience after you have taken some notes.

- **Ask questions.** Think of questions about your experience such as What happened? Who was there? How did it happen? When and where did it happen? Why did it happen? Make a chart and fill in the details that answer each question.

COMPUTER
TIP

To help you concentrate more intensely on your thoughts and feelings, free-write on a word processor with the monitor screen turned off. Then turn the screen on to see what you have written and what you want to change or add.

One Student's Process

Alissa Hamilton chose to write about the time a tree fell on her family's truck. She explored her memory of the incident by making this chart.

Who	Me, Mom, my sister, my cousin Anthony.
What	Tree fell on truck. Mom cut it up with a chain saw. Rode down mountain in the rain. Made sign for truck window.
When	Last summer on a Sunday.
Where	At the cabin on Cedar Mountain, Utah.
Why	Gusty winds blew tree down. Couldn't move truck without moving tree first. Truck looked awful afterwards—I was afraid someone would see us!
How	Mom used a chain saw for the first time —we watched and cheered her on. Even though the truck was wrecked, the engine still worked so we drove it home.

Writing from
Personal Experience   **33**

DRAFT AND DISCOVER

1. Begin drafting. You can use your freewriting as you begin a draft about your experience. Just start writing the part of the experience that interests you most. You can add missing information and put the pieces together later.

 Writer's Choice Do you want to do some planning before you start writing your draft? You could list the main idea or feeling you want to get across, details you want to include, and maybe even the order you want to present them in. Would you rather wait to see where the drafting takes you? You decide.

2. Make the experience seem real. Show what you saw, heard, felt, tasted, and smelled. These details from your senses will help your readers experience the event as if they had been there themselves. Notice that Nadja Salerno-Sonnenberg does not just tell readers that she played a duet with her mother. Instead, she lets us hear it for ourselves: "So Mama played her vamp; *um-cha, um-cha, um-cha, um-cha.* Then I came in *eeh, eeh, eeh . . .*"

3. Show why the experience was meaningful. Whether you're retelling a funny story or exploring a difficult situation, feel free to explain why the experience was important to you. For example, Alissa Hamilton learned an important lesson about her mother's character, and she says so in the first paragraph.

4. Consider using dialogue. Ask yourself if having people speak to each other will help you tell about your experience. Sometimes a well-chosen bit of conversation can say more than many sentences of description. For example, Alissa included her cousin's simple words "Uh-oh, Aunt Rusty! Your truck!" early in her writing. These words made readers wonder what had happened and want to read on.

5. Think about your draft. Read through your draft. Do the pieces of the story seem to be fitting together as you write? Do you want to ask a classmate for responses, or would you rather just keep working alone? The questions on page 35 may help you review what you have written.

PROBLEM
S O L V I N G

"How can I untangle my draft?"

For help with organizing and clarifying your writing, see

- Handbook 7, "Ways of Organizing," pages 238–242

- Handbook 13, "Unity," pages 266–269

- Handbook 14, "Coherence," pages 270–274

Questions for Yourself
- How can I make sure my readers understand why this incident is important to me?
- What have I left out? What other details could I add to show what happened?
- Are the events in my story in the right order? Would my story be more interesting if I started it in the middle of the action?

Questions for Your Peer Readers
- Which part was most interesting to you? What made it interesting?
- What parts confused you or seemed out of place?
- What would you like to know more about?
- Why do you think I wrote about this experience?

One Student's Process

Here is part of Alissa's first draft. She asked one of her classmates to read and respond to it. How would you have responded to Alissa's draft?

My family and I have a cabin on Cedar Mountain in Utah that we visit every weekend during the summer. Actually, we usually stay home when the Fourth of July holiday falls on a weekend. I love it up there. I remember one event really well. It was a frightening yet silly incident but I learned a lot about my mom. One weekend my dad had to stay in town and work, so the rest of us were alone on the mountain. On Sunday morning we were all upstairs. Mom was cleaning, and the rest of us were putting a puzzle together. It was windy outside and some gusts were getting up to sixty miles per hour. Suddenly, we heard a huge crash!

Peer Reader Comments

I like the way you begin. Do you need this part about July 4th?

Why do you like being at the cabin?

These details really help me see what's going on!

REVISE YOUR WRITING

1. Review your responses. Decide what you like best about your draft. Then go over your readers' comments. Do the comments help you see your draft in new ways? Did your readers suggest any specific changes you want to make?

2. Get off to a good start. Your opening should draw people into your story and make them want to read more. Try using one of these beginnings:

- an interesting bit of dialogue
- an exciting incident
- a vivid description of the setting or a character

Notice how Nadja Salerno-Sonnenberg draws readers into her story with a vivid description of her music teacher. Alissa Hamilton began her story with a description of the setting. However, she could have begun her story differently. For example, she could have started in the middle of her story with the falling tree or with some dialogue.

 Paragraphs at Work When you tell about a personal experience, you often describe a chain of events. Paragraph breaks can help show when one idea ends and another begins. Remember to begin a new paragraph at these times:

- When you start to describe a new incident
- When the setting changes
- When the story jumps forward or backward in time
- When a new speaker says something in a dialogue

3. Create an ending that works. Don't just stop at the end of your experience. You might answer any questions your readers still have about what happened or tell why the experience was important to you, as Salerno-Sonnenberg did. Notice that Alissa avoided ending with a corny "moral of the story" by repeating a quotation she used earlier.

One Student's Process

Alissa thought about the beginning of her draft and her classmate's comments. She decided to clarify what her story was about and why it was important to her.

, however, that was not so peaceful and quiet.

My family and I have a cabin on Cedar Mountain in Utah that we visit every weekend during the summer. ~~Actually, we usually stay home when the Fourth of July holiday falls on a weekend.~~ I love it up there. because it is so peaceful and quiet. I remember one event really well. It was a frightening yet silly incident ~~but I learned a lot about my mom.~~ One weekend my dad had to stay in town and work, so the rest of us were alone on

my mom, my sister, my cousin, and I

the mountain. On Sunday morning we were all upstairs. Mom was cleaning, and the rest of us were putting a puzzle together. It was windy outside and some gusts were getting up to sixty miles per hour. Suddenly, we heard a huge crash!

that showed me that my mother was determined and self-reliant.

P ROOFREAD

1. Proofread your work. Correct any errors in grammar, capitalization, punctuation, and spelling.

Using Specific Words

Your experiences spring to life when you use words that appeal to all of the senses. You don't have to use lots of flowery adjectives, though. Instead, choose specific nouns and verbs that show the reader exactly what you mean. Notice how Alissa replaced two vague nouns and a dull verb with precise, vivid words:

Original

To my mom's horror, a tree had fallen on our truck.

Revised

To my mom's horror, a sixty-foot aspen had been whipped down onto our Toyota 4 x 4, smashing it.

For more information about using precise nouns and verbs, see Handbook 23, "Meaning and Word Choice," pages 310–311.

2. Make a clean copy of your writing. Are you satisfied with your work? Do you want to prepare it for publication now? If so, do a final check of your writing, using the Standards for Evaluation listed in the margin. Then make a final copy.

P UBLISH AND PRESENT

- **Have an authors' party.** Get together as a group and take turns reading your writing aloud. Offer helpful comments to each other. Discuss what you discovered as you wrote.

Standards for Evaluation

PERSONAL
WRITING

A personal narrative

- starts with an image or idea that makes readers want to find out more
- explores one personal experience
- gives a good sense of time, place, and characters through vivid, sensory details and, possibly, dialogue
- helps readers follow the order of events in time
- shows why the experience was important to the writer
- concludes in a satisfying way

- **Share your experience with a friend or relative in a letter.** Send your personal narrative to a friend or relative. You might especially like to share it with the people who experienced the event with you. Ask them if they remember the event the same way. Is there another side to your story?

- **Create a class anthology.** Gather class members' writings into a book of memorable experiences. Save the book to read at graduation or maybe at a class reunion.

REFLECT ON YOUR WRITING

WRITER TO WRITER

A good writer uses words to discover, and to bring that discovery to other people.

Donald Hall, poet and critic

1. Add your writing to your portfolio. You have now read about two writers' personal experiences and have written about one of your own. In a note to yourself or to your teacher, answer these questions about your writing process. Then, attach your note to your final draft.

FOR YOUR
PORTFOLIO

- What part of retelling a personal experience did I like best?

- How did I find a personal experience to write about?

- What did I discover about myself or others as I explored a personal experience in writing?

- What was hardest about doing this kind of writing?

- What techniques from my own writing or from the personal experiences I've read did I especially like? Which of these would I like to use in other things I write?

2. Explore additional writing experiences. See the suggestions for creating a collage on pages 42–44 and Springboards on page 45.

Collage

Viewing a
COLLAGE

Every person is a unique collection of interests, talents, ambitions, and feelings. One way you can express some of those many aspects of yourself is through a collage—an artistic arrangement of visual images.

As you look at this collage, think of what each image says about the boy's personality. In what ways is this boy like you? In what ways is he different?

Think & Respond

Which image in the collage caught your eye first? What seems to be this boy's strongest interest? Why do you think the boy is near the center of the collage?

INVITATION
— **TO** —
Write

A collage is more than pictures, shapes, and colors. It is a piece of art that shows the creator's thoughts and feelings. Creating a collage allows you to express yourself in pictures as well as in words.

Assemble a collage that visually expresses your feelings or tells the viewer something about you.

EXPLORING YOUR VISION

1. Track down ideas.   Begin thinking of the important things about yourself that make you who you are. An "idea" funnel may help. First list broad headings like "Pet Peeves," "Dreams," or "Heroes." List as many ideas as you can under each heading. Then list more specific ideas under each of those ideas.

2. Collect images.   Gather photos, cartoons, drawings, and words from magazines, newspapers, junk mail, empty food packages, and so forth. Even if you don't have an idea for a collage yet, collect images of objects that appeal to you. Look for images of specific objects as well as images that suggest moods or emotions. For example, the smiling face and bright colors in the collage suggest that the boy is a happy, outgoing person.

3. Choose one or several aspects of yourself to express in your collage.   Look over your idea lists and your collection of images. Try to figure out what they seem to be saying about you. Choose the idea or ideas that represent you best. For example, the boy included several different images in his collage to emphasize his strong interest in magic. He also used images that show his many other interests and activities.

Writer's Choice Would you like to design a collage for a friend, perhaps as a birthday gift? If so, think of images that reflect your friend's qualities, interests, or hobbies.

CREATING YOUR COLLAGE

1. Select your best images. Look through the images you've collected and pick the ones that express your ideas and feelings best. If none seems right, you might ask classmates if you can search through the images they don't need.

2. Arrange your images. Try several layouts, or ways of arranging your images on a piece of posterboard. You might want to use

Sarah Emerson, Sunrise Middle School, Scottsdale, AZ.

clusters of images, each telling something different about you, or maybe even two sets of opposite images to express mixed feelings or uncertainty. Don't fix the images in place yet, however. You may still change your mind.

3. Name your collage. Pick a title for your collage. The boy might have titled his collage "All the Me's That Everyone Sees" or, to tie in with his interest in magic, "Now You See Me, Now You Don't."

PROBLEM
SOLVING

"How can I make my writing match my artwork?"

To create writing as expressive as your images, see

• Handbook 23, "Meaning and Word Choice," pages 310–311

4. Write a caption. Write a short explanation of your collage. You might mention which feelings or ideas you are expressing. You could also explain how your images relate to those ideas. This explanation can be in any form: a paragraph, a story, or perhaps even a poem. Tape your caption to the back of your collage. That way viewers can compare the message they got from your collage with what you were trying to say.

REVIEWING YOUR COLLAGE

1. Share your collage. Have classmates respond to your layout. You might ask specific questions like, "Which word or phrase sums up the main impression you get?" or "What goes through your mind as you view the collage?" Reflect on their answers and on your own feelings about your collage.

2. Put the finishing touches on your collage. Make final changes, adding or deleting images and arranging them in the way that satisfies you best. Then fix your images in place, using a glue stick, library paste, or other adhesive. You may want to paint or spray a thin coat of sealant over the entire collage and attach a hook or wire to the back so you can hang it on a wall.

PUBLISHING AND PRESENTING

• **Present your collage to your class.** Explain what it expresses about you, and maybe talk about a few of the main images. Ask classmates to tell you which images make the strongest impression on them.

• **Turn a school corridor into an art gallery.** Invite members of other classes to view your work. You might want to display the collages without the creators' names and have the viewers guess who did each one.

• **Share your collages with the community.** Exhibit collages from your class where schoolmates or community members can see them. You may get permission to display your collages in your local library or civic center.

Lisa Apostalides, Sunrise Middle School, Scottsdale, AZ.

Spring boards

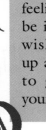

MUSIC   Write song lyrics to express feelings that are important to you. These can be in the form of a very simple poem. If you wish, make up a melody to go with your lyrics.

Social Studies
Write or tell orally some of your favorite stories about your family members or your family's experiences.

General Interest   Tell or write about a time when the light went on in your head—when an idea in science, math, history, or some other subject that had baffled you finally made sense.

Geography   Describe a trip you took or a place you once lived that has special meaning for you. Give enough details so your readers can picture the place themselves and can understand why it is important to you. You might want to include photographs, postcards, drawings, or a map with your narrative.

Make a Catch at Huntington Beach, Cal.

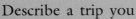

LITERATURE Choose a character from a novel or short story you have read. Write a set of journal entries from that character's point of view. Use words that capture the character's personality and feelings.

45

Sentence

Imitating Sentences

You can learn new ways to compose, structure, and punctuate your writing by imitating sentences written by professional writers. Professional writers add variety and interest to their writing by crafting sentences with care. Notice how the writer of the description below varied his sentences.

Model A   He waited on the stoop until twilight, pretending to watch the sun melt into the dirty gray Harlem sky.

Model B   Up and down the street, transistor radios clicked on and hummed into the sour air.

Model C   Men dragged out card tables, laughing.

Robert Lipsyte, *The Contender*

▶ **ON THE MARK**   Use commas to set off information that interrupts the flow of a sentence.

A. Chunking Sentence Parts   People read and write sentences in meaningful "chunks." By dividing each sentence into sentence parts, or chunks, you can see how the parts work together to express a complete thought. Choose the sentence in each pair below that is divided into meaningful chunks. Be prepared to explain how each chunk relates to the other chunks in the sentence.

1. **a.** He waited on the stoop / until twilight, / pretending / to watch the sun melt / into the dirty gray Harlem sky.
   b. He waited on the stoop until / twilight, pretending to / watch the / sun melt into the dirty / gray Harlem sky.

2. **a.** Up and / down the street, transistor / radios clicked / on and hummed into the sour / air.
   b. Up and down the street, / transistor radios clicked on / and hummed into the sour air.

3. **a.** Men dragged out / card tables, / laughing.
   b. Men dragged / out card / tables, laughing.

B. Identifying Imitations   Which of the sentences in each pair below can be divided into chunks that match the chunks in the models on page 46?

1. Choose the sentence that imitates Model A.
   a. Marie propped up her doll in front of the fireplace, and its eyes twinkled with the fire's reflection.
   b. Chuck ran down the hill near the stream, trying to make the tire roll down the winding country path.

2. Choose the sentence that imitates Model B.
   a. Throughout the morning, the squirrel scampered around and darted over the roof's shingles.
   b. After the game, the JV coach announced a victory party to be held at the Pizza Palace.

3. Choose the sentence that imitates Model C.
   a. Suddenly jumping on him, the puppy licked the boy's face.
   b. Pirates climbed down the rigging, yelling.

C. Unscrambling and Imitating Sentences   Unscramble each set of sentence chunks below to create a sentence that matches one of the models on page 46. Then write a sentence of your own that imitates each model.

1. Write sentences that imitate Model A.
   hoping / to make the baby sitter agree / the boy pouted in the family room / for twenty minutes / to his request

2. Write sentences that imitate Model B.
   and chewed on his pencil / once or twice each hour / Rick looked up

3. Write sentences that imitate Model C.
   the fluffy clouds / Helen studied / daydreaming

Grammar Refresher   To learn more about sentence parts and how they work together, see Handbook 37, "Understanding Sentences," pages 374–375.

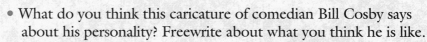

- What do you think this caricature of comedian Bill Cosby says about his personality? Freewrite about what you think he is like.

- Draw a caricature of your best friend, emphasizing his or her strongest features. Then make a cluster about your friend, focusing on his or her personality traits.

- Imagine that a city could have a personality. Describe the character of New York, New Orleans, Los Angeles, or your own city or town.

Show, Don't Tell

You can show a character's personality through clothing, mannerisms, and actions. Try turning one of these *telling* sentences into a *showing* paragraph by using these kinds of details.

- She was a sports fanatic.
- He was the quiet type.

Observation and Description

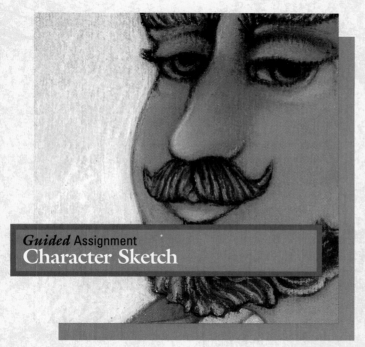

Guided Assignment
Character Sketch

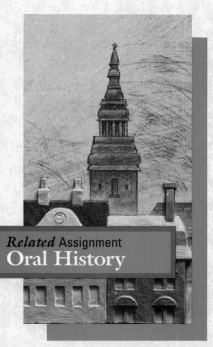

Related Assignment
Oral History

Who are the people you know? What makes them different from each other? What makes them different from you? How have they influenced you? The experiences you share with others during your life affect who you are and who you become.

In this workshop you will learn how writing about other people can help you learn about your world and about yourself. The guided assignment asks you to describe someone you know well. In the related assignment, you'll learn to prepare an oral history, another person's experience told in his or her own words.

Character Sketch

When you think about the people you know, you remember the details: the twinkle in their eyes, the calluses on their hands, the gentleness of their voices, or the smell of their clothes. You also remember their personal qualities, such as honesty, loyalty, or a sense of humor. Read this character sketch by writer Rudolfo Anaya. How does this portrait of Anaya's grandfather make you feel?

Abuelo [1]

BY RUDOLFO ANAYA

MY GRANDFATHER WAS a plain man, a farmer from the valley called Puerto de Luna on the Pecos River. He was probably a descendant of those people who spilled over the mountain from Taos, following the Pecos River in search of farmland. There in that river valley he settled and raised a large family.

Bearded and walrus-mustached, he stood five feet tall, but to me as a child he was a giant. I remember him most for his silence. In the summers my parents sent me to live with him on his farm, for I was to learn the ways of a farmer. My uncles also lived in that valley, there where only the flow of the river and the whispering of the wind marked time. For me it was a magical place.

I remember once, while out hoeing the fields, I came upon an anthill, and before I knew it I was badly bitten. After he had covered my welts with the cool mud from the irrigation ditch, my grandfather calmly said: "Know where you stand." That is the way he spoke, in short phrases, to the point.

One very dry summer, the river dried to a trickle; there was no water for the fields. The young plants withered and died. In my sadness and with the impulse of youth I said, "I wish it would rain!" My grandfather touched me, looked up into the sky and whispered, "Pray for rain." In his language there was a difference. He felt connected to the cycles that brought the rain or kept it from us. His prayer was a meaningful action, because he was a participant with the forces that filled our world; he was not a bystander. . . .

These are the things I remember, these fleeting images, few words.

I remember him driving his horse-drawn wagon into Santa Rosa in the fall when he brought his harvest produce to sell in the town. What a tower of strength seemed to come in that small man huddled on the seat of the giant wagon. One click of his tongue and the horses obeyed, stopped or turned as he wished. He never raised his whip. How unlike today, when so much teaching is done with loud words and threatening hands.

I would run to greet the wagon, and the wagon would stop. *"Buenos días le de Dios, abuelo,"*[2] I would say. . . . *"Buenos días te de Dios, mi hijo,"*[3] he would answer and smile, and then I could jump up on the wagon and sit at his side. Then I, too, became a king as I rode next to the old man who smelled of earth and sweat and the other deep aromas from the orchards and fields of Puerto de Luna.

We were all sons and daughters to him. But today the sons and daughters are breaking with the past, putting aside *los abuelitos.*[4] . . .

"They don't make men like that anymore," is a phrase we hear when one does honor to a man. I am glad I knew my grandfather. I am glad there are still times when I can see him in my dreams, hear him in my reverie. Sometimes I think I catch a whiff of that earthy aroma that was his smell. Then I smile. How strong these people were to leave such a lasting impression.

So, as I would greet my *abuelo* long ago, it would help us all to greet the old ones we know with this kind and respectful greeting: *"Buenos días le de Dios."*

1. **Abuelo** (ä bwe′ lô) *Spanish:* grandfather.
2. **Buenos días le de Dios, abuelo** (bwe′ nôs dē′ äs lā dā dyôs ä bwe′ lô) *Spanish:* God give you a good day, grandfather. (greeting of respect)
3. **mi hijo** (mē ē′ hô) *Spanish:* my son.
4. **los abuelitos** (lôs ä bwe lē′ tôs) *Spanish:* the grandparents.

Think & Respond

What do you think Anaya most wanted his audience to know? Which words or details make a strong impression on you? Where does Anaya use physical description and personal memories to create a vivid picture of his grandfather?

One Student's Writing

When Eric Gould was a student in Northborough, Massachusetts, he wrote this character sketch about a very special friend he made at summer camp when he was nine years old. Like Rudolfo Anaya, Eric cares deeply about his subject. How does Eric show his readers how important Phil's friendship was to him?

Phil
by Eric Gould

I never thought that anything bad would happen to anyone close to me. When it did, my whole perspective changed. . . . I still could not accept the fact that Phil was dead. Not only was he one of my best friends, he was the first friend I had made at overnight camp. He was only twelve and he was always smiling. I kept thinking about all of the good times we had together and I could not understand why he had to die so early in his life.

I first met Phil when I was nine years old. It was summer vacation and my first day at overnight camp. I was practically shaking with nervousness. I missed my parents already even though they had just left me a few minutes earlier. I had an empty feeling inside of me. For the first time in my life, it seemed that I was all alone. I was sitting on my bed when Phil came up to me and introduced himself. He was small with short black hair. He had a friendly grin that made me feel instantly comfortable. He was not as nervous as I was because it was his third year at camp. He asked me if I would like to play a game. We played games and talked for a long time and I was happy to have a friend.

With each summer, it seemed that Phil and I got closer and closer. We enjoyed the same things, like sports and comic books. We also shared many laughs together. We especially loved to play pranks on other people and each other. Whenever Phil became the victim of a prank, he would never get upset, but would just laugh with the rest of us and accept the joke. I especially remember the time that Phil needed to take a shower and all of his towels were outside on the clothesline. Everyone was either waiting in line to take a shower or relaxing on the beds. Phil asked the people sitting in the bunk to get a towel for him, but, as a joke, none of them would go. With a devilish smirk, Phil ran outside to get his towel. He was completely naked. Everyone laughed since this was a coed camp, but Phil was a good sport and had the best laugh of all.

Phil had other positive traits besides being good-natured. He could be trusted. We would talk every night and tell each other secrets that we never told anyone else. We talked about people that we liked and disliked, especially girls. We shared opinions about day-to-day life at camp. From our relationship, it was easy for me to understand why everyone who knew Phil wanted to be his friend.

That summer, just before Phil died, our relationship grew even closer than it had ever been. We were best friends. . . . After I had been home for about a week, I got a call from our counselor saying that Phil was dead. He had developed pneumonia after camp and died unexpectedly. . . .

Now that the years have passed, I still think about Phil and what a wonderful and special friend he was. My summer days continue to be spent at camp and my bunkmates and I still talk about Phil and remember the good times we shared together.

Think & Respond

Respond as a Reader

▶ Why do you think Eric decided to write about Phil?

▶ What do you think Eric learned about himself by writing about his friend?

Respond as a Writer

▶ How does Eric show rather than tell about Phil's personal qualities?

▶ What adjectives and other modifiers does he use to describe his friend?

INVITATION
— TO —
Write

A character sketch is like a portrait. It is a picture, in words, of what someone is like, inside and out. A good character sketch shows how a person looks, acts, thinks, and even feels. Well-chosen details—like the ones used by Rudolfo Anaya and Eric Gould—breathe life into a character sketch.

Think of someone you admire or find interesting or amusing. Then write a character sketch that will paint a vivid portrait for your readers.

PREWRITE AND EXPLORE

1. Think of a person you wish others could meet. Who are the people you care most about? You may already know whom you would like to write about. If you're not sure, try one or more of the following activities.

Exploring Topics

- **Family snapshots** Look through family photo albums to find a photo of someone you admire. **Freewrite** about the person, writing what you know or remember.

- **Who's who?** Divide your paper into columns. At the top of each column, write a category. Some possibilities include "Funny people," "People I respect," "People who stand out from the crowd," or "People who drive me crazy." In each column, list the names of people you know that fit the description. Freewrite about the person who interests you most.

- **Familiar strangers** Although you may not know them personally, famous people are possible candidates for a character sketch. Make a **cluster** about a famous person. Include what you know about the person and how he or she has influenced you.

2. Get to know your subject.   If you're having trouble choosing a subject, talking with friends about your ideas may help you decide. The following activities can help you gather information and details about your subject to include in your sketch.

- **What makes your subject unique?**   Explore what you know about your subject by making a **cluster,** or **spider map.** Tell what makes the person special by including details about his or her physical appearance and personality traits.

- **See with your mind's eye.**   Close your eyes and bring your subject to mind. Experience the person with all your senses. Then make notes about him or her in your journal.

- **Ask questions.**   Interview your subject, or talk to people who know him or her. Find out what makes the person "tick."

TIP

In addition to clusters, graphic organizers like observation charts and idea trees can help you explore your ideas and remember details. See Handbook 2, pages 226–230, for more information on using graphic organizers.

One Student's Process

Eric Gould chose to write about one of his best friends, Phil. Although Phil had died, Eric still remembered the many personal qualities that made this friend so special. The following cluster shows Eric's memories of Phil.

- towel on clothesline
- introduced himself first day of camp
- played pranks
- good-natured
- outgoing and friendly
- loved to laugh
- PHIL
- loved to sleep late
- always missed breakfast
- trustworthy and honest
- appearance
- great smile
- small
- short black hair

PROBLEM

S O L V I N G

"I can't decide what I most want my readers to know about the subject of my character sketch."

To help you find a reason for writing, see

- Handbook 3, "General Purpose and Specific Goals," pages 231–232

3. Find a focus.   Look over the information and details you've gathered. What do you most want your readers to know about your subject? After Eric made his cluster, he decided to focus on how good-natured Phil was and how close he felt to him. Setting a goal like this early on may help you stay focused as you draft and revise. Remember, however, that you are free to change your mind—and your focus—at any time during the writing process.

DRAFT AND DISCOVER

1. Begin drafting.   If you take another look at all your prewriting notes, you'll be ready to start writing your first draft. As you write about your subject, keep in mind the main impression you want to leave with your readers. If you're not sure what that impression is, drafting may help you find it.

2. Show rather than tell.   We learn about other people from what they do and say. When you write a character sketch, then, let the subject's own actions and words tell the story. Include the stories and details that best reveal your subject's personality. Notice how Rudolfo Anaya lets the deeds of his grandfather show how strong yet gentle his grandfather was.

> What a tower of strength seemed to come in that small man huddled on the seat of the giant wagon. One click of his tongue and the horses obeyed, stopped or turned as he wished. He never raised his whip.

 Writer's Choice   Sometimes writers create fictional characters based on people they know. Would you like to add some fictional elements to your character sketch? If so, give your subject a new name.

3. Let your character speak.   Your subject's own words may show aspects of his or her personality. Anaya, for example, quotes his grandfather in his sketch. He even comments on the way his grandfather spoke. "My grandfather calmly said: 'Know where you stand.' That is the way he spoke, in short phrases, to the point."

4. Try different patterns of organization.   Most character sketches include physical description and personal qualities, or character traits. They also include anecdotes, or stories, that illustrate those qualities. Here are two ways to present the information.

PROBLEM

SOLVING

"How can I use dialogue naturally to make my subject sound real?"

For more information on creating dialogue, see

• Handbook 27, pages 320–323

- First paragraph: physical description
- Second paragraph: character trait followed by an anecdote that illustrates it
- Third paragraph: another character trait followed by an anecdote that illustrates it
- Conclusion

- First paragraph: physical description
- Second paragraph: general description of several character traits
- Third paragraph: one or two anecdotes that show those character traits at work
- Conclusion

Generally, Eric Gould's story follows the first pattern of organization, but Rudolfo Anaya organized his sketch differently. He did not begin with physical description. Instead, he included those kinds of details throughout his sketch. You can try different methods, too.

5. Think about your draft.   Read over what you have written. Are you ready to share your sketch with others? Perhaps you'd rather make some changes before showing it to someone else. Use the following questions to help you and your readers review your draft. The answers may help you decide how to revise your sketch.

REVIEW YOUR WRITING

Questions for Yourself
- What part of my character sketch means the most to me?
- Where did I use description particularly well?
- What examples or details can I add to make the person seem more real? What should I take out?
- How can I best organize my sketch?

Questions for Your Peer Readers
- What makes the character most memorable to you?
- What else would you like to know about this person?
- What parts are confusing or unclear to you?
- Why do you think I wrote about this person?

COMPUTER TIP

A computer can make it simpler for you to experiment with your organization. You can save each draft as a separate document and then go back to the one that works best for you.

Writing TIP

When you come back to your writing after a break, begin by reading aloud what you have already written. This will help you get focused once again. At the same time, you may notice things you want to change.

You must really miss him.
You guys were such good
friends.

I'm confused here. Do you
need this information about
baseball and basketball?

How did Phil act when
someone played a prank
on him? Can you give an
example?

One Student's Process

Here is part of a draft of Eric's sketch. Notice the peer reader
comments. How would you have responded to this draft?

With each summer, it seemed that Phil and me
got closer and closer. We enjoyed the same
things. He was always talking about baseball
when he wasn't actually playing it. I like basketball better, but I know a lot about baseball too.
He had a lot of comic books. So did I. We also
shared many laughs together. We especially loved
to play pranks on other people and each other.
He was always a good sport when he was the
victim of a prank.

REVISE YOUR WRITING

1. Review your responses.   Think about how you can use the
answers to the questions on page 57 to guide your revision. Did
your readers get a clear picture of your subject's appearance and
personality? If they didn't, what details could you add—or
change—to make the picture clearer?

2. Think about your introduction.   Will your opening sentences catch a reader's interest? If you begin with a description,
use vivid nouns, verbs, and adjectives to engage your readers and
get them thinking about your subject. You might also begin your
sketch with some dialogue or an interesting anecdote. Rudolfo
Anaya identifies his subject and provides background information
about his grandfather in the first paragraph of his sketch.

3. Take another look at your ending.   Do you sum up the person's personality or achievements, or do you leave your readers
with unanswered questions? Anaya wanted to leave his readers
with a piece of advice, something important to think about. Eric
Gould's conclusion shows his readers that the memory of his
friend continues to be important for him.

PROBLEM

S O L V I N G

**"How can I make my
character seem more
real to my readers?"**

To learn how descriptive
details can show a char-
acter's personality, see

- Handbook 12, "Show Not
Tell," pages 262–265

Paragraphs at Work   Each paragraph in a character sketch should have a single focus. You might use a separate paragraph for each personality trait you describe. When you revise, check the content of each paragraph.

- Make sure that each paragraph has a single focus.
- Make sure that every sentence in a paragraph is related to the focus.
- Delete sentences or details that don't belong, or move them to other paragraphs.

One Student's Process

Eric thought about his draft and considered how he might answer his peer reader's questions. He decided to take out unrelated information and to add details that support his focus. Here is how he changed one part of his draft.

With each summer, it seemed that Phil and ~~me~~ I got closer and closer. We enjoyed the same things, like sports and comic books. ~~He was always talking about baseball when he wasn't actually playing it. I like basketball better, but I know a lot about baseball too. He had a lot of comic books. So did I.~~ We also shared many laughs together. We especially loved to play pranks on other people and each other. ~~He was always a good sport when~~ Whenever Phil became the victim of a prank,

he would never get upset, but would just laugh with the rest of us and accept the joke. I especially remember the time that Phil needed to take a shower and all of his towels were outside on the clothesline.

PROOFREAD

1. Proofread your work. Correct any errors in grammar, capitalization, punctuation, and spelling.

LINKING MECHANICS AND WRITING

Using Commas to Combine Sentences

Combining sentences is one way to make the connections between your ideas clear. Notice how the simple sentences below can be combined with *but* to form a compound sentence. Remember that in a compound sentence, a comma comes before the coordinating conjunction.

Original

Everyone laughed at the ridiculous outfit. Phil was a good sport and had the best laugh of all.

Revised

Everyone laughed at the ridiculous outfit, but Phil was a good sport and had the best laugh of all.

For more information on using commas in compound sentences, see Handbook 47, "Punctuation," pages 648–650.

2. Make a clean copy of your sketch. Is your writing ready to share? If so, make one last check using the Standards for Evaluation in the margin. Then make a final copy.

PUBLISH AND PRESENT

- **Hold an "exhibition" of your sketches.** Draw or paint a portrait of the subject of your character sketch, or exchange papers and draw the person someone else described. Then display the essays and artwork in a "portrait gallery."

Standards for Evaluation

DESCRIPTIVE WRITING

A character sketch

- gives a clear portrait of someone's appearance and personality
- uses anecdotes to illustrate the person's character traits
- shows why the person was important to the writer
- has a strong introduction and conclusion

- **Share your sketch with people who know your subject.**
Friends, relatives, or classmates who know the subject of your
character sketch might enjoy reading your work.

- **Arrange an oral reading.** Join with other students to give a
public reading of your sketches. You might do this at your
school or public library.

REFLECT ON YOUR WRITING

1. Add your character sketch to your writing portfolio.
By now, you've had enough experience with character sketches
to give other writers some advice. Make
some notes about your experience and
attach them to your final draft. Ask yourself these questions to help you gather your
thoughts:

FOR YOUR
PORTFOLIO

- How did I select a person to write
about?

- What did I learn about myself
in the process of writing about
someone else?

- What was the hardest part about
writing my character sketch? How
did I work through my difficulties?

- How did peer comments help me
evaluate and revise my work?

2. Explore additional writing ideas.
For more ideas, see the suggestions for
writing an oral history on pages 64–66 and
Springboards on page 67.

Oral History

Have you learned about other times or other cultures by listening to your parents or grandparents talk? One exciting way to learn about history is to listen to people describe what their lives were like in another time or place. An oral history, like this one by Grete Rasmussen, is the story of a person's experiences told in his or her own words. Grete was a teenager in Denmark during World War II. What else do you learn about her by reading her oral history? What do you learn about the place and time in which she lived?

FROM DENMARK, 1950

as told by GRETE RASMUSSEN

I WAS A STUDENT NURSE during World War II. It was a gruesome time, and that's the reason I am a pacifist. I was in the school, down in a big gymnasium, when they just came in, the Germans. It looked like a scene from a movie. It was a scary experience.

We had to give up the army. Our king said, "There's a better way of fighting," and right away the young people started going underground. First of all, we heard about Norway being invaded. We knew that the Norwegians were fighting in the mountains and everywhere else. We were concerned about the Norwegians. The talk was in the university, "How can we help them? We must do *our* part." That's when they started blowing up the railroads. I was not in the underground right away. I didn't feel like I could be in it, being a nurse.

When Hitler said all the Jewish people had to wear the star, the next day, who's the first one to show up with the star but the king. And then everybody did that, and the Germans said, "What can we do with people like that?"

Then Hitler told us that we had to give the names of Jews. That Sunday—I'll never forget—when he said that all the Danish people

were to give up the names of Jewish people, all the church bells started ringing at eleven o'clock. I remember going to church. The minister went up to the pulpit and he said, "We are Danish people. We will never give up our brothers and sisters. We are going to be behind them and help them. Every Dane is going to." That was in every church in Denmark. And the Germans couldn't do anything, because it was too unified. They couldn't shoot everybody.

I was almost seventeen and I was working nights sometimes to earn extra money, in a little pension place, where old people had a home. There was such an old, sweet lady, I just adored her. I remember the night the Nazi Gestapo came in and they asked for her. When I saw them take her, I think something happened to me. I opened that window and looked out and saw them take her and throw her in the big truck. And that was the day I said, "Now I'm ready to go in the underground. I'm going to help anywhere I can. I'll help get the Jews off to Sweden."

Many times we had them hide in the hospital. It was one or two on a floor. The doctors put them in traction, or we put oxygen on them; we'd do all kinds of things. We sure had to do a lot of work to write up charts on so many people. Sometimes there was a raid in the hospital, when we were held up with guns, and they went through the charts. . . .

It was hard not to hate. Very, very hard. I had a time where I really struggled with this. I remember coming home once. There was no train running, and I had to bicycle home. And every time I saw a German, it was just that hate came over me. I said to myself, "You're making yourself sick." And when I was home, my mother said, "You know, I don't care if he's your enemy. You must not hate for your own sake—because they are human, God's children." I said, "I don't care. Spit on them!" Until one day a little German soldier came in with a big gun he almost couldn't carry. He didn't look more than fifteen or sixteen. He looked white and he said, "Could I just buy a little milk? I haven't had food, and I can't walk another step." My mother looked at me and she said that was her salvation, because I not only gave him milk and egg and bread, I gave him a whole bagful of food. From that day I couldn't hate anymore.

Think & Respond

Discuss with your classmates how Grete Rasmussen's description of her wartime experiences made you feel. What words would you use to describe her? Look back over the oral history and write down two or three questions Grete's interviewer may have asked her.

INVITATION
━ TO ━
Write

How can you find out what it was like to live in another place or time? Ask someone! People everywhere, like Grete Rasmussen, have stories to tell that can provide you with a look at history as it was being made.

Interview someone you know, or someone you would like to know better, who has an interesting story to tell about his or her past. Write your interview as an oral history.

CONDUCTING THE INTERVIEW

1. Find someone with a story to tell.   Do you know someone who might have experienced an exciting event in your community's past, such as an earthquake or a visit from the President? Did a parent or neighbor serve in the military during a war? Do you know someone whose life as a teenager might have been totally different from your own? Make a list of people you might interview, then make some notes about what makes them interesting or appealing to you. Select the person who interests you most.

2. Interview your subject.   Good interviews don't just happen. They take careful planning and preparation.

- Contact your subject and set up a date, time, and place for an interview.
- Think about what you most want to learn during the interview. What stories do you want your subject to tell? Make a list of open-ended questions that allow your subject to answer with more than just yes or no. If you ask someone, "Was it fun to be a teenager in the 1950s?" you might not get as much information as if you had asked, "What did you do for fun when you were a teenager in the 1950s?"

PROBLEM
S O L V I N G

"I've never interviewed anyone, and I'm nervous about it! Where can I find some tips for successful interviewing?"

To learn more about interviewing, see

- Handbook 34, "Interviewing Skills," page 357

- Ask for more information. Don't be afraid to ask the person you're interviewing to repeat something you don't understand or to give more details. Before you end the interview, ask if there's any information he or she would like to add.

3. Tape-record your interview.   An oral history should be written using the person's own words as much as possible. If you tape the interview, you can accurately copy down the words later.

DRAFTING YOUR ORAL HISTORY

1. Get in focus.   Listen to the recorded interview several times, and look for a focus, or main point, for your oral history. What main idea comes through from the speaker's words? Did the person focus on the topic you originally asked about, or did the interview take an unexpected turn? Try to express the main idea in a single sentence. Let this sentence guide you as you organize your notes and write your draft.

2. Organize your notes.   Once you're familiar with the entire interview, listen to it again and take notes on index cards. On separate cards, briefly summarize each point the speaker makes. Review the note cards and arrange them in an order that makes sense. Set aside those note cards that do not relate to the focus of the interview.

3. Assemble the oral history.   Since an oral history tells a person's story in his or her own words, you need to transcribe the parts of the taped interview you want to use. This means you must start and stop the tape frequently, writing down what the speaker says word for word. Once you have the words on paper, decide how the sentences should be grouped into paragraphs. Begin a new paragraph when the speaker changes the subject or begins a new part of the story.

4. Introduce your speaker.   You may wish to write a brief introduction to your oral history. Include such information as the person's name, age, occupation, and anything else that might help readers know who he or she is.

Writing TIP

When you take notes from the tape recorder, write down the number that appears on its counter, if it has one. This number will help you find that particular part of the interview when you're ready to transcribe the tape.

Writing TIP

Don't include every word the speaker says in your final oral history. Feel free to omit any "umms" or "wells" or stories that don't relate to the main focus of the interview.

R EVIEWING YOUR WRITING

1. Capture the flavor of your subject's speech. Read your oral history aloud. Do the words sound natural? Can you hear the voice of the person you interviewed? Remember, people often express their ideas in fragments, and their speech may not follow the rules of written grammar. This is true in Grete Rasmussen's oral history. She said, "Many times we had them hide in the hospital. It was one or two on a floor." Although "We hid one or two on a floor" would have been grammatically correct and expressed the same meaning, the writer used Grete's exact words to show you what Grete sounded like.

2. Go right to the source. If possible, review your work with the person you interviewed. Ask if you've told his or her story accurately or if you need to make corrections or additions. You may also wish to share the oral history with a peer reader. Ask your reader what kind of impression the subject of your oral history made on him or her. Review your reader's responses and make any changes you feel are necessary.

3. Proofread your work. Play the tape one more time and compare the spoken words with the ones you wrote down. Make sure you've recorded the words accurately. Then reread what you've written and correct any spelling errors.

P UBLISHING AND PRESENTING

- **Publish an "Oral History" magazine.** Link several histories together on the basis of theme, age, or occupation. Distribute a new magazine each week for a month or two.

- **Donate copies of oral histories to your community's public library.** Collect those histories that provide information about your community and its past and present leaders.

- **Give dramatic readings of your oral histories.** You may wish to read your oral histories aloud in front of your class or during a school assembly.

Grammar
TIP

How do you punctuate something you've only heard? Use a comma when your speaker pauses in the middle of a sentence. Use a period at the end of a complete thought.

Springboards

Drama   Give a dramatic reading based on an oral history interview. Use your voice and body language to reflect your subject's mannerisms, attitude, and speaking style.

Science   Conduct some research on a famous scientist, such as Albert Einstein, Marie Curie, or Margaret Mead. Look for sources that provide information about their personal lives as well as their greatest achievements. Write a character sketch about the scientist you select.

LITERATURE   Who is the most fascinating character you have read about in literature? Working in pairs, imagine that you are a literary character and tell your story—your history—to a classmate. Have your classmate tell you his or her character's story. Then write each other's oral history and work together to revise your drafts.

Art   Create a visual character sketch of someone you know personally or of a famous actor or musician you admire. You might draw, paint, sculpt, photograph, or even make a collage of images to represent your subject.

Sentence

Sentence Openers

Experienced writers sometimes open sentences with a word or phrase that calls attention to certain details. Notice the types of details the sentence openers below add to each sentence.

Model A	At the <u>front door</u>, Mother and Father and Mr. and Mrs. Matsui bowed and murmured. **Monica Sone, "The Japanese Touch"**
Model B	<u>Eagerly</u>, we settled onto the muddy forest floor and waited. **Mildred D. Taylor, *Roll of Thunder, Hear My Cry***
Model C	<u>Then, obeying my mother's voice</u>, I hunted for a spot of earth and buried the stiff kitten. **Richard Wright, *Black Boy***

▶ **ON THE MARK**   Remember that sentence openers are usually followed by a comma.

A. Combining Sentences   Combine the following sets of sentences and begin each new sentence with the underlined words. Write the complete sentence, putting a comma after the sentence opener.

1. The wind blew. It blew <u>on the prairie</u>.

         Dorothy M. Johnson, *The Day the Sun Came Out*

2. He would hear a sniff or a coarse gurgle, and that made him angrier than ever. He heard this <u>occasionally</u>.

         Leon Hugo, "My Father the Hippopotamus"

3. The pony climbed at last upon the marshy shore of the mainland. The pony was <u>dripping with cold water</u>.

         Ellis Credle, "Betsy Dowdy's Ride"

4. He lay down to take a nap. He was <u>satisfied with his meal</u>.

         Lin Yutang, "The Tiger"

5. She could see a huge jagged slab of ice sticking up from the snow. She saw it <u>outside the window</u>. It was <u>in the blue moonlight</u>.

         Susan Fromberg Schaefer, *Time in Its Flight*

B. Unscrambling and Imitating Sentences   Unscramble each set of sentence chunks below to create a sentence that matches one of the models on page 68. Then write a sentence of your own that imitates each model. Be sure each of your sentences starts with a sentence opener.

1. Write sentences that imitate Model A.
   ghosts and goblins / at midnight / awoke and roamed / and Dracula and Frankenstein

2. Write sentences that imitate Model B.
   and won / quickly / Delvon dashed / toward the finish line

3. Write sentences that imitate Model C.
   and landed the giant starship / Captain Reardon searched for a clearing in the trees / later / scanning the ground below

C. Expanding Sentences   Use your imagination to add a sentence opener, followed by a comma, where the caret appears in each sentence below.

1. ∧ Thomas ate two portions of meat, nothing else.

   Hal Borland, *When the Legends Die*

2. ∧ He got control of his nerves.

   Arthur C. Clarke, *Dolphin Island*

3. ∧ Romey folded his hands in his lap and closed his eyes.

   Bill and Vera Cleaver, *Where the Lilies Bloom*

4. ∧ They had moved into a rotting old farmhouse two miles north of town, long abandoned.

   Ambrose Flack, "The Strangers That Came to Town"

5. ∧ The streets looked beautiful to her.

   Celestine Sibley, "The Girl Who Hated Christmas"

Grammar Refresher   Many sentence openers are prepositional phrases. To learn more about using prepositional phrases at the beginning of sentences, see Handbook 43, "Using Prepositions, Conjunctions, and Interjections," pages 543–544.

- Write a few paragraphs from a story that could include the picture and the two sentences shown below.
- Freewrite about the scariest thing that ever happened to you or the incident that made you happiest or angriest.

MR. LINDEN'S LIBRARY

He had warned her about the book.
Now it was too late.

Show, Don't Tell

You can show suspense in a story by using sensory details that reveal a growing tension. Practice on one of these *telling* sentences.

- They knew they were in trouble.
- They were taken by surprise.

3

Narrative and Literary Writing

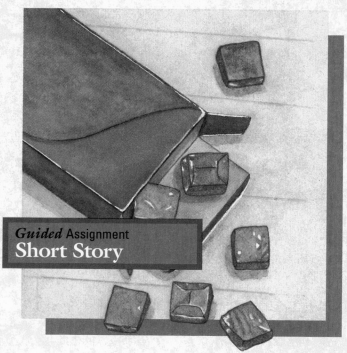

**_Guided_ Assignment
Short Story**

**_Related_ Assignment
Children's Book**

How do you make sense of what happens around you and share your experience with other people? One way is to write a story. You can write about something that really happened, something that might never happen, or something that hasn't happened but that you wish would. You can tell about the world you know, or you can create whole new worlds.

In this workshop you will write a short story about anything you choose—a story only *you* can write. In a related assignment, you will have the chance to write and illustrate a book for children.

71

Short Story

Starting from LITERATURE

Have you ever been surprised to find out what the people closest to you really feel? Do you sometimes forget how much you mean to those who care about you?

As you read Cynthia Rylant's story, think about the kind of real-life experiences that may have prompted her to write it.

Papa's Parrot

by Cynthia Rylant

Though his father was fat and merely owned a candy and nut shop, Harry Tillian liked his papa. Harry stopped liking candy and nuts when he was around seven, but, in spite of this, he and Mr. Tillian had remained friends and were still friends the year Harry turned twelve.

For years, after school, Harry had always stopped in to see his father at work. Many of Harry's friends stopped there, too, to spend a few cents choosing penny candy from the giant bins or to sample Mr. Tillian's latest batch of roasted peanuts. Mr. Tillian looked forward to seeing his son and his son's friends every day. He liked the company.

When Harry entered junior high school, though, he didn't come by the candy and nut shop as often. Nor did his friends. They were older and they had more spending money. They went to a burger place. They played video games. They

shopped for records. None of them were much interested in candy and nuts anymore.

A new group of children came to Mr. Tillian's shop now. But not Harry Tillian and his friends.

The year Harry turned twelve was also the year Mr. Tillian got a parrot. He went to a pet store one day and bought one for more money than he could really afford. He brought the parrot to his shop, set its cage near the sign for maple clusters and named it Rocky.

Harry thought this was the strangest thing his father had ever done, and he told him so, but Mr. Tillian just ignored him.

Rocky was good company for Mr. Tillian.

When business was slow, Mr. Tillian would turn on a small color television he had sitting in a corner, and he and Rocky would watch the soap operas. Rocky liked to scream when the romantic music came on, and Mr. Tillian would yell at him to shut up, but they seemed to enjoy themselves.

The more Mr. Tillian grew to like his parrot, and the more he talked to it instead of to people, the more embarrassed Harry became. Harry would stroll past the shop, on his way somewhere else, and he'd take a quick look inside to see what his dad was doing. Mr. Tillian was always talking to the bird. So Harry kept walking.

At home things were different. Harry and his father joked with each other at the dinner table

as they always had—Mr. Tillian teasing Harry about his smelly socks; Harry teasing Mr. Tillian about his blubbery stomach. At home things seemed all right.

But one day, Mr. Tillian became ill. He had been at work, unpacking boxes of caramels, when he had grabbed his chest and fallen over on top of the candy. A customer had found him, and he was taken to the hospital in an ambulance.

Mr. Tillian couldn't leave the hospital. He lay in bed, tubes in his arms, and he worried about his shop.

New shipments of candy and nuts would be arriving. Rocky would be hungry. Who would take care of things?

Harry said he would. Harry told his father that he would go to the store every day after school and unpack boxes. He would sort out all the candy and nuts. He would even feed Rocky.

So, the next morning, while Mr. Tillian lay in his hospital bed, Harry took the shop key to school with him. After school he left his friends and walked to the empty shop alone. In all the days of his life, Harry had never seen the shop closed after school. Harry didn't even remember what the CLOSED sign looked like. The key stuck in the lock three times, and inside he had to search all the walls for the light switch.

The shop was as his father had left it. Even the caramels were still spilled on the floor. Harry bent down and picked them up one by one, dropping them back in the boxes. The bird in its cage watched him silently.

Harry opened the new boxes his father hadn't gotten to. Peppermints. Jawbreakers. Toffee creams. Strawberry kisses. Harry traveled from bin to bin, putting the candies where they belonged.

"Hello!"

Harry jumped, spilling a box of jawbreakers.

"Hello, Rocky!"

Harry stared at the parrot. He had forgotten it was there. The bird had been so quiet, and Harry had been thinking only of the candy.

"Hello," Harry said.

"Hello, Rocky!" answered the parrot.

Harry walked slowly over to the cage. The parrot's food cup was empty. Its water was dirty. The bottom of the cage was a mess.

Harry carried the cage into the back room.

"Hello, Rocky!"

"Is that all you can say, you dumb bird?" Harry mumbled. The bird said nothing else.

Harry cleaned the bottom of the cage, refilled the food and water cups, then put the cage back in its place and resumed sorting the candy.

"Where's Harry?"

Harry looked up.

"Where's Harry?"

Harry stared at the parrot.

"Where's Harry?"

Chills ran down Harry's back. What could the bird mean? It was like something from *The Twilight Zone.*

"Where's Harry?"

Harry swallowed and said, "I'm here. I'm here, you stupid bird."

"You stupid bird!" said the parrot.

Well, at least he's got one thing straight, thought Harry.

"Miss him! Miss him! Where's Harry? You stupid bird!"

Harry stood with a handful of peppermints.

"*What?*" he asked.

"Where's Harry?" said the parrot.

"I'm *here*, you stupid bird! I'm here!" Harry

yelled. He threw the peppermints at the cage, and the bird screamed and clung to its perch.

Harry sobbed, "I'm here." The tears were coming.

Harry leaned over the glass counter.

"Papa." Harry buried his face in his arms.

"Where's Harry?" repeated the bird.

Harry sighed and wiped his face on his sleeve. He watched the parrot. He understood now: someone had been saying, for a long time, "Where's Harry? Miss him."

Harry finished his unpacking, then swept the floor of the shop. He checked the furnace so the bird wouldn't get cold. Then he left to go visit his papa.

Think & Respond

Do the events of this story seem true to life? What details in this story tell you most about Mr. Tillian? about Harry? about the parrot?

One Student's Writing

Mind's Flight
Adam Baughman

Reading a
STUDENT MODEL

What do you love to do most? Run? Play baseball? Sing? How do you think you would feel if you couldn't do that activity any longer?

As a junior high school student, Adam Baughman imagined a character in that situation. He turned his imaginings into a short story.

As you read Adam's story, think about how it makes you feel. How do your feelings change as the story progresses?

It was about 2:30 P.M., just before his doctor's appointment. Kit was looking about his room to see if he had forgotten anything. He came across his image in the mirror. He sat down and took a good long look at himself.

All at once, he started seeing other images in the mirror. Clouds bigger than he'd ever seen went whizzing by at tremendous speeds. He could smell the fragrance of oil and steel about him, the smell of power! Then, he started spinning and turning and diving; he had never felt so free in his life. He rolled over and caught a glimpse of a familiar sight—it was earth! He was flying—what a feeling! Looking down, he saw what he had imagined and read so much about, the controls to this mechanical marvel. He looked at the altimeter and found he was at about 1,000 feet. The airspeed indicator read 250 knots. It was wonderful!

All of a sudden, he heard it. It was a noise unrivaled by any he had ever heard. It made his body feel so fragile and weak, yet his mind so large and powerful. It was like being in the clouds of a thunderstorm and hearing the thunder roar up close. It was the engine, the propelling factor to this aircraft.

Now, getting used to this, his hands ventured out and touched the sticks that were on both sides of him. They felt as if they were custom-fitted to his hands. He began to feel the seat of the cockpit and the cushioned lump behind his back—the parachute. Even if he was about to crash and was staring death in the eye, he would not use the chute for love of what he was doing.

He seized control of the massive metal beast. Now he controlled the spinning, turning, and diving. Never had he felt so unbounded and in charge of his own destiny! Then he heard the crackling of the air boss's voice over the squawk box. He couldn't really make out what the boss was saying, but even if he could, he would not understand it for lack of knowledge of flight terminology.

Looking out the canopy, he realized that he was all alone. He looked back to see who the RIO (Radio Intercept Officer) was but discovered that he was in a one-seater. Normally, he would be afraid—but not this time. No way, not this time. This was the fantasy of a lifetime come true, and he was not about to let it pass him by.

As he thought back, Kit reviewed all his knowledge of jet aircraft and concluded that he was flying an F-16 Falcon. Everything fit—the sticks being on the sides, the bubble canopy, and the single engine. He remembered that this plane's nickname was the "Electric Jet" because it is controlled by electricity.

The sun was big and bright and shone down on the familiar landscapes of earth. While trying to figure out where he was, he jetted over a mountain and finally saw it, the base! He had been there so many times before with his father. Of course—his father! That's where he was, in his father's plane. His father, the renowned pilot on the famous United States Air Force Flight Demonstration Team, the "Thunderbirds."

The Thunderbirds! Wow, what an experience! Here he was, in the position that every kid dreams of. The lead man. He had always wanted to be there. Watching his dad at the air shows had always made him jealous, but now it was his turn to shine.

"Bird Two in place," crackled his radio. "Bird Three in place. Bird Four in place." The crew! Looking out to his sides, Kit saw the red, white, and blue patterns on the magnificent ships of flight. They had just completed their famous "Diamond" formation where Kit's plane was about twenty inches away from the two wing men's. Everything fit perfectly; it had to!

Suddenly, he heard something. Over the roar of the engine and the radio, he heard it. The sound grew stronger and stronger and sounded like a familiar voice. It seemed to be pulling at him, nagging and tugging. "Kit! . . . Kit!" All of a sudden, reality reconvened, and he was once again sitting in his room, staring at his reflection in the mirror.

"Kit, will you please come on, Kit! We're late already!" called his mother.

Splashing down, the tear of a crushed and yearning body fell upon its metallic bonds. Kit rose, still wobbly, on his new artificial leg. With a hunger in his heart and a curse on his tongue, he flipped off the light to his room.

First appeared in *Merlyn's Pen: The National Magazine of Student Writing.*

Think & Respond

Respond as a Reader

▶ What is the most important moment in this story for you?

▶ What, if anything, puzzles you or seems mysterious about the story?

Respond as a Writer

▶ What details does Adam use to make the scenes in the story seem real?

▶ Why do you think he ends the story the way he does?

INVITATION
— TO —
Write

Both Cynthia Rylant and Adam Baughman explored an idea that was important to them by writing a short story. Each writer created a slice of life that readers can experience as if they were there.

Now write your own short story about anything you like. Your story can be set in any time and place, and the events can be real or imaginary, serious or funny.

PREWRITE AND EXPLORE

1. Look for story ideas. Ideas can spring from your experiences, reading, or imagination. A story needs just four elements:

- characters—who takes part
- conflict—a problem to be solved
- plot—what happens
- setting—where the action occurs

To discover a story you really want to tell, try the following activities.

Exploring Topics

- **Being there** In your mind, relive interesting, funny, or sad experiences you have had. Take notes on what you see, hear, smell, taste, and feel.

- **What if** Alone or with a friend, **brainstorm** a list of questions that begin, "What if . . .?" For example, What if time ran backwards? One of these questions could suggest a plot.

- **Reading literature** Reread your favorite short stories or read stories recommended by friends. See if the characters, plots, or settings spark ideas. **Freewrite** about your thoughts.

2. See where your story idea leads. Once you have an idea for a story, you can begin to explore it. You might want to just start writing and see what happens. On the other hand, you could begin by thinking about the key elements of your story and by gathering details that will make these elements come alive. The key is to "be there" in your mind. The following activities may help you explore and expand your story idea.

- **Talk it out.** Meet with a friend or group of friends to discuss and respond to each other's story ideas. Ask for the specific help you need—for example, what a character would look like or how the story might end.

- **Use a graphic device.** Use a cluster diagram or other graphic device to come up with details like these:

  characters—appearance, language, ambitions, worries
  conflict and plot—what happened, where, when, and how
  setting—what you see, hear, smell, touch, and taste

PROBLEM
S O L V I N G

"How can I find details for my story?"

For hints on how to expand your ideas, see

- Handbook 11, "Elaboration," pages 254–260
- Handbook 12, "Show Not Tell," pages 262–265

One Student's Process

Finding ideas can be the hardest part of writing a short story. Here's a passage of freewriting for "Mind's Flight":

How am I ever going to think of an idea for a story? All my thoughts keep coming back to the same thing—my injured eye and the end of my dream. For so long, all I ever thought about was flying. From the time I was a little kid, I wanted to follow in my grandfather's footsteps—or jet trails. I was going to be an Air Force pilot just like him. Now that I don't have 20/20 vision any more, the Air Force won't take me. I don't know what I'm going to do. I still go to air shows every chance I get—my head's in the clouds most of the time, I guess. I just feel so sad—kind of trapped. Sometimes I think this is just a bad dream and I'll wake up with perfect vision and a pilot's life ahead of me.

1. Begin drafting. If you did some freewriting already, looking it over may help you get started on your draft. You can begin by writing any part of your story that you're interested in and have ideas about. This might be the opening or closing scene, the setting, a character, or any event in the plot.

2. Keep writing. Where are the characters and events of your story leading you? Just add details as you think of them, and follow your story as it unwinds. Feel free to change the plot, setting, or characters as much as you like. For example, Adam Baughman had an injured eye. However, he decided to give his character, Kit, an injured leg instead. As you write, ask yourself:

- What are my goals in writing this story?
- Who will my readers be?

3. Walk through the action of your story. Will your readers be able to understand how the action moves from one point to the next? For example, notice how Adam brings readers into Kit's imaginary world by having Kit look in the mirror. If you need to fill in missing details, you can either do it at this point or make notes to yourself and fill the details in later.

4. Let your characters talk. Think about whether having your characters talk to each other will help you tell your story. If you're not sure, you can try writing some dialogue and see if it works. If you decide to use dialogue in your story, remember that each character should sound like a unique individual.

Notice how Cynthia Rylant uses dialogue between Harry and the parrot very effectively. The parrot talks like only a parrot would. It keeps repeating Harry's father's words, "Where's Harry? Miss him." Finally, Harry gets the message.

Writer's Choice Do you want to tell the story from the point of view of a character who takes part in the action (first person)? Maybe you would rather use a narrator who does not take part in the action (third person). You might want to experiment before you decide.

COMPUTER TIP

If you think of an idea for another part of your story as you draft, just switch to "all caps" and type it in. When you review your draft, you can decide what to do with the idea and then delete the capitalized note.

PROBLEM SOLVING

"How can I make my characters sound more natural?"

For hints on writing realistic dialogue, see

- Handbook 27, "Creating Dialogue," pages 320–322

5. Think about your draft.   Read through what you have written. Are you ready to share your rough draft, or do you want to make some changes in your story first? You may want to get responses by reading your draft to a friend or having your friend read it silently or aloud. Asking questions like the following may help you review your story.

R E V I E W   Y O U R   W R I T I N G

Questions for Yourself
- What part of this story is most important to me?
- What can I do to make my characters seem more real?
- What details can I add to help show the scene?
- How can I make the story flow smoothly and naturally?

Questions for Your Peer Readers
- How did my story make you feel? What parts made you feel that way?
- What part did you find most important? Why?
- Whom or what do you want to know more about?

One Student's Process

Adam was excited about his story idea, but it was still unclear in his mind. He did know how he wanted the story to end, though. He decided to start writing the conclusion and to ask his classmates for comments and ideas.

Looking out to his sides, Kit saw the red, white, and blue patterns on the magnificent ships of flight. They had just completed their famous "Diamond" formation. It reminded me of the time I saw the Blue Angels do their incredible formations at the county air show. They were so close they could have touched each other. Suddenly, he heard something. The sound grew stronger and stronger. He was once again sitting in his room, staring at his reflection in the mirror.

Peer Reader Comments

You lost me here. I'm not sure who "I" is or who's telling the story.

I like this—it's weird! He was having a dream, right?

1. Review your responses.   Go over your own and your peer readers' reactions to your first draft. Review what you want to accomplish in writing your story, and make changes that will help you reach your goals. Remember, you can make any changes you want. You can create new characters, invent a different ending, or even turn a funny story into a serious one.

2. Think about point of view.   Who is telling your story? If your narrator takes part in the action, the story is told from the first person point of view. You should use the pronoun *I* in describing the action. If the narrator is not part of the action, but just explains what is happening, the story is told from the third person point of view. In that case, you should use the pronouns *he* and *she*. Whatever point of view you use, be sure to stick with it throughout your story.

For example, notice how the narrator in Adam's story does not take part in the action. The story is told from the third person point of view using the pronoun *he*.

Paragraphs at Work   Creating paragraphs in your story will help your readers follow the information about your characters, plot, and setting. Correct paragraphing will also help readers to follow a conversation between characters and to know when the scene changes. Remember to begin a new paragraph in your story at these times:
- When a different character begins speaking
- When there is a change in the action
- When the scene changes

3. Look for ways you can show, not tell, your story.   Review your story from a reader's point of view. Remember that your writing should make readers feel that they are experiencing the events right along with the characters. Close your eyes and go into the story. See, hear, smell, and feel what is happening around you. For example, could you reveal your characters' feelings by showing them acting a certain way rather than by telling how they felt?

Notice that Cynthia Rylant doesn't just say that Harry felt like a stranger going into the shop when his father was in the hospital. She shows it by using vivid details. "In all the days of his life, Harry had never seen the shop closed after school. Harry didn't even remember what the CLOSED sign looked like. The key stuck in the lock three times, and inside he had to search all the walls for the light switch."

One Student's Process

Adam reread his draft and thought about his classmates' comments. He realized that he needed to make it clear who was telling the story. He also decided to add details to help explain what was happening. These are some of the changes he made.

where Kit's plane was about twenty inches away from the two wing men's.

and sounded like a familiar voice. It seemed to be pulling at him, nagging and tugging. "Kit! Kit!" All of a sudden, reality reconvened, and

Looking out to his sides, Kit saw the red, white, and blue patterns on the magnificent ships of flight. They had just completed their famous "Diamond" formation. ~~It reminded me of the time I saw the Blue Angels do their incredible formations at the county air show. They were so close they could have touched each other.~~ Suddenly, he heard something. The sound grew stronger and stronger. He was once again sitting in his room, staring at his reflection in the mirror.

¶"Kit, will you please come on, Kit! We're late already!" called his mother.

PROOFREAD

1. Proofread your work. Check your work for errors in grammar, capitalization, punctuation, and spelling. Pay particular attention to the use of quotation marks.

LINKING
MECHANICS AND WRITING

Using Quotation Marks

When you write dialogue, be sure to enclose the speaker's words in quotation marks. Begin the speaker's words with a capital letter, and put commas and periods inside the closing quotation marks. When a sentence of dialogue is divided into two parts by a phrase such as "he said," begin the second part with a small letter. Notice how Adam corrected his use of quotation marks.

Original

"Bird Two in place, crackled his radio. "bird Three in place. Bird Four in place."

Revised

"Bird Two in place," crackled his radio. "Bird Three in place. Bird Four in place."

For more information about using quotation marks correctly, see Handbook 47, "Punctuation," pages 648–652.

2. Make a clean copy of your work. Does your story read exactly the way you want it to? Would you like to prepare it for publication now? If so, do a final check of your work using the Standards for Evaluation in the margin. Then make a final copy.

PUBLISH AND PRESENT

• **Publish your class's stories as a book.** You might group the stories by type (autobiography, science fiction, humor) or by subject matter (animal stories, adventure stories).

Standards for Evaluation

NARRATIVE
WRITING

A short story

• holds the reader's interest

• allows the reader to experience what is happening

• uses natural-sounding dialogue

• maintains a consistent point of view

• presents events in an order that is clear to readers

- **Dramatize your story.** With others, write a script for part or all of your story. Use dialogue from your writing, and create props and settings. Perform the skit for your classmates.

- **Present your story orally.** Read or tell your story to your class or to other classes in your school. You might want to get together with classmates and present your stories in a Readers Theater. You will need a narrator and people to read the part of each character.

- **Submit your story to a writing contest.** The publications *Market Guide for Young Writers* and *Writer's Market* list magazines that sponsor contests for young writers.

REFLECT ON YOUR WRITING

WRITER TO WRITER

Why do storytellers start to tell one story and then tell another?

Life is a speeding train. Storytellers get derailed too.

Ann Beattie, novelist

FOR YOUR PORTFOLIO

1. Add your writing to your portfolio. Now that you have read two stories and have written one of your own, think about your writing process. Write your thoughts in a letter to your teacher or to yourself and attach it to your story. The following questions may help you.

- What surprised me as I wrote my story?
- What was easiest about writing my story? What was hardest?
- Which responses from my peer readers helped me most?
- What kind of help would I ask for next time?
- What techniques did Cynthia Rylant or Adam Baughman use that I would like to try myself?

2. Explore additional writing ideas. See the suggestions for writing a children's book on pages 88–89 and Springboards on page 90.

Children's Book

Starting from LITERATURE

What were your favorite books when you were a child? What thoughts would you like to share with children? Aruna Chandrasekhar, a young writer, said, "I feel so sad when I read how oil spills threaten the lives of animals." She turned this sadness into a story that she hoped would teach children how important it is to protect wildlife and our environment.

As you read the opening pages of her story, look for ways that it might appeal to children.

Oliver was a sea otter pup who lived in the ocean. He and his mother were part of a large group of otters called a *raft*.

Every day Oliver and the other pups splashed about and played in the water. They liked to swim among the leafy stalks of kelp that grew up from the ocean floor.

6

From OLIVER and the OIL SPILL

written and illustrated by
ARUNA CHANDRASEKHAR

The mother otters stayed busy too. They dived many times to the bottom of the ocean to hunt for shellfish to eat.

Before the mothers dived, they always wrapped long strands of kelp around their pups. They did not want the pups to drift away and get lost in the big ocean.

7

Think & Respond

How do you feel about the otters? What do you think might happen to them? What makes the illustrations appropriate for young children?

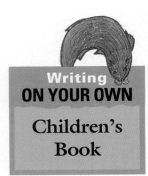

**Writing
ON YOUR OWN**

Children's Book

**INVITATION
TO
*Write***

A children's book can tell a story about the real world, as *Oliver and the Oil Spill* does, or it can create an imaginary world in words and pictures. A children's book can also teach a lesson, such as why something happens or what the colors of the rainbow are.

Write and illustrate a children's book that tells a story or teaches a lesson.

Writing
TIP

You might begin exploring your story idea by drawing pictures. Sketch characters, the setting, or any action that comes to mind.

EXPLORING A CHILD'S WORLD

1. Remember being a child. In small groups, brainstorm about your childhoods. What were you interested in? Which books did you enjoy? If you have younger brothers and sisters, observe what interests them. Freewrite about any ideas that appeal to you.

2. Read children's books. Ask your librarian or the owner of a children's bookstore which children's books are the most popular. You might choose a subject from one of those books that interests you. Then use this subject as the basis of a cluster.

CREATING YOUR
CHILDREN'S BOOK

1. Begin putting your ideas on paper. You can start writing any part of your story that you have ideas about. Just begin to write and see where your ideas lead. Doing a drawing of the setting or the characters may help get your words flowing.

2. Keep your audience in mind. Use ideas and language that your readers can understand. Aruna wrote her story for third and fourth graders, but it can also be read to younger children.

Writer's Choice   Do you want to write your story in rhyme? Rhyming books can be fun to write as well as to read.

3. Don't forget the pictures.   Art is a very important part of children's books. As you write, be thinking of pictures that can help explain your story and support the words you use. You don't have to be an artist; you can make simple drawings or cutouts, or use photographs or pictures from magazines.

Notice how Aruna's drawings support her words in two ways. They show readers what kelp looks like, and they illustrate the otters' playfulness.

REVIEWING YOUR BOOK

1. Try it out.   Read or show the draft of your book to several children of the appropriate age. What do they like best? What do they want to know more about?

2. Decide what changes to make.   Read your book over and think about the children's reactions to it. You might ask several friends to respond to it as well.

3. Don't forget the cover.   The cover of your book should be colorful and lively so that it makes readers want to open it. A clever title can also help catch your readers' attention.

PUBLISHING AND PRESENTING

- **Present your book to a group of children.**   As a class or in small groups, visit a local children's hospital or the primary classes in your school. Read your stories to the children, or have a child volunteer to read them aloud.

- **Take a class field trip to the library.**   Make arrangements to read your books to the children who come for story hour.

- **Publish your book.**   Send your book to a company that publishes children's books. Check *Market Guide for Young Writers,* which is available at your local library, for a list of these companies.

COMPUTER TIP

The computer can help you illustrate your book. Many computer programs include ready-made "clip art." You can also add your own images to the computer file with a scanner.

Spring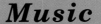boards

History

Imagine that you go back in time and take part in any event in history. Tell the story of that event from your own point of view. Be sure to describe the setting, the other participants, and the action. You might want to do some research on the event itself and get background information on the styles, speech, and daily life of the time.

A guard stands at what is left of the wall that separated him from his countrymen for almost thirty years.

Music

Write and perform a rap. Think about how to best use words, rhythm, and action to tell your story. You can play the parts of several characters yourself or work together with a friend.

SCIENCE

Create a book for young children that explains a concept in science or mathematics in simple terms. You might explain thunder, animal camouflage, subtraction, or fractions. Include colorful illustrations to help get your point across.

Media

Create a teaching videotape for young children. For example, you might create a tape teaching the alphabet by photographing things in nature that begin with each letter of the alphabet. You might also make a tape that teaches about flowers, buildings, or people. Use your imagination!

Your Passport, Please

English gives you a ticket to travel, especially when it comes to things you eat and wear. Let's say you pull on some jeans, meet your friends at the mall, and stop for a hamburger. In terms of language you're already something of a world traveler.

That word *mall* comes from an Italian game, *pallamaglio,* meaning ball and mallet. The English played the game on quiet little streets called pall mall lanes. Soon these "malls" became nice places to stroll and shop and find a bite to eat.

Those jeans you're wearing got their name from Genoa, Italy, the origin of the strong fabric used in jeans. A similar fabric was made in Nîmes, France, so cloth from Nîmes (*de Nîmes* in French) was called—you guessed it—denim. Still another variety of this tough cloth was made in India, in a place called Dhungaree. Got it? If you call your dungarees "levis," however, you owe the word to Levi Strauss, who started making work clothes in California in the 1870s.

Shopping in a mall, you might see anything from a tuxedo to a bikini. You'd see cashmere, suede,

cardigans, argyles, leotards—the list goes on. Each of these items, a dictionary will tell you, is named after a person or place.

Foods, too, get their names from all over the map. Think of Cheddar cheese, turkey, or French dressing. In England, the fourth Earl of Sandwich wanted to eat at

the table while playing cards. Guess what he came up with. Then try looking up *hamburger, frankfurter, wiener, bologna, mayonnaise, tangerines, lima beans.*

Now you've been all over the world, and you haven't even left the mall.

Sentence

Sentence Openers That Tell Time

Good writers sometimes use clauses as sentence openers to tell when something happened. Notice that each of the sentence openers below has a subject and a verb and answers the question *when*.

Model A   While Teruo was out to lunch, Mr. Sasaki called us aside. (Tells when Mr. Sasaki called them aside)

Toshio Mori, "Say It with Flowers"

Model B   When she heard footsteps on the stairs, she stepped back quickly, closing the door. (Tells when she stepped back quickly)

Mary Lavin, "One Summer"

Model C   As the cool stream gushed over one hand, she spelled into the other the word *water,* first slowly, then rapidly. (Tells she spelled the word)

Helen Keller, "The Most Important Day"

▶ **ON THE MARK**   Use a comma after an introductory clause that tells time to separate it from the rest of the sentence.

A. Combining Sentences   Make a new sentence by putting the underlined part of the second sentence into the first sentence as a sentence opener. Write the complete sentence, putting a comma after the sentence opener.

1. I reached down and picked him up by the neck. I did this when the big fellow didn't show any fight.   **Jesse Stuart, "Old Ben"**

2. It was getting light. This happened by the time Solly reached the highway.
    Lorenz Graham, "Hitchhiker"

3. The carton wobbled, and there was a scratching noise. This happened as she approached her chair.   **E. B. White, *Charlotte's Web***

4. She was snoring gently. Her snoring began before he could dish up the food.
    Flannery O'Connor, "A Good Man Is Hard to Find"

5. Mother asked me if I had enjoyed it. She asked me this after the little party was over and they had all gone home.   **Christy Brown, *My Left Foot***

B. Unscrambling and Imitating Sentences   Unscramble each set of sentence chunks below to create a sentence that matches one of the models on page 92. Then write a sentence of your own that imitates each model. Be sure each of your sentences starts with a sentence opener that contains a subject and a verb and tells time.

1. Write sentences that imitate Model A.
   the captain took us / on deck / while the ship's crew worked up / below

2. Write sentences that imitate Model B.
   we rushed forward anxiously / on the field / joining the crowd / when we saw the teams

3. Write sentences that imitate Model C.
   first fearfully, then cheerfully / as the roller coaster plunged / toward the ground / we screamed / our reaction / into the air

C. Expanding Sentences   Use your imagination to add a sentence opener that tells time to each sentence below. Start your openers with words such as *while, when, before,* and *after.*

1. ∧ Each of the ladies had a chocolate moustache on her upper lip.
   Ray Bradbury, "The Whole Town's Sleeping"

2. ∧ I was starving to death.   **Jean McCord, "The Long Way Around"**

3. ∧ I had awful nightmares about it.   **Mary Whitebird, "Ta-Na-E-Ka"**

4. ∧ Rollie ran back to get her to play with him.
   Dorothy Canfield Fisher, "The Apprentice"

5. ∧ Oz sent word to his people that he was going to make a visit to a great brother Wizard who lived in the clouds.
   L. Frank Baum, *The Wizard of Oz*

Grammar Refresher   Clauses that tell time are examples of subordinate clauses. To learn more about subordinate clauses, see Handbook 44, "Using Compound and Complex Sentences," pages 565–569.

- Why is the snake on the left laughing? Freewrite in your journal about the problem the snake's invention solved.

THE FAR SIDE   By GARY LARSON

Put 'er there, Rob... Ha ha ha ha ha ha!..

© 1987 Universal Press Syndicate

Snake inventors

1·29

- Have you ever come across something you didn't recognize—something that made you ask, "What's this for?" Find a tool or gadget you've never seen or used before (kitchen drawers or hardware stores are good places to look), and write a description of the problem you think the gadget is supposed to solve.

- Draw or paint a picture of a problem you face. It may be a problem in your personal life or something in society you wish you could change.

Show, Don't Tell

When you explain a problem, you can use a true story to show how important the problem really is. Try turning one of the *telling* sentences below into a *showing* paragraph. Use an anecdote or example to explain the particular problem.

- My allowance just doesn't cover my expenses anymore.
- People sometimes think the wrong thing about me.

4

Informative Writing: Explaining *How*

Guided Assignment
Problems and Solutions

Related Assignment
Group Discussion

Writing is a great way to discover and understand what you think about your world. Do you have a problem? Exploring it in writing may lead you to a good solution. Are you faced with a tough decision? Writing about it can help you make the choice that's right for you. The guided assignment in this workshop will show you how to explain problems and explore solutions. The related assignment offers you the opportunity to discuss an important subject with your classmates and then write about your thoughts and feelings.

Problems and Solutions

Starting from LITERATURE

You will face many problems throughout your life. Everyone does. Mark Salzman realized he had a big problem on his hands when a drawing he gave to a Chinese family as a gift led to a clash of cultures. How does his solution make everyone happy?

From

IRON & SILK

by
Mark Salzman

I had walked along the river many times since meeting the fisherman that day in winter, but I did not see him again until spring. It was late afternoon, and I had bicycled to a point along the river about a mile downstream from where we had met, hoping to find a deserted spot to draw a picture. I found a niche in the sloping flood wall and started drawing a junk[1] moored not far from me. Half an hour passed, and just as I finished the drawing, I heard someone calling my Chinese name. I looked down to see Old Ding scrambling up the flood wall, his boat anchored behind him. . . . He squatted down beside me and . . . asked me what I was doing. I showed him the drawing, and his face lit up. "Just like it! Just like the boat!" He cupped his hands to his mouth and yelled something in the direction of the junk, and

1. **junk**—a flat-bottomed boat used in China and other Asian countries.

right away a family appeared on deck. "Let's show it to them!" he said, and dragged me down to the water. He exchanged a few words with the family, and they leapt into action, the women going into the sheltered part of the junk to prepare food and the men rowing out to meet us in one of two tiny boats lashed to the side. We got in the little boat and returned with them to the junk. We ate a few snacks of different kinds of salted fish, had tea, and then I showed them the drawing. They seemed delighted by it, so I tore the sheet out of my block. I handed it to the oldest member of the family, a man in his sixties, who opened his eyes wide with surprise and would not take it, saying, "How can I take this? It is a work of art; what do I have to offer you in return?" I laughed, saying that it was only a drawing, and I would be happy if he would take it just for fun. But he was serious; when at last he accepted it, putting it down carefully on the bed, he began negotiating with Old Ding to choose an appropriate gift for me.

Fifteen minutes of vigorous discussion, all in dialect, produced a decision: they would give me one of the rowboats. I looked at Old Ding and said that that was absolutely ridiculous, that of course I would not take a boat from a poor fisherman's family in return for a charcoal sketch. . . . I realized that the situation was serious, for if I refused and left, they would no doubt carry the rowboat to my house and lay it on the front porch. . . . "That is a very fine gift, it is worth thousands of drawings like that one, but we Americans have a custom, and that is we speak directly. If we want something, we say so. . . . The boat is very fine, but there is something I want more." They all smiled and nodded and said that of course I could have whatever I wanted, but I could see they were deeply nervous. . . . "In my country, we have a superstition. If someone gives you a piece of art, like a painting or a poem, you must give him a piece of art in return, or the feeling will be spoiled. If I take the boat, I will feel sad. I would prefer that a member of your family sing a folk song from your hometown." The family, almost hysterical with relief, cheered my decision, saying it had "true spirit," and each of them sang something for me.

Think & Respond

Does the kind of problem Mark Salzman describes remind you of a problem you faced? What effect does Salzman's use of dialogue have on you as you read the story?

One Student's Writing

THE BUGLE

Letters to the Editor

Play Ball!

My friends are already asking each other, "What're you going to do this summer?" Well, I know what I won't be doing. Even though I love baseball, I won't be going to any major-league games, and I won't be rooting for the local major-league team. The reason is simple. There is no local major-league team in North Dakota. There's none in South Dakota or in Montana or even in Wyoming. The closest major-league team is the Minnesota Twins, and that's over 300 miles away!

When I'm old enough to drive, I'll probably go watch the Twins at least once a summer. Right now, though, my parents can't take off work for two days to drive me to the other side of Minnesota and back, and none of my friends' parents can either. We'll all probably do what we do every summer—yell our heads off for the Cardinals, the local semipro team. We'll also drive 90 miles into Fargo to watch the North Dakota State University Bisons play. We'll have fun, but I can't help thinking how great it would be if there were just one major-league team somewhere between Minneapolis and Seattle.

The problem is that getting a major-league team costs money. Any city that wants a team has to have enough money to build a stadium. The city also has to have a big enough population to support the team. Fargo is the biggest city in North Dakota, and it only has about 74,000 people. That's not enough to support a major-league franchise. Sports stadiums often hold more people than Fargo has!

Even though the towns around here aren't exactly huge, there are a lot of die-hard baseball fans like me and my friends. So here's my plan. Why couldn't a couple

"Well, it's not the Twins but it's all we have."

of towns get together to build a stadium and start a team? For example, Moorhead, Minnesota, is right next to Fargo. They already share the same airport and the metropolitan area has about 150,000 people. That might be enough to support a team. If it's not, then maybe Grand Forks, or even Aberdeen, could join in too.

People might say you'd have a problem naming a team that was supported by cities in two or three different states. I think baseball fans would be so happy to have a team, they wouldn't really care what it was called. We could just call the team the Northern Stars, or something like that, and everyone would be happy.

People also might have a problem spending so much money on a baseball team when times are so hard. It's true that a lot of people here are struggling, and they need all the help they can get. However, a major-league team actually might bring in more money. The people from out of town who came to see the team play would have to eat in local restaurants, sleep in hotels, and buy gas and other things. It would be good for business.

Let's think about my plan. If enough people wrote to the Fargo and Moorhead city governments, maybe the idea could be put on a ballot. Big-league baseball is supposed to be our national pastime. Shouldn't we be able to be a part of it too?

BLAIR NYGARD,
JEFFERSON JUNIOR HIGH SCHOOL

Think & Respond

Respond as a Reader

▶ What do you think of Blair's ideas?

▶ Why do you think Blair's solution will or won't work?

Respond as a Writer

▶ How does Blair introduce the problem she wants to solve?

▶ How does Blair address the objections people might have to her solution?

INVITATION
— TO —
Write

Mark Salzman and Blair Nygard wrote about problems
they faced and cared about. Writing about problems and
solutions and sharing your ideas with others is often a
first step toward making real change.

**Think of a problem that interests you or bothers
you. Write about the problem, and tell your readers
how it might be solved.**

PREWRITE AND EXPLORE

1. Think about problems. You can get ideas for writing by
noticing what's on your mind right now. Are you having problems
getting along with a friend or family member? Is there something
at school or in your neighborhood that you would like to change?
Try one or more of the following activities to help your thinking.

Exploring Topics

- **Journal search** Does some problem keep reappearing in
  your journal? It might be an issue to write about. You might
  also jot down two or three new issues and try **freewriting**
  about one of them.

- **If you ruled the world** What would you change if you had
  the power? Try **brainstorming** with classmates about problems related to school, the community, or the world.

- **Reading literature** Think about the characters in short
  stories and novels you've read. What problems did they face?
  What advice could you give them? Write notes in your
  journal about the character that interests you most and his or
  her problem.

2. Explore a problem.   Sift through your ideas and decide which problem you most want to write about. Then use these activities to explore it further:

- **Examine the problem.**   The "5 W + H" questions can help you find out what you know—and what you want to know—about a problem. Try writing answers to questions such as these: What causes the problem? When did it start? Whom does it affect? Where is it a problem? Why should something be done about it? How have people tried to solve it?

- **Get ideas from others.**   Form small discussion groups to explore problems further. Ask each other questions about the problems and try out possible solutions. Afterwards, **freewrite** about any thoughts sparked by your discussion.

- **Look for answers.**   You may need to dig deeper to find information about the problem and possible solutions. Would **library research** help you find answers you need? Is there an expert you could interview? Take notes on your findings.

PROBLEM SOLVING

"What am I trying to accomplish by writing about this problem?"

For help with understanding your purpose and personal goals, see

- Handbook 3, "General Purpose and Specific Goals," pages 231–232

One Student's Process

Blair Nygard used the "5 W + H" questions to explore a problem that was important to her. She knew that some of the answers she uncovered could be useful as she drafted her piece.

<u>Who's affected?</u> Me. My friends. Baseball lovers.

<u>Where is the problem?</u> Everywhere between Washington state and Minnesota; there's no team between those two states.

<u>What causes the problem?</u> No money, no big cities.

<u>When did it start?</u> I don't know. Maybe it doesn't matter.

<u>Why should something be done?</u> It would be fun. Baseball's the national pastime. We shouldn't miss out.

<u>How have people tried to solve the problem?</u> They haven't. I'd like to see people think about it, write letters, maybe even vote on it.

1. Begin drafting. You've already done some writing while thinking about the problem you've chosen. Now you can begin a draft, following where your ideas lead. Start where you feel comfortable—with the introduction, with an explanation of the problem, with a possible solution, or even with the conclusion. If you run out of ideas, it's all right to jump to another part. You can work out the order and smooth out the jumps when you revise.

Most problem-solution writings end up with these parts:

- **An introduction** This part should catch your readers' attention. Blair Nygard uses a quotation in her introduction; Mark Salzman begins with a personal anecdote. You might start by directly telling readers why they should care about the problem, or you could use a statistic, a description, or an example to introduce the problem.

- **An explanation of the problem** If you didn't state the problem directly in your introduction, do it now. You can then explain the problem's causes, its effects, or its importance. Be sure to support your ideas with specific facts, examples, anecdotes, or other details.

- **A proposal for a solution** This part tells what you think would solve the problem, and why the solution would work. Blair offers a plan in the fourth paragraph. She then backs up her ideas by addressing the specific objections some people might have to her proposed solution.

- **A conclusion** The conclusion can take different forms. Mark Salzman's conclusion shows how his problem was actually solved. Blair Nygard's conclusion, however, urges readers to take action and support her proposal. A conclusion may also warn what will happen if the solution is ignored.

2. Let your draft suggest a form. Problem-solution writing can take many forms. Mark Salzman chose to tell a story. Blair Nygard wrote a letter to the editor. You might choose one of these options, or you might write a letter of advice, an opinion piece for the editorial page of a newspaper, or a proposal.

PROBLEM

S O L V I N G

"How can I best explain why this problem is important?"

For tips on supporting your ideas, see

- Handbook 11, "Elaboration," pages 254–260

Writer's Choice   Do you want to write an explanation of your problem and your solution? Would you rather write a persuasive piece, convincing others that your solution is the best one? Choose the form that meets your personal goals.

3. Think about your draft.   When you feel "written out," read over your draft and share it with peer readers when you're ready. These questions can help guide your review.

REVIEW YOUR WRITING

Questions for Yourself
- Which part of my draft do I feel most satisfied with? Why?
- What sections of my draft feel unfinished or need further elaboration?

Questions for Your Peer Readers
- What interested you most in my draft?
- What questions do you have or what additional information do you need to understand the problem better?
- What are *your* views on the problem I've written about?
- What objections can you think of to the solution I've offered?

One Student's Process

Here is part of Blair's first draft. Read the comments one friend made. What would you have said about this part of Blair's draft?

The problem is that getting a major-league team costs money. Anyone who wants a team has to have enough money to build a stadium. A city also has to have a big enough population to support the team. Even though the towns around here aren't exactly huge. There are a lot of diehard baseball fans like me and my friends. So here's my plan. Why couldn't a couple of towns get together to build a stadium and start a team?

Peer Reader Comments

I like that you take on a big problem—one that is important to you.

Isn't Fargo big enough?

Which towns could work together?

1. Look over your responses. Is your message getting across? Your readers' comments and your own responses to the questions on page 103 can help you find ways to revise your writing. If your readers miss your point, you might add more specific examples to elaborate on your explanation. If readers disagree with you, look for ways to win them over. Keep in mind, though, that this is your writing. Make the kinds of changes you think will improve your presentation of the problem and solution.

2. Look at the problem again. Now that you've written more about the problem, you probably understand it better. What additional facts, opinions, statistics, anecdotes, or examples could make your explanation even stronger? Also, look back over your early freewriting. It may contain phrases or ideas you want to add now.

3. Check your solution. Is your solution well thought out and complete? Remember, some people might oppose your solution, but that doesn't mean it isn't good. Just be sure you have noted and responded to the objections that others would make.

LINKING
GRAMMAR AND WRITING

Using Adverbs

When you write about problems and solutions, be careful not to overstate your case. Adverbs such as *usually, often, frequently,* and *sometimes* help limit or qualify statements.

Original
> Sports stadiums hold more people than Fargo has! (Not <u>all</u> stadiums are that large.)

Revised
> Sports stadiums <u>often</u> hold more people than Fargo has!

For more information on adverbs, see Handbook 42, "Using Adverbs," pages 516–530.

Paragraphs at Work   Limit each paragraph in your problem-solution composition to one key section or idea. For example, you might write separate paragraphs for your introduction, your explanation of the problem, your solution, possible objections, and your conclusion. The breaks between paragraphs show when you are moving on to a new idea. Remember these tips.

- Start a new paragraph whenever you start a new idea.
- Limit each paragraph to one main idea.
- Develop each paragraph with sentences that support and explain the main idea.

One Student's Process

Blair thought about her draft and about her friend's comments. Then she made these changes.

Fargo is the biggest city in North Dakota, and it only has about 74,000 people. That's not enough to support a major-league franchise. Sports stadiums often hold more people than Fargo has!

The problem is that getting a major-league team costs money. ~~Anyone who~~ Any city that wants a team has to have enough money to build a stadium. ~~A~~ The city also has to have a big enough population to support the team.   ¶Even though the towns around here aren't exactly huge, There are a lot of die-hard baseball fans like me and my friends. So here's my plan. Why couldn't a couple of towns get together to build a stadium and start a team?

For example, Moorhead, Minnesota, is right next to Fargo. They already share the same airport and the metropolitan area has about 150,000 people.

Problems and
Solutions   **105**

PROOFREAD

1. Proofread your work. After revising, you can check your work for errors in grammar, spelling, punctuation, and capitalization. Use a dictionary and Handbook 19, "Proofreading," pages 288–290, to help you proofread.

Watch for usage errors too. Have you written "you and me" as a subject when you should have written "you and I"? Do your verbs agree with your subjects? Is it always clear which nouns your pronouns are referring to?

2. Make a clean copy of your composition. Once you are satisfied with your work, you can use the Standards for Evaluation, shown in the margin, for one last check. Then make a final copy.

PUBLISH AND PRESENT

- **Hold "Lunchtime Soapbox" presentations.** Take turns making short presentations to your class about the problems and solutions you've written about. You may wish to bring in additional materials, such as books, photographs, and magazines.

- **Put your ideas in the mail.** If you've written about a school, community, or worldwide problem, let others know about your solution. Send your writing to your school or local newspaper or to a magazine that specializes in the subject you've written about. You might want to change the form of your writing from a composition to an editorial or a letter to the editor.

- **Transform your writing into a letter of advice.** Have you written about a personal problem that you think other students might also be facing? If so, you can turn your composition into a general letter of advice that shows others how you suggest solving the problem.

- **Share your ideas with a professional.** Get together with classmates who wrote problem-solution compositions on the same topic you did. Then invite a social worker, community advocate, or local political leader to visit your school. Share your writing and your ideas with him or her.

R EFLECT ON YOUR WRITING

1. Add your writing to your portfolio. Now that you have completed your problem-solution assignment, think about what you have accomplished and how you did it. Write your thoughts in a note to yourself and attach it to your final draft. These questions may help you focus your thoughts.

FOR YOUR
PORTFOLIO

- How did I find a problem to write about? What strategies did I use to come up with a solution?

- What did I learn about the problem I chose? Did it seem simpler or more complicated once I started writing about it? How did my feelings about the problem change as I explored it in writing?

- Did my peer readers understand the point I was making? What kind of helpful advice did my peers offer? Did they suggest any other solutions to the problem?

- What are the special strengths of this piece of writing? What was the easiest part about writing it?

- How does this assignment compare to other types of writing I have done, such as narrative or descriptive writing? Is one easier or more difficult for me? Which type of writing do I enjoy most or find most satisfying?

2. Explore additional writing ideas. See the suggestions on pages 110–111 for participating in a group discussion, and see Springboards on page 112.

Group Discussion

Can you imagine what it would be like to find yourself suddenly without a home? Where would you sleep at night? How would you eat, wash your clothes, and keep yourself clean? Suppose everywhere you went people avoided you, or told you to go somewhere else? Many people in the United States—men, women, and children—face such problems every day. As you read Katie Monagle's article about the homeless, ask yourself, "How would I solve this problem?"

Homeless
in the
United
States

BY KATIE MONAGLE

No issue more vividly symbolizes the problems facing America's cities than homelessness. Over the last ten years, the number of homeless has grown to tremendous proportions, with an estimated 3 million people living in the streets or in crowded shelters.

But as the numbers have increased, the sympathy of many city dwellers has diminished. They have grown tired of seeing the homeless everywhere— sleeping or panhandling in public places. They've also grown weary of government inability to deal with the homeless.

City governments are responding by "getting tough" with homeless people. In New York, the police are kicking homeless people out of bus and subway stations, where they have traditionally sought shelter in winter. In San Francisco, the homeless are being swept out of parks and public beaches. Beleaguered mayors say that

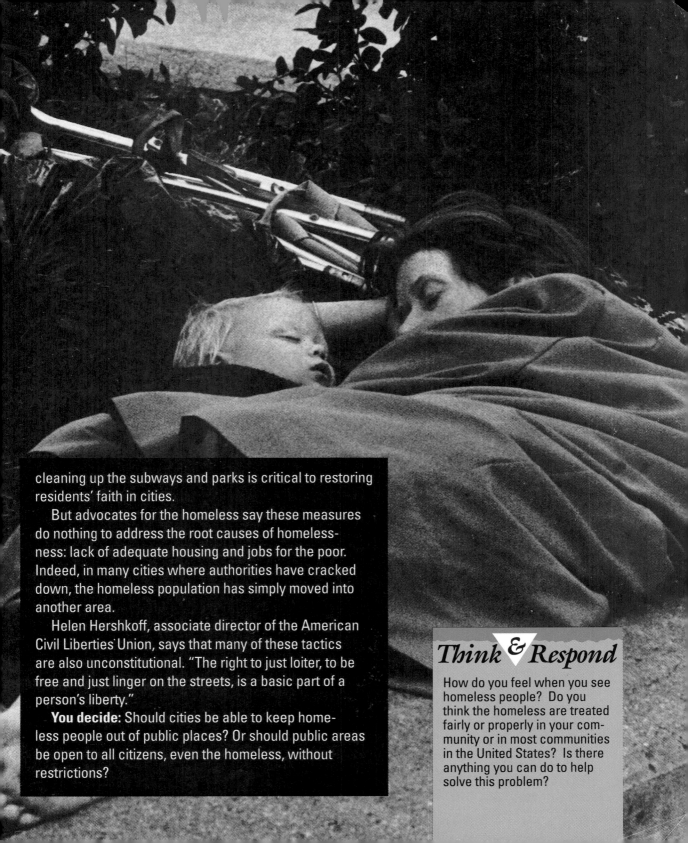

cleaning up the subways and parks is critical to restoring residents' faith in cities.

But advocates for the homeless say these measures do nothing to address the root causes of homelessness: lack of adequate housing and jobs for the poor. Indeed, in many cities where authorities have cracked down, the homeless population has simply moved into another area.

Helen Hershkoff, associate director of the American Civil Liberties Union, says that many of these tactics are also unconstitutional. "The right to just loiter, to be free and just linger on the streets, is a basic part of a person's liberty."

You decide: Should cities be able to keep homeless people out of public places? Or should public areas be open to all citizens, even the homeless, without restrictions?

Think & Respond

How do you feel when you see homeless people? Do you think the homeless are treated fairly or properly in your community or in most communities in the United States? Is there anything you can do to help solve this problem?

INVITATION
━━ TO ━━
Write

When it comes to solving problems, no one has all the right answers. In fact, one of the best ways to find solutions to difficult problems like homelessness is to get together with others and talk things over. When people share ideas, they also share different ways of looking at the world. Such sharing can lead to creative solutions.

Take part in a group discussion about the problem Katie Monagle presents. Look for effective solutions to that problem.

Holding a Discussion

1. Gather your thoughts. Begin by thinking about the problem of homelessness. How did Katie Monagle's article make you feel? Have you thought about the problem before now? You might freewrite to explore your thoughts. You also might want to research the problem before you meet with your discussion group.

2. Assign roles. It may help to select a chairperson to lead the discussion, to encourage everyone to take part, and to keep the discussion orderly. You also might choose someone to be the recorder, a person who takes notes on what is said.

3. Begin the discussion. The chairperson should introduce the problem and state the purpose of the discussion. In this case, you are meeting to discuss possible solutions to the problem of homeless people seeking shelter in public places. Everyone in the group will want to keep these suggestions in mind:

- **Speak up.** Present your ideas clearly and confidently. Support them with whatever facts or examples you may have. Don't be afraid to say things that others might disagree with. The goal of the discussion is to examine the problem from all sides.

- **Listen actively.**   Active listening means more than just listening politely. It means thinking about what you hear. Hold off responding to what someone has said until you are sure you understand—and can summarize—what he or she was trying to say. Active listeners also respect the opinions of others.

- **Look for other points of view.**   Has your group examined the problem from more than one angle? Who else might have an opinion about the issue you've discussed? To look at the problem in a new way, try taking on another person's point of view. For example, what would a homeless woman with children say to you about her many difficulties?

4. Sum up the discussion.   To end the discussion, the chairperson might give a brief summary of key ideas or solutions that have been discussed. The recorder, having taken notes, can add any important points the chairperson might have missed.

REVIEWING THE DISCUSSION

1. Share discussion notes.   The recorder should share his or her notes with the group. Group members can clarify points or share ideas that they may have jotted down during the discussion. Note which comments were particularly helpful in making the discussion fruitful and respectful.

2. Write a summary.   You can work as a group to write a summary of the discussion. The summary should state the problem, explain the group's feelings about the problem, and present any solutions or proposals the group has developed.

PUBLISHING AND PRESENTING

- **Share your summary.**   Send your summary to an organization working on the problem. You can attach a letter introducing your group and explaining the purpose of your discussion.

- **Write a letter.**   You might turn your summary into a letter to the editor of a school or community newspaper, or you might write to your mayor or another local politician.

Spring boards

Science
Think about great scientific discoveries that have been made. Imagine you were the laboratory assistant for a scientist who made a great breakthrough. Describe the problem the scientist faced and how he or she solved it (with your help, of course).

Journalism
You have been chosen to write a new advice column for teenagers. Choose a problem faced by people your age, and write about it in your first column.

Speaking and Listening
What would you say if you were called to Washington, D.C., to tell the government how to solve a national problem? Prepare a speech you could give to a Congressional committee presenting your solution.

History
Imagine you are living in some earlier time in history. Think about the events happening throughout the world at that time. Write about a problem and suggest a solution. For example, imagine that you are the fifteenth century navigator Christopher Columbus. You might write a letter to Queen Isabella of Spain telling her about the need to find a faster sea route to the Orient. Your suggestion? Sail west! Ask the queen to finance your voyage.

THE FAR SIDE

By GARY LARSON

NINA — EAT OUR WAKE PINTAHEADS!

PINTA

SANTA MARIA

LITERATURE
Science fiction often looks into the future. Now *you* try looking ahead in time. What new inventions do you see? Write about a future gadget that would solve a problem people face today.

My Hot Water Fossil Is Extinct

Young children often have their own very special understanding of what words mean. A nursery school teacher sent some of her students' definitions to newspaper columnist Jack Smith.

Accident—Whenever you did something that your mother doesn't like what you did.

Analogy—You sneeze and stuff.

Cheap—You don't have to give the store man all your money.

Cheap—A bird.

Extinct—When something's not working.

Family—A thing that you live with.

Family—Where animals and people live together.

Florist—Puts the floor on.

Fossil—The wet sand and something on top of it like a dead fish or a dead man and it turns into a fossil when it dries up and the man doesn't even know it.

Fossil—It makes hot water come out of it.

Fun—Walking up a slide in tennis shoes.

Germ—Like someone breathes at you.

Moisture—My sister found a moisture and she found a pearl in it.

Problem—Someone wants you to do what you don't want to do.

Secret—Only letting yourself know.

Surprise—You can't wait and you don't know what it is but you want it.

Terminate—Someone comes and sprays around your house.

Trouble—You go to your room and stay for a year. It rains and you can't go out and your sister can.

Sentence

Subject-Verb Splits: Phrases

Professional writers sometimes add phrases or clauses between the subject and verb of a sentence. These subject-verb (S-V) splits provide additional information about the subject of the sentence. Each of the S-V splits in the sentences below is a phrase that adds details about the subject.

Model A   One of the dogs, <u>the best one</u>, had disappeared.
Fred Gipson, *Old Yeller*

Model B   Taran, <u>hunched against a tree root</u>, pulled his cloak closer about his shoulders.   **Lloyd Alexander, *The Book of Three***

Model C   Professor Kazan, <u>wearing a spotlessly white tropical suit and a wide-brimmed hat</u>, was the first ashore.
Arthur C. Clarke, *Dolphin Island*

▶ **ON THE MARK**   Use commas to set off a phrase used as a S-V split.

A. Combining Sentences   Make a new sentence by putting the underlined part of the second sentence into the first sentence at the caret (∧) as a S-V split. Write the complete sentence, putting commas before and after the S-V split.

1. The others ∧ yelled for something to happen. They were <u>clapping hands</u>.
Ray Bradbury, *The Martian Chronicles*

2. The nest ∧ didn't show from the road. The nest was <u>high in a double-topped pine at the foot of the hill</u>.   **Ruth E. Hampton, "Diaries Are for Secrets"**

3. Mr. Jamison ∧ was putting some papers into his briefcase. He was <u>sitting next to Big Ma</u>.   **Mildred D. Taylor, *Roll of Thunder, Hear My Cry***

4. A crow ∧ attracted the eye and nose of a fox. The crow was <u>perched in a tree with a piece of cheese in his beak</u>.   **James Thurber, "The Fox and the Crow"**

5. Mr. Lema ∧ greeted me and assigned me a desk. He was <u>the sixth-grade teacher</u>.   **Francisco Jiménez, "The Circuit"**

B. Unscrambling and Imitating Sentences Unscramble each set of sentence chunks below to create a sentence that matches one of the models on page 114. Then write a sentence of your own that imitates each model. Be sure each of your sentences has a S-V split.

1. Write sentences that imitate Model A.
the tallest player / was fouled / one of the starters

2. Write sentences that imitate Model B.
dressed like a miniature Robin Hood / Delvon / with a bright green mask / covered his face completely

3. Write sentences that imitate Model C.
the sci-fi movie / seemed outdated now / predicting space travel and a fully computerized house

C. Expanding Sentences Use your imagination to add a phrase as a S-V split where the caret appears in each of the following sentences. Set off each phrase with commas.

1. George ˄ frowned as he thought.

John Steinbeck, *Of Mice and Men*

2. The Scarecrow ˄ thanked Oz warmly and went back to his friends.

L. Frank Baum, *The Wizard of Oz*

3. Walters and Williams ˄ looked grimly at each other, and tried not to laugh.

Edward Everett Hale, "The Man Without a Country"

4. The kitchen ˄ had a rich, bold, musty smell.

Elizabeth Enright, "Nancy"

5. One of the men ˄ began to speak, grinning a little.

Ursula K. Le Guin, *Tehanu*

Grammar Refresher Some S-V splits are appositives. To learn more about punctuating appositives, see Handbook 47, "Punctuation," pages 634–636.

- What two words were combined to form the term *hozone?* What other silly word combinations can you make up to define a place or an object?

- Make up a word to capture the character of each of these things: the hook on the end of a tape measure, the sound a revolving door makes as it turns, and the smell of freshly cut onions.

- Write a poem that defines Saturday afternoon.

"Hozone"

Show, Don't Tell

Telling someone what a word means isn't always the best way to get your message across. Showing what the word means with an example or series of examples helps others understand the meaning. Try turning one of these *telling* sentences into a *showing* paragraph using examples.

- A *best friend* is more than just a friend.
- *Cool* is a popular word.

5

Informative Writing: Explaining *What*

Guided Assignment
Informing and Defining

Related Assignment
Comparison and Contrast

"What is that?" You have been asking that question in one form or another since you were a young child. You will probably continue asking it as long as you live. Why? Simply because at school, at work, and at play, people always want to understand the world around them. In this workshop, you will explore two different ways of answering the question "What is that?" Both will help you explain the world to others, and perhaps to yourself as well.

Informing and Defining

Starting from LITERATURE

When you want to know the meaning of a word or term, you can look it up in the dictionary. Often, though, the brief dictionary definition doesn't tell you everything you want to know. That is why people often explore things and ideas in longer articles. Marjorie Jackson wrote the following article to teach others about *wayang kulit* performances. As you read, notice the different ways she describes her subject to show its unique characteristics.

BY MARJORIE JACKSON

After sundown in the island country of Indonesia, crowds gather in front of white screens to watch *wayang kulit* performances, the dramatic shadow puppet plays that have been a part of Indonesian culture for many hundreds of years. Cymbals clang and drums thump as fanged giants lumber across the screen. Everyone laughs to see clowns argue and bite each other's noses, or watch monkeys soar in wild games of leapfrog.

Wayang kulit is one of the most popular and entertaining arts of Indonesia. The plays are often staged in open courtyards, and once the music begins, the whole village stops to watch. Children perch in trees, and others sit on mats, but important guests are given chairs. Even today a *wayang* performance is thought to work a special magic. A powerful *dalang,* or puppet master, is said to bring protection and good fortune to all who attend. Long ago, kings sponsored frequent *wayang* performances hoping to keep their country safe. At that time, the *dalangs'* skills were secrets they passed on only to sons or grandsons.

Today, schools teach the necessary skills. It takes years of training for *dalangs* to learn to work the puppets for the eight or nine hours needed to complete a play. A three-foot-high puppet

FROM
SHADOW PUPPETS of INDONESIA

weighs as much as five pounds and must be held slightly above the head at arm's length for minutes at a time. Learning to twirl the control rods smoothly is what gives the illusion of life to the *wayang* puppet. Students are also expected to memorize all of the stories from beginning to end and be able to sing and speak in many different voices. . . .

Today, a full set of *wayang kulit* might contain six hundred puppets, but usually only forty or fifty are needed at one performance. The *dalang* arrives wearing a printed sarong and headcloth. He sits cross-legged next to the screen, on the side away from the audience, and takes his puppets from their box. He then spreads incense over them. A bright coconut oil lamp hangs overhead to cast the puppets' shadows onto the screen. . . . The *dalang* gently shakes the puppets to make them move. The puppet master moves new characters quickly on or off stage so that his hands won't cast shadows. A figure appears to grow in size when he moves it toward the screen, and then it blurs when he pulls it away. At the moment of blurring, the *dalang* can exchange two puppets, giving the illusion of changing a beautiful maiden into an ogre, or a lion into a knight. . . .

At sunrise the last battle has been won, and the final gong is sounded. Some of the crowd are caught napping. The puppets fade from the screen and are folded into their box. Everyone has laughed and cried, and now they will go home content. The *wayang kulit* performance was a success. It has been "written in the world," as the Indonesians say, and its goodness will be lasting.

Think & Respond

How would you explain *wayang kulit* to someone else? What types of details does Marjorie Jackson use to explain her subject? What aspect of American culture—perhaps a special event or celebration—could you compare to the Indonesian *wayang kulit*?

One Student's Writing

Marjorie Jackson defined and explained a subject that would be unfamiliar to most readers. Even familiar subjects, however, sometimes need to be explained. Jeff Nichols, thirteen, who keeps a snake for a pet, was frustrated by the strange ideas his friends had about snakes. He wrote this article to clear up some of the misconceptions.

The Truth About Snakes
by Jeff Nichols

Do you think snakes are evil, slimy, scary creatures? Many people do. Throughout history, people have feared snakes because of their strange appearance and the reputation of deadly poisonous snakes. However, many fears really are the result of false stories and false ideas.

Snakes are members of the reptile family. Like other reptiles, they are coldblooded and their bodies are covered with scales. Unlike most other reptiles, they don't have any legs, movable eyelids, or outside ear openings. Their appearance is probably their most interesting feature. They look like long stuffed socks or slinky cylinders. They can have many different colors and designs on their skins.

People have many false ideas about snakes. They often think snakes are slimy, like eels, but snakeskin is smooth and dry. Many people also believe all snakes are poisonous. However, most snakes are harmless. Another myth is that snakes can slither across the ground at high speeds. In fact, most snakes only go about one mile per hour.

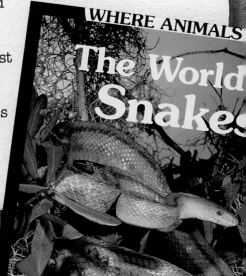

WHERE ANIMALS
The World
Snakes

Legends and myths about snakes are passed on from generation to generation. Most of them contain incorrect information. In 1855 a newspaper published an article about a gigantic snake. The article said this about the snake: "fifty-nine feet, eight inches in length . . . slime a quarter of an inch thick covers the body . . . head the size of a full-grown calf." The story was just a hoax, but stories like this are still repeated today. Another myth tells about the hoop snake, which is supposed to form a hoop by taking its tail in its mouth. Then it rolls down a hill and flings itself at its enemy, stinging the enemy with its deadly tail. Herpetologists, scientists who study snakes and other reptiles, say no such snake exists.

Despite these frightening images, snakes are actually useful animals. Farmers use them to control pests such as mice and rats. In some parts of the world, including Japan, China, and even the United States, people eat the meat of snakes. It is said that snake meat tastes something like chicken. Even the venom of poisonous snakes isn't all bad. It is used in medicines and for medical research.

People sometimes dislike or fear things they don't understand. Snakes are a victim of this lack of knowledge. Most snakes are harmless to people and helpful to the environment. Instead of fearing snakes, we should learn to appreciate them.

Think & Respond

Respond as a Reader

▶ What new information about snakes did you learn from Jeff's essay?

▶ Do you think Jeff accomplished his purpose? Why?

Respond as a Writer

▶ What details did Jeff include to show that snakes can benefit people?

▶ What features of Jeff's opening and closing paragraphs are particularly effective?

INVITATION
═ TO ═
Write

Marjorie Jackson wrote an explanation of *wayang kulit* to inform others about one aspect of Indonesian culture. Jeff Nichols wrote about snakes to clear up misconceptions about them. Often a good way to explain something new is to include a definition.

Write a composition that informs and defines a subject that interests you. Write so that your readers will learn how to look at something in a new way.

PREWRITE AND EXPLORE

1. Look for ideas. What special knowledge would you like to share with others? Would you like to explain something about your culture or about a favorite hobby or sport? Perhaps you'd rather write about an idea, such as friendship or courage. Try one or more of these activities to help you find a topic.

Exploring Topics

- **UFO's** Imagine you are an alien who lands on Earth and knows nothing about the Earth's environment, its people, or its many cultures. What would puzzle you most about this new planet? Get together with classmates and **brainstorm** some questions an alien visitor might ask about planet Earth.

- **Shades of gray** What things or ideas do people view differently? You might think spiders are fascinating, for example, while someone else might think they're hideous. Review your **journal** for topics you can explore further.

- **Reading literature** Think about characters in stories you have read. What special qualities did they have? Were they brave, fearful, sly, or clumsy? Use your ideas to **freewrite** a passage that begins with a phrase like "Bravery is . . ."

2. Choose a topic. Choose a topic and freewrite about it. Discover what you know and what you still need to find out.

Writer's Choice Would you like to use humor in your writing? For example, you might poke fun at an idea like popularity or athletic skill, or make an activity like football or dating look ridiculous.

3. Gather information. When you write to inform and define, you need to figure out what is most important for others to know. "Check out" your topic by trying some of these activities:

✔ **Check your dictionary and other reference works.** Look up your subject in a dictionary, encyclopedia, or other reference work. What do you learn that you didn't know before? Take notes on the background or history of your subject.

✔ **Check your senses.** Depending on your subject, you might make a chart of what your subject smells, sounds, tastes, looks, or feels like. Use these sensory details when you write your draft.

✔ **Check your subject's parts.** If you are defining an object or an event, you might make a list of its parts. Marjorie Jackson, for example, describes the most important parts of a *wayang kulit* performance in her article.

PROBLEM

SOLVING

"I just can't seem to find a topic I care about."

To find a meaningful topic, see

• Sketchbook, page 116

• Springboards, page 135

• Handbook 1, "Finding Writing Ideas," pages 218–224

One Student's Process

Jeff Nichols wanted to inform others about snakes, so he made this chart of sensory details to gather his thoughts.

Sight	unlike other animals; like long stuffed socks or slinky cylinders; many different colors
Sound	like nothing I know of; except for rattlesnakes, they don't make noise unless their movement rustles leaves, etc.
Taste	supposed to taste like chicken
Smell	generally no smell at all
Feel	smooth and dry, not slimy

1. Begin your draft. Now it's time to start drafting. Use your prewriting notes to help you explain the unique qualities or characteristics of your subject. Don't worry about where to start or how your writing looks. You don't need to worry about your spelling or grammar, either. You can take the time to polish your writing later.

2. Think about your audience. By now you have done quite a lot of thinking—and writing too—about your topic. Take a moment to think about who is going to read your work. For example, are you writing to a friend in another part of the country or to the readers of your school newspaper? Jot down a few notes to yourself about how much your readers are likely to know about the subject you've chosen.

3. Examine your subject from different angles. You might present a variety of information about your subject. Consider beginning your piece with a brief definition or description of the subject, and then expanding from there.

Notice how Marjorie Jackson organizes her article. First, she briefly states what *wayang kulit* performances are—"the dramatic shadow puppet plays that have been a part of Indonesian culture for many hundreds of years." Next, she describes the setting of a performance, explains the equipment and training needed, and then tells how the puppet master puts on the play. Marjorie Jackson's conclusion chronicles the end of a performance and the dawn of a new day.

Similarly, Jeff Nichols first introduces the topic of his composition. Then, he gives a physical description of snakes. Next, he talks about the misconceptions people have about snakes. Finally, he explains how snakes actually benefit people. Experiment to discover the best way to arrange the details you have gathered.

PROBLEM SOLVING

"I can't decide how to arrange my ideas."

For help organizing your writing, see

• Handbook 7, "Ways of Organizing," pages 238–242

4. Think about your draft.   Are you ready to share your draft with peer readers, or do you want to make some changes first? Here are some questions to ask yourself and your peer readers about your writing.

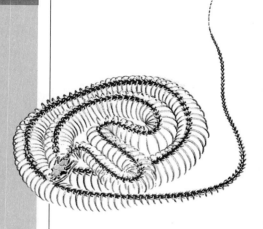

R E V I E W   Y O U R   W R I T I N G

Questions for Yourself
- What is the most important thing I want readers to know about my subject? How can I best show this?
- What examples or details can I add to make my definition clearer? Can I compare my subject to something that is more familiar to my readers?
- What is the best way to organize my information?

Questions for Your Peer Readers
- What stands out most in your memory about my draft?
- Are there places where my writing seems confusing?
- What would you change to make my writing clearer?
- What else do you want to know about my subject?

One Student's Process

Here is part of Jeff's first draft. Notice how one peer reader has responded to the draft.

People have many false ideas about snakes. But I've had a pet snake for more than three years, and I know the truth about snakes. My snake's name is Granger, and he's a great pet. I like to tell people that the myths people beleive about snakes just aren't true.

Legends and myths about snakes are passed on from generation to generation. Most of them contain incorrect information. In 1855 a newspaper published an article about a gigantic snake. The story was just a hoax, but stories like this are still repeated today.

Peer Reader Comments

What kind of false ideas?

Do you really need this information about Granger? It seems out of place.

I'd like to know more about the gigantic snake. Did the paper describe how it looked?

Informing and Defining

1. Review your responses. Look over your own responses and those of your peer readers to see what changes you want to make. Remember, you don't have to make every change suggested to you. Just make the changes that strengthen your piece.

2. Make a comparison. To make your explanation clearer, you might compare and contrast your subject with something more familiar. Jeff Nichols, for example, writes that snakes "look like long stuffed socks or slinky cylinders." He also contrasts snakes' dry skin with the slimy skin of eels.

3. Check your introduction and conclusion. Your introduction should grab your readers' attention. Notice how Marjorie Jackson draws in readers with a vivid, sensory description of a *wayang kulit* performance, complete with clanging cymbals, thumping drums, and laughing spectators. Your introduction may also clearly state your topic. Your final paragraph should provide the reader with a satisfying ending to your writing. In his conclusion, Jeff Nichols tries to convince his readers that snakes are helpful and worthy of our appreciation.

Paragraphs at Work When you write to inform and define, you might discuss a separate aspect of your subject in each paragraph. Follow these guidelines for paragraphing as you revise your writing.

• Each paragraph should elaborate on a key characteristic.
• Support the main idea of each paragraph with specific details and examples; strive to show instead of tell.
• Take out any information that is not related to the main idea of the paragraph.

4. Replace general words with specific ones. Are there some ho-hum places in your writing? Marjorie Jackson doesn't just say that people watch the *wayang kulit* performance. She *shows* when she says "children perch in trees, and others sit on mats." Look for places in your writing where you have used flat, ordinary nouns and verbs and replace them with exciting language that helps your readers see, hear, and feel.

GRAMMAR AND WRITING

Using Appositives

Use an appositive to define or explain a word or term within a sentence. An appositive is often set off from the rest of the sentence with commas.

Original

Herpetologists say no such snake exists. Herpetologists are scientists who study snakes and other reptiles.

Revised

Herpetologists, <u>scientists who study snakes and other reptiles,</u> say no such snake exists.

For more information about using appositives, see Handbook 47, "Punctuation," pages 634–636.

Writing
TIP

Make your writing smoother by using appositives to combine sentences. For more information about when to use appositives, see Handbook 22, "Sentence Combining," pages 300–309.

One Student's Process

Here's how Jeff changed his draft. He made more changes later.

People have many false ideas about snakes. They often think snakes are slimey, like eels, but snake-skin is smooth and dry. People believe snakes are poisonous. However, most snakes are harmless.

Legends and myths about snakes are passed on from generation to generation. Most of them contain incorrect information. In 1855 a newspaper published an article about a gigantic snake. The story was just a hoax, but stories like this are still repeated today.

The article said this about the snake: "fifty-nine feet, eight inches in length . . . slime a quarter of an inch thick covers the body . . . head the size of a full-grown calf."

PROOFREAD

1. Check for correctness. By now you should feel good about what you have written. Now polish your writing by solving grammar, usage, and punctuation problems and correcting misspelled words.

One technique you can use to discover misspelled words is to read your writing backward, one word at a time. Start at the end and read right to left. This will help you slow down and look at each word separately. Use a dictionary to check the spelling of any words you are unsure about.

You may also want to re-examine sentences with appositives to make sure that you have set off the appositives with commas when necessary.

2. Make a clean copy of your writing. Are you ready to prepare your work for presentation or publication now? Use the Standards for Evaluation in the margin for one last check, and make additional changes if necessary. Then make a final copy.

PUBLISH AND PRESENT

- **Make a mini-encyclopedia.** Publish the explanations written by your class as a booklet. You might even think about preparing special volumes on individual themes—inventions, holiday celebrations, hobbies, or personal qualities, for example.

- **Make a bulletin board display.** You might look for photographs of your subject and include them in your display. If you've explained an abstract idea or concept, sketch or paint a picture of what that idea means to you.

- **Deliver a speech.** Turn your written composition into a speech, making note cards to help you remember what you want to say. Then deliver your speech to another class or to an organization that would be interested in your topic.

- **Stage mock television or radio talk shows.** In class, take turns having one student interview another about his or her subject. Invite the "audience" to participate by asking follow-up questions.

REFLECT ON YOUR WRITING

1. Add your writing to your portfolio. Reflect on your experience by writing a note to yourself or to your teacher and attaching it to your final piece. Answering the following questions may help you focus your thoughts.

- How did I find my subject?
- What did I learn about myself or my subject? What did I discover? What surprised me?
- What was the biggest problem I had with this writing assignment? How did I solve it?
- What advice did my peers offer? Did I use their suggestions?
- What would I advise someone else who is doing this kind of writing?

2. Explore other writing ideas. See the suggestions for writing a comparison-contrast composition on pages 132–134 and look at Springboards, page 135.

FOR YOUR
PORTFOLIO

Informing and
Defining

129

Comparison and Contrast

Sometimes the best way to explain or define a subject is by comparing it to something else. That way, you can show how your subject is similar to and different from a related subject. The following article by Jim LiSacchi appeared in a guidebook to the Space Center at Chicago's Museum of Science and Industry. As you read, notice the similarities and differences between space travel today and three decades ago.

LIVING IN OUTER SPACE

BY JIM LISACCHI

Ten . . . nine . . . eight . . . The date is December 21, 1968.

Seven . . . six . . . five . . . Alongside a launch gantry at Cape Kennedy, Florida, a huge Saturn V rocket stands fueled and ready for blastoff, hydrogen vapor steaming from its eleven rocket motors.

Four . . . three . . . two . . . At the top of the rocket sits the Apollo 8 command module, the capsule that will ferry astronauts Frank Borman, James A. Lovell, Jr., and William A. Anders to the moon and back.

One . . . zero . . . Liftoff! The Saturn's powerful engines roar to life, and another exciting chapter in the history of the United States space program begins.

Today, that same Apollo 8 command module is one of the most popular attractions at the Henry Crown Space Center at the Museum of Science and Industry in Chicago. For six days in 1968, this cone-shaped capsule was home to the first humans to leave the security of Earth's orbit and venture out to visit another heavenly body.

Museum visitors, especially young people accustomed to space travel in the shuttle era, are often amazed at the cramped quarters within the capsule, and they wonder just how three adults lived for six days in such a compact environment. Space travel has come a long way since those pioneering days of the 1960s.

Today's shuttle crews have both a flight deck and a lower crew-quarters deck in which to move around. The Apollo crews, however, were pretty much confined to their metal-and-fabric flight couches, although there was a little stretching room beneath the couches and around the hatch area that led to the Lunar Excursion Module.

Basic hygiene also has progressed a great deal since the era of Apollo. The space shuttles, for instance, are equipped with vacuum toilets and simple, hand-held vacuum showers. In contrast, the Apollo astronauts had to make do with Defecation Collection Kits. Needless to say, there were no shower facilities aboard the Apollo craft, and astronauts often reported that the quality of the air within the capsules suffered greatly as a result.

Mealtime is a highlight of anyone's day, including an astronaut's. Early space travelers were limited to puréed foods squeezed out of toothpaste tubes, juices in plastic bags, and some freeze-dried food that was reconstituted with water. Shuttle crews, on the other hand, enjoy a much more appetizing diet. It's still not exactly fine dining, but at least the food is served on trays, eaten with utensils, and includes healthy snacks, like fresh fruit.

At the end of a working "day" in space, the astronauts are ready for some rest. In Apollo, the crew simply drifted off to sleep on their couches. Aboard the shuttle, crew members sleep in special sleep restraints. Some sleep horizontally, while others opt for a vertical snooze. In zero gravity, position doesn't matter!

During the next decade, the United States intends to build and permanently staff a space station in Earth orbit. Plans have also been drawn up for experimental bases on the moon. The lessons learned during the past three decades of space flight will make life in the alien environment beyond the Earth's atmosphere much more pleasant for future space explorers.

Think & Respond

Imagine you had been an Apollo astronaut. Would the excitement of traveling to the moon have made the uncomfortable conditions in your spaceship easier to put up with? Which words and phrases in the article signal the differences between space travel in the 1960s and today?

Comparison and Contrast

INVITATION
═ TO ═
Write

Jim LiSacchi explained what modern space travel is like by comparing it with space travel thirty years ago. Your world is filled with things to compare—people, ideas, objects, and concepts. How are the people and things that make up your world alike? How do they differ?

Write about a subject that interests you, explaining how it is similar to and different from something else.

E XPLORING IDEAS

1. Look for things or ideas to compare and contrast. Which are better, mountain bikes or racing bikes? How do you feel when you're with one friend versus being with a group? Which baseball league do you prefer, the National League or the American League? How would you compare living in this country with living somewhere else?

Answering each of these questions involves comparison and contrast. What subject would you enjoy explaining through comparison and contrast? Gather ideas by brainstorming with a group of classmates. List all the ideas your group thinks up.

2. Choose a topic. Think about the list of ideas you created in your group. Which ideas interest you most? Spend some time freewriting in your journal about your favorite topics, and then choose one to explain.

3. Explore your subjects. Before you start writing, you will need to discover the ways your subjects are the same and the ways they are different. Try making a comparison-and-contrast chart. Notice how the chart on the next page shows the differences between the subjects being compared.

	Apollo	**Space Shuttle**
Living Space	cramped, little room to move, metal/fabric couches	spacious, plenty of room to move, two flight decks
Hygiene	no showers or bathroom facilities, poor air quality	vacuum showers and toilets
Food	toothpaste-tube mush, juice in plastic bags, freeze-dried snacks	regular food, fresh fruit, utensils

PROBLEM
S O L V I N G

"How can I find more details for my comparison?"

For more help using charts to gather information, see

• Handbook 2, "Using Graphic Devices for Writing," pages 226–230

WRITING YOUR COMPARISON

1. Start drafting. Get as many ideas as you can on paper in one sitting. Don't worry about correct spelling or punctuation now; just write. If unexpected ideas creep into your draft, that's great! Sometimes just sitting down and writing can help you find something new to say or a different way to say it.

2. Introduce your subject to your readers. Reread what you wrote and pay special attention to your opening paragraphs. Will it be clear to your readers what subjects you are comparing and contrasting?

3. Organize your comparison. Try using subject-by-subject or feature-by-feature order to organize your comparison. For **subject-by-subject** order, first discuss the characteristics of one of your subjects. Then discuss the characteristics of the other subject. For **feature-by-feature** order, compare and contrast the characteristics of each subject, one characteristic at a time.

The outline on the next page shows how Jim LiSacchi used feature-by-feature order to organize his comparison. Each Roman numeral shows a different characteristic of space travel, then and now.

Comparison and Contrast

133

I. Living space
 A. Apollo: cramped
 B. Shuttle: spacious
II. Hygiene
 A. Apollo: no basic hygiene facilities
 B. Shuttle: vacuum showers and toilets
III. Food
 A. Apollo: mush, freeze-dried
 B. Shuttle: more appetizing, fresh fruit
IV. Sleeping quarters
 A. Apollo: couches
 B. Shuttle: special sleep area, restraints

R EVIEWING YOUR WRITING

1. Think about your audience.   How much will your readers know about your subject? Do you need to define or explain any jargon or key terms that are specific to your subject? Make sure that your language is clear and easy to understand.

2. Show, don't just tell.   Use plenty of facts, examples, or incidents in your comparison to bring your writing to life. Close your eyes and try to experience your subject with all your senses. Go there in your mind's eye. For example, Jim LiSacchi takes his readers with him to the launch site of Apollo 8 in his opening paragraphs.

3. Check your organization.   Read your draft again. If you chose one of the organizational patterns described on page 133, check to be sure you followed that pattern from beginning to end.

S HARING YOUR COMPARISON

- **Make a poster.**   Attach your writing to a large piece of poster board. Add graphic aids such as bar charts or circle graphs to display your information. You may also wish to use photography or your own illustrations to make your poster more interesting.

- **Hold a class discussion.**   After each student presents his or her writing, discuss the subject being compared. What other means of comparison could the writer have used?

Spring**boards**

History

Use dialogue to compare two historical figures. Choose two people with similar roles in history, such as Civil War generals Ulysses S. Grant and Robert E. Lee, or nineteenth-century inventors Eli Whitney and Elias Howe. Write a conversation between them. Let each figure discuss the same elements or ideas. The result will be an interesting comparison of their thinking and their achievements. Choose a classmate to help you read the dialogue aloud to your class.

LITERATURE

Writing poetry is one way to explore your emotions. Write a poem that defines an emotion that is important to you.

Speaking and Listening

What does freedom or liberty or equality mean to you? Suppose you were asked to give a speech at an Independence Day celebration about a principle that is important to democracy. Choose a principle and write a speech that explores its meaning.

Mathematics

Explain a mathematical operation, such as multiplying fractions, by walking your readers through the steps. You might even include a short quiz to make sure that your readers understand your explanation.

Art

Create a drawing, painting, cartoon, or collage to illustrate or define a subject that interests you. Write an explanation to accompany your artwork and post the writing alongside the artwork.

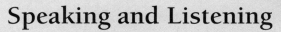

Alexander Calder, *Ostrich*, 1970.

Sentence

Subject-Verb Splits: Clauses

You can add a clause that begins with *who, whose,* or *which* between the subject and verb of a sentence to tell more about the subject. Each clause used as a S-V split in the sentences below has its own subject and verb and adds information about the subject.

Model A Stockton, who had played a little football in high school, blocked Mrs. Barrows as she made for Mr. Martin.

James Thurber, "The Catbird Seat"

Model B Gwydion, whose eyes were everywhere at once, caught sight of them instantly. **Lloyd Alexander, *The Book of Three***

Model C His black hair, which had been combed wet earlier in the day, was dry now and blowing. **J. D. Salinger, "The Laughing Man"**

▶ **ON THE MARK** Use commas to set off a clause if the clause just provides additional information about the subject of a sentence. If the clause provides information that is needed to understand the meaning of the sentence, do not set it off with commas.

A. Combining Sentences Make a new sentence by putting the underlined part of the second sentence into the first sentence at the caret (∧) as a S-V split. Write the complete sentence, putting commas before and after the S-V split.

1. The boy ∧ came and stood at her knee, asking questions with his eyes. The boy was the one <u>who was five years old and only an inch or so taller than the horseweeds</u>. **Hal Borland, *When Legends Die***

2. The tomboy in her ∧ seemed to loathe to be put away forever in skirts. The tomboy in her was the part <u>which was big</u>. **William Allen White, "Mary White"**

3. The palace itself ∧ gradually assumed proportion and form for Anna. The palace was a building <u>which at first had seemed too complex to be understood</u>. **Margaret Landon, *Anna and the King of Siam***

4. The tree ∧ had been cut down because the housewives complained that wash on the lines got entangled in its branches. The tree was the one <u>whose leaf umbrellas had curled around, under, and over her fire escape.</u>

Betty Smith, *A Tree Grows in Brooklyn*

5. King Haggard ∧ fell down through the wreckage of his disenchanted castle like a knife dropped through clouds. King Haggard was the one <u>who was quite real.</u>

Peter S. Beagle, *The Last Unicorn*

B. Unscrambling and Imitating Sentences   Unscramble the sentence chunks below to create sentences that match a model on page 136. Then write sentences that imitate each model. Be sure each sentence has a S-V split.

1. Write sentences that imitate Model A.
just before the car burst into flames / who had arrived right after the accident / the paramedics / removed the driver

2. Write sentences that imitate Model B.
cried out for them ceaselessly / the child / whose parents were out of sight

3. Write sentences that imitate Model C.
was lower now and hissing / which had been cackling loudly / the sea serpent's voice

C. Expanding Sentences   Add a clause as a S-V split to each sentence. Begin your clauses with *who, whose,* or *which,* and set them off with commas. Remember that in most cases *who* and *whose* refer to people and *which* refers to things.

1. Eva ∧ turned on her lively imagination.   **James Thurber, "What Happened to Charles"**

2. Jacques ∧ understood.   **Quentin Reynolds, "A Secret for Two"**

3. Grandfather gave the signal; and Yoshi's cousin Take ∧ poled their boat away from the shore.   **Eve Bunting, "Magic and the Night River"**

Grammar Refresher   Remember that clauses positioned between the subject and verb do not affect subject-verb agreement. For more on interrupting words and subject-verb agreement, see Handbook 45, "Understanding Subject and Verb Agreement," pages 578–594.

- Freewrite in your journal about how this photograph makes you feel. Do you agree with its message? Is there another side to the story? What do you think?

- What if Congress wanted to charge admission to the nation's free monuments and museums in Washington, D.C., to raise money for the federal government? How would you feel, for example, if you had to pay to visit the Lincoln Memorial or the National Gallery of Art? What action would you take to encourage or discourage lawmakers from going ahead with this plan? Freewrite about your thoughts and feelings.

Show, Don't Tell

When you want to persuade someone, show him or her the reasons why you feel the way you do. Choose one of these *telling* sentences and write a paragraph that *shows* the reasons why you think the statement is true.

- Watching TV is (or is not) a waste of time.

- People should (or should not) have to wear helmets when they ride their bikes.

6

Persuasion

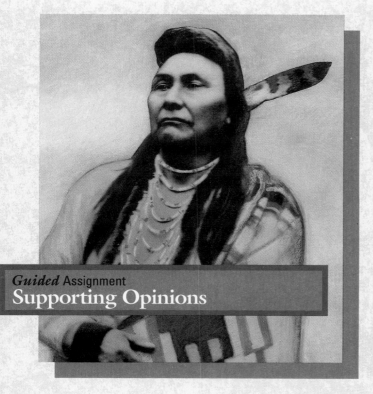

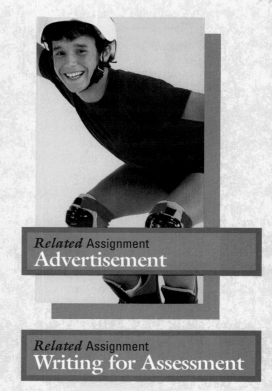

Related Assignment
Advertisement

Guided Assignment
Supporting Opinions

Related Assignment
Writing for Assessment

Have you ever been in an argument? Have you ever tried to change somebody's mind? Have you ever tried to sell anything, argue for a candidate, prove that one team is better than another, defend your actions, or complain about a person or product or situation? If you have done any of these things—and almost everyone has—you have used language to persuade.

In this workshop you will learn to use persuasive writing to take a stand on some issue that is important to you. In a related assignment you will learn to write an effective advertisement.

Supporting Opinions

Think of a time you were treated unjustly. Try to remember how you felt. How did you express your feelings? Did you argue? Did you fight?

As you read this selection, notice the language Chief Joseph uses to express his deep feelings and convince people to feel as he does.

In the late 1800s, the United States government took over the land of the Nez Percé Indians and ordered them to live on reservations far from their homes. Chief Joseph refused to accept this order and set out for Canada with a small band of his people. However, thirty miles from the Canadian border the U.S. Army surrounded them, and they were forced to surrender. The chief traveled to Washington, D.C., and tried to persuade President Hayes to set his people free.

Chief Joseph Speaks

I have seen the Great Father Chief [the President], the next Great Chief [Secretary of the Interior], . . . and many other law chiefs [members of Congress], and they all say they are my friends, and that I shall have justice; but while their mouths all talk right, I do not understand why nothing is done for my people. I have heard talk and talk, but nothing is done.

Good words do not last long unless they amount to something. Words do not pay for my dead people. They do not pay for my country, now overrun by white men. They do not protect my father's grave. . . . There has been too much talking by men who had no right to talk. Too many misrepresentations have been made, too many misunderstandings have come up between the white men about the Indians.

If the white man wants to live in peace with the Indian, he can live in peace. There need be no trouble. Treat all men alike. Give them the same law. Give them all an even chance to live and grow.

All men are made by the same Great Spirit Chief. They are all brothers. The earth is the mother of all people, and all people should have equal rights upon it. You might as well expect all rivers to run

backward as that any man who was born a free man should be contented when penned up and denied liberty to go where he pleases. If you tie a horse to a stake, do you expect he will grow fat? If you pen an Indian up on a small spot of earth and compel him to stay there, he will not be contented, nor will he grow and prosper.

I have asked some of the great white chiefs where they get their authority to say to the Indian that he shall stay in one place, while he sees white men going where they please. They cannot tell me.

I only ask of the Government to be treated as all other men are treated. If I cannot go to my own home, let me have a home in some country where my people will not die so fast. I would like to go to Bitter Root Valley [on the Idaho-Montana border]. There my people would be healthy; where they are now, they are dying. Three have died since I left my camp to come to Washington. When I think of our condition, my heart is heavy. I see men of my race treated as outlaws and driven from country to country, or shot down like animals.

I know that my race must change. We cannot hold our own with the white men as we are. We only ask an even chance to live as other men live. We ask to be recognized as men. We ask that the same law shall work alike on all men. If an Indian breaks the law, punish him by the law. If a white man breaks the law, punish him also.

Let me be a free man—free to stop, free to work, free to trade where I choose, free to choose my own teachers, free to follow the religion of my fathers, free to think and talk and act for myself—and I will obey every law or submit to the penalty.

Whenever the white man treats an Indian as they treat each other, then we shall have no more wars. We shall all be alike—brothers of one father and mother, with one sky above us and one country around us and one government for all. Then the Great Spirit Chief who rules above will smile upon this land and send rain to wash out the bloody spots made by brothers' hands from the face of the earth. For this time the Indian race are waiting and praying. I hope that no more groans of wounded men and women will ever go to the ear of the Great Spirit Chief above, and that all people may be one people. . . .

Think & Respond

What is your reaction to Chief Joseph's message? What sentence or paragraph affects you the most? **Freewrite** about your reactions in your journal and share your thoughts with your friends.

One Student's Writing

November 24

Reading a STUDENT MODEL

Chief Joseph spoke with great feeling about the injustices done to Native American people. Like Chief Joseph, each of us has issues that concern us.

Paul Ryan, thirteen, read a magazine article about a boy who bought a valuable comic book from an inexperienced clerk for much less than it was worth. Paul wrote about his feelings in this letter to the editor of the magazine. As you read the letter, notice the arguments Paul uses to support his case.

Dear <u>Comic Book Monthly</u>:

I'm concerned about the argument between the store owner and the boy about the rare copy of <u>Superhero</u> that the boy bought for twenty dollars. I know that when you buy something, you have a right to keep it. But I think the boy tricked the clerk and should give the comic back.

The store where that happened is in my town, and I read about the case in our local newspaper. The young girl working there was not the regular clerk. A group of kids who were collectors were in the store. They were asking her a lot of questions and were making her nervous. They asked her the price of the <u>Superhero</u> comic. She said, "It's twenty dollars."

The kids all laughed at her and asked, "Are you sure?"

She answered, "Yes, it is."

One of them said, "I'll take it." They walked away laughing. Then the manager came in, found out what had happened, and yelled, "That was a two-thousand-dollar comic book, not a twenty-dollar book! How could you be so stupid?" The girl ran out crying.

One reason that I think the boy should give the comic book back is because he tricked the girl. Some people might say that the girl made the mistake and must take all the blame, but I don't agree. I think the boy tried to get her to make a mistake on purpose. He and his friends kept asking her questions about comics. Probably the girl didn't even know that a comic could be worth two thousand dollars. He knew how much it was worth, but he still pretended that he thought the price was twenty dollars. She walked right into the boy's trap.

In addition, his trickery might have other bad results. I have been at many comic-book shows, and most of the dealers seem honest. They want a fair price, but they aren't trying to rip off the collectors. If collectors act dishonest, some dealers might start trying to trick them. Both dealers and collectors will be suspicious. Therefore, nobody will have any fun at comic-book shows.

Most important, honesty is at stake. The boy should give the comic book back just because he used trickery and deceit to get it. He knew how much it was worth. If he was honest or good in any way, he would have told her the value and would not have bought it. Even now, he can give it back and make thirty dollars, since the store owner has offered him fifty dollars for the comic. However, the boy wants the value listed in your price guide, which, of course, is two thousand dollars. That, to me, seems dishonest and greedy.

The boy took advantage of someone and got what he wanted—a great comic book. Was it really worth cheating someone to get it, though?

Sincerely,

Paul Ryan

Supporting Opinions

INVITATION
TO
Write

Chief Joseph and Paul Ryan used persuasion to communicate their feelings and opinions to others. You, too, use persuasion all the time—whenever you try to get other people to agree with you, or at least to understand your point of view.

Think of an issue that you feel strongly about. Write a piece that will persuade people to see why you feel the way you do.

PREWRITE AND EXPLORE

1. Look for issues.   What bothers you? Maybe you'd like to change a policy in your school or tackle a problem in your neighborhood. Try using one or more of the following activities to discover issues you feel strongly about.

Exploring Topics

- **Pet peeves**   Get together with two or three classmates and share your pet peeves. Appoint one member of your group to **list** all the things that annoy you.

- **Mirror, mirror**   What do you argue about with your friends? Look in your journal to see what has been bothering you. **Freewrite** about an issue you discover there.

- **News watch**   Browse through newspapers and newsmagazines to find articles about controversial subjects. Which issues spark responses in you? Discuss your ideas with some classmates. Then pick the idea you're most interested in.

2. Explore your issue.   Freewrite or do a cluster or idea tree to see what you already know about your issue. Then start collecting facts, examples, observations, and opinions that will enable you to

---

PROBLEM
SOLVING

"I still can't find an issue."

To find more writing ideas, see

- Springboards, page 161
- Sketchbook, page 138
- Handbook 1, "Finding Writing Ideas," pages 218–224

support your position. Here are two activities that can help you find the information you need.

- **Make lists.** Write a list of facts, opinions, and examples that support your point of view and a list of those that oppose it.
- **Do some research.** Ask your librarian to recommend books, newspapers, and newsmagazines that will have the most up-to-date information on your topic. Also ask about experts on the issue whom you could interview.

One Student's Process

You read Paul Ryan's letter to the editor about the comic-book dealer who was taken advantage of by a collector. Paul read about the case in the magazine *Comic Book Monthly*. That really got him thinking, because he collects comic books himself and also knows several dealers. He wanted to write to the editor of the magazine but wasn't sure exactly what he wanted to say. He thought it might help to sketch out some ideas and see how they were connected.

I can see both sides of this issue. Which is right?

$2,000 <u>SUPERHERO</u> COMIC FOR $20

The dealer

The collector

Wants the comic back

The collector knew it was worth $2,000.

Wants to keep the comic— clerk made the mistake

What a <u>cheat</u>!

What a <u>deal</u>!

It'll get even more valuable.

Reprinted with special permission of King Features Syndicate, Inc.

3. Think about your audience. Who will read your writing? Will it be your classmates and teacher, adults in the community, or some other group of people? Knowing who your readers are will help you decide what you need to tell them in your writing. Ask yourself these questions:

- How much do my readers already know about this issue?
- Do they care about it?

DRAFT AND DISCOVER

1. Begin your draft. Start getting your ideas on paper. Some ways to get started are to state your position in one sentence or to tell a story that makes your point. Then give reasons to support that position. You can also just begin with any thought about your issue and see how the idea develops as you write. Look at your freewriting and prewriting notes to help you develop your draft.

2. Support your position. As you write, ask yourself "Why do I believe this is true?" Then give the reasons. You can use both facts and opinions to support your ideas. **Facts** are statements that can be proved. The statement "The first *Superhero* comic was published in 1948 and is worth twenty thousand dollars" is a fact. **Opinions** give personal feelings or beliefs. The opinions of experts can be especially strong support. The statement "One bookstore owner said that Superhero is the best comic-book character ever created" contains an opinion. When you present your own opinions, be sure to support them with facts.

You can use several kinds of facts to support your position.

- **Statistics** Use a fact that involves numbers. For example, "He bought that comic two years ago for fifty dollars, and now it's worth seventy dollars."
- **Incidents and examples** Tell about an event or give an example. For instance, "One day when I was looking for a tennis racket in the closet, I found an old comic book. I thought it might be valuable, so I checked with a dealer. It was worth one hundred dollars! I've been collecting comics ever since."

Grammar
━TIP━

If you quote experts directly in your writing, be sure to use quotation marks correctly. For help, see Handbook 47, "Punctuation," pages 648–650.

3. Think about how people might oppose your position.
Try to guess objections people might have to your point of view.
Then answer those objections. Notice how Paul did this in his
letter to the editor: "Some people might say that the girl made the
mistake and must take all the blame, but I don't agree. I think the
boy tried to get her to make a mistake on purpose."

4. Shape your draft.   There is no right way to organize
persuasive writing. One way that often works well is to start with
your weakest argument and build to your strongest. Both Chief
Joseph's speech and Paul Ryan's letter to the editor are organized
this way. You might try organizing your material differently—
maybe by starting with ideas your audience will agree with and
moving to ones they might oppose. Feel free to try more than one
type of organization and see which you like best.

COMPUTER
━ TIP ━

If you are writing your draft
on a word processor, copy
your work into several
separate documents. That
way, you can try out
different ways of organizing
the material and choose the
best one.

Writer's Choice   Persuasive writing can take many
different forms. For example, you could write an
essay, a letter to the editor, a speech, or a petition.
Which form is best for the issue you have chosen?

5. Think about your draft.   Once you are satisfied with your
draft, put it aside for a few hours or a day. Then reread it when
your mind is fresh. You might also ask your peer readers to
respond to it, if you wish. Questions such as these may help you
review your work.

R E V I E W   Y O U R   W R I T I N G

Questions for Yourself
- How can I state the issue and my position on it more clearly?
- What reasons have I given to support my position?
- How have I answered objections to my views?

Questions for Your Peer Readers
- How would you restate my position in a sentence or two?
- What other ideas can you offer to support my position?
- What do you disagree with?
- Where is my paper strongest? weakest?

That's a good reason, but it <u>was</u> her mistake. Can you give some details?

This confused me. How does your comic fit in here?

Aren't you a little hard on him? It <u>was</u> tempting.

One Student's Process

Here is part of Paul's first draft. Notice his peer readers' responses on the side. What comments would you add?

One reason that I think the boy should give the comic book back is because he tricked the girl. He and his friends kept asking her questions about comics. She walked right into his trap.

The boy should give the comic book back just because he used trickery and deceit to get it. He knew how much it was worth. I have one comic that is worth seven hundred dollars. If he was honest or good in any way, he would have told her the value and would not have bought it.

REVISE YOUR WRITING

1. Review your responses. Think about your own reactions to your draft and the comments of your peer readers. Which changes will you make to strengthen your writing?

2. Check your reasoning. Look over your writing to make sure that your arguments are logical. Pay special attention to your language. It should help your audience think clearly about the issue, not confuse them. Beware of the following traps.

PROBLEM
S O L V I N G

"I'm not sure my arguments are logical."

To check your reasoning and use language effectively, see

- Handbook 23, "Meaning and Word Choice," pages 310–311
- Handbook 29, "Applying Thinking Skills," pages 332–334

- **Vague terms**—words such as *right* or *wrong* that may mean different things to different people

- **Loaded language**—words such as *disgusting* that play on people's emotions without providing real information

Paragraphs at Work In persuasive writing, you state an opinion and then back it up with convincing reasons. You can help readers by explaining each supporting reason in a separate paragraph. In addition, remember . . .

- You can explain the reason in a topic sentence.
- All the sentences in a paragraph should relate to the reason you're explaining.

3. Look back at the beginning of your writing. Look for a "hook" to grab your readers' interest. Would a dramatic incident or a powerful statistic make an exciting beginning?

4. Write a powerful conclusion. Try to find a strong closing for your piece—one that will stick in readers' minds. Paul ended his letter with a question that challenged his audience to think about the issue and come to their own conclusions.

5. Decide which changes you want to make. Remember that you alone decide what changes—if any—to make in your draft.

One Student's Process

These are the changes Paul made after he and his friends reviewed his draft. He would make even more changes later.

> One reason that I think the boy should give the comic book back is because he tricked the girl. Some people might say that the girl made the mistake and must take all the blame, but I don't agree. I think the boy tried to get her to make a mistake on purpose. Probably the girl didn't even know that a comic could be worth two thousand dollars. He knew how much it was worth, but he still pretended that he thought the price was twenty dollars. She walked right into the boy's trap.

> The boy should give the comic book back just because he used trickery and deceit to get it. He knew how much it was worth. ~~I have one comic that is worth seven hundred dollars.~~ If he was honest or good in any way, he would have told her the value and would not have bought it.

> Even now, he can give it back and make thirty dollars, since the store owner has offered him fifty dollars for the comic.

Writing
TIP

As you revise, try writing changes and additions on separate pieces of paper. Then attach them over the old copy (flaps) or at the sides or bottom of the page (kite tails).

1. Proofread your work. Check your work for errors in grammar, capitalization, punctuation, and spelling.

LINKING
GRAMMAR AND WRITING

Using Transitional Words

To make your writing as persuasive as it can be, be sure that you express the relationships between ideas clearly. Use words and phrases such as *however, therefore, in addition,* and *on the other hand* to make the connections, or transitions, between ideas obvious to your readers. Transitional words are usually used at the beginning of a sentence, but they can also appear in the middle or at the end of a sentence. They are always set off by commas.

Notice how Paul clarified the relationship between two ideas in his writing by adding a transitional word. Look for other transitional words in Paul's writing.

Original

> Both dealers and collectors will be suspicious. Nobody will have any fun at comic-book shows.

Revised

> Both dealers and collectors will be suspicious. Therefore, nobody will have any fun at comic-book shows.

For more information on using transitions, see Handbook 14, "Coherence," pages 270–274.

2. Make a clean copy of your piece. Are you satisfied with your work now? Do you want to prepare it for publication? If so, do a final check of your piece using the Standards for Evaluation listed in the margin. Then make a final copy.

Standards for Evaluation

PERSUASIVE
W R I T I N G

- has a strong introduction
- clearly states the issue
- explains the writer's position
- presents ideas logically
- supports ideas with facts or experts' opinions
- answers opposing viewpoints
- ends with a strong argument or summary or a call for action

- **Write a letter to the editor.**   Submit your writing to a school or community newspaper.

- **Present your writing as a speech.**   Identify a group that might be interested in the issue you have addressed and ask to give a speech to the group.

- **Create a leaflet or brochure.**   Add headlines and illustrations to your work. Then distribute your work to interested people.

- **Start a campaign.**   Use your writing as a starting point for a campaign in support of your position. Distribute your writing to interested people and ask them to work with you to get results.

REFLECT ON YOUR WRITING

FOR YOUR
PORTFOLIO

WRITER TO WRITER

A writer's material is what he cares about.
John Gardner, novelist and essayist

1. Add your writing to your portfolio.   Now that you have completed a persuasive paper and read two others, think about your experience. Then write your thoughts in a paragraph or two and attach it to your paper. These questions may help you focus your thinking.

- What did I learn about myself or my beliefs as I wrote?

- What was hardest and easiest for me—finding support for my position? organizing my ideas? choosing the right language?

- What comments from my peers were most helpful?

- What did I enjoy most about my writing? What didn't I like?

- What did I do in my own writing that I'd like to try again?

2. Explore additional writing ideas.   See the suggestions for writing an advertisement on pages 154–156 and Springboards on page 161.

Advertisement

Blade through

Start your day off on the right foot with the newest cereal to hit the streets. This unique blend of supersoluble oat bran and corn gives you all the nutrition and energy you need to glide through the day and perform your best. And the taste leaves other breakfast cereals by the side of the road.

Healthy Whole Grain Flakes

Roller BRAN

Cholesterol Free
Low Sodium

PROVIDES 10 ESSENTIAL VITAMINS AND MINERALS

NET WT. 12 OZ. (340 GRAMS)

Watch for Roller Bran on your grocer's shelf.

the day with Roller Bran

And grab it
while you can—
this cereal's on
the move.

Think & Respond

What audience was the adver-
tiser trying to reach? Do you
think you would buy the cereal?
Why? What words or pictures
in the ad are most persuasive?

INVITATION
━━ TO ━━
Write

This advertisement implies that you'll be on the fast track if you eat Roller Bran cereal. Ad writers are the superstars of persuasion. They use only a few words and pictures to get people to do or buy something.

Now create your own advertisement persuading people to buy, believe, or do something.

PLANNING YOUR ADVERTISEMENT

1. Decide what you will advertise. You can create an ad for a product you really use or you can "invent" a new product—like Roller Bran cereal—and develop an ad for it. Maybe you prefer thinking about people or ideas. If so, you can create an ad to get people to vote for a candidate or to volunteer to coach a T-ball team.

2. Target your audience. What kinds of people will be interested in your product or idea? Think about both who will be using the product and who will be buying it. For example, the Roller Bran ad is aimed at young people who will be eating the cereal and probably persuading their parents to buy it. If your ad is for actual Rollerblades, though, you might want it to appeal more to adults. These skates are more expensive than cereal, so parents will want to know that they are safe and long lasting. Be sure to stress those points in your ad.

3. Choose an advertising medium. Will you write your ad for television or radio, or for a newspaper or magazine? TV lets you use both action-packed images and appealing sounds. Radio has no visual images, but you can use catchy words and melodies to "hook" the listener. Newspapers and magazines can be looked at over and over. When choosing the medium for your ad, think about your audience's interests and habits.

4. Consider advertising "tricks." Read or watch several ads and think about the "tricks" that the advertisers use. Here are some common ones:

- famous-person endorsement—"Michael Jordan says . . ."
- snob appeal—"Be a step ahead of the crowd with . . ."
- bandwagon appeal—"Everyone's trying . . ."
- patriotism—"All good Americans . . ."

For example, the cereal ad makes good use of both snob appeal and bandwagon appeal. The ad promises that eating Roller Bran will put you on the fast track, but that you'd better hurry, because everyone else is buying it too. In writing your own ad, think about the things that are important to your audience and try to appeal to those values.

CREATING YOUR ADVERTISEMENT

1. Decide on the main point of your ad. What message do you want to get across in your ad? State this message clearly in a single sentence. For example, the main point of the cereal ad is "Roller Bran is easy to eat, healthful, and tasty—a cereal designed for people on the move."

2. Make your message short, simple, and direct. In advertising, less definitely is more. Just identify your product and state its benefits simply. If you are telling a story in your ad, make sure that the information is very clear.

3. Use strong images that catch your audience's attention. Both words and pictures should be crisp, clear, and memorable. Also, make sure that the vocabulary and style match your audience's knowledge and experience. For example, in the Roller Bran ad, notice the crisp adjectives and active verbs that are connected with Rollerblading—"hit the streets," "glide," "on the move." Remember, too, that people love to laugh! Use humor if you can.

Grammar TIP

Advertisers sometimes use single words or sentence fragments to make their message seem like everyday conversation.

PROBLEM SOLVING

"What words best express my feeling?"

To find the best word, see

• Handbook 23, "Meaning and Word Choice," pages 310–311

• Handbook 25, "Using Language Imaginatively," pages 314–317

1. Make sure that your words and pictures create the same feeling. Underline the key words in your ad and see if they send a strong message. You might read these words to a partner and ask what feeling or image comes to mind. For example, both the words and pictures in the cereal ad are bold, simple, and direct. Like skating on Rollerblades, they give the sensation of fast, clean motion.

2. Show your ad to someone who might buy the product. Does the ad catch the person's interest? Is your message easy to understand? Is he or she convinced to buy the product or to act on your advice? Ask the person reviewing your ad to tell you what is most appealing or convincing about it.

PUBLISHING AND PRESENTING

• **Create a complete setting for your ad.** Write a script that tells how the sound and visual effects of your ad fit together. For a print ad, make a final layout showing the arrangement of words and pictures on the page.

• **Record your ad.** Make a cassette or videotape of your ad. You might want to have your classmates take part in the recording.

• **Display your ad.** Post your ad on the bulletin board or submit it to the school newspaper. If you have access to a photocopying machine, you might want to distribute copies to your friends.

Writing for Assessment

As a student, there's one thing you know for sure: taking tests will be part of your school year. You may be asked to take two kinds of tests that involve writing. One such test asks questions about what you've learned in various school subjects. You respond by writing essays of one or more paragraphs. Another kind of test asks you to respond to a writing prompt. This test evaluates your writing skills by asking you to show how well you can express your thoughts on a particular subject.

Here are two essay-test questions and two writing prompts that might appear on a general writing assessment test. What does each essay question or prompt ask you to do? Who is the audience for each piece of writing? What form does each prompt suggest?

- **History** Explain why people were eager to make the difficult journey west over the Oregon Trail in the mid-1800s. What were they hoping to find in the new territory?

- **Science** Write a detailed description of photosynthesis, including a discussion of why photosynthesis is necessary for the survival of plant and animal life. For extra credit, draw a diagram of the process.

- **Writing Test** Imagine that you've received a letter from a friend who is feeling sad about something. How can you cheer up your friend? Write your friend a letter in which you examine his or her problem and describe a solution.

- **Writing Test** Imagine that your principal and teachers have been discussing ways to combat cheating in your school. They are looking for input from students about what causes the problem and what can be done to stop it. Write an editorial for your school newspaper that expresses your opinion about the problem of cheating—its causes and its effects. What should happen to students who are caught cheating?

INVITATION
TO
Write

Test taking can be a nerve-racking experience if you're unprepared. If you know what to expect, however, taking a test can be a golden opportunity to show others what you know. Knowing how to respond to different kinds of questions can help you do better on all tests that involve writing.

Follow the directions in the last writing prompt and write an editorial that expresses your views.

ANALYZING THE PROMPT

A writing prompt usually gives you three pieces of information:

- your topic (migration, photosynthesis, cheating)
- your audience (your teacher, a friend, your classmates)
- your format (an essay, a letter, an editorial)

Writing prompts also include key words that give you clues about what kind of information to present in your answer. The following are some key words and the strategies you should use as you write.

Key Words	Strategy
Describe, define	Identify main characteristics and provide specific information or sensory details about each one.
Narrate, tell *how,* trace the steps, describe the process	Give sequence of events or steps in a process, in the order in which they occur.
Explain, analyze, compare, contrast, explore, discuss, examine	Focus on a topic and its main points. Develop each point with facts, examples, or other specific details.
Persuade, convince, give the reasons, express your opinion	State your point of view and give reasons to support it. Use facts, examples, anecdotes, or other specific details.

PLANNING YOUR RESPONSE

When you plan your response, follow these steps.

1. Budget your time.   For example, on a thirty-minute writing test you might give yourself ten minutes to plan, fifteen minutes to write, and five minutes to revise and proofread your work.

2. Make notes.   Focus and organize your ideas by making a cluster or a list. Keep in mind the strategy suggested by the prompt. If you are asked to express your opinion, list your reasons and the facts or examples you will use to support them.

3. Put your ideas in order.   Make an informal outline or list your main ideas, numbering them from most to least important.

One Student's Process

Sophia Perez planned her response to the third test question.

<u>Topic:</u> What cheers me up; <u>Audience:</u> A friend; <u>Form:</u> Letter; <u>Strategy:</u> Give an example of what I do
— General opener about exercise
— Specific details: run to the park with my dog
  • getting ready
  • playing Frisbee or fetch
— How I feel afterwards

DRAFTING YOUR RESPONSE

1. Get right to the point.   You may be able to begin your response with a one-sentence answer. Continue with specific details, facts, or reasons to make your response more complete.

2. Let your notes guide you as you draft.   Remember that each paragraph should focus on a single main idea. Every sentence in a paragraph should relate to that idea. Using transitions between paragraphs will help you link your ideas.

3. End with a strong conclusion.   You may be able to finish your answer by restating your main idea.

PROBLEM SOLVING

How can I connect my ideas?

For more information on using transitions, see

• Handbook 14, "Coherence," pages 270–274

Writing for
Assessment   **159**

R EVIEWING YOUR RESPONSE

1. Reread the prompt. Have you answered the question completely, including all the points you wanted to make? Add any additional details you need.

2. Proofread your work. You won't have time to make a clean copy, so make corrections in the margin or between the lines.

One Student's Process

Here's how Sophia's response looked when she had finished.

Dear Cathy,

    I'm sorry you're feeling down. Sometimes it feels like everything bad happens at once and everyone thinks you can go on like nothing happened.

    What do I do when I feel bad? Exercise! It can be hard to get started, but it always makes me feel great. I forget all my problems—at least for a little while.

    I put on my most comfortable sneakers and sweats and strech out in my room. Then I grab a Frisbee or a tennis ball and take my dog Shawn for a run. The park is about a mile and a half away. Once we get there, we play fetch for a while and then run home. I pretty much forget about whatever's bothering me when I'm running. Maybe exercise would help you too? Riding your bike or swimming might have the same affect. Anyway, I hope you're better—let me know if this works.

                   Your friend,

                   Sophia Perez

Spring**boards**

CONSUMER EDUCATION

Imagine you are on the staff of a magazine that evaluates consumer products. Choose a product you use and write an evaluation of it for the magazine. Be sure to mention the important qualities or features this type of product should have. Then rate the product. Recommend that your readers either purchase the product or not.

History

Choose a leader in world history who interests you. Assume you were that person, and write an editorial to a newspaper of the time persuading people to support your cause.

Art

Make a poster about an issue facing your school or community. For example, you might feel strongly about the homeless, school dress codes, or special provisions for people with disabilities. Use strong language and images to make your position clear.

SPEAKING AND LISTENING

Imagine that a television station will give an award to one student at your school based on his or her personal qualities and concern for others. Write a speech that you might give nominating a student for this honor.

Media

Write a review of a movie, play, or television show. Give your opinion about the performance and present evidence to persuade readers to see or not see it themselves.

Sentence

Sentence Closers: Phrases

Professional writers sometimes draw attention to details by adding phrases to the ends of their sentences. These phrases, called sentence closers, may add information about the words directly before them or about the sentence as a whole.

Model A   It rolled and somersaulted forward, <u>completely out of control</u>.
Nancy L. Robison, "A Space-Shuttle Trip"

Model B   The snow grew thicker, <u>falling to the ground in large, whirling flakes</u>.
Isaac Bashevis Singer, "Zlateh the Goat"

Model C   The monster was a whale shark, <u>the largest shark and the largest fish known in the world today</u>.   **Thor Heyerdahl, *Kon-Tiki***

▶ **ON THE MARK**   Use a comma to set off a sentence closer from the rest of the sentence.

A. Combining Sentences   Make a new sentence by putting the underlined part of the second sentence into the first sentence at the caret (∧) as a sentence closer. Write the complete sentence, setting off the sentence closer with a comma.

1. She walked alone ∧ . She was <u>slowly thinking</u>.
Frances Hodgson Burnett, *The Secret Garden*

2. Deep down here by the dark water lived old Gollum ∧ . Gollum was <u>a small slimy creature</u>.   **J.R.R. Tolkien, *The Hobbit***

3. There he was ∧ . He was <u>sitting with a fish pole in his hand</u>.
Sherwood Anderson, "Stolen Day"

4. The night was very long ∧ . It was <u>longer than the night before</u>.
Scott O'Dell, *Island of the Blue Dolphins*

5. For almost half an hour, Mrs. Scott stood at the front of the room ∧ . She was <u>reading poems and talking about the lives of the great poets</u>.
Toni Cade Bambara, "Geraldine Moore the Poet"

B. Unscrambling and Imitating Sentences   Unscramble each set of sentence chunks below to create a sentence that matches one of the models on page 162. Then write a sentence of your own that imitates each model. Be sure each of your sentences has a sentence closer.

1. Write sentences that imitate Model A.
   and looked around / the police officer stopped / totally out of breath

2. Write sentences that imitate Model B.
   echoing through the stadium / the cheers became louder / in a sharp, booming roar

3. Write sentences that imitate Model C.
   by Margaret Mitchell / the famous movie and best-selling book / the story was *Gone with the Wind*

C. Expanding Sentences   Use your imagination to add a sentence closer, preceded by a comma, where the caret appears in each sentence below.

1. She sat quietly in a kitchen chair ∧ .

   Harper Lee, *To Kill a Mockingbird*

2. Up in her bedroom, behind her closed door, the thirteen-year-old stamped her foot in rage ∧ .

   Dorothy Canfield Fisher, "The Apprentice"

3. Soon they could hear the flap of the goblin feet ∧ .

   J.R.R. Tolkien, *The Hobbit*

4. The monster came quietly ∧ .

   Thor Heyerdahl, *Kon-Tiki*

5. Because she was twelve years old, Araminta Morley was perhaps just the age to be cynical ∧ .

   Celestine Sibley, "The Girl Who Hated Christmas"

Grammar Refresher   Some sentence closers are appositives. To learn more about punctuating appositives, see Handbook 47, "Punctuation," pages 634–636.

SKETCH BOOK

WRITING WARM-UPS

Andrew Wyeth (1917–). *Wind from the Sea,* 1947. Tempera; Mead Art Museum, Amherst College. Gift of Charles and Janet Morgan EL1984. 51.

- Close your eyes and imagine yourself sitting next to an open window. What would you most like to see out the window when you open your eyes? Draw or write about your vision.

- Listen to jazz or classical music and freewrite about the images and feelings the music brings to mind.

Show, Don't Tell

You can show others what a poem means to you by relating it to your experiences. Read the following short poem and the *telling* sentence that follows it. Then write your response, *showing* what the poem means to you.

Dreams

Here we are all, by day; by night we are hurled
By dreams, each one into a several world.   **Robert Herrick**

- Although we share experiences during the day, our nighttime dreams take us to places no one else could understand.

7

Responding to Literature

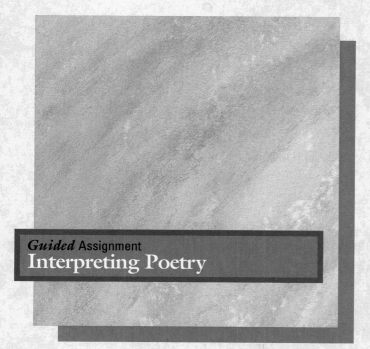

Guided Assignment
Interpreting Poetry

Related Assignment
Focusing on Media

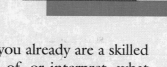

Y ou may not have thought about it, but you already are a skilled interpreter. Every day you make sense of, or interpret, what happens in your world—for instance, what other people do and what they say.

In this workshop you will learn to apply your skills to help you interpret a poem. In a related assignment you will interpret the look and content of a magazine. You will then have a chance to create a plan for your own magazine.

Interpreting Poetry

Starting from LITERATURE

Read the poems on this page several times. Then listen to your teacher read them aloud. Each time, notice what strikes you—especially things that you didn't notice before. Think about why these poems require several readings before you begin to understand them.

OUTDISTANCED

This man of canes is in my way, snailing
Over three-quarters the girth of the sidewalk—
A wrinkled road-hog menacing
The speed of youth. I'll jet past
That wooden gentleman, with flashing
Countenance and polite excuses, the way
The sun outstrips the stars. Should
Grandfathers turn to lumber above their graves?
I'll pass him now; I'll look. He has my face.

                                        Larry Rubin

The Dream Keeper

Bring me all of your dreams,
You dreamers,
Bring me all of your
Heart melodies
That I may wrap them
In a blue cloud-cloth
Away from the too-rough fingers
Of the world.

                    Langston Hughes

WOMAN WITH FLOWER

I wouldn't coax the plant if I were you.
Such watchful nurturing may do it
*   harm.*
Let the soil rest from so much digging
And wait until it's dry before you water
*   it.*
The leaf's inclined to find its own
*   direction;*
Give it a chance to seek the sunlight for
*   itself.*

Much growth is stunted by too careful
*   prodding,*
Too eager tenderness.
The things we love we have to learn to
*   leave alone.*

                    Naomi Long Madgett

Think & Respond

What do you think each of
these poems is about? How
does each poem make you
feel? What words or images
in each poem make you feel
that way? Freewrite about
your reactions, and discuss
them with friends.

One Student's Writing

Sita Raiter

Understanding "Outdistanced"

"Outdistanced" by Larry Rubin is a poem about a young boy who learns something about himself by seeing part of his future. What he first sees as an elderly man in the way, soon becomes an experience of a lifetime. Reading the poem helped me see my own life differently too.

The poem starts with the boy walking along on the sidewalk, and an old man is in the way. The boy has no respect for the man and speeds past him. When the boy turns and looks at the old man, he sees that both of them have the same face.

The poem really isn't as simple as that. There are several sentences in the poem that I don't quite understand, and I feel that there is another message behind it.

I think that the title of the poem, "Outdistanced," has a lot to do with the main points of the story. The poem is told by the youth the whole way through. It starts with the youth describing the old person. He calls the old man, "A wrinkled road-hog menacing / The speed of youth" and, "That wooden gentleman." The old man is seen as an obstacle. I could really understand those lines well because I get impatient with old people, too, sometimes. Then the youth describes himself. He says, "I'll jet past / That wooden gentleman . . . the way / The sun outstrips the stars." He sees himself as the speedy great one. In these lines of the poem, the youth outdistances the old man because of his physical ability. He is faster and stronger than the slow and frail old man.

One statement that was interesting to me was "the way / The sun outstrips the stars." I thought about this and realized that the sun really is a star. Our sun just stands out to us more than other stars. This is like how the young one stands out to us more and seems to have more to offer than the old one. Stars get old and then fade. This is how we feel about the old man in the poem. The youth is supposed to be the bright, new star, and the man is the faded, old star from the youth's point of view.

Another sentence that puzzles me is, "Should / Grandfathers turn to lumber above their graves?" There are several meanings to the word <u>lumber</u>, but in this case I think it means "wood." Lumber is trees that have been chopped down and killed. Although the trees are not growing anymore, they are still in existence. Maybe this means the same thing in the poem. The old man is not growing or doing many things, but he is still in existence. This sentence from the poem is a sarcastic remark. I think of it as, "Should grandfathers turn stiff above their graves?"

At the end of the poem, when the boy realizes that the old man has the same face as he, it changes the whole poem. Without that part, it would just be a poem about the way a boy sees an old man. Because of this sentence, I have realized that the old man and the boy are the same person. I think that the boy is seeing himself as an old man. In that sense he has outdistanced himself in time.

The main idea of this poem is a boy seeing himself as an old man. I just hope when I am old that I will remember what it was like to be young.

Writing ON YOUR OWN

Interpreting Poetry

INVITATION TO *Write*

In her interpretation of "Outdistanced," Sita Raiter offered readers one way to make sense of the poem. She also came to understand both the poem and herself more clearly.

Select a poem that interests you and write an interpretation of it for other readers.

PREWRITE AND EXPLORE

1. Choose a poem and begin to explore it. Reread the poems on pages 166–167 or other poems. Then read them aloud to yourself. Choose one that puzzles or says something special to you and reread it several times. Then try any or all of the following activities.

Exploring Topics

- **Writing it down** Each time you read and reread your poem, you may find new meanings in it. **Freewrite** about your reactions in a **double-entry journal.** In one column write phrases or lines from the poem that interest or puzzle you. In the other column write your responses, reactions, or questions.

- **Sketching it out** Explore your reactions to the poems visually. For example, you could draw a large circle with ears to represent the head of a character in or a speaker of the poem. Then you could fill in the circle with drawings or symbols of the character's thoughts and feelings.

- **Talking it through** In pairs or small groups, share what you think, feel, wonder, or notice about the poem. Feel free to change your mind as you discuss what the poem means.

2. Gather your ideas. After you have explored your poem, review your journal, freewriting, and drawings to see what you might want to write about. You could discuss the meaning of the whole poem or of any interesting or puzzling part. You might also decide, like Sita, to do both in your interpretation.

One Student's Process

Sita Raiter decided to write about "Outdistanced" because she didn't understand it completely and kept finding new meanings every time she read it. She explored her ideas about the poem in a double-entry journal.

Lines from Poem	My Interpretation or Questions
• "This man of canes is in my way"	• Man is a wooden lump boy must speed around. • Why are old people so stiff and why do they just trudge along? • I get so impatient with old people, too, sometimes.
• "turn to lumber above their graves"	• Could this mean lumber as in wood? • Maybe this means the old man is stiff and ready for death, yet he is still alive. He is preparing for death.
• "I'll pass him now; I'll look. He has my face."	• Boy realizes that he will be old and won't want to be treated badly. • He realizes that old man was young at one time, too. • When I'm old, I hope I remember what it was like to be young.

Paula Modersohn-Becker, *Old Bredow*, 1899.

COMPUTER
TIP

Try using the split-screen function on your word processor to do your double-entry journal. Type the lines from the poem on one screen and your reactions on the other screen.

Writing
— **TIP** —

As you draft your interpretation, be honest about what you do and do not understand about the poem. Try to work out what puzzles you.

1. Start drafting.   You might begin by expanding your freewriting or passages from your double-entry journal. Just start getting your thoughts on paper. Don't worry yet about how logical they sound or whether they fit together.

2. Begin thinking about organization.   You don't have to work out all the details yet, but remember: most interpretations include three parts—an introduction, a body, and a conclusion. Here are some suggestions for writing each of these parts.

- **Introduction**   Give the facts about the poem—the author and title and a brief summary of what happens or what the poem is about. You might also tell why you chose to interpret this particular poem.

- **Body**   Explain in your own words what the poem means, what puzzles you, or what you learned from it. Be sure to give reasons, examples, or quotations from the poem to support your statements.

- **Conclusion**   Summarize your interpretation. You could also mention any questions you still have about the poem or why you thought its message was important.

Notice how Sita gave nearly all of the important facts about "Outdistanced" in her introduction. In the body of her paper she explained what the poem meant to her and mentioned several lines that still puzzled her. Her conclusion briefly and simply summarized her interpretation of the poem.

PROBLEM
S O L V I N G

"How can I briefly tell my readers what the poem is about?"

For help writing summaries, see

- Handbook 31, "Writing Paraphrases and Summaries," pages 341–343

 Writer's Choice   You might develop more than one interpretation of a poem. Do you want to mention the other interpretations and explain why the one you chose makes more sense?

3. Remember your audience.   Remind yourself who will be reading your interpretation. How well do your readers know the poem? What ideas or words in it might be unfamiliar to them? Be sure to give readers all the background information they need to understand what you are saying.

4. Think about your draft. Put your draft aside for a while and then reread it. You might also want to show it to one or more of your classmates and ask for their responses. The following questions may help you review your writing.

One Student's Process

Here is part of Sita's first draft. Since several lines in the poem still confused her, she decided to ask some classmates to respond to her interpretation. Look at their comments and think about how you would have responded.

I think that the title of the poem, "Outdistanced," has a lot to do with the main points of the story. The poem is told by the youth the whole way through. It starts with the youth describing the old person. Then the youth describes himself. He says, "I'll jet past / That wooden gentleman . . . the way / The sun outstrips the stars." He sees himself as the speedy great one.

Peer Reader Comments

How does the boy describe the old man?

Oh, I see what you mean. He "outdistances" the old man, right?

1. Review your responses. Make sure your draft includes the most important things you want to say about the poem. You may even want to reread it at this point. Then think about your peer readers' responses and your own reactions to your interpretation. What changes will help you improve your draft?

Paragraphs at Work When you write an interpretation, creating well-developed paragraphs can help readers understand your ideas. Begin a separate paragraph for each important idea or part of the poem you are discussing. So remember . . .

- start a new paragraph for each idea or part of the poem
- consider summarizing your interpretation in a topic sentence
- support your interpretation with examples and reasons

2. Show readers how you found meaning in the poem. Your interpretation should help readers understand how you interpreted the poem the way you did, not just tell them *what* your interpretation was. Here are three ways you can show rather than tell:

- Quote lines from the poem itself
- Draw on your own experience—ideas, people, and events
- Explain how you reached your conclusions

Notice how Sita explained the line "Should / Grandfathers turn to lumber above their graves?" by showing how she understood the word *lumber.*

PROBLEM
S O L V I N G

"How can I make sure I've given good reasons for my interpretation?"

For help with thinking clearly, see

- Handbook 29, "Applying Thinking Skills," pages 332–334

These senior surfers have been riding Pacific Coast waves since 1935.

One Student's Process

Sita reread both the poem and her draft and thought about her peer readers' comments. She realized that she needed to show more about how she arrived at her interpretation. She made these changes:

> He calls the old man, "A wrinkled road-hog menacing / The speed of youth" and "That wooden gentleman." The old man is seen as an obstacle. I could relate to those lines because I get impatient with old people, too, sometimes.

I think that the title of the poem, "Outdistanced," has a lot to do with the main points of the story. The poem is told by the youth the whole way through. It starts with the youth describing the old person. Then the youth describes himself. He says, "I'll jet past / That wooden gentleman . . . the way / The sun outstrips the stars." He sees himself as the speedy great one.

> In these lines of the poem, the youth outdistances the old man because of his physical ability.

Standards for Evaluation

Pᴿᴼᴼᶠᴿᴱᴬᴰ

1. Proofread your writing. Check your writing for errors in grammar, capitalization, punctuation, and spelling. Pay special attention to any lines you have quoted from the poem. Make sure that they are exactly as they appear in the original. Also check the spellings of all proper nouns.

L I N K I N G
MECHANICS **ᴬᴺᴰ** WRITING

Quoting Lines of Poetry

When you quote lines from a poem in your writing, enclose the lines, including end punctuation, in quotation marks. Use a slash (/) to show the end of a line as it appears in the poem. Use ellipsis points (. . .) to show where you have left out words that were in the original. Be sure to capitalize any words that are capitalized in the poem.

Notice how Sita revised her writing to make it clear to her readers that she was quoting lines directly from the poem.

Original

> One statement that was interesting to me was the way the sun outstrips the stars.

Revised

> One statement that was interesting to me was "the way / The sun outstrips the stars."

For more information on using quotation marks, see Handbook 47, "Punctuation," pages 648–652.

---

2. Make a clean copy of your interpretation. Have you accomplished what you wanted to in this piece of writing? Are you ready to prepare it for publication? If so, read it over a final time, thinking about the Standards for Evaluation shown in the margin. Then make a final copy.

- **Have a "poetry chat."** Get together with three or four of your classmates who interpreted the same poem. Have a volunteer read the poem aloud. Then share your interpretations and discuss how they differ.

- **Create a poster or bulletin board display.** Put a copy of the poem in the center and surround it with quotations from the interpretations of that poem. Make a display for each poem interpreted by students in your class.

- **Establish a class "Literature Response" file.** Group the interpretations of particular poems together in a file. This can become a permanent reference for other students.

REFLECT ON YOUR WRITING

WRITER TO WRITER

Understanding is joyous.

Carl Sagan, astronomer and author

1. Add your interpretation to your writing portfolio. Think about what you have learned from reading one student's interpretation of a poem and writing your own. Then write your thoughts in a letter or note and attach it to your interpretation. The following questions may help you focus your thoughts.

- How did writing about the poem help me understand it?
- What connections did I make to my own life?
- What was the hardest thing about writing my interpretation? What was easiest?
- What skills that I have used in other types of writing were helpful to me? What new skills did I learn?

2. Explore additional writing experiences. See the suggestions for focusing on media on pages 180–181 and Springboards on page 182.

FOR YOUR PORTFOLIO

Focusing on Media

Starting from
LITERATURE

Much of your information about the world comes from the media—sources such as magazines, newspapers, television, radio, and movies. Like poems, the media have a message you must interpret. Media writers must know and appeal to their audience's interests to make sure that their message gets across.

As you look at the magazine pages shown here, think about whether or not you would want to read the magazine and why.

Inside Action!

Volume 5 • No. 3 • March 1994

FEATURES

ATTACK OF THE *ISMS!*
by JUDITH ROSSEN • How you can combat racism, sexism and ageism...**30**

RECLAIMING OUR NEIGHBORHOODS
by PETE ONO • Teen activists turn abandoned homes into affordable housing...**38**

KEEPING THE *FUN* IN FUND-RAISING
by JO WASHINGTON • Thanks to Comic Relief, there *is* such a thing as a free lunch...**53**

DEPARTMENTS

LETTERS...**11**

SUCCESS STORIES • *by* BETH JOBSON
Two Kids + One Petition = Recycling in Twenty-five Schools...**12**

ACTION SKILLS • *by* NIK SHANKS
Letter to Leaders: Getting *Your* Voice Heard in Our Nation's Capitol...**18**

CONSUMER SPOTLIGHT
by SHERRY CLARK • Dolphin-Safe Tuna Makes a Big Splash!...**21**

SPEAK OUT: THE *ACTION!* SURVEY
compiled by MICHELLE JOHNS
Displaying the Flag: What's Right? What's Wrong?...**46**

In Our Next Issue...

FASHION ATTACK!
Are Your Clothes Hazardous to the Environment? And much more!

Action!

March 1994 · $2.50

RECLAIMING OUR NEIGHBORHOODS

KEEPING THE FUN IN FUND-RAISING

ATTACK OF THE ISMS!

Think & Respond

What do you like most about what you see here? least? What specific words or pictures tell you whom this magazine is written for and what its message is? What other features or articles would you have included?

INVITATION
═ TO ═
Write

The magazine pages you just looked at were designed to show people your age they can have an impact on the world. What do you like about the magazines you enjoy reading? Notice the articles, language, and pictures.

Write a plan for your own magazine. Decide who your audience will be, describe the goals and content of your magazine, and tell how it will appeal to readers and get your message across.

E XPLORING YOUR PLAN

1. Decide on your audience.   Do you want to plan a magazine for your peers, for young children, or for another group? You might want to brainstorm ideas as a class or in small groups.

2. Think of a subject or theme for your magazine.   What issues interest your audience—for example health, the environment, or old cars? Browsing through the magazine section of your local library may help spark ideas.

Writer's Choice   Do you want to treat your subject humorously or seriously? For example, you might want to do a cartoon-strip parody like those done in *Mad* magazine.

3. Think about features, special articles, and advertisements. Will features such as horoscopes or movie reviews appeal to your readers? What articles and ads will be of interest? What products or services should be advertised? Remember that these must work together to help readers interpret your message.

4. Imagine the overall look of your magazine.   Choose type styles, colors, and pictures that create the look and feel you want. Examine magazines written for your audience for ideas.

CREATING YOUR MAGAZINE PLAN

1. Name your magazine.   Like *Action!,* your title should immediately appeal to your audience and tell them the subject and tone or feeling of the magazine.

2. Organize your ideas.   Collect the ideas that will interest your audience and help get your message across. Here is one way to present them in your plan:

- **Identification**   Give the name of the magazine, and describe its audience and theme or subject.

- **Description**   List a few sample articles, the regular features, and one or two suggested advertisers. Describe the use of type, color, and pictures.

- **Explanation**   State why the magazine will appeal to its audience and how it will communicate your message.

REVIEWING YOUR MAGAZINE PLAN

1. Get feedback on your plan.   Show your plan to several people in your intended audience. Ask if they understand your message and would want to read the magazine.

2. Revise your plan.   Make any changes that you think will strengthen your magazine and make it more appealing.

PUBLISHING AND PRESENTING

- **Create a mock-up of your magazine.**   Design the cover and table of contents page. Submit them to a publisher listed in *Market Guide for Young Writers,* along with your plan.

- **Present your plan orally.**   Read your plan and show sample pages of your magazine to your intended audience.

- **Produce an entire issue of your magazine.**   As a class, write the articles, features, and advertisements and choose or create the art for one issue of your magazine.

Springboards

MUSIC Write your personal interpretation of a piece of instrumental music. Be sure to take notes as you listen to the piece. Explain the mood or feeling you think the composer was trying to create and list specific passages or rhythms that made you feel that way.

Physical Education Watch a sports event and notice when a call by an official is challenged by a player or coach. Explain how each person interpreted the event. How can an instant replay help resolve the conflict?

fine Arts

Do a drawing, painting, or collage that presents your interpretation of a story or poem. Write a paragraph that explains your interpretation.

History Choose a period of history that interests you. Then create a newsmagazine, similar to *Time* or *Newsweek,* for a particular week during that time. Show how events were interpreted by the people who took part in them. Include advertisements and features that would have interested the magazine's audience.

A Terribly Nice Oxymoron

If *civil* means polite, what is a *civil war?* How could something get *freezer burn?* What on earth is an *industrial park?* How could there be *plastic silverware?* Who would want to go to a *work party?* If a host and a guest are different, what is a *guest host?*

Then again, if *jumbo* means large, and a shrimp is something small, how big is a *jumbo shrimp?* If news is supposed to be new, what is *old news?* For that matter, what is an *original copy?*

Why would anybody say "Good grief"?

All of these expressions seem to make sense, even though each seems to be going in two directions at once. The English language contains hundreds of such expressions. You might not notice the contradictions unless you look closely, however.

Sometimes writers contradict themselves on purpose, because it's the best way to make a point. For example, have you ever known a *wise fool?* Have you ever experienced *cruel kindness?* How about when somebody says a lot by saying nothing—an *eloquent silence?*

There's a word for this way of using language. The word is *oxymoron*—a figure of speech that

combines opposite terms. Sometimes it's a good way of expressing mixed feelings. Think of Juliet, saying good night to Romeo:

> Good night, good night!
> Parting is such *sweet sorrow,*
> That I shall say good night
> till it be morrow.

Sentence

Sentence Closers: Clauses

To tell more about a noun that comes at the end of a sentence, you can add a clause that begins with *who, whose,* or *which* as a sentence closer. Notice that each sentence closer below is a clause that has its own subject and verb, and that adds information about the noun preceding it.

Model A   I looked at the lady, who waited for an answer.

Francisco Jiménez, "The Circuit"

Model B   Thoroughly frightened, she telephoned Mr. Link at his store, which was not too far from his house.

Harper Lee, *To Kill a Mockingbird*

Model C   The boy fell on the back of the dog, whose snarling jaws had pushed into the daylight between the boy's legs.

William H. Armstrong, *Sounder*

▶ **ON THE MARK**   Use a comma to set off a clause if the clause just provides additional information at the end of a sentence. If the clause provides information needed to understand the meaning of the sentence, do not set it off by a comma.

A. Combining Sentences   Make a new sentence by putting the underlined part of the second sentence into the first sentence at the caret (∧) as a sentence closer. Write the complete sentence, putting a comma before the sentence closer.

1. The man on the loudspeaker begins calling everyone over to the track for the first event ∧ . It is the event which is the 20-yard run.

   Toni Cade Bambara, "Raymond's Run"

2. My father was thirty-six when he married my mother ∧ . It was my mother who was then twenty-five.   **Anne Frank, *The Diary of a Young Girl***

3. My hands are wrapped in an old towel ∧ . It is the towel which I also use to wipe the sweat from my face.   **Richard E. Kim, *Lost Names***

4. There was silence except for the ticking of the old wall clock $\wedge$. It was the clock <u>whose face showed the phases of the moon.</u> **John Christopher, *The Guardians***

B. Unscrambling and Imitating Sentences   Unscramble the sentence chunks below to create sentences that match a model on page 184. Write your own sentences that imitate the models. Be sure each sentence has a sentence closer.

1. Write sentences that imitate Model A.
   on the children / the baby sitter checked / who slept in the bunk beds

2. Write sentences that imitate Model B.
   which was totally filled with balloons / Jason greeted his friends in the rec room / completely surprised

3. Write sentences that imitate Model C.
   on the tip of his baton / the conductor nodded / whose attention was focused / toward the young members of the orchestra

C. Expanding Sentences   Add a sentence closer, preceded by a comma, to each sentence below. The first word of the sentence closer is provided for you.

1. His most noticeable feature was his fine tail, which. . . .   **John Muir, *Stickeen***

2. Stunned, Jem and I looked at each other, then at Atticus, whose. . . .
Harper Lee, *To Kill a Mockingbird*

3. The goat had learned to visit the houses of the neighbors, who. . . .
Isaac Bashevis Singer, "Shrewd Todie and Lyzer the Miser"

4. He had a permanent case of sun itch, which. . . .
Robert Heinlein, *The Green Hills of Earth*

5. Then she made Colin a cup of beef tea and gave a cup to Mary, who. . . .
Frances Hodgson Burnett, *The Secret Garden*

Grammar Refresher   Remember to use the subject form *who* as the subject of a clause. Use *whom* if the pronoun is functioning as a direct object in a clause. For more on *who* and *whom,* see Handbook 43, "Using Prepositions, Conjunctions, and Interjections," pages 541–542.

- Have you ever been caught in a major storm or natural disaster, such as a tornado, hurricane, or earthquake? Have you heard about a horrible accident—such as the sinking of the *Titanic?* Freewrite in your journal, telling what happened.

- Tell everything you know about one of these people or things: Charlie Chaplin, John F. Kennedy, fingerprints, or cholesterol. Jot down some questions about things you would like to know more about.

Show, Don't Tell

When you write a report, use facts and examples to show what you know about a specific topic. Add information to one of these *telling* sentences and write a paragraph that *shows* what you know.

- The fads of yesterday are the fashions of tomorrow.
- There are many superstitions about good luck and bad luck.

Informative Writing: Reports

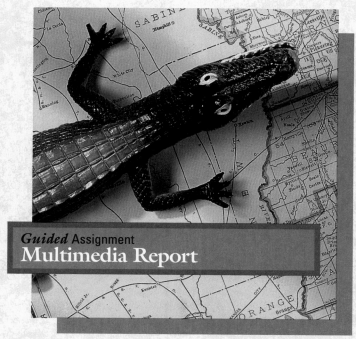

Guided Assignment
Multimedia Report

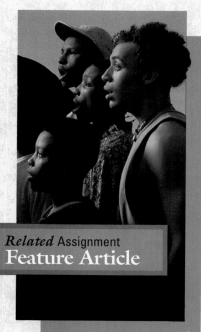

Related Assignment
Feature Article

Like a detective working on a case or a reporter following up on a story, you can conduct an investigation to get to the bottom of things. By using research skills, you can dig into subjects you want to learn more about.

In this workshop you will have a chance to research a subject that interests you and to report on what you learn. You will be able to use a variety of media to present your information. A related assignment will help you apply your research skills to writing a feature article.

Multimedia Report

Reading a STUDENT MODEL

Have you ever eaten Cajun dishes, such as gumbo or jambalaya? Cajun cooking—like Cajun culture—is a spicy mix of ingredients. Linda Leverenz, a junior high school student, decided to make her report about the Cajuns a spicy mixture too. She added music and photos and brought samples of Cajun food to class. As you read her multimedia report, think about how these "extras" make her report more interesting.

A new day dawns in Cajun country.

The Louisiana bayou

The Cajun Experience

What do you think of when you hear the word <u>Cajun</u>? Most people probably think of a spice or maybe a kind of cooking. I think of the wonderful music and food my great-grandmother talked about from her girlhood in Louisiana and the exciting music I heard at a folk festival. However, <u>Cajun</u> means more than just those things. It is actually the name of a group of people who have settled in the United States and have their own special history and culture.

Henry Wadsworth Longfellow wrote about these people in his famous poem <u>Evangeline</u>. He told about the search of a group called the Acadians for a new home after they were driven out of Canada. Many of these people traveled down the Mississippi River to Louisiana, where they found their new home. The poet called them "the shipwrecked / Nation . . . / Bound by the bonds of a common belief and a common misfortune. . . ." (Longfellow 86).

The Acadians were settlers from France who founded the colony of Acadia in Canada in 1604. It was located in the area that is now Nova Scotia. In the eighteenth century, the British took control of the area. They demanded that the Acadians pledge allegiance to Britain. The ones who refused were forced to leave. About fifteen thousand Acadians left to search for a new home, taking with them only what they could carry on their backs. Thousands died of hunger and disease, and many people became separated from their families. About four thousand survivors ended up in Louisiana, where the Spaniards gave them land. This became the home of the Cajuns (Kent 25). The word <u>Cajun</u> is a shortening of <u>Acadian</u>. Over

Fresh seafood—a staple of Cajun cooking

Cajun gumbo tastes as good as it looks.

Cajun Cuisine
Recipes from the Louisiana Bayou

time, the way people pronounced <u>Acadian</u> gradually changed. It became <u>Cadian</u> and finally <u>Cajun</u> (Smith 45).

The Cajuns settled on the prairies and marshy areas—bayous—of southern Louisiana. On the prairies they planted rice and started cattle ranches. In the bayous they fished, trapped, and gathered moss, and they raised sugar cane, cotton, and corn. Many of their descendants carry on the same way of life today ("Cajuns" 19). About 500,000 Cajuns now live in Louisiana. The southern part of the state, west of the Mississippi River, is called Acadiana because of the strong influence of the Cajun culture. This culture includes its own language, food, and music.

The Cajuns speak a unique dialect of French. The original Acadians spoke French, but when the people came to Louisiana, they began to mix in English, Spanish, German, African, and Native American words. At the beginning of the century, Louisiana's government prohibited Cajun children from speaking French in school, but now schools teach French so the Cajuns can hold on to their heritage (Anderson and Anderson 115).

Cajun cooking is famous worldwide. The Cajuns use the unique things they catch where they live. Alligator and crayfish are favorite ingredients. Two Cajun specialties are gumbo and jambalaya. Gumbo is a meat or seafood stew with peppers, tomatoes, onions, okra, and hot spices. Jambalaya is a chowder of rice and seafood (Kent 88; Burton 82).

The most unusual part of Cajun culture is the music. Cajun music is becoming known around the world. The songs are usually sung in French, and they are loud and high-pitched so they can be heard over the sound of dancing feet. The music is played on fiddles, triangles, accordions, guitars, and drums. It really makes you want to get up and dance too (Smith 56). Groups of musicians go from town to town. They perform at all-night dances called <u>fais-dodos</u>. The words literally mean "go to sleep." Whole families come to these dances, and the babies fall asleep there. The songs go back to the time when the Acadians came to Canada from France. However, some of the lyrics are about modern problems. One song tells about the vicious mosquitoes of the Louisiana bayous: "The mosquitoes have eaten up my sweetheart! They have left only two big toes!" (Kent 85).

Two hundred and fifty years ago, the Acadians found their new home in Louisiana. This is how Longfellow described the land that they found:

> Beautiful is the land, with its prairies
> and forests of fruit trees;
> Under the feet a garden of flowers,
> and the bluest of heavens
> Bending above, and resting its dome
> on the walls of the forest.
> They who dwell there have named it
> the Eden of Louisiana! (88)

Today, the Cajuns still live in the prairies, forests, and bayous of southern Louisiana, adding the beauty of their culture to their special part of the world.

No Cajun band would be complete without a fiddler.

MICHAEL DOUCET
BeauSoleil

à V

Works Cited

Anderson, Jim, and Carlotta Anderson. "The Good Times Are Rolling in Cajun Country." _Smithsonian_ Feb. 1988: 112-124.

Burton, Marda. "A Country Called Cajun." _Saturday Evening Post_ Sept. 1987: 82-84.

"Cajuns." _Academic American Encyclopedia_. 1991 ed.

Kent, Deborah. _Louisiana_. Chicago: Childrens, 1988.

Longfellow, Henry Wadsworth. _The Poetical Works of Longfellow_. Boston: Houghton Mifflin, 1975.

Smith, Griffin, Jr. "The Cajuns: Still Loving Life." _National Geographic_ Oct. 1990: 41-65.

Think & Respond

What did you learn about Cajun culture that you hadn't known before? How do the Cajun songs and food enrich Linda's report? What sources of information do you think Linda used in researching her report?

Writing

ON YOUR OWN

Multimedia Report

INVITATION
═ TO ═
Write

Linda Leverenz used not only words but also pictures, music, and food to present information about Cajun culture. Writing a report is a way to learn new facts, fit them in with what you already know, and try out ways of presenting them. Using a mixture of different media can also make your report memorable for others.

Create a report on a topic you would like to learn more about. Use more than one medium, or method of communication, to present your work.

PREWRITE AND EXPLORE

PROBLEM
S O L V I N G

"Where can I get more help finding a topic I want to report on?"

To discover more writing ideas, see

• Sketchbook, page 186

• Springboards, page 211

• Handbook 1, "Finding Writing Ideas," pages 218–224

1. Look for a topic that interests you. If you can choose your own topic, look for something that you feel connected with and want to learn more about. If your teacher assigns a broad topic, find an aspect of it that interests you. For example, if you have to report on Latin American culture, and you enjoy music, you could focus on bossa nova or salsa. The activities below can help you find a subject and a focus for your report.

Exploring Topics

• **Looking inward** What do you care most about? **Freewrite** about interests—maybe a favorite author, sport, or type of music—you want to explore and share with others.

• **Visiting wonderland** What have you always wondered about? Why people dream? How static electricity works? Whether Alice in *Alice in Wonderland* was based on a real person? **Brainstorm** a list of questions with several friends.

• **Raiding the magazine rack** Browse through magazines and newspapers for stories that make you want to know more, such as how to interpret a stock market report, or what recycling methods your town uses. **List** the ideas that you find.

2. Choose a topic. Of the topics you have come up with, which do you care most about? Try freewriting or brainstorming with others about your interests if you are having trouble finding a topic that you really connect with. You might want to look up one or two of your favorite topics in an encyclopedia to see which is more interesting to you. Also remember that you can change topics at any time.

One Student's Process

Linda Leverenz had been assigned a report on some aspect of modern American culture. She was having a hard time finding a topic that was interesting to her, however. She decided to look through some magazines at the local library. Then she did some freewriting about the ideas that she found.

> That article about Cajun music in the folk music magazine reminded me of the musicians I saw at the folk festival last summer. I'd never heard anything like their music before—it was loud and kind of twangy, but I liked it. The musicians used a different kind of speech, too, when they introduced the songs.
> Wait a minute! I just remembered how my great-grandmother from Louisiana used to talk about the wonderful Cajun food and music that was popular where she grew up. Now I really want to find out who these Cajuns are.

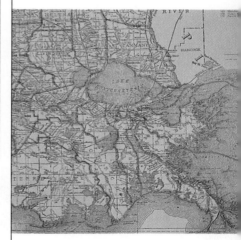

3. Zoom in on your topic. Once you find a topic that you can really get involved with, make sure that it is broad enough to include interesting details but narrow enough to be covered in a short report. For example, although Linda's original interest was in Cajun music, she realized that that topic was too narrow. She decided to include information about other aspects of the culture as well. On the other hand, if your topic has many different aspects, you need to focus on a few that you can present in some detail. Linda chose to focus on the Cajun language, cooking, and music.

Hold on to all your prewriting notes. As your report evolves, you may want to change direction and go back to some ideas you had earlier.

Once you have a topic that is the right size, try freewriting about it. First write about what you know. Then write about what you want to find out.

4. Imagine different ways you can present your report. Your teacher may want you to do a written report, but you can use other materials to make your presentation even more interesting. You might create a photo essay with detailed captions; a videotaped interview with comments and background information; an oral presentation with maps, photos, illustrations, or demonstrations; or an audiotape with a pamphlet. You don't have to decide how to present your report yet. Just keep the options in mind as you proceed with your research and writing.

Writer's Choice Do you want to interview people to get information for your report? If so, you might want to use a tape recorder during the interview. You might also want to tape-record the information you gather from books and even do some "freetalking" about your thoughts on the topic.

RESEARCH YOUR TOPIC

1. Begin gathering material about your topic. The library is a good place to start your research. Handbook 33, "Using the Library," on pages 347–356 can help you learn to use library materials, and a librarian can also give you advice. Don't forget other sources, however. There may be experts or eyewitnesses you can interview or events at which you can tape-record sounds and conversations or videotape people. Also consider visiting museums or searching for things you can sketch, map, or photograph.

2. Keep a list of your sources. In your report, you will need to list the sources you used, so keep track of them while you do your research. For each source, make an index card listing the important information about it. This information is given in the guidelines on the next page. Give each source card a number.

Guidelines for Source Cards

- **Book** author or editor, last name first; book title; city of publication; publisher; copyright date; library call number
- **Magazine or newspaper** author, if given; article title; name and date of magazine or newspaper; page numbers
- **Encyclopedia** author, if given; entry title; encyclopedia name; year of publication
- **Interview** name of person interviewed; type of interview (personal or telephone); date
- **Television program** name of program; narrator or other person providing information; network; date
- **Recording** artist; title of recording; manufacturer; year

COMPUTER TIP

Try entering the information on your source cards in a computer file. Then you can add, organize, and call up sources easily.

Linda made these source cards as she did research for her report.

Book

> ④
>
> Kent, Deborah. Louisiana.
>   Chicago: Childrens, 1988.
>
> School Library   J976.3
>   Kent

Encyclopedia Entry

> ②
>
> "Cajuns." Academic
>   American Encyclopedia.
>   1991 ed.
>
> Public Library

Magazine Article

> ③
>
> Smith, Griffin, Jr. "The
>   Cajuns: Still Loving Life."
>   National Geographic Oct.
>   1990: 41–65.
>
> School Library

Recording

> ⑥
>
> BeauSoleil. Cajun Conja.
>   R.N.A., 1991.
>
> Public Library

3. Take notes. Record the information you find on index cards or paper. Index cards are useful because you can shuffle them to try different ways of organizing information. Record important facts, anecdotes, or statistics you think you will use in your report. Use a separate card for each key idea.

4. Put the information in your own words. When you write a report, **paraphrase,** or put the information in your own words. Paraphrasing helps you to avoid plagiarism, the wrongful use of someone else's words and ideas. If you want to use a quotation, copy it exactly, put it in quotation marks, and credit the source.

5. Begin organizing your material. Look for the main points you want to present. You might want to make an outline, either rough or more formal, depending on your needs and class requirements. You also could write a **thesis statement**—a sentence or two that gives the overall purpose of your report.

PROBLEM
S O L V I N G

"How can I put things in my own words without losing important ideas?"

For help with taking notes from source material, see

- Handbook 31, "Writing Paraphrases and Summaries," pages 341–343

PROBLEM
S O L V I N G

"How do I make an outline?"

For more on outlining, see

- Appendix, page 668

One Student's Process

Linda made this rough outline to help her organize her report. She realized that this was only a tool to help her get started and that her final report might turn out very differently.

I. History
    A. Acadians in Canada
    B. Search for a new home
    C. Origin of <u>Cajun</u>
II. Geography
III. Culture
    A. Language
    B. Cooking
    C. Music
        1. Musicians
        2. Performances

How I learned about the Cajuns
—folk festival
—great grandmother
(WHERE CAN I PUT THIS IN MY REPORT?)

6. Think about other media to use in your report. Note where and how you can use sources such as maps, illustrations, demonstrations, audiotapes, and videotapes in your presentation.

For example, Linda thought she might bring a map, play a recording of Cajun music, and maybe even bring in some Cajun food for the class to sample.

DRAFT AND DISCOVER

1. Start writing.   Now you can begin expanding any freewriting you have done, adding material from your research notes. Your outline can help, but you don't need to follow it strictly. Just start writing any part of the report. As you write, new ideas may occur to you. Follow them to see where they lead.

2. Credit your sources.   Whenever you use someone else's ideas or words, you need to credit the source. One way is to put the source in parentheses at the end of the sentence, as Linda did in her report. The following guidelines will help you.

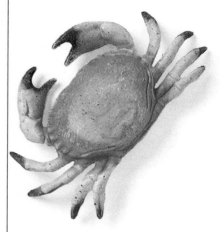

Crediting Sources

- **Work by one author**   At the end of your sentence, put the author's last name and the page number in parentheses. (Smith 58). If you have mentioned the author's name in the sentence that introduces the material you are crediting, put only the page number in parentheses.

- **Work by more than one author**   Put all the last names and the page number in parentheses. (Wright and Brown 63).

- **One of two or more works by the same author**   Put the author's name, a comma, the work's title, and the page number in parentheses. (Lorenz, <u>King Solomon's Ring</u> 82); (Lorenz, <u>Behind the Mirror</u> 25).

- **Works with no author (such as encyclopedias)**   Put the title of the work, article, or entry, or a shortened version of the title, and the page number in parentheses. ("Fossil Find" 24).

- **Nonprint works**   For personal interviews, television programs, or recordings, put the name of the person interviewed, the program, or the recording in parentheses. (Wilson).

COMPUTER
——— TIP ———

Remember, if you have used a computer information service to locate sources, you credit the book or magazine—not the name of the information service.

PROBLEM
S O L V I N G

"How can I show how all my information fits together?"

For help organizing your draft, see
• Handbook 7, "Ways of Organizing," pages 238–242

3. Organize your draft. You can use your outline to identify the main points of your report, but you may need to experiment to find the best way to arrange your information. You may even need to change your outline to fit in new ideas you discovered while drafting. You also may have found different ways of understanding and explaining information that puzzled you. Here are some types of organization you can try.

• Chronological order—the order in which events happened
• Order of importance—from the most important to the least important point, or the other way around
• Order of familiarity—from information readers will be familiar with to new information

You may find that you need to use a combination of these or other approaches to present the information in your report. For example, Linda used chronological order to present the information about the history of the Cajuns. She then presented details about the culture in the order of their importance to her.

4. Create a strong introduction and conclusion. One good way to make your report memorable is to begin and end it strongly. Think about using a question or a quotation, as Linda did. Remember that your introduction should clearly show what your report is about. Your conclusion might sum up the importance of your topic, point out what is still not known about it, or suggest ideas for future research.

PROBLEM
S O L V I N G

"How can I write an exciting beginning and ending?"

For help with writing introductions and conclusions, see
• Handbook 15, "Introductions," pages 275–277
• Handbook 16, "Writing Conclusions," pages 278–280

 Writer's Choice Do you want to make your own recordings, videotapes, photographs, illustrations, or other materials to go along with your report? You could also consider using photographs and illustrations from books or using commercially produced recordings and videotapes to add interest.

5. Look over your draft. Read over what you have written and think about how your report seems to be shaping up. Do you want to share your work and get some feedback on it at this point, or do you want to keep working on your own? The questions on the next page can help you review your draft.

REVIEW YOUR WRITING

Questions for Yourself
- How can I help readers share my interest in my topic?
- What information do I still need to research?
- How can I organize my material so it is as clear as it can be to readers?
- How can I use other media in my presentation to bring it to life?

Questions for Your Peer Readers
- Which part of my report do you like best? Why?
- What do you want to know more about?
- What parts, if any, confuse you or don't seem to belong?
- What additional materials would make my report more interesting to you?

One Student's Process

When Linda had finished the part of her report about Cajun music, she asked several classmates to read and comment on her draft. What would you have said to Linda about her report?

The most unusual part of Cajun culture is the music. The Cajuns have an unusual way of singing, and they use interesting instruments. Groups of musicians go from town to town. They perform all-night dances called fais-dodos. The musicians play songs that go back to the time when the acadians came to Canada from France. However some of the lyrics are about modern problems, One song tells about the vicious mosquitos of the Louisiana bayous: "The mosquitoes have eaten up my sweetheart! They have left only two big toes!" (Kent 85).

Peer Reader Comments

Can you tell me more about what the music is like?

What does fais-dodos mean?

This made me laugh! Do you have a recording of the song?

1. Review your responses. Think about your own reactions to your draft and about your peer readers' comments. If parts of your report need more explanation, look over your notes. Have you already collected information that you could add, or do you have to go back to your sources to find more details? Are there unnecessary details that you can eliminate? Also consider if including pictures, charts, maps, or music would make parts of your report clearer. Remember that this is *your* report, and it is up to *you* to make the final decision about what to change.

Paragraphs at Work In a report, paragraphs help your readers understand how the many ideas you are presenting are related. Each main idea of your outline should probably be covered in one or more paragraphs. One way to make sure that the main idea of each paragraph is clear is to state it in a topic sentence. Be sure to use transitional words that show how your ideas are connected. Remember these tips.

- Cover each main idea of your outline in one or more paragraphs.
- Make sure that the main idea of each paragraph is clear.
- Use transitions to show the connection between paragraphs.

2. Double-check your facts. This is the time to make sure that your information is accurate. Also check to see that you have written your report in your own words, that you have used quotation marks when necessary, and that you have credited your sources correctly.

3. List your sources. Attach a list of your sources in a Works Cited section at the end of your report. Include only the sources you actually used in your writing. Arrange them alphabetically by authors' last names. If no author is given, use the first word in the title. (Do not use *A* or *The* for alphabetizing.) Present the information in the form recorded on your source cards. Leave two spaces after each period and double-space the list. Indent five spaces to continue entries that are longer than one line.

"When do I start a new paragraph?"

For help with paragraphing, see

- Handbook 10, "Using Paragraphs," pages 251–253

PROBLEM

S O L V I N G

"I don't know whether to use quotation marks or underlining when I write the titles of my sources."

For help with punctuating titles, see

- Handbook 47, "Punctuation," page 651

Notice on page 193 how Linda arranged the sources in her report and the format she used. The encyclopedia article titled "Cajuns" followed the name Burton and came before the name Kent.

One Student's Process

After reading her peer readers' comments, Linda realized that she needed to add details to her report. She also decided to look for a recording of the Cajun song about mosquitoes to include in her presentation.

The most unusual part of Cajun culture is the music. Cajun music is becoming known around the world. The songs are usually sung in French, and they are loud and high-pitched so they can be heard over the sound of dancing feet. The music is played on fiddles, triangles, accordions, guitars, and drums. It really makes you want to get up and dance too (Smith 56).

Groups of musicians go from town to town. They perform at all-night dances called <u>fais-dodos.</u> The musicians play songs that go back to the time when the <u>acadians</u> came to Canada from France. However, some of the lyrics are about modern problems. One song tells about the vicious mosquitos of the Louisiana bayous: "The mosquitoes have eaten up my sweetheart! They have left only two big toes!" (Kent 85).

The words literally mean "go to sleep." Whole families come to these dances, and the babies fall asleep there.

Writing **TIP**

As you revise your draft, you can cut out sections and tape them in a different place. You can also tape on a "flap" (as Linda did) to replace a section or add new material on a "kite tail" at the bottom of your paper.

1. Proofread your written material. Carefully check the spelling of names, places, and other unfamiliar words. Also, make sure that your grammar, capitalization, and punctuation are correct.

LINKING
MECHANICS **AND** WRITING

Using Direct Quotations
In writing a report, clearly indicate when you are using someone else's words. Quotes shorter than four lines go in quotation marks in the text. Indent longer quotes ten spaces from the left margin. Do not use quotation marks. Here is Linda's revision.

Original

This is how Longfellow described the land that they found. "Beautiful is the land, with its prairies and forests of fruit trees; / Under the feet a garden of flowers, and the bluest of heavens . . . / They who dwell there have named it the Eden of Louisiana!" (88)

Revised

This is how Longfellow described the land that they found.

> Beautiful is the land, with its prairies and forests of fruit trees;
> Under the feet a garden of flowers, and the bluest of heavens . . .
> They who dwell there have named it the Eden of Louisiana! (88)

For more information on when to use quotation marks, see Handbook 47, "Punctuation," pages 648–650.

2. Prepare your presentation. When your report satisfies you, check the Standards for Evaluation and make a clean copy.

Standards for Evaluation

INFORMATIVE
W R I T I N G

A multimedia report
- has an interesting introduction that makes the topic clear
- conveys the writer's interest in the topic
- contains specific information to support general statements
- presents ideas in a logical order
- credits sources correctly and includes a source list
- is presented using several media
- has a strong conclusion

PUBLISH AND PRESENT

- **What equipment will I need?** All tape recorders, projectors, screens, and VCRs should be available and working. Load and set up the equipment before your presentation.

- **How will I arrange the room?** Decide where to hang pictures, posters, or maps so everyone can see them. Clear space for any demonstrations you will be doing.

- **When will I present my multimedia material?** Clearly mark your written report to show when to present each item.

REFLECT ON YOUR WRITING

WRITER TO WRITER

It doesn't matter which leg of your table you make first, so long as the table has four legs and will stand up solidly when you have finished it.

Ezra Pound, poet, editor, and critic

1. Add your writing to your portfolio. You have just read a multimedia report and created one of your own. Now think about what you have learned and write a paragraph or two about it. Attach this statement to your report. These questions may help you reflect on your writing.

FOR YOUR
PORTFOLIO

- How did I manage to get interested in my topic?
- What did I discover as I created and presented my report?
- What did my audience like best about my report? Why?
- Which sources helped me most? Which were disappointing?
- What will I do differently the next time I write a report?

2. Explore additional writing ideas. See the suggestions for writing a feature article on pages 208–210 and Springboards on page 211.

Feature Article

Starting from LITERATURE

What subjects in the news fascinate you? A sports hero? A tragic or exciting event? Newspapers and magazines are full of feature articles—special news stories that examine a topic in depth. As you read this excerpt from a feature article in *YSB* magazine about the Harlem Boys Choir, jot down the information that interests you the most.

FROM

HARLEM BOYS CHOIR
VOICES
RISE HIGH AS THE LISTENING SKIES

BY JAMES EARL HARDY

THE BOYS CHOIR OF HARLEM [is] one of the most famous youth choirs ever. For over two decades, this posse of thirty brothers, ranging in age from eight to eighteen, have been lifting their voices in song, spreading messages of faith and inspiration all over the world. As twelve-year-old choir member Lamond Lane tells it, "Music is a universal language. You can reach so many people and say so much with a song. . . ."

But the boys get more from the choir than just a chance to nurture their artistic talent. As Jose Suazo, thirteen, explains, "I am discovering who I am, what I'm capable of, and where I can go in life." This, says Dr. Walter Turnbull, the group's founder and director, is the choir's ultimate goal. "In an area where dreams often die before they are born," he says, "we try to instill in the boys that they are important and can do anything they set their minds to."

Turnbull, a native of Greenville, Mississippi, remembers the impact singing in a choir had on his own life. "There is definitely a sense of belonging—of family. You feel important and see that what you're doing is important." When Turnbull came to New York City at twenty to pursue a career performing opera, he saw that young boys in Harlem needed a similar outlet. So he started a choir in the basement of the Ephesus Church in 1968, with ten boys. Little did Turnbull know this small group would one day tour the world.

Today, the Boys Choir is a Harlem institution. On two floors of what used to be a school, the choir conducts its business—and that means not only rehearsals, but career and college counseling, academic tutoring, sports, and other recreation. The boys even have their own school there. . . .

While the choir is twenty-four years old, its members' voices were virtually unheard by the national media until a few years ago, after the choir received rave reviews for its concerts in Japan, Italy, Germany, and England. Suddenly the choir became a media darling—it was profiled on TV shows such as *60 Minutes, Nightline,* and *20/20.* . . .

For some of the boys, the choir entered their lives at just the right time. "I was a rebel; I did things to get attention," says Christopher Brown, fifteen, a freshman at Graphic Communications High School in Manhattan. "If I hadn't joined the choir when I did, I'm afraid to think about what I may have become." Of friends who didn't think joining the choir was cool, Brown says, they now "look up to us. They see us as role models. . . ."

The dedication to self and community upliftment doesn't end for choir members with their graduation. Nathan G. Simmons, twenty-six, joined in 1980 when he was a high school freshman. . . . Today, he is an assistant director there, teaching voice.

"It may seem like I can't get enough of this place, but I'm just giving back what I've gotten," Simmons says. . . .

When people around the world meet Boys Choir members, [Tracey] Sydnor says, they're "surprised to find out where we're from, but they shouldn't be. We've proven that just because you may be poor, or from Harlem, doesn't mean you can't succeed. It doesn't mean you can't dream."

Think & Respond

What impression did you get of the people in the choir? How do you think Hardy gathered information for this article? Why do you think he uses so many quotations from choir members?

INVITATION
TO
Write

James Earl Hardy had a strong interest in the Harlem Boys Choir. He shared his enthusiasm by writing an informative and entertaining article. Writing a feature article is a chance to explore a subject firsthand and to share what you learn and how you feel about it.

Research and write a feature article about a subject that interests you.

R ESEARCHING YOUR

FEATURE ARTICLE

1. Find feature articles in your favorite magazines. Share them with your classmates. Which ones interest you most?

2. Choose a person, place, or event that touches you. Writing a feature article is an opportunity to investigate something that you really care about. What interests you most?

3. Explore your subject. First, write down what you already know about your subject. Then, list questions that you or your readers might have. Remember that your article should answer these questions: *who, what, when, where, why,* and *how.*

4. Gather information. A good first stop is often the library, where you can gather background information about your subject. Then you can do some firsthand reporting using these tools:

- **Interviews** Talk to people who know about your subject. Take notes as they speak, listening for interesting statements you can quote word for word. Notice how Hardy brings both the choir and its members to life by using direct quotations.

- **Observation** Take notes about all the details you see, hear, feel, smell, and taste as you collect your information.

PROBLEM
S O L V I N G

"How can I get the people I interview to tell me what I want to know?"

For help with conducting interviews, see

- Handbook 34, "Interviewing Skills," page 357

Writer's Choice Do you want to write your feature article about something you know well, such as a hobby or a favorite place? Would you rather investigate something or someone you'd like to learn more about, such as a local celebrity? The choice is up to you.

WRITING YOUR ARTICLE

1. Think about what you want your readers to learn. As you gather your notes and begin to draft, you might ask yourself, "What things do I most want to tell readers?" or "How do I want readers to feel about my subject?" Your answer will help you decide the focus, or angle, of your article. For example, you might want readers to become concerned about the plight of homeless people in your community.

One goal of Hardy's article was to show how being in the Harlem Boys Choir affected the lives of its members. To get this point across, he quoted several choir members directly.

2. Decide how to organize your article. Once you have a focus, you can decide how to organize your article. Here are some possibilities:

- **Chronological order** Tell a story, describing things in the order that they happened. Look at how Hardy used this technique in his article (works well for events or people).

- **Order of importance** Tell readers what is most important or interesting to you and then describe less important ideas (works well for people or scenes).

- **Spatial order** Describe something as you see it—for example, from far to near, inside to outside, top to bottom, or left to right (works well for scenes).

3. Write a strong lead, or opening. A feature article should be entertaining, so look for a lead that will catch your readers' attention. You might start with a quotation, a story, or a question—anything to get readers interested in your subject. Hardy used a catchy title and a powerful quotation to draw readers into his article.

Writing
━━━ **TIP** ━━━

Follow the practice of newspapers and magazines and use mostly short paragraphs in your feature article.

PROBLEM
S O L V I N G

"How can I make my lead more interesting?"

For help getting your article off to a good start, see

- Handbook 15, "Introductions," pages 275–277

PROBLEM SOLVING

"How can I show readers what I mean?"

To make your writing more lively, see

• Handbook 12, "Show Not Tell," pages 262–265

Grammar TIP

When you use a person's exact words, be sure to put them in quotation marks.

REVIEWING YOUR ARTICLE

1. Think about your audience. Remember that feature articles are written for an audience of general readers. Think about whether you need to explain terms or ideas that might be unfamiliar to your readers. You might want to share your draft with some of your classmates to see if anything is unclear to them.

2. Show, don't just tell, readers what you're describing. Look over your notes to see if there are details you can add to make your description of the people, places, and events in your article more vivid. Revisit the scene in your mind, if necessary, to come up with more details. Also check to see that you use precise verbs and modifiers in your descriptions.

3. Check for accuracy. Like a research report, a feature article needs to be accurate. Double-check to make sure that your facts, statistics, dates, names, quotations, and other details are correct. Then revise your report based on your own reactions and any comments from your peers that you want to respond to.

SHARING YOUR FEATURE ARTICLE

• **Display your article.** Ask for permission to post your article in a display case or on a bulletin board at your local library or community center. You might include photographs or illustrations as part of your display.

• **Send your article to a newspaper or magazine.** Submit your article to your school or local newspaper or to a specialty magazine. The publication *Market Guide for Young Writers* lists magazines you might consider. Your teacher can help you prepare your article for publication and write a cover letter to go with it.

• **Create a video based on your article.** You might use your article to create a video like the feature stories on TV news shows. You could film your subject on videotape and have a friend act as newscaster, reading your article as you present the filmed footage.

Springboards

Music Find out as much as you can about your favorite musician or musical group. Prepare a report that uses both words and music.

LITERATURE Think of a different place or time that you might like to use as the setting for a novel or short story. Do research about that place or time and write an opening paragraph to set the scene for your story. Use details from your research to make the setting realistic.

PEANUTS reprinted by permission of UFS, Inc.

Science Report on an interesting phenomenon you have observed in nature, such as the annual fall meteor shower. Write a detailed description of your observations, do research to learn more about the phenomenon, and include photographs, diagrams, or sketches if you can.

Journalism Congratulations! You have just been made lead sportscaster for the evening news. Prepare a feature story about your favorite team. If possible, interview a player or team member to get an insider's viewpoint.

Social Studies

Research a person or event from history, using as many primary sources as you can find—journals, letters, autobiographies, old photographs, eyewitness accounts in old newspapers, or interviews with people who were involved in the event. Then write a report and present it along with audiotapes of interviews and copies of your primary sources.

Sentence

Reviewing Sentence Composing Skills

In the preceding Sentence Composing exercises, you have studied how professional writers use sentence openers, subject-verb splits, and sentence closers to add detail, emphasis, and variety to their writing.

Sentence Opener	<u>At the front door</u>, Mother and Father and Mr. and Mrs. Matsui bowed and murmured. **Monica Sone, "The Japanese Touch"**
S-V Split	Stockton, <u>who had played a little football in high school</u>, blocked Mrs. Barrows as she made for Mr. Martin. **James Thurber, "The Catbird Seat"**
Sentence Closer	The monster was a whale shark, <u>the largest shark and the largest fish known in the world today</u>. **Thor Heyerdahl, *Kon-Tiki***

A. Identifying Sentence Composing Skills   The sentences below are from the stories and novels of Lloyd Alexander, who writes about a fantasy land called Prydain. Each sentence illustrates one or more of the sentence composing skills you have studied. For each sentence, write the letter identifying the skill or skills illustrated in the underlined parts.

a. sentence opener
b. S-V split
c. sentence closer
d. sentence opener and S-V split

e. sentence opener and sentence closer
f. S-V split and sentence closer
g. sentence opener, S-V split, and sentence closer

1. The book, <u>which had seemed to weigh so little</u>, now grew so heavy that his pace faltered, and he staggered under the burden.   **"The Foundling"**

2. His cheeks, <u>once full and flushed with youth</u>, were now hollow and wrinkled, <u>half hidden by a long, gray beard</u>.   **"The Foundling"**

3. <u>Now, grown a little stout around the middle and much lacking in hair on the crown of his head</u>, he had taken to farming.   **"Coll and His White Pig"**

4. <u>At the sight of Maibon</u>, the dwarf squeezed shut his bright red eyes and began holding his breath.   **"The Stone"**

5. When Princess Anharad of the royal house of Llyr came of an age to be married, her mother, Queen Regat, sent throughout the kingdom to find suitors for her daughter's hand. **"The True Enchanter"**

6. He handed his old shuttle to the traveler, who popped it into the leather sack and without another word left the weaving shed.
"The Smith, the Weaver, and the Harper"

7. When Rhitta was crowned King of Prydain, the great sword Dyrnwyn, fairest ever wrought, was given him in token of his kingship. **"The Sword"**

8. As Dallben watched, the enchantress, the hag named Orddu, unlocked an iron-bound chest and rummaged inside, flinging out all sorts of oddments until there was a large heap on the floor. **"The Foundling"**

9. As he spoke, he stretched out his open hands, and all the court fell silent, marveling. **"The True Enchanter"**

10. Gurgi snatched the food, thrust it between his teeth, and scuttled up a tree trunk, leaping from tree to tree until he was out of sight. *The Book of Three*

B. Matching and Imitating Sentences Divide each sentence below into chunks that match those of a sentence in Exercise A. Write the number of the sentence in Exercise A that the sentence imitates. Then write your own imitation.

1. When Alice was named the student of the year, a standing ovation, the loudest ever heard, was given her in recognition of her accomplishment.

2. While the tourists stared, a baboon, the selfish one called Willy, chased the other baboons and scurried about, gathering up all the food of the others until there was a giant pile in his dish.

3. While Mr. Blakestone talked, he fingered the report cards, and all the students looked nervous, waiting.

4. Robin's hair, once long and straight to her shoulders, was now short and curly, loosely coiled in a bouncy, blond perm.

5. Afterward, feeling quite chilled from the snow and much regretting the plunge down the hill, he had lain in the snowbank.

This yarn painting is an example of the artistry of the Huichol people, who live in a mountainous region of central Mexico. The deer, cow, cactus, and sun symbols commonly appear in Huichol textiles.

Writing Handbook

MINI-LESSONS

SKETCH BOOK

> *Writers write about things that other people don't pay much attention to. For instance, our tongues, elbows, water coming out of a water faucet, the kind of garbage trucks New York City has, the color purple of a faded sign in a small town.*
>
> Natalie Goldberg
> WRITING DOWN THE BONES

- How would you describe a strawberry to someone who has never seen or tasted one before? Be as creative as you can.
- What objects do you pass on your way to school every day? Describe one object in detail.
- What surprises have you had lately?

Writing Process

Wherever you look there are ideas just begging to be written about. From the crowds and color and excitement of a parade to a single ripe strawberry hanging on a vine, the possibilities are endless.

Of course, you may hate parades or have nightmares about monster strawberries. Writing is one way to share your own unique view of the world. So pick up a pencil and join the community of writers. Everyone can write—but nobody can do it just like you.

217

How Can I Find Ideas?

Finding Writing Ideas

A song, a daydream, books, a photograph—anything can lead to a writing idea. Of course, finding an idea you like can take detective work. However, once you know how to discover interesting ideas, you can track down appealing topics any time.

FINDING A TOPIC

Just as detectives have their fingerprint powders and other crime-solving tools and techniques, writers have tools and techniques for figuring out what to write about. You can use these tools and techniques to find topics that interest and excite you.

Personal Techniques

Experienced writers often advise beginners to "write about what you know." In other words, first look for writing ideas among your personal experiences, interests, and observations.

Recalling   Think back on your experiences, the people you've known, and the places you've been. Try doing the following:

- Look through your journal, photo albums, and scrapbooks for entries or pictures about events, people, or places.

- Think back to "firsts" in your life—your first friend or first pet.

- Look around your room to see what you've saved. Do any items bring to mind experiences or interests to write about?

- Talk to a friend or family member about shared experiences.

WRITER TO WRITER

Ideas often strike me when I see an object such as an apple. I give it a mind and tell how it would feel getting picked or baked in an apple pie.

Bonny Grabowski, student, Kenosha, Wisconsin

Identifying Your Interests   What do you like to do? What do you like to read about? Look at the subjects and activities you already know you like. Ask yourself questions like these:

- What is my favorite book or movie?
- What do I like to watch on television?
- What activities do I enjoy?
- What am I really good at doing?
- Whom do I admire? Why?

Using Trigger Words   Sometimes a word can trigger thoughts and images that lead to writing ideas. Pick a word, any word, from a dictionary, novel, thesaurus—anything. Focus on that word. Then jot down all the words, ideas, and images that come to mind. Write until you've generated several interesting ideas.

Here is how one student used the word *travel* to trigger ideas.

Trigger Word: Travel
the trip my family took last year to the Grand Canyon
the first time I flew in an airplane
exploring outer space or even "inner space"
going back in time or visiting the future

Images can also trigger ideas. Try using the image on this page to trigger writing ideas by jotting down what comes to mind.

Questioning   Good detectives ask *who, what, where, when, why,* and *how* questions to gather information. You can use the same questions to get writing ideas. Start with a general topic such as bicycles. Develop a list of *who, what, where, when, why,* and *how* questions about your topic like those on the next page. Decide which

Student
MODEL

questions you really want to answer. Find the answers to them. Then ask more questions about those answers.

- Who set the record for the longest jump on a bicycle?
- What kinds of stunts can you do on a bicycle?
- Where could I learn about bicycle racing?
- When should you wear a helmet?
- Why are mountain bikes so popular?
- How do you tell whether a bicycle is right for you?

Gleaning   The world around you is full of writing ideas. All you have to do is to **glean,** or collect, those ideas. To try gleaning, jot down whatever you see, hear, read, do, think, or feel that catches your attention. You might describe a crazy outfit you saw or something you heard. Keep your notes in a folder or a journal.

Sharing Techniques

Sometimes working with others can help you generate ideas. When people work together, ideas seem to multiply.

Brainstorming   When you want to generate many ideas quickly, try brainstorming. **Brainstorming** is like a game in which people bat around ideas instead of a ball. To brainstorm, do this:

- Get together with a small group of classmates or friends.
- Select a note keeper to jot down all the ideas.
- Decide on a topic.
- Start suggesting ideas related to this topic.
- Build on one another's suggestions.
- Don't stop to judge ideas.

This should produce a long list of related ideas. Here is part of the list of ideas that a group of students generated about flight:

flying fish	How do you become	hang gliders
flying jets and	an astronaut?	hoverboards
helicopters	How do you	*Star Trek*
sky writing	become a pilot?	space shuttle

Discussion   Talking with others can also spark ideas. Trying to explain an idea can help you focus your thoughts. Hearing other people's ideas can also trigger fresh ideas of your own.

In a discussion, try to give each member of the group an opportunity to speak about his or her ideas. Also try to get everyone to share reactions to what others have said.

Writing Techniques

Ask writers the world over how to find writing ideas, and you'll get the same advice. You find writing ideas by writing. "I write because I don't know what I think until I read what I say," said short-story writer Flannery O'Connor. Poet Mekeel McBride explains, "Writing . . . is a process of discovery, and you don't know what you're going to learn about yourself or what you're going to learn about the world until you're through." Great, but where and how do you begin? Read on to find out.

Freewriting   When you **freewrite,** you give your thoughts freedom to roam. Start by choosing a topic you want to explore or by writing the first thing that comes to mind. Then keep writing. Don't worry about grammar, spelling, or punctuation, and don't stop to read what you've written. Do give yourself a time limit—say three minutes. At the end of that time, look at what you've written, and identify ideas you want to explore further.

Here's how one student used freewriting to generate ideas:

Student
MODEL

> What will I write about? I don't know. Here I am stuck in class when I'd rather be out skateboarding. That new skateboard park that just opened. Wow, I'd like to try out those ramps. Wonder how they design those things. Wonder how they first came up with skateboards. Maybe I could write about that. Or about how I feel when I'm skateboarding.

Listing   You can also use listing to come up with writing ideas. Pick a topic. Then quickly list all ideas related to the topic that occur to you. On the next page is one student's list of ideas related to the topic of communication. Her next steps would be to read over the list, pick an interesting item, and make a new list. A string of topics can come out of this process.

Using a Journal   Whatever you put in your journal is just for you. When you're writing in it, feel free to explore your thoughts and feelings, record experiences and observations, and try out new ways of writing. Above all, be yourself. Write the way you talk or the way you communicate in letters to friends. Allow yourself to think aloud on paper.

You may also use your journal as a clip file. A clip file is a collection of items—quotes, magazine or newspaper articles, cartoons, photographs—you have found interesting. Notebooks with pockets make good journals to use as clip files.

Here are some suggestions for starting and keeping a journal.

- Pick a notebook that feels comfortable to you. Many people like spiral notebooks and loose-leaf binders. Some writers select blank paper on which they can draw as well as write.

- Keep your journal handy. If you carry your journal around with you, you can jot down ideas as they occur to you.

- Write in your journal regularly. Try to make an entry at least every other day. Writing is a skill, like learning to play the guitar or to kick a field goal. It takes practice.

- Date your journal entries. Doing this will make finding specific entries easier.

Using Graphic Devices   Sometimes you need to "see" your thoughts to figure out what you're thinking, to come up with new ideas, or to organize details. That's when graphic devices come in handy. For example, a two-column chart might help you generate ideas for a comparison-and-contrast composition. To learn more about how to use graphic devices, see Handbook 2, "Using Graphic Devices for Writing" (pages 226–230).

Calvin and Hobbes
by Bill Watterson

DO YOU HAVE AN IDEA FOR YOUR STORY YET?

NO, I'M WAITING FOR INSPIRATION.

YOU CANT JUST TURN ON CREATIVITY LIKE A FAUCET. YOU HAVE TO BE IN THE RIGHT MOOD.

WHAT MOOD IS THAT?

LAST-MINUTE PANIC.

Drawing   Drawing a picture can also help you "see" your thoughts. For example, if you need to describe the way a character looks, try drawing the character in different clothing or at different ages. Sketching a picture can also give you ideas for settings.

LIMITING A TOPIC

Suppose you have a three-page report to write and you choose *theater* as a topic. Then you discover that there's too much information to cover in three pages. What do you do? You narrow your topic to something that you can cover well in three pages. You might write on "how to age a person with theater makeup." To limit a topic, use questioning, brainstorming, or a graphic organizer.

Questioning

You can narrow a topic by asking *who, what, where, when, why,* and *how* questions. Here are some questions you might ask to limit the topic of earthquakes:

- Who invented a device to measure the strength of earthquakes?
- What should you do when an earthquake happens?
- Where do earthquakes occur most often?
- When might the next big earthquake occur in San Francisco?
- Why do earthquakes take place?
- How have people tried to "earthquake proof" buildings?

Brainstorming

Brainstorming can help you discover topics of interest to you. If, after brainstorming, the ideas are still too broad to cover in the paper you plan to write, pick an appealing idea and brainstorm again to come up with a still narrower focus.

Here is how one group narrowed the general topic of movies:

action films	cartoons	special effects
horror films	animation	*E.T.*
thrillers	*Fantasia*	Steven Spielberg
comedies	computer graphics	George Lucas

Graphic Devices

Graphic devices, such as cluster maps and idea trees, are great aids to limiting topics. In both kinds of graphics, you begin with a main idea and then branch off into more limited ideas and details. On a cluster map, the ideas farthest from the center are the narrowest in focus. To learn more about graphics, see Handbook 2, "Using Graphic Devices for Writing" (pages 226–230).

Practice Your Skills

A. Choose a topic of your own or one from the list below. Use recalling, questioning, freewriting, or listing to find writing ideas.

friendship	dinosaurs	volcanoes	homework
museums	baseball	Saturdays	cooking

B. Open a dictionary, and with your eyes closed, point to a word. If you don't know the word, read its definition. Write the word on a piece of paper. Then use it as a trigger word, jotting down whatever it brings to mind. Keep writing until you've noted several topics that appeal to you.

C. Practice gleaning by writing anything you notice around you in the next five minutes. Reflect on what you have collected. Circle observations that might make good starting points for writing.

D. In a small group, choose one of the topics listed on this page and brainstorm to come up with several writing ideas related to it.

E. Use your journal, a drawing, or a graphic device to come up with some writing ideas related to one of the topics below.

art	sports	heroes	vacations
careers	music	fears	hobbies

F. Use questioning, brainstorming, or a graphic device to limit a topic below to something you could write about in two pages.

pets	inventions	videos	transportation
family	weather	exploring	mysteries

on the LIGHT side

Headline Horrors

LAWMAKER BACKS
TRAIN THROUGH IOWA
Des Moines Register, 1/24/91

Town to Drop School Bus When Overpass Is Ready

Quarter of a Million Chinese Live on Water

2 SISTERS REUNITED
AFTER 18 YEARS IN
CHECKOUT COUNTER

DEALERS WILL HEAR
CAR TALK FRIDAY NOON

LARGE HOG FARMERS
ARE MORE EFFICIENT
Sentinel-Tribune (Bowling Green, Ohio), 6/29/91

Tuna Biting Off
Washington Coast

BALD
EAGLES
RAISING
NEBRASKA
BABY
*Omaha World-Herald,
6/21/91*

Man Held Over Giant L.A. Brush Fire

LAWYERS
GIVE POOR
FREE LEGAL
ADVICE

Iraqi Head
Seeks Arms

Unattributed headlines are from
Anguished English by Richard Lederer

How Can Graphic Devices Help Me?

Using Graphic Devices for Writing

It's not always easy to find ideas for writing—or to sort out those ideas once you've found them. Sometimes "seeing" your ideas on paper can make both of these writing activities easier. Using a graphic device—a graph or chart—can help.

Some graphic devices are particularly well suited for exploring ideas. Others are especially useful in organizing ideas. However, you can use any of these devices in any way that works for you and at any time in your writing process.

DEVICES FOR EXPLORING IDEAS

Graphic devices that are good for exploring ideas include cluster maps, idea trees, and observation charts.

Clusters   Creating a cluster can help you generate ideas or limit a topic. To make a cluster, write down your general idea or topic in the center of a sheet of paper and circle it. Jot down related ideas around this circle as they occur to you. Circle each one and draw a line connecting it to the main idea or to one of the other new ideas you have added. Continue adding ideas to the cluster until you have found one you'd like to write about. Turn to page 259 to see an example of a cluster.

Idea Trees   An idea tree works the same way as a cluster to help you generate ideas. It just takes a different form on paper. To make an idea tree, write your general topic at the bottom or top of a sheet of paper. Then think of ideas that are related to the main idea and write them on "branches" connected to it. Add new ideas that branch out from any of your ideas as you think of them.

In doing an idea tree about her memories, one student discovered how many ideas and feelings she had about her dog's death. The idea tree helped her choose a topic for her personal narrative.

Idea Tree

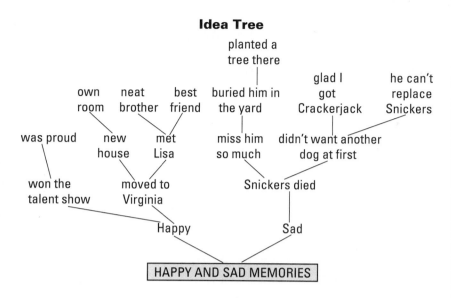

Observation Charts   An observation chart can help you generate details or writing ideas about a person, place, or experience. It is a handy way to organize information you gather through your senses.

To make an observation chart, first decide on your main idea or topic. Then make a chart with the five senses as column headings. Remember or imagine what you see, hear, smell, taste, and touch when you think about your subject. Write each detail in the appropriate column.

Here's how one student used an observation chart to generate ideas for a short story about a major league baseball game.

Observation Chart

Major League Baseball Game				
Sight	**Sound**	**Touch**	**Taste**	**Smell**
green grass	cheers and	hard seats	salty peanuts	steaming
white lines on	boos	crunch of	tangy	hot dogs
field	cries of	peanut shells	mustard	roasted
fireworks	"Peanuts!"	cold, sweaty	sweet	peanuts
fans	"Hot dogs!"	drink cup	soft drink	sunscreen
flashing	crowd singing	hot sun		lotion
scoreboard	"Take Me			
tiny figures of	Out to the			
players	Ballgame"			

Graphic devices that can help you organize the details for your writing include idea-and-details charts, story maps, classification frames, compare-and-contrast charts, and Venn diagrams.

Idea-and-Details Charts This type of graphic device can help you sort out your main ideas and supporting details. By numbering the details, you can show their order of importance.

Notice how one student used this type of chart to sort out his ideas for a report on a space camp he planned to attend.

Idea Chart—Space Camp

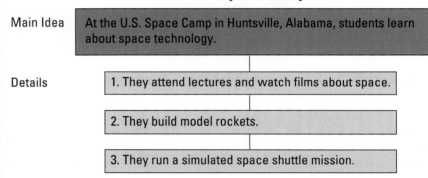

Main Idea
At the U.S. Space Camp in Huntsville, Alabama, students learn about space technology.

Details
1. They attend lectures and watch films about space.

2. They build model rockets.

3. They run a simulated space shuttle mission.

Story Maps A story map can help you organize the elements of a story you are writing. It can also show you what information you still need to work out.

A story map helped one student realize that she still had some holes in her plot.

Story Map

Characters	Junior high basketball players: Juanita, Doris Basketball coach: Mrs. Michaels
Setting	School gym
Plot	
Background	The two girls are friends. Both want to be starting guard. The coach will judge the girls during two weeks of practice.
Event 1	Juanita and Doris argue about who should be chosen.
Event 2	Juanita runs off in a huff and Doris runs after her.
Event 3	(I'M NOT SURE WHAT HAPPENS NEXT.)
Ending	The two friends make up.

Classification Frames   In many types of writing you will be grouping things into categories. A classification frame can help you picture these groupings. It might also give you ideas for other groupings you may not have thought of before.

One student did a classification frame as she was preparing for an oral presentation on musical instruments. She decided to classify the instruments by an important characteristic—how they are played.

Classification Frame

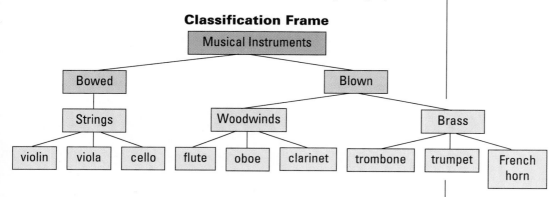

Compare-and-Contrast Charts   If your writing involves examining the similarities and differences between several things, a compare-and-contrast chart can help you organize your ideas. You can then use the chart as you structure your writing.

One student made the following compare-and-contrast chart as he was working on a persuasive paper about payment for chores:

Compare-and-Contrast Chart—Chores

| Characteristics | Subjects Being Compared | |
	Set weekly chores for set allowance	Individual chores for individual fees
Amount of work done	set amount	varies
Amount of money earned	set amount	depends on number of chores completed
Flexibility	must complete all chores to get allowance	can adjust chores to other activities and to meet expenses
Problems	some weeks other activities make chores hard to do	can't count on a set amount of money each week

Venn Diagrams   A Venn diagram is another graphic device you can use to compare and contrast subjects visually. To make a Venn diagram, draw two overlapping circles. Write the characteristics that are common to both subjects in the overlapping area. Write the characteristics that are unique to each subject outside this area.

Notice how a student used a Venn diagram to sort out the similarities and differences between in-line skating and roller-skating.

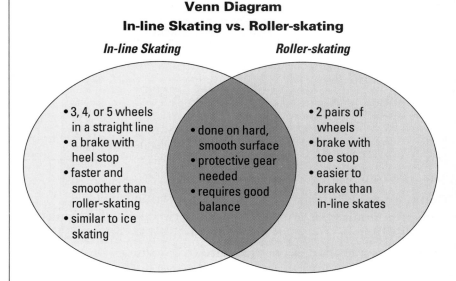

Venn Diagram
In-line Skating vs. Roller-skating

In-line Skating

- 3, 4, or 5 wheels in a straight line
- a brake with heel stop
- faster and smoother than roller-skating
- similar to ice skating

- done on hard, smooth surface
- protective gear needed
- requires good balance

Roller-skating

- 2 pairs of wheels
- brake with toe stop
- easier to brake than in-line skates

Practice Your Skills

A. Choose one of the topics listed below and use a cluster map, idea tree, or observation chart to generate writing ideas.

movies	Olympics	heroes	archaeology
Japan	pets	music	fears

B. Write which graphic device or devices would be most helpful in organizing information about each of the topics listed below.

the reasons you need to have your own telephone
the types of sports shoes available
a ghost story
cold climates vs. warm climates

What Is My Reason for Writing?

General Purpose and Specific Goals

If you know your purpose and specific goals, you can decide what to write and how to write it. Your **purpose** is your general reason for writing. Your **specific goals** are the things you hope your writing will achieve for your readers and for yourself.

PURPOSE

Of course, you often write to complete a paper your teacher has assigned. Sometimes, however, you have other purposes for writing. For instance, you may write to convince someone that your community should build a new recreation center. You may write to share an amusing story. At other times, you may feel a deep need to pour out your thoughts and feelings in your journal.

There are four main purposes, or general reasons, for writing: **to express yourself, to entertain, to inform,** and **to persuade.** Some pieces of writing have a single purpose. For example, you might write a report to inform your classmates about aquanauts living in undersea laboratories. Other pieces of writing, however, have more than one purpose. For instance, a report giving information about recycling might also persuade readers to buy products that come in recyclable containers.

Sometimes you will have a clear sense of purpose before you begin to write. Often, though, you discover your purpose by drafting and exploring your topic. You may even find your purpose changing as you write. Also, as you revise, your purpose may change along with some changing ideas.

To focus on your purpose, try asking yourself the following questions:

- What effect do I want my writing to have on my readers?
- What is my reason for choosing this topic?

Writing
TIP

Remember that your purpose may change as you draft. That's fine. Simply start a fresh draft with a new focus.

General Purpose and
Specific Goals   **231**

SPECIFIC GOALS

Besides thinking about purpose, consider also your specific goals for writing. For example, imagine that your topic is juvenile diabetes. Your purpose is to inform your classmates about the illness. Your specific goal, however, may be to show that a person with this illness can still play sports. You may also want to help a friend who has this illness to see it differently. In another piece of writing, you might give advice about the best way to gain a friend. Your purpose may be to entertain. Your specific goal may be to explore your feelings about friendship.

Thinking about specific goals helps you understand your personal connection with your topic. In general, the more you care about your topic, the more interesting your writing will be. To help identify your specific goals, ask yourself the following questions:

- What aspect of this topic has special appeal to my readers? to me?
- What do I hope my writing will achieve for my readers and myself?

Practice Your Skills

A. For each of the following topics, suggest a possible purpose and some specific goals for writing.

1. letter to the school newspaper about hot lunches
2. report about the Statue of Liberty
3. journal entry about a movie you saw
4. magazine article about nutrition and exercise
5. feature story about an exhibit of Aztec art at a local museum
6. historical novel about the Civil War
7. political cartoon
8. short story about baby-sitting
9. ad for athletic shoes
10. magazine article describing a new video game

B. Choose a piece of writing from your writing portfolio or choose a topic you want to explore. Write a statement of your purpose and your specific goals for writing.

Who Are My Readers?

Audience

Imagine a comedian telling jokes in an empty room, a magician performing tricks in a deserted theater, or a rock group recording music no one will hear. To do effective work, writers, like performers, need an audience.

CONSIDERING YOUR AUDIENCE

Your **audience** is the people with whom you share your writing. Often your audience is chosen for you. For example, if your teacher assigns a report on Chinese festivals, your teacher and classmates are your audience. Sometimes you may choose your audience. For instance, if you decide to write a story for a teen magazine, you are choosing an audience that shares many of your interests. If you write a letter to your local newspaper, your audience may be readers of all ages who share a concern about your community.

Thinking about your audience will help you make better decisions as a writer. You will find it easier to think about your purpose and personal goals, and about what to say and how to say it. Suppose you are writing promotional material about recycling. To an audience of adults, you might write the following sentence:

> If all citizens of our community cooperate, our recycling program will be a success.

For an audience of primary school children, however, you might use simple words, short sentences, and a warm tone:

> You and I have an important job. We must do our best to recycle paper, cans, and bottles. Let's be recycling winners.

Sometime before you finish writing, think about your readers. Try asking the following questions about them:

- What background information do my readers need?
- What part of my topic will interest my audience most?
- How can I best get the attention of my audience?

A graphic organizer like the one below can help you consider your purpose, goals, and audience.

Topic: Chinese New Year Celebration

Purpose (mark possibilities)	Audience	
☐ to express myself ☐ to entertain ☒ to inform ☐ to persuade ☐ other _____	Who is my audience? *my classmates*	
	What is their age level? *11 to 13*	
What are my specific goals? *to relive my excitement and to help non-Chinese people understand the celebration*	What do they already know about the subject? *Some students may have seen highlights of the Chinese New Year parade on TV.*	
	What might interest them in my topic? *They might be interested in the colorful dragon featured in the parade.*	
	What do I want them to know about my topic? *the rich traditions this celebration reflects*	

Practice Your Skills

Revise the following paragraphs so that they appeal to an audience of third-grade children. Consider making changes in word choice, sentence length, and tone.

The highlight of the New Year celebration is the big parade in Chinatown. To scare away evil demons, people set off firecrackers and strike cymbals, drums, and gongs. Decorated floats and performing bands go by. Lion dancers perform.

A huge dragon nearly a block long breathes out fire and smoke. Dozens of dancers inside make the dragon twist and writhe down the street. To the Chinese the dragon is not a monster but a kind, supernatural being that brings rain, which is a symbol of life and rebirth. The dragon is also a symbol of the Emperor. According to legend, the dragon awakens and appears on earth at the New Year.

What Is Drafting?

Drafting as Discovery

   Imagine that you have been asked to come up with ideas for a new playground in your neighborhood. You've listed crowd pleasers, such as swings and ropes. You've suggested some equipment with unusual designs as well: a slide slipping off a giant football helmet, a pretzel pole, and a wooden castle. Now you're ready to try putting all these pieces together in a sketch. In other words, you're ready for drafting.

   Drafting is the process of trying out ideas on paper. It's the same process whether you're sketching out a playground or writing a composition. You explore. You make discoveries. You rearrange. In the process, your castle might become an ark. You might decide to add a pond, only to replace it later with a fountain.

Model for a new playground by Vito Acconci, 1983.

KINDS OF DRAFTING

   You can draft adventuresomely or carefully. You can also try a combination of these two extremes.

Adventuresome Drafting

   When you follow the adventuresome approach to drafting, you write freely, letting your ideas and imagination take you where they may. Adventuresome drafting can be particularly useful for expressing thoughts and feelings in a journal or for developing a poem or short story.

Careful Drafting

   When you follow the careful approach to drafting, you plan what you will write. Then you use that plan, or outline, to help you organize your ideas. Careful drafting can be especially good for report writing or any kind of writing in which you need to explain a subject clearly and completely.

Writing
— TIP —

At the drafting stage, you might want to set a five-minute rule. That is, give yourself five minutes to solve any problem, then move on. This will help you keep your ideas flowing.

Trying out ideas on paper and making discoveries in the process is what drafting is all about. Just express yourself in writing. Later, once you've gotten your ideas down on paper, you can focus on improving the way you've expressed them. At that point, though, drafting really becomes a revision process.

Knowing When to Stop

When you like a draft well enough to want to share it, stop. Reread what you've written. Consider asking a friend to read it too. Note in the margins any revision ideas—that is, ideas for improving your draft. Then put the draft aside for a few hours or even a few days to help you see your work more clearly.

> ### W R I T E R   T O   W R I T E R
>
> *I don't know how to get started, so I just start anywhere. You can brainstorm and just write anything. You can add or take away anything.*
>
> **Tiffany de Jesus, student, Clovis, California**

Practice Your Skills

Choose an item you've written that you especially like. It may be one from your writing portfolio or perhaps a journal entry. Recall how you went about drafting it. Then ask yourself the following questions and note your answers in your writing log.

- Why did I write about this particular topic?
- How did my prewriting—or lack of prewriting—affect my drafting process?
- In what ways did my plans or ideas change as I drafted?
- Was my drafting style adventuresome or careful?
- What feelings did I experience as I drafted this piece?
- What discoveries did I make? What surprised me?
- How did I know when I was ready to stop drafting?

What Form Should My Writing Take?

Choosing a Form

What do advertisements, announcements, letters, limericks, and recipes have in common? Each is a form of writing. A **form** of writing is a particular shape or structure that the writing takes.

FORMS OF WRITING

Your purpose will often determine which form you use to express your ideas. If you wanted to complain to a manufacturer about a defect in your new gym shoes, you would probably write a letter. If you wanted to announce yourself as a candidate for student council, however, you might create a poster.

Sometimes, though, you'll just want to try out a form. That's fine. In fact, the more forms you learn to use, the better your chances of finding a form that suits your purpose and your personality. There are many forms of writing. Here are a few of the most common ones.

Forms of Writing		
advertisement	poem	newspaper article
joke	book review	short story
play	letter	instructions
announcement	editorial	movie review
journal entry	cartoon	speech

Save our forests. Recycle.

Practice Your Skills

Suggest a suitable form for writing about each of these topics.

1. What happens when two enemies get lost in the woods together
2. How to steer a canoe using the J-stroke
3. The best movie you saw all summer
4. The intramural game between the Sharks and the Raiders
5. The need for more stoplights in your community

How Do I Organize My Ideas?

Ways of Organizing

Have you ever gotten separated from your friends or family in a crowded museum, sporting event, or shopping mall? Do you remember the feeling of not knowing where you were or where to go next? Writing that is not well organized can make readers feel that same kind of frustration.

How can you organize your ideas so your readers can follow them easily? There *is* no one best way. Different types of writing need to be organized differently. There is also no best time to organize your writing. Sometimes you might want to plan everything out in your head first. Other times you might just start writing and fit the pieces together as you revise. Use the method and type of organization that work best for you. Here are some ways of organizing ideas that you can experiment with.

MAIN IDEA AND SUPPORTING DETAILS

Many times you will be writing about a topic that you can organize into main ideas and details that support those ideas. For example, in the following paragraph, the writer stated her main idea in the first two sentences, telling what *pandau* are. The other sentences in the paragraph explain how these decorated cloths are used.

Student
MODEL

Supporting detail

Supporting detail

> The Hmong people from Southeast Asia are famous for their colorful *pandau,* which means "cloth made beautiful like a flower." Without using patterns or machines, Hmong women have been creating complicated designs on cloth for centuries. They turn the finished *pandau* into clothing, home decorations, and wraps for babies. Large *pandau* even tell the whole history of the people in tiny stitches and colorful cloth and threads.

ORDER OF IMPORTANCE

Sometimes you might want to present details in order of their importance. Notice how the writer of the following paragraph started with the least important reason for wanting karate included as part of the school gym program and ended with the most important. She used transitional words to clearly point out each reason.

> I think our school should offer karate as part of the gym program. There are several reasons this is a good idea. **First,** karate is fun, and anyone can learn to do it. Many students who want to learn martial arts can't afford to because private lessons are so expensive. Karate is **also** a great form of exercise. It improves strength, coordination, and grace. The **most important** reason, though, is that learning karate makes students more confident and gives them skills that can help them throughout life.

Student
MODEL

Least important reason

More important reason

Most important reason

You can use this type of organization in many ways. For example, you might start with the most important detail and end with the least important. You can also order ideas based on any quality —most to least familiar or inexpensive to expensive, for example.

CHRONOLOGICAL ORDER

Many types of writing—stories, histories, biographies, news reports, and explanations of a process—describe events that take place over a period of time. The natural way to present these events is in the order that they occurred, or chronological order. In the following paragraph about Harriet Tubman's escape from slavery, the writer presents events in chronological order. Notice how she links events with transitional words.

> **Suddenly** she felt afraid. It was too dangerous to be out on the road. She turned and ran into the woods. **Moments later** two horsemen galloped past, shouting and laughing. **Then** the road was quiet again, but Harriet stayed in the shadowy woods.   **Jeri Ferris, *Go Free or Die***

Literary
MODEL

Transitional words show time relationships.

CAUSE-AND-EFFECT ORDER

Often in stories, reports, or persuasive writing, you will be explaining why or how things happen. A natural way to present ideas like these is to use cause-and-effect order. You can talk about the causes first and then describe their effects, or the other way around. Notice the cause-and-effect organization in the following paragraph.

Professional
MODEL

Cause
Effect
Cause
Effect
Cause/Effect

Oil spills are especially dangerous to sea otters. Otters spend most of their time on the water's surface, where the oil lies. Soon after the spill people began finding large numbers of dead or dying otters. The mucky oil was matting their fur. The cold water then could reach their skin, **causing** the otters to freeze to death. Otters were also dying from poisoning. The animals groom frequently, licking their fur. They were swallowing the poisonous goo they licked off.

"Sea Otter Rescue," *National Geographic World*

SPATIAL ORDER

If you are writing about a place or an object, you might want to describe the details the way they are arranged in space. Starting at a specific spot, you might move from left to right, front to back, top to bottom, or inside to outside. In the following paragraph, notice how the writer uses inside to outside order to describe the layout of a castle.

> The space **in the center** of the castle was called the inner ward. It was enclosed by a high wall called the inner curtain. The area **around the outside** of the inner curtain was called the outer ward, and it was enclosed by a lower wall called the outer curtain. Rounded towers were located along both walls, making it possible for soldiers to observe **the entire perimeter** of the structure.
>
> **David Macaulay, *Castle***

CLASSIFICATION

Often you will be describing different ideas or objects in your writing. One way to organize this kind of writing is to classify things—to sort them into groups or categories based on certain characteristics. For example, you might classify schools as public or private. You could group animals by species. In the following paragraph, fish are classified according to their physical structure.

> [Scientists] divide fish into two main groups: (1) *jawed* and (2) *jawless.* Almost all fish have jaws. The only jawless species are lampreys and hagfish. Jawed fish are further divided into two groups according to the composition of their skeletons. One group has a skeleton composed of a tough, elastic substance called *cartilage.* Sharks, rays, and chimaeras make up this group. The other group has a skeleton composed largely or partly of bone. Members of this group, called *bony fish,* make up by far the largest group of fish in the world.
>
> ***The World Book Encyclopedia, "Fish"***

Comparison and Contrast An important part of classifying things involves looking at their similarities and differences. For example, the writer of the encyclopedia article describes how fish are classified based on their physical differences.

Writers can also use similarities and differences to explain or describe something. Notice how these writers help you understand Eskimo clothing by contrasting it with winter clothing you are probably more familiar with. They make the differences obvious by introducing them with clear transitional words.

> Eskimo clothing was extremely efficient. It was lightweight, comfortable, warm, and allowed the wearer to move around easily. A complete winter outfit weighed only about ten pounds. **By contrast,** an average Minnesota businessman wears twenty to thirty pounds of clothing on his way to work in winter; if caught in a sudden blizzard, he would be in danger of freezing to death. Getting dressed takes him about fifteen times as long as it took an Eskimo—an important consideration at temperatures below freezing.
>
> **Charlotte and David Yue, *The Igloo***

Practice Your Skills

List the type of organization you would use for each set of details. Then write a paragraph based on those details.

1. not enough lifeboats on board   over 1,500 passengers die
   ship hits iceberg   the *Titanic* sinks
2. Daydreaming: can spark new ideas, way to resolve conflicts,
                          can be beneficial, way to deal with fears
3. Spanish: Romance language, pronunciation closely follows
                    spelling, many words come from Latin
   English: Germanic language, pronunciation often departs
                    from spelling, many words come from Latin
4. Basic food groups:

Meat group	turkey	beef
Milk group	corn bread	green beans
Vegetables/fruit group	cottage cheese	yogurt
Bread/cereals group	bananas	oatmeal

What Is a Paragraph?

Understanding Paragraphs

The volleyball comes skimming over the net. The person behind you smacks it back up into the air. Another teammate springs it off her fingertips. Then, as the ball falls toward you, you spike it back over the net. That's teamwork.

Like players on a volleyball team, the sentences in a paragraph also work together to accomplish a purpose. Each sentence joins other sentences to communicate an idea.

WHAT IS A PARAGRAPH?

A **paragraph** is a group of related sentences that develop a single main idea or accomplish a single purpose. Usually paragraphs are part of longer pieces of writing, such as a short story or essay. Sometimes, however, a paragraph stands alone. For example, a single paragraph could answer an essay question on a test.

Each paragraph that follows has a single main idea or purpose. In the model below, the first sentence states the main idea.

> The wolf never kills for fun, which is probably one of the main differences distinguishing him from man. It is hard work for a wolf to catch and kill a big game animal. He may hunt all night and cover fifty or sixty miles of country before he is successful—if he *is* successful even then. This is his business, his job, and once he has obtained enough meat for his own and his family's needs he prefers to spend the rest of his time resting, being sociable, or playing.
>
> **Farley Mowat, *Never Cry Wolf***

Literary
MODEL

These sentences support the idea that the wolf does not kill for fun.

In the next paragraph, no one sentence states the main idea. However, all the sentences work together to achieve a specific purpose. That purpose is to vividly describe a scary situation.

> The wide wooden floorboards were cold against her feet. Wind blew in the crevices about the window frame, in spite of the protection the storm sash was supposed to offer. She could hear wind howling in the chimneys. From all the way downstairs she could hear Fortinbras, the big black dog, starting to bark. He must be frightened, too. What was he barking at? Fortinbras never barked without reason.
>
> **Madeleine L'Engle, *A Wrinkle in Time***

WHAT MAKES A GOOD PARAGRAPH?

All good paragraphs share two characteristics: unity and coherence. In a paragraph with **unity,** all the sentences are related to the main idea or purpose of the paragraph. In a paragraph with **coherence,** all the sentences in the paragraph follow each other in logical order and are clearly connected.

Read the following paragraph. Is it unified?

> When I was ten years old, I got the best birthday present I'd ever had. He was a black cocker spaniel, and I named him Midnight. One time he ran away from home and I went after him. Soon the whole neighborhood was searching for both of us. He was a bundle of energy. When he wagged his tail his whole body shook like a shaggy black rug.

The purpose of this paragraph is to introduce the reader to the dog Midnight. However, the sentences about the time Midnight ran away from home don't help to accomplish this purpose. Therefore, the paragraph is not unified. Here is a more unified version:

> When I was ten years old, I got the best birthday present I'd ever had. He was a black cocker spaniel, and I named him Midnight. He was a bundle of energy. When he wagged his tail his whole body shook like a shaggy black rug.

Now read the paragraph below. Is it coherent? That is, do the sentences follow a logical order?

> Sixty-five million years ago, the dinosaurs, who had roamed the earth for millions of years, mysteriously disappeared. What happened to them? Some scientists now think that a huge cloud of dust blocked the sun. A giant meteorite had crashed into the earth. This lowered the temperature of the earth for many years. The cold-blooded dinosaurs could no longer survive.

Can you tell what happened and when?

The purpose of this paragraph is to explain a theory about the extinction of dinosaurs. However, the ideas in the paragraph are not presented in a logical order, nor are they clearly connected. Thus, the paragraph lacks coherence. Here is a more coherent version:

> Sixty-five million years ago, the dinosaurs, who had roamed the earth for millions of years, mysteriously disappeared. What happened to them? Some scientists now think that a giant meteorite crashed into the earth. **This impact** created a huge cloud of dust that blocked out the sun and lowered the temperature of the earth for many years. **As the climate grew colder,** the cold-blooded dinosaurs could no longer survive.

Student
MODEL

Events reordered to follow a more logical, cause-and-effect sequence

Transitions added

Practice Your Skills

For each paragraph that shows both unity and coherence, write "No revision needed." For each that has a problem, identify that problem and then revise the paragraph to correct it.

1. When you want to buy a bicycle, there's one question you should ask yourself first: What kind of riding do I plan to do? More than 105 million cyclists ride the roads in the United States. If you just want to zip around town, you might choose a racing bike. If you want to go on long-distance rides, you might pick a touring bike instead. You can see a lot of beautiful country touring. If, however, you dream of dirt roads and steep trails, a mountain bike is for you.

2. Some animals that hunt at night rely on sharp eyesight to spot their prey. The rattlesnake, however, has a different approach. This nocturnal hunter has a secret weapon located just below its eye. It's called a pit, and it detects heat. The snake can thus sense the presence of a living creature even on the darkest night. The snake then glides silently toward the unsuspecting victim and strikes with lightning speed.

3. I shoved my books into my locker and slammed it shut. I was furious with Angela. How could she have told her brother about our plan? She had been my best friend since we started junior high. I had thought I could trust her. Now I realized you can only trust yourself.

4. On September 7, 1960, Wilma Rudolph made history. Rudolph had been crippled by polio when she was four years old. For many years, she could walk only with the aid of a heavy metal leg brace. Competing in the Summer Olympics, this young runner from Tennessee became the first woman from the United States to win three gold medals in a single Olympics. However, her win marked an even more important personal victory. Through physical therapy and some-times-painful exercise, Rudolph eventually was able to walk and run without the brace. She went on to become a high school basketball and track star and finally, in the 1960 Olympics, "the fastest woman on earth."

5. For more than three hundred years the *Atocha* lay undiscovered on the sea floor. In 1622 the Spanish ship *Atocha* set sail from Cuba, bound for Spain. The ship was loaded with a vast treasure of gold and silver from the New World. But the *Atocha* never reached Spain. A powerful hurricane sank the ship soon after it left port. Hurricane winds can blow nearly two hundred miles an hour. Finally, divers found the ship and hauled up a fortune worth nearly 400 million dollars.

How Do I Develop a Paragraph?

Constructing Paragraphs

Have you ever wondered how Steven Spielberg learned to make motion pictures? As a boy he experimented with home movies. He tried out various characters, action, and settings. He examined what he was doing bit by bit and part by part. He learned about lights, scenes, and special effects—improving his art by improving each small aspect of it.

Similarly, one way to improve your writing is to learn how to craft the smaller parts—the paragraphs. As you examine your paragraphs, keep in mind what you learned in "Understanding Paragraphs" on pages 243–246: a paragraph is a group of related sentences that develops a main idea or accomplishes a single purpose. A good paragraph is organized in a clear and logical way.

KNOWING YOUR GOAL

Before you begin to write, you need to decide what you want your paragraph to do. Do you want to use your paragraph to answer a question, explain an idea, describe something, or tell a story? Try to summarize your goal in a few words. Then, as you write, make sure each sentence helps you achieve this goal.

USING A TOPIC SENTENCE

In a well-written paragraph, the main idea or purpose is clear to readers. One good way for a writer to accomplish this is by including a topic sentence. A **topic sentence** states the main idea or purpose of a paragraph. It lets readers know what to expect from the rest of the paragraph. On the following page, for example, are three topic sentences. Can you imagine the paragraph that each sentence might introduce?

At the dress rehearsal, everything that could go wrong did.

Space probes, like *Voyager 2,* have helped scientists unlock the secrets of the solar system.

The *Titanic* was the largest, most luxurious ship of its day.

Creating Interest

A good topic sentence does more than just state the main idea of a paragraph, however. A good topic sentence catches readers' interest, making them want to read on. Which of the following topic sentences make you want to continue reading?

People are killing off ocean life.

The most dangerous predators in the ocean today are humans, not great white sharks.

What will astronauts find on Mars?

I am going to tell you about what astronauts think they will find on Mars.

If you're like most people, you were probably more interested in the second and third sentences than the first or last. The first and last sentences are dull. How were they improved?

There are several ways to make topic sentences more interesting. The following are good techniques you might try.

1. **Include an unusual fact or an interesting detail.**
   The jungle in Cancun, Mexico, is so dense that you could be standing next to an ancient pyramid and not see it.

2. **Ask a question.**
   What is wrong with being labeled a couch potato?

3. **Address the reader.**
   Imagine your worst nightmare.

4. **Set a scene.**
   It's 130° F., and all you can see are rolling red sand dunes. Welcome to Australia's Great Sandy Desert!

Grammar **TIP**

Try using different kinds of sentences as topic sentences. Statements, commands, questions, and exclamations can all make effective topic sentences.

DEVELOPING THE PARAGRAPH

A paragraph does not consist of a topic sentence alone. A paragraph is also made up of details that support its main idea or help to accomplish its purpose. Here are a few types of **elaboration,** or supporting details, you can use to develop a paragraph.

Types of Elaboration

Type	Definition	Example
Facts/ Statistics	Statements that can be proved	Meteor Crater in Arizona is a mile wide.
Sensory Details	Words that appeal to the five senses	The wet wood crackled, popped, and hissed as it burned.
Incidents	Events that illustrate a main idea	Without José we never would have won. In the final seconds, he scored the winning points by sinking a basket from half court.
Examples	Specific cases or instances that illustrate a main idea	Picking wildflowers and leaving behind garbage are two ways that people ruin national parks.
Quotations	The words of an expert or authority	"It's better to be fit than thin," said Dr. Greene.

PROBLEM
SOLVING

"I still don't understand elaboration."

To find help, see
• Handbook 11, "Elaboration," pages 254–260

A paragraph is well developed if it answers most of the questions it raises. Consider if the paragraph below is well developed.

> Archaeologists are now using space technology to look for ancient ruins on earth! They use pictures taken by satellites. The pictures show scientists where to look for "lost cities."

What kinds of satellites? How do they work? What have they found? Since the above paragraph fails to answer any of the questions it raises, it is not well developed. On the next page is a much better developed draft of this same paragraph.

Facts and examples support the topic sentence and answer readers' questions.

> Archaeologists are now using space technology to look for ancient ruins on earth! Using technology known as remote sensing, special cameras aboard satellites take pictures of the earth's surface. The cameras can detect minor details in the landscape that are otherwise invisible. Scientists then examine the satellite images to discover lost cities. Already, the satellite photos have helped scientists find a city buried in the Arabian desert and hidden ruins along the Silk Road in China.

Practice Your Skills

A. Read each of the following topic sentences. If a topic sentence is fine as is, write "No revision needed." Revise any weak topic sentences to make them clearer and more interesting.

1. This is a story about two friends.
2. How would you like to change places with your parents?
3. The movie theater seemed eerily silent.
4. I am going to explain how a jet engine works.
5. My topic is rock music.

B. Act as a peer reader and review the following paragraph. Does it begin in an attention-getting way? Does its main idea or purpose come across clearly? Is it well developed? On a separate sheet of paper, note any ideas you have for improving the paragraph. Then revise the paragraph, using your suggestions.

> It was lunchtime and the school cafeteria was crowded. It was really busy and noisy. You couldn't even hear yourself think. There were people everywhere. I had to wait in a long line, and then it was hard to find a seat.

C. Write a paragraph on one of the topics below or on a topic of your choice. Develop the paragraph by using one or more of the techniques listed on the preceding page.

1. An incident that taught you something about yourself
2. How to play a sport you enjoy
3. A place that has special meaning for you

Using Paragraphs

What if a sentence just went on and on without stopping and with nothing to tell you where one thought ended and another began would you find it confusing most people would.

Whew! Ideas that run together are difficult to follow. That's why writers organize ideas into separate sentences and paragraphs.

WHY CREATE PARAGRAPHS?

Grouping related details together makes the idea or point they support easier for your readers to grasp. Since each paragraph is a cluster of details that support the same idea or purpose, a new paragraph acts as a signal to readers that a new idea is starting.

When you begin drafting, you probably will not know exactly how many paragraphs you will write or what each paragraph will be about. Instead, paragraphs will develop from the ideas you are trying to express. As you draft and revise, follow these guidelines.

Guidelines for Paragraphing

As you draft . . .

- **Look for related details.** Group them together as a paragraph.
- **Look for changes in content.** Start a new paragraph with each new idea.
- **Recognize changes in setting or speaker.** Whenever the setting or speaker changes, begin a new paragraph.

As you revise . . .

- **Look for paragraphs overloaded with ideas.** Break these down into smaller paragraphs, each focusing on one main idea.
- **Make sure the main idea of each paragraph comes across clearly.** Add topic sentences where necessary.
- **Identify unrelated details.** Delete or move such details.
- **Check paragraphs for coherence.** Make sure details appear in a logical order and are connected by appropriate transitions.

Now look at how one writer used these guidelines to revise a composition. Notice especially why she creates new paragraphs.

I need a more interesting topic sentence.

These details are all about what's in the museum. So it would make more sense to present them in a paragraph of their own after I explain how the museum works.

I don't need this unrelated fact.

How the museum works is a new topic and so should be in a new paragraph.

I need transitions to make the order clear.

Would you like to sit down in front of a television screen and watch your favorite episode of your favorite TV show? There's a place where you can do just that.

~~There's a new museum in New York City.~~ It's called the Museum of Television and Radio. ¶You can watch your favorite cartoons, comedy shows, historic news events, even a collection of commercials. ~~One~~ Some of the most popular requests ~~is~~ are the 1969 moon landing and the Beatles' and Elvis's first appearances on the Ed Sullivan Show. Located in New York City, This new museum ~~cost $50 million. It's~~ is actually more like a library. Instead of books, though, it houses a vast collection of old television and radio shows. Chances are good that you'll find what you're looking for, because the museum has forty thousand programs on tape.

¶Here's how the museum works. You pay five dollars to enter. You then use a computer to help you choose the shows you want to see. Next You go to a special carrel where a museum assistant will bring you the clips you've chosen. It's as simple as that.

Practice Your Skills

Read through the following composition. Decide where it should be broken into paragraphs. Put the paragraphs in logical order and add any transitions you need to make the connections between them clear. Finally, eliminate any unrelated details.

Imagine a bird so fast that it can reach a speed of nearly two hundred miles an hour as it dives for its prey. That bird is the peregrine falcon, and it's considered to be the fastest creature on earth. The falcon is related to the hawk. I saw a hawk once when we were on a camping trip. They're huge. To help save the falcons, a group of scientists started a project called the Peregrine Fund. Researchers carefully gathered fragile falcon eggs from wild nests and hatched them in the safety of the laboratory. They fed the falcon chicks, using hand puppets painted to look like adult falcons. You have to be careful with falcons, though, because they have sharp talons and a fierce grip. Then they released the young falcons back into the wild. Just twenty years ago, scientists feared that these amazing birds were headed for extinction. There were only a few nesting pairs of peregrines left in the entire United States. Falcons usually nest in high places, like cliffs. The major reason for their disappearance was DDT, a pesticide that had once been widely used in farming. The falcons ate birds and other animals that had eaten the DDT.

The pesticide then caused the falcons' eggshells to become thinner and thinner. Since the thin shells broke easily, few falcon chicks were hatched. Thus, the falcon population dwindled. The birds were listed as an endangered species in 1973. The project has proven to be so successful that the peregrine falcon may no longer be an endangered species in the United States. In fact, peregrines have now been seen diving after pigeons and nesting atop skyscrapers in New York City.

How Do I Develop Ideas?

Elaboration

Have you ever given someone directions? If so, you've probably discovered that ideas expanded with details come across more clearly and strongly than vague statements. "Look behind you at that guy in the green sweater!" is easier to follow than "Look!" How do you develop ideas? Use elaboration, or details, to support your ideas.

TYPES OF SUPPORT

You can use several kinds of details to elaborate an idea. However, try to select those details that fit your purpose, audience, and topic. Asking these questions can help:

- What details would help me accomplish my purpose?
- What details would make my idea clearer or stronger?
- What might my audience want to know about this topic?

Facts and Statistics

A **fact** is a statement that can be proved by observation, experience, checking in a reference work, or consulting an authority. "Baseball was played by soldiers during the Civil War" is a fact. You can find it in an almanac or encyclopedia. A **statistic** is a fact that involves numbers, such as "Cy Young won 511 games as a major-league pitcher." This statement, too, can be found in a reference work. In the following paragraph, facts support the main idea.

Professional
MODEL

The facts in this paragraph support the idea stated in the first sentence.

> If there was ever a record for the shortest major-league career by a pitcher, it surely belongs to a right-handed pitcher named Henry Heitman. On July 27, 1918, Heitman started a game for the Brooklyn Dodgers. He faced the St. Louis Cardinals. The first four batters all hit safely. Heitman was sent to the showers. He promptly enlisted in the United States Navy and never played major-league baseball again.
>
> **Howard Liss, "Short Stay"**

Sensory Details

When you show the way something looks, sounds, smells, tastes, or feels, you are providing sensory details. Such details help your readers to more completely imagine the characters, or the scene, or the events you are writing about.

To provide sensory details, use words in your writing that vividly communicate the sensations you want to share. Such words are often specific nouns, active verbs, adjectives, or adverbs.

Now read the following paragraph to see how Laurence Yep uses sensory details of sight and sound to describe San Francisco after the great earthquake of 1906.

Houses on Howard Street after the San Francisco earthquake of April 18, 1906.

> A strange, eerie silence hung over the city. The bells had stilled in their steeples, and houses had stopped collapsing momentarily. It was as if the city itself were holding its breath. Then we could hear the hissing of gas from the broken pipes, like dozens of angry snakes, and people, trapped inside the mounds, began calling. Their voices sounded faint and ghostly, as if dozens of ghosts floated over the rubble, crying in little, distant voices for help.
>
> **Laurence Yep, *Dragonwings***

Literary
MODEL

The topic sentence sets the stage for the sensory details that follow.

Suppose Yep had written, "The earthquake was over. Many people were trapped in the ruins." The fully elaborated description in the model helps you *see* the ruined city and *hear* the ghostly voices.

W R I T E R   T O   W R I T E R

What I dislike the most about writing is dull, boring facts. I don't mind if they're facts, but I do if it's not enjoyable to read.

Brittney Brodie, student, Clovis, California

Writing TIP

When first drafting an incident, focus on telling what happened. Then, in later drafts, try adding sensory words and images to bring the story to life.

Literary MODEL

Notice that an incident has a beginning, a middle, and an end.

Incidents

When you tell a friend about the time you missed the bus, you are relating an incident. An **incident** is a happening, or occurrence. Retelling an incident is sometimes a good way to help explain a main idea. Just make sure the event you choose to describe makes your point.

In the paragraph below, the narrator tells about his visit to the Navajo reservation that his father had left years earlier. This incident helps to explain the feeling presented in the first two sentences.

> I felt nervous and out of place. My aunt and uncle have always been nice to me, but we've never stayed long enough for me to get very well acquainted with them or with my cousins. My one memory of playing there is when Alex let me ride his bike without telling me the brakes didn't work. I wasn't used to reservation roads anyway, and in my panic at not being able to slow down, I crashed into a boulder, finally bouncing into a nearby sagebrush. Alex and the other kids laughed like crazy and talked in Navajo, retelling my mishap again and again. I knew they were talking about it because of their gestures and sound effects. That was one time when I didn't mind it when Dad called, "Let's go."
>
> **Paul Pitts, *Racing the Sun***

Examples

Charlie Chaplin, Mary Pickford, and Douglas Fairbanks are examples of silent movie stars. An **example** is an instance of something. When you want to supply an example, look for lively, interesting items that support your main idea or help explain it. Also keep the needs and interests of your audience in mind. You might use school examples to an audience of teachers, for instance.

The paragraph at the top of the next page shows how two writers have used examples to explain what they mean when they talk about "EcoKid power" and how to turn it on. As you read the paragraph, notice how the examples relate to the intended audience.

EcoKid power is all over the USA. It's your cousins. It's your friends. It's you. What can EcoKid power do? Plenty! You just have to know how to turn it on! When you write a letter to the president that says "Ban ivory! I want elephants around when I grow up!" show it to your friends. They'll want to write to the president, too. When you decide not to buy food that comes in Styrofoam, tell other kids. They'll stop buying Styrofoam, too. When you want to learn about the ozone hole or acid rain, ask your teacher a question. Other kids will want some answers, too. And when your friends tell you what they're doing to spread the word, help them by spreading it, too.

Randy Hacker and Jackie Kaufman,
50 Simple Things Kids Can Do to Save the Earth

Professional
MODEL

The examples in this paragraph also serve as a list of suggestions for action.

Quotations

If someone else has said something that perfectly supports your point, you can use what they said as a **quotation.** When you use a quotation, copy it exactly and credit its author.

The paragraph below is about tennis star Althea Gibson. In 1950 she was the first African-American woman to play in the U.S. National Tennis Championship at Forest Hills, New York. In 1958 she ranked number one in women's tennis. Notice how the quotation helps explain the importance of Gibson's achievements.

Today, Gibson still teaches tennis professionally and plays frequently. After so many years in the spotlight, she has settled into a quiet life, but her achievements remain as dazzling as ever. She occupies a permanent place in both the history of sports and the history of civil rights. As tennis writer Stan Hart put it, "You mention Althea Gibson and you also think of Martin Luther King, Jr., and Jackie Robinson." Like Jackie Robinson, Gibson opened doors for blacks in her sport and showed how hard work and dedication can lead to outstanding achievement in any field. And like Dr. Martin Luther King, Jr., Althea Gibson, through her dignity, courage, and sheer talent, opened the world's eyes to the senselessness and injustice of racism.

Tom Biracree, *Althea Gibson*

Professional
MODEL

The writer notes that the quotation comes from an expert source.

Once you've decided on the types of elaboration that may be best suited to your purpose, audience, and topic, you still need to include specific information. Here are some methods and sources you can use to gather this information.

Questioning

Ask yourself questions. Questioning is a handy technique for quickly discovering what you know and don't know about your topic. The most useful questions to ask yourself are *who, what, when, where, why,* and *how.*

To begin questioning, write the words *who, what, when, where, why,* and *how* down the left side of a sheet of paper. Then see what questions about your topic each of these words inspires. Beside the appropriate words, write the questions you have.

After you've generated a list of questions under each word, freewrite or brainstorm to explore answers to your questions. Then try finding answers to any remaining questions by doing library research.

Exploring

Recalling, brainstorming, freewriting, listing, using a journal—in Handbook 1, "Finding Writing Ideas" (pages 218–224), you learned many ways to find ideas. These same methods can help you find details for elaborating a specific idea.

Try listing, for example. Write your main idea at the top of a sheet of paper. Then, list all the details that come to mind when you think about your idea. Last, choose those details that will best help you get your main idea across.

Research

To find details on some topics, you will need to do library research. The library contains many reference works that are good sources of facts. Use the library catalog to find these resources. You might ask a librarian to help you find good books or magazine articles about your topic. Then, as you read, note any details you find that support your main idea.

Experts are also good sources of facts. You can get baseball facts from a baseball coach or medical facts from a doctor or nurse. Think about the experts you know who might supply information about your topic. Then set up an interview. Make a list of questions you want answered. Finally, during the interview, write down all the information you get and ask follow-up questions to clarify anything you don't understand. If you take careful notes, you may be able to use a quotation from the expert in your writing.

Graphic Devices

Another good way to find details is to use one of the graphic devices you learned about in Handbook 1, "Finding Writing Ideas" (pages 218–224), or Handbook 2, "Using Graphic Devices for Writing" (pages 226–230). These devices include clustering, charting, and using an idea tree.

Clustering, for example, can help you find details closely related to your topic. This technique can even help you discover ways to organize your details. Look at the following cluster diagram to see how you might organize details on skateboard safety.

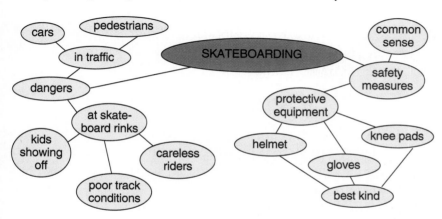

Practice Your Skills

A. Choose two of the following main ideas. Then elaborate each idea in a brief paragraph by following the suggestions in parentheses.

1. The fire engine screamed down the busy street.
   (*Suggestion:* Provide sensory details or tell about an incident. The incident can be real or one you make up.)
2. People act in strange ways on the day of an important test.
   (*Suggestion:* Give examples. If you wish, include sensory details that describe people's actions.)
3. People don't go to the movies anymore. They watch tapes on their VCRs.
   (*Suggestion:* Research the topic by interviewing classmates. Include a quote from one of them.)
4. Hockey (or football, boxing, or wrestling) is a violent sport.
   (*Suggestion:* Choose one of the sports. Give examples or tell about an incident.)
5. Many teenagers dress the way their favorite rock stars dress.
   (*Suggestion:* Provide examples or statistics. You can gather statistics by counting the number of students in some public place who are dressed like rock stars.)
6. The problem of homelessness (or hunger, drug abuse, or air pollution) is growing worse.
   (*Suggestion:* Choose one of the problems. Support the statement with facts or statistics from a recent article in a newspaper or magazine. Remember to tell where you found your facts.)

B. Imagine that you have to elaborate each of the following main ideas to produce a lively or informative piece of writing. For each idea, name an appropriate method of finding details.

1. The person who has most influenced my life is _____.
2. Here are the steps in making a pizza.
3. Today's Olympics have ancient Greek roots.
4. Adults tend to worry a lot more than children do.
5. There are several ways to raise money for our team's trip to Washington, D.C.
6. In 1895 William Morgan invented the game of volleyball.

on the LIGHT side

Outrageous Breakers

When the *breakers* get *gnarly,* they *grunt, growl, hiss,* and *howl.* But a *wimpy mushburger* might just *dribble* and *let down.* Using terms like these, according to *Surfing* magazine, surfers can describe just about any kind of wave they run into.

Try describing a wave yourself. Choose one of each part of speech from the lists below, and insert the words into a sentence like the following.

"Look out—that *(adjective) (noun)* is going to *(verb)*!"

Then try to imagine what you've described!

Ways waves are (adjectives): all-time, big, brutal, classic, clean, fast, fat, filthy, flat, flawless, gnarly, gutless, heavy, hideous, hollow, insane, juicy, long, lumpy, mindless, outrageous, powerful, radical, righteous, rugged, scary, shifty, slack, sloppy, sluggish, spooky, tasty, thick, unreal, wimpy.

Kinds of waves (nouns): ankle-snapper, barrel, beachbreak, billow, bluebird, boomer, bowl, breaker, cloudbreak, comber, cracker, creamer, cylinder, dumper, foamie, greenback, grinder, groundswell, groveler, heavy, looper, mushburger, peeler, reefbreak, ripple, rivermouth, roller, screamer, shorebreak, spiller, tube, tunnel, wall, wedge, windswell, zipper.

Things waves do (verbs): back off, blast, boom, bowl, crank, crumble, curl, dredge, dribble, dump, feather, go round, go square, grind, growl, grunt, gutter, heave, hiss, howl, kick, let down, line up, lob, mush out, peel, pinwheel, pitch, pump, scream, shift, slam, smoke, spin, spit, stack, stand up, steamroll, thump, thunder, toss, warp, wrap.

How do you know he had energy? What was he wearing? What was he looking at?

How Can I Use Elaboration Techniques in My Writing?

Show Not Tell

Which of the two paragraphs below is more interesting to read? Why? What does the second paragraph do that the first paragraph does not?

Telling

I saw an old man who had a lot of energy. He walked near the pool. He was dressed nicely, and he walked around, looking this way and that.

Showing

Just then I noticed a small, oldish man walking briskly around the edge of the pool. He was immaculately dressed in a white suit, and he walked very quickly with little bouncing strides, pushing himself high up onto his toes with each step. He had on a large creamy Panama hat, and he came bouncing along the side of the pool, looking at the people and the chairs.

Roald Dahl, "Man from the South"

The first paragraph *tells* what happened in general terms. With an opportunity to revise, the writer can add details to make the passage more interesting. The second paragraph, then, *shows* you what happened. Descriptive details about the old man's clothing and the way he walks allow you to experience the man for yourself. You can almost *see* him as he walks around the pool.

In "Elaboration" (pages 254–260), you learned about different kinds of details that can be used to support your ideas. Depending on the kind of writing you are doing, you may use sensory details (like the ones Roald Dahl uses to describe the man's clothing and gestures), facts or statistics, examples, incidents, or quotations to support your ideas and to construct good *showing* paragraphs. Asking yourself questions like the ones in the margin above can help you find the details that will bring your writing to life.

Ways to Show, Not Tell

Showing a Character's Personality   Along with physical descriptions, you can use character traits or specific incidents to show what someone is like. Notice how Leslie Norris uses typical actions in the model below to reveal a friend's personality.

> **Telling**
>   My friend was unique.

> **Showing**
>   Maldwyn had been my friend as long as I could remember. . . . He had great advantages as a friend. Not only could he laugh more loudly than anyone else, he was so awkward that with him the simplest exercise, just walking up the street, was hilarious chaos.
>   **Leslie Norris, "The Wind, the Cold Wind"**

Showing a Scene or Place   When you're writing about a personal experience or crafting a short story, you might include details that describe the setting and create the mood. Sentences that tell about a scene can be rewritten to show the scene instead. Look at the following example.

> **Telling**
>   Her father works in a small jewelry store. You can see him from the sidewalk. There are boxes of jewels in the window.

> **Showing**
>   Her father's store was on the same block as the Blue Moon, but two doors from the main street and in a much better location. It was a narrow store with precious jewels in velvet boxes placed in the window. Beyond the window was her father's workbench, and when you walked along the sidewalk you could see her father working there, his head bent over the tiny watches, and his big brown hands hovered as carefully as butterflies.
>   **Carson McCullers, *The Member of the Wedding***

What made your friend different from everyone else?

Literary
MODEL

Where was this jewelry store? What did it look like? What kind of work was the father doing?

Literary
MODEL

Showing a Problem or Solution When you write about a problem or defend your opinion about how to solve it, use facts, examples, anecdotes, or reasons to support your ideas. Notice how the student writer uses vivid examples in the model below to show a problem and suggest a solution.

Where is pollution especially bad? What sort of illness does it cause? What kinds of changes can people make?

Student
MODEL

> **Telling**
>   Air pollution is making people sick. To solve the problem, people need to change their ways.

> **Showing**
>   Air pollution is so bad in some areas of North America that breathing has become a health hazard. Experts say that three out of five people may suffer lung damage from breathing ozone-polluted air. In the worst areas, such as Los Angeles and Mexico City, people's lungs are aging prematurely, and some people even have severe lesions, or damage in their lung tissue.
>   We can all help clean up the air by making changes in our lifestyles. We should walk, ride bikes, or take public transportation instead of driving. In addition, to keep ozone-depleting CFC's from reaching the atmosphere, we should use fans instead of air conditioners. Finally, we should encourage our lawmakers to pass much stricter emission-control laws.

Showing Why When you're writing a report, you will want to support your statements by showing why something is true. The telling sentences below give important, yet general, information about Henry David Thoreau, an American writer who lived for two years in solitude at Walden Pond. Notice, however, that the showing paragraph provides specific evidence or reasons that show why the statements are true.

Why didn't Thoreau feel lonely? What took the place of people?

> **Telling**
>   Thoreau never felt lonely when he was by himself at Walden. He felt at home with nature and with the world around him.

> ### *Showing*
> Thoreau . . . never felt lonely when he was by himself at Walden. All around him he heard the rustling and bustling of nature. Squirrels chattered; blue jays scolded. How could he feel lonely when he had for company the friendly stars which spangle the midnight sky, the warm moon rising through the Walden pines to pave a path across the pond?
> **Sterling North,** *Thoreau of Walden Pond*

Practice Your Skills

A. Rewrite the following telling sentences to turn them into showing paragraphs. Use the writing strategies in parentheses.

1. I was in a good mood. (Show your mood through actions and inner feelings.)
2. He was nervous. (Show this character by using physical details and actions.)
3. She cared only about herself. (Show this character through examples or incidents.)
4. The room was finally quiet. (Show the setting using descriptive details.)
5. Good athletes practice good sportsmanship. (Show the meaning of good sportsmanship by giving examples.)
6. Teenagers should (should not) be permitted to wear what they want to school. (Show reasons to support your argument.)
7. Bumper stickers say a lot about today's society. (Show the meaning behind some bumper stickers.)

B. Write a showing paragraph for each sentence.

1. I was sitting on the edge of my seat.
2. The cafeteria was like a circus.
3. The hospital waiting room was somber.
4. The "F" grade should be abolished.
5. She had real style.
6. Mondays are miserable.
7. A student's life is hard.
8. Every rule has an exception.

She had real style.

How Do I Stay on the Subject?

Unity

A spinning Ferris wheel, screaming rollercoaster riders, offers to "Step right up," peanuts, popcorn, music—start heading toward any attraction in an amusement park and at least a dozen others will beckon you in their direction. The same thing tends to happen when you write. Start following one idea, and other ideas occur to you—ideas that may seem even more tempting to explore. So what do you do?

As you explore your ideas, try to stay focused on your overall purpose. Make sure that each paragraph and composition you write is unified. A paragraph has **unity** if all of its sentences support the same main idea or purpose. A composition has unity if all of its paragraphs work together to achieve the same goal.

UNITY IN THE PARAGRAPH

To achieve unity in your paragraphs, start a new paragraph each time you begin a new main idea. Try not to let any sentence stray from the paragraph's main idea or goal. Even one unrelated sentence can confuse readers. To see how confusing including unrelated sentences can be, read the following paragraph about the kind of movies that may soon be coming to a theater near you.

Main idea

Unrelated sentence

Unrelated sentences

Do you ever wish you could fast forward films in the movie theater? I use fast forward a lot when I watch movies at home. Well, if researchers at the Massachusetts Institute of Technology's Media Laboratory are successful, you'll come close to getting your wish. At M.I.T., researchers are working on developing motion pictures that actually watch audience members and respond to their reactions. For example, if a lot of people were to yawn during a particular scene, the movie would cut that scene short. If only people could take a hint from a yawn or two, conversations would be a lot more interesting. It would be great if people would stop talking during movies, too.

Now look at how much easier it is to follow these ideas when the unrelated sentences are taken out.

Student
MODEL

> Do you ever wish you could fast forward films in the movie theater? Well, if researchers at the Massachusetts Institute of Technology's Media Laboratory are successful, you'll come close to getting your wish. At M.I.T., researchers are working on developing motion pictures that actually watch audience members and respond to their reactions. For example, if a lot of people were to yawn during a particular scene, the movie would cut that scene short.

Topic Sentences

One good way to achieve unity in a paragraph is to state the main idea in a topic sentence. Then make sure that all the other sentences develop this main idea. The topic sentence helps the writer focus on the most important idea, and it helps the reader understand what the paragraph is about. The topic sentence can come at different places in the paragraph, but often it is stated first. To learn more about topic sentences, see "Constructing Paragraphs" on pages 247–250.

In the following paragraph, the first sentence is the topic sentence. The other sentences provide details that support the paragraph's opening statement about the character's beauty.

Literary
MODEL

> The Goober was beautiful when he ran. His long arms and legs moved flowingly and flawlessly, his body floating as if his feet weren't touching the ground. When he ran, he forgot about his acne and his awkwardness and the shyness that paralyzed him when a girl looked his way. Even his thoughts became sharper, and things were simple and uncomplicated—he could solve math problems when he ran or memorize football play patterns. Often he rose early in the morning, before anyone else, and poured himself liquid through the sunrise streets, and everything seemed beautiful, everything in its proper orbit, nothing impossible, the entire world attainable.
>
> **Robert Cormier, *The Chocolate War***

Details of appearance, feelings, and thoughts support the main idea.

Specific Events

Narrative paragraphs are often unified in yet another way. They usually just present related events in chronological order.

As you read the following passage, notice that each paragraph focuses on a different set of actions taken by a stranger. Also notice that the details are related in chronological order as noticed by two fascinated observers.

▼

Literary
MODEL

First set of actions

Next set of actions

Final details before departure

> Father and I watched him dismount in a single flowing tilt of his body and lead the horse over to the trough. He pumped it almost full and let the horse sink its nose in the cool water before he picked up the dipper for himself.
>
> He took off his hat and slapped the dust out of it and hung it on a corner of the trough. With his hands he brushed the dust from his clothes. . . . Taking a comb from his shirt pocket, he smoothed back his long dark hair. All his movements were deft and sure, and with a quick precision he flipped down his sleeves, reknotted the handkerchief, and picked up his hat.
>
> Then, holding it in his hand, he spun about and strode directly toward the house. He bent low and snapped the stem of one of mother's petunias and tucked this into the hatband. In another moment the hat was on his head, brim swept down in a swift, unconscious gesture, and he was swinging gracefully into the saddle and starting toward the road.
>
> **Jack Schaefer, *Shane***

Achieving Unity

You can check the unity of your paragraphs by making sure you have

- deleted unrelated sentences
- made all sentences relate to the main idea
- presented details in chronological order in a narrative paragraph

W R I T E R T O W R I T E R

Stick on one topic at a time. Don't jumble your words around and add something that doesn't belong.

Megan Shumard, student, Charleston, Illinois

Practice Your Skills

A. The following paragraph lacks unity. Identify by number the sentences that do not belong in this paragraph.

> [1]If you think luge racing looks exciting, why not try this high-speed sport for yourself? [2]All you'll need is a luge, a course, some coaching, and courage. [3]A luge is a four-foot long sled built for one or two persons. [4]You've probably seen toboggans, which are built to carry four people. [5]The course is an icy track with high walls that looks very similar to an open-air waterslide. [6]You might want to try watersliding before you take up luging. [7]The coaching is a necessity if you want to steer safely down the perilous path. [8]As for the courage, it, too, is essential, since a luge can rip down the track at 90 m.p.h.

B. Revise the paragraph below to make it unified. Create a more interesting topic sentence and eliminate unrelated sentences.

> One day when the electricity went out my dad taught us how to play an old-fashioned game called "Ringer." Lightning struck a tree behind our house, causing the tree to knock down the power lines. To set up Ringer, you draw a circle ten feet across on the ground. In the middle of the circle, you place thirteen marbles three inches apart in the shape of a cross. Then you take turns trying to knock the marbles out of the circle with a special marble called a "shooter." My shooter was a milky blue marble. The person who knocks out the most marbles wins. There's one catch though: you can only fire your shooter from outside the circle.

C. Create a narrative paragraph about one of the following topics. Include only those events related to the topic you have selected. Also, arrange the events in chronological order.

1. getting ready to go someplace (school, a job, to meet friends)
2. meeting somebody for the first time (friend, teacher, relative)
3. trying something new (dancing, making pasta, doing the laundry)
4. a big event (moving, giving a recital, getting braces)

In luge racing, competitors lie on their backs and race feet first down the ice-covered course.

How Can I Make My Writing Flow Smoothly?

Coherence

> She began to make the American Sign Language gestures that Dr. Patterson had been forcing her hand to shape. She understands over one thousand spoken words. She is able to carry on intelligent conversations by signing over six hundred words in American Sign Language. All she did before was bite Dr. Patterson. Just who is she? She's Koko, a lowland gorilla.

The paragraph you just read was probably a little difficult for you to follow. The order of ideas does not quite make sense, and it's hard to see how one sentence relates to the next. Now read a revised version of the paragraph.

> *At first* all she did was bite Dr. Patterson. *After a while,* however, she began to make the American Sign Language gestures that Dr. Patterson had been forcing her hand to shape. *Now* she understands over one thousand spoken words and is also able to carry on intelligent conversations by signing over six hundred words in American Sign Language. Just who is she? She's Koko, a lowland gorilla.

The revised version of the paragraph is **coherent:** that is, all of its details are connected logically to one another. Here are two good ways to make sure your paragraphs are coherent:

- Check that the sentences are arranged in a logical order.
- When necessary, link sentences with connecting words that help make the order of the ideas clear.

Koko signs "mad."

USING TRANSITIONS

Transitions are the connecting words that let readers know how the details in a paragraph are related. Some common transitional words show relationships of time and space. Others point out comparison and contrast and other logical relationships. The chart below lists some of the words most commonly used as transitions.

PROBLEM SOLVING

"What is the best way to organize my ideas?"

For information on logical ways to organize details, see

• Handbook 7, "Ways of Organizing," pages 238–242

Transition Words and Phrases

Time Order	before last yesterday first	after then during second	next later meanwhile third
Spatial Order	above around inside on top of	below to the left outside along the edge	behind to the right in front of in the center
Order of Importance	first second third	most important less important least important	strongest most significant weakest
Comparison	as similarly neither . . . nor	than in the same way either . . . or	like by comparison also
Contrast	yet unlike nevertheless	but instead on the contrary	however in contrast on the other hand
Cause and Effect	because if . . . then consequently due to	therefore thus as a result accordingly	for this reason so since owing to

Time Order   Transitions that indicate time order, such as *after* and *next,* can link several events together while also helping to make the order of those events clear. Read the paragraph on the next page about a woman's first week in a fortune cookie factory. Notice how the transitions link the events and show day-by-day changes in the woman's behavior.

After the first day, I suffered ten red fingers. This was not a job for a stupid person. You had to learn fast or your fingers would turn into fried sausages. *So the next day* only my eyes burned, from never taking them off the pancakes. *And the day after that,* my arms ached from holding them out ready to catch the pancakes at just the right moment. *But by the end of my first week,* it became mindless work and I could relax enough to notice who else was working on each side of me.   **Amy Tan, *The Joy Luck Club***

Spatial Order   Transitions such as *in the center, in front of,* and *to the right* can help you locate objects in space. For example, transitions showing spatial relationships in the paragraph below help readers to locate the objects in a room more precisely.

The room was quiet—too quiet. *To my left* loomed the big white refrigerator. *To my right* squatted the gas stove, blue pilots glowing. *Straight ahead* sat the huge island. Cutting board, knife, and half-chopped carrot lay abandoned upon it now. Stepping cautiously *to the right* of the island, I came into view of the oven. That's where I froze. The oven door was open. A faint, white light pulsed and flickered *high in one corner.*

Order of Importance   When you organize details by their degree of importance, transitions such as *most significant, less important,* and *least important* can help you show each detail's rank. Look for the transitions that reveal the importance of each detail in the following paragraph.

Alligators, flesh-eating piranha, snakes, thick jungle undergrowth—the rain forest of South America's Amazon has never been a very easy place to live. However, gold miners have recently brought to the region some of the most deadly problems people there have ever faced. *The worst of these new problems* is malaria. This disease is spreading like wildfire. Malnutrition, another terrible killer, is fast becoming *almost as bad.* The introduction of guns in tribal warfare may actually be *the least of the new problems,* even though it, too, is taking a terrible toll in lives.

Comparison and Contrast   Use transitions that introduce points of comparison—*like, as, similarly*—to let readers know when to look for similarities. Introduce points of contrast with transitions such as *unlike, but,* and *nevertheless* to signal differences. Notice how transitions in the first paragraph below signal comparison and contrast. In the second paragraph, the writer uses time transitions to contrast her later understanding with earlier self-doubts.

Professional MODEL

> The magazines told me that to be normal and happy I had to look good and have a boyfriend. *But* I wasn't as pretty or thin as the models. I wasn't dating yet *either.* Every time I read another article on how to deal with your boyfriend, I would feel as if there was something wrong with me. The feeling that I didn't quite measure up stayed with me for years.
>
> *Eventually* I matured and realized that I was perfectly normal and that the magazines were giving me a wrong message. *Looking back,* I'm glad that I didn't start dating *then.*
>
> **Irma Johnson, *New Youth Connections***

Cause and Effect   To show that a cause-and-effect relationship exists between details, use transitions such as *consequently* and *as a result.* Also, try to put the cause before the effects. Look at the following paragraph to see how cause-and-effect transitions may be used to introduce effects.

Student MODEL

> A volcanic eruption can cause severe damage. *As a result* of the deafening noise of Krakatoa's eruption in 1883, sailors as far as twenty-five miles away lost their hearing. *Another consequence* of this eruption was that it created waves so huge that they swept over nearby islands, killing some thirty-six thousand people.

Practice Your Skills

A. Identify the way in which the details in the following paragraph are arranged. Then supply a transition for each blank.

Papier mâché pig.

> Papier mâché sculpture can be made from just a few items. (1)_____, cut newspaper into one- or two-inch strips. (2)_____, dip the paper into a mixture of water and white paste (use equal parts of each). (3)_____, mold the strips over a box, a hanger, or wadded newspaper. The shape you create will (4)_____harden.

B. The following pairs of sentences are related by order of importance, comparison, contrast, or cause and effect. Rewrite the second sentence in each pair so that it begins with a transitional word or phrase that shows how it is related to the first sentence. The first item has been done for you.

1. Days in the desert are hot. Nights in the desert are cold.
   By contrast, nights in the desert are cold.

2. I came down with the flu. I missed the math test.
3. Jeff plays the guitar and sings. Ursula is very musical.
4. The most important task when setting up camp is to build a fire. Look for water.

C. Revise the following paragraph to improve its coherence. Feel free to rearrange and combine sentences in addition to adding transitions.

> I tuned out everything else but the ball. I discovered that I could actually see which pitch would be good. Watching the pitches and waiting for a good one became a fun game. Best of all, though, I felt like I could do anything I put my mind to doing—anything! I watched and waited. I let two more balls fly by. I saw my pitch coming. I swung at it. The rest was perfect—like in the movies. I heard the earsplitting crack of the ball connecting with wood. I heard the wild cheers as I raced around the bases to beat the scrambling outfielders. I heard the bat plunk and roll on the ground as I took off running.

How Do I Begin My Writing?

Introductions

Imagine you are flipping through TV channels and a show catches your eye. How long would you pause before moving on? a minute? two minutes?

Readers become interested or bored by a piece of writing just about as quickly. That's why writers try to create introductions that not only tell what the writing is about but also capture the reader's attention.

TYPES OF INTRODUCTIONS

How do you write an introduction that will hook your audience? Try beginning in one of the following ways.

Startling or Interesting Facts

Put unusual information first to get your reader's attention.

> The University of Rochester's checker-playing robot is a good sport. When it loses to a person, it doesn't knock over the board. Instead it says, in a distinct machine voice, "Con-grat-u-la-tions. You win."　**"King Me,"** *Discover*

Vivid, Detailed Description

Whether you're writing or painting, you can snare people's imaginations with vivid details that appeal to their senses.

> I am up to my knees in squishy mud. It gurgles as I lift up my right leg; then it sucks from somewhere in Middle earth and pulls my rubber boot clean off. My left one is buried so solid that I can't hop to regain my balance; I lurch to the side, put my left foot down with an instant sense of doom. It slips down and down and I slap face-first into the muck. I figure at least it's clean dirt.
>
> **Tom Dworetzky, "Touring the Jungle"**

Writing
—TIP—

You don't have to write the introduction first. Try starting in the middle or even at the end of your piece. Then write the introduction after your ideas begin to flow.

Professional
MODEL

Professional
MODEL

Active verbs and concrete nouns help to bring this description to life.

Introductions　　**275**

Questions

Do you wonder what is happening beyond these open doors? Everyone is curious. Writers and artists often use that curiosity to get readers and viewers interested in their work. Ask your readers a question and they will usually want to read on.

> What happens when two cultures collide? Some things will change, but others will persist for a long, long time. Take clothing fashions.
>
> **"Clothing Styles Adapt as Two Cultures Meet,"**
> *National Geographic*

Incidents or Anecdotes

Most people like a good story—especially an interesting or humorous one. That's why incidents and anecdotes make good introductory material.

> It was game 2 of the 1986 World Series, the Boston Red Sox were battling the New York Mets, and Sox fan Henry Yuen set his VCR to record the contest. Or so he thought. Yuen, a research scientist who holds degrees in mathematics, applied mathematics and law, played his tape later that evening only to find a fuzzy haze where his game was supposed to be.   **"Taming the #!*?@!! VCR,"** *People*

Professional
MODEL

This incident sparks the reader's curiosity and provides a starting point for an article about an invention to improve VCR programming.

Quotations

Starting with a quotation can also spark enough curiosity or interest to get someone to read on.

> It was a sparkling Florida morning—March 19, 1989— when Gillian Mueller, 14, who was visiting her grandmother in Ocala, called home to Long Island, N.Y., and announced, "Hi, Mom. I'm off for my first swim as a tall person."
>
> **Kim Hubbard and Giovanna Breu, "Long on Courage"**

Professional
MODEL

The *who, what, where,* and *why* information supplied by the writers helps to bring the quotation to life.

Practice Your Skills

A. Search through the literary models and student models in the Writer's Workshops until you have found and noted five introductions that grab your attention. Then, identify how each introduction sparked your interest.

B. Following are five weak introductions. Choose three of them and rewrite each one to make it more interesting.

1. Black widow spiders are poisonous. They also do bad things.
2. The costume party was very colorful and enjoyable. My friends arrived in the strangest costumes you could imagine. I couldn't even guess who some of the people were.
3. I tried to give my dog [cat, other pet] a bath, but all I managed to do was to make a big mess.
4. I think my cat is silly. He's always doing silly things.
5. Sometimes the words from a song tell just how I feel. When my best friend moved away, the words to this one song summed up my feelings perfectly.

How Do I Finish My Writing?

Writing Conclusions

Writing a conclusion is somewhat like saying goodbye. Think about the kinds of things you say at the end of a conversation. Do you repeat the idea you want remembered: "Thanks again. I really had a nice time"? Do you tag on a reminder: "Don't forget to pick me up from school"? Perhaps you conclude with the point you've been trying to make: "So if anyone calls, be sure that you take a message." Writing a conclusion can be as easy as ending a conversation.

TYPES OF CONCLUSIONS

Just as there are many ways to end a conversation, there are many ways to conclude a piece of writing. Here are four types of endings to try.

Repeating the Main Idea

When you want to be sure your reader will remember your main idea, repeat it in your conclusion. You might also want to restate the main points you used as support. In the following model the first sentence states the main idea. The other sentences in the paragraph all support that idea. The main idea and supporting details in this concluding paragraph repeat the main points covered in the article.

Professional
MODEL

> Win or lose, most people race sled dogs for fun. Racing is too demanding and too costly, and the cash prizes are too few and too small, for people to race for any other reason. Sled dog racing is not for everyone, but it's a truly unique and exciting sport for people who like the winter outdoors and who love dogs.
>
> **Michael Cooper,** *Racing Sled Dogs: An Original North American Sport*

Making a Recommendation

You can use your conclusion to make a recommendation—to tell readers what you want them to think or to do. The economist who wrote the following piece argues that the penny has outlived its usefulness.

> Let's get penny-wise and abolish the 1¢ piece. The idea is so logical, so obviously correct, that I am sure the new Congress will enact it during its first days in office.
> **Alan S. Blinder, "Abolishing the Penny Makes Good Sense"**

Professional
MODEL

The first sentence is a call to action.

Ending with the Last Event

Many pieces of writing, such as news reports, personal narratives, feature articles, or stories, end by telling the last thing that happened. When you tell what happened last, try to bring the final moments to life by using vivid, concrete language. Also try to show what was most important or meaningful about the event to you or to your audience.

> I watched the closing ceremonies, realizing that our Olympic dreams were now just memories. Athletes from all over the world spilled into the stadium. Some held hands forming long chains; others embraced in tearful good-byes; all were swaying with the intoxicating music in a sea of bright colors. Fireworks exploded overhead. The scoreboards flashed "Farewell." Then the music and lights faded, and all eyes watched as the Olympic torch dimmed, flickered, and died.   **Pat Connolly,** *Coaching Evelyn*

Literary
MODEL

Connolly first explains what is meaningful to her about these final moments. Then she shows the moments.

WRITER TO WRITER

I find that, when writing, you don't have to write in order. For instance, if you have an idea for the ending of a story, you should write down that idea no matter what part of the story you are on.
Jason A. Taylor, student, Flint, Michigan

Using a Quotation

Quotations from eyewitnesses, participants, and experts make especially strong conclusions. The following quotation from a member of a cheerleading squad helps to make the writer's point: a "no-cuts" policy for school activities may be a very good idea.

> Just before she was to perform at a basketball game, this girl told me: "I'm going to high school next year, and I know I won't make the cheerleading squad there. I know there are a lot of girls who are better at it than I am. But at least I got to have the experience. And that's something I can remember all my life."
>
> **Michael Ryan, "Here, Everybody Gets to Play"**

Practice Your Skills

A. Below are five weak conclusions. Choose two of them and rewrite each one to make it stronger. Use the techniques you have just learned.

1. So, in conclusion, I think that cats make better pets than dogs.
2. In order to create a more friendly atmosphere at our school, we might want to try smiling at each other more, don't you think?
3. You don't have to devote your life to cleaning up the environment in order to make a difference. However, sometimes we all should put more energy into recycling.
4. Then it was my turn at bat. What I did would decide the outcome of the game. I swung and missed at the first two pitches. I hit the third. It went out of the park. We won.
5. So, I think skateboarders should wear helmets and knee and elbow pads. You shouldn't worry about how you look. I once had an accident and I know how important such protection can be.

B. Choose a piece you have written that has a conclusion you would like to revise. Then rewrite the conclusion, using what you have learned in this lesson.

Peer Response

"What kind of movie do you like?"
"Which brand of peanut butter do you prefer?"
"Where do you shop for your clothes?"
Each year business people pay millions of dollars to get answers to questions like these. That's because feedback from their customers lets them know how to improve their products and services and how to get their messages across better.

Feedback is just as valuable to writers—but you can get it free from a peer reader. **Peer readers** are friends or classmates who read and respond to your writing. Their comments and suggestions on your writing can give you encouragement and support. Peer readers can also provide new ideas, and they can let you know how well you've gotten your ideas across.

WHAT TO ASK YOUR PEER READER

You can ask a peer reader for a response to your writing at any stage in its development. What you ask will depend on where you are in the process. If you want feedback on a rough draft, ask your peer reader to focus on your ideas rather than your choice of words. You might ask the questions listed below.

- Can you sum up in a sentence what you think I'm saying?
- Which parts did you like best?
- What would you like to hear more about?
- Which parts, if any, were confusing?

After you've done some revising, you might get more feedback by asking your peer reader questions like these:

- Which words or phrases do you particularly remember?
- What comes across as my main point?
- How did you feel as you read this piece?
- Is the organization clear? How can I improve it?

How to help your peer reader

You can help your peer reader in several ways:

- Tell your reader whether your writing is a rough draft or a more finished piece.
- Tell your reader the questions or issues you would like him or her to address.
- Allow enough time for a thoughtful response.
- Listen to what your peer reader says without defending your writing or apologizing for it.

Keep in mind that you are the one asking for feedback. If you want a response to your organization and some new ideas to use as examples, it's fine to say that. Then, if your peer reader starts commenting on your word choices, you could say, "For now, I'd like to get your reactions just to my ideas and organization. Since this is a first draft, I'm not concerned with word choices yet."

How to respond to the writing of others

Put yourself in the place of the writer when you act as a peer reader. Give the kinds of responses that you would find helpful.

- Be respectful as well as considerate of the writer's feelings.
- Give yourself enough time to respond thoughtfully. You will probably want to read the piece at least twice.
- Tell what you liked and what you hear the writer saying.
- Don't give criticism or advice without checking whether the writer wants this kind of feedback.

Writing
TIP

Remember that you decide which of your peer reader's suggestions to use. Consider all ideas. Then make your decision about what to change.

- Always use "I" statements. Say "I found this confusing" rather than "This paragraph was confusing."
- Be specific. You might write in the margins or use stick-on notes to tie your comments to specific passages and ideas.

Here is an example of a weak peer response.

> Your story doesn't have a clear main point. It just goes on and on. Who cares about these characters anyway?

Notice the "I" statements in this improved response.

> I liked your main point about friendships always changing. But I got kind of confused when you started talking about your dog. It would help me if you would explain what this has to do with your main point.

Ways of Responding

When acting as a peer reader, you may find such techniques as *pointing, summarizing, telling,* and *identifying problems* helpful. Read the following paragraphs from a student's first draft. Then look at the comments that follow.

Student
MODEL

> Would you like to travel back in time? In Italy there's a place where you can do just that. It's called Pompeii.
> Here you can see the city just as it was in A.D. 79 when Mt. Vesuvius erupted and buried it under fifteen feet of lava and ash. Graffiti, campaign slogans, and advertisements are still on the walls of buildings. An uneaten meal of fish and eggs sits on a table in a temple. In a bakery, loaves of bread lie in the ovens where they were left to bake centuries ago.

Pointing   Point to words and phrases and ideas that you liked or that you found memorable.

> I liked your opening question. It got me interested.

Summarizing   Briefly sum up what you understood as the main idea. Ask the writer if that was what he or she intended.

> At Pompeii you can see what life was like in A.D. 79. Is that your main idea?

"I'm not sure I understand how peer response works."

For more information on peer response techniques, see

• Appendix, pages 666–667

Citizens of Pompeii, Italy, as they were when Mt. Vesuvius erupted in A.D. 79.

Telling   Describe what happened to you as you read. For example, tell the effect characters, events, and details had on you.

> When you described the meal and the loaves of bread, I understood how swiftly everything must have been buried. But I also wanted to know how big the city was.

Identifying Problems   Identify passages that you found confusing or other difficulties that you encountered during your reading.

> I didn't understand how you could see a city that was buried under so much lava and ash. Was it uncovered? If so, how and when? Also, what happened to the people of Pompeii? Did they escape?

Practice Your Skills

A. Read each of the following peer responses. Rewrite the ones that are negative or not specific enough.

1. Your story is boring.
2. I was confused by this paragraph. If you use transitions, the order of events would be clearer for me.
3. Your argument isn't convincing at all.

B. Respond to the following beginning of the first draft of a short story. Write one of each kind of comment: *pointing, summarizing, telling,* and *identifying problems.*

> "Ready?" asked Roberto. "Lead on," I replied. My heart was pounding hard. I had never explored a cave before.
>
> I felt blindfolded by the darkness. I heard the plip-plip-plip of dripping water and the scuff and crunch of Roberto's footsteps. Caves have odd rock formations. Then, "Time for flashlights," said Roberto.
>
> I was so amazed by the sights of this eerie world that I don't know when I stopped hearing Roberto's footsteps. All I know is that suddenly I felt very, very alone.

C. Choose something you have written recently. Read it and make changes if you wish. Then ask a classmate to respond to it.

How Do I Improve My Draft?

Revising

Even the best writers revise their writing again and again. **Revising** means "re-seeing," or looking at a draft with a fresh eye. When you revise, you bring new ideas, interesting details, exciting language, and improved form to your writing.

Revising doesn't mean just recopying a draft. Instead, keep asking questions as you work: Do I like the direction my writing is taking? What is really important to me about my subject? Are my ideas coming across clearly? The answers to these questions will help you to "re-see" and revise your draft.

Revision can happen at any time during the writing process. Some writers revise as they draft. Other writers draft quickly, then revise. Use whichever method works best for you.

TYPES OF REVISION

Two basic types of revision are **revising for ideas** and **revising for form.** When you revise for ideas, you look at the content of your draft. When revising for form, you check your organization and presentation. The following charts will help you solve problems as you work.

Revising for Ideas

Concern:

- Is my opening lively?
- Have I clearly stated my most important point?
- Is each idea thoroughly developed?
- Are there any confusing or unnecessary details?
- Does my ending tie my writing together?

Try this:

- Start with a fact, story, or quotation.
- State the main idea in a sentence near the beginning.
- Look for gaps in thought. Add details to provide missing links.
- Look for sudden switches in thought. Delete those sentences.
- Restate the main idea near the end.

Revising for Form and Language

Concern:	Try this:
• Have I broken my writing into paragraphs?	• Start a new paragraph for each main idea and for each change of setting or speaker.
• Does each paragraph develop one thought?	• Move or delete details not related to the main idea.
• Do the paragraphs follow in a logical order?	• Make an outline, a time line, or a flow chart. See whether anything is out of place.
• Do ideas flow smoothly?	• Use transitions such as *now, later, then, next,* and *finally* to link sentences.
• Are any words or ideas repeated unnecessarily?	• Combine sentences. Use synonyms to avoid repetition.
• Is the language precise?	• Make sure the words state exactly what you want to say.

COMPUTER TIP

You can easily insert, delete, or move words, sentences, and paragraphs when revising your writing on a word processor.

The following passage is from José's first draft. Notice the changes he made in revising the draft.

Student **MODEL**

Details added.

Told more about the top of the shell.

Moved sentence to next paragraph.

A new paragraph begins here.

This sentence is off the point.

A transition makes the contrast clear.

The turtle's shell is protective. [as] The shell has two parts, the plastron and the carapace. [as a suit of armor] [strong, bony] The plastron is the bottom part of the shell. The carapace is the [domed] top. There are openings where the head, legs, and tail poke out. A freshwater turtle can pull its entire body into its shell whenever it senses danger. The shell protects the soft body of the turtle. Sea turtles have flippers instead of legs. A sea turtle [, however,] cannot pull into its shell. Its head, legs, and tail remain outside the shell.

Practice Your Skills

A. Revise the passage below. Make any changes in ideas and form you think are needed.

An erupting volcano is a terrifying sight. Carbon dioxide and other hot gases billow from the vent in the mountain. Ancient peoples feared volcanoes. Huge stones are shot like pebbles into the air. A lot of molten rock called lava flows down. The lava brings fire and destruction to every house and tree. Clouds of gray ash from the vent block sunlight and turn night into day. It's as if a dam has broken and the inside of the earth is pouring out. A major eruption leaves its mark on the entire planet. A fine cloud of particles circles the globe for months. This haze can be thick enough to lower average temperatures worldwide by about one degree. Many scientists have found links between volcanoes and weather conditions thousands of miles away.

B. Choose a piece of writing you have recently completed or one from your writer's portfolio. Revise it for ideas and for form, using the charts as a guide. Then work with several classmates. Discuss the reasons for the changes you made.

How Do I Correct My Writing?

Proofreading

Before you go out in the morning or go somewhere special, you probably stop for a moment to see how you look. You don't want to walk down the street or into a classroom wearing a belt of the wrong color or with your pockets hanging out. You want to make a good impression, so you check your appearance in a mirror. Your eye takes in a number of small details, and perhaps you make some corrections.

In the same way, before you present your writing to the public, you need to consider the impression it will make. Look for mistakes such as misspelled words and missing or incorrect punctuation. Also check such things as run-on sentences, incorrect verb tenses, errors in pronoun usage, and other errors in grammar. Such flaws confuse your readers, distracting them from the good things you have to say. Good proofreading allows your work to look its best.

STRATEGIES FOR PROOFREADING

Here are some strategies that can help you become an expert proofreader:

- **Proofread several times.** Read your work several times, looking for a different kind of mistake each time. You are most likely to catch errors if you do this careful reading after you have laid your paper aside for a while.

- **Proofread for end punctuation.** Pause where you think each sentence ends. Find the subject and verb. Make sure you have a complete sentence. Also be sure that you have used the right punctuation mark—a period, a question mark, or an exclamation point—for that type of sentence.

- **Proofread for initial capitals.** Skim to find each end punctuation mark. Check to see that the next word begins with a capital letter.

COMPUTER TIP

Use the spelling check feature on your word processor to find misspelled words. Note, however, that it will not catch mistakes like *to* instead of *too* or *led* instead of *lead*.

- **Proofread for commas within sentences.** Read your writing aloud to yourself. Notice where you pause briefly. Check to see that a comma is there and add one if not. Also make sure you haven't used commas unnecessarily.

- **Proofread for other punctuation.** Use a list of rules to check that you have correctly inserted punctuation marks in abbreviations, dates, and addresses and around direct quotations. Look ahead to see that you have both opening and closing quotation marks.

- **Proofread for spelling.** To keep from reading too quickly, start with the last word and read backward, one word at a time. If the word is a name, be sure it starts with a capital letter. Pay special attention to words like *there* and *their*—be certain you have used the right one. Circle the spellings you're unsure of. After you finish reading, check them in a dictionary.

Proofreading Checklist

Step 1. Check the forms of words.

Did I use the correct forms of verbs to show tense?
Did I use any adjectives where I should have used adverbs?
Did I use *-er/-est* and *more/most* correctly in comparisons?
Did I use all forms of *be* and other irregular verbs correctly?
Did I use the correct forms of pronouns?

Step 2. Check sentence structure and agreement.

Are there any run-on sentences or sentence fragments?
Do all verbs agree with their subjects?
Do all pronouns agree with their antecedents?
Did I keep all verb tenses consistent?

Step 3. Check capital letters, punctuation, and spelling.

Are all first words capitalized?
Are all proper nouns and proper adjectives capitalized?
Does each sentence have the correct end mark?
Are all words, including possessive forms, spelled correctly?
Did I use commas correctly?

Proofreading Symbols

∧ Add letters or words.	/ Make a capital letter lowercase.
⊙ Add a period.	¶ Begin a new paragraph.
≡ Capitalize a letter.	∽ Switch the positions of letters or words.
‿ Close up space.	
⌄ Add a comma.	— or ⌿ Take out letters or words.

Note the corrections in the following passage.

> ¶Three volcanic mountains rise from the floor of the
> ~~the~~ Pacific ocean to form ^the^ island of hawaii⊙ some
> volcanos are ~~active~~ still there and parts of the
> island are covered by lava flows and volcanic ash.

Practice Your Skills

A. Proofread the passage below for mistakes in grammar, mechanics, usage, and spelling. Rewrite the passage correctly.

When my parents were growing up, No one owned a VCR. People went to the movies in a movie theater. They buyed pop corn and candy. They sat with a gang of there friends. Going to the movies was a major event that they looked forward to all week. Some saturdays they even set through a double feture. "Those were the good old days" said uncle George. "I still have'nt learned how to use the VCR yur folks bought for me, Uncle George may be one of the last people in the world who don't know how to use a VCR. Most households in the US. now owns VCR's. Over forty percent of new VCR purchases this year were for hi-fi VCRs—the next generation of machines. Things have shur changed in twenty years.

B. Select a paper from your writing portfolio and proofread it.

How Can I Present My Writing?

Sharing and Publishing

If you've just done a job you're proud of, you usually want others to know. You show off your medal from the race, the new paint job in your bedroom, a fresh tray of muffins, or a poem or essay you have written. You feel good when other people appreciate something you've done.

Some of what you write, of course, will be private, for your eyes only. Often, though, you'll want to share your writing with someone. This can happen *during* the writing process, as you get reactions or suggestions from a friend or teacher who reads your draft. Sharing can also happen when your writing is finished and you want to celebrate your writing by presenting it to others.

WAYS TO SHARE YOUR WRITING

Here are ways to share, or publish, your completed work:

- Show your writing to friends or relatives who might be interested in the topic.
- Read your work aloud in your writing group or at an Author's Day celebration in your school or classroom.
- Send what you've written to a magazine that publishes student writing or enter it in a writing contest.
- Tape record your work for the class's listening corner.
- Send your piece to your school newspaper or to the editor of the young adult page in your local newspaper.
- Display your writing on a bulletin board in the classroom or hallway or in the school's writing showcase.
- Arrange a special presentation if your work is for a specific audience, such as first graders.
- Present your work as a poster with illustrations or photos.
- Give a public performance if your work is a song or a play.
- Create a special bound copy for the classroom library.

Sketch Book

WRITING WARM-UPS

- What can you guess about each of these people from the clothes they wear? Where might they live? What foods might they like? What music might they listen to? Write a short character sketch about one of them.

- What does your haircut say about you?
- Freewrite about what the world would be like if everyone looked alike.

Style

You express your personality in everything you do. Your clothes, shoes, hairstyle, friends, and activities all tell people something about who you are and what you believe in.

The words you use and the way you put them together also tell people about you. As you continue to write and to grow as a person, you will develop a personal writing style that is uniquely your own.

How Do I Improve My Sentences?

Correcting Problem Sentences

Pascal, the French philosopher and mathematician, once said, "Please excuse me for writing this long letter; I do not have time for a short one." Writing clearly and concisely takes time and effort. With practice, though, identifying and improving problem sentences becomes easier. The strategies presented in this handbook will help you write more smoothly and clearly.

CORRECTING FRAGMENTS

AND RUN-ONS

Both sentence fragments and run-on sentences confuse the reader. The sentence fragment leaves something out. The run-on sentence combines ideas that should be separate.

Correcting Fragments

A **sentence fragment** is a group of words that does not express a complete idea. A sentence fragment leaves out something important, such as the subject, the verb, or sometimes both. Sometimes you can correct a fragment by supplying what is missing so that a complete idea is expressed.

Fragment At the side of the road *(What happened?)*
Sentence   At the side of the road lay a wrecked motorcycle.

Sometimes you can add the fragment to a complete sentence.

Sentence   The bus was late.
Fragment Because traffic was heavy
Revised   The bus was late because traffic was heavy.

For more help with revising sentence fragments and run-ons see Handbook 37, "Understanding Sentences," pages 394–396.

Correcting Run-Ons

A **run-on sentence** occurs when two or more sentences are incorrectly written as one. Sometimes, the writer simply forgets to separate the sentences with a period. At other times, a comma is incorrectly used. To correct a run-on sentence, add the proper end mark and capitalize the first letter of the next sentence.

Run-on   The outfielder ran back the ball sailed over his head.
Correct   The outfielder ran back. The ball sailed over his head.

Run-on   The bus skidded to a halt, we raced out the door.
Correct   The bus skidded to a halt. We raced out the door.

Practice Your Skills

A. Revise each sentence fragment by completing the thought.

1. The stories of baseball heroes
2. The crowd at the stadium
3. A feeling of joy and relief
4. Can still buy hot dogs and popcorn
5. Holds the record for most home runs
6. Good hitting record but a weak throwing arm

B. Correct each of the following run-on sentences.

1. The pet shop is a popular spot, many teenagers visit it.
2. A girl stood at the window she was looking at the kittens.
3. A young boy wanted a rawhide bone for his dog, he rummaged through the bins.
4. I studied a tank of exotic fish, their colors were eye-catching.
5. Didn't you hear me don't tap on the fish tank.
6. One of the helpers fed the puppies, they barked excitedly.

Ron Cohen, *Willie Mays*, 1978.

Correcting Problem
Sentences   **295**

A **stringy sentence** contains too many ideas connected loosely by the word *and*. Stringy sentences are difficult to follow. The reader must sort out the ideas and their relationships.

Stringy   Melissa needed money for a new bike, and she started baby-sitting, and after three months, she had saved enough money, and the bike was hers.

The sentence merely strings together ideas with *and's*. To revise the sentence, first find each of the ideas it expresses.

> Melissa needed money for a new bike.
> She started baby-sitting.
> After three months, she had saved enough money.
> The bike was hers.

Then ask yourself how the ideas are related. Finally, combine the ideas again, adding words that show the relationships among the ideas. Try using words from the following list:

because	as	although	later
when	until	then	soon
after	before	next	meanwhile

You also may reorder or reword the ideas to sharpen the meaning.

Revised   Melissa started baby-sitting because she needed money for a new bike. After three months, she had saved enough money. The bike was hers.

Practice Your Skills

Rewrite these stringy sentences, making the relationships between ideas clear.

1. The car had a flat tire, and the driver pulled over to the side of the road, and the driver changed the tire.
2. The dam broke, and water flooded through the break, and a work crew brought sand bags, and the town was saved.
3. Isabel had a collection of dolls, and she donated it to a children's hospital, and the children there were thrilled.

4. I approached the door, and my heart was in my throat, and I started to knock, and then the door opened.

5. The bell rang, and the entire girls' team raced to the gym, and the other team was already practicing its shots.

CORRECTING EMPTY SENTENCES

Empty sentences are weak because they don't provide enough useful details. There are two types of empty sentences. One type simply repeats an idea. The other type makes a claim that is not supported with a fact, reason, or example.

Stating Ideas Clearly

When revising a draft, check to see if you have said the same thing twice. If you have, delete the repeated idea or look for ways to combine sentences.

1. Portable tape recorders are inexpensive and don't cost much.

   Problem   *Don't cost much* means the same as *inexpensive*.
   Revised   Portable tape recorders are inexpensive.

2. The crowd cheered when the team appeared. The fans were happy. The band played loudly.

   Problem   These sentences can be combined to state one idea.
   Revised   The crowd cheered and the band played loudly
                    when the team appeared.

Adding Supporting Details

Do not leave your reader asking, "Why?" Statements that are not supported by facts or examples produce empty writing.

Unsupported   I like Wonder skates because they are the best.

The writer needs to fill out the sentence by explaining why Wonder skates are special. Giving a reason, a fact, or an example will improve this sentence.

Revised   I like Wonder skates because the wheels have more ball bearings than do other skates.

TIP

Ask a peer reader to help you think of details to support your ideas.

Practice Your Skills

Rewrite the sentences below. Delete or combine repeated ideas or add details to unsupported statements.

1. A newspaper route doesn't pay well, and the carriers don't make much money.
2. Milk is a healthier food than soft drinks.
3. The doctors in the emergency room treat everything from broken bones to severe hemorrhages. They treat all sorts of cases at a moment's notice.
4. I like dogs more than cats because they make better pets.
5. Our social studies class is going on a field trip to the county courthouse. The whole class will go on the trip to see the county courthouse.

CORRECTING PADDED SENTENCES

A **padded sentence** contains words or phrases that do not contribute to its meaning. The padding is like the extra stuffing in a clown suit: it slows the sentence down and makes it seem lumpy and a little silly.

Some padding consists of extra words or phrases that repeat ideas. Other padding consists of word groups that can be reduced to smaller phrases without changing the meaning of the sentence.

Taking Out Extra Words

Padded sentences clutter your writing and keep your reader from fully understanding what you are trying to say. Sentences are smoother when you take the padding out.

Padded   The coach was upset **on account of the fact that** her two star swimmers broke training.

Revised   The coach was upset because her two star swimmers broke training.

Padded   **What I want to say is that** training rules for athletes make sense.

Revised   Training rules for athletes make sense.

The chart below lists some phrases that contain extra words. Notice how these common phrases can be shortened effectively.

Padded	Shortened
because of the fact that	because, since
on account of the fact that	because, since
in spite of the fact that	although
call your attention to the fact that	remind you
what I want is	I want
what I mean is	(Just say it!)
what I want to say is	(Just say it!)

Simplify Word Groups

Often, you can simplify word groups that begin with *who is* or *which is* by eliminating those words.

Wordy   The video store, **which is** around the corner, rents only science-fiction movies.

Revised   The video store around the corner rents only science-fiction movies.

Wordy   Nan Perez, **who is** the owner, is a sci-fi fan.
Revised   Nan Perez, the owner, is a sci-fi fan.

Practice Your Skills

Shorten the following padded sentences wherever you can.

1. What the U.S. Constitution says is that all of the people must be counted every ten years.
2. The reason why a census is needed is that representatives to Congress are elected on the basis of population.
3. It was the United States that was the first nation in history to make a census part of its constitution.
4. It is a fact that the first census was taken in 1790 and has been taken every ten years since then.
5. The Census Bureau, which is the agency that does the counting, must hire thousands of workers to count the people.
6. I want to point out that it is very important to fill out the census form when it arrives at your home.

How Do I Avoid Boring Sentences?

Sentence Combining

A simple cheese pizza has three essential elements: crust, tomato sauce, and cheese. You would soon grow bored eating pizza made only with these ingredients. However, if you top each pizza you make with a combination of other foods, such as green peppers, mushrooms, or spinach, you would change something simple and ordinary into something deliciously different.

A sentence also has essential elements: a subject and a verb. If every sentence you write contains only these elements, however, your writing will be just as plain as that simple cheese pizza. You can make your writing more interesting and exciting by combining related sentences.

COMBINING SENTENCES
AND SENTENCE PARTS

You can join complete sentences or parts of sentences using **conjunctions,** such as *and, but,* or *or.*

Combining Complete Sentences

When two sentences contain ideas that are similar and equally important, combine them using a comma and the word *and.*

Separate   The tires on this bike are worn.
               The rims are bent out of shape.
Combined   The tires on this bike are worn, **and** the rims are
               bent out of shape.

When two sentences are on the same topic but contain contrasting ideas, combine them using a comma and the word *but.*

Separate   Racing bikes have narrow tires.
               Mountain bikes have fat tires.
Combined   Racing bikes have narrow tires, **but** mountain bikes
               have fat tires.

When two sentences offer a choice between ideas, use a comma and the word *or* to join the sentences.

Separate	Can you still enter the bike race? Has the deadline already passed?
Combined	Can you still enter the bike race, **or** has the deadline already passed?

Combining Sentence Parts

Sometimes ideas in two sentences are so closely related that words are repeated. Combine such sentences by dropping the repeated words or ideas and using *and, but,* or *or* to join them. Do not use commas. In the examples, the repeated words or ideas are italicized.

Separate	Riding over potholes can damage your bike. *Riding over* bumpy roads *can damage your bike.*
Combined	Riding over potholes **and** bumpy roads can damage your bike.
Separate	The repair shop mended the tire. *The shop* could not fix the rim.
Combined	The repair shop mended the tire **but** could not fix the rim.
Separate	Will you buy a new wheel? *Do you need to buy* a new bike?
Combined	Will you buy a new wheel **or** a new bike?

Practice Your Skills

A. Rewrite each pair of sentences as one sentence. Drop repeated words or ideas and use the word in parentheses to combine the sentences. Add commas where necessary.

1. Volcanoes shape the surface of the earth. Earthquakes shape the surface of the earth. (*and*)
2. Did you feel a rumble? Was it just my imagination? (*or*)
3. The buildings shook. They did not fall. (*but*)
4. We called the police. We also called the fire department. (*and*)
5. Repair crews searched carefully. Crews found no damage. (*but*)

Grammar
TIP

Always use a comma before the conjunction that joins two complete sentences. See Handbook 44, pages 556–564, for more information on using compound sentences.

B. Rewrite the following passage. Combine sentences using *and, but,* or *or.* Add commas where necessary.

¹Fans crowded the sidewalks. Curious onlookers also packed the sidewalks. ²Limousines pulled up to the curb. They dropped off glamorous people. ³Was Meryl Streep in that car? Had she already entered the movie theater? ⁴A TV crew carried a camera. The crew carried sound equipment. ⁵People waved into the camera. The camera crew hardly noticed. ⁶The crew was searching the crowd for famous faces. They found none. ⁷The stars were inside the theater. The film was about to begin.

ADDING WORDS AND WORD GROUPS

Combining sentences with *and, but,* or *or* is only one way to avoid repetition and connect related ideas. You can also make your writing livelier and more precise by taking the important details from two or more sentences and joining them in a new sentence.

Adding Single Words

You can combine sentences by moving an important word from one sentence into another. Omit the rest of the words.

Separate	Computers have many uses. *The uses are* different.
Combined	Computers have many **different** uses.
Separate	Computers may be small enough to fit in a briefcase. *They are* lap-top *computers.*
Combined	**Lap-top** computers may be small enough to fit in a briefcase.
Separate	A computer can store millions of files. *A computer is* powerful. *The files are* important.
Combined	A **powerful** computer can store millions of **important** files.

Sometimes you will need to add a comma or the word *and* when you move more than one word into the main sentence.

Separate	The horse's hooves left marks in the mud.
	The mud was soft.
	The mud was squishy.
Combined	The horse's hooves left marks in the **soft, squishy** mud.
Separate	The horse trotted at the trainer's command.
	The horse trotted quickly.
	The horse trotted gracefully.
Combined	The horse trotted **quickly and gracefully** at the trainer's command.

Sometimes you can put the words you've added in more than one place in the new sentence.

Combined	**Quickly and gracefully,** the horse trotted at the trainer's command.

Adding Words That Change Form

Sometimes you must change the form of a word before you can move it to another sentence. For example, you may have to add *-y* to the end of the word.

Separate	The sports car sped down the road.
	The road was covered with dust.
Combined	The sports car sped down the **dusty** road.

Sometimes you must use the *-ed* form of a word when you add it to the main sentence.

Separate	The driver of the car wore a jacket.
	The jacket had stripes.
Combined	The driver of the car wore a **striped** jacket.

Sometimes you must use the *-ing* form of the word.

Separate	He saw the blue lights of a police car.
	He saw blue flashes.
Combined	He saw the **flashing** blue lights of a police car.

Grammar
═ TIP ═

You don't always need a comma between two adjectives. See Handbook 47, pages 630–631, for more information about when to use commas with two or more adjectives.

You may also need to add *-ly* to a word when you move it to another sentence.

Separate   The traffic light glowed in the darkness.
               The glow was bright.

Combined   The traffic light glowed **brightly** in the darkness.

Words ending in *-ly* can sometimes go in more than one place in the sentence. Choose the place that best fits your meaning.

Separate   The car stopped. *The stop was* sudden.

Combined   The car stopped **suddenly.**
               The car **suddenly** stopped.
               Suddenly, the car stopped.

Whenever you change the form of a word, be sure you have spelled the new word correctly.

Adding Groups of Words

You can also combine sentences by moving groups of words from one sentence to another.

Separate   The nurse wheeled the patient out of the emergency room.
               She wheeled him into the X-ray lab.

Combined   The nurse wheeled the patient out of the emergency room **and into the X-ray lab.**

Practice Your Skills

A. Combine each group of sentences. Omit the words in italics and follow any other directions that are given in parentheses.

1. A dog ran on the beach. *The beach was full of* rocks. (Use *-y.*)
2. A boat cruised across the lake. *It was* swift. (Use *-ly.*)
3. A motorboat pulled a water skier. *The boat was* noisy. *The water skier was* on a tow line.
4. The water skier rode the wake of the boat. *The skier's actions were* skillful and courageous. (Use *-ly.*)
5. Mothers waded into the lake with their toddlers in their arms. *The toddlers* giggled. (Use *-ing.*)
6. A lifeguard watched the swimmers. *He had a* tan. (Add *-ed.*)

B. Combine the following sentences by omitting unnecessary words. You may need to change the form of words you add to another sentence.

1. The flea market promised many bargains. The flea market was huge. It was outdoors.
2. One woman was selling arrangements of flowers in pretty baskets. The flowers were silk.
3. A jewelry maker displayed her finest earrings. She was proud of her display.
4. A group of people enjoyed the antics of a clown. The clown made the people laugh.
5. Bargain hunters explored every table and booth. They were cheerful and thorough.
6. Later they looked for a bench and a drink. The bench should be in the shade. The drink should be cool.
7. A woodcarver was selling handmade mirrors and fancy boxes. The woodcarver was tall. He was friendly.
8. I saw someone buy a model of an engine. The model works.

C. Rewrite the passage below, combining sentences to avoid repetition and to create variety. Add the ending -*y, -ly, -ed,* or -*ing* if you need to change the form of a word.

Wayne Thiebaud,
Coconut Cake.

¹Everyone brought food to Aiko's party. The food was delicious. ²Jorge brought loaves of fresh bread. They gave off steam. ³Simon and Sue brought pizzas. The pizzas were small. They were frozen. ⁴Sal baked trays of cookies. The trays were enormous. The cookies had a nice taste. ⁵Ella remembered the birthday cake. That was thoughtful. ⁶Aiko took a breath and blew out candles. Her breath was deep. There were fourteen candles.

COMBINING WITH *WHO*, *THAT*, AND *WHICH*

If you introduce a person, place, or thing in one sentence and then provide details about the person, place, or thing in another sentence, you can combine the sentences using *who, that,* and *which.*

Using *Who*

When you combine sentences to add details about people, use *who.* The word *who* replaces *he, she, they,* or other words that name people.

Separate   Professional athletes earn extra money.
               They endorse commercial products.
Combined   Professional athletes **who endorse commercial products** earn extra money.

The combined sentence above includes all the information expressed in the two separate sentences. The words *who endorse commercial products* are essential. They identify the subject, *athletes.* Therefore, these words are inserted without commas.

Separate   Ryne Sandberg is one of the best second basemen in baseball.
               He plays for the Chicago Cubs.
Combined   Ryne Sandberg**, who plays for the Chicago Cubs,** is one of the best second basemen in baseball.

Here, the added words simply provide extra information about Ryne Sandberg. Therefore, the added words are set off by commas.

Using *That* or *Which*

When you combine sentences by adding details about a place or a thing, use *that* or *which.* The word *that* or *which* replaces the words that name the place or thing in the original sentence.

Use *that* when you want to add an essential detail that identifies or explains the place or thing you're writing about. Do not use commas when you're combining with *that.*

Separate	My parents gave me a camera. *The camera* takes pictures under water.
Combined	My parents gave me a camera **that takes pictures under water.**

Use commas and *which* when you are merely adding information to the sentence. You could leave this information out, and readers could still identify the place or thing you're writing about.

Separate	The world's tallest tree is a California redwood. *The world's tallest tree* is 367 feet tall.
Combined	The world's tallest tree, **which is 367 feet tall,** is a California redwood.

Using Appositives You have seen that you can combine sentences using commas and *who* or *which,* taking extra information from one sentence and adding it to another. Instead of always combining with *who* or *which,* however, you can use an appositive instead.

An **appositive** is a noun or a phrase that identifies or explains the person or thing preceding it. An appositive that adds extra information is set off from the rest of the sentence with commas. Do not use commas with appositives that add essential information to a sentence.

Separate	James Earl Jones will sign autographs today. *He* is a famous actor.
Appositive *with Commas*	James Earl Jones, **a famous actor,** will sign autographs today.
Appositive *without Commas*	The famous actor **James Earl Jones** will sign autographs today.

Note that the first combined sentence is about James Earl Jones. The fact that he is famous is simply additional information. The second combined sentence is about a famous actor. The name of the actor is essential for us to understand which actor will sign autographs.

Remember to place commas around groups of words that provide additional information. Use no commas when the information is essential to understanding the sentence.

Practice Your Skills

A. Combine the following sentences. Omit the words in italics and follow the directions that are given in parentheses.

1. The shoe store just hired an excellent salesperson. *She* knows all about athletic shoes. (Use *who.*)
2. The model railroad club has invited the public to an open house this month. *The club* is looking for new members. (Use *which* and commas.)
3. The nature center has a display about local wildlife. *This display* will interest visitors of all ages. (Use *that.*)
4. Our swimming coach has many years of experience. *She* also coaches at the high school. (Use *who* and commas.)
5. The girl is the editor of our class paper. *She* won the writing contest. (Use *who.*)
6. Some commercials feature cartoon characters. *These characters* are familiar to many children. (Use *that.*)
7. The school newspaper needs a new sports reporter. *A sports reporter* will write about all the home games. (Use *who.*)
8. My bicycle helmet protects me from head injuries. I wear *my helmet* whenever I ride. (Use *which* and commas.)
9. The Pueblo people make beautiful silver jewelry. *The Pueblo people* live in New Mexico. (Use *who* and commas.)
10. This jacket did not keep me warm enough today. *It* was a gift from my aunt. (Use *which* and commas.)

B. Combine each pair of sentences using *who, which,* or *that.* Add commas if needed. Omit any unnecessary words.

1. The two boys bring their own power mower. They take care of our lawn.
2. The tree bears Red Delicious apples. It provides shade for the doghouse.
3. The roller-skating rink is a popular place among the town's teenagers. The rink stays open all year.
4. A figure skater choreographed the ice show. She once won an Olympic gold medal.
5. Last night I held a baby. She had just come home from the hospital.

6. Bowling is a sport the whole family can enjoy. Bowling appeals to both young and old.
7. This copy of *Winnie the Pooh* is finally showing signs of wear and tear. It has been in my family for years.
8. I can't find the gloves. The gloves were in my pocket.

C. Combine the following pairs of sentences using appositives. Add commas where you need them. Do not use *who* or *which*.

1. Amber romped in the park, chasing squirrels and sparrows. Amber is a golden retriever.
2. Mrs. Sparks watched from a park bench. Mrs. Sparks is the dog's owner.
3. Mrs. Sparks chased the dog when he ran toward the edge of the pond. She is a strong runner.
4. Another dog joined in the chase. This dog was a German shepherd.
5. The German shepherd knocked Amber into the water. The German shepherd was a big, friendly dog.

D. Revise the following passage. Use *who, which,* or *that* to combine sentences. Use at least one appositive, omitting *who* or *which* and adding the words that explain or define a word in another sentence. Use commas where you need them.

¹The airplane taxied to the gate. The aircraft was a large 747. ²Excited vacationers hurried down the walkway. They had saved their money all year for this trip. ³Luggage circulated on the carousel in the baggage claim area. It had been taken off the plane. ⁴Seventy-eight passengers waited impatiently for their bags. They had been on the flight from Oklahoma City. ⁵The suitcases did not belong to these passengers. The luggage kept going round and round. ⁶The Oklahoma City airport staff loaded the plane with the wrong luggage. They were tired from working overtime. ⁷The passengers were disappointed and frustrated by this mishap. They had been so excited about their trip.

What's the Best Word for Me to Use?

Meaning and Word Choice

Is the friend you're writing about *peculiar* or *unusual? Funny* or *silly?* With more than a million English words to choose from, how do you decide which to use? That will depend on what you want to say, on the situation, and on who will read your writing.

DENOTATION AND CONNOTATION

Words have two kinds of meaning. **Denotation** is the dictionary definition of a word. **Connotation** includes all the emotions and thoughts that come into people's minds when they hear a word. For example, which would you rather wear—a *cheap* jacket or an *inexpensive* one? Both words have the same denotation—low in price. *Cheap,* however, has some negative connotations; *inexpensive* has more positive ones. Here are other examples:

You're *stubborn;* I'm *strong-minded.*
She's *sloppy;* I'm *casual.*

A **dictionary** tells you what a word means. A **thesaurus** lists a word's *synonyms*—other words with similar meanings. For example, if you looked up *inexpensive* in a thesaurus, you might find words such as *low-priced, economical, reasonable, shabby,* or *cheap.* Then you could choose the exact word you need.

AUDIENCE

When choosing words, think about your **audience**—the people who will read or hear the words. First, consider the age of your audience. You probably wouldn't use teen slang with senior citizens or difficult words in a children's story. Second, what does your audience know about your subject? You may need to explain more to an audience unfamiliar with your subject. (For more information on audience, see Writing Handbooks 3 and 4.)

COMPUTER TIP

Some word-processing programs have special "Grammar Checkers" that not only check grammar but also check for informal language and slang.

Finally, consider where and when your words are to be used. Would you wear jeans to a fancy wedding? Probably not. Likewise, you wouldn't use informal language on a formal occasion.

Formal and informal language are types of **standard English.** That is, both use correct grammar, usage, and mechanics. **Formal English** is suitable for dignified occasions, legal documents, and scholarly writing. Formal English has a serious tone and an advanced vocabulary. **Informal English** is better suited for casual situations such as everyday conversation or a class discussion; it's also used in newspapers and magazines. Informal English has a more casual tone than formal English, with simpler words, shorter sentences, and contractions such as *you'll* and *she's.*

Sometimes informal English includes **slang**—the very informal language of a particular group. **Nonstandard English** usually consists of spoken language that breaks the rules of grammar and usage. You could use it for the speech of a fictional character, but otherwise you should avoid it in your writing. Note these examples:

Formal	John's prevarications are believed to be habitual.
Informal	John doesn't tell the truth a lot of the time.
Slang	What a snow job—he burned me again.
Nonstandard	I ain't gonna believe nothin' he says.

Practice Your Skills

A. Choose a word in parentheses to complete each sentence.

1. Shakespeare (croaked, died) in 1616. [audience: teacher; occasion: report in English class]
2. The team members were (miserable, displeased) when they lost the championship. [audience: students; occasion: school newspaper sports column]
3. Some (creep, miscreant) (misappropriated, ripped off) my lunch. [audience: a friend; occasion: conversation]

B. In a book or magazine, find one example of informal language and one of formal language. Rewrite the formal example to make it informal. Rewrite the informal one to make it formal.

Writing
— TIP —

Dialogue in a short story should sound real. Most people in real life would not say, "I shall be there momentarily," but rather "I'll be right there."

Meaning and
Word Choice

311

How Can I Make My Writing Sound Like Me?

Personal Voice

Your voice sounds a little different every time you speak. Sometimes you sound angry, sarcastic, joking, loving. Sometimes you talk in a formal way, sometimes in an informal, casual way. Your friends recognize you in all these different ways of speaking—even over a bad phone connection. If you try to put on a style or mood that doesn't fit you, however, most listeners will recognize it and tell you to stop pretending.

So it is with writing. You can use various styles, but you can still sound like yourself. Problems come when you try to use a style that you're not comfortable with or that doesn't feel natural. Then readers will usually sense a problem, and they will tend to pay less attention to your words.

BE YOURSELF

When you write, try to use words that come naturally to you—words that sound like you. Sometimes writers are afraid to sound like themselves. They want to sound impressive, so they write long, complex sentences in stiff, colorless language. Here is one student's first draft of a paragraph in an opinion piece:

> It is in the interests of all concerned to pass laws that will ensure the safety of African elephants. These majestic beasts will otherwise most certainly be slaughtered to extinction by hunters who care only for the profit to be made from ivory. This would be unthinkable.

When he reread the piece, the student noticed the wordy sentences and the dull vocabulary. As he continued drafting and revising, he created a version much closer to his natural speech.

> Unless we act soon to stop the ivory trade, African elephants may be hunted to extinction. These mighty animals are being killed in huge numbers just for their ivory tusks. Only when the demand for ivory stops will the killing end.

Writing
═ **TIP** ═
If you have trouble expressing yourself in your own voice, try drafting your writing as a letter to a friend.

BE HONEST

When you write about your real feelings and thoughts, your ideas and writing voice will tend to come across clearly and strongly. On the other hand, when you write what you think others want to hear, your words will tend to sound forced and false. For example, a student writing what she thought her teachers wanted to hear drafted the following:

> Although the principal canceled the field trip just because one student behaved inappropriately, we know that the principal had our very best interests at heart.

When that same student then decided to write about what she really believed, her words carried the strength of her beliefs.

> I was upset when the principal canceled the field trip because one student misbehaved. It seemed unfair. My friend and I decided to ask Mrs. Berkson to meet with us to try to work out a solution.

To discover your own natural and honest writing voice

- freewrite often
- use your journal regularly to record your thoughts, feelings, and interests
- write letters to your friends about things you care about
- read the writing of many different authors
- read your writing out loud to yourself and to your friends

Practice Your Skills

Read the paragraph below. Then rewrite it using a voice that would be more natural to you.

> There is an inadequate amount of time for students' lunch period. It is unfortunate that students must accelerate their mealtime activities—getting in line, obtaining a meal, consuming it, tidying up, and returning to the classroom—in order to return to their classes in a mere fifteen minutes.

How Can I Find New Ways to Express My Ideas?

Using Language Imaginatively

> Summer rains came, soft at first, with mists that lay like lace over the meadows. When the sky grew darker and the rain steady, Grandma sent us out to gather peonies. Grumbling, we carried dripping pink and white armfuls into the house, filling all the pitchers we could find and a washtub in the kitchen. The smell filled the house, and so did the ants that crawled down from the blooms, crisscrossing the house like sightseers. **Patricia MacLachlan, *Journey***

Can you picture the "lacy" mists, the "dripping" peonies, and the "sightseer" ants? The figurative language in this paragraph helps make these images vivid and alive.

Figurative language is the imaginative and poetic use of words to create pictures and sensations. For example, MacLachlan compares mists to lace to help create a particular image and feeling. She compares ants to tourists to add a light touch to the description.

TYPES OF FIGURATIVE LANGUAGE

Three figurative devices are particularly useful for emphasizing important details of a subject. These devices are **similes, metaphors,** and **personification.** Each is a different way of making a comparison.

Simile

A **simile** is a comparison that uses the word *like* or *as* to compare two things. For example, "His face was as round as the moon" is a simile. It emphasizes roundness. What does the next simile emphasize?

> Great green and yellow grasshoppers are everywhere in the tall grass, popping up like corn. . . .
>
> **N. Scott Momaday, "The Way to Rainy Mountain"**

To create the simile, Momaday chose an important detail about grasshoppers: jumping. He then thought of something else that shares the characteristic of jumping: popcorn. His simile compares the two things using the word *like* and gives us an unforgettable image. You can use this pattern to create your own similes.

Metaphor

A **metaphor** also makes a comparison, but without using the word *like* or *as*. This metaphor compares a whale to a mountain.

> The whale was a mountain so high she could not see the cliffs beyond, only the sunlit clouds.
>
> **Jean Craighead George, *Julie of the Wolves***

To create a metaphor, you can begin by choosing an important characteristic. George chose the huge size of the whale. Next identify something else that shares that characteristic. In this metaphor, George selected a mountain. Then describe the first thing as if it were the second—*without* using the word *like* or *as*.

Personification

Personification is figurative language that gives human qualities to nonhuman things such as plants, animals, objects, and ideas.

> The sun crept slowly across the bedclothes, as if nervous of what it might find among them, slunk down the side of the bed, moved in a rather startled way across some objects it encountered on the floor, toyed nervously with a couple of motes of dust, lit briefly on a stuffed fruit bat hanging in the corner, and fled.
>
> **Douglas Adams, *The Long Dark Tea-Time of the Soul***

Using Language
Imaginatively   **315**

To personify a subject, first identify the human quality you want to give it. Adams, for example, wanted to suggest that the sun is nervous. Then emphasize that quality as you describe your subject. Adams achieved this by describing the sun's movements with verbs that would fit the movements of a nervous person: *crept, slunk, encountered, toyed, lit,* and *fled.*

A VOIDING CLICHÉS

Cold as ice, busy as a bee, slow as molasses in January, dull as a doorknob—what impressions do these common expressions create? As you read them, did you find yourself imagining the coldness of ice, the busyness of a bee, the slowness of molasses, or the dullness of a doorknob? Probably not. An overused expression, or **cliché,** usually fails to bring to mind any image at all. So, if you find a cliché in your writing, brainstorm to come up with an alternative image to replace it.

cliché	happy as a lark
alternative	happy as a child on a snow day
cliché	quiet as a mouse
alternative	quiet as moonglow

S OUND DEVICES

Similes, metaphors, and personification use meanings of words to create images. Devices such as **onomatopoeia, alliteration,** and **assonance** use the sounds of words to enrich writing.

Onomatopoeia

Onomatopoeia is the use of words such as *crack, buzz,* and *hiss* whose sounds suggest their meanings.

> If you listen to recordings of owls you will hear an eerie babel of *moans* and *cackling, snores* and *screeches.*
>
> **Scott Sanders, "Listening to Owls"**

Writing
—**TIP**—

To keep your ideas flowing as you draft, you may find yourself using clichés. You can always go back and replace them during the revision stage of writing.

Professional
MODEL

Alliteration

Alliteration is the repetition of a consonant sound at the beginning of words. It can link words and create a mood.

> The old aunts lounge in the *w*hite *w*icker armchairs, *f*lipping open their *f*ans, *s*napping them *sh*ut.
>
> **Julia Alvarez, *How the Garcia Girls Lost Their Accents***

Assonance

Like alliteration, assonance involves the repetition of sounds. **Assonance** is the repetition of a vowel sound within words.

> Once up*o*n a midn*i*ght dr*ea*ry, wh*i*le *I* p*o*ndered, w*ea*k and w*ea*ry,
> Over many a quaint and curious volume of f*o*rgotten l*ore*,
> Wh*i*le *I* nodded, nearly n*a*pping, suddenly there came a t*a*pping,
> *A*s of some one gently r*a*pping, r*a*pping at my chamber door.
>
> **Edgar Allan Poe, "The Raven"**

Practice Your Skills

A. Identify each of the following as a simile, a metaphor, or personification. For each simile or metaphor, tell what two subjects are compared and the characteristic that is emphasized.

1. The dancer moved with the grace of a cat.
2. The snow had frozen in fluffy peaks like whipped cream.
3. The half-open gate invited the boys to enter.

B. Identify every example of onomatopoeia, alliteration, and assonance that appears in the following sentences.

1. Brakes squealing and tires screeching, the car skidded to a halt.
2. The graceful gull glided over the water.

C. Use figurative language or sound devices to describe each of the following subjects.

    a train   a beach   bacon frying

"Benny," the talking car, from the movie *Who Framed Roger Rabbit.*

WRITING
HANDBOOK
26

Who Tells My Story?

Point of View

Imagine you have just laced up a pair of Rollerblades for the first time. You feel nervous and self-conscious. Tipping left and right to keep your balance, you head unsteadily for the park. Suddenly, your feet shoot out in opposite directions and you grab madly for a lamppost to keep from falling.

If you were to write about this experience from your own point of view, you would probably discuss your feelings of fear and embarrassment. Now imagine you are a passerby watching the unfortunate skater. How would you describe the experience? Would the whole situation suddenly seem a lot funnier? Any story can change dramatically when told from different points of view.

DIFFERENT POINTS OF VIEW

Point of view is the vantage point, or angle, from which a story is told. There are three basic points of view: first-, third-, and second-person.

When the narrator is someone who takes part in the action of a story, the writer is using the **first-person point of view.** A first-person narrator uses pronouns such as *I, me, my, we,* and *our* to describe the action and to tell about thoughts and feelings.

Literary
MODEL

First-person point of view

> When I went to bed that night, I thought about how bad it was in my house, how much I loved Stuart, and how glad I was that Smedley and Ms. Finney were at school.
>
> **Paula Danziger, *The Cat Ate My Gymsuit***

When the narrator is someone who observes the action of a story but doesn't take part in the events, the writer is using the **third-person point of view.** Pronouns such as *he, she, him, her, they,* and *them* usually signal the use of third-person point of view. The third-person narrator describes the action and the characters but does not include his or her own experience.

> When Meg woke to the jangling of her alarm clock the wind was still blowing but the sun was shining; the worst of the storm was over. She sat up in bed, shaking her head to clear it.
>
> **Madeleine L'Engle, *A Wrinkle in Time***

The **second-person point of view** is one in which the narrator addresses the reader using the pronoun *you*. Directions and instructions often use this point of view: for example, "After you have chosen the materials, you can begin designing the costume."

Your teacher may ask you to use only first-or third-person point of view in your writing, so be sure to get approval before using second-person and addressing your readers directly with the pronoun *you*.

Practice Your Skills

A. Read the following paragraph. Identify the point of view from which it is told.

> Heavily bundled against antarctic cold, Lisa Zidek and Jackie McCray walk over slippery rocks on a barren coast, carrying buckets of fish and a clipboard. Suddenly the water is torn by penguins, zooming up onto shore as if they'd been fired from submarine cannons. Opening their beaks wide and pointing them straight up, they waddle quickly up to the women.
>
> **David Berreby, "Where the Wild Things Are"**

B. The following paragraph is written in third-person. Rewrite it as a first-person narrative.

> The young boy slipped the mask and snorkel over his face, took a deep breath, and dove into the cool green water. After the morning's snorkeling lesson, he was eager to explore the coral reef. As he swam along the rocky ledge, he spied a pair of brightly colored parrot fish. Below him a manta ray fluttered across the ocean floor. The boy felt a shiver of fear as he watched it. Then in the shadows along the reef, he spotted something larger and more ominous. He recognized it instantly—a shark!

How Do I Write Conversation?

Creating Dialogue

Which passage is livelier and tells you more about the character?

> Jody told the others that she was really tired of working in the bean patch and suggested that they all go fishing.

> "I'm sick and tired of hoeing beans," cried Jody. "Let's go fishin'!"

Writers use **dialogue,** the actual speech of people, in all kinds of works—stories, poems, plays, essays, and letters. As you saw in the passage above, dialogue adds life and interest to the writing.

DIALOGUE IN FICTION

Good dialogue does several things at once. First, it moves the story along. In the passage about Jody, we learn what she wants, and we read on to hear what her friends will say. Second, dialogue makes a story more interesting. It puts us right in that bean field. Third, dialogue helps us understand the characters by showing how they speak—sometimes by including informal language and slang. Jody's words give us an idea of her personality.

In the following example, the author uses dialogue to move the story along and to help us understand the characters. Speaker's tags—*I asked, he said*—identify who is speaking. When it is clear who is speaking, such tags need not be used.

Literary
MODEL

> "Where are the pictures?" I asked.
> "What?" asked Grandfather. "What pictures?"
> "The pictures of Papa and Mama and me. And Cat. When we were babies like Emmett? When I was on Papa's knees?"
> Grandfather looked down at the floor.
> "There weren't many," he said.
> "I don't need many."
> Grandfather sighed.
> "They're gone," he said.
>
> **Patricia MacLachlan, *Journey***

Sometimes dialogue can be a quick way to present information. What do you learn about the Hintons in the following passage?

> "Dollie Hinton's got a healthy girl baby," were Mom's first words as she sat down for a cup of coffee.
> "What did they name the baby?" Glenna asked.
> "They've not named her yet," Mom said. "I think they plan to call her Ethel. They're tickled to death. Three boys and now a girl!"
>
> **Jesse Stuart, "The Clearing"**

DIALOGUE IN PLAYS AND SKITS

Plays and skits are made up almost entirely of dialogue. The dialogue must sound natural, yet it must show what is happening offstage and it must reveal what the characters are thinking and feeling. The speeches of characters appear—without quotation marks—after their names. **Stage directions,** in brackets, give information about setting and tell how the characters move or look. In this example the dialogue and stage directions show several characters reacting to a strange event. The narrator's words at the end help move the action forward.

> STEVE. What was that? A meteor?
> DON. *[Nods]* That's what it looked like. I didn't hear any crash though, did you?
> STEVE. *[Shakes his head]* Nope. I didn't hear anything except a roar.
> MRS. BRAND. *[From her porch]* Steve? What was that?
> STEVE. *[Raising his voice and looking toward porch]* Guess it was a meteor, honey. Came awful close, didn't it?
> MRS. BRAND. Too close for my money! Much too close.
> *[The camera pans across the various porches to people who stand there watching and talking in low tones.]*
> NARRATOR'S VOICE. Maple Street. Six-forty-four P.M. on a late September evening. *[A pause]* Maple Street in the last calm and reflective moment . . . before the monsters came.
>
> **Rod Serling, *The Monsters Are Due on Maple Street***

Grammar TIP

You can use adverbs like *happily, tearfully, uncertainly,* and *hopefully* to show how something is said: "Thanks, but no thanks," Rico said sarcastically.

Writing TIP

Don't overuse speaker's tags. Instead, let the speaker's words *show* how he or she is feeling.

Guidelines for Writing Dialogue

Good dialogue sounds realistic. Like real conversation, it often contains slang, informal language, and sentence fragments. When you write dialogue, be sure to read it aloud. Does it sound like something a person might actually say? Here are some other guidelines to keep in mind when writing dialogue:

1. Use speaker's tags—such as "he said" and "I whispered"—to identify the speaker and to tell how things are said.

   "Skiing is fun!" Felicia said excitedly.

2. Put quotation marks only around the characters' exact words.

   Felicia announced that she wanted to try it again. "Let's start higher up this time," she suggested.

3. Capitalize the first word of a quotation. Also capitalize the first word of a new sentence within a quotation.

   "**N**o," said Hector. "**It**'s too dangerous. **Let**'s just go halfway up."

4. Place commas and periods inside quotation marks. Place question marks or exclamation points inside quotation marks if they belong to the quotation itself. Place question marks and exclamation points outside the quotation marks if they do not belong to the quotation.

   "Do you think so?" asked Felicia. "It looks safe to me!"
   How scary to hear, "The trail has six sharp turns"!

5. Begin a new paragraph each time the speaker changes.

   "Up higher, there are lots of rocks just below the snow," Hector explained. "It's really not safe!"
   "OK. Halfway up is fine."

Practice Your Skills

Using dialogue, rewrite a portion of the following scene as it might appear in a short story.

> Imagine two close friends. One is shy, the other outgoing. A music star is holding an audition. This performer needs extras to be part of a background crowd in a new video. The more talkative of the two friends convinces the other to go to the audition. They arrive at the studio, but they are a day early. To their surprise, the star comes out and greets them. What do the three people say to one another?

The Cliché Expert Testifies

Almost fifty years ago, humorist Frank Sullivan made fun of the clichés, or overused expressions, that kept turning up in sports writing and broadcasting. Are many of these tired old phrases still around today?

knuckle-Ball Artists

veteran hurlers, powerful sluggers, knuckle-ball artists, towering first basemen, key moundsmen, fleet base runners, ace southpaws, scrappy little shortstops, sensational war vets, ex-college stars, relief artists, rifle-armed twirlers, dependable mainstays, doughty right-handers, streamlined back-stops, power-hitting batsmen, redoubtable infielders, . . . veteran sparkplugs, sterling moundsmen, aging twirlers, and rookie sensations.

Q—What other names are rookie sensations known by?
A—They are also known as aspiring rookies, sensational newcomers, promising fresh-men, ex-sandlotters, highly touted striplings, and young-sters who will bear watching.

Q—You are an expert in the clichés of baseball—right?
A—I pride myself on being well versed in the stereotypes of our national pastime.

Q—Well, we'll test you. Who plays baseball?
A—Big-league baseball is custom-arily played by brilliant outfielders,

Q—What's the manager of a base-ball team called?
A—A veteran pilot. Or youthful pilot. But he doesn't manage the team.

Q—No? What does he do?
A—He guides its destinies.

Frank Sullivan

The Trivia Game
1. Who invented plaids?
2. Who made the first necklace?
3. When did sunglasses come into being?
4. When were pockets added to clothes?
5. What French queen invented "big hair"?

- What have you always wondered about? Make a list of several questions you'd like to have answered, such as, Why is yawning contagious?

- What creative explanations can you come up with to answer your questions?

- Do some research to find the real answer to one of your questions.

Academic Skills

What a fascinating world we live in! Although few of us see it through fanciful sunglasses, we each have unique interests and questions that come from our own special point of view.

The skills presented in these handbooks can help you learn about, interpret, and enjoy the things you see and hear around you. These skills can also help you have an impact on your world.

How Do I Improve My Vocabulary?

Strengthening Vocabulary

One of the simplest things you can do to help you succeed in school—and in life—is to improve your vocabulary. After all, you spend much of your time expressing yourself through speech and writing. The more words you have at your command, the more likely you will be to communicate your ideas clearly and effectively.

Also, the more words you know, the better able you will be to understand the ideas of others when you hear them in speeches or you read them in books, magazines, or newspapers. A good vocabulary is like mental muscle. Fortunately, there are some fairly simple ways to build that muscle.

DEVELOPING YOUR VOCABULARY

One of the good things about vocabulary development is that you can do it on your own—you don't even need a teacher or a textbook. The first key to improving your vocabulary is to read as much as you can. Reading tends to increase your stock of words.

The second key to building vocabulary is to keep your own word lists. Simply save a part of your notebook or learning log as a Vocabulary Bank. There, jot down new words that you hear or read. Later, look up these words in a dictionary. Think of sentences in which the words could be used. Jot these sentences down. Try working the new words into your conversation. Also, don't be afraid to stop someone and say, "What does that word mean?"

COMPUTER
=== TIP ===

A computer file is a good place to store your personal vocabulary lists.

WRITER TO WRITER
You should use creative words, but not words you don't understand yourself.

Kristina Lace, student, Flint, Michigan

Using Context Clues

When you come across an unfamiliar word, look for clues to the meaning by examining the way the word fits into the text. These **context clues** may provide hints about the word's meaning. Often such clues surround a word and can lead to an obvious answer. Types of context clues to look for include **definitions and restatements, examples,** and **comparisons and contrasts.**

Using Definitions and Restatements

Sometimes a writer simply tells you what a word means. The writer may define the word directly or restate its meaning in different words. Consider this example:

> *Hieroglyphics,* the symbols used in ancient Egyptian writing, covered the walls of the tomb.

The sentence tells you that *hieroglyphics* means the symbols used in ancient Egyptian writing. Here's another example:

> Jimmy Alvarez lives near the *marina,* where the local sailboats are docked.

The sentence tells you that a *marina* is a place "where the local sailboats are docked." In other words, it is a place for docking boats. As you read, be aware of definitions and restatements. They are often signaled by words and phrases such as *in other words, that is, or,* and *this means.*

Using Examples

Sometimes examples serve as clues to the meaning of an unfamiliar word.

> Chandra told us about the *couture* of India—the silk wraps, sandals, shawls, and nontraditional dresses.

Couture is a difficult word. However, from the examples you can figure out that couture is something like "clothing" or "fashions." Be on the lookout for examples in your reading. They are often signaled by words and phrases like *for instance, like, especially, for example, such as, these,* and *to illustrate.*

Grammar
TIP

One way to spot a definition or restatement clue is to look for certain punctuation marks. A dash, a comma, or parentheses will often signal one of these clues.

Grammar
TIP

When a restatement appears just after a word, it is called an **appositive,** and it is usually set off by commas.
   One famous constellation, or group of stars, is Ursa Major, the Great Bear.

Using Comparison and Contrast

Another common type of context clue is comparison or contrast. Here is a typical comparison clue:

Like her *punctual* sister, Sarah was always on time.

The sentence says the behavior of the two sisters was similar, so you can figure out that *punctual* means "on time."

Here's an example of a contrast clue:

Sean decided that instead of spending money so wastefully, he would try to be more *frugal*.

The sentence tells you that being *frugal* means the opposite of spending money wastefully. Comparisons and contrasts are common in all types of writing, so watch for them. They are signaled by words and phrases such as *similarly, like, as, but, unlike, instead of,* and *on the other hand.*

Inferring from General Context

Sometimes you cannot figure out, or **infer,** the meaning of a word from either the sentence in which it appears or from the neighboring sentences. Sometimes you need to examine the whole paragraph to discover the meaning of a word. Here is an example:

Suddenly we came upon an *ominous* sight. There, looming before us in the mist, stood the castle. It was deserted now, and it looked pitch-black inside. There seemed to be something sinister about the place, some shadowy threat lurking within. We had the feeling someone was watching us. Everything seemed deathly quiet; even the birds had stopped singing. I was worried now; I felt that something evil was about to happen.

At the beginning of that paragraph you may not know what the word *ominous* means. Many clues, however, suggest the meaning. The castle is dark and deserted; it "looms" in the mist. A "shadowy threat" is "lurking" within; it seems "sinister." Things are "deathly quiet" as if "something evil" will happen. These clues suggest that an *ominous* sight is one that is threatening or menacing.

Writing
TIP

When you write, use context clues to help your readers understand unfamiliar or unusual words.

Practice Your Skills

A. Using the context clues given in the sentences, write the meanings of the italicized words.

1. *Dissension,* or strong disagreement, arose among the delegates to the political convention.
2. The water had frozen in the pipes and caused them to *rupture.* Water was flowing everywhere.
3. I am not here to *disparage* Caesar. Quite the contrary, I'm here to praise him.
4. Victoria was interested in playing *percussion instruments,* such as drums, chimes, and cymbals.
5. The loss by the United States hockey team made Lamont sad for days. Mavis was *melancholy* too.
6. The message from headquarters was *terse* and to the point; it was only eleven words long.
7. When she sang, Leontyne Price was accompanied by an *octet,* a group of eight musicians.
8. Willie was always a *precocious* child. He walked earlier, talked earlier, and learned to read earlier than other children.
9. Maria was smart, ambitious, cheerful, and well liked; she seemed to have all the *requisites* to succeed.
10. Earlier in the year the classroom had been full of noisy excitement and confusion; now it seemed much more *tranquil.*

B. Rewrite each of these sentences. Add a context clue to each to help readers understand the meaning of the italicized word. Use no more than three restatements. Consult a dictionary as necessary.

1. Kamaria needs to see an *ophthalmologist.*
2. Andre put the *condiments* on the table.
3. Jobelle has a good deal of *gumption.*
4. The snake's skin looked *iridescent.*
5. Kate showed *ingenuity.*
6. Anthony is a *novice* at downhill skiing.
7. As the two girls left, Carmen's expression was *grave.*
8. At the zoo, Sarah wanted to see the *marsupials.*
9. The king's troops were thought to be *invincible.*
10. The stars *scintillated* in the black sky.

Words are often made up of elements known as **word parts**. If you know the meanings of word parts, you can figure out the words that contain the parts. For example, the word part *re-* means "again." The word part *-ment* means "the act of." So *reappointment* means "the act of appointing again." *Appoint* is the basic word to which these other word parts have been added. It is called a **base word**.

Understanding Prefixes

A **prefix** is a word part added to the beginning of a word. Here are some common English prefixes and their meanings.

Prefix	Meaning	Examples
anti-	not	antiwar, antifreeze
extra-	beyond, outside	extraordinary
il-, im-, in-, ir-	not	illegal, informal
mis-, mal-	wrong, bad	misplace, maladjusted
non-	not	nonfiction, nonsense
pre-	before	preschool, preflight
re-	again	rebuild, retell
super-	above, more than	superpower, superman
un-	not	unwise, unexplored

Understanding Suffixes

A **suffix** is a word part added to the end of a base word to form a new word. A suffix usually changes the part of speech of the word. Sometimes when a suffix is added to a base word, a letter is changed, dropped, or doubled. Examples are beauty + *-ful* = *beautiful* and create + *-or* = creator.

Noun suffixes turn words into nouns.

Suffix	Meaning	Examples
-er, -ist, -or	one who does	believer, cyclist, governor
-ship, -ment, -ness, -hood	state of, act of, process of	friendship, government, dryness, childhood

Verb suffixes turn words into verbs.

Suffix	Meaning	Examples
-ate, -en, -fy, -ize	to make	activate, darken, terrify, glamorize

Adjective suffixes turn words into adjectives.

Suffix	Meaning	Examples
-able	capable of	readable
-ful, -ous	full of	thoughtful, dangerous
-ish	relating to	childish
-less	without	worthless

Practice Your Skills

A. Make a chart with four columns. Label the columns *Prefix, Base Word, Suffix,* and *Meaning.* Then, write the parts of the following words and the meanings of the parts. Finally, write the meaning of each word. Here is an example:

Prefix	Base Word	Suffix	Meaning
sub- (under)	marine (sea)		under the sea

1. submarine
2. extralegal
3. nonswimmer
4. predetermine
5. superhuman
6. biologist
7. loneliness
8. lighten
9. glorify
10. useless

B. Form a new word in each of the following sentences by adding the correct prefix to the base word given in parentheses. Write the new word on your paper.

1. Joe retyped the letter because he had (spelled) three words.
2. "Using taxpayer dollars to get (elected) is (moral)," said the senator, "and no one running for a second term should do it."
3. Arturo's story about the flying saucers sounded (believable).
4. A group of (nuclear) protesters gathered outside the plant.
5. Leaving your skateboard on the sidewalk, where someone could slip on it, was (responsible).

How Can I Be Sure My Thinking Is Sound?

Applying Thinking Skills

"All the popular kids are wearing Neon jeans." "Either you wear Skyjumpers basketball shoes or you might as well stay off the court." "Iron Man Steve, the famous wrestler, drinks milk." You are presented with statements like these every day in television commercials, in magazine ads, and from your friends and classmates. Not everything you read or hear, though, is true. Whether you accept statements like these or question their value depends on your ability to think critically.

Critical thinking involves judging the value or truth of statements. Knowing how to evaluate what you read or hear can help you gain more confidence in your own ideas and opinions.

ERRORS IN REASONING

Some writers mislead their readers with information that is not complete or not true. As you learn to recognize errors in reasoning, you can judge the ideas of others and avoid problems in your writing. Here are some common errors in reasoning.

- **Overgeneralization** "Everybody likes a good comedy show." ***Think about it.*** This statement is an overgeneralization—a statement that is so broad that it could not possibly be true. Words such as *everyone, no one, everybody, nobody, always,* and *never* often tell you that a statement is an overgeneralization.

- **Circular Reasoning** "The practice of adding commercials to the beginning of rental movies is unfair because it's not right for advertisers to put commercials at the beginning of a movie." ***Think about it.*** We do not learn why it is unfair to put commercials on rental movies. The only proof given is a restatement of the main idea in different words. The statement is therefore circular.

- **Either/Or Argument**   "Either we buy a computer or I won't ever be able to learn how to use one."
  Think about it. Either/or arguments imply that there are only two choices, when actually more exist. Perhaps the person could enroll in a computer training course or find some other such means to learn.

- **False Cause-and-Effect Statement**   "Our governor suggested new taxes, then he left for Hawaii. Why should we pay for his vacation?"
  Think about it. Does the governor's vacation really depend on new taxes? Although one event comes before another in time, the first event does not necessarily cause the second.

IMPROPER APPEALS TO EMOTION

Improper appeals to emotion can be just as misleading as errors in reasoning. Learn to spot these unfair tactics.

- **Bandwagon Appeal**   "Don't be the last one in your neighborhood to watch the new Weird Eddie TV series shown on Thursday nights."
  Think about it. This appeal suggests that you should do or believe something to be like everyone else. Consider what is right for you, not what others are doing.

- **Snob Appeal**   "Only the most popular people wear the new Skinny Jeans."
  Think about it. This kind of statement is the opposite of a bandwagon appeal. Instead of being like everyone else, it suggests you will be part of a special "in" group if you use specific products or accept certain ideas.

- **Loaded Language**   "Our coach is confident and supportive." "Our coach is arrogant and pushy."
  Think about it. These statements contain loaded language, that is, words with strong positive or negative associations that can influence you. Think about these two coaches. Which one would you rather play for?

- **Name-Calling** "Everyone knows that Sally, the candidate for class treasurer, is lazy and irresponsible."
  Think about it. Name-calling statements attack or criticize someone. Attacks on a person are one means of getting you to dismiss that person's ideas without examining them. Perhaps Sally really spends money wisely and has good ideas and skills.

- **Weak Testimonial** "Famous fashion model Cynthia Jackson buys Jaxx cars. Shouldn't you?"
  Think about it. Testimonials from famous individuals can provide strong support for an argument—unless those people have no connection to the product or idea. A testimonial is strong only if it comes from an expert.

Practice Your Skills

A. Identify the error in reasoning or the improper emotional appeal in each statement and then rewrite to eliminate the problem.

1. With all the new CD equipment on the market, nobody buys record albums anymore.
2. Ed is such a slob, so why should I listen to his ideas about raising money for the school play?
3. Vegetables are healthy foods because they are good for you.
4. Either our team wins its opener or the whole season will be ruined.

B. Read the following paragraph from an article about the Plains Indians. Identify the loaded language and describe the impression of the army and of the Indians the writer wanted to convey.

> A good part of the army's work was simply keeping peace among the Indian tribes, for these savages lived for intertribal warfare. Only after the Civil War did the victorious North, its troops free for duty on the frontier, launch a grand offensive to conquer the Indians and tame the West. Before this was done, the army had fought more than 1,000 battles with the enemy, and 2,571 white men—both soldiers and civilians—had been murdered. No one knows exactly how many Indians died, but the number is estimated at 5,500.

Study and Research Skills

"Work smarter, not harder," say people in the business world. That idea can apply to your schoolwork, too. The way you study can be as important as how hard you study. Strategies for studying smarter range from managing assignments to keeping a learning log to learning specific reading skills. By mastering study skills, you can take charge of your schoolwork and your future.

MANAGING ASSIGNMENTS

One secret to success in school is keeping track of assignments. The following guidelines will help you:

1. Keep an assignment log. Write down all assignments in a special notebook or folder.

2. Write down the important information about the assignment. Include what needs to be done, what materials you'll need, what form your final product should take, and when it is due.

3. Keep a weekly schedule. Write down all your assignments on a single weekly calendar that you can check at a glance. Update your calendar every time you get a new assignment.

4. Break long assignments into parts. If you're writing a report, for example, list what you need to do each day: find a topic, write an outline, get books from the library, take notes.

COMPUTER TIP

If you work on a personal computer at home, try keeping your weekly schedule on your computer, where it's easy to update.

Calvin and Hobbes

by Bill Watterson

TAKING NOTES

Taking notes is an important part of your job as a student. Good notes help you remember what you hear in class and what you read. There are many effective ways of taking notes. Find the one that works best for you. Here are some guidelines:

1. Keep your notes in a single place. Use a separate folder, notebook, or notebook section for each subject. Write the date on each page of notes.

2. Use a modified outline form, not complete sentences.
Jot down main ideas. Write related ideas beneath the main ones. Indent the related ideas. Here is an example of a modified outline:

> Native Americans of Eastern Woodlands
> > Types of houses
> > > —bark-covered wigwam
> > > —longhouse (large, many families in one place)
> > > —clay & wattle (wattle = sticks woven together)
> > Foods
> > > —game (deer, pigs)
> > > —crops (corn, squash, pumpkin, beans)

3. Look and listen for key words. Don't try to write down everything. Look for key points, such as names, important facts and ideas, main points of outlines. Key words that signal important information include *first, most important, for these reasons, remember, finally.*

4. Use abbreviations and symbols. Make up your own abbreviations if you like. The following are some of those in common use:

&	and	=	equals	y	why
w/	with	Eng	English	~	approximately
w/o	without	def	definition	re	regarding

5. Go back over your notes. Review your notes as soon as you can. Revise or add to them if necessary, perhaps by underlining key points or grouping related ideas together.

USING KWL

More and more students use the KWL study method, because they find it an efficient and enjoyable way to learn. Here's how it works. As you study, ask yourself these three questions about your subject:

K: What do I already **know** about it?
W: What do I **want** to know?
L: What did I **learn?**

To answer the first question, list what you already know about the subject. (You may be surprised at the length of your list!) At this stage you are brainstorming and taking notes. Then, with the help of your list, think of what you want or need to know about the subject. Write down questions you'd like answered. As you study, look for the answers. Finally, after you've studied, list the things you've learned.

You can use the KWL method for many different types of studying. For example, you can use it to study a chapter in a text-book, to do a research report, or to work on a class project. You can use it alone or with classmates. The KWL method helps you take charge of your own learning.

USING A LEARNING LOG

A good way to use the KWL approach is with a learning log. In fact, keeping a learning log is a good way to keep track of your subject no matter how you study. A learning log is simply a note-book or journal where you note down whatever seems important or interesting as you learn about something.

Let's say that you plan to study tropical rain forests. Using KWL, you first jot down what you already know about rain forests and what you might like to know. Any notes you take in class go in the log too. So do any stray ideas or unanswered questions you might have. Later, based on your questions or an assignment, you might do some library research or conduct an interview if possible. Again, the results go in the learning log.

Day by day, you keep track of the rain forest project. When the project is complete, you jot down your reactions and what you've learned. Now it's all there in your log—what you've thought, learned, and felt about a subject. Over time, you will develop a really interesting document—a kind of diary of your mind.

Learning logs can also help you with your reading. Suppose your teacher asks you to read Mark Twain's *Adventures of Tom Sawyer.* As you read, you jot down notes about whom you like or dislike in the story, what you don't understand, what you think will happen next. You even write about what it might be like to live on the Mississippi River or to have a friend like Huck Finn.

Whether the subject is rain forests or Tom Sawyer, keeping a log puts you in charge of what you know. Here are some of the things you can put into your log:

1. Freewriting about anything that interests you
2. KWL lists—what you know, want to know, and have learned
3. A WILT list—"What I Learned Today," updated daily
4. Questions about an assignment or anything else
5. Possible writing topics, listed in a special part of your log
6. Reactions to whatever you're reading at the time
7. Notes on group projects—progress, problems
8. Rough drafts or outlines for future writing
9. Summaries of things you've heard or read
10. Personal hopes or goals for each of your classes
11. Plan for the future—even daydreams

READING SKILLS

Good reading skills will last you all your life. Here are some tricks that many good readers have found helpful.

Previewing Your Reading   Look over the material to get an idea of what it's about. Read titles and headings. Glance at charts and illustrations and read the captions. If you're previewing a chapter, read the first two paragraphs and the first sentence of each paragraph that follows. Read the last two paragraphs. All this should give you an accurate impression of the whole.

Adjusting Your Reading Rate   Don't read everything the same way. Sometimes you may need only a general idea of the material. Other times you will skim to find a particular piece of information. Often you will need to read slowly and carefully.

Reading Actively   Good reading is more like having a conversation than listening to a lecture. Don't just move your eyes across the page. Instead, read with a pencil in your hand. As you read, respond in writing (or even aloud) to what you are reading. A learning log is a good place to record your reactions.

Asking Questions   Previewing the reading may raise questions in your mind. As you read, look for answers and write down additional questions that may come to you.

Making Predictions   Especially when reading fiction, it's fun to make predictions, or guesses, about what might happen next.

Looking for Main Ideas and Key Terms   These often appear in beginning and ending paragraphs—and in the topic sentences of paragraphs in between. Jot down main points in your learning log, along with any important terms and definitions.

Reacting to What You Read   Think about what the author says. Do you agree or disagree? Why or why not? Do you have questions? Write your own ideas and opinions in your learning log.

Reviewing Your Notes   Organize your ideas while the material is fresh in your mind. In your log, list what you have learned.

The experimental Impact may be one of the first mass-produced electric cars.

Practice Your Skills

A. Practice making a learning log entry using the KWL study method. First, choose one of the following topics, or choose another topic that interests you.

blues singers	mummies	pueblo living
soap operas	Nile River	comets
Mars	plague	electric cars

Write the topic at the top of a piece of paper. Then make two columns. Label the left-hand column "What I already know."

Label the right-hand column "What I want to learn." In the columns, list what you know about the topic and what you would like to learn about it.

B. Take notes based on the following passage.

In 1956, the year before the Soviet Union launched *Sputnik I,* a group of scientists met to discuss how to explore a different frontier—one that contained mystery, danger, and possibly, alien life. They were planning a voyage to the bottom of the sea.

The lakes, seas, and oceans hold 99 percent of earth's living space. But the deep ocean, sometimes called the abyss, contains huge expanses of uncharted territory. Its great depth and harsh conditions make it nearly impossible to explore. In some places, the water temperature is barely above freezing. There is no light. In the deepest spots, you could sink Mount Everest to the bottom, and it still would be covered by a mile of water. The air pressure reaches eight tons per square inch, enough to compress a Styrofoam coffee cup to a size not much larger than a thimble.

The scientists knew that they were going to need a very special vehicle to explore the deep ocean. Like a spacecraft, it would have to provide an air supply, light source, pressurized environment, and a communications life line. The result was not *Apollo* or *Viking,* or even *Discovery.* It was *Alvin.*

Alvin was a submersible, or submarine, maintained and operated by the Woods Hole Oceanographic Institution of Woods Hole, Massachusetts, to provide a way for scientists to study the ocean floor. It measured eight by twenty-two feet—not much larger than a car.

Odyssey, January-February, 1992

C. With a small group of classmates, respond to the passage about *Alvin.* Choose one group member to read it aloud. At the end of the reading, discuss what its main idea is and develop several questions about the topic. Make a prediction about what the rest of the article will be about.

How Do I Put Things in My Own Words?

Writing Paraphrases and Summaries

Suppose you read an exciting eyewitness report about the tearing down of the Berlin Wall. You are so interested that you begin reading about the terrifying history of the wall, the people who built it, and those who opposed it. You have the right report topic, but you must put the information you have collected into manageable shape. The skills of paraphrasing and summarizing will help you draft your report.

PARAPHRASING

When you **paraphrase,** you rewrite a passage in your own words. Your paraphrase should be about as long as the original passage. These steps may help:

1. **Find the main idea.** Read a passage carefully. Determine the writer's main idea and rewrite it in your own words.

2. **List supporting details.** In your own words, write down all the details, points, and arguments that support the main idea of the passage.

3. **Simplify the language.** Try to simplify the material by replacing difficult words with more familiar ones. Keep the tone—the excitement, seriousness, or humor—of the original article.

4. **Revise your paraphrase.** Make sure you have included key ideas and details. Proofread for spelling, punctuation, capitalization, and grammar. Check that you have given credit to authors whose ideas you use.

For example, suppose you are writing a report about the Cajuns whom you learned about in Workshop 8. You read the paragraph on the next page about Cajun music:

COMPUTER TIP

The on-line thesaurus in some computers can help you find synonyms to use in your paraphrase.

A very different form of music unique to Louisiana is the accordion music of the Cajuns. Groups of musicians travel from town to town performing at all-night dances called *fais-dodos* (literally, "go to sleep"). A Cajun band usually consists of a fiddle, guitar, accordion, and set of steel triangles. Many of the rollicking tunes came from France in the early 1700s. But the songs, though usually sung in French, are often distinctly American in theme. Even the vicious bayou mosquitoes are a worthy subject: "The mosquitoes have eaten up my sweetheart! They have left only two big toes!"

Deborah Kent, *America the Beautiful: Louisiana*

You might paraphrase the paragraph as follows:

According to Deborah Kent, a distinct type of music is found in Louisiana. Cajun bands that travel through Louisiana towns play accordion music at all-night dances. The bands feature instruments such as a fiddle, a guitar, an accordion, and a set of steel triangles. Many of the lively tunes they play came from France in the early 1700s. The songs, sung in French, usually concern American subjects, such as the unbelievable fierceness of swamp mosquitoes.

SUMMARIZING

To **summarize,** express the main ideas of a passage in your own words, leaving out details. A summary is usually about one-third as long as the original. Follow these steps:

Writing a Summary

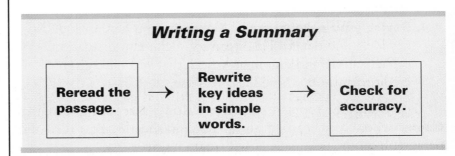

Reread the passage.	→	Rewrite key ideas in simple words.	→	Check for accuracy.

Here is a summary of the paragraph about Cajun music:

> In Louisiana, Cajuns play lively accordion music. Many tunes came from France in the 1700s, but today's lyrics, usually sung in French, have strong American themes.

Student
MODEL

AVOIDING PLAGIARISM

Like other creative people, writers deserve credit for their words and ideas. When you write reports, credit your sources. Avoid **plagiarism**—presenting someone's words or ideas as your own.

You need not credit a source that provides general information that you rewrite in your own words. You must credit a source, however, when you quote exact words or you paraphrase or summarize original ideas. Not to do so is dishonest.

To credit a source, follow the guidelines in Workshop 8, "Reports," page 199. Observe these rules for avoiding plagiarism.

- **Credit all direct quotations.** Use quotation marks and copy the source word for word. You might introduce the quotation with words like, *As Kent said, . . .*

- **Credit all original ideas.** If you didn't think of it, and you haven't heard of it or read it in more than one source, then give your source credit.

Practice Your Skills

Working with a partner, write a paraphrase of this paragraph. Then use your paraphrase to write a summary.

> The beauty of the mountain bike is that it brings riders to territory that was previously available mainly to motorcyclists—but it does so without tearing up fragile wilderness areas. It would take dozens of off-roaders doing their worst to equal the damage inflicted by an off-road motorcycle, for which high-power wheel spin is the big kick. Even horses do more damage than these mountain bikes.
>
> **Walton and Rostaing, *Bill Walton's Total Book of Bicycling***

Writing Paraphrases
and Summaries   **343**

How Can I Learn from Charts and Graphs?

Understanding Graphic Aids

Graphic aids are pictures or visual devices that present a lot of information in a small amount of space. Graphic aids often appear in newspapers, textbooks, reference books, and other similar kinds of writing. The chart below is one kind of graphic aid. It summarizes the features of three *other* kinds of graphic aids.

Comparing Graphic Aids		
Graphic Aid	**How It Looks**	**What It Shows**
Pie chart	Circle divided into sections	Parts of a whole
Bar graph	Horizontal or vertical bars	Numerical information
Line graph	Line connecting points on a graph	Trends or changes over time

READING GRAPHS

Pie Charts   In a **pie chart,** or **circle graph,** the circle represents 100 percent, or the whole, of something. The "slices" of the "pie" show the parts or percentages of the whole.

These circle graphs tell what percentage of the total immigrant population came to the United States from various parts of the world during two different periods.

Changes in U.S. Immigration

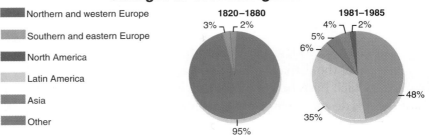

Northern and western Europe
Southern and eastern Europe
North America
Latin America
Asia
Other

1820–1880
3% ⌐ 2%
95%

1981–1985
4% ⌐ 2%
5%
6%
48%
35%

Bar Graphs   A **bar graph** uses separate bars to show numerical information. Usually, numbers run along one side of the graph, and words run along another side. The length of each bar on the graph shows what number is associated with each word or name. The bars allow you to compare the facts presented. The bar graph below, for example, shows the amount of time teens spend on various activities.

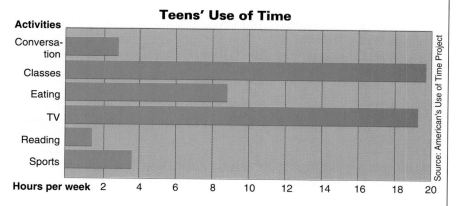

Teens' Use of Time

Source: American's Use of Time Project

Line Graphs   A **line graph** shows the increases or decreases in something over time. The line connecting specific points plotted on the graph shows trends and allows you to make predictions. This line graph shows that voter turnout has generally been declining since 1960.

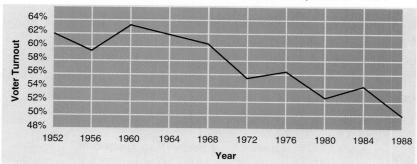

Voter Turnout for Presidential Elections, 1952–1988

Sometimes symbols, or pictures, are used instead of bars or lines. A graph that uses pictures instead of bars or lines is known as a **picture graph.**

Writing
TIP

Try creating your own graphic aids when you write reports or articles for your school paper.

Many computer programs can help you create graphs and tables. Ask your computer teacher about them.

Guidelines for Reading Graphic Aids

- Read the title or caption of the graphic aid to learn what information is covered.
- Read the key to the symbols or abbreviations, if there is one.
- Read any headings along the top, bottom, and sides of the graph or chart.
- Find specific information by making a connection between the numbers on the graph and the points on the line, the bars, or the sections of the circle.

Practice Your Skills

A. Based on the graphs shown on the preceding pages, answer the following questions.

1. What percentage of immigrants came to the United States from northern and western Europe between 1820 and 1880? between 1981 and 1985?
2. Between 1981 and 1985, nearly half of the immigrants to the United States came from what continent?
3. About how many more hours do teenagers spend eating each week than they spend engaging in sports activities?
4. What percentage of eligible voters cast their ballots in the 1988 presidential election?

B. Use the information from the table below to draw a bar graph. Along the left side of the graph, write the numbers 0 to 100 in increments of 10, starting with 0 at the bottom. Along the bottom of the graph, write the names of the countries listed. Don't forget to write the title and headings in the appropriate places.

Aluminum Can Recycling, 1990

Countries	Recycling Rates, %
United States	64
Italy	10
Britain	6
Japan	42

Where Can I Find Information?

Using the Library

Today's libraries are more like community resource centers than simply collections of books. At your local library, you'll find books, to be sure, shelves and shelves of them. You also may find magazines, posters, videotapes, audiocassettes, films, filmstrips, CDs, computers, and works of art. Some libraries present concerts, movies, plays, puppet shows, classes in arts and crafts, and other special events. You can still go to the library to do research and to study, but you can also go there to explore whatever interests you. So check out your local library. You'll find yourself checking out more than just books.

THE ORGANIZATION OF THE LIBRARY

Because there's so much going on in libraries, they can be confusing places. Learning about how libraries are organized will help you to find just what you're looking for.

Sections of the Library

Most libraries are organized into sections to help their patrons find materials. The following list briefly describes some of the most common sections:

- **The Stacks**   The shelves where you can find fiction and nonfiction books are called *the stacks.*

- **Catalogs and Indexes**   Catalogs and indexes, which might be kept in card files, books or folders, or on-line computer files, help you locate materials in the library.

- **The Reference Section**   Encyclopedias, dictionaries, and other materials are kept here.

- **The Periodicals Section**   You can find magazines, newspapers, and journals in the periodicals section of your library.

- **The Audiovisual Section**   In some libraries, audiovisual materials such as videotapes, audiocassettes, and CDs, and even projectors and tape players are available for use or checkout.

- **The Young Adult and Children's Section**   Books and other materials especially for young people and children are often shelved in a special section.

- **Special Services Section**   Many libraries present special events such as story times for children, book readings, art displays, and lectures. The special services section might also provide space for local government services, community bulletin boards, computers, and classes.

The Arrangement of Books

Libraries arrange books by the type of material they cover. Most libraries separate books into at least four types: **fiction, nonfiction, biography and autobiography,** and **reference.**

Fiction   You will find novels, collections of short stories, and other fiction arranged on shelves in alphabetical order by the author's last name. These shelves make up the fiction section. To find *The Pigman* by Paul Zindel, for example, find the fiction section and look for books by authors whose last name begins with *Z.*

Nonfiction   For books that provide factual information on almost any subject, look to the nonfiction section. Most libraries organize nonfiction books by using the Dewey Decimal System, which classifies books into the following groups by their subject:

000–099	General Works	500–599	Science
100–199	Philosophy	600–699	Technology
200–299	Religion	700–799	Fine Arts
300–399	Social Science	800–899	Literature
400–499	Language	900–999	History

Each major group is further divided into smaller categories. For example, the 700s are divided into separate sections on music (780), sports (790), and so on. Nonfiction books are shelved in the stacks in the order of their Dewey Decimal numbers.

Biography and Autobiography   A **biography** is a nonfiction book about someone's life. In an **autobiography,** a writer tells the story of his or her own life. Biographies and autobiographies are assigned Dewey Decimal numbers in the 920s. In some libraries, you'll find these books shelved in numerical order with other nonfiction. At other libraries, you will find them in a separate biography section. In either case, biographies and autobiographies are arranged in alphabetical order by the last name of the person the book is about. For example, to find a biography of the Olympic hero Jesse Owens, you would look in the biography section or in the 920s under the letter *O*.

Reference Books   When you research a report topic, an encyclopedia and other reference books may be the first places you look for information. Many libraries keep these books in a separate reference section. Usually reference books cannot be checked out, so you will have to use them at the library.

Locating Materials

Each library book has a special code of letters and numbers printed on its spine. This code indicates where the book belongs on the library shelves.

Call Numbers   Nonfiction books are marked with a **call number.** Under the Dewey Decimal System, the first part of the call number is the Dewey Decimal number of that book. Books with the same Dewey number are shelved together.

Following or beneath a book's Dewey number you might find another code, based on the author's name, called the **cutter number.** The cutter number helps you locate a specific book among all the books that have the same Dewey number. Such books are arranged according to the first letters of the cutter number.

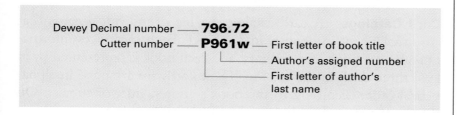

Dewey Decimal number —— **796.72**
Cutter number —— **P961w** —— First letter of book title
—— Author's assigned number
—— First letter of author's last name

Section Letters On the spines of some books you might see one or more **section letters,** which identify different sections of the library. Section letters might appear before or above a call number for nonfiction works. Books such as biographies or mystery novels might have only section letters, or section letters and the biography subject's or the author's initial. These materials would be shelved alphabetically by the subject's or the author's last name. Here are some commonly used section letters:

R, REF = Reference	B, BIO = Biography
C, CHILD = Children's	X, J, JUV = Juvenile
X, Y, YA = Young Adult	F, FIC = Fiction
AV = Audiovisual	P, PER = Periodicals
SF = Science Fiction	MYS = Mystery

LIBRARY CATALOGS

The easiest way to find materials in a library is to use a library catalog. Library catalogs list the books and other materials the library owns. There are several kinds of catalog systems in use. Whatever kind of catalog system your library has, it will provide you with the information you need to identify the book you want and to find it in the stacks.

Kinds of Catalogs

Two of the most common types of library catalogs are card catalogs and on-line computer catalogs. These resources can provide you with titles of all the library's books on a specific subject or by a particular author. Catalogs can also give you author and subject information for a specific title.

Card Catalogs A card catalog is a file of individual cards that are usually kept in drawers in a cabinet. Each card gives information about a book in the library, and each book is represented by at least three cards in the catalog. These cards are arranged in alphabetical order according to the book's author, title, or subject. On the next page is an example of a subject card for a book on science.

On-line Computer Catalogs   Many public libraries and some school libraries now have their catalogs on computer. You can search for materials by typing in key words, such as the author's name, the title, or the subject. The computer matches what you have entered against the information it has about the library's collection. The computer screen then shows the information you asked for, displaying the information in a form similar to that of a card in a card catalog. Look on the next page for an example of a computer-catalog entry. Computer-catalog systems differ from library to library. If your library has a computer catalog, ask your librarian how to use it.

Catalog Entries

Library catalogs include separate title, author, and subject entries to make book searches easy. Each kind of entry gives the same information about the book, but in a different arrangement. So no matter what information you begin with, the catalog will lead you to the books you want.

Subject Entries   Suppose that you need a topic for a science report on energy, and you want to write about your favorite topic, sports. How could you tie sports into a report about energy? To find out, you could look under *Science, Energy,* or *Sports* in the library catalog to find subject entries for books that might help you. You might find a card catalog entry like the one shown. Notice that the book's call number appears on the entry to tell you where to locate the book in the stacks.

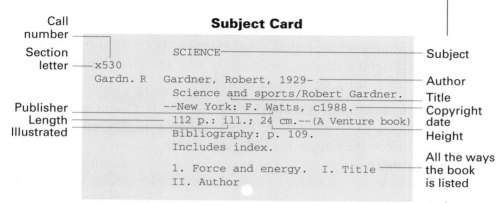

Subject Card

Call number
Section letter
Publisher
Length
Illustrated

```
              SCIENCE                                    Subject
    x530
    Gardn. R   Gardner, Robert, 1929-                    Author
               Science and sports/Robert Gardner.        Title
               --New York: F. Watts, c1988.              Copyright date
               112 p.: ill.; 24 cm.--(A Venture book)    Height
               Bibliography: p. 109.
               Includes index.
                                                         All the ways
               1. Force and energy.  I. Title            the book
               II. Author                                is listed
```

COMPUTER TIP

Many computer catalogs allow you to narrow your search by using key words that combine an author's name and a subject. For example, you could look for all books by an author named Brown on the subject of Space Flight.

Author Entries Imagine that you've enjoyed reading a book by Nat Hentoff. You want to find another one of his books. To do that, you can look under *H* in the catalog and find author entries with the name *Hentoff* on them. A card catalog would have a separate card for each book by Nat Hentoff. An on-line catalog might show a screen with all of the library's books by that author. Here is a sample of a single entry you might see under *Hentoff* in a computer catalog. Notice that this computer entry provides the same kinds of information that the card-catalog entry does.

Computer Catalog Author Entry

```
    AUTHOR:   Hentoff, Nat
     TITLE:   Jazz Country
 PUBLISHER:   New York, Harper & Row [1965]
  SUBJECTS:   Jazz musicians--Fiction.
African-Americans--Fiction.


## ----Call number ------Volume Material  Location  Status
1        Fiction/ H                Adult Book MAIN STX Available


Enter: F          to see Full title record.
>>                          Enter ? for HELP.
```

Title Entries Now imagine that a friend says to you, "I just read a great book called *The Martian Chronicles.* You ought to check it out." However, your friend can't remember the name of the author. That's no problem. Simply look up the title *The Martian Chronicles* in the library catalog. If a title begins with *A, An,* or *The,* the entry is alphabetized by the next word in the title. So you would look under the *M*'s for *Martian.* The title entry would be similar to the entries shown above, but the title would appear at the top.

Cross-reference Entries Another kind of catalog entry can help you find information. Cross-reference entries tell you where to look in the catalog for additional books on a subject. For example, under *Astronomy,* you might find a cross-reference entry that says, "See also: Space." If nothing appears under *Astronomy,* there might be an entry that says, "Astronomy. See Space."

Jacob Lawrence,
The Library, 1960.

Reference Works

Wouldn't it be great if you could hire a thousand experts to help with your homework? Well, using the reference section of a library is like having all those experts at your command. The answer to almost any question can be found there simply by looking it up. The reference sections of libraries contain hundreds of different kinds of works. Here are some reference works that are often used by students:

Encyclopedias   These are collections of informational articles written by experts. The articles are arranged alphabetically. Some encyclopedias are contained in one volume, and others include many volumes. General encyclopedias, like *The World Book Encyclopedia,* cover a wide range of topics. Specialized encyclopedias, like *The Encyclopedia of Sports,* deal in depth with a specific topic.

Almanacs and Yearbooks   These books are usually published once a year and present current facts and statistics on topics such as government, population, sports, and entertainment. *The Guinness Book of World Records* and *The World Almanac* are two examples.

Atlases   Atlases are books of maps. They provide information about highways, populations, governments, tourist attractions, climates, place names, and such land features as bodies of water, mountains, valleys, deserts, and forests.

Vertical File   You will find small, loose materials on many subjects in the vertical file, including pamphlets, handbooks, booklets, photos, and newspaper or magazine clippings.

Periodicals   Periodicals are materials that are published at various times throughout the year. Newspapers, magazines, and journals are periodicals. Recent periodicals are usually kept in the open, on shelves. Older periodicals are often stored in a special place. Ask your librarian to help you find them. See below for information about periodical indexes—reference works that will help you locate specific articles in magazines.

Microforms   Many libraries save space by storing some materials on pieces of film called **microforms.** If the film comes in rolled strips, it is called **microfilm.** If the film comes in cards, it is called **microfiche.** Special machines must be used to read microforms.

Periodical Indexes

A **periodical index** lists articles from magazines, newspapers, and journals. The articles are listed by subject and sometimes by author. You can use a periodical index in much the same way as you use a library catalog.

The Readers' Guide to Periodical Literature   Perhaps the most widely used periodical index in schools is the *Readers' Guide to Periodical Literature.* This is a monthly list of articles that have appeared in well-known magazines. At the end of the year, the information in the monthly guides is combined into one book. So

to find articles about the space shuttle that were published in 1990, you would look in the 1990 volume of the *Readers' Guide*. An excerpt from a page of the *Readers' Guide* appears below.

Excerpt from the *Readers' Guide*

VIDEO GAMES
  See also
    Computer games
    Nintendo video games
    Time Traveler (Game)
  Games for grown-ups [special section] il *Popular Mechanics* 168:72+ D '91
  World of electronic games [special section] il *Omni (New York, N.Y.)* 14:93–4+ N '91
  The world of electronic games [special section] il *Compute* 13:95–6+ N '91
      Exhibitions
  Vid news [Consumer Electronics Show] J. Champion and others. il *Compute* 13:116 O '91
      Political use
  The electric body politic. G. Keizer. il *Omni (New York, N.Y.)* 14:100 N '91

Notice that much of the information in the *Readers' Guide* is abbreviated. You will find explanations of these abbreviations in the front of the guide. The following diagram shows the parts of a typical entry.

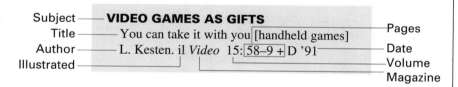

Subject — **VIDEO GAMES AS GIFTS**
Title — You can take it with you [handheld games]
Author — L. Kesten. il *Video* 15:58–9 + D '91
Illustrated
Pages
Date
Volume
Magazine

Computerized Indexes Some libraries use computerized periodical indexes such as *Infotrac* and *Uncover*. These indexes are much like the *Readers' Guide*. They list periodical articles by subject and sometimes by author. However, they are not divided into separate indexes for each year. Instead, in one search you can find articles from as many years as you want. If your library has such a computerized index, ask your librarian to show you how to use it.

Practice Your Skills

A. Use the card catalog or computer catalog in your library to find a listing for each of the following books. For each book, write the title and the author, and include the call number for nonfiction works.

1. a book about the Aztecs
2. a book about television
3. a collection of science fiction short stories
4. a novel by S. E. Hinton
5. a biography of Martin Luther King, Jr.

B. Refer to the list of Dewey Decimal System numbers on page 348. Tell where in the Dewey Decimal System you would find books on the following topics:

1. a book about painting in watercolors
2. a book about robots
3. a collection of poetry by African Americans
4. a book on the Hindu religion
5. a history of the Civil War

C. Write this *Readers' Guide* entry on your paper and label the following parts of the entry: subject, title, author, magazine, page, and date.

> **DOGS**
> Guide to getting the right dog. D. Arden. il *Good Housekeeping* 213:224 O '91

D. Which reference works in your library would you use to find answers to the following questions? Write the type of reference work you would use: encyclopedia, almanac, atlas, and so on.

1. What is the population of the country of Brazil?
2. In which part of Africa is Zimbabwe located?
3. Who won the Academy Award for Best Actress last year?
4. What are the names of two paintings by Pablo Picasso?
5. What was the weather like in Tokyo yesterday?

How Can I Get Firsthand Information?

Interviewing Skills

Suppose you are writing a report about emergency first aid. You might interview a paramedic, an expert in this field. Interviewing can help you gather firsthand information for assignments such as writing character sketches, oral histories, or reports.

GUIDELINES FOR INTERVIEWERS

Planning an Interview

1. Contact the person. Set a time and place to meet.
2. Prepare. Do some background reading on the subject. Learn about the expert and his or her field so you can ask good questions.
3. Plan questions that require more than a *yes* or *no* answer. For example, instead of asking, "Do you like working as a paramedic?" ask, "What do you find challenging about your work?"
4. Gather paper and pencils, and perhaps a cassette recorder.

Conducting an Interview

1. Listen carefully and take accurate notes.
2. Ask questions to clear up anything you don't understand.
3. If you need more time, ask the person to repeat answers.
4. Ask follow-up questions.
5. Go over your notes immediately after the interview.

Practice Your Skills

Rewrite the following questions so that they require more than a *yes* or *no* answer.

1. Do you like being a surgeon?
2. Was medical school difficult?
3. Do you have any hobbies?
4. Were you nervous when you performed your first operation?
5. Do you ever think about a different career?

Caricature of Samuel L. Clemens, "Mark Twain" (1835–1910).

How Can I Improve My Speaking Skills?

Making Oral Presentations

Mark Twain was a lively and amusing speaker, but even he once said, "It usually takes me more than three weeks to prepare a good impromptu speech." To him preparation was the key to effective speaking.

This handbook will show you how to prepare a short talk. For example, you may want to make an announcement, introduce a speaker, or give a "how-to" talk. You may want to share the oral history you created in Workshop 2 or the report you wrote for Workshop 8. As you learn to speak clearly and confidently, you will develop skills that you can use again and again.

PREPARING A TALK

Preparing a talk is very much like creating a piece of writing. As in writing, you choose a topic and consider your audience. You gather information and organize ideas.

After writing out a talk, you transfer it into note form. You can simply jot down brief notes—key facts or ideas—on cards. As you practice and later deliver your talk, you can use your notes to jog your memory.

PRACTICING AND PRESENTING A TALK

Practice your talk several times. Practicing will help you spot areas for improvement, and it will help you feel confident during your presentation. As you practice, you might want to get feedback from a friend to help you identify any trouble spots. The way you present a talk can be as important as what you say. Here are some guidelines for practicing and presenting a talk effectively.

Guidelines for Practicing and Presenting a Talk

Practicing

1. Read your notes several times. Know your material.

2. Practice your talk out loud. Speak distinctly and stress key points. Tape-record your talk if possible so you can listen for areas you may want to improve. You may also want to watch yourself in a mirror.

3. Practice using visual aids. If you are using visual aids, such as posters or charts, practice getting comfortable using them.

4. Present your talk to family members or friends. Ask for useful suggestions.

Presenting

5. Stand straight and look natural. To help yourself relax, try taking a deep breath before you begin. Use good posture.

6. Look at your listeners. Make each person in the audience feel you are speaking directly to him or her.

7. Use your voice effectively. Speak distinctly and loudly enough to be heard. Don't speak too slowly, or your listeners may get bored. Don't speak too quickly, or they may miss a key point.

8. Pause when appropriate. Pause briefly for emphasis after making a key point.

9. Use natural gestures and facial expressions. For example, don't smile when telling a sad story. Don't look glum when saying something funny.

Practice Your Skills

A. Prepare a short talk based on one of the following topics or on a written assignment already completed. Jot down key ideas on note cards.

how to make a pizza	an issue you care about
your favorite movie	an explanation of a solar eclipse
popular music	a book your classmates would enjoy

B. Practice the talk you prepared in Part A. Then present the talk in front of your classmates.

How Can I Improve My Test Scores?

Test-Taking Skills

Like Peppermint Patty, do you sometimes wonder if a test question contains a special challenge? You'll know what to do on all kinds of tests if you learn to analyze the questions and to do some advance planning. This handbook will show you some strategies to use when taking classroom tests and standardized tests.

CLASSROOM TESTS

These tests cover topics studied in a class. In social studies class, for example, a test might cover the Crusades or the American Revolution. To prepare for a classroom test, follow these steps:

1. **Find out what the test will cover.**   Know what to study.

2. **Make a study plan.**   Organize your time to prevent last-minute cramming.

3. **Review your materials.**   Study by reviewing your class notes, skimming chapters you have already read, and going over questions and answers you explored.

4. **Memorize key facts.**   Find a way to memorize key names, terms, dates, events, and vocabulary items.

5. **Rest and relax.**   Get plenty of sleep the night before a test.

Classroom tests often feature objective questions, short-answer questions, or essay questions.

Objective Questions

An objective question has a single, short correct answer. The following are some types of objective questions:

True-false questions ask you to tell whether a statement is true or false. Use these strategies with true-false questions.

• If part of the statement is false, the whole statement is false.

- Words such as *all, always, every, never, none,* and *only* often appear in false statements.
- Words such as *generally, probably, some, usually, often,* and *most* often appear in true statements.

1. T (F) U. S. presidents always serve for four years.
2. (T) F The president must be at least 35 years old.

Matching questions ask you to connect items in one column with items in a second column. These strategies may help you.

- Match the items you know first. This will leave fewer choices.
- Check to see if some items are used more than once and if some items are not used at all.

Write the letter of the body part next to its body system.

___D___ **1.** circulatory system   **A.** bone
___C___ **2.** respiratory system   **B.** stomach
___B___ **3.** digestive system   **C.** lungs
___A___ **4.** skeletal system   **D.** heart

Multiple-choice questions ask you to choose the best answer from three or more possible answers. Use these strategies.

- Read all choices.
- Eliminate incorrect answers.
- Choose the answer that is most complete or accurate.

1. Which of the following books did Gwendolyn Brooks write?
   A. *Annie Allen*   **C.** *A Street in Bronzeville*
   B. *The Bean Eaters*   (D.) all of the above

Fill-in-the-blank (completion) questions ask you to fill in the missing word or phrase. Try these strategies.

- First fill in the answers of which you are certain.
- Then go back and complete the other sentences.
- Make sure that your answers fit grammatically.

1. By agreeing to the Louisiana Purchase in 1803, President ___Jefferson___ doubled the size of the United States.

Short-Answer Questions

Short-answer questions ask you to provide a short answer for each question. Always read the directions first to find out whether you must use complete sentences.

> Write a complete sentence to answer the question.

> **1.** What are the three branches of the United States government?

> *The three branches of government are the legislative, the*
>
> *executive, and the judicial branches.*

Essay Questions

Essay questions ask you to write a paragraph or more in answer to a question. In your social studies class, for example, you may be asked to describe the kinds of houses lived in by settlers on the Great Plains in the 1860s. In your science class, you may be asked to explain what causes a volcanic eruption.

To test your writing skills, you may be asked to write a composition in response to a **writing prompt.** Here are some examples of prompts:

> **1.** Describe your favorite holiday memory in an essay for a family magazine.
>
> **2.** In an editorial for your school newspaper, explain your views on the best ways to get students to do their homework.

Understanding the Question   Make sure you understand exactly what the essay question or writing prompt asks you to do. For example, you may be asked to describe something, to outline events, or to narrate an incident. As you prepare to write, look for the following:

- the topic
- the approach, indicated by key words such as *compare, explain, describe, identify,* or *discuss*
- the form, such as a letter to the editor
- the audience, such as other students

Writing the Response As you write, keep these strategies in mind:

1. **Outline** your main points and list supporting details on scrap paper.
2. **Answer** all parts of the essay question.
3. **Follow instructions** in the writing prompt. Pay careful attention to the audience and purpose specified in the prompt.
4. **Proofread** your essay by checking for correct spelling, grammar, usage, and mechanics.
5. **Add an important point** by writing it in the margin and drawing an arrow to indicate where the idea should go.

Practice Your Skills

Choose one of the following writing prompts. Use the strategies presented in this handbook to help you write your answer.

1. Recall an interesting exhibit you have seen at a museum, an aquarium, a zoo, or any other place. Write a description of that exhibit for a local newspaper. Include specific sensory details to make your writing come alive.
2. People of different ages often have different tastes in music, clothes, and movies. Choose something very popular among young people today. Then write a letter to an older person explaining why the item you chose is so popular.

Standardized tests measure your understanding of a variety of subjects, such as mathematics, vocabulary, reading comprehension, grammar and language skills, science, and social studies. Standardized tests are sometimes called **achievement tests,** because they try to find out what you have learned in all your years at school. You will find it helpful to know the types of questions to expect and to develop strategies for answering them. The following sections cover some common types of questions. Many are similar to the questions on classroom tests.

Reading Comprehension

Reading comprehension questions test how well you understand something you have read. You first read a passage and then answer questions about it. For example, you may have to state the main idea, recall a detail, or draw a conclusion. Read the directions carefully. Then follow these steps:

1. **Preview the questions** before reading the passage.

2. **Read the passage quickly but carefully,** looking for answers to the questions.

3. **Read all answer choices first** and then choose the best, most complete answer.

Read the following passage and answer the questions. The questions may have one, two, or three correct answers.

> In the middle of the last century, more than a hundred thousand Chinese men and women came to the United States of America. They worked primarily as miners, lumberjacks, fishermen, and farm laborers. They also laid track for railroads. Chinese workers helped build the Transcontinental Railroad, the first railroad to span the United States.

1. At what jobs did the early Chinese immigrants work?
   A. They worked as miners and lumberjacks.
   B. They worked on telephone lines.
   C. They worked as fishermen and farm laborers.
   D. They built railroads.

Vocabulary

Two types of vocabulary questions often appear on standardized tests. **Synonym questions** ask you to find words that are similar in meaning. **Antonym questions** ask you to find words that are opposite in meaning.

Choose the word most similar in meaning to the underlined word.

1. a <u>tardy</u> student

   A. eager   **B.** punctual   **C.** late   **D.** restless

Choose the word opposite in meaning to the underlined word.

2. a <u>tense</u> situation

   A. calm   **B.** nervous   **C.** angry   **D.** unhappy

Analogies

Analogies ask you to think about how items are related.

Puppy is to *dog* as *kitten* is to _____.

This analogy compares two pairs of things. You are to decide how the items in the first pair, *puppy* and *dog,* are related. The items in the second pair are related in the same way. Make a sentence out of the first pair of words that explains their relationship.

A *puppy* is a young *dog.*

Now take your sentence and substitute the incomplete pair (*kitten* and _____) for the first pair.

A *kitten* is a young _____.

The correct answer is *cat.*

Some analogy questions ask you to fill in the blank. Others ask you to choose the right answer from three or four possible answers.

1. Japan → Asia : Germany → _____

   A. Europe   **B.** China   **C.** France   **D.** Cuba   **E.** Berlin

The correct answer is *A. Europe.* Japan is a nation in Asia. Germany is a nation in Europe.

Grammar, Usage, and Mechanics

This type of question measures language skills. You are given a sentence with certain parts underlined. You are asked to tell whether there is an error in grammar, usage, punctuation, or capitalization—or no error at all.

<u>Robert <u>louis</u> Stevenson <u>wrote</u> *Treasure Island.* <u>No error</u>
    A   **(B)**   **C**   **D**

The error occurs in Part B. The name *Louis* must be capitalized.

TAKING THE TEST

You can use the following steps when taking tests:

1. **Skim the test.** Look over the whole test to see what types of questions it has and how long it is.

2. **Judge the time.** Read all the directions first. You may decide that you need more time for some sections. You may need the most time for a section of essay questions.

3. **Read all directions carefully.** Ask questions if you do not understand directions. Follow the directions exactly.

4. **Read each test item carefully.** Be sure to read all the choices provided for answers.

5. **Answer easy questions first.** Then go back to harder ones.

6. **Review your answers.** Make sure you have not left out any answers. Change unreadable or confusing answers.

When taking a standardized test, be careful to mark the answer sheet correctly. Usually, machines score the answer sheets. Do two important things when filling in an answer sheet:

1. **Keep your place.** Mark the part of the answer sheet that matches the test part you are working on. Make sure you are marking the correct item number as well.

2. **Mark neatly; erase completely.** If your marks go far outside the lines or circles provided, the scoring machine may misread them. The machine may also read partial erasures as answers. Erase carefully. Never cross out. Never use a pen.

Correctly marked Answer Sheet

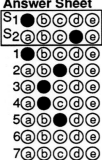

Incorrectly marked Answer Sheet

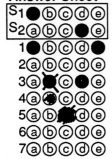

Practice Your Skills

A. Read the following passage and then answer the questions about what you have read. More than one answer may be correct.

> Merlin and Arthur rode for a long while through lonely paths and giant forests. Then, through a clearing, Merlin pointed to a strange and wonderful sight. A great lake stretched out as far as the eye could see. They rode out into the middle of the lake in a small boat. Suddenly an arm clothed in white and holding a beautiful sword reached out of the lake toward Arthur. Merlin explained that the Lady of the Lake herself was offering Arthur the most powerful sword in all of Britain—Excalibur.

1. The selection is mainly about how—
   A. Merlin betrays Arthur
   B. the Lady of the Lake tricks Arthur
   C. the Lady of the Lake presents a sword to Arthur
   D. Arthur betrays the Lady of the Lake

2. The sword Excalibur—
   A. once belonged to Merlin   **C.** is little help in battle
   B. is offered to Arthur   **D.** may give Arthur power

B. Choose the word or phrase that is most similar in meaning to the underlined word.

1. petrified wood
   A. polished   **B.** rotten   **C.** painted   **D.** turned into stone
2. a confidential letter
   A. handwritten   **B.** secret   **C.** typed   **D.** forged

C. Complete the following analogies:

1. carpenter → hammer : painter → _____
   A. painting **B.** masterpiece **C.** gallery **D.** brush **E.** canvas
2. lion → den : sparrow → _____
   A. bird **B.** feeder **C.** feathers **D.** flight **E.** nest
3. shepherd → flock : general→ _____
   A. lieutenant **B.** war **C.** orders **D.** troops **E.** battle

Anne Comfort Morrell, *Seasons of My Life*, 1981–1982. This pieced, appliqué, and embroidered quilt has scenes of family life in Nova Scotia, Canada, surrounding a fabric painting of a farm. The artist has embroidered a brief family history above and below each square on the quilt.

368

Grammar and Usage Handbook

MINI-LESSONS

*Skills*

Directions   One or more of the underlined sections in the following sentences may contain an error in grammar, usage, punctuation, spelling, or capitalization. Write the letter of each incorrect section; then rewrite the item correctly. If there is no error in an item, write *E*.

Example   <u>The lands</u> that Gulliver <u>visited</u> in *Gulliver's <u>Travels. Included</u>*
               A   B   C
Brobdingnag, where there were <u>giants</u> sixty feet tall.   <u>No error</u>
                                 D   E

Answer   C—*Travels* included

---

1. By <u>its</u> first <u>birthday,</u> a blue-whale calf will have <u>growed</u> to a <u>weight</u> of about
      A   B   C   D
 twenty-nine tons.   <u>No error</u>
                      E

2. <u>America's</u> favorite fresh fruit is the <u>banana, although</u> we use more <u>apples</u> and
    A   B   C
 oranges, they are not <u>necessaryly</u> used as fresh fruit.   <u>No error</u>
                      D   E

3. A violinist once left his $250,000 violin in a <u>New York</u> taxicab. <u>He</u> felt <u>badly</u>
                                      A   B   C
 until the valuable instrument was returned by the <u>cabs'</u> next customer.
                                                    D
 <u>No error</u>
   E

4. <u>Thomas Edison's</u> <u>famousest</u> invention was the light <u>bulb, but</u> he also invented
          A   B   C
 <u>hundreds</u> of other things, including a talking doll.   <u>No error</u>
     D   E

5. Probably the <u>oldest</u> form of money is the shell of a <u>cowrie a</u> <u>small, delicately</u>
               A   B   C
 tinted mollusk native to the shores of the Indian and <u>pacific oceans.</u>   <u>No error</u>
                                             D   E

6. The <u>most hardest</u> of all <u>gems, the diamond,</u> is ninety times <u>harder than</u> the next
         A   B   C
 <u>hardest</u> mineral.   <u>No error</u>
    D   E

7. The Venus' flytrap, a truly unusual flower, can <u>eat flies,</u> <u>however,</u> <u>it</u> prefers <u>ants.</u>
A   B   C   D
<u>No error</u>
E

8. Although formed by volcanic action, the <u>Hawaiian Islands</u> <u>has</u> <u>few</u> active
A   B   C
<u>Volcanoes.</u>   <u>No error</u>
D   E

9. One of the founders of the <u>Boy Scouts of America</u> was <u>Charles Alexander</u>
A   B
<u>Eastman,</u> a <u>well-known</u> Santee Sioux doctor and writer whose Indian name was
B   C
<u>Ohiyesa,</u> meaning "winner."   <u>No error</u>
D   E

10. As each bowler <u>takes</u> <u>their</u> <u>stance, be</u> very <u>quiet.</u>   <u>No error</u>
A   B   C   D   E

11. Because of a childhood illness, Scott Hamilton never <u>grew</u> beyond
A
5 feet 3 inches <u>tall; but</u> he <u>became</u> a <u>world champion</u> ice skater.   <u>No error</u>
B   C   D   E

12. The amount <u>spent</u> on <u>advertising</u> in the United States <u>is</u> <u>greater</u> than the gross
A   B   C   D
national product of Ecuador or Kenya.   <u>No error</u>
E

13. <u>Ray Bradbury's</u> novel about censorship and book burning is called
A
Fahrenheit 451, a reference to the <u>temprature</u> at which <u>pages</u> of a book
B   C
<u>catches</u> fire.   <u>No error</u>
D   E

14. Nobody <u>hits</u> <u>their</u> stride in the first mile of a <u>Marathon.</u> <u>It's</u> usually much later
A   B   C   D
in the race before that happens.   <u>No error</u>
E

15. The <u>gazelle and the cheetah</u> <u>are</u> both very fast <u>animals,</u> but of the two the
A   B   C
cheetah is <u>fastest</u>.   <u>No error</u>
D   E

Sketch Book

WRITING WARM-UPS

- What do you think these characters are saying to each other? Write a dialogue to go along with this scene from a silent movie.

- Create a brief story, but leave blanks for several key words. Ask a friend to guess words for the missing parts of speech, such as nouns, verbs, or adjectives. Then read the completed story aloud.

- Create a secret code by substituting letters for other letters or words for other words. Exchange messages with a classmate and try to break each other's codes.

Understanding Sentences

The world can sometimes be a puzzling place. To make sense of it, we need to communicate our ideas and feelings in a way that other people can easily understand.

In this handbook, you will learn about the pieces that make up the key unit of communication—the sentence. You will discover how to fit those pieces together to express your ideas clearly.

Understanding
Sentences   **373**

A **sentence** is a group of words that expresses a complete thought. A sentence must have a subject and a predicate.

A sentence expresses a complete thought. It may make a statement about something. It may ask a question or tell someone to do something. It may also express strong feeling. Every sentence always has two parts. One part tells whom or what the sentence is about. That is the **subject.** The second part tells something about the subject. This is the **predicate.** Subjects and predicates can be short or long, as you can see from the following examples:

Subject (Who or what)	Predicate (What is said about the subject)
The magician	performed his famous trick.
A purple scarf	turned into a white bird.
It	amazed me.
Everyone in the audience	clapped.

One way to understand the parts of a sentence is to think of a sentence as telling who did something or what happened. The subject tells *who* or *what.* The predicate tells *what was done* or *what happened.* You can divide sentences, then, in this way:

Who or What	What Was Done or What Happened
Magic	fascinates me.
I	borrowed a book on it from the library.
People and objects	don't really disappear.
The magician	creates an illusion.

Practice Your Skills

A. CONCEPT CHECK

Subjects and Predicates   Write the following sentences. Draw a vertical line between the subject and the predicate.

Writing Theme
Magicians and
Illusions

1. The Chinese magician Ching Ling Foo came to America in 1899.
2. He wore a flowing silk robe during his act.
3. His most famous trick involved an enormous bowl of water.
4. The bowl appeared from behind a cloth.
5. It weighed one hundred pounds.
6. The water filled more than three buckets.
7. He did this trick with the help of special equipment.
8. This equipment included a harness, a cord, and a hook.
9. The harness fitted over his shoulders.
10. A cord with an unusual hook hung from the harness.
11. The huge bowl attached to the hook.
12. Ching Ling Foo's robe hid the bowl.
13. First he bent his legs slightly.
14. Then the bowl touched the stage.
15. Finally the hook released the bowl.

B. DRAFTING SKILL

Drafting Sentences   As a writer you construct complete thoughts from bits and pieces of ideas. Combine each subject or predicate in column **A** with a predicate or subject from column **B**. Each subject and predicate will be used only once. Add end marks to the sentences you form. Your completed sentences will form a paragraph.

A	B
16. Sleight-of-hand	do an amazing trick with a ball
17. did tricks with many kinds of special equipment long ago	The equipment appeared as two
18. Cards and handkerchiefs	The audience
19. I once saw a performer	The magician's agile fingers
20. included a plain rubber ball	are often used in modern tricks
21. A metal shell	
22. could see the shell	held the ball and shell apart
23. removed the shell from the ball	covered the ball
	The ancient Egyptians
24. Then he	involves skilled hand
25. Finally one ball	movements

FOR MORE PRACTICE
See page 398.

Understanding
Sentences   **375**

SIMPLE SUBJECTS AND PREDICATES

> The **subject** of a sentence tells *whom* or *what* the sentence is about. The **predicate** of a sentence tells what the subject *does* or *is*.

In every sentence there are a few words that are more important than the rest. These key words form the basic framework of the sentence. In the following examples the key words are printed in boldface type.

Subject	Predicate
The happy, excited **fans**	**cheered** for Jim Abbott.
Fans	**cheered.**

The subject of the first sentence is *The happy, excited fans.* The key word in this subject is *fans.* You can say *Fans cheered for Jim Abbott.* You cannot say *happy cheered for Jim Abbott.* Nor can you say *excited cheered for Jim Abbott.*

The predicate in the first sentence is *cheered for Jim Abbott.* The key word is *cheered.* Without this word you would not have a sentence.

The key word in the subject of a sentence is called the **simple subject.** It is the **subject** of the verb.

The key word in the predicate is called the **simple predicate.** The simple predicate is the **verb.** Hereafter, this book will use the word *verb* rather than the phrase "simple predicate."

The verb and its subject are the basic framework of every sentence. All the rest of the sentence is built around them. To find this framework, first find the verb. Then ask *Who?* or *What?* This will give you the subject of the verb.

> The talented young pitcher threw a supersonic fastball.
> *Verb:* threw *Who threw?* pitcher
> *Subject of verb:* pitcher

Sentence Diagraming   For information on diagraming subjects and verbs, see page 677.

Practice Your Skills

A. CONCEPT CHECK

Simple Subjects and Verbs   Write each verb and its subject.

1. Many athletes triumph in sports despite physical disabilities.
2. Jim Abbott played baseball with only one hand.
3. Jim overcame his disability early in life.
4. He hurled fastballs as a Little League pitcher.
5. Hard work on slow curve balls strengthened his skills.
6. Jim set a number of records.
7. This talented athlete stunned crowds at the Olympics.
8. Another pitcher returned to baseball after cancer surgery on his arm.
9. Dave Dravecky's pitches flew as fast as ever.
10. However, he reinjured the arm.
11. Doctors amputated the arm at the shoulder.
12. Dave fought back.
13. He turned his attention to golf.
14. Amazingly, this courageous athlete played in a pro-am tournament in California.
15. Dave's determination redefined the meaning of the word *disability*.

B. REVISION SKILL

Precise Word Choice   Act as a peer reader for the writer of the passage below. Suggest replacements for any subjects or verbs that can be made more lively or precise. First, write and label the *Subject* and *Verb* from each sentence. Then, when needed, write a suggested replacement for either the subject or the verb.

    16The famous inventor Thomas Edison got partially deaf as a child. **17**Once an inconsiderate conductor moved the boy onto a train by his ears. **18**At that very moment, the boy had a snap inside his head. **19**His deafness happened at that moment. **20**The problem became worse and worse. **21**Doctors offered an operation. **22**Edison said no. **23**He liked the silence. **24**It made him concentrate. **25**However, many of his inventions involved sound. **26**He liked the phonograph best of all his inventions. **27**He put it with a camera. **28**That was a motion picture with sound. **29**Edison also made the dictaphone. **30**People like sound more because of this deaf man.

FOR MORE PRACTICE
See page 398.

Understanding
Sentences   **377**

> A **verb** expresses an action, states that something exists, or links the subject with a description.

To understand a sentence, you must find the verb. Here are some guidelines that tell you what verbs do. These guidelines can serve as clues to help you find the verb in a sentence.

Some verbs tell about action:

> The Lighthouse of Alexandria *stood* for fifteen hundred years.
> It *rose* from a stone platform.
> A fire at the top *provided* light.

Sometimes the action shown by the verb is an action you cannot see:

> People *marvel* at the size of the pyramids.
> We *enjoy* their elegant beauty.
> They *remind* us of the glory of ancient Egypt.

The Sphinx (Egypt) is considered by many to be one of the Great Wonders of the World.

Some verbs tell about a *state of being* rather than an action. These verbs link a subject to words that tell what it is or describe it.

> The Colossus of Rhodes *was* a huge bronze statue.
> Rhodes *is* an island in the Aegean Sea.
> The Hanging Gardens of Babylon *looked* beautiful.
> Their exact location *remains* unknown.

Practice Your Skills

A. CONCEPT CHECK

Verbs   Write the verb in each sentence. It may express an action you can see, an action you cannot see, or a state of being. Label each verb *Action* or *State of Being*.

Writing Theme
Wonders of
the World

1. The Great Wall of China is the longest structure in the world.
2. It stretches almost four thousand miles across northern China.
3. Around 210 B.C., Emperor Shi Huangdi planned the Great Wall.
4. He was afraid of invaders.
5. Construction became a major undertaking.
6. Over 300,000 workers built the wall by hand.
7. The wall seemed secure.
8. In A.D. 1234, however, Genghis Khan, the conqueror of China, crossed the Great Wall.
9. The modern Chinese rebuilt parts of the wall.
10. Today the Great Wall remains a major tourist attraction.

B. DRAFTING SKILL

Finding the Best Word   Make this writing stronger by replacing each italicized word or word group with a precise and colorful verb from the word bank.

stretched	longed	spanned	gushed
strengthened	retells	dazzled	linked
astonished	burst	constructed	raised
overlooked	treasured	attracted	

   [11]Nebuchadnezzar *took* Babylon to new heights of glory. [12]The mighty ruler *made* the city's walls *stronger.* [13]A beautiful bridge *went across* the width of the River Euphrates. [14]An impressive palace *looked down on* the city. [15]The Hanging Gardens *had* many admirers from miles around. [16]A legend *states again* the story of the Hanging Gardens. [17]Nebuchadnezzar's wife, Semiramis, *wished* for the hills of her homeland. [18]Babylon *was flat* as far as the eye could see. [19]Nebuchadnezzar *made* a hill for her. [20]The hill *pleased* the eye. [21]Soaring terraces *surprised* many visitors. [22]Gleaming marble staircases *went between* the terraces. [23]Stone-circled flower beds *came into bloom.* [24]Water *poured* from fountains. [25]The queen *liked* her artificial hill.

FOR MORE PRACTICE
See page 398.

Understanding
Sentences   **379**

A **helping verb** helps the main verb make a statement or express action.

There are certain words you can count on to be verbs.

Words that are always verbs

am	was	has	do
is	were	have	does
are	be	had	did

Sometimes these words are used alone. Sometimes they are used as **helping verbs** with a **main verb.**

> The Kiowa Indians *have created* many fascinating myths.
> The myths *were retold* from generation to generation.

A verb may consist of a main verb and one or more helping verbs. A main verb and its helping verbs are called a **verb phrase.**

> These myths *had been told* orally for many years.
> They *have been written* down now.

Sometimes the main verb ends in *-ing:*

> The Kiowa *have been living* in the Southern Plains of North America for years.
> Stories of their bravery *are becoming* legendary.

How to find the verb in a sentence

1. Look for a word that tells the main action, expresses a state of being, or links the subject with a description.

2. Look for helping verbs. Examples are *is, am, are, was, were, be, been, have, has, had, do, does, did, shall, will, should, would,* and *could.*

3. Look for all the verbs that make up the verb phrase.

Practice Your Skills

A. CONCEPT CHECK

Main Verbs and Helping Verbs   Make two columns on your paper. Label them *Helping Verbs* and *Main Verbs*. Write the helping verbs from the following sentences in the first column. Write the main verbs in the second column.

1. A Kiowa myth about the origin of storms has been on my mind.
2. I had heard it first during a thunderstorm.
3. The Kiowa were creating a horse.
4. They were fashioning it out of clay.
5. No one could have guessed the result.
6. The horse had begun twisting out of control.
7. The wind was howling all around.
8. Many creatures had begun swirling in the confusion.
9. Soon, the chaos had swallowed even the mighty buffalo.
10. A mighty storm had been created.

B. APPLICATION IN LITERATURE

Identifying Subjects and Verb Phrases   Write the verb and its simple subject from the following sentences. If there is a helping verb and a main verb, write both of the verbs.

[11]The whole sky was blazing with light. [12]Heavy smoke filled the air. [13]After many hours, the fire had burned itself out. [14]Then the frightened villagers returned to their huts. [15]Their abandoned supplies of food were burned completely. [16]Their hunger was stronger than their disappointment, however. [17]Surprisingly, the food tasted much better than their usual uncooked food. [18]The fire had also not destroyed their clay pots and cooking vessels. [19]Actually, the clay utensils had been hardened by the heat. [20]Ever since then, people have been "firing" their earthen pots for strength and durability.

African Myth—The Finding of Fire

C. APPLICATION IN WRITING

Paragraphs   In a paragraph, write your own myth describing how something in nature came into being. For example, think about how giraffes might have gotten their long necks. Make your writing interesting by using helping verbs.

FOR MORE PRACTICE
See page 399.

Separated Parts of a Verb

Sometimes the parts of a verb are separated by words that are not verbs. In the sentences below, the verbs are printed in bold type. The words in between are not part of the verb phrase.

Ships carrying treasure **have** often **been wrecked.**
People **do**n't always **know** where a ship went down.

Notice that *not* and the ending *-n't* in contractions are not part of the verb even though they do change its meaning.

Practice Your Skills

A. CONCEPT CHECK

Verb Phrases   Write the complete verb for each sentence.

1. Mike Wilson had often dived below the waters near Sri Lanka.
2. During one dive, he was exploring the sea with two friends.
3. They were suddenly looking into the mouth of a small cannon.
4. The three explorers couldn't have been more excited.
5. They were soon brushing away sand and debris.
6. Shiny objects were glinting in the murky light.
7. The explorers didn't have much time.
8. Other divers would shortly be searching for this treasure.
9. They had soon collected two hundred pounds of valuables.
10. No one else would ever find a trace of the sea's bounty here.

B. REVISION SKILL

Sentence Variety   One way to vary your writing is to reposition, or move, words that split a verb. Write the main verb and helping verb in each sentence. Then rewrite sentences 11, 12, 13, 14, and 19 by moving the separating word or words to another part of the sentence. See the example. (Think about which version of the sentence sounds better.)

EXAMPLE   Many activities can now be performed under water.
can be performed
Now many activities can be performed under water.

11. People have for centuries been diving beneath the sea.
12. Divers can only go to certain depths without special equipment.
13. Several types of breathing aids are currently being used.

14. Divers can comfortably wear air tanks on their backs.
15. The diver can also breathe through a hose. It is attached to air pumps on a boat.
16. Divers can be totally enclosed in a submersible vehicle for extremely deep descents.
17. One type of submersible is commonly known as a bathyscaph.
18. Since 1960 the bathyscaph *Trieste* has proudly held the record for the deepest dive.
19. In that year, it had actually descended 35,800 feet into the Pacific Ocean.
20. That record will be long remembered.

C H E C K ✔ P O I N T
MIXED REVIEW · PAGES 374–383

Write the subject and complete verb in each sentence. Label the subject *S*, the helping verb *HV*, and the main verb *MV*.

Writing Theme
Modern Motion Pictures

1. Disaster films captured public attention in the 1970s.
2. These films were very popular with audiences.
3. The lives of some characters were threatened by terrible fires.
4. Others couldn't escape violent storms at sea.
5. Comic-strip fantasies were also becoming popular as movie themes.
6. Overnight, Superman had become a folk hero.
7. Fans of Popeye were rooting for his triumph over Bluto.
8. Films about space later played to eager crowds in many theaters.
9. By 1982 E.T. had become familiar to many viewers.
10. Audiences were enthusiastically talking about that movie for months.
11. Studios were soon encountering a new problem, however.
12. The creation of the special effects in these disaster and fantasy films was very expensive.
13. Studios could produce only two or three of these films a year.
14. For example, *Terminator 2* cost its studio millions of dollars.
15. Studios might not make these expensive films in the future.

COMPOUND SUBJECTS AND COMPOUND VERBS

A **compound subject** or a **compound verb** has two or more parts.

Look at these two sentences. How do they differ?

Louise saw Bigfoot.   Louise and her friend saw Bigfoot.

In the first sentence, the subject is *Louise*. In the second sentence, both *Louise* and *her friend* are subjects. Two or more subjects joined together are called a **compound subject.** The word *compound* means "having more than one part." Notice how using a compound subject can help make your writing precise. It also makes your writing more efficient. You can tell about Louise and her friend in the same sentence, not in two different sentences.

Verbs can be compound too. How do these sentences differ?

Bigfoot growled.   Bigfoot snarled and growled.

In the first sentence the verb is *growled*. In the second, the **compound verb** is *snarled* and *growled*. Again, the second sentence is more precise and efficient than two separate sentences.

The word *and* joins the parts of the compound subject and the parts of the compound verb above. Words that join words and groups of words in this way are called **conjunctions.** The word *and* is a conjunction.

Sentence Diagraming For information about diagraming compound subjects and compound verbs, see page 677.

Writing
—— **TIP** ——

To make your writing more efficient, try combining simple sentences into sentences with compound subjects or compound verbs.

Practice Your Skills

A. CONCEPT CHECK

Compound Subjects and Verbs Make two columns on your paper. Label them *Subjects* and *Verbs*. Write the subjects from the following sentences in the first column. Write the verbs in the second column.

1. According to one report, Louise Baxter was driving her car one day and felt something strange.
2. She suspected a flat tire and stopped the car.
3. Louise walked around the car and checked the right front tire.
4. An uneasy feeling and a vague fear crept over her.
5. Ms. Baxter turned around and saw Bigfoot.
6. Bigfoot was about ten feet tall and had gigantic shoulders.
7. Its arms hung down to its knees and were covered with fur.
8. Her account and other stories like it have puzzled scientists.
9. Photographs and movies of Bigfoot reveal few details.
10. The legends of Bigfoot and the mystery of its identity still fascinate people.

B. DRAFTING SKILL

Sentence Combining Combine the following sentence pairs into sentences with either compound subjects or compound verbs.

11. The Abominable Snowman supposedly lives on Mount Everest. The Abominable Snowman has also been sighted in China.
12. Yeti is a native name for the creature. Metoh Kangmi is also a native name for the creature.
13. Explorers have seen the creature from a distance. Explorers have sighted footprints in the snow.
14. The footprints are huge. The footprints may be bear tracks.
15. The tracks could melt in the snow. The tracks would then appear larger.
16. The footprints could also be fake. The reports of sightings could also be fake.
17. Fake feet could be built. Fake feet could be used to make prints.
18. No one has seen the Abominable Snowman up close. No one has gathered any real proof of its existence.
19. Scientists have spent years searching for the creature. Ordinary people have spent years searching for the beast.
20. The stories are intriguing. The legends are intriguing.

FOR MORE PRACTICE
See page 399.

There are four kinds of sentences: **declarative, interrogative, imperative,** and **exclamatory.**

You use language for several different purposes. Sometimes you want to tell something. Other times you might want to ask a question or tell someone to do something. Sometimes you just want to show how strongly you feel about something. There is a different kind of sentence to use for each purpose. A **declarative sentence** is a sentence that makes a statement. An **interrogative sentence** asks a question. An **imperative sentence** tells or requests someone to do something. An **exclamatory sentence** expresses strong feeling. Following is a list of the four kinds of sentences with examples of each kind:

1. A sentence that makes a statement is called a declarative sentence.

    Willow warblers travel five thousand miles in the fall.

    Some fish migrate too.

    The barn swallow winters in the Southern Hemisphere.

2. A sentence that asks a question is called an interrogative sentence.

    Why do animals migrate?

    How do they find their destination?

    Are scientists studying this subject?

3. A sentence that tells or requests someone to do something is an imperative sentence.

    Read about migration in the encyclopedia.

    Study the navigational systems of animals.

4. A sentence that expresses strong feeling is an exclamatory sentence.

    What beautiful colors the monarch butterfly has!

    How far it travels!

Rules for Punctuating Sentences

1. Use a period after a declarative sentence.
2. Use a question mark after an interrogative sentence.
3. Use a period after an imperative sentence.
4. Use an exclamation point after an exclamatory sentence.

Practice Your Skills

A. CONCEPT CHECK

Kinds of Sentences   Identify each of the following sentences as *Declarative, Interrogative, Imperative,* or *Exclamatory.* Then write the punctuation mark that belongs at the end.

1. Why do birds migrate south in the winter
2. Birds follow an internal clock
3. Observe birds before a long flight
4. What an enormous amount of food they eat
5. Their body weight may increase by 30 percent
6. Do you know how long some species can fly nonstop
7. A sustained flight of over 100 hours is possible
8. Try to imagine yourself walking for that long
9. Birds can cross vast oceans or deserts
10. What an incredible feat this is

B. REVISION SKILL

Sentence Variety   Using various types of sentences can make your writing more interesting. In the following passage, rewrite sentence 11 as an imperative sentence, sentences 13 and 14 as interrogative sentences, and sentences 12 and 20 as exclamatory sentences. Change the punctuation marks as needed.

   [11]You should find someone who can tell you about the remarkable whistling swan. [12]These birds can fly at speeds up to fifty miles per hour. [13]Between October and April, flocks of whistling swans fly southward. [14]Their two homes are very far apart. [15]The Hudson Bay area near the Arctic Ocean is their summer nesting spot. [16]They winter as far south as the Carolinas. [17]Their nests are very large. [18]They are made from water plants. [19]The birds line the nests with down from their bodies. [20]A nest may be two feet wide and six feet high.

Writing Theme
Migration

FOR MORE PRACTICE
See page 400.

The subject does not always come at the beginning of a sentence.

You won't have to look far in this book or in any other book to discover that the subject does not always come before the verb in a sentence. Occasionally placing the verb before the subject will make your writing more interesting and give emphasis to what you say.

Usual order   Elizabeth Kenny rode through the lonely outback area of Australia.

Unusual order   Through the lonely outback area of Australia rode Elizabeth Kenny.

Practice Your Skills

A. CONCEPT CHECK

Usual or Unusual Order   Tell whether the subject and verb in each sentence are in *Usual Order* or *Unusual Order*. Then write the subject and verb.

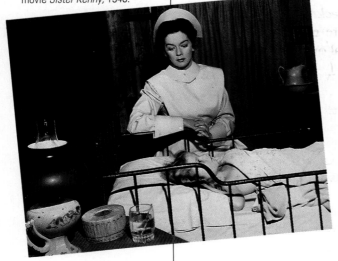

Writing Theme
Women in Medicine:
Elizabeth Kenny

Rosalind Russell's portrayal of Elizabeth Kenny in the movie *Sister Kenny,* 1946.

1. Elizabeth Kenny rode to the MacNeil's house.
2. Like lightning dashed her horse.
3. In the house lay a very sick girl.
4. Amy MacNeil's leg was twisted by polio.
5. Elizabeth gently worked on the leg.
6. In her hands was the promise of a miracle.
7. She wrapped the affected muscles with warm strips of wool.
8. Amy's muscles gradually relaxed with the heat.
9. Elizabeth had invented a new treatment for polio.
10. How fortunate was this discovery!

B. REVISION SKILL

Sentence Variety   Add variety to the sentences in the paragraph below by rewriting sentences 11, 14, 15, 17, 19, and 20. In sentences 11, 14, and 19, place the verb before the subject. In sentences 15, 17, and 20, leave the subject and verb in the usual order. (See the examples.)

EXAMPLE   Elizabeth Kenny peered into the ward.

Into the ward peered Elizabeth Kenny.

EXAMPLE   She drew back in horror.

In horror she drew back.

¹¹The polio victims lay in their hospital beds. ¹²Nurses had put the patients' arms and legs in casts. ¹³Elizabeth was opposed to casts for treatment. ¹⁴A thought came into Nurse Kenny's head. ¹⁵She would open her own hospital in Queensland. ¹⁶Elizabeth would use heat in her method of treatment. ¹⁷Full recovery could be achieved with the addition of an exercise program. ¹⁸Elizabeth's dream became a reality. ¹⁹The children came from all over Australia. ²⁰They poured into Elizabeth's hospital.

FOR MORE PRACTICE
See page 400.

C H E C K ✔ P O I N T
MIXED REVIEW · PAGES 384–389

Identify the kind of sentence by writing *Declarative, Interrogative, Imperative,* or *Exclamatory.* Then rewrite each declarative sentence so the subject and verb are in unusual order.

Writing Theme
Robots

1. ROBOT T6R4: Have you heard the news?
2. A new generation of robots lurks in the engineers' lab.
3. ROBOT Y9V3: What will our replacements look like?
4. ROBOT T6R4: Sit down.
5. This news may blow your circuits!
6. Lasers and tiny TV cameras lie under their shiny exteriors.
7. ROBOT Y9V3: How lucky those robots are!
8. Our usefulness ends so quickly.
9. ROBOT T6R4: An idea surges through my circuits.
10. ROBOT Y9V3: Tell me how we can have our old parts replaced.

Understanding
Sentences

QUESTIONS, EXCLAMATIONS, AND COMMANDS

> Questions, exclamations, and commands often change the order of the subject and verb.

Some interrogative sentences are written in the usual order, with the subject first and the verb second.

> Which explorer found a cave in Borneo in 1977?
> (*Explorer* is the subject; *found* is the verb.)

Often, questions change the order of the subject and verb.

> Did Eavis find the cave by accident?
> (The subject *Eavis* falls between the two parts of the verb.)

Some exclamatory sentences also change the order.

> Are those formations beautiful!   Is that cave breathtaking!

A sentence with the subject and verb in changed order can be either a question or an exclamation, depending on how it is spoken.

> Were we deep underground?   Were we deep underground!

To find the subject and verb in a question or exclamation, try rewording the sentence as a declarative sentence.

> Do you know the story of the discovery?   Is it incredible!
> You do know the story of the discovery.   It is incredible.

Imperative sentences, or commands, usually begin with the verb. There doesn't seem to be any subject. However, the subject in the sentence is *you*, even though it is not expressed. We say that the subject *you* is understood.

> (you) Begin the story.   Don't (you) leave out any details.

Imperative sentences sometimes consist of only one word—the verb: *Stop. Look. Listen.* These are single-word sentences. The subject is the same: *(you) Stop. (you) Look. (you) Listen.*

Sentence Diagraming   For information on diagraming questions, exclamations, and commands, see page 677.

Practice Your Skills

A. CONCEPT CHECK

Subjects in Questions, Exclamations, and Commands   Write the subject and verb for each of the following sentences. If the subject is understood, write (*you*).

Writing Theme
Caves

   1. LYDIA: Are these cave passageways narrow!
   2. BRAD: Can we get through?
   3. LYDIA: Watch your head.
   4.   Does that painful bump answer your question?
   5. BRAD: Stop for a second.
   6.   Do you see something ahead?
   7. LYDIA: Such a beautiful cavern that is!
   8.   Get your camera ready.
   9. BRAD: Will this be a great picture!
   10.   Say "Stalagmite."

B. CONCEPT CHECK

Subjects and Verbs   People use a variety of sentence types in conversation. Identify the subject and verb in each sentence. If the subject is understood, write (*you*). Then write the last word of the sentence and add the appropriate end mark.

FOR MORE PRACTICE
See pages 400–401.

   11. CARLOS: Do you remember that spectacular cave in Austria
   12. SYLVIA: Remind me about which one
   13. CARLOS: Wasn't it called Adelsburg
   14. SYLVIA: Of course it was
   15.   What do you know about the cave
   16. CARLOS: Just look at these pictures of its speleothems
   17. SYLVIA: What in the world are speleothems
   18. CARLOS: Would you believe that's just another name for rock formations
   19. SYLVIA: Tell me the depth of the cave
   20. CARLOS: It descends an incredible 115 feet into the earth

Understanding
Sentences   **391**

SENTENCES THAT BEGIN
WITH *THERE*

> When **there** is used to begin a sentence, it usually serves just to get the sentence moving.

Study these sentences. What are the simple subjects?

> There are exciting plans for the colonization of Mars.
> There will be many difficult problems.

The word *there* is not the subject of these sentences. The subjects are *plans* and *problems*.

> There *are* exciting *plans* for the colonization of Mars.

> There *will be* many difficult *problems*.

Study the following sentences. Notice that the subject is not first when *there* comes near the beginning of the sentence. What are the subjects?

> **Will** there **be** enough breathable **air?**
> There **is** very sophisticated **equipment** available.
> **Is** there a **date** for the first flight yet?

Practice Your Skills

A. CONCEPT CHECK

Sentences Beginning with *There*   Write the subjects and verbs from the following sentences.

1. Can there be exploration of Mars in the twenty-first century?
2. There are several expeditions planned.
3. There is special equipment being developed for supporting the astronauts.
4. Will there be any effects of this exploration on the planet itself?
5. There may be an increase in the surface temperature on Mars from -76° F to -40° F.
6. Will there be breathable air?

7. There will be factories for the measurement and improvement of air quality.
8. Can there ever be enough oxygen and moisture for plants?
9. There have been predictions of lush green patches on the red planet.
10. There may be human residents on Mars in the future, too.

B. DRAFTING SKILL

Drafting Sentences Write sentences using the following beginnings. Each sentence should be about something you think will happen in the future. Underscore each subject and verb and add correct punctuation at the end of each new sentence.

11. Were there . . .
12. There has been . . .
13. There has never been . . .
14. Has there ever been . . .
15. Will there be . . .
16. There is . . .
17. There would often be . . .
18. There will be . . .
19. Have there been . . .
20. Would there ever be . . .

C. APPLICATION IN WRITING

Paragraphs Scientists speculate that by the year 2170, Mars may be very much like Earth. The atmosphere may be like ours, and there may be large cities with businesses and high-tech industries. Write a paragraph or two describing a typical day you might spend on Mars in 2170. Vary your sentences and begin several with *there*.

FOR MORE PRACTICE
See page 401.

SENTENCE FRAGMENTS AND RUN-ON SENTENCES

> A **sentence fragment** is a group of words that does not express a complete idea.
>
> A **run-on sentence** occurs when two or more sentences are written as one.

Both sentence fragments and run-on sentences confuse the reader. The fragment leaves something out. The run-on sentence combines ideas that should be separate.

Sentence Fragments

A group of words that is not a sentence is called a **sentence fragment.** A fragment is only part of something. Avoid sentence fragments in your writing.

A sentence fragment leaves out something important. Sometimes it leaves out the subject. Sometimes it leaves out the verb. As you read a fragment, you may wonder either *What is this about?* or *What happened?*

Fragment   The first portable radio *(What happened?)*
Sentence   The first portable radio worked differently than table models.

Fragment   Received signals *(What is this about?)*
Sentence   Inside the portable radio a coil received signals.

Practice Your Skills

A. CONCEPT CHECK

Sentence Fragments   Write *Sentence* or *Fragment* for each of the following.

1. Rain can make people very uncomfortable
2. Many funny inventions
3. Special eyeglasses with wiper blades
4. The frame contains a small motor and switch
5. Worry about electrocution

6. Another invention was a raincoat with a drain
7. A trough at the bottom edge of the coat
8. A spout drained the water from the trough
9. Are not really practical
10. Have you ever seen anyone wearing these

B. REVISION SKILL

Correcting Sentence Fragments   Read the following letter. Rewrite the letter, turning the fragments into sentences.

Dear Sirs:
[11]Please accept this application for a patent on the hen exerciser. [12]Who wants unhealthy poultry? [13]Don't get enough exercise. [14]My invention combines two activities. [15]Can eat and run at the same time. [16]Consists of a disk in front of a feeding box. [17]Onto the disk hops. [18]The weight of the hen tilts the disk. [19]Must run up the disk again and again. [20]Is unquestionably a major advance in poultry management.

Sincerely yours,
William Jared Manly

C. APPLICATION IN WRITING

Business Letter   Write a formal letter asking for a patent on a clever or humorous invention for handling garbage. Turn these fragments into sentences in your letter.

for taking out the garbage   eliminates the walk to the garbage can
the dreaded daily chore   a special chute to the outside

FOR MORE PRACTICE
See page 401.

Run-on Sentences

When two or more sentences are written incorrectly as one, the result is a **run-on sentence.** Sometimes there is no end mark at the end of the first thought. At other times, a comma is used incorrectly. Here are some examples:

Incorrect   The dirigible was a balloon Zeppelin invented it.
Correct   The dirigible was a balloon. Zeppelin invented it.

Incorrect   The dirigible has motors, a glider does not.
Correct   The dirigible has motors. A glider does not.

Readers don't know which words go together in run-on sentences. Without a period and a capital letter to guide them, they believe they are following one thought. Suddenly the words stop making sense, and readers have to back up to find the start of a new idea. You can correct a run-on sentence by adding the proper end mark and capitalizing the first letter of the next sentence.

Practice Your Skills

A. CONCEPT CHECK

Run-on Sentences   Find the run-on sentences. For each one, write *No End Mark* or *Comma Error* to show what is wrong with it. Write *Correct* if the sentence is correct.

1. Air crosses the parts of an airplane wing at different speeds.
2. Pressure above the wing is low, pressure below it is high.
3. High pressure pushes low pressure pulls.
4. The action of the air on the wing lifts the airplane.
5. A large wing creates more lift than a small wing, a wing tilted up also provides more lift.
6. A wing tilted down creates less lift, the plane will descend.
7. Flaps create a curved wing surface they also provide lift.
8. Great differences in pressure on the wing surfaces create whirlpools of air this causes drag.
9. The plane slows, it may stall.
10. A plane at too great an angle loses lift it also may stall.

B. REVISION SKILL

Correcting Run-on Sentences   If a sentence is a complete sentence, write *Sentence.* If it is a run-on, rewrite it correctly.

11. Helicopters can fly horizontally they fly vertically too.
12. Rotors lift helicopters, the blades are above the fuselage.
13. A rotor may have four blades, these blades rotate on a hub.
14. Vertical propellers on the tail prevent tipping.
15. The tilt of the rotor determines the direction of flight.
16. Helicopters are adaptable, they can land in a small space.
17. Very slow flight is possible hovering is another feature.
18. Helicopters are good for rescues, maneuvering is easy.
19. They are used for the inspection of pipes and telephone wires.
20. Patrolling forests is another use in cities they patrol the highways.

C. PROOFREADING SKILL

Proofread the following paragraph. Then rewrite it, correcting all errors in grammar, capitalization, punctuation, and spelling. Pay particular attention to run-on sentences. (10 errors)

An interesting careers assembly last week. An airplain pilot explained. How to fly a plane. He told us about the planes three basic movements, *pitch, roll,* and *yaw.* Pitch describes the plane's nose moving up or down, roll describes the tipping of the wing. Yaw refers to the plane's nose turning left or right. Showed us a diagram of the plane's controlls and instruments flying a plane is quiet complicated.

C H E C K ✔ P O I N T
MIXED REVIEW · PAGES 390–397

A. Write the subject and verb in each sentence.

A. Write the subject and verb in each sentence.

1. HEATHER: Where was the first automobile race held?
2. VINCE: That exciting event had its debut in France.
3. HEATHER: Guess the number of cars and year of the race.
4. VINCE: There were one hundred cars participating in 1894.
5. Were the spectators thrilled!
6. HEATHER: There also was a race in Chicago in 1895.
7. VINCE: Had any event like that been held in America before?
8. HEATHER: That was the first time.
9. VINCE: Name a popular race today.
10. HEATHER: Many people would vote for the Indianapolis 500.

B. Label each sentence as *Correct, Fragment,* or *Run-on.* Rewrite each fragment or run-on.

[11]The dragster roared down the track Darrell Gwynn was driving.[12]Was approaching 240 miles per hour. [13]Suddenly something terrible. [14]Bright orange flames engulfed the car. [15]Fought for his life. [16]He was rushed to the hospital, he did survive. [17]Darrell was paralyzed he lost an arm. [18]Didn't lose his ambition, though. [19]He attended the U.S. Nationals in 1990. [20]From a wheelchair he signed autographs, the fans cheered.

Writing Theme
Automobile Racing

Writing Theme
Birds, Bugs, and
Beasts

A. Finding Subjects and Predicates   Copy the following sentences. Draw a vertical line between the subject and the predicate.

1. Honeybees have a kind of language.
2. A form of dance is used for communication.
3. A worker bee discovers a source of food.
4. The other members of the hive must know the location.
5. The worker rushes back to the hive.
6. He begins an important dance.
7. The kind of dance tells the distance of the food source.
8. A round dance means a very short trip to the food.
9. The more complicated sickle dance indicates food at a distance of about twenty to sixty feet.
10. The tail-wagging dance indicates greater distances.

B. Simple Subjects and Verbs   Write the verb and its subject in each of the following sentences.

11. An African bird gathers food in an unusual way.
12. The brown bird goes by the name of honey guide.
13. It has a strange fondness for beeswax.
14. The honey guide cleverly locates a beehive.
15. Then it gives a high-pitched call.
16. The call signals a need for help.
17. The little bird has wit but not strength.
18. A badgerlike partner arrives.
19. The ratel's long claws rip the hive open.
20. The two creatures feast on the wax and honey.

C. Finding Verbs   Write the verb in each sentence. Write whether it expresses *Action* or *State of Being*.

21. A tiny sea turtle hatchling heads straight for the sea.
22. The newborn plunges into the surf.
23. Even in total darkness it swims a correct course.
24. In a vast ocean with no landmarks, it navigates perfectly.
25. Migrations of over a thousand miles are common for adults.
26. The females return to the exact beach of their birth.
27. The cycle begins again.
28. Apparently magnetism is the basis of this accurate navigation.
29. In the water the reptiles' bodies become like compass needles.
30. Even delicate flight instruments aren't so reliable.

D. Main Verbs and Helping Verbs Find the main verbs and helping verbs in each sentence.

31. Do you ever think about your brain?
32. Scientists have recently been studying dolphins' brains.
33. They have certainly learned some interesting things.
34. The covering of the brain has been described as very wrinkled.
35. The number of wrinkles may possibly indicate intelligence.
36. Dolphins have often been taught difficult tricks.
37. They will never collide with each other.
38. Their clicking sounds are continuously acting like radar.
39. Have you ever heard a dolphin whistle?
40. With a special signature whistle, a dolphin can identify itself to others of its kind.
41. A low-pitched whistle will often signal distress.
42. Dr. Lou Herman, a professor at the University of Hawaii, has been using sign language as a means of communication with dolphins.
43. Apparently, they can understand simple sentences.
44. They have also given Herman answers to simple yes–no questions.
45. For successful communication, Herman must use correct grammar and a limited vocabulary.

E. Finding Compound Subjects and Verbs Make three columns on your paper. Label them *Subjects, Verbs,* and *Conjunctions.* Fill the appropriate columns for each sentence.

46. Many animals, birds, and insects have some system of communication.
47. The male spider approaches and signals to its lady love.
48. Otherwise, he and a crumb, a fly, or any morsel might become her dinner.
49. Fiddler crabs wave or gesture to one another.
50. A crab and its relatives identify each other in this way.
51. Female wolves and cubs communicate with facial expressions.
52. A stiff tail and a growl also send a message.
53. A robin's song marks and protects its territory.
54. Apes and monkeys scream and chant at each other.
55. Danger, anger, or affection may be the cause.

F. Identifying Kinds of Sentences
Write *Declarative, Interrogative, Imperative,* or *Exclamatory* to identify each of the following sentences. Write the correct end mark.

56. Look very carefully at the world at your feet
57. What amazing things you can see
58. A tiny farmer plants and fertilizes a crop
59. Another harvests mushrooms
60. Small workers build roads and towns
61. A general leads an army of soldiers into battle
62. An officer gives orders to marchers in formation
63. Will the conquered become slaves
64. One injured soldier lives forty-one days with his head cut off
65. Imagine an army that can devour everything in sight
66. Look They just took on a foe one hundred times their size
67. Beware of these busy creatures
68. Who are they
69. Do they come from outer space
70. No, they are ants

G. Subjects and Verbs in Unusual Order
Write the subjects and verbs in the following sentences.

71. Onto the field files a stream of ants.
72. Away goes all vegetation but the rice plants.
73. Into their homes parade the workers with the rice seeds.
74. In the dark sprout the small seeds.
75. Out march the ants again.
76. Into the ground plop the tiny seedlings.
77. Up pop the new rice plants.
78. From far and near come the families for harvest.
79. On and on continues the cycle.
80. Tirelessly toil these little farmers.

H. Questions, Exclamations, and Commands
Write the subject and verb for each of the following sentences. If the subject is understood, write (*you*).

81. Have you ever heard stories about dragons?
82. Picture a yellow-speckled, olive-green creature with short yellow spines down the center of its back.

83. Look!
84. Does it have a third eye on top of its head?
85. Indeed it has!
86. Meet the tuatara, one of the rarest creatures on earth.
87. Where does it live?
88. Travel to the islands near New Zealand for a meeting.
89. Would I be scared!
90. Don't be afraid of this two-and-a-half-foot-long lizard.

I. Sentences with *There* Write the subjects and verbs in the following sentences.

91. There is a lion lurking in the tall grass.
92. By the water hole there stands a solitary zebra.
93. Is there an ostrich nearby?
94. Then there is no danger for either ostrich or zebra.
95. What reason can there be for this strange partnership?
96. There are special qualities belonging to each creature.
97. There may be no animal with keener sight than an ostrich.
98. Wouldn't there also be a need for sensitive hearing and smell?
99. There will be a warning, thanks to the zebra's keen ears and nose.
100. There is little hope for the lion.

J. Writing Complete Sentences Add words to the following fragments to make them complete sentences. Then write the complete sentences.

101. was stung by a bee
102. as sticky as honey
103. turtle at the aquarium
104. as good a sense of direction as the sea turtle
105. could communicate with animals
106. have a wolf as a pet
107. ant farm as a birthday present
108. horse with stripes
109. long, shaggy mane
110. playful lion cubs

GRAMMAR
HANDBOOK
37

Writing Theme
The Romance of the
Old West

A. Identifying Subjects and Verbs   Write each sentence. Draw a vertical line between the complete subject and complete verb. Underline the simple subject once and the verb twice.

1. "Buffalo Bill" Cody's Wild West Show brought the excitement of the Old West to the eastern United States and Europe.
2. Performers demonstrated their skills with guns and horses.
3. Annie Oakley starred as a sharpshooter in the show.
4. Annie's abilities with a weapon made her a main attraction.
5. People at the show called Annie "Queen of the Rifle."
6. This expert with a gun formed lacy patterns of bullet holes in airborne playing cards.
7. She often shot coins out of the hands of her assistants.
8. Once Germany's crown prince was her assistant.
9. People all over the world knew Annie as a figure of the West.
10. Her home during her youth was, in truth, the East.

B. Identifying Verbs   Write the verb in each sentence and label it as *Action* or *State of Being*.

11. The Old West created many larger-than-life folk heroes.
12. Wyatt Earp was an example of such a hero.
13. Earp wore the badge of peace officer in several Old West towns.
14. He remained the deputy marshal in Dodge City for two terms.
15. At that time Dodge City was a wild town at the end of a cattle trail.
16. Law enforcement became nearly impossible.
17. After a while, Earp left Dodge City for Tombstone, Arizona.
18. There he joined two of his brothers in a famous showdown.
19. The gun battle at O.K. Corral is now legendary.
20. From these events, Earp gained a place in the folklore of the West.

C. Identifying Compound Sentence Parts   On your paper, write the compound parts of each sentence. Then label each as a *Compound Subject* or *Compound Verb*.

21. Joseph F. Glidden's invention of barbed wire improved and complicated life at the same time.
22. Farmers in the Old West bought and used barbed wire for fences.
23. At first, farmers and ranchers had many heated disagreements about the fencing.
24. Both the open range and cattle trails were enclosed.
25. Before long, however, ranchers accepted and used the fencing.

D. Sentence Types   Write and label each sentence as *Declarative, Interrogative, Imperative,* or *Exclamatory.* Add the correct end mark. Underline the subject once and the verb twice. Write (*you*) for an understood subject.

26. Imagine a deserted town somewhere in the West.
27. Vacant buildings cast long eerie shadows
28. Down the streets blow tumbleweeds
29. Wow! This must be a ghost town
30. Where have all the people gone
31. Here is a clue
32. On the ground lies the sign for an assayer's office
33. There must be a mine nearby
34. Once, through the streets was heard a famous cry
35. Gold! I found gold

E. Identifying Fragments and Run-ons   For each sentence, write *Sentence, Sentence Fragment,* or *Run-on Sentence.*

36. Virginia City was a famous mining town, it is in Nevada.
37. After the discovery of gold and silver in the hills of Nevada.
38. Virginia City grew thousands came to mine the Comstock Lode.
39. Virginia City became the most prosperous city in the West.
40. When gold and silver eventually ran out.

F. Correcting Fragments and Run-ons   Rewrite each item to correct sentence fragments and run-ons.

41. Some of the most glorified heroes of the Old West
42. Cowhands seemed to have exciting lives, in fact they had a very difficult, lonely way of life
43. They worked hard they spent long hours in the saddle
44. Throughout the year, the main job of the cowhand
45. The cowhands rounded up the cattle, they branded the calves
46. A big event in their lives was the trail drive for many years it was the only way to get cattle to market
47. They led the cattle on a long journey it took months
48. Greatest dangers on the drive
49. The cowhands had to stop stampeding cattle, they would race ahead of the cattle and turn them back
50. The drive ended at a cow town there the cowhands were paid

Persuasion

A persuasive essay reflects the opinions and feelings of the writer. (See Workshop 6.) When you revise persuasive writing, be sure that you have stated the issue and your position on it clearly. Your statements should be supported with facts and examples. Correct any sentence fragments or run-on sentences that may confuse your readers and weaken your argument.

Revise and proofread the following draft of an editorial for a school newspaper. Begin by following the directions at the bottom of the page. As you proofread, pay particular attention to sentence fragments and run-ons. Also look for other errors in grammar, capitalization, punctuation, and spelling.

¹The school board will soon vote on a "no-cuts" policy for after-school activities. **²**I'd like to attend the meeting, but it's only for school board members. **³**With a no-cuts policy, anyone who wants to join an activity may. **⁴**For example, all students who want to be in the Band can join. **⁵**Even if they cannot play an instrument very good. **⁶**Ability is not as important as intrest. **⁷**There are advantages to a no-cuts policy. **⁸**Everyone will have the opportunity to particepate, as a result, involvment in after-school activities will increase. **⁹**They also have more self-confidence. **¹⁰**Plainfield middle school adopted a no-cuts policy, and now over half of its eight hundred students take part in after-school activities. **¹¹**The students have more school spirit more importantly, they are having fun. **¹²**You might argue that Sports Teams won't be competitive. **¹³**If the school adopts this policy. **¹⁴**However that has not been the case at plainfield. **¹⁵**its time for us to support no-cuts too it will be great fun for everyone!

1. In sentence 1, tell which school board by inserting the phrase "of Jefferson Middle School."

2. Move sentence 9 to a more appropriate position.

3. After sentence 14, add the following detail about the performance of Plainfield's sports teams: their no-cuts sports teams won eight championships last year.

4. Delete the sentence that doesn't belong.

5. Divide the editorial into three paragraphs.

Punctuation—Old and New

Who invented punctuation, and how do you suppose people wrote questions before question marks were invented? In Roman times, writers simply put the Latin word *questio* at the end of a sentence. You can see what problems that might cause, though. A whole word takes up a lot of space. So some writer long ago shortened the word *questio* to *QO*. That was a good idea, but it had one drawback: some people thought the letters *QO* were part of the last word in a sentence. Then someone had the clever idea of putting the *Q* over the *O*. You can imagine what finally happened. The *Q* turned into a squiggle over a period—a question mark. See?

Exclamation points, on the other hand, started with the Latin expression of excitement—*IO*. Again, the writers wanted to save space, so they put the *I* above the *O*. Right then and there, the exclamation point was born. Amazing!

Recently, people have been inventing new punctuation. Some advertising copywriters, for example, were looking for a mark that would be even stronger than an exclamation point. What did they come up with? The *flabbergasterisk* ⁑ Then, looking for a still bigger and more spectacular effect, they produced the *stupendapoint* ⁑

Meanwhile, the march of progress continues. For example, what if you feel like asking a question and making an exclamation at the same time? Easy—just combine the two marks, and you have an *interrobang*. Can you believe it ⸘

Sketch Book

- If you were a one-person circus act, what would you look like? Draw yourself and label the drawing.

- Describe your room as precisely as you can. For example, give the titles of books and magazines in your room, the kinds of shoes in your closet, and the items on your dresser or bed.

- Doodle a collection of hats—every kind you can imagine. Make up a name for each hat and write it under the sketch.

Using Nouns

- **What Is a Noun?**
- **Nouns Used as Subjects**
- **Nouns Used as Direct Objects**
- **Nouns Used as Indirect Objects**
- **Predicate Nouns**
- **The Plurals of Nouns**
- **Possessive Nouns**

Can't you almost feel the warm summer breeze, smell the damp freshness of newly mown grass, see the stars appearing as darkness falls, and hear the strains of the music and the conversations of the crowd? You could almost be at this concert yourself.

To paint a scene in words as vivid as this picture or as fanciful as a one-person band, you must use precise nouns to name the people, places, things, and ideas that are a part of the experience. This handbook will show you how.

A **noun** names a person, place, thing, or idea.

All words may be classified into groups. These groups are called **parts of speech**. A **noun** is the part of speech that names a person, place, thing, or idea. You use nouns every day when you speak and write. Notice how you find them everywhere—even in a list of things you plan to do. Nouns are italicized in the list below.

To do today

Art supply *store*—buy *paints* and *paper.*
Call *Jim* and *Teresa*—*library?*
Find *books* about *artists* from *1875* to *1900.*
Start *report* for *class.*
Ask *Mom* to read first *draft.*

Remember that nouns name persons, places, or things. These nouns name things you can see.

Persons	Places	Things
artist	New York	paintbrush
sister-in-law	gallery	paper
teacher	museum	canvas
Picasso	France	picture

Nouns also name things you cannot see. These nouns name ideas, feelings, or characteristics.

Ideas	Feelings	Characteristics
freedom	hunger	patience
honesty	joy	intelligence
democracy	shyness	kindness
time	jealousy	stubbornness
philosophy	hope	talent

Some nouns are one word, others are written as two words, and some are hyphenated. In this handbook you will learn to recognize different kinds of nouns, and to use nouns to add interest and precision to your writing.

Mary Cassatt, *The Letter,* 1894.

Practice Your Skills

CONCEPT CHECK

Nouns Find and write the nouns in the following sentences. Then label each noun *Person, Place, Thing,* or *Idea.* Use the label *Idea* for nouns that name feelings or characteristics.

1. Mary Cassatt was born in the United States in 1844.
2. Her education began at an academy in Pennsylvania.
3. Cassatt left the U.S., however, to study art in Europe.
4. The young artist lived in Italy, Spain, and Belgium and then moved to Paris.
5. The French artist Edgar Degas asked Mary Cassatt to join a group of painters called impressionists.
6. The impressionists were not like traditional French artists.
7. These adventurers wanted to explore new and different artistic styles.
8. With enthusiasm Cassatt agreed to try their methods.
9. For some time Cassatt was unsure about her paintings.
10. However, the support and friendship of such artists as Degas, Pissarro, Monet, Sisley, and Renoir gave Cassatt the courage to experiment.
11. Her paintings were included in several important exhibitions.
12. The shows brought Cassatt great success and honor.
13. Critics raved about the color and light on each canvas.
14. Her portraits of women and children became a trademark.
15. Members of her family were often the models for her paintings.

Common Nouns and Proper Nouns

Nouns are called either common nouns or proper nouns. A **common noun** is a general name for a person, place, thing, or idea. A **proper noun** is a specific name for a person, place, or thing. Proper nouns always begin with capital letters. Like other nouns, proper nouns may be made up of more than one word.

Common Nouns	Proper Nouns
writer	Thomas Paine
state	Rhode Island
brother	George
city	Lexington
river	Delaware River

Writing Theme
Artist Mary Cassatt

FOR MORE PRACTICE
See page 423.

Writing TIP

In your writing, use a specific noun that says what you mean. Say *rose* instead of *flower,* or *Baltimore Orioles* instead of *baseball team.*

A. APPLICATION IN LITERATURE

Common Nouns and Proper Nouns   Write the italicized words from each sentence and identify each as a *Common Noun* or a *Proper Noun*. Be sure to capitalize the proper nouns.

¹In the late *summer* shortly after *tom* and *eb* left, there was *news* of another *defeat* for the *north;* it was closer to *home* this time—at *wilson creek* in *missouri.* ²There were *boys* from *illinois* at *wilson creek,* and the *war* for many *people* in *jasper county* had suddenly become a sorrowful *reality.* ³It was at *wilson creek* that the . . . *commander, nathaniel lyon,* was killed. . . . ⁴*Sumter* and *bull run* had been far away, but *wilson creek* and the conflicting *passions* of *missouri* were very close. . . . ⁵*jethro* listened with *fascination* to the new *names* of *men* and *places.*

Irene Hunt, *Across Five Aprils*

B. REVISION SKILL

Using Precise Nouns   Rewrite the following sentences. Substitute a proper noun for each italicized common noun. You may need to omit the articles *a, an,* or *the.*

6. A *man* rode into the *town.*
7. He stopped at a *shop* on the *street.*
8. Then he asked a *woman* for directions to an *inn.*
9. The *innkeeper* brought the *man* food.
10. He read a *book* while he waited for a *friend.*

C. PROOFREADING SKILL

Correct Noun Forms   The following paragraph is historical fiction based on fact. Write the paragraph, correcting all errors in grammar, capitalization, punctuation, and spelling. (16 errors)

My name is Phillis wheatley. As a child, i was brought to the united states from Africa I was a Slave in the Household of wealthy boston merchants? The wheatleys encouraged me to study and write. I composed poetry Mrs. Wheatley had my Poems published in london, and I became a celebrity. I visited england in 1773. When I returned to Boston. The Wheatleys gave me my Freedom.

FOR MORE PRACTICE
See page 423.

Writing Theme
History in Literature

Nouns Used as Subjects

> A **noun** may be used as the *subject* of a sentence.

The **subject** of a sentence tells whom or what the sentence is about. Nouns are often used as subjects.

> The girls stopped at the library. (Who stopped? The girls. The noun *girls* is the subject of the verb *stopped*.)
> Up the steps walked Jessie and Becca. (Who walked up the steps? Jessie and Becca. The nouns *Jessie* and *Becca* are subjects of the verb *walked*.)

In many sentences, the subject and the verb are next to each other. In other sentences, as in the example below, additional words may separate the subject from the verb.

> The books on the third shelf fell to the floor. (What fell? The books. The noun *books* is the subject of the verb *fell*.)

Practice Your Skills

CONCEPT CHECK

Nouns as Subjects   Write the nouns used as subjects in the following sentences. Some sentences have more than one subject.

1. In 1957 Ray Bradbury wrote *Dandelion Wine,* a novel based on his childhood memories.
2. Decades later, children and adults are still choosing this book as their favorite novel.
3. Readers always remember the setting of Green Town, Illinois, and the main character, Douglas Spaulding.
4. Twelve-year-old Douglas loves summer.
5. A pair of sneakers in the window of Sanderson's Shoe Emporium catches Douglas's eye.
6. The boy asks his father for the shoes.
7. Mr. Spaulding tells the boy to save his money.
8. Into Douglas's mind pops a better idea.
9. The boy cleverly persuades Mr. Sanderson to make a trade.
10. In exchange for the special sneakers, Douglas will run errands for Mr. Sanderson.

Writing Theme
Ray Bradbury

FOR MORE PRACTICE
See page 423.

NOUNS USED AS DIRECT OBJECTS

A **noun** used as a *direct object* receives the action of the verb.

Julia picked the *flowers*.   Joe helped *her*.

The noun *flowers* and the pronoun *her* are direct objects. They answer the questions *picked what?* and *helped whom?* In other words, they receive the action of the verbs *picked* and *helped*.

A sentence may have more than one direct object.

Maria grows *tomatoes* and *cucumbers* in her garden.

Remember, direct objects always answer the questions *what* or *whom,* and they are always nouns or pronouns.

Sentence Diagraming   For information on diagraming direct objects, see page 678.

Practice Your Skills

A. CONCEPT CHECK

Nouns as Direct Objects   Write the direct object or objects.

1. You can grow fresh herbs indoors.
2. You don't need an outdoor garden.
3. You need only a planter, soil, and herb seeds.
4. First, put the soil into the planter.
5. Then, thoroughly sprinkle the soil with water.
6. Plant a few herb seeds in the moist soil $\frac{1}{4}$-inch deep.
7. Put the planter in a sunny window so the seeds will grow.
8. Don't overwater your seedlings.
9. The sun should dry the top of the soil between waterings.
10. Soon you can season your meals with fresh chives or thyme.

B. REVISION SKILL

Achieving Precision   Write the following sentences, replacing the vague italicized direct objects with more precise nouns.

11. Every summer my family flies to California to visit *a person*.
12. She owns *a place* in the San Joaquin Valley.

Writing
TIP

Remember that pronouns may sometimes be used instead of nouns. For more information on pronouns used as direct objects, see Handbook 39, pages 437–439.

Writing Theme
Gardening

13. Our friend lives in the country and plants *crops* on several acres of her land.
14. She also grows *vegetables* in her backyard garden.
15. In the evening, we make delicious *food* from the vegetables we picked in the morning.
16. We also eat the *fruit* from the trees in front of the house.
17. This year we will help her plant *flowers* in the garden.
18. The flowers will attract *insects*.
19. Our friend feeds the *birds* that nest in her trees.
20. Since she grows more than she can eat, she takes the extra *things* from the garden to neighbors down the road.

FOR MORE PRACTICE
See page 424.

CHECK ✓ POINT
MIXED REVIEW · PAGES 408–413

Writing Theme
Holography

Write the nouns from the sentences. Identify each noun as *Common* or *Proper*. Label it as *Subject, Direct Object,* or *Neither*.

1. A hologram creates an amazing three-dimensional image out of light.
2. Dennis Gabor invented holography in 1947.
3. These days, holograms are created with the beams of lasers.
4. Theodore Maiman and other scientists built the first workable laser in 1960.
5. Emmett Leith and Juris Upatnieks made the first holograms from lasers at the University of Michigan in 1961.
6. The illusions made by modern holograms are remarkable.
7. All sides of the object in the image are visible.
8. Holograms serve many useful purposes.
9. Holography can produce three-dimensional images of objects that can be seen through a microscope.
10. Mechanics can examine the wings of airplanes more thoroughly with the aid of holograms.
11. Credit cards have holograms. As a result, people cannot make counterfeits.
12. In addition, holograms often decorate book jackets and compact disk covers.
13. Artists create beautiful holographic images.
14. Hologram pendants, badges, and postcards make popular souvenirs.
15. The U.S. Postal Service even put a hologram on an envelope.

NOUNS USED AS INDIRECT OBJECTS

> The **indirect object** of the verb generally tells to whom or for whom an action is done.

A sentence may contain an indirect object only if the sentence also has a direct object. The indirect object comes before the direct object and tells to whom (or to what) or for whom (or for what) something is done. Note that an indirect object never appears in any phrase beginning with the words *to* or *for*.

Subject	Verb	Indirect Object	Direct Object
Alice	gave	*Mom*	a card.
Kenny	brought	*Mrs. Jones*	the magazine.

A sentence may contain more than one indirect object.

William sent *Beth* and *Andy* T-shirts from Australia.

In the example above, *Beth* and *Andy* form a compound indirect object.

Sentence Diagraming   For information on diagraming indirect objects, see page 678.

Practice Your Skills

A. CONCEPT CHECK

Nouns as Indirect Objects   Write the indirect objects in the following sentences. Some sentences may have more than one indirect object. Remember that indirect objects do not appear in phrases beginning with *to* or *for*.

1. Mom promised my brother a Halloween party on his birthday.
2. Tim sent twelve friends invitations.
3. The invitations gave the kids instructions to wear costumes.
4. I lent Tim my hockey uniform for a costume.
5. As guests arrived, they handed Mom and Tim their coats.
6. As the first activity, Tim gave his guests pumpkins to carve.
7. We awarded Perry and Tanya prizes for the strangest pumpkins.

Writing
═ TIP ═

Vary your sentence structure by using a mixture of indirect objects and prepositional phrases beginning with *to* or *for*.

Writing Theme
Celebrations and Gift-Giving

8. Then Mom served the hungry carvers pumpkin pie and hot cider.
9. Finally Mom gave Tim the signal to open his presents.
10. Tim's friends brought Tim some great gifts, including a monster mask, fake fangs, and a long gray wig.
11. After that, Perry offered his friends a challenge.
12. Each guest would tell the others his or her favorite ghost story.
13. The listeners would award the winner the title of best storyteller.
14. Shawna's story gave the guests goosebumps.
15. Mom quickly made Shawna a certificate labeled Best Teller of Ghost Stories.

B. REVISION SKILL

Sentence Variety   There are various ways to arrange sentences to express an idea. In the following paragraph, write the indirect object for each sentence. If a sentence does not have an indirect object, rewrite the sentence, changing the appropriate phrase to an indirect object.

> EXAMPLE   On New Year's Day, visitors brought cake *to their neighbors.*
> On New Year's Day, visitors brought *their neighbors* cake.

[16]People in many cultures give New Year's gifts to their friends. [17]In ancient Rome, citizens gave friends gold-covered nuts and coins. [18]During the 1500s, English subjects presented expensive jewelry and gloves to Queen Elizabeth I in celebration of the New Year. [19]French tradespeople presented New Year's gifts such as breads, chickens, or other gifts of their trade to their customers and friends. [20]On a Hindu New Year, people offer their family members, as well as their cows, a special treat of rice boiled in milk.

C. APPLICATION IN WRITING

Lists   Write a list of ten people. You may include friends, family members, and fictional or historical characters. Think of something you would like to give each person. Write a sentence for each name on your list, using the following form: "I would give (name of person) (name of gift) because (reason)." You can be as practical or as fanciful as you wish with your gifts.

FOR MORE PRACTICE
See page 424.

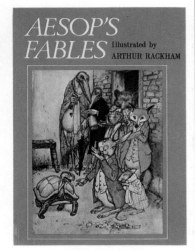

AESOP'S FABLES Illustrated by ARTHUR RACKHAM

The hare and the tortoise.

Writing Theme
The Storytellers

PREDICATE NOUNS

Predicate nouns are nouns in the predicate that explain or identify the subject.

When a linking verb connects the subject of a sentence with a noun in the predicate, that noun is a **predicate noun.**

A crow is a large black *bird.*   Aesop was a Greek *storyteller.*

Bird and *storyteller* are predicate nouns. They mean the same thing as the subject or explain the subject in some way.

A sentence can also have a compound predicate noun, as in the following example.

Today, our storytellers are *Li Chan* and *Greta Knappen.*

Note that the predicate nouns *Li Chan* and *Greta Knappen* identify or rename the subject *storytellers.*

Sentence Diagraming   For information on diagraming predicate nouns, see page 678.

Practice Your Skills

A. CONCEPT CHECK

Predicate Nouns   For each sentence, identify the subject and the predicate noun by writing this equation: subject = predicate noun. If a sentence does not have a predicate noun, write *None.*

EXAMPLE   That story is a fable.   story = fable

1. Aesop was a storyteller and a slave in ancient Greece.
2. His stories were fables with a moral, or lesson, at the end.
3. Most characters in fables are animals or plants that talk.
4. Their characteristics are reflections of human weaknesses.
5. His tales have long been a popular kind of entertainment.
6. One Aesop fable is the account of *The Grasshopper and the Ant.*
7. The characters are a hard-working ant and a lazy grasshopper.
8. At the start of winter, the ant is prepared with food and a home.
9. The grasshopper, however, becomes a cold, hungry creature.
10. The fable teaches the importance of hard work and preparation.

B. CONCEPT CHECK

Recognizing Predicate Nouns   Write the sentences below. Then underline the subject once and the predicate noun or nouns twice. Note that not every sentence has a predicate noun.

11. Minstrels were often historians as well as storytellers in the Middle Ages.
12. They were popular entertainers.
13. Their performances were a welcome escape from daily chores.
14. They set stories, news, and history to music.
15. Their songs could be folk tales, legends, or original stories.
16. Repetition of well-known tales and ballads helped preserve stories and songs over time.
17. The minstrels' theaters were marketplaces and kings' courts.
18. Minstrels were known by different names in different places.
19. In Ireland, minstrels were bards; in France, minstrels were troubadours; and in Germany, minstrels were minnesingers.
20. The late 1400s was the last active period of the minstrels.

FOR MORE PRACTICE
See pages 424–425.

C H E C K ✔ P O I N T
MIXED REVIEW • PAGES 414–417

Write the underlined noun or nouns in the sentences and identify them as *Predicate Noun, Direct Object,* or *Indirect Object.*

1. Matt gave Cassie and Pat a ride home from the airport.
2. In the car, the girls described the sights and experiences of their trip to Washington, D.C.
3. They had sent home postcards and photographs of their trip.
4. In Washington, D.C., they visited the Smithsonian Institution.
5. In 1829, James Smithson left the United States his fortune.
6. Congress used the money to set up the Smithsonian.
7. Important parts of the institution are its museums and zoo.
8. One museum is the National Museum of American History.
9. The First Ladies exhibit is a popular attraction there.
10. Recently museum officials gave that exhibit a new look.
11. The exhibit now emphasizes the first ladies' involvement in social issues more than it did before.
12. The previous exhibit gave their fashions more emphasis.
13. The museum provided Pat and Cassie insights into our culture.
14. Pat's favorite exhibits were sports items and TV props.
15. Cassie's favorites were the quilts and the old toys.

Writing Theme
At the Smithsonian

Using Nouns   **417**

A **singular noun** names one person, place, thing, or idea.
A **plural noun** names more than one person, place, thing, or idea.

Many writers have trouble spelling the plural forms of nouns. For example, they may know how to spell the singular form of the word *alto*. They may not be sure whether the plural form is spelled *altos* or *altoes*. Seven guidelines for forming plural nouns are listed below.

Writing TIP

Use the dictionary to check your spelling of plural nouns.

1. **To form the plural of most nouns, add -s.**
   drums   violins   songs   concerts   notes

2. **When a singular noun ends in s, sh, ch, x, or z, add -es.**
   classes   dishes   speeches   boxes   buzzes

3. **When a singular noun ends in o, add -s.**
   pianos   radios   sopranos   piccolos   studios

   For a few nouns ending in *o*, add *-es:*
   echoes   heroes   vetoes   potatoes   tomatoes

4. **When a singular noun ends in y with a consonant before it, change the y to i and add -es.**
   harmony—harmonies   melody—melodies

   When a vowel (*a, e, i, o, u*) comes before the *y*, just add *-s.*
   toy—toys   way—ways   key—keys
   valley—valleys   journey—journeys   play—plays

5. **To make the plural of nouns ending in f or fe, change the f to v and add -es or -s.**
   leaf—leaves   half—halves   self—selves
   knife—knives   life—lives   wife—wives

   For some nouns ending in *f,* add *-s* to make the plural.
   roof—roofs   cuff—cuffs   chief—chiefs

6. **Some nouns have the same spelling in the singular and the plural.**
   deer   tuna   sheep   trout   moose

7. For some nouns, the plural is formed in a special way.

foot—feet   child—children   tooth—teeth

man—men   woman—women   mouse—mice

Practice Your Skills

A. CONCEPT CHECK

Plurals of Nouns   Rewrite the sentences, changing the nouns in the parentheses to their plural forms.

1. People enjoy music on (holiday) and at (ceremony) and (festivity).
2. For example, on the Fourth of July, many people attend (parade) or (concert).
3. There they are sure to hear patriotic songs and military (march).
4. Listeners clap their (hand) and stamp their (foot) in time with the music and join in singing the (chorus).
5. Some wave flags or (scarf) to the music.
6. (Orchestra) and bands play marches with slower (tempo) at (graduation) and weddings.
7. Music is always important at (party).
8. Some school (dance) have (jukebox) that play popular (tune).
9. Others feature disc (jockey) who play current recordings.
10. A formal dance might even have a band that plays (waltz).

B. PROOFREADING SKILL

Correct Plural Forms   Rewrite the following paragraph, correcting all errors in grammar, capitalization, punctuation, and spelling. (15 errors)

Some modern composers write classical peices, such as concertoes and symphonys. Others compose popular music. Most composers, however, use a system called musicle notation to write there melodies and harmoneys. They use special paper. Have you ever seen paper printed with staves, or sets of five paralell lines running across the page. Composers place symbals called notes. At specific places on these lines. The notes show what pitchs should be played. Musician's know how long to hold each pitch by looking at the shape of the note for example, an empty oval is a whole note and an empty oval with a stem on it is a half note. A Musician would give a whole note the same time value as two halfes.

Writing Theme
Making Music

FOR MORE PRACTICE
See page 425.

POSSESSIVE NOUNS

A **possessive noun** shows who or what owns something.

You can express possession in different ways. For example, you might say "the toy of a child." However, it is more concise, or shorter, to say "the child's toy."

A **possessive noun** shows who or what owns a thing or a quality. In the example above, *child's* is the possessive noun.

Forming the Possessive of Singular Nouns

To form the possessive of any singular noun, add an apostrophe and *s*.

> Chris's wishes   the lion's paw   Cinderella's slipper

Forming the Possessive of Plural Nouns

To form the possessive of a plural noun that ends in *s*, simply add an apostrophe.

> candles' wax   sisters' dresses   the Simpsons' house

To form the possessive of a plural noun that does not end in *s*, add an apostrophe and *s*.

> geese's flight   women's team   children's books

Sentence Diagraming   For information on diagraming possessive nouns, see Adjectives on page 678.

Practice Your Skills

A. CONCEPT CHECK

Using Possessive Nouns   Rewrite the following sentences to make them more concise. You may need to omit some words as you use possessive nouns to replace "of" phrases.

1. Even though the wishes of people may not always come true, they still make them again and again.
2. Many people wish on the first star of the night.

Writing
━ TIP ━

Using possessive nouns can help make your writing less wordy. For example, you can say "bird's nest" instead of "nest of a bird."

Writing Theme
Wishful Thinking

3. There are people who make a wish as they blow wispy seeds of dandelions.
4. Others wish on the first frog of spring they see or hear.
5. In England, the hopeful wish on the first fruit of a new season.
6. Citizens of Sweden wish as they break a gingersnap cookie.
7. Filipinos wish when they see beautiful colors of rainbows.
8. In Japan, the written wishes of children are hung on trees.
9. Tourists visiting Italy wish as they toss coins in a famous fountain of Rome.
10. Wouldn't it be wonderful if the wishes of everyone could come true?

B. DRAFTING SKILL

Possessive Nouns   Decide how to use possessive forms to make each phrase more concise. Then use each possessive form in a sentence.

11. dreams of children
12. leaf of a clover
13. whiskers of a mouse
14. guess of James
15. turn of a Ferris wheel
16. tails of foxes
17. wish of Charles
18. eggs of geese
19. gown of a princess
20. wings of fairies
21. family of deer
22. garden of the Smiths
23. face of a jack-o'-lantern
24. elves of Greenglas
25. throne of a prince
26. banks of rivers
27. hands of a clock
28. morals of stories
29. dresses of Deloris
30. shells of eggs

C. PROOFREADING SKILL

Correcting Possessive Nouns   Rewrite the following paragraph, correcting all errors you find. Pay special attention to possessives. (15 errors)

Folk and farey tales are often about a persons wishes. According to legend, Aladdins lamp grants wishes when it is rubbed. A Russians gold ring grants his wish to marry the king's daughter. Cinderellas fairy godmother helps cinderella get ready for the princes ball. A charmed fish grants the wishs of the fishermans wife untill she asks for too much then, the fish reverses the wifes wishes that he had already granted. In fairy tales. Some people use there wishes carefuly, while others do not.

FOR MORE PRACTICE
See page 425.

C H E C K ✔ P O I N T

Writing Theme
Scientific Facts
and Fiction

A. Write the plural of each underlined word below. You may wish to consult a dictionary.

1. Every year, <u>person</u> on <u>beach</u> around the world hold seashells to their <u>ear</u> to hear the <u>sound</u> of the ocean.
2. <u>Belief</u> such as that have been passed down through <u>generation</u>.
3. Some of these <u>story</u> are based on fact, others are <u>legend</u> or fanciful tales that attempt to explain <u>mystery</u>.
4. One popular myth for <u>child</u> tells about <u>reindeer</u> that can fly.
5. However, <u>scientist</u> have yet to find <u>deer</u> with flying <u>ability</u>.
6. Legends tell of <u>unicorn</u>, but <u>naturalist</u> have never found one.
7. Perhaps people confused <u>rhinoceros</u> or antelopes such as <u>bongo</u> or <u>oryx</u> with these fabled <u>beast</u>.
8. <u>Dolphin</u> are real animals that humans find especially appealing.
9. These sea creatures were considered sacred in some ancient <u>culture</u> and are still <u>sign</u> of good luck to sailors.
10. There are true <u>tale</u> of these sea <u>mammal</u> nudging the <u>body</u> of drowning swimmers toward shore.
11. The <u>life</u> of dolphins and humans seem alike in many <u>way</u>.
12. For example, both live in <u>family</u> and care for their <u>offspring</u>.
13. Dolphins enjoy people, and some <u>study</u> show that swimming with dolphins can make people feel better about themselves.
14. Dolphins at <u>zoo</u> and <u>park</u> perform remarkable <u>trick</u>.
15. They can find tiny objects under water by sending out several <u>series</u> of sounds and listening for the returning <u>echo</u>.

B. Write the possessive form of each underlined word below.

16. The full <u>moon</u> glow shines brightly in the clear night sky.
17. Yet <u>Earth</u> moon generates no light of its own.
18. It reflects the <u>sun</u> rays.
19. The moon has inspired <u>people</u> imaginations for centuries.
20. In some ancient <u>cultures</u> religions, there was a moon god.
21. The goddess Diana was one of <u>Rome</u> three moon goddesses.
22. The Romans thought that the crescent moon and moonbeams looked like <u>Diana</u> bow and arrows.
23. The <u>Babylonians</u> most powerful god was the moon god Sin.
24. <u>Egypt</u> ancient culture honored the moon god Khonsu.
25. <u>Astronomers</u> discoveries have changed <u>men</u> and <u>women</u> beliefs.

Writing Theme
Award Winners

A. Identifying Nouns   Write the nouns in the following sentences. Capitalize each proper noun.

1. joseph pulitzer was born in hungary in 1847.
2. This young man came to the united states to fight in the civil war.
3. pulitzer later moved to st. louis, missouri, and became a reporter for a newspaper.
4. Eventually, pulitzer owned and managed several newspapers, including *the world,* new york city's daily newspaper.
5. His publishing empire made joseph pulitzer very wealthy.
6. By 1887, pulitzer had unfortunately lost his sight and had also become very sensitive to noise.
7. He needed the quiet of his yacht to direct his two newspapers.
8. In his will, pulitzer left two million dollars to columbia university to establish a journalism school.
9. The pulitzer prizes were also created with this money.
10. These awards are given for achievements in journalism, literature, drama, and music.

B. Identifying Nouns as Subjects   Write the nouns used as subjects in the following sentences.

11. The Special Olympics began in 1968.
12. The Joseph P. Kennedy, Jr., Foundation sponsors the program.
13. The Olympic Games are the model for the Special Olympics.
14. The Special Olympics program has twenty-two official sports.
15. Both children and adults compete in the games.
16. Summer and winter sports are included in the program.
17. Gymnastics and swimming are featured in the summer games.
18. Ice-skating and skiing are included in the winter games.
19. Wheelchair events are an important part of the games.
20. Competitors can train in year-round games, meets, and programs.
21. Age and ability determine the competitor's level.
22. Gold, silver, and bronze medals are awarded to the winners.
23. At the local, state, and chapter levels, the Special Olympics are held every year.
24. Every four years, International Special Olympic Games are held in both summer and winter.
25. In the Special Olympics, athletes benefit from team sport competition.

C. Identifying Nouns as Direct Objects Write the direct object in the following sentences.

26. The Swedish chemist Alfred Nobel invented dynamite.
27. This invention made Nobel a very wealthy man.
28. The chemist established the Nobel prizes with his money.
29. These prizes honor people. Their work benefits humanity.
30. Some prize winners have made important discoveries or inventions in physics, chemistry, medicine, or economics.
31. Other winners have written inspiring literature.
32. Still other prize winners promote international peace.
33. Every year, the Nobel prize winners receive their awards on December 10.
34. Each gets a medal and a cash award of about $190,000.
35. The winners join a very respected group. The group includes Albert Einstein, Marie Curie, and Martin Luther King, Jr.

D. Identifying Nouns Used as Indirect Objects Write the indirect objects in the following sentences. Write *None* if a sentence does not have an indirect object.

36. In 1950, Mother Teresa founded a religious order called the Missionaries of Charity in Calcutta, India.
37. The order provides the neediest members of the community with food, shelter, and clothing.
38. The missionaries offer men, women, and children help and love.
39. City officials provided Mother Teresa with a building.
40. The shelter gave patients with terminal illnesses a place to die with dignity.
41. Word of Mother Teresa's work spread around the world.
42. Individuals everywhere send her organization donations.
43. The Missionaries of Charity have branches in many countries.
44. The Nobel committee awarded Mother Teresa the Peace Prize in 1979.
45. She had sent the world a message about caring for others.

E. Finding Predicate Nouns Write the predicate nouns in each sentence. Write *None* if a sentence does not have a predicate noun.

46. The Newbery Medal is an award for children's literature.
47. Authors of outstanding children's books are the recipients of the award.

48. The founder of the award named the medal for John Newbery.
49. Newbery was a British bookseller and publisher in the 1700s.
50. He was the first person to print and sell children's books.
51. In 1922, Hendrik van Loon was the first Newbery Medal winner.
52. The title of his award-winning book is *The Story of Mankind*.
53. Elizabeth G. Speare is the author of two award-winning books.
54. She received the award in 1959 and again in 1962.
55. Many other fine authors have been proud winners of this award.

F. Forming Plurals of Nouns   Write the correct plural form of the underlined nouns in the sentences below.

56. The Academy <u>Award</u> ceremony is a televised annual event that honors <u>filmmaker</u> for their <u>achievement</u>.
57. The <u>trophy</u>, or Oscars, are given in many <u>category</u>.
58. <u>Drama</u> and <u>comedy</u> have often won the best film award.
59. Two of the <u>actress</u> in the 1991 movie *Fried Green <u>Tomato</u>* had won Oscars in previous years.
60. Nervous laughter and sweaty palms are common <u>reflex</u> for <u>nominee</u>.
61. Most Oscar <u>winner</u> give lengthy acceptance <u>speech</u>.
62. They often say this is the best night of their <u>life</u>.
63. Commercials also cause many <u>delay</u> in the ceremony.
64. The <u>man</u> usually wear <u>tuxedo</u>, while <u>woman</u> wear fancy <u>dress</u>.
65. The <u>flash</u> of bulbs light up the room where <u>photo</u> are taken.

G. Forming the Possessives of Nouns   Write the possessive form of each underlined noun in the sentences below.

66. Each year, some <u>people</u> bravery or service to the community may be rewarded with decorations or medals of honor.
67. The <u>medals</u> sizes and shapes vary.
68. Many <u>ribbons</u> colors and designs correspond to a <u>country</u> national colors or to qualities such as bravery or virtue.
69. <u>Congress</u> approval is needed for some awards.
70. The <u>United States</u> highest military decoration is the Congressional Medal of Honor.
71. <u>Citizens</u> outstanding service to the country and the world is awarded with the Presidential Medal of Freedom.
72. This is the <u>nation</u> highest civilian honor.
73. President <u>Kennedy</u> administration set up the award in 1963.

GRAMMAR
HANDBOOK
38

A. Identifying Nouns   Write the underlined word or words in each sentence and identify them as *Subject, Direct Object, Indirect Object,* or *Predicate Noun*.

1. In 1587 a <u>group</u> of English colonists settled on Roanoke Island off the coast of what is now North Carolina.
2. John White, who became the colony's governor, brought his <u>daughter</u> and <u>son-in-law</u> with him.
3. Virginia Dare was his <u>granddaughter</u> and the first English <u>baby</u> born in the new colony.
4. <u>White</u> returned to England for more food and supplies.
5. Then <u>England</u> and <u>Spain</u> went to war for three years.
6. When <u>White</u> brought the <u>colonists</u> supplies in 1590, the people were gone.
7. They had left the <u>governor</u> only one clue.
8. The clue was the <u>word</u> *Croatoan* carved on a tree.
9. The Croatans were <u>Indians</u> who lived on a nearby island.
10. Perhaps the <u>colonists</u> went to live with the Croatans.
11. Some descendants of the Croatans, known as Lumbee Indians, have the same last <u>names</u> as the missing colonists.
12. To this day, no one has solved the <u>mystery</u> of the Lost Colony.

B. Forming Plurals   Write the plural of each of these nouns.

13. clue
14. decoy
15. key
16. question
17. thief
18. detective
19. hunch
20. motto
21. knife
22. glass
23. mummy
24. diary
25. dish
26. radio
27. sheep
28. chef
29. salmon
30. fungus

C. Forming Possessives   Write the possessive form of each underlined word. If the underlined word is plural, be sure to use the plural possessive form.

31. Monarch butterflies are among <u>nature</u> mysterious creatures.
32. The <u>monarchs</u> orange-and-black wings look fragile.
33. Yet the <u>butterflies</u> wings carry them great distances.
34. In summer, monarchs visit <u>gardens</u> colorful flowers and flit through a <u>woods</u> sunlit clearings.
35. As summer days shorten, however, flocks of monarchs leave behind the northern <u>regions</u> cold weather and migrate south.

36. The insects mass migration begins as far north as Canada and ends in Mexico, Florida, or California.
37. In a single day journey, they can cover eighty miles or more.
38. A typical monarch flight could be two thousand miles long.
39. Amazingly, each flock destination is the same year after year.
40. One tree branches may be home to hundreds of butterflies.
41. A butterfly life is short; very few live more than one year.
42. They do not survive long enough to guide their young migration the next year.
43. Naturalists wonder how the offspring destinations can match the parents choices exactly.
44. How do each year newcomers know which trees to choose?
45. Is it the species instinct? We do not know!

D. Using Plural and Possessive Forms Correctly   Rewrite the sentences, correcting errors in the plural and possessive forms.

46. Strange rings, called *crop circles,* have been appearing in Englands farmlands' among growing crops and sheafs of grain.
47. Something is bending the stalkes of grain close to the ground.
48. Aerial photoes show massive patterns where the land looks as if it might have been blasted by intense winds or heat.
49. The strange appearances have spread beyond Britains' countryside, reaching twenty other countrys.
50. The shapes's origins have puzzled experts worldwide and are one of the most interesting mysteries of the time's.
51. Local groups set up watchs to discover what causes the rings, and many have storys about flashs of light and buzzing sounds.
52. Peoples' explanations vary depending upon their believes.
53. Some credit aliens spaceshipes, and electrical engineer Colin Andrews' studyes suggest some kind of intelligent being.
54. One physicists' theory involves weather phenomena such as whirlwindes.
55. In 1991, two British artist's claimed they created southern Englands' crop circles.
56. The Englishmens' technique required simple tools, such as a plank and string, to bend the plants stems.
57. They claimed imitators made some of the other patterns'.
58. Were they really responsible for the circle's existence?
59. If so, they created one of this centuries great hoaxs.
60. They could become heros in the futures' folk tales.

WRITING CONNECTIONS

Elaboration, Revision, and Proofreading

Informative Writing: Explaining *What*

Writing to inform and define is a very straightforward way of explaining something. (See Workshop 5.) When you revise, make sure that your information is presented in a logical order. Also be sure you have included specific details about your subject. When you write, use precise nouns to provide concrete examples. Nouns will also help you compare or contrast your subject with things that are familiar to your reader.

On your paper, revise the following draft. Follow the directions at the bottom of the page. Proofread your revision, looking especially for errors in the use of nouns as well as for errors in grammar, capitalization, punctuation, and spelling.

¹Have you ever found one thing when you were looking for another? ²Or not looking for anything at all? ³That is called <u>serendipity.</u> ⁴Horace wallace invented the word. ⁵he took it from a persian fairy tale. ⁶The word <u>Serendipity</u> first appeared in 1754. ⁷The princes' in the story discovered by acident things that they were not looking for.

⁸Serendipity can happen to anyone at any time but there are some famous examples of this accidental good fortune. ⁹For instance think of the little yellow papers people use to stick notes on things. ¹⁰Art Fry, a worker at 3M Company, had been irritated by bookmarks that fell out of his books. ¹¹He remebered a glue that was not permanent that his company had developed. ¹²Fry invented Post-it notes. ¹³By using the glue to solve the problem with the bookmarks. ¹⁴He had not been looking for a better bookmark, but he found a removable marker that would stay in place. ¹⁵By serendipity!

1. Add this definition of *serendipity* to sentence 3: "the good luck to make an important discovery by accident." Add a comma after *serendipity.*

2. Add the appositive, "an English writer," to sentence 4. Place a comma before and after the appositive.

3. Add the title of the tale, *The Three Princes of Serendip,* to sentence 5. Add a comma after the word *tale.*

4. Move sentence 6 to a more logical position.

5. Be more precise by replacing the wordy phrase "the little yellow papers people use to stick notes on things" with the proper noun "Post-it Notes."

Watch Your English

We'll begin with a box, and the plural is boxes;
But the plural of ox is oxen, not oxes.
Then one fowl is a goose, but two are called geese,
Yet the plural of moose should never be meese!
You may find a lone mouse or a whole nest of mice,
But the plural of house is houses, not hice!
If the plural of man is always called men,
Why shouldn't the plural of pan be called pen?
If I speak of a foot, and you show me your feet,
And I give you a boot—would a pair be called beet?
If one tooth, and a whole set are teeth,
Why should not the plural of booth be called beeth?
Then one may be that and three would be those,
Yet hat in the plural would never be hose;
And the plural of cat is cats, not cose!
We speak of a brother, and also of brethren,
But though we say mother, we never say methren!
Then the masculine pronouns are he, his and him,
But imagine the feminine, she, shis and shim!
So English, I fancy, you all will agree
Is the funniest language you ever did see!

Author Unknown

- What is in store for the people you know? Write fortune-cookie slips for several of your friends or family members.

- What will your life be like twenty years from now? Write a brief description of your future.

- Do you believe in luck? List several lucky things that have happened to you or to people you know.

Using Pronouns

- **What Is a Pronoun?**
- **Subject Pronouns**
- **Object Pronouns**
- **Possessive Pronouns**
- **Pronoun Problems**
- **Reflexive and Intensive Pronouns**
- **Pronouns and Their Antecedents**
- **Indefinite Pronouns**

Do you worry about your future? You can consult fortune cookies, the Chinese calendar, or a horoscope, or you can just wait and see what happens. One thing you can't do, however, is talk or write about the future, the present, the past—or anything else that has to do with people or things—without using pronouns.

This handbook explains what you need to know about these useful words.

Calvin and Hobbes
by Bill Watterson

A **pronoun** is a word that is used to take the place of a noun or another pronoun.

Like nouns, pronouns are used to refer to people, places, things, and ideas. Unlike nouns, pronouns change form according to their use. Study these pairs of sentences.

Nouns	Pronouns
Ira passed the ball.	*He* passed the ball.
Mrs. Stein coached *Ira*.	Mrs. Stein coached *him*.
Mrs. Stein is *Ira's* mother.	Mrs. Stein is *his* mother.
The *uniforms* came today.	*They* came today.
Mr. Salas ordered the *uniforms*.	Mr. Salas ordered *them*.

The Forms of Pronouns

Pronouns have three forms: *subject, object,* and *possessive.*

She won. (*She* is the subject.)
I watched *her*. (*Her* is the direct object.)
The trophy is *hers*. (*Hers* is possessive.)
It is *her* trophy. (*Her* is also possessive.)

The pronouns listed below are called **personal pronouns.** Each has a subject, object, and possessive form.

Forms of the Personal Pronouns

	Subject	Object	Possessive
Singular	I	me	my, mine
	you	you	your, yours
	she, he, it	her, him, it	her, hers, his, its
Plural	we	us	our, ours
	you	you	your, yours
	they	them	their, theirs

Substituting Pronouns for Nouns

The form that a pronoun takes depends on its use. Subject pronouns are used as subjects. Object pronouns are used as direct objects, indirect objects, and objects of prepositions. Possessive pronouns are used to show possession.

The players are here. *They* practice daily. (subject)
The coach came later. Yuki greeted *him*. (direct object)
Darryl warmed up. Sam gave *him* advice. (indirect object)
The players are ready. *Their* spirits are high. (possessive)

Practice Your Skills

A. CONCEPT CHECK

Pronouns   Write *Subject, Object,* or *Possessive* to identify the italicized pronoun in each sentence.

1. Most athletic coaches have an important influence on *their* players.
2. Coaching is demanding, and *it* is sometimes a thankless job.
3. However, *I* have discovered some interesting information about a few important coaches.
4. The fact that John Heisman was both a football coach and a Shakespearean actor surprised *me*.
5. Many football players owe *their* lives to Heisman.
6. In 1906 *he* introduced the forward pass.
7. *It* eliminated the hazardous mass formations that had caused eighteen deaths in 1905.
8. Often *we* remember the name of the athlete but not that of the coach.
9. For example, *you* may not recognize the name Bela Karoli.
10. Yet, the names of *his* pupils Nadia Comaneci and Mary Lou Retton are probably very familiar.
11. Pat Connolly devoted *her* efforts to runner Evelyn Ashford.
12. *She* guided Evelyn to her first two Olympic gold medals and a world championship.
13. As a result of Ashford's astounding running times, the press called *her* the "fastest woman in the world."
14. Pat, the first female track-and-field coach at UCLA, has written *her* first book.
15. She titled *it Coaching Evelyn.*

Writing
TIP

Pronouns help a writer avoid repetition of the same nouns and link ideas between sentences and paragraphs. Notice how Nadja Salerno-Sonnenberg uses pronouns in her narrative on pages 28–29.

Writing Theme
Coaches and Teams

B. REVISION SKILL

Eliminating Repetition Rewrite the following sentences, changing the italicized proper nouns to pronouns. Follow the directions in parentheses.

> EXAMPLE   Soccer goalies and players must be skillful, but *goalies* and *players* must also have a positive attitude. (Use one pronoun.)
> Soccer goalies and players must be skillful, but they must also have a positive attitude.

16. Sherry and Shelly both wanted to join the soccer team, but *Sherry* and *Shelly* did not know which positions would suit them best. (Use one pronoun.)

17. *The coach* was undecided. (You are the coach. Use a pronoun.)

18. Joel is the captain, and *Joel* was undecided too. (Use a pronoun.)

19. In the tryout games, Sherry dribbled well and *Sherry* shot accurately. (Use a pronoun.)

20. However, *Sherry's* blocking needed improvement. (Use a pronoun.)

21. Joel gave *Sherry* praise for handling the ball well and for faking opponents out of position. (Use a pronoun.)

22. Therefore, *Joel* and *the coach* asked Sherry to be a forward. (Use one pronoun. Remember, you are the coach.)

23. Shelly, on the other hand, was a good blocker and a fast attacker, but *Shelly's* dribbling and shooting skills were just average. Shelly would make a great goalie! (Use a pronoun.)

24. After talking with *the coach,* Joel was confident that Sherry and Shelly would do well in their positions. (Use a pronoun.)

25. Happily, *Joel's* and *the coach's* position assignments turned out to be very wise ones— the team was undefeated! (Use one pronoun. Remember, you are the coach.)

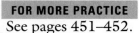
FOR MORE PRACTICE
See pages 451–452.

SUBJECT PRONOUNS

The pronouns *I, you, he, she, it, we,* and *they* are **subject pronouns.** Use these pronouns as subjects of a sentence or after linking verbs.

The subject form of a pronoun is used when the pronoun is the subject of a sentence or is a predicate pronoun following a linking verb in a sentence. A **predicate pronoun** is a pronoun that renames, or refers to, the subject. Consider the following examples of pronouns in subject form:

Subject	Predicate Pronoun
He and *she* ran.	The runners were *he* and *she.*
You and *I* flew the kite.	The contestants were *you* and *I.*
They and *we* watched.	The observers were *they* and *we.*

Predicate pronouns are used in speaking and writing to rename people and things: The pilot was *she.*

To identify predicate pronouns, remember these points:

1. Predicate pronouns follow linking verbs. The verb *be* is the most common linking verb. The verb *be* can take many forms, such as *am, is, are, was, were, have been, shall be,* and *will be.*
2. The predicate pronoun renames, or refers to, the subject of the sentence.
3. A sentence with a predicate pronoun will usually still make sense if the subject and the predicate pronoun are reversed.

Study the following examples:

Subject	Verb	Predicate Word
The designer	was	he.
He	was	the designer.
The stunt fliers	were	Julie and I.
Julie and I	were	the stunt fliers.
The judges	are	they.
They	are	the judges.

Practice Your Skills

A. CONCEPT CHECK

Subject Pronouns   Write the correct form of the pronouns given in parentheses. After each pronoun, write *S* if it is used as a subject pronoun or *P* if it is used as a predicate pronoun.

1. Eun Lee and (I, me) built a kite for the annual Shirone kite-fighting competition in Shirone, Korea.
2. However, the actual designers were Sun Ja and (I, me).
3. Most likely Eun Lee and (she, her) will fly it.
4. Proud owners of an o-dako, or giant kite, are (we, us).
5. While making our kite, (we, us) learned that kites have a long history.
6. (They, Them) were very practical devices in ancient times.
7. (We, Us) in Asia, along with the people in the United States, used kites for weather observations until balloons were invented.
8. In 1752 Ben Franklin experimented with kites; an "electrifying" scientist was (he, him).
9. A story is also told about a Korean general. (He, Him) hung a lantern from a kite to inspire his troops.
10. Kite fliers with a proud history are Eun Lee, Sun Ja, and (I, me).

B. REVISION SKILL

Using Pronouns for Precision   Substitute a pronoun for the word or words printed in italics in the following sentences.

[11]Stunt kite flying is becoming a popular competitive sport. *The sport* involves "pilots" who fly their kites in required and in freestyle patterns. [12]*The pilots* compete individually and in teams. [13]Don Tabor is a champion pilot, and quite a kite designer is *Don* as well. [14]*Don* designed the Super Hawaiian kite. [15]*The Super Hawaiian kite* was named the "Best New Manufactured Kite" of 1983. [16]Don was proud of his award-winning kite, because *the kite* had new and creative stability and control features. [17]*Don* now operates a factory that manufactures the Super Hawaiian. [18]My best friend, Gina, just bought one of the kites—apprentice kite fliers are *Gina and I!* Gina and I have watched Super Hawaiian teams. [19]*The teams* are made up of three or four pilots and perform such stunts as cascades, star bursts, and team ballet. [20]Gina now wants to join a Super Hawaiian team. What an enthusiast is *Gina!*

FOR MORE PRACTICE
See page 451.

> The pronouns *me, you, him, her, it, us,* and *them* are
> **object pronouns.** Use them as objects of the verb or as
> objects of a preposition.

Look at the examples below. They illustrate the uses of object
pronouns.

Direct Object	Dwayne met *them* at the airport.
Indirect Object	The tour guide gave *us* brochures.
Object of Preposition	Did the tour bus leave without *me?*

You will learn about prepositions on pages 536–545.

Pronouns in Compound Objects

A compound object may consist of two pronouns joined by
and, or, or *nor.* It may also consist of a noun and a pronoun. The
object form of pronouns is used in all compound objects.

Direct Object	Thai artifacts interest *Ochi* and *me.*
	He will drive *you* and *me* to Bangkok.
Indirect Object	Please send *Luis* and *me* a schedule.
	I gave *him* and *her* our itinerary.
Object of Preposition	The guide traveled with *him* and *me.*
	It was a great trip for *Ochi* and *me.*

Thai women in Bangkok wearing ceremonial costumes.

Speakers and writers often make errors in the
use of compound objects. If you are unsure which
pronoun form to use in a compound construction,
follow this simple rule: Look at each pronoun
object separately, as in the following examples.

> Gilda showed (he, him) and (I, me) slides of
> Thailand.
> Gilda showed *him* slides of Thailand.
> (not *he*)
> Gilda showed *me* slides of Thailand. (not *I*)

Practice Your Skills

A. CONCEPT CHECK

Object Pronouns Write the correct pronouns given in parentheses in the following sentences. Label the pronouns *Direct Object, Indirect Object,* or *Object of a Preposition*.

1. Su Linn and Tranh told (we, us) about Thailand, their native land.
2. My family had invited (she and he, her and him) to visit us.
3. We wanted to learn about Thailand from (they, them).
4. Su Linn gave my parents and (I, me) some books about Thailand.
5. Tranh told (we, us) the former name of Thailand, Siam.
6. According to Su Linn and (he, him), the name changed in the 1930s.
7. The name *Siam* was familiar to my family and (I, me) because of the movie *The King and I.*
8. We showed (they, them) the movie, which is about King Mongkut and the English governess of his children.
9. Su Linn talked about the king and said that the Thai people had great respect for (he, him).
10. King Mongkut had given (they, them) freedom and prosperity.

B. REVISION SKILL

Avoiding Repetition Revise the following passage by replacing the italicized nouns with object pronouns.

[11]Many Asians consider bird's-nest soup a delicacy. Cooks use the nests of small birds called swiftlets to make *the soup.* [12]Some people believe that the soup can keep *people* healthy. [13]Even though this soup is very expensive, they are willing to pay high prices for *the soup.* [14]High on cliffs inside caves in Thailand, the little birds build their nests. The location of the nests makes *the nests* hard to reach and contributes to the high cost of the soup. [15]After I learned that Grandfather collected swiftlet nests, I admired *Grandfather* more than ever. [16]I once watched as Grandfather scaled a cliff and climbed bamboo poles. He finally reached the nests and carefully placed *the nests* in a pouch. [17]The danger never discouraged *Grandfather* because he was used to *the danger.* [18]To protect Grandfather, Grandmother gave *Grandfather* a charm to wear. [19]According to *Grandmother,* the charm will keep *Grandfather* safe. [20]Grandfather wears *the charm* so that Grandmother will not worry.

FOR MORE PRACTICE
See page 452.

C H E C K ✔ P O I N T

MIXED REVIEW · PAGES 432–438

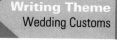
Write the correct pronoun given in parentheses for each sentence. Label the pronoun *Subject* or *Object*.

1. Wedding traditions have never interested (I, me) until recently.
2. In fact, my friends and (I, me) think some of the customs are silly.
3. (They, Them) are based on old-fashioned ideas.
4. However, since my sister will be a bride soon, (she, her) and (I, me) have been investigating some of these customs.
5. (We, Us) have discovered that many of today's practices are really ancient traditions.
6. Some of (they, them) are supposed to bring luck.
7. Today the bride and groom have rice thrown at (they, them).
8. My sister and (I, me) learned that rice was a symbol of prosperity and growth to the ancient Hindus and Chinese.
9. (They, Them) threw rice at couples for good fortune.
10. My sister, a bird lover, has told (we, us) to throw birdseed instead.
11. At the wedding, Jeff, the bridegroom, will give (she, her) a ring.
12. (She, Her) said that the giving of rings is an Egyptian custom.
13. Brides wear (they, them) as a symbol of eternal love.
14. (They, them) are worn on the left hand because it was believed that a vein runs from that hand to the heart.
15. (She, Her) and Jeff are going on a honeymoon.

16. Their destination is known only to (he, him) and (she, her).
17. At the hotel, (he, him) will carry her over the threshold.
18. (She, Her) says this is an ancient custom.
19. The groom carries the bride so that evil spirits cannot trip (she, her) and spoil her happiness.
20. A few of these customs still seem silly to my friends and (I, me), but (I, me) do like helping with the wedding plans.

POSSESSIVE PRONOUNS

> **Possessive pronouns** are personal pronouns used to show ownership or belonging.

Like nouns, pronouns have special possessive forms. The possessive form of a noun is made with an apostrophe. Study the chart. Note that possessive pronouns do not have apostrophes.

Possessive Pronouns

Singular	Plural
my, mine	our, ours
your, yours	your, yours
his, her, hers, its	their, theirs

Possessive Pronouns and Contractions

Writers often confuse the possessive forms of some pronouns with the contractions they resemble.

its—it's   your—you're   their—they're

The first word in each pair is a **possessive pronoun.** It shows possession, or ownership. The second word is a contraction made from a pronoun and a verb.

The dolphin enjoys *its* freedom. (possessive pronoun)
It's free to roam the ocean. (contraction: *it is*)

May I sign *your* petition? (possessive pronoun)
You're very persuasive. (contraction: *you are*)

The teams donated *their* time. (possessive pronoun)
They're playing for charity. (contraction: *they are*)

Remember that if the word you are using takes the place of two words, it is a contraction. Also remember that a possessive pronoun does not contain an apostrophe. If you understand the difference between the two, you will be able to write more precisely.

Practice Your Skills

A. CONCEPT CHECK

Possessive Pronouns and Contractions   Write the correct possessive pronoun or contraction from the words given in parentheses and label it *Pronoun* or *Contraction*.

Writing Theme
Success Stories

1. (Its, It's) always encouraging to hear success stories.
2. This one about dolphins will win (your, you're) praise.
3. Some students in Aurora, Colorado, set (their, they're) goal to help save dolphins.
4. Since a dolphin is a mammal, it must frequently make (its, it's) way to the surface for air or it will drown.
5. Some tuna companies were accidentally trapping dolphins in (their, they're) nets.
6. As a protest, the students convinced (their, they're) local school board to change (its, it's) policy and ban tuna.
7. It would not be served in (their, they're) school cafeteria.
8. Many consumers applauded this effort and (its, it's) results.
9. Perhaps you and (your, you're) friends joined the boycott.
10. In response to consumer concerns, some companies have changed (their, they're) policies and are using new fishing methods.
11. In addition, (their, they're) labeling (their, they're) tuna cans as "dolphin safe."
12. As a result, (your, you're) able to buy dolphin-safe tuna.

B. PROOFREADING SKILL

Correcting Pronoun Errors   Rewrite the following paragraph, correcting errors in grammar, capitalization, punctuation, and spelling. Pay special attention to pronoun usage. (15 errors)

   The unsighted cannot see, but their able to read. Its possible for them to read because of Louis Braille. As a young child, Braille was in an accidant that blinded him. He wanted to be able to read as well as sighted people? At the time, however, blind people read by running they're fingers over large indented letters. It was a verry slow method, and so Braille invented a code. Its a system of tiny raised dots that stand for leters, numerals, and punctuation marks. The Braille code let's the unsighted read quickly with they're figners. If your ever on an elevator, look at the Control panel. Your likely to see Braille near the numerals.

FOR MORE PRACTICE
See page 453.

Using Pronouns   **441**

We is always the subject form; **us** is the object form. **Who** is the subject form; **whom** is the object form.

The pronouns *we* and *us* are often used with nouns. To decide whether *we* or *us* is correct, say the pronoun alone with the verb.

> (We, Us) students performed in a play.
>   (Subject form: *We* performed)
> The director asked (we, us) actors to bow.
>   (Object form: Asked *us*)

The **interrogative pronouns** *who* and *whom* are used to ask questions. *Who* is the subject form, and *whom* is the object form.

> Who will play the lead? (*Who* is the subject of *will play*.)
> Whom do you see? (*Whom* is the direct object of *do see*.)
> From whom do we buy tickets? (*Whom* is the object of the preposition *from*.)

Practice Your Skills

CONCEPT CHECK

Pronoun Problems   Write the correct pronouns from those given in parentheses.

1. (We, Us) performers in Shakespeare's acting company love the theater!
2. (Who, Whom) does not enjoy the sound of applause?
3. A chance at any role delights (we, us) inexperienced actors.
4. To (who, whom) will go the part of Romeo?
5. (We, Us) competitors are jealous of that lucky man.
6. To (who, whom) do all the roles in Elizabethan theater go?
7. All the roles are played by (we, us) males.
8. (Who, Whom), then, will play Juliet?
9. One of (we, us) younger actors will probably play Juliet.
10. (We, Us) younger actors always get the female roles.
11. There are many roles for (we, us) fencers too.
12. (Who, Whom) is not entertained by a good sword fight?

Writing Theme
Theater

FOR MORE PRACTICE
See page 453.

REFLEXIVE AND INTENSIVE PRONOUNS

> Pronouns that end in **-self** or **-selves** are either intensive or reflexive pronouns.

The reflexive and intensive pronouns are *myself, yourself, herself, himself, itself, ourselves, yourselves,* and *themselves.*

A **reflexive pronoun** refers to an action of the subject of a sentence. The sentence's meaning is incomplete without the pronoun.

> Lila reminded *herself* to buy film. (Without *herself,* the meaning of the sentence is incomplete.)

An **intensive pronoun** adds emphasis to a noun or another pronoun. The meaning of a sentence is complete without it.

> Rex took that photo *himself.* (Even without *himself,* the meaning of the sentence remains complete.)

Practice Your Skills

CONCEPT CHECK

Reflexive and Intensive Pronouns   Write the following sentences with the correct reflexive or intensive pronoun. Then identify each pronoun as *Reflexive* or *Intensive.*

1. I _____ enjoy learning about history.
2. We owe it to _____ to preserve our history.
3. We should not deprive _____ of learning opportunities.
4. The photographer Mathew Brady _____ taught this lesson.
5. At the outbreak of the Civil War, Brady had a corps of photographers, and they _____ recorded the battle scenes.
6. Through the photographs you feel that you _____ are experiencing the Civil War.
7. However, Brady gave _____ the credit for all the pictures.
8. This problem of picture credit never resolved _____.
9. Brady seemed to be saying, "Consider _____ lucky to work for me!"
10. As a result, many found _____ other jobs.

Writing Theme
Mathew Brady

FOR MORE PRACTICE
See page 454.

CHECK ✔ POINT

MIXED REVIEW · PAGES 440–443

A. Write the correct pronoun given in parentheses.

1. (We, Us) readers enjoy Jacob and Wilhelm Grimm's stories.
2. However, (who, whom) knows much about the brothers?
3. (Their, They're) mostly known for collections of fairy tales.
4. (Its, It's) difficult to find out much more about them.
5. (Who, Whom) can you ask about them?
6. Libraries have some information about (their, they're) lives.
7. (Your, You're) research will show that Jacob was the older.
8. Some of (we, us) researchers have learned that they came from a large family.
9. The brothers worked hard to support (their, they're) poor family.
10. In fact, (we, us) careful readers can see how hard work and generosity play a part in some of the brothers' stories.
11. (Who, Whom) doesn't know their story "The Shoemaker and the Elves"?
12. (Its, It's) story line tells about some clever, hardworking elves.
13. (Their, They're) skill as cobblers makes a poor shoemaker rich.
14. The shoemaker repays (their, they're) kindness with clothes.
15. From the story, (your, you're) sure to learn about giving.

B. Complete each sentence with a reflexive or intensive pronoun.

16. The Brothers Grimm collected hundreds of folk tales _____.
17. We have long convinced _____ that they gathered their tales from peasants.
18. This belief _____ has proven to be a myth.
19. We should remind _____ that not everything we hear is true.
20. You can give _____ credit if you realized this.
21. I _____ was not aware of how stories were passed on.
22. Most of the storytellers _____ were well-educated people.
23. Wilhelm's wife, Dortchen, could rank _____ among them.
24. These people offered to tell stories they had heard _____.
25. Don't kid _____ that the tales were only for children.
26. German culture revealed _____ in these stories.
27. Later, Wilhelm Grimm gave _____ the task of editing them.
28. He _____ made the tales more suitable for children.
29. I find _____ amazed by the amount of work that took place.
30. The edited stories _____ have endured for generations.

Illustration from the Brothers Grimm fairy tale "Rumpelstiltskin."

PRONOUNS AND THEIR ANTECEDENTS

The **antecedent** of a pronoun is the noun or other pronoun for which the pronoun stands.

Note the pronouns in the following sentences. The pronouns all have **antecedents,** or words for which the pronoun stands.

> *Aretha* came today and brought *her* slides.
> (*Aretha* is the antecedent of *her*.)

> *Leo* and *Toshiro* watched intently. Then *they* asked questions.
> (*Leo* and *Toshiro* are the antecedents of *they*.)

The antecedent usually appears before the pronoun. Sometimes, as in the second example, the antecedent is in the sentence before it.

Practice Your Skills

A. CONCEPT CHECK
Understanding Antecedents   Write the pronouns from the following sentences and the antecedent for each pronoun.

Writing Theme
Coyotes

EXAMPLE   Humans fear the coyote. They do not understand it.

Pronouns	Antecedents
They	Humans
it	coyote

1. Does the word *predator* mean something slightly different to each person who hears it?
2. Because coyotes are considered predators, they are feared by some people.
3. However, Laurence Pringle defends coyotes in his book.
4. He points out that people do not fear or dislike robins, toads, and ladybugs, although these creatures are predators.
5. Such animals, however, are not known for their cunning.
6. Coyotes, on the other hand, are most cunning when they hunt.

7. For example, a prairie rodent makes its burrow under the ground and builds a berm, a mound of dirt, at the entrance.

8. When hunting the rodent, a female coyote will bide her time.

9. The clever creature knocks away the berm and lets the water from a rainstorm flush out her dinner.

10. Pringle suggests that not all predators are as fierce or clever as people think they are.

B. REVISION SKILL

Eliminating Repetition   Using pronouns can eliminate repetition in your writing. Rewrite the following passage, changing many of the repeated nouns to pronouns. Underline the antecedent of each pronoun.

[11]Mr. Andros spotted a coyote in Mr. Andros's back yard. [12]Mr. Andros's yard is not in a remote area; the yard is in a city in the Midwest. [13]Recently, coyotes have surprised Chicagoans by appearing in the Chicagoans' city. [14]People came in contact with an adult male coyote when the coyote was captured by the people in Lincoln Park. [15]A short time later, a female coyote, perhaps the male's mate, was also captured. [16]The male and the female were removed; the male and the female were taken to a distant forest. [17]Usually, the coyote wants to keep the coyote's presence secret. [18]For example, coyotes are known for coyotes' howling, but in urban areas, coyotes have learned to be silent. [19]Some experts have a theory; they think a coyote is so cunning that even if a coyote lived close to humans, people would probably never see the coyote. [20]Unless a female coyote is disturbed while the female coyote is caring for the female coyote's pups, people need never fear an attack by a coyote.

FOR MORE PRACTICE
See pages 454–455.

City coyote returns to true nature

By George Papajohn

Lincoln Park's fur-bearing yuckie — a young urban coyote who had taken up residence on the tony lakefront — was returned to a less fashionable but more traditional neighborhood Monday.

He didn't seem to mind the change, especially since his release into a forest preserve near Willow Springs ended a four-day stay in captivity at the Chicago Animal Care and Control Department.

"Last we saw him, he was loping off into the woods," said Peter Poholik, executive director of animal control.

Tribune photo by John Irvine

A stray coyote found in Lincoln park springs to his freedom after being released from an animal-control van Monday.

Agreement of Pronouns and Antecedents

Use a singular pronoun for a singular antecedent. Use a plural pronoun for a plural antecedent. This is called agreement in number. When you write and speak, be sure that each pronoun agrees in number with its antecedent.

> The *Hawaiian* language (singular) was once endangered. *It* (singular) is now being taught in schools.
> Many *children* (plural) are learning *their* (plural) native language and customs.

Practice Your Skills

CONCEPT CHECK

Agreement with Antecedents Complete the following sentences with pronouns that agree with their antecedent in number.

1. Eyak is a native Alaskan language. _____ is endangered and soon may vanish, however.
2. Two elderly women are the last speakers of Eyak. When _____ die, the language will die too.
3. Michael Krauss, a specialist in language study, says that in _____ opinion over half of the world's six thousand languages are endangered.
4. In the Western Hemisphere alone, three hundred out of nine hundred languages may disappear. _____ will never be spoken again.
5. In Turkey, researchers found only one woman who spoke Ubykh. Unless _____ teaches this language to other people, _____ will disappear too.
6. If the world loses a language, _____ loses all the knowledge of that culture.
7. The Basques of Spain are fortunate; _____ have saved _____ language and culture.
8. One way to save a language is to record _____ in writing and on audio tapes.
9. We should learn to value and fight for _____ languages as much as we do for _____ environment.
10. People can lose _____ heritage if _____ lose _____ language.

Writing Theme
Endangered
Languages

FOR MORE PRACTICE
See pages 454–455.

INDEFINITE PRONOUNS

> An **indefinite pronoun** is a pronoun that does not refer to a particular person or thing.

Certain pronouns, such as *everybody* or *no one*, do not refer to a definite person or thing. They are called **indefinite pronouns.**

Singular Indefinite Pronouns

another	each	everything	one
anybody	either	neither	somebody
anyone	everybody	nobody	someone
anything	everyone	no one	something

Use *his, her,* and *its* with singular indefinite pronouns.

Neither likes *her* part.   Everyone said *his* or *her* lines.

Plural Indefinite Pronouns

both	few	many	several

Use the plural possessive *their* with plural indefinite pronouns.

Both have *their* tickets.

His or her may be used when the person referred to could be either male or female. To avoid awkward agreement problems, you may use a plural noun instead of an indefinite pronoun.

Each of the actors knew *his or her* lines. (indefinite pronoun)
The *actors* knew *their* lines. (plural noun)

The pronouns *all, some, any,* and *none* may be singular or plural, depending on their meaning in the sentence.

Some of the creatures had glitter on *their* wings.
Some of the glitter had lost *its* shine.

Practice Your Skills

A. CONCEPT CHECK

Understanding Indefinite Pronouns   Label two columns *Possessive Pronouns* and *Antecedents*. Write the correct possessive pronouns in the first column and their antecedents in the second column.

1. Everyone has (his or her, their) eyes on the conductor's baton.
2. No one will begin (his or her, their) part until the signal to start is given.
3. All of the musicians have carefully tuned (his or her, their) instruments.
4. Each has carefully studied (his or her, their) score.
5. Many of the players began (his or her, their) study of music at a very early age.
6. Nobody denies the importance practice and training have on (his or her, their) ability to play well.
7. Both have (its, their) role in a musical career.
8. The baton moves, and everybody in the violin section moves (his or her, their) bow.
9. At the end of the performance, some of the spectators are on (his or her, their) feet.
10. All of the effort has had (its, their) effect on the audience.

B. CONCEPT CHECK

Agreement with Indefinite Pronouns   Choose the correct possessive pronouns given in parentheses in the following sentences.

11. Many of today's actors don't do (his or her, their) own stunts.
12. Few want to risk (his or her, their) neck crashing a car.
13. So each has (his or her, their) own stunt person.
14. Anyone who does stunt work plans (his or her, their) stunts carefully and practices them repeatedly.
15. Everyone learns to make (his or her, their) falls correctly.
16. Some know how to make (his or her, their) fights look real.
17. Several will use (his or her, their) skills as well as special materials to do fire stunts.
18. One can make (his, their) car roll, jump, and spin.
19. Another performs (her, their) stunts while riding a horse.
20. Most of the stunt people say common sense is more important than (his or her, their) physical abilities.

Writing Theme
Actors and Musicians

FOR MORE PRACTICE
See page 455.

Complete each sentence with a pronoun that agrees with the antecedent in number.

1. Many people have pinned _____ hopes on finding lost treasure.
2. Gold with _____ great value has long attracted people.
3. Several treasure tales have _____ origins in Aztec culture.
4. The Aztecs are believed to have had some of _____ gold mines in the region that is now Arizona.
5. Anybody with a dream in _____ heart can hunt for gold.
6. But few have succeeded with _____ search.
7. In fact, many have lost _____ lives looking for gold.
8. Nobody should start _____ treasure hunt without a plan and extensive research.
9. A treasure hunter may find a map and study _____ carefully.
10. But maps and old mines keep _____ secrets well.
11. Some may discover _____ gold by accident, but that is a rare occurrence.
12. Robert Jones claimed _____ found gold when _____ fell into a cavern in the Arizona mountains.
13. Later, when he returned for the gold, he couldn't find _____.
14. "I know the gold is there," said Jones, "because I held _____ in _____ own two hands!"
15. Perhaps someone, during _____ exploration of the region, found the gold and took _____.
16. One can also include ancient records in _____ search for lost treasure.
17. A man named De Estine Shepherd searched records in Mexico for clues to Aztec mines and _____ locations.
18. He said he found a mine in Arizona with gold dust in _____.
19. But he died shortly after making _____ discovery.
20. Shepherd and Jones never reached _____ goals.
21. Both failed to realize _____ dream of wealth.
22. Each had told other people about _____ treasure hunt.
23. Could either have told _____ tale to other treasure hunters?
24. After all, many would like to spend _____ lives in comfort and luxury.
25. Somebody may have used _____ wits and grabbed the gold.

A. Using Subject Pronouns Write the correct pronouns given in parentheses in the following sentences.

1. A good friend and (I, me) recently received a very special invitation.
2. (She, Her) and (I, me) were invited to a Native American sweat lodge.
3. As newcomers, (we, us) did not know the group gathered there.
4. Curious about the ancient rite of the sweat lodge, (we, us) and others met our host, Dan Highwater.
5. (He, Him) and his family invited the group to experience a traditional ceremony of many Native American cultures.
6. What gracious and friendly people were (they, them).
7. For generations, (they, them) and their ancestors have used the sweat lodge for purification and meditation.
8. My friend and (I, me) entered the low sweat lodge with the other guests.
9. (She, her) and (I, me) sat down in a place where long ago a shaman, or medicine man, would have prepared for the ceremony.
10. With the help of the warriors, (he, him) would have placed heated rocks on the ground in the center of the lodge.
11. When (he, him) poured cold water on the rocks, steam would fill the lodge.
12. After sitting in the steam, some warriors would dive into a cold river. What brave men were (they, them)!
13. During our visit, (we, us) and our host repeated the ceremony in the sweat lodge four times.
14. (He, Him) and (we, us) took breaks to cool off between turns in the lodge.
15. What a hot and sweaty group were (we, us)!
16. At first, my friend and (I, me) had trouble breathing in the steam.
17. In a short time, though, (she, her) and (I, me) grew accustomed to it.
18. (We, Us) and the other guests in the sweat lodge began to feel very good.
19. (We, Us) were all happy and calm visitors.
20. Our host simply smiled, because (he, him) knew all along that (we, us) would find the visit to the sweat lodge a wonderfully relaxing experience.

GRAMMAR
HANDBOOK
39

Writing Theme
Native Americans

B. Using Object Pronouns Write the correct pronouns given in parentheses in the following sentences.

21. For (I, me) and other history buffs, time travel would be a wonderful adventure.
22. It would show (we, us) glimpses of life in the past.
23. The French artist Jacques Le Moyne de Morques has given (we, us) the next best thing—his drawings and firsthand accounts.
24. In 1564 the government of France sent (he, him) to map the coast of what is now Florida and to observe the native peoples there.
25. The artist met the native Timucuas and made friends with (they, them).
26. Unfortunately, little remains that helps (we, us) learn about (they, them).
27. Sadly, the native peoples could not survive diseases, such as chickenpox, that Europeans brought with (they, them).
28. That is why the drawings and writings of Le Moyne de Morques are so important to (we, us).
29. We can learn a great deal from (they, them).
30. For example, his notes and paintings tell (we, us) how the Timucua chief took a wife.
31. He chose (she, her) from among the daughters of the highest subchiefs.
32. The chosen woman was brought to (he, him) on a litter.
33. Trumpeters blowing horns of bark announced (she, her) and the procession.
34. At the wedding, tribal subchiefs and villagers arrived to honor (he, him) and (she, her).
35. The chief and his bride welcomed (they, them).
36. The nobles sat on both sides of (he, him) and (she, her).
37. The chief then told (she, her) why she had been chosen.
38. She, in turn, answered (he, him) warmly.
39. Afterwards, young maidens danced as the spectators watched (they, them).
40. Le Moyne de Morques watched the spectacular ceremony, which impressed his companions and (he, him) greatly.
41. Le Moyne's records show (we, us) a proud and sensitive people.
42. Scholars have praised (he, him) for the details he has provided (we, us) about the Native Americans of his time.

C. Using Problem Pronouns
Write the sentences, using the correct pronoun or contraction given in parentheses.

43. If (your, you're) a visitor to the Northwest, (your, you're) likely to hear about the Northwest Indian fishing industry.
44. (Its, It's) very important to the Northwest Native Americans.
45. (Their, They're) fishing traditions began centuries ago.
46. Moreover, (their, they're) still fishing today.
47. Every spring, salmon make (their, they're) run upstream.
48. (Their, They're) prized for (their, they're) delicious meat.
49. (Its, It's) a tradition of the Northwest people to give thanks for (their, they're) first salmon catch of the year.
50. You would, too, if (your, you're) existence depended on fishing.
51. The people built weirs; (their, they're) like long, open fences across a river.
52. The people found that the weirs made (their, they're) job easier.
53. A weir lets river water continue on (its, it's) course.
54. (Its, It's) designed, however, to corral the fish.
55. In this way (its, it's) easier to catch the fish.
56. If you were a male in (their, they're) group, you would fish.
57. If you were a woman, (your, you're) job would be to clean and dry the fish.

D. Correcting Pronoun Problems
Write the following dialogue, correcting errors in using *we, us, who,* and *whom.* If a sentence contains no error, write *Correct.*

58. INEZ: Who do I ask about the False Face Society?
59. JOE: Who around here is an expert on Iroquois customs?
60. MARIA: Dr. Zola from the museum once gave a demonstration for we students.
61. Some of we class members helped dramatize an Iroquois healing ceremony.
62. We volunteers felt a little strange wearing the wooden masks.
63. He also showed us listeners the corn husk masks worn by the Shuck Faces, or medicine men.
64. Us observers had no trouble believing those masks frightened the little children watching a healing ceremony.
65. Us students heard that Dr. Zola moved away recently.
66. INEZ: From who can I get his address?
67. JOE: Let me see! Who do I know at the museum?

E. Identifying Reflexive Pronouns and Intensive Pronouns

Write *Reflexive* or *Intensive* to identify the italicized pronoun in each sentence below.

68. Many Native American cultures pride *themselves* on their great artistry.

69. Last week at an art fair, I bought *myself* a beautiful rug.

70. A Navaho woman from the Southwest wove the rug *herself.*

71. The Plains Indians prided *themselves* on their beadwork.

72. Their beadwork was *itself* a beautiful art form.

73. At first, the Plains Indians used porcupine quills in their beadwork, but later some found *themselves* using glass beads.

74. You *yourself* might be surprised by the weight of a beaded shirt, which could weigh as much as three or four pounds!

75. Inuit women traditionally adorned *themselves* with finger masks during special ceremonies.

76. My mother recently decided to try to make *herself* a finger mask.

77. She made the mask *herself* from fur and feathers.

78. Like my father, I find *myself* unable to do the simplest craft.

79. Dad thought of *himself* as a great artisan as he built a canoe.

80. Mom and I enjoyed *ourselves* watching him work.

81. We also enjoyed *ourselves* as we teased him about the canoe.

82. Even Dad *himself* had to see the humor in his leaky dugout.

F. Finding Antecedents

Make two columns: *Pronouns* and *Antecedents*. Write the pronouns from the following sentences in the first column. Write their antecedents in the second column. Note that an antecedent may be in a preceding sentence.

83. Marcy and Louise did their report on George Catlin's paintings of the dances of the Plains Indians.

84. The Plains Indians wanted to bring game to their hunting grounds, so they would dance to attract the buffalo.

85. George Catlin wrote his observations of one dance.

86. He had watched a buffalo-calling dance performed in its entirety.

87. The dancers in their buffalo costumes continued dancing for days until they spotted a herd of buffalo.

88. If a dancer fell, the onlookers would drag him out of the ring by his heels.

89. If a herd of buffalo appeared, there was no doubt the dance had done its job.
90. While the men were hunting, the women and children remained in the village with only meager rations to sustain them.
91. The people used the entire buffalo, from its tail to its horns.
92. The Plains Indians were models of conservation and lived in harmony with their environment.

G. Using Indefinite Pronouns   Write the indefinite pronoun from each sentence. Then write the correct possessive pronoun given in parentheses that agrees with the indefinite pronoun.

93. Anyone who studies Native Americans will learn about their games in (his or her, their) investigations.
94. Several games played by Native American peoples required everyone to use (his or her, their) skills.
95. Many of the young Chippewa braves tried (his, their) hand at corncob darts.
96. Everybody made (his, their) own darts and tossed them at a target on the ground.
97. In the game of chunkey, one of the players rolled a stone, and then (his, their) team and opponents threw poles at it.
98. Everyone tried to get (his, their) pole closest to the stone.
99. Another of the Native American games was played by two women at a time. (Its, Their) name was the bowl game.
100. In the bowl game, one of the two players tossed playing pieces into the air, and (her, their) score depended on the number of pieces that fell face up on the ground.
101. Both players recorded (her, their) score by using counting sticks.
102. Neither wished to lose to (her, their) opponent.
103. One group of Native Americans played a game of kickball in which no one could claim (his or her, their) team had won.
104. As a matter of fact, nobody scored points for (his or her, their) team.
105. Instead of achieving a high score, the goal was for everyone to demonstrate (his or her, their) skill by controlling the ball for as long as possible.
106. From playing this and other games, each of the players developed (his or her, their) coordination.

GRAMMAR
HANDBOOK
39

Writing Theme
Partnerships

A. Subject and Object Pronouns For each sentence, write the correct subject or object pronoun given in parentheses.

1. Many of (we, us) have heard of Abbott and Costello.
2. What a funny comedy team (they, them) were!
3. Did you know that (they, them) became partners by accident?
4. Costello's partner became ill, and (he, him) could not perform.
5. As a favor, Abbott replaced (he, him) as the straight man in the comedy routine.
6. From that day on, Costello and (he, him) were partners.
7. Audiences laughed at (they, them) and their hilarious comedy routines.
8. People everywhere enjoyed (they, them) on stage, radio, television, and in the movies.
9. Years ago, fans considered one routine a favorite; (they, them) enjoyed the famous routine "Who's on First?" and (we, us) are still amused by it today.
10. Such lucky people (we, us) are to have their recordings!

B. Possessive Pronouns and Contractions Write the correct possessive pronoun or contraction given in parentheses.

11. (Its, It's) surprising that the scientific team Katherine Bell and Emily Dixon survived (their, they're) partnership.
12. These women risked (their, they're) lives for botany.
13. (Your, You're) probably not familiar with a plant called *Kobresia bellardi,* which is found in the Colorado Rockies.
14. (Its, It's) a plant that stays green during the winter.
15. Katherine and her assistant, Emily, made (their, they're) way to the Colorado Rockies to study the plant one winter.
16. If you were Emily, would you have offered (your, you're) services to spend a cruel winter in the wilderness?
17. The harsh Colorado climate did (its, it's) best to discourage them.
18. (Its, It's) true that they underwent many hardships in that forbidding environment.
19. (Their, They're) friendship was tested during that cold, dark winter.
20. Yet, (their, they're) still friends today.

C. Reflexive and Intensive Pronouns and Pronoun Problems
Use the clue in parentheses to complete each sentence.

21. In his youth, Richard W. Sears supported _____ by selling watches. (reflexive pronoun)
22. With _____ did he become partners? (who, whom)
23. You _____ could guess the answer! (intensive pronoun)
24. Around 1890, Mr. Sears and Mr. Roebuck benefited _____ by forming what was to become a successful partnership. (reflexive pronoun)
25. _____ bought their merchandise? (who, whom)
26. _____ mail-order shoppers did! (we, us)
27. For a number of years, early in the partnership, Sears, Roebuck and Company _____ was only a mail-order business. (intensive pronoun)
28. Retail stores, as we know them today, _____ did not appear until 1925, long after both men had left the company. (intensive pronoun)
29. Now the stores are where most of _____ shoppers buy. (we, us)
30. Today, both the name Sears, and the stores, are known to _____ consumers worldwide! (we, us)

D. Antecedents and Pronoun Agreement
Write the following sentences and correct all errors in pronoun agreement. If a sentence has no errors, write *Correct*.

31. People often enjoy cartoons during his or her youth.
32. Hasn't everyone seen Woody Woodpecker cartoons on their television?
33. Walter Lantz and Grace Stafford certainly hoped so. They both became "partners" with this lovable animated character.
34. Neither anticipated their great success with Woody.
35. One of Grace's talents was her remarkable voice.
36. Walter did the animation and received an Academy Award for their efforts.
37. Both of them were loyal to their feathered partner.
38. Each put their own ego aside.
39. Woody's performances captured the hearts of their fans.
40. Only one of the three made their home in a tree, though.

Observation and Description

A good way to share your understanding of a person is to describe the person in a character sketch. (See Workshop 2.) When you revise a character sketch, make sure that you have identified the person and have included specific details that make him or her come alive for readers. Look for repeated nouns that you can replace with pronouns to make your writing flow more smoothly, and make sure all pronoun references are clear and correct.

On your paper, revise the following character sketch by using the directions given. Proofread the passage for errors in the use of pronouns and for other errors in grammar. Also check for correct capitalization, punctuation, and spelling.

¹Josh was really something else. ²The first time I saw Josh was the day we moved into the Neighborhood. ³Josh was walking down the sidewalk on his hands. ⁴My brother tried to teach me to walk on my hands once, but I kept falling over. ⁵When I introduced myself to Josh, he stuck his foot out I didn't know what else to do so I shook the foot. ⁶It seemed so strange. ⁷When I finally talked to Josh face to face I found out that all the peopel in Josh's family were circus performers they were acrobats animal trainers or clowns. ⁸Josh was training to do a special act. ⁹He loved to make people laugh. ¹⁰Me and him always had fun when we was together. ¹¹The best freind I ever had. ¹²My family moved away two year's later, but Josh gave me a going-away present I'll never forget. ¹³He taught me to walk on my hands.

1. In sentence 1, replace the vague phrase "something else" with specific words that describe Josh.

2. Replace the vague pronoun *it* in sentence 6 with the noun phrase "shaking a foot instead of a hand."

3. Following sentence 8, add the following details about the clown act: Josh wears an upside-down clown suit and walks on his hands. Nobody is supposed to realize that he's not right side up until the act is over.

4. Delete the sentence that doesn't belong.

5. Divide the passage into two paragraphs.

on the LIGHT side

Can You Supply References?

Do you find this news flash confusing?

Although her mother was in it, thieves stole a suitcase containing jewelry and clothing from the car of Mrs. Vanya Koskis yesterday.

Question: Where was the mother —in the car or in the suitcase?

If a pronoun's antecedent—the noun it refers to—isn't clear, a sentence can say something hilariously different from what the writer meant. Here are more errors of pronoun reference collected by language expert Richard Lederer.

- About two years ago, a wart appeared on my left hand, which I wanted removed.

- After Governor Baldwin watched the lion perform, he was taken to Main Street and fed twenty-five pounds of raw meat in front of the Cross Keys Theater.

- Two cycles belonging to girls that had been left leaning against lampposts were badly damaged.

- Antinuclear protestors released live cockroaches inside the White House Friday, and these were arrested when they left and blocked a security gate.

- The driver had a narrow escape, as a broken board penetrated his cabin and just missed his head. This had to be removed before he could be released.

- My mother wants to have the dog's tail operated on again, and if it doesn't heal this time, she'll have to be put away.

- Jerry Remy then hit an RBI single off Haas's leg, which rolled into right field.

Skills

Directions   One or more of the underlined sections in the following sentences may contain an error in grammar, usage, punctuation, spelling, or capitalization. Write the letter of each incorrect section; then rewrite the item correctly. If there is no error in an item, write *E*.

Example   People in the <u>United State's</u> <u>eat</u> enough <u>ice cream</u> and
                                              A   **B**   **C**
sherbet each year to fill the <u>Grand Canyon</u>.   <u>No error</u>
                                              D   **E**

Answer   A—United States

---

1. When two <u>horses</u> breathe <u>gently</u> at each other as they meet, <u>their</u> <u>giveing</u> each
              A   **B**   **C**   **D**
   other a friendly welcome.   <u>No error</u>
                                              E

2. Before <u>they</u> finally <u>got</u> married, Octavio Guillen and Adrian Martinez <u>were</u>
              A   **B**   **C**
   engaged for sixty-seven <u>years?</u>   <u>No error</u>
                                        D   **E**

3. Van Gogh and <u>him</u> both used very bright <u>colors, but</u> of the two artists, I like
                          A   **B**
   <u>Gauguin's</u> colors <u>best.</u>   <u>No error</u>
        C   **D**   **E**

4. If smoke rises <u>straight</u> <u>up. The</u> <u>winds'</u> speed is <u>probably</u> less than one mile per
                          A   **B**   **C**   **D**
   hour.   <u>No error</u>
                  E

5. Captain <u>Hook's</u> an evil pirate in J. M. Barrie's <u>Peter Pan Darth</u> Vader and <u>him</u>
                    A   **B**   **C**
   would probably get along very <u>well.</u>   <u>No error</u>
                                              D   **E**

6. If <u>you're</u> right-handed, your right <u>hands'</u> <u>fingernails</u> grow <u>faster</u> than those on
            A   **B**   **C**   **D**
   your left hand.   <u>No error</u>
                              E

7. <u>Cicadas</u> may live as long as seventeen <u>years, they</u> <u>spend</u> most of <u>their</u> life under-
      A   **B**   **C**   **D**
   ground.   <u>No error</u>
                      E

8. Robinson Jeffers once <u>said,</u> <u>"Lend</u> me the stone strength of the past, and <u>i</u> will
A   B
lend you the <u>wings</u> of the future." <u>No error</u>
           D   E

9. <u>It's</u> a wet world. The water in the <u>earth's</u> <u>seas</u> and oceans could cover the <u>whole</u>
A   B   C   D
world and still be two miles deep. <u>No error</u>
                            E

10. Everyone has <u>their</u> own favorite <u>author.</u> Agatha Christie must be at the top of
                 A   B
many <u>lists,</u> since about 2 million of her books are <u>sold</u> each year. <u>No error</u>
     C   D   E

11. <u>Whom</u> shall <u>we</u> invite to the <u>New Year's Eve</u> <u>party?</u> <u>No error</u>
     A   B   C   D   E

12. The Cincinnati <u>Red's</u> four straight wins in the 1990 <u>World Series</u> shocked the
                   A   B
defending <u>champions,</u> the Oakland <u>Athletics.</u> <u>No error</u>
         C   D   E

13. Charlotte and <u>her</u> both <u>wrote</u> under pen <u>names Emily</u> wrote poetry in addition
                  A   B   C
to her novel, *Wuthering Heights.* <u>No error</u>
               D   E

14. One <u>Chinese</u> typewriter <u>has</u> 5,700 <u>characters</u> on <u>its</u> keyboard. <u>No error</u>
        A   B   C   D   E

15. <u>Georgia O'Keeffe</u> is a favorite of <u>we</u> art students. It was <u>she</u> who painted such
     A   B   C
<u>beautifull</u> flowers. <u>No error</u>
   D   E

16. <u>To who</u> do all lovers of detective fiction owe a debt of gratitude? Well, many of
     A
the first detective <u>stories</u> <u>were</u> written by <u>Edgar Allan Poe.</u> <u>No error</u>
                   B   C   D   E

17. During his <u>career. Gordon</u> Parks, one of this <u>country's</u> outstanding photogra-
               A   B
phers, <u>have</u> also been a film <u>writer, director, and</u> producer. <u>No error</u>
     C   D   E

18. <u>Wolfs</u> in the wild almost never attack <u>humans.</u> People who have stumbled into
     A   B
wolf dens <u>have</u> suffered only injuries caused by <u>their</u> fall. <u>No error</u>
        C   D   E

Sketch Book

SHOE by Jeff MacNelly   Reprinted by permission: Tribune Media Services.

- What is your favorite activity? Write directions describing how to do that activity.
- Recall the most exciting moment in sports you've ever seen. Write a short sportscast reporting the event.
- What famous person would you like to change places with for a day? Freewrite about what the experience would be like.

Using Verbs

- **What Is a Verb?**
- **Verbs and Direct Objects**
- **Transitive and Intransitive Verbs**
- **Linking Verbs and Predicate Words**
- **Verb Phrases**
- **Tenses of Verbs**
- **The Principal Parts of Verbs**
- **Choosing the Right Verb**

Without a verb, a sentence would be as lifeless as an empty basketball court or an unfinished sports broadcast. The ball would just hang in the air forever and never get any closer to the basket. The sportscaster would never announce who beat whom.

This handbook will help you use verbs to give life, movement, and interest to your writing.

> A **verb** expresses an action, states that something exists, or links the subject with a word that describes or renames it.

The verb is the most important part of every sentence. Without a verb, a sentence cannot be complete or make sense.

Action Verbs

An action verb says what the subject of the sentence does, as in "The skaters *raced* around the park." The action may be one that you cannot see, as in "Shana *knew* the winner." What verbs could you use to describe the action in the picture below?

An artist's interpretation of skating wheels that were first used in Germany in 1870. Some historians believe these wheels may have been the forerunners of roller skates.

Linking Verbs

A linking verb links the subject of the sentence with a word or words in the predicate that modify the subject. A linking verb expresses a state of being. It does not refer to an action.

Yes, I *am* on time. (emphasizes state of being)
My skates *are* fast. (links *skates* with *fast*)

The most common linking verbs are the following: *am, are, were, being, is, was, be,* and *been.*

Other familiar linking verbs include *look, appear, seem, become, remain, feel, sound, taste, grow,* and *smell.* Many linking verbs can also be used as action verbs.

The skates *looked* new. (linking verb)
Ricardo *looked* at the skates. (action verb)

Practice Your Skills

A. CONCEPT CHECK

Verbs   Write the verbs from the following sentences. Label each verb either *Action* or *Linking*.

Writing Theme
Roller-skating

1. Rollerblade in-line skates feature four plastic wheels in a row.
2. These skates are much faster than traditional roller skates.
3. These flashy skates seem very modern to most people.
4. In-line skates, however, appeared long ago, in the 1700s.
5. In fact they probably were the world's first roller skates.
6. Traditional skates, though, dominated the sport for years.
7. In 1980 this situation changed dramatically.
8. A twenty-year-old hockey player started the Rollerblade company in a Minnesota garage.
9. The new skates quickly became a popular item.
10. Now, millions of people enjoy the sport of blading.

B. REVISION SKILL

Using Vivid Action Verbs   In your writing, always look for opportunities to replace weak verbs with stronger ones. In this paragraph, replace the italicized verbs with livelier action verbs.

[11]On your in-line skates, at top speed, you *go* down the hill. [12]The wind *is* against your cheek. [13]Your skates almost *put* you into orbit. [14]Suddenly, a cyclist *moves* into your path out of nowhere. [15]You *say,* "Watch out!" but she doesn't hear. [16]You're afraid you may *run* into that oncoming bike. [17]If you swerve, you'll *push* that jogger into the bushes. [18]You decide you'd better *get* onto the grass, and you hope you won't hit a tree while you're going at this speed. [19]Now you're in midair, and the landscape *moves* by. [20]Finally, as you *get* up out of the ditch, you say to yourself, "I'd better learn how to use those brakes."

FOR MORE PRACTICE
See page 486.

VERBS AND DIRECT OBJECTS

> The **direct object** is the noun or pronoun that receives the action of the verb.

The subject and verb often can express a complete thought.

Subject	Verb
Winter	came.

In some sentences, though, the thought is not complete until one or more words have been added after the verb.

Snow covered   The police closed

You wonder what the snow covered and what the police closed. Suppose you complete the sentences.

Snow covered the *mountain*. The police closed the *road*.

The words *mountain* and *road* receive the action of the verbs. *Mountain* and *road* are direct objects of the verbs.

Recognizing Direct Objects

To find the direct object in a sentence, ask *what* or *whom* after the verb. The word that answers *what* or *whom* is the direct object. If you cannot answer *what* or *whom* after the verb, there is no direct object in the sentence. (Don't confuse direct objects with adverbs that tell *how, where, when,* or *how much*.)

Workers removed the snowdrifts. (Removed what? *snowdrifts*)
They cleared the roads and bridges. (Cleared what? *roads and bridges*)

Practice Your Skills

A. CONCEPT CHECK

Verbs and Direct Objects   Write and label each *Verb* and *Direct Object*. If a sentence does not contain a direct object, write *None*.

1. In July 1863, Union and Confederate armies fought a terrible battle at Gettysburg, Pennsylvania.
2. Thousands of soldiers died in that conflict.

3. Four months later, President Lincoln visited the site.
4. Lincoln gave a dedication speech for a national cemetery there.
5. Lincoln's speech followed an address by Edward Everett.
6. That popular speaker delivered a two-hour oration.
7. In contrast, Lincoln spoke for only two minutes.
8. Lincoln's brief address, though, greatly moved his audience.
9. The words captured a nation's feelings about the war.
10. The Gettysburg Address lives on today in people's hearts.

B. DRAFTING SKILL

Using Direct Objects   As you have learned, direct objects make your writing more precise by providing needed information. For each of the following sentences, write a direct object for the verb.

[11]Every four years, the nation elects a _____. [12]Obviously, only one candidate wins the _____. [13]To gain attention, candidates buy _____ on radio or TV. [14]They write _____ to voters, asking for support. [15]All this costs _____. [16]So candidates seek financial _____. [17]Meanwhile, public speaking is still an important skill, since candidates frequently deliver _____ to audiences. [18]They express their _____ to various groups. [19]Along the way, they answer _____. [20]If they are honest, they tell the _____.

FOR MORE PRACTICE
See page 486.

C H E C K ✔ P O I N T
MIXED REVIEW · PAGES 464–467

On your paper write the verb from each of the sentences below. Label each verb *Action* or *Linking*. For each action verb write the direct object. If there is no direct object, write *None*.

1. Tropical seas often contain coral reefs.
2. Coral reefs are limestone formations.
3. They grow in warm, shallow water.
4. Some of these reefs grow very large.
5. Millions of tiny marine animals secrete a stony substance.
6. That substance becomes the framework of a reef.
7. The tiny creatures live together in huge colonies.
8. Many other tropical sea animals also find homes there.
9. They all lend their brilliant colors to the reef.
10. Coral reefs, with their lagoons, often look quite beautiful.

Writing Theme
Coral Reefs

TRANSITIVE AND INTRANSITIVE VERBS

A verb that has a direct object is called a **transitive verb.**
A verb that does not have a direct object is called an
intransitive verb.

The following are examples of transitive and intransitive verbs.

> The storyteller *told* a folk tale. (*Told* is transitive; *tale* is the direct object.)
> The story *amused* the audience. (*Amused* is transitive; *audience* is the direct object.)
> The happy listeners *applauded*. (*Applauded* is intransitive; it has no direct object.)
> They *rose* to their feet. (*Rose* is intransitive; it has no direct object.)

Recognizing Transitive and Intransitive Verbs

To determine whether a verb is transitive or intransitive, first determine whether the sentence contains a direct object. If the sentence has a direct object, the verb is transitive. If there is no direct object, the verb is intransitive. Remember that a direct object tells *what* or *whom;* it does not tell *when, where,* or *how.*

> Laura saw a snake. (tells what)
> The snake moved quickly. (tells how)

Some verbs, like the word *find,* are always transitive. They must always take a direct object. Other verbs, like the word *look,* are always intransitive. Most verbs can be used with or without direct objects. They can be transitive in one sentence and intransitive in another. An example is *see.* Here are some examples of verbs that can be either transitive or intransitive.

Transitive	Intransitive
Ian shouted a warning.	He shouted loudly.
The snake opened its jaws.	The reptile exhibit will open soon.

Practice Your Skills

A. CONCEPT CHECK

Transitive and Intransitive Verbs   Write the verbs in the following sentences. Label each verb *Transitive* or *Intransitive*. If a verb is transitive, write its direct object.

Writing Theme
Snakes and Folklore

1. Snakes frighten the average person.
2. Most people lack real knowledge about these reptiles.
3. As a result, some peculiar beliefs and superstitions exist.
4. For example, no snake rolls along the ground like a hoop.
5. Some snakes climb trees, however.
6. Snakes hear—although not very well.
7. They usually detect motion quite well.
8. Milk snakes do not milk cows.
9. However, they kill mice.
10. In fact, in spite of all the folklore about snakes, our natural world benefits greatly from their presence.

B. APPLICATION IN LITERATURE

Using Transitive and Intransitive Verbs   Write the italicized verbs in the passage. Label each verb *Transitive* or *Intransitive*. If a verb is transitive, write the direct object of the verb.

I began hitting the snake with the hoe. **11**He *thrashed* around. **12**He *bit* the hoe handle a couple of times. **13**Finally, I *killed* him. **14**I *hung* him on the fence. . . .

15Two weeks *passed*. **16**One day I *took* a walk through my cornfield. **17**A huge new log *lay* at the end of my fence. **18**I *looked* closer. **19**I *recognized* that hoe handle! **20**It still *had* the poison in it, and had grown as big as a tree trunk.

Appalachian Folk Tale, "The Snakebit Hoe Handle"

C. APPLICATION IN WRITING

Imagine you are walking in the woods and you suddenly see a snake a few feet away. Using at least five of the verbs listed, describe what you might see and what you might do. Make three of the verbs transitive and two intransitive.

see	wait	glisten	strike
crawl	freeze	cringe	slither
yell	surprise	run	frighten

FOR MORE PRACTICE
See page 487.

LINKING VERBS AND PREDICATE WORDS

> A **linking verb** connects, or links, the subject with a word in the predicate that modifies or renames the subject.

A **linking verb** connects the subject with a word in the predicate. The word that follows the linking verb describes or renames the subject.

The battle *grew* fierce.   The king *looked* confident.
Victory *was* his.   The prize *was* a kingdom.

The adjective *fierce* says something about *battle;* the adjective *confident* says something about *king.* The pronoun *his* is linked with *victory,* and the noun *kingdom* is linked with *prize.*

The words that follow linking verbs and modify or rename the subject may be adjectives, nouns, or pronouns. Because they appear in the predicate, these words are called **predicate words.**

Do not confuse a linking verb with a transitive verb. A transitive verb has a direct object. A linking verb connects the subject with a word in the predicate that says something about the subject. A predicate word may identify, rename, explain, or describe the subject.

The roast smelled delicious. (*Delicious* is a predicate word that says something about the subject, *roast; smelled* is a linking verb.)

The king tasted the meat. (*Meat* is the direct object of *tasted. Tasted* is a transitive verb.)

The knights were tired and hungry. (*Tired* and *hungry* are predicate words that say something about the subject, *knights; were* is a linking verb.)

Remember, the words *am, is, are, was, were,* and *be* are often used as linking verbs. Other words used as linking verbs are *seem, look, appear, become, smell, taste, feel, sound, remain, grow, turn,* and *stay.*

Detail of "January" from *Très riches heures du duc de Berry* ("The Very Rich Hours of the Duke of Berry"), an illuminated manuscript by the Limbourg brothers, early 1400s.

Practice Your Skills

A. CONCEPT CHECK

Linking Verbs Identify each verb as *Linking* or *Transitive*. Write the predicate word(s) for each linking verb.

1. Henry VIII of England became king at age seventeen.
2. He chose Thomas Wolsey as his chief administrator.
3. Under their rule England grew prosperous.
4. King Henry became a patron of the arts.
5. Poets, painters, and musicians visited the royal palace.
6. Henry himself wrote songs and poems.
7. Henry VIII's early reign seemed "golden."
8. His later years were more difficult, however.
9. Over the course of his reign, he had six wives.
10. His many marriages caused religious conflicts.

Writing Theme
Kings and Queens

B. PROOFREADING SKILL

Write the following paragraph, correcting errors. (10 errors)

Lady Jane Grey, one of historys youngest queens took the throne at sixteen her riegn lasted only nine days. Jane was the great-neice of Henry VIII of england, whose son King Edward VI, was dying. Some politicians had Jane named queen so they could controll the country Then Henrys daughter Mary became queen, and Jane was beheaded.

FOR MORE PRACTICE
See page 487.

C H E C K POINT
MIXED REVIEW · PAGES 468–471

Label each verb *Transitive* or *Linking*. Write each predicate word.

1. The Mexican general Santa Anna is famous for many reasons.
2. Santa Anna's army defeated the Texans at the Alamo.
3. Later, his defeat by Sam Houston gave Texas its independence.
4. After his defeat, Santa Anna entered the United States.
5. Staten Island, near Manhattan, was his home.
6. He brought with him some chicle, the sap of the sapodilla tree.
7. This tasteless chewing gum remained the general's favorite treat.
8. Thomas Adams, a neighbor, became curious about the substance.
9. Adams eventually marketed the chicle as Adams New York Gum.
10. With flavorings, Santa Anna's gum tasted good to millions.

Writing Theme
Invention of
Chewing Gum

VERB PHRASES

> A **verb phrase** consists of a main verb and one or more helping verbs.

Often the **main verb** of the sentence appears with one or more helping verbs. A main verb with one or more helping verbs is called a **verb phrase.** The most common helping verbs are forms of *be, have,* and *do.* These and other helping verbs are shown below in italics.

will wear	*must* wear	*is* wearing
could wear	*does* wear	*has* worn
might wear	*did* wear	*have* worn

A verb phrase may consist of a main verb and two helping verbs. Some form of the verb *be* or some form of *have* is often the middle word of a three-word verb phrase.

will have worn   *will be* wearing   *has been* wearing

The words that make up a verb phrase are not always together. Sometimes the helping verbs and the main verb are separated by words that are not verbs. Notice that *not* and its contraction, *n't,* are not verbs.

can hardly *wait*   *could* not *have danced*   *did*n't *fit*

Practice Your Skills

A. CONCEPT CHECK

Verb Phrases   On your paper make two columns labeled *Helping Verbs* and *Main Verbs.* Write the helping verbs in the following sentences in the first column. Write the main verbs in the second column.

1. The Cinderella tale may be the most famous story in the world.
2. People have been telling versions of this story for over one thousand years.
3. Scholars have often suggested China as the story's place of origin.
4. It might have first appeared there about A.D. 850.

5. In the Chinese tale, a girl is mistreated by her stepmother.
6. Like Cinderella, this girl cannot escape her stepmother's cruel treatment without the help of magic.
7. Also like Cinderella, she does lose her slipper at a party.
8. Could people in Europe have somehow heard this story?
9. European traders may have brought the tale home with them.
10. No one knows how many changes may have been made by the time of the tale's arrival in Europe hundreds of years later.

B. APPLICATION IN LITERATURE

List all the verbs and underline the helping verbs in the following passage. Some of the sentences have more than one verb.

Cinderella at the Prince's ball; engraving from an 1875 edition of Charles Perrault's fairy tale.

11Some time later, the king's son gave a ball and invited all the most stylish people for miles around. **12**The two sisters were invited too. **13**Right away they chose their gowns and petticoats as well as their hair ornaments and slippers for the ball. **14**This made Cinderella's work still harder, for she was constantly starching their linen and pleating their ruffles. **15**All day long the sisters would talk about nothing but their clothes for the ball.

16One night Cinderella was dressing their hair. **17**The elder sister said to her, "Cinderella, wouldn't you like an invitation to the ball?"

18"Please, sisters, do not mock me," she said. "How could I ever dream of such a thing?"

19"You are right," they answered. "People would surely laugh at a Cinderwench at the ball."

20Over the next two days the sisters were still more excited. **21**They could hardly eat. **22**They laced themselves into their gowns and paraded before the looking glass.

23At last the evening of the ball had come. **24**The sisters left for the court as Cinderella watched. **25**When she had lost sight of them, she sat down and wept.

Adapted from "Cinderella" by Charles Perrault

FOR MORE PRACTICE
See page 487.

> Different forms of the verb are used to show the time of an action or of a state of being. These forms are called the **tenses** of the verb.

A verb has different forms called **tenses** to indicate whether an action takes place or a condition exists in the present, past, or future. The tense of the verbs you use tells your readers clearly when something happened or when a condition existed.

The **present tense** places the action or existing condition in the present.

> I *live* in the United States.   I *am* a citizen.

The **past tense** places the action or condition in the past.

> I *visited* Egypt last year.   I *was* a tourist.

The **future tense** places the action or condition in the future.

> I *will* write to my Egyptian friend.   I *will be* a pen pal.

Tense changes are made in three ways:

1. By a change in an ending: *invent, invented*
2. By a change in spelling: *know, knew, known*
3. By a change in a helping verb: *has started, will start*

Tenses of Verbs

Present Tense	she explores	they learn
Future Tense	she will explore	they will learn
Past Tense	she explored	they learned
Present Perfect Tense	she has explored	they have learned
Past Perfect Tense	she had explored	they had learned

You can see that three different tenses may be used to show the time of a past action or condition: the *past,* the *present perfect,* or the *past perfect.* You will learn two things about these tenses.

1. The past tense form of the verb is used alone. It is never used with a helping verb.

    we learned   you wrote   I was

2. The present perfect tense is formed by using the helping verb *has* or *have* with the main verb. The past perfect tense is formed by using the helping verb *had* with the main verb.

    he has learned   they have written   she had been

Some verbs, such as *write,* take a different form in the past tense than in the perfect tenses. You will learn more about these verbs in the next section of this handbook.

Practice Your Skills

A. CONCEPT CHECK

Verb Tenses   For each of the following sentences, write the verb and identify its tense.

1. A colossal structure rises from the Egyptian desert near Cairo.
2. It has been there for forty-five centuries.
3. The ancient Greeks regarded it as one of the Seven Wonders of the World.
4. It will amaze future generations.
5. The structure is called the Great Pyramid of Khufu.
6. Scientists have studied this pyramid's structure.
7. It is a mass of $2\frac{1}{2}$-ton blocks of stone.
8. Somehow, without heavy machinery, the Egyptians piled more than 2 million of those huge blocks into a pyramid almost forty stories high.
9. In preparation for building, they had smoothed thirteen acres of land into a perfectly level surface.
10. They had also dragged the stone blocks from quarries on sleds.
11. Today, all of the blocks still fit together perfectly.
12. After many centuries, nobody has quite figured out the Egyptian techniques.
13. Probably the Great Pyramid will remain mysterious forever.
14. In spite of all the difficulties, the ancient Egyptians erected many of these pyramids.
15. They wanted some really fancy graves for their kings.

Writing
━━━ **TIP** ━━━

When you write about two past actions, use the past perfect tense to show that one action precedes the other.

Writing Theme
Ancient Egypt

B. DRAFTING SKILL

Using Verb Tenses   Write the following sentences using the verb form given in parentheses.

16. Queen Cleopatra of Egypt (present—be) a fascinating figure.
17. For many people she (future—remain) one of the great romantic heroines of all time.
18. In her youth, Cleopatra (past—share) the Egyptian throne with her brother.
19. Later, the Roman general Julius Caesar (past—help) her fulfill her ambitions.
20. Always, she (past perfect—want) more political power.
21. History (present—tell) of her influence upon Caesar.
22. They (past—sail) down the Nile on her 300-foot barge.
23. Soon she (past perfect—decide) to go with Caesar to Rome.
24. After Caesar's murder, Cleopatra (past—depart) from Rome.
25. She (past—travel) to Asia to ask for Mark Antony's help.
26. Together with Mark Antony, she soon (past—struggle) with Caesar's nephew, Octavian, for control of the whole empire.
27. Octavian's defeat of Antony and Cleopatra (present—remain) a turning point in history.
28. Her legend (present perfect—survive) for two thousand years.

FOR MORE PRACTICE
See page 488.

C H E C K ✔ P O I N T
MIXED REVIEW · PAGES 472–476

Writing Theme
Amusement Parks

Label three columns *Helping Verbs, Main Verbs,* and *Verb Tense.* Write the parts of the verb phrase in columns 1 and 2 and the verb tense in column 3. Not all of the verbs have helping verbs.

1. Amusement parks first appeared about a century ago.
2. Outdoor entertainment centers, with rides, games, and shows, have been constructed in many countries.
3. However, most large parks are located in the United States.
4. By 1900, "trolley parks" had been established in many areas.
5. These were placed outside towns, at the end of trolley lines.
6. Coney Island, New York, is the site of a famous amusement park.
7. It has entertained summer visitors since 1895.
8. Theme parks, like Disneyland, have become popular recently.
9. By the late 1940s, attendance at traditional parks had declined.
10. Amusement parks in some form will probably always have appeal.

THE PRINCIPAL PARTS OF VERBS

> Verb tenses are made using the three **principal parts** of verbs: the **present,** the **past,** and the **past participle.**

The different tenses of a verb are all made from three basic forms of that verb. Those forms are called the **principal parts** of the verb. They include the **present, past,** and **past participle.**

Another form, the **present participle,** is sometimes called the fourth principal part. The present participle is formed by adding *-ing* to the present: *tell—telling.* The present participle is often used with one or more helping verbs to make a verb phrase, such as *is telling* or *will be telling.*

Regular Verbs

Most English verbs are **regular.** To make the past form of a regular verb, add *-ed* or *-d* to the present. For all regular verbs, the past form and the past participle form are spelled the same. The past participle form is always used with a helping verb.

Present	Past	Past Participle
talk	talked	(have) talked
hope	hoped	(has) hoped

Irregular Verbs

Verbs that do not form the past and past participle by adding *-d* or *-ed* are called **irregular verbs.** In some cases, the past and the past participle forms of an irregular verb are spelled the same:

Present	Past	Past Participle
bring	brought	(was) brought
say	said	(had) said

Often, the past and past participle are not the same:

Present	Past	Past Participle
sing	sang	(have) sung
go	went	(has) gone

Writers and speakers often make mistakes in using verb forms. To form verbs correctly, remember the following rules:

1. The past form of the verb is used alone, without a helping verb: Someone *stole* the sun god's cattle.

2. The past participle is used with a helping verb: Hermes *had stolen* Apollo's cattle.

Refer to this list of common irregular verbs, or a dictionary, whenever you are unsure about which form to use. Remember that the past participle is always used with a helping verb, such as *have, has, had,* or *was.*

Irregular Verbs

Present	Past	Past Participle	Present	Past	Past Participle
begin	began	(have) begun	ride	rode	(have) ridden
break	broke	(have) broken	ring	rang	(have) rung
bring	brought	(have) brought	rise	rose	(have) risen
choose	chose	(have) chosen	run	ran	(have) run
come	came	(have) come	say	said	(have) said
do	did	(have) done	see	saw	(have) seen
drink	drank	(have) drunk	sing	sang	(have) sung
eat	ate	(have) eaten	speak	spoke	(have) spoken
fall	fell	(have) fallen	steal	stole	(have) stolen
freeze	froze	(have) frozen	swim	swam	(have) swum
give	gave	(have) given	take	took	(have) taken
go	went	(have) gone	teach	taught	(have) taught
grow	grew	(have) grown	throw	threw	(have) thrown
have	had	(have) had	wear	wore	(have) worn
know	knew	(have) known	write	wrote	(have) written

Practice Your Skills

A. CONCEPT CHECK

Principal Parts of Verbs On your paper write the correct form of each verb in parentheses.

1. No one knows when the myths of Scandinavia (began, begun).
2. They were told by people who (spoke, spoken) the Norse language.
3. Until the 1200s, no one had ever (wrote, written) them down.

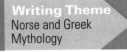

Writing Theme
Norse and Greek
Mythology

4. The German composer, Richard Wagner, (chose, chosen) some of these myths for the plots of his operas.
5. So, exciting stories can (teach, taught) us about Norse gods.
6. Asgard, the home of these gods, was completely (froze, frozen).
7. The sun never (rose, risen) over this chilly place.
8. Nothing ever (grew, grown) there either.
9. Odin, the chief god, (wore, worn) two ravens on his shoulders.
10. These birds (gone, went) around the world each day.
11. The ravens (bring, brought) the news of the day to Odin.
12. By their return they had (seen, saw) all the day's events.
13. They told him everything that humans had (did, done) that day.
14. Odin's female attendants (have, had) the name Valkyries.
15. The Valkyries had been (gave, given) a very important role.
16. From earliest times, the Valkyries had always (chose, chosen) which of the dead would be honored as heroes.
17. Often, they (rode, ridden) alongside humans in battle.
18. Many brave warriors (fell, fallen) in combat.
19. The maidens (took, taken) only the bravest of the dead to Valhalla, the most magnificent palace in Asgard.
20. Here, the heroes (came, come) for feasts.
21. Moody Odin (give, gave) lavish banquets.
22. The Valkyries helped with the bread that was (broke, broken).
23. Odin himself rarely (say, said) or (eat, ate) anything.
24. He often just (threw, thrown) food to the wolves at his feet.
25. According to myth, each morning the dead heroes (rode, ridden) into battle, but no matter how badly they were wounded, they had (rose, risen) by noon to feast again.

An illumination from a thirteenth-century Icelandic manuscript showing the Norse god Thor battling a serpent.

B. DRAFTING SKILL

Using the Principal Parts of Verbs   A writer can use verb tenses to show a variety of relationships or points in time. Complete the following by using the principal parts of the verb to form the tense named in parentheses. Write the complete sentences on your paper.

26. For centuries, poets (present perfect—sing) the praises of the gods of Greek mythology.
27. These gods (past—inhabit) a magical realm.
28. The Greeks (past—call) this realm Olympus, after a mountain.
29. Unlike the Norse gods, the Greek gods (past—choose) their home for its comfort and beauty.
30. The gods (past—come) to this site for its warmth and splendor.
31. No rain ever (past perfect—fall) on Olympus.

FOR MORE PRACTICE
See page 488.

32. Likewise, cold never (past perfect—freeze) its waters.

33. No mortal (past—see) the daily activities of the gods.

34. But the poets imagined and (past—write) about the gods' adventures on their mountain home.

35. Some (present perfect—describe) the sounds, smells, and tastes of Olympus.

36. In these poems, the sounds of Apollo's lyre are (present participle—ring) sweetly through the halls.

37. The gods (present—eat) wonderful ambrosia.

38. They (present—drink) delicious nectar.

39. According to myth, consuming ambrosia and nectar (past—give) the gods their immortality.

40. In some tales, mortals (past—steal) this nectar.

41. Woe, however, (past—come) to any mortals who (past perfect—break) the laws of the gods.

42. Repeatedly we mortals (present—read) these stories.

43. For as long as myths (present—give) us pleasure, these gods (future—exist).

44. Poseidon, the god of the seas, (future—swim) eternally in his watery realm.

45. Each dawn, Apollo, the sun god, (future—ride) off from Olympus in his chariot.

46. With him (future—go) the sun.

47. As long as Apollo (present—ride) the sun (future—rise).

C. PROOFREADING SKILL

Correct Forms of Verbs Proofread the following paragraphs. Rewrite each paragraph, correcting all errors in grammar, capitalization, punctuation, and spelling. (15 errors)

The anceint Greeks have wrote about Artemis. The goddess of the moon and the hunt. They knowed she could become angryer than other gods. One story taught just how angry artemis could be.

in this tale, a hunter named actaeon came to close and stealed a look at Artemis. Furious, she ran after the young man she changed him into a deer. Then she had the hunters' own hounds turn on him and eat him.

Not all hunters felt the Wrath of Artemis. For some, she brung good luck. She was also known for watching over and protecting all yuong things.

FOR MORE PRACTICE
See page 488.

CHECK ✔ POINT

MIXED REVIEW · PAGES 477–480

Writing Theme
Endangered and
Extinct Species

A. Rewrite the following sentences, using the verb form given in parentheses.

1. Creatures can (present—become) extinct for many reasons.
2. Often, their habitats (present perfect—become) unlivable.
3. During the Ice Age, for example, dinosaurs lost the habitat they (past perfect—grow) accustomed to.
4. Dinosaurs could not survive in a habitat that (past perfect—freeze).
5. Such changes often (present—begin) naturally.
6. Others (present perfect—come) from human interference.
7. For centuries the Great Plains Indians (past perfect—see) and hunted vast herds of bison.
8. Then millions of bison (past—fall) to the guns of European settlers.
9. Settlers also (past—carve) the plains into farms.
10. Soon, the humans (past participle—run) most of the bison from the plains.

B. For each sentence write the correct form of the verb in parentheses.

11. Recent events have (thrown, threw) the future of the Simien jackal into doubt.
12. For thousands of years, this animal has (sung, sang) nightly in the Bale Mountains of Ethiopia.
13. Many observers have (wrote, written) about the mournful sounds.
14. Some have (say, said) the sounds resemble the call of a fox.
15. For years, these jackals (have, had) no enemies.
16. Suddenly, though, deaths among the Simien have (risen, rose) sharply.
17. Apparently, a virus (broke, broken) out among their population.
18. At the same time, lawless herders (began, begun) attacks on the jackals.
19. The Simien jackal population (fell, fallen) dramatically.
20. As a result, this animal has (became, become) the rarest member of the dog family.

The use of certain pairs of verbs can cause confusion. These verbs include **let** and **leave, lie** and **lay,** and **sit** and **set.**

Sometimes people confuse one verb with another one. For example, they do not know whether to say, "Let me see the animals" or "Leave me see the animals."

In this lesson, you will study several pairs of verbs that often cause difficulty. Notice the correct way to use these verbs.

Using *Let* and *Leave*

1. *Let* means "to allow" or "to permit."

   EXAMPLE   *Let* the smaller fish go free.

2. *Leave* means "to depart" or "to allow to stay or be."

   EXAMPLE   *Leave* your bait in the water longer.

These are the principal parts of the verbs *let* and *leave.*

let, let, let

Present	The Paysons *let* us hike on their property.
Past	They *let* us use their boat yesterday.
Past Participle	They have *let* us watch the wildlife.

leave, left, left

Present	*Leave* nothing behind you in the woods.
Past	Other hikers *left* litter behind.
Past Participle	We have *left* nothing but footprints.

Practice Your Skills

CONCEPT CHECK

Let and *Leave*   Write the correct verb for each sentence.

1. That mother duck has (let, left) her ducklings to go find food.
2. She has probably never (let, left) them alone before.
3. She cannot (let, leave) the young birds search for food yet.
4. Like most birds, she won't (let, leave) them permanently for some time.

5. Be sure you (let, leave) those baby ducks remain undisturbed!
6. Ducks don't (let, leave) anyone near their ducklings.
7. If you touch one, the mother may not (let, leave) it return.
8. Then the baby must (let, leave) the flock and may not survive.
9. Like birds, mammals also don't (let, leave) their young go off on their own too soon.
10. Young bears, for example, don't (let, leave) for three years.

Using *Lie* and *Lay*

1. *Lie* means "to rest" or "to recline." It does not take an object.

   EXAMPLE   I often *lie* on the ground in my yard to watch the birds.

2. *Lay* means "to put or place something." It takes an object.

   EXAMPLE   The hawk *laid* its prey on the top of the cliff.

These are the principal parts of the verbs *lie* and *lay*.

lie, lay, lain

Present	Big cats *lie* around all day long.
Past	The leopard *lay* for hours under the tree.
Past Participle	The sleepy cat *has lain* there all day.

lay, laid, laid

Present	The photographer *lays* the camera on a branch.
Past	A bird *laid* her eggs in a nest near the camera.
Past Participle	The bird *has laid* four tiny eggs.

Practice Your Skills

CONCEPT CHECK

Lie and Lay   Write the correct verb for each sentence.

11. Mike (lay, laid) his gear on the ground.
12. Tired from his hike, he (lay, laid) down to rest .
13. Matted grass showed where an opossum had (lain, laid) earlier.
14. An opossum (lies, lays) on the ground to play dead.
15. Mike had not (laid, lain) there long when he heard something.
16. In a nearby stream, a bear (lay, laid) its paw on a fish.
17. Soon the fish (lay, laid) wriggling on the bank near Mike.
18. A large stick was (lying, laying) nearby, and he picked it up.
19. He moved cautiously from where he had (lain, laid) his gear.
20. The bear strolled away, and Mike (lay, laid) back down in relief.

Using *Sit* and *Set*

1. *Sit* means "to be in a seat" or "to rest." It does not take an object.

    SMALLCAPS EXAMPLE   The circus train *sat* on the track.

2. *Set* means "to put or place something." It takes an object.

    EXAMPLE   The lion tamer *set* the chair in the cage.

    These are the principal parts of the verbs *sit* and *set*.

sit, sat, sat

Present	Bareback riders *sit* on horses.
Past	One clown *sat* on another.
Past Participle	I *have* never *sat* in the front row.

set, set, set

Present	The trainer carefully *sets* the lion's food in the cage.
Past	Yesterday he *set* it a little too close.
Past Participle	Workers *have set* barricades in front of the animal cages.

Practice Your Skills
CONCEPT CHECK

Sit **and** *Set*   Write the correct verb for each sentence.

21. Crew members carefully (sat, set) the net in place below the high wire.
22. Far above the circus ring, a tightrope walker (sits, sets) on a tiny platform.
23. For several minutes, the audience has (sat, set) waiting, expectant and excited.
24. A performer (sits, sets) one foot slowly before the other.
25. His partner (sits, sets) at the other end of the rope, watching.
26. One small child has (sat, set) his popcorn aside to watch.
27. Has the aerialist (sat, set) his foot too far to one side?
28. Moments later the acrobat is (sitting, setting) safely in the net.
29. After momentarily jumping to their feet, the audience has (sat, set) down again.
30. What if the net had not been (sat, set) in place?

Writing Theme
Circus

FOR MORE PRACTICE
See page 489.

C H E C K ✓ P O I N T

Write the correct form of the verb given in parentheses.

Writing Theme
Indianapolis
500 Race

1. Track attendants (sit, set) aside the sawhorses that are in front of the gates, and a day at the Indy 500 begins.
2. A mechanic has (laid, lain) under the slightly elevated car for an hour making delicate adjustments.
3. A pit crew has just (lay, laid) the fuel hose aside after filling the forty-gallon nylon tank with flammable methyl alcohol.
4. For reasons of safety, officials (let, leave) only a few specially trained people come into this area.
5. Some fans have (sat, set) for hours in the infield watching the preparations and holding their hard-to-come-by viewing positions.
6. Other more fortunate ticket holders (sit, set) in the stands.
7. Spectators tell stories about the tar-and-gravel track of 1909; 3,200,000 bricks were (lain, laid) over that original surface.
8. Those bricks now (lie, lay) under a coating of asphalt, but the speedway is still called "the Brickyard."
9. A driver pulls into position and (sits, sets) in the tiny cockpit waiting for the famous checkered flag.
10. "(Let, Leave) your hand off the turbocharger control lever until it's really needed," she thinks.
11. The lever (lets, leaves) air into the engine, causing a burst of speed.
12. A good driver, however, will (lie, lay) his or her desire for speed aside, if necessary, so that the engine does not become overstrained and break down.
13. Instead of saying "(Let, Leave) the race begin," someone says, "Ladies and gentlemen, start your engines."
14. The starter (lets, leaves) the flag drop, and the race begins.
15. For the more than thirty competitors, the finish line will (lie, lay) in view in about $3\frac{1}{2}$ hours, slightly over half the time of the first Indy.

In 1992 Lyn St. James was the second woman in the history of the Indianapolis 500 to qualify for and finish the race.

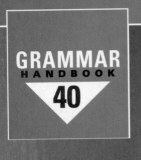

GRAMMAR
H A N D B O O K
40

Writing Theme
Virginia

A. Identifying Verbs Write the verbs in each of these sentences. Label each verb *Action* or *Linking*.

1. One of the nicknames for the state of Virginia is Mother of Presidents.
2. Virginia gave the United States four of its first five presidents.
3. Washington, Jefferson, Madison, and Monroe claimed this state as a birthplace.
4. A second nickname of Virginia also seems appropriate.
5. The western territory of Virginia eventually became all or part of eight other states.
6. So, some people call Virginia the Mother of States.
7. In the seventeenth century, Charles II of England named it Old Dominion.
8. Loyalty to England during a civil war earned this title.
9. Sir Walter Raleigh was probably responsible for the name Virginia.
10. Surely, he gained the favor of the Queen as a result.

B. Recognizing Direct Objects Write and label each *Action Verb* and *Direct Object* in the following sentences.

11. England founded its first permanent North American settlement in 1607.
12. Settlers steered three ships up the James River in present-day Virginia.
13. The ships carried 105 hopeful English colonists.
14. One of them described the many "tall trees" in Virginia.
15. Most colonists, however, sought gold and silver.
16. The Virginia Company, an English investment group, paid the expenses for the journey.
17. The English landed their ships at a small peninsula.
18. They named their new town after King James I.
19. Unfortunately, they chose a terrible place for their settlement.
20. First, swamp water flooded their farms.
21. Then a drought parched the land.
22. Bad drinking water caused much sickness.
23. Extreme seasonal changes added more problems.
24. Chief Powhatan and his tribe also posed a threat.
25. Within two years, disease, hunger, and hostilities killed two-thirds of the settlers.

C. Recognizing Transitive and Intransitive Verbs   Write the verbs from the following sentences. Label them *Transitive* or *Intransitive*. If a verb is transitive, write its direct object.

26. John Smith took control of the Jamestown settlement in 1608.
27. The settlement's luck quickly improved after his appointment.
28. Smith governed skillfully.
29. He encouraged the colonists to plant practical crops.
30. Even more important, he made peace with the natives.
31. He bought corn from Chief Powhatan and his people.
32. In 1609, after a bad accident, Smith returned to England.
33. There he wrote a book of attractive descriptions of the colony.
34. After his departure, the colony suffered its worst winter ever.
35. The name of that terrible winter became "the starving time."

D. Identifying Linking Verbs   Write and label each *Subject, Linking Verb,* and *Predicate Word* in the following sentences.

36. The early settlers often were wrong about life in Virginia.
37. The land looked new and fertile to them.
38. Beauty and promise were everywhere.
39. In their eyes, everything seemed possible.
40. Their first attempts at industry, however, were failures.
41. Their grapes tasted terrible.
42. The trees for silkworms grew scrawny.
43. Virginia did not appear suitable for silkworms or grapes.
44. Some products, though, were right for that climate.
45. The colony became successful with tobacco and other crops.

E. Identifying Main Verbs   Make two columns on your paper. Label them *Helping Verbs* and *Main Verbs*. Write the helping and the main verbs from the following sentences in the correct column.

46. The following story may not be true.
47. Captain John Smith could have invented it.
48. Smith had been captured by Powhatan, a Native American chief.
49. At one point Captain Smith was facing certain death.
50. The chief was raising his stone war club against him.
51. Pocahantas, however, had been standing nearby.
52. She may have jumped between the two men.
53. Because of her plea for mercy, Powhatan did spare Smith's life.

54. Rumors about Pocahantas' love for Smith probably have been exaggerated.

55. She eventually was married to John Rolfe, another settler.

F. Recognizing Tenses   Write the verbs from the following sentences. Beside each verb write its tense.

56. The state of Virginia is named after a queen of England.

57. Elizabeth I (1533–1603) had been known as the Virgin Queen.

58. Many historians have described Elizabeth's quarrels with her half-sister, Queen Mary I of England.

59. Elizabeth also defended herself against followers of her cousin, Queen Mary of Scotland.

60. At her death, Elizabeth had ruled for forty-five years.

61. Today, people remember her reign as the Elizabethan Age.

62. Elizabeth's greatest triumph came in 1588.

63. King Philip II of Spain had sent a mighty fleet against England.

64. The defeat of this fleet has been a source of pride for England.

65. The English will always think of Elizabeth as a great monarch.

G. Recognizing Principal Parts   Write the verbs from the following sentences. Identify the parts that have been used by labeling them *Present, Past,* or *Past Participle.*

66. People have usually celebrated their harvest time with a feast.

67. Both the United States and Canada have a Thanksgiving Day.

68. In New England the Thanksgiving custom began in 1623.

69. For the Plymouth settlers, the first winter had been terrible.

70. However, more plentiful corn crops had brought new hope.

71. Governor Bradford decreed a time of prayer and thanks.

72. The colonists prepared a meal of fish, duck, goose, corn bread with nuts, and succotash.

73. Native Americans contributed wild turkeys and deer meat.

74. That pleasant gathering remains a part of American culture.

75. Thanksgiving today is a time of big dinners and happy family reunions.

H. Using Irregular Verbs   Write the following sentences with the correct form of the verb given in the parentheses.

76. Mardi Gras has always (take) place on Shrove Tuesday.

77. This is the last day before Lent (begin).

78. Before the Christian era, the Romans (have) a similar custom.

79. In ancient France, people (eat) a fat ox before holidays.

80. This old custom has (give) us the name Mardi Gras, or Fat Tuesday.

81. For many years New Orleans has (have) a festive Mardi Gras.

82. Each year, thousands of visitors (go) there.

83. Before New Orleans became known for Mardi Gras, Biloxi, Mississippi, and Mobile, Alabama, had also (throw) big festivals.

84. In fact, Mardi Gras parades first (begin) in Biloxi.

85. Since the mid-1800s, societies called krewes have (run) the huge parades in New Orleans.

86. Krewe members have always (wear) special costumes and (ride) on spectacular floats.

87. "Kings" and "Queens" are (choose) for the event.

88. Some merrymakers dance, and others (sing) Cajun songs.

89. Cajun is a language that was (bring) to Louisiana by a group of French settlers from Acadia, an area in Canada.

90. A more traditional form of French had been (speak) before they came.

I. Choosing the Right Verb Write the correct verb given in parentheses.

91. The year is 1400 and servants (sit, set) flaming torches along the castle walls.

92. "(Let, Leave) the feast begin!" cries the host.

93. A long board has been (lain, laid) between trestles in the middle of the room and covered with a floor-length cloth.

94. The cloth hides the Duke's dogs (lying, laying) under the table eagerly waiting for scraps.

95. Guests will (sit, set) on a long bench on one side of the table.

96. A serving maid (lies, lays) joints of meat and steaming bowls of soup on a smaller side table.

97. At the end of this table (sits, sets) a water container, or *aquamanile,* for hand washing.

98. Since all the diners will (let, leave) their hands touch the food, cleanliness is very important.

99. Servers (let, leave) each guest take a trencher, or thick square slice of four-day-old bread.

100. Trenchers take the place of plates, and some of the feasters have already (lain, laid) chunks of meat on their trenchers.

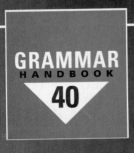

GRAMMAR
HANDBOOK
40

A. Identifying Linking Verbs   Write the linking verbs and the predicate words from the following sentences.

1. Islands are an attraction to many adventure seekers.
2. A faraway island—as an escape—sounds wonderful.
3. South Sea islands, in particular, seem ideal as romantic vacation places.
4. For many people, life on a tropical isle has become a kind of dream.
5. For example, the climate on this imaginary island stays pleasant forever.
6. The nights never turn cold.
7. On such an island, rare tropical fruits always taste fresh and delicious.
8. The lifestyle remains easy, with graceful palm trees, white beaches, and blue lagoons.
9. An actual tropical island, however, could look quite different from the imaginary one.
10. The grim reality could be humidity, spiders, and crowds of tourists.

B. Identifying Action Verbs   Make columns on your paper for *Transitive Verbs, Intransitive Verbs,* and *Direct Objects.* Write the verbs from the following sentences in the correct column. Write the direct objects of the transitive verbs in the third column.

11. Thousands of islands, large and small, exist on this planet.
12. Oceans, lakes, and rivers contain these bodies of land.
13. Various occurrences can create an island.
14. Sometimes a continent loses a large piece of itself.
15. In Europe, for example, rising sea levels long ago isolated the British Isles.
16. Sometimes a volcano suddenly builds an island in the middle of an ocean.
17. Iceland began this way, millions of years ago.
18. Sometimes ocean waves and winds pile sediment offshore, as with Hatteras Island, North Carolina, and Padre Island, Texas.
19. In shallow tropical waters, coral formations turn slowly into islands.
20. The earth will probably develop more new islands in years to come.

C. Identifying Verb Tenses   Make two columns on your paper, labeled *Verbs* and *Verb Tenses.* Write the verbs from the following sentences in the first column, and write their tenses in the second column.

21. Certain islands have become famous for one reason or another.
22. These include both real and imaginary places.
23. Readers will always enjoy Daniel Defoe's famous novel, *Robinson Crusoe.*
24. In that story a man is stranded for many years on a remote desert island.
25. Jules Verne wrote *The Mysterious Island,* another exciting novel about castaways.
26. *Treasure Island,* by Robert Louis Stevenson, also used the idea of an island as a place of adventure.
27. Year after year, new readers of that book learn about Captain Kidd, Long John Silver, and the search for buried treasure.
28. Ellis Island, a real place in New York Harbor, has become a symbol of new opportunities.
29. It was a processing site for twelve million immigrants over a period of sixty years.
30. On nearby Liberty Island, stands an even more familiar monument, the Statue of Liberty.
31. "The Rock"—Alcatraz Island in San Francisco Bay—had been, before 1963, a maximum-security federal prison.
32. Now Alcatraz Island will receive sightseers as a National Recreation Area.
33. Until 1945 Devil's Island, off the northeast coast of South America, had been a prison for French political offenders.
34. It will be remembered forever as a frightful place.
35. Islands like these have always inspired some kind of emotion: hope, fear, romance, or adventure.

D. Using Irregular Verbs   Complete the following sentences with the verb form given in parentheses. Write the complete sentences.

36. One of William Shakespeare's most interesting plays (present— take) place on an island.
37. *The Tempest* may (present perfect—be) the last of his plays.
38. He may (present perfect—write) it around 1610.

39. In the play, the magician Prospero (present perfect—bring) his daughter, Miranda, to a magic island.
40. Miranda never (present perfect—see) any man except her father.
41. Prospero (past tense—teach) Miranda himself.
42. The play (present tense—begin) with a fierce storm.
43. Great waves (present participle—break) up a ship.
44. Several nobles (past perfect—ride) on that ship.
45. They (present tense—swim) to the nearby shore of Prospero's island.
46. Soon, Miranda (present perfect—fall) in love with one of these nobles.
47. She never (past perfect—know) anyone like him.
48. By the end, everybody except Caliban, a monster, (present perfect—leave) the island.
49. Later, this story (past—become) the basis for a famous science fiction movie, "The Forbidden Planet."
50. In the movie, the Prospero character (past perfect—build) an empire on a distant world.

E. Choosing the Right Verb   Write the correct verb given in parentheses.

51. Easter Island (lays, lies) in the South Pacific, 2,200 miles west of Chile.
52. Giant, mysterious stone heads are (sit, set) on the hillsides of this island.
53. Some of the heads (sit, set) upright.
54. Others (lie, lay) on the ground.
55. Could these strange monuments have been (lain, laid) that way on purpose?
56. The builders of the statues on Easter Island (let, left) behind other mysteries.
57. Those unsolved mysteries have not (let, left) the scientists rest.
58. What sort of people could (sit, set) up these strange fifty-ton statues?
59. What of the bodies that (lie, lay) in burial chambers in the ground beneath?
60. Most of all, what people (let, left) the mysterious statues on this remote island?

WRITING CONNECTIONS

Elaboration, Revision, and Proofreading

Revise the following introduction of a short story by using the directions at the bottom of the page. Also proofread the passage, looking especially for errors in the use of verbs and for other grammatical mistakes. Check capitalization, punctuation, and spelling as well.

¹The Sandler house has stood vacant for years when mom and dad decided to buy and remodel the drafty old building. ²As we begin to rebuild various rooms, we were often surprised by hiden stairs and narrow, long halls for passing from one place to another. ³The house seemed to have a mysterious past. ⁴That we hadn't uncovered yet. ⁵A clue to this past was revealled to us on a quite saturday afternoon. ⁶Thats when we find papers in an old sack that had been put into the small space behind the brick. ⁷Torn and crumbled, the papers were yellow with age. ⁸They apeared to be a handwritten will left by someone. ⁹According to the will, the house holds a secret. ¹⁰It's writer had left gold coins in an unobvious place somewhere in the house. ¹¹Old Mr. Sandler had lived in the house alone for over forty years.

1. Delete the sentence that does not belong.

2. Insert the following sentence after sentence 5 to set the scene for the discovery: "Mom and I had just started to scrub the fireplace in a back bedroom when a loose brick crashed to the floor."

3. Replace the phrase "narrow, long halls for passing from one place to another" with a precise noun.

4. In sentence 6, replace the verb *put* with a stronger, more precise verb.

5. Replace the verb phrase "left . . . in an unobvious place" in sentence 10 with a precise verb.

Narrative and Literary Writing

The elements of a short story—characters, plot, conflict, and setting—work together to amuse, frighten, or educate readers. (See Workshop 3.) When you revise a short story, make sure that you have clearly established the characters and setting. Check that your verb tenses help readers understand the sequence of events. Also look for chances to create memorable images by replacing weak verbs or verb-modifier combinations with precise, strong verbs.

Sketch Book

- Write a postcard to a friend describing a breathtaking scene. Use words that capture what you see, hear, feel, smell, and, possibly, taste.

- Do you dream in color? Freewrite about a vivid dream that you remember.
- Think of an object you see every day, for example, a can opener or a doorknob. Describe the object in detail—without naming it. Have a friend read your description and try to guess what the object is.

Using Adjectives

- **What Is an Adjective?**

- **Predicate Adjectives**

- **Adjectives in Comparisons**

- **Possessive Pronouns May Be Used as Adjectives**

- **Demonstrative Adjective or Demonstrative Pronoun?**

The sun is setting.

Well, yes. But what does it look like? How does it make you feel? To be effective, writing must paint a word picture as colorful and lifelike as this photograph.

One good way to add color to your writing is by using precise adjectives. That's what this handbook will help you do.

WHAT IS AN ADJECTIVE?

An **adjective** is a word that modifies a noun or pronoun.

Adjectives are words that modify or clearly define the nouns and pronouns you use in your speaking and writing. Adjectives add important details and make what you say more meaningful. Notice the difference between the two sentences below.

The spaceship landed in the meadow.
The silver spaceship landed in the grassy meadow.

You can usually tell whether a word is an adjective by deciding if it answers the questions *what kind, which one,* or *how many.*

broken robot	*magnetic* shield
those wires	*experimental* procedure
two technicians	*second* time

Some words that can be used in other ways can also function as adjectives. The examples below are adjectives because they answer *what kind, which one,* or *how many.*

rocket ship	*sealed* package
leading scientist	*one* satellite
Toni's experiment	*that* astronaut

Proper Adjectives

Adjectives can be made from nouns, and like nouns, adjectives can be common or proper. **Common adjectives,** those formed from common nouns, are not capitalized. When adjectives are made from proper nouns, they are called **proper adjectives,** and they are always capitalized.

A proper noun can become an adjective when it is used to describe another noun, as in the examples *June day* or *Friday night.* However, sometimes an ending such as *-an, -ian, -n, -ese,* or *-ish* must be added to the proper noun to make it an adjective. In this way, the proper nouns *Italy* and *China* become the proper adjectives *Italian* and *Chinese.*

Writing
TIP

Adjectives make writing more vivid and interesting. They help the reader "see" what is being described.

Articles

The words *a, an,* and *the* are special adjectives called **articles.** *The* is the **definite article.** It points out one specific person, place, thing, or idea. *A* and *an* are **indefinite articles.** They are less specific.

When you speak or write, you refer to specific persons, places, things, and ideas with the word *the.* When you want to be less specific, use *a* or *an.*

Tom wished upon *the* falling star. (a specific falling star)
Tom wished upon *a* falling star. (any falling star)

Sentence Diagraming For information on diagraming adjectives, see page 678.

Practice Your Skills

A. CONCEPT CHECK

Understanding Adjectives On your paper, write the adjectives found in each of the following sentences. Then label each adjective *Common* or *Proper.* Do not write articles.

Writing Theme
Science Fiction

1. Futuristic novels often include imaginary inventions, time travel, and life on other planets.
2. One novel is set on Mars in the twenty-first century.
3. An expedition of sixteen American space travelers lands on the red planet.
4. They expect to find a hot, barren Martian landscape.
5. Instead, the surprised travelers find a curious scene that resembles a Midwestern town.
6. A tall brown Victorian house with an old swing on the front porch stands on a quiet shady street.
7. Is this some clever plot?
8. Did dangerous Martians create this homelike scene as a trap for the space travelers?
9. Indeed, the Martians have remarkable mental powers.
10. They created this environment based on the fond memories of home of the travelers.
11. In the morning sun, sixteen new graves were dug, and the landscape returned to normal.
12. Blue sand and winding canals replaced the shady lawns.

B. APPLICATION IN LITERATURE

Recognizing Adjectives   Notice how Ray Bradbury uses adjectives to create vivid, interesting images in the selection below. For each sentence in the paragraph, write the adjectives and the words they modify. Do not include articles. If there are no adjectives in the sentence, write *None.* You should find a total of twelve adjectives.

> [13]They set foot upon the porch. [14]Hollow echoes sounded from under the boards as they walked to the screen door. [15]Inside they could see a bead curtain hung across the hall entry, and a crystal chandelier and a Maxfield Parrish painting on one wall over a comfortable Morris chair. . . . [16]You could hear the tinkle of ice in a lemonade pitcher. [17]In a distant kitchen, because of the heat of the day, someone was preparing a cold lunch.
>
> **Ray Bradbury,**
> ***The Martian Chronicles***

C. APPLICATION IN WRITING

A Description   Imagine that you are writing a script for a science fiction play. Write a brief description of the scene as the main character walks on stage. What does he or she see, hear, and feel? Use five of the adjectives listed below in your description.

shimmering	weird	immense
purple	American	cold
quiet	slimy	happy
nervous	three	several
dark	first	long
one	steamy	Plutonian

FOR MORE PRACTICE
See page 509.

PREDICATE ADJECTIVES

A **predicate adjective** is an adjective that follows a linking verb. It describes the subject of the sentence.

Adjectives usually come before the words they modify.

A *strong, cold* wind blew down from the North.

For variety, adjectives may be placed after the words they modify.

The wind, *strong* and *cold,* blew down from the North.

In some sentences, the verb separates an adjective from the word it modifies:

The sky looks *stormy. (stormy* modifies *sky)*

The wind is *strong. (strong* modifies *wind)*

The day is *cold* and *damp. (cold* and *damp* modify *day)*

In these sentences, the adjectives *stormy, strong, cold,* and *damp* are **predicate adjectives** because they are in the predicate of each sentence. Each one of these adjectives modifies the subject of its sentence. Each one is linked to the subject it modifies by a linking verb.

Sentence Diagraming   For information on diagraming predicate adjectives, see page 678.

Practice Your Skills

A. CONCEPT CHECK

Predicate Adjectives   Write the following sentences. Circle each predicate adjective. Then underline the subject it modifies once and underline the linking verb twice. There may be more than one predicate adjective in a sentence.

1. For part of the year, the Arizona desert is hot and dry.
2. In the summer, the sun's rays grow intense.
3. By June the heat seems unbearable.
4. In such heat, even the smallest shady spot looks inviting.

Saguaro cactus during
a desert storm.

5. In July and August, the
thunderstorms are frequent
and dangerous.
6. The rain feels refreshing and
welcome before the return of
the burning desert heat.
7. After the summer ends, the
weather grows mild.
8. Shortly before winter, the
desert becomes cool and rainy.
9. The weather turns warm
again in spring.
10. With its multicolored wildflowers, the desert looks
breathtaking.

B. DRAFTING SKILL

Creating Mood   Write each predicate adjective found in the
following paragraph. If a sentence has no predicate adjective, write
None. Then rewrite the paragraph, replacing the predicate
adjectives with others to create a different mood.

> [11]I woke up and looked out the window that morning. [12]The
> day seemed promising. [13]The sky was cloudless. [14]By noon,
> however, the wind had become chilly and biting. [15]The air felt
> harsh. [16]As the afternoon wore on, the temperature grew
> colder. [17]The weather forecast on the radio certainly sounded
> terrible. [18]I was really disappointed. [19]I never realized before
> how much the weather affected my mood. [20]I felt tired and
> grouchy. [21]I wondered whether it would remain ugly for long.
> [22]Then suddenly the sky turned clearer. [23]The breeze became
> milder. [24]The air grew softer. [25]As the weather changed, I felt
> cheerful again.

C. APPLICATION IN WRITING

A Description   Write ten sentences to describe an experience
you've had with the weather. You might describe a storm or tell
about unusual weather conditions. Use adjectives that tell what
you remember touching, smelling, seeing, hearing, or tasting. Use
a predicate adjective in each sentence.

FOR MORE PRACTICE
See page 509.

ADJECTIVES IN COMPARISONS

> Use the **comparative form** of an adjective to compare two things.
>
> Use the **superlative form** of an adjective to compare more than two things.

Adjectives are often used to compare two or more people or things.

> Golden Delicious apples are *sweeter* than Granny Smith apples.
>
> Red Delicious apples are the *sweetest* apples at the market.

When adjectives are used in comparisons, they have special forms or spellings.

The Forms of Adjectives in Comparisons

When you compare one thing or person with another, use the **comparative form** of the adjective. When you compare a thing or person with more than one other, use the **superlative form.**

Short adjectives, like *sweet* and *fresh,* change their forms by adding *-er* for the comparative and *-est* for the superlative. Notice that adjectives ending in *y* change the *y* to *i* before adding these endings.

Adjective	Comparative Form	Superlative Form
hot	hotter	hottest
ripe	riper	ripest
creamy	creamier	creamiest
spicy	spicier	spiciest

Longer adjectives, like *peppery* and *delicious,* use *more* for the comparative and *most* for the superlative.

Adjective	Comparative Form	Superlative Form
fragrant	more fragrant	most fragrant
well-done	more well-done	most well-done
flavorful	more flavorful	most flavorful

Writing
— **TIP** —

Using comparative forms correctly helps you show relationships more clearly.

Use only one form of comparison at a time. Do not use *more* and *-er* together, or *most* and *-est* together.

Incorrect   Steak is the most easiest meat to barbecue.
Correct   Steak is the *easiest* meat to barbecue.

Incorrect   My soup is much more hotter than yours.
Correct   My soup is much *hotter* than yours.

The Forms of *Good* and *Bad*

The comparative and superlative forms of some adjectives are totally different words, as in the examples that follow.

Adjective	Comparative Form	Superlative Form
good	better	best
bad	worse	worst

Practice Your Skills

A. CONCEPT CHECK

Adjectives in Comparisons   For each of the following sentences, write the correct form of the adjectives given in parentheses.

1. Chinese cooking often offers a (greater, more greater) variety of dishes than many people realize.
2. Some people think that Cantonese food is the (better, best).
3. Cantonese food is the (more popular, most popular) of all Chinese food in the United States.
4. In China, Cantonese chefs make the (most fine, finest) pastries.
5. Chefs in Szechwan province cook the (most hottest, hottest) foods.
6. They claim the (spicier, more spicy) the food, the warmer people will stay in the damp mountain air.
7. Szechwan is the province (farther, farthest) from the sea.
8. That's why seafood is (uncommoner, more uncommon) there than in Canton province.
9. Food from Shanghai is (milder, mildest) than food from Szechwan.
10. Shanghai chefs make the (most tastiest, tastiest) vegetables.
11. Beijing's weather is (colder, more cold) than Shanghai's.
12. Therefore, food from Beijing is (heavier, heaviest) than food from Shanghai.

B. PROOFREADING SKILL

Correct Comparative Forms Proofread and write the following paragraph, correcting errors in grammar, capitalization, punctuation, and spelling. Pay special attention to the use of comparative forms. (10 errors)

FOR MORE PRACTICE
See page 510.

The United States has one of the most richest cooking traditions in the world. Santa Fe cooking is a cheif example. Its a blend of at least four traditions. The older tradition comes from Native Americans. Their more important contributions are the corn tortilla and chilies. Then the Spanish arrived they brought fruit from their homeland. Later, mexicans settled in the area, bringing New spices and sauces. People from other parts of the United States were the recenter arrivals. Together these cultures have made Santa Fe cooking among the wonderfullest anywhere.

CHECK ✔ POINT
MIXED REVIEW · PAGES 496–503

Write the italicized adjectives in each sentence. Then label each adjective as either *Common* or *Proper*. Label any predicate adjectives *Predicate Adjective*. In addition, if an adjective is used in a comparison, label it as either *Comparative* or *Superlative*.

Writing Theme
Dog-Sled Racing

[1]In March 1925, a *serious* epidemic of diphtheria broke out in Nome, Alaska. [2]The *winter* snows hampered rescue attempts. [3]*Alaskan* dog-sled drivers loaded their sleds with *medical* supplies and mushed their teams from Anchorage to Nome. [4]*Each* March since then, the *Iditarod Trail* dog-sled race has been run to commemorate that rescue. [5]The race is very *long*, about 1,100 miles, and takes between eleven and fifteen days for the *best* drivers to complete. [6]Only the *most experienced* mushers dare attempt the Iditarod at all. [7]*March* weather may be *severe*, and conditions can get *worse* as the race proceeds. [8]There may be no competitive sport in the world *more grueling* than this one.

POSSESSIVE PRONOUNS
MAY BE USED AS ADJECTIVES

> Sometimes **possessive pronouns** stand alone and sometimes they modify nouns. When a possessive pronoun modifies a noun, it functions as an adjective.

Mine, ours, yours, hers, his, its, and *theirs* are possessive pronouns that can stand alone. When the possessive pronouns *your, my, our, her, his, its,* and *their* are used to modify nouns, they function as adjectives.

> *Yours* is the prettiest painting. (*Yours* is a possessive pronoun that stands alone.)
> Did he like *your* painting? (*Your* is a possessive pronoun that modifies painting. It functions as an adjective in the sentence.)
>
> The charcoal sketches are *mine*. (*Mine* is a possessive pronoun that stands alone.)
> I'll put the sketches in *my* portfolio. (*My* is a possessive pronoun that modifies portfolio. It functions as an adjective in the sentence.)

Practice Your Skills

A. CONCEPT CHECK

Possessive Pronouns Used as Adjectives   For each of the following sentences, write the possessive pronoun and the word it modifies.

1. The apprentice artist listened to his instructions eagerly.
2. "Your first task," the master said, "is to grind limestone, ocher, and other minerals to make paint."
3. The apprentice's master was also his father.
4. Their family had painted the Pharaohs' tombs for generations.
5. "Soon," the apprentice thought, "I will get my chance to paint."
6. "Now hold this bronze reflector so its light strikes the wall," the master commanded.

Writing
— **TIP** —

Remember, the possessive adjectives *its* and *your* do not take an apostrophe, unlike the contractions *it's* and *you're*.

Writing Theme
Artists

7. "Our art is difficult when we work in this dark pyramid."
8. The apprentice held the reflector so that its surface reflected light onto the painting of the Pharaoh's wife.
9. "Her hair must be painted just so," the master mumbled.
10. "I must be sure the Pharaoh is pleased with my work."

B. PROOFREADING SKILL

Correcting Errors with Possessive Pronouns   Proofread and write the following paragraph, correcting errors in grammar, capitalization, punctuation, and spelling. Pay particular attention to the use of possessive pronouns. (10 errors)

Martha Graham was one of the founders of modern dance. She introduced new ways of using the body in dance that are now part of every dancers' technique. Traditionally, dancers had been taught to move to they're left and right or foreword and backward. Graham began encourageing her students to move up and down also. When dancers were showing saddness, she taught them to slump or even fall to the floor. Graham also beleived that dancing should involve more than just you're arms and legs the back could be very expressive. Graham helped dancers discover how to use their backs and torsos. She developed exercises for them to strengthen there backs. Graham's contributions gave modern dance much of it's character and identity.

FOR MORE PRACTICE
See page 510.

C. APPLICATION IN WRITING

A Description   Look at the picture on the right, or think of a painting, sculpture, dance, theatrical performance, musical concert, or some other work of art. Describe it in a brief paragraph. Use at least five possessive pronouns as adjectives in your description.

Thomas Hart Benton, *Rural Family Life and Law* (detail), 1936.

DEMONSTRATIVE ADJECTIVE OR DEMONSTRATIVE PRONOUN?

A **demonstrative pronoun,** such as *this, that, these,* or *those,* points out a specific person or thing. When such a word is used as a modifier, it becomes a **demonstrative adjective.**

The words *this, that, these,* and *those* can be used to modify nouns or pronouns.

This elephant is from Africa, but *that* one is from Asia.

When used as modifiers, *this, that, these,* and *those* are called **demonstrative adjectives.** They tell *which one* or *which ones* about the words they modify. When used by themselves, *this, that, these,* and *those* are called **demonstrative pronouns.**

Demonstrative Adjective	Demonstrative Pronoun
I like *this* wild animal park.	I like *this.*
Did you hear *that* coyote?	Did you hear *that?*
These animals are endangered.	*These* are endangered.

Using Demonstrative Adjectives Correctly

This, That, These,* and *Those   *This* and *that* modify singular nouns. *These* and *those* modify plural nouns.

> *this* owl   *these* owls   *that* bear   *those* bears

Kind* and *Sort   The demonstrative adjectives *this* and *that* may be paired with the singular nouns *kind* and *sort.* The demonstrative adjectives *these* and *those* may be paired with the plural nouns *kinds* and *sorts.*

> *this* kind   *these* sorts   *that* sort   *those* kinds

Never use *there* or *here* with demonstrative adjectives.

Incorrect   I saw that there goat.
Correct   I saw *that* goat.

Writing
— TIP —

Use *this* or *these* to refer to things that are close by. Use *that* or *those* to refer to things that are farther away.

Practice Your Skills

A. CONCEPT CHECK

Demonstrative Adjectives and Demonstrative Pronouns

For each of the following sentences, write *Demonstrative Adjective* or *Demonstrative Pronoun* as you label each one.

1. A hundred years ago, this country declared war on wolves.
2. To ranchers at the time, these were killers who attacked livestock.
3. The government hired trappers to destroy these wolves.
4. The trappers even killed those in Yellowstone National Park.
5. Those government hunters were very effective.
6. By the 1950s, this effort had eliminated wolf packs in the Rockies.
7. Later, people began to realize this had been a bad idea, and the government made the killing of wolves illegal.
8. Some people wanted these animals reintroduced into the wild.
9. Others did not want that.
10. Nevertheless, in the 1980s, wolves began coming south out of Canada and living again in those places where they had roamed a century ago.

Gray wolf howling.

B. PROOFREADING SKILL

Correcting Demonstrative Adjectives and Demonstrative Pronouns

Proofread and write the following paragraph, correcting errors in grammar, capitalization, punctuation, and spelling. Pay special attention to the use of demonstrative adjectives and demonstrative pronouns. (10 errors)

"This here is a long-nosed bat," said the naturalist. "Out here in the dessert, these bats help Cactuses survive." He pointed to too kind of cactuses. "These kind, the organ-pipe cactus and the saguaro, have flowers that open at night. These bats poke their long noses into those there flowers to drink the nectar. When the bats do this, there heads get dusted with pollen. As the bats feed. They transfer pollen from this flower to that. This process helps the flower's produce fruit and seeds. Later, these bats return, eat the cactus fruit, and scatter the seeds, which will produce new cactuses."

FOR MORE PRACTICE
See page 510.

C H E C K ✓ P O I N T

MIXED REVIEW • PAGES 504–507

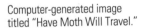

Writing Theme
Entertainment

A. In each sentence below, find one of the following and label it as: *Possessive Pronoun, Possessive Pronoun as Adjective, Demonstrative Pronoun,* or *Demonstrative Adjective.*

1. One of the most amazing advancements in sound technology of our time is the compact disc, or CD.
2. Play one of yours over and over, and it will never wear out.
3. A CD does not scratch easily, and its sound is unmatched.
4. How is this possible?
5. Such scientific breakthroughs are often the work of those electrical engineers who study sound.
6. Theirs was the discovery that the laser could be used in digital recording.
7. Manufacturers use laser beams to record a pattern of pits on their discs.
8. These patterns represent musical sounds.
9. A laser beam from the CD player reads these.
10. When your CD player is on, the laser beam strikes the disc.
11. The beam bounces off those pits on the CD.
12. Inside your CD player, a sensor reads the reflected beam.
13. This sensor changes the information into electrical signals.
14. These signals create electrical waves.
15. Your amplifier turns electrical waves into sound waves.

B. Rewrite each sentence that contains a mistake in pronoun use, correcting the error. If a sentence has no error, write *Correct.*

16. You're favorite actor killed the movie's insect monster.
17. Special effects were used in filming these kind of scene.
18. The director used a model for this here insect monster.
19. These kind of model is filmed one movement at a time.
20. That there model was shot hundreds of times for one scene.
21. It's legs were moved many times to complete one step.
22. The crew worked for hours just to see this monster walk.
23. There's was no easy task.
24. Those sort of scenes with real people were shot separately.
25. Then those two film sequences were combined to create a battle between a person and a monster.

Computer-generated image titled "Have Moth Will Travel."

A. Identifying Adjectives   For each of the following sentences, write the adjectives and the words they modify. Do not write articles.

Writing Theme
Transportation

1. Sailing ships have been used for thousands of years.
2. Some early sailing vessels were built by the Egyptians.
3. The Egyptian ships had square sails.
4. The boats were also equipped with long oars.
5. Many Egyptian boats were made of bundles of reeds.
6. The Egyptians did not travel far in the fragile reed boats.
7. They built wooden ships for traveling greater distances.
8. However, the Egyptians lacked a supply of suitable wood for building ships.
9. The nearby Phoenicians could build sturdy ships from their strong cedar trees.
10. The Phoenicians traveled and traded throughout the Mediterranean area.
11. The Greeks designed and built the first large ships that had wooden frames.
12. They developed a way to attach planks to the frame to make a seaworthy craft.
13. The Romans improved on the Greek design.
14. They built the first modern ships that could sail great distances and carry heavy cargoes.

B. Identifying Linking Verbs and Predicate Adjectives
Write each of the following sentences. Underline the subject once and the linking verb twice. Circle the predicate adjectives.

15. In the nineteenth century, clipper ships became famous.
16. Clipper ships looked graceful.
17. They were tall and slender.
18. Other ships appeared clumsy in comparison.
19. The first clipper ships were small.
20. Later they became longer.
21. At 335 feet in length, the *Great Republic* was immense.
22. The clippers also were fast.
23. *The Champion of the Seas*'s 1854 speed record appeared unbeatable.
24. At that time, steamships seemed slow next to clippers.

C. Identifying Correct Comparative and Superlative Forms
Write the correct form of the adjectives given in parentheses.

25. Airships, or dirigibles, provided the (earliest, most earliest) transatlantic passenger air service.
26. They were (most popular, popularest) during the 1920s and 1930s.
27. They were filled with gas and were (lightest, lighter) than air.
28. At first, people thought hydrogen was the (goodest, best) gas for dirigibles.
29. Then helium replaced hydrogen because helium was (more safe, safer).
30. The (most big, biggest) airships were the zeppelins.
31. Some were (longer, more long) than eight hundred feet.
32. The (most fast, fastest) zeppelins flew eighty miles per hour.

D. Identifying Possessive Pronouns and the Words They Modify   For each of the following sentences, write the possessive pronoun and the word it modifies.

33. Our modern helicopter has a very long and interesting history.
34. The Chinese wrote about its design in A.D. 320.
35. The idea may have been inspired by one of their toys, a flying top.
36. Leonardo da Vinci drew his plans for a helicopter in 1483.
37. Its wings were made of stiff cloth.
38. Early helicopters were difficult for their pilots to control.
39. Today a pilot can move his or her craft safely and easily in any direction.

E. Identifying Demonstrative Adjectives and Demonstrative Pronouns   Write each of the following sentences on your paper, deleting any unnecessary words. Not every sentence requires a change. Then underline the demonstrative adjectives once and the demonstrative pronouns twice.

40. It took years to develop these here bicycles.
41. Have you seen those old bicycles with five-foot-high wheels?
42. Can you imagine riding one of those?
43. That there kind was practical on rough, muddy roads.
44. These bikes are better suited to riding today.

Writing Theme
The Anasazi

A. Identifying Adjectives   For each of the following sentences, write the adjectives and the words they modify. Label each *Predicate Adjective*. Do not identify articles.

1. In the Southwest, ancient cities perch on sheer cliffs.
2. These old stone dwellings resemble modern apartment buildings.
3. They were built into natural caves in the cliff walls.
4. The dwellings were generally quite small, but they held one or two families.
5. A few are huge and once housed large numbers of people.
6. The rock houses were constructed eight centuries ago by the Anasazi.
7. You may be familiar with their later name, the Pueblo.
8. The Pueblo lived in the Southwest for a long time before European settlers came to this continent.
9. River valleys and mesas were also common sites for Anasazi towns.
10. The Anasazi left their cliff towns in the thirteenth century.
11. A long drought is one reason they had to leave.
12. Early ancestors of these people built village settlements.
13. The ancestors lived in pit houses during the first century.
14. These buildings were partly underground.
15. Such homes were remarkably cool in summer and comfortably warm in winter.
16. Few ruins of these dwellings remain today.
17. However, many examples of the cliff dwellings do survive.
18. They are found in various places in the Southwestern states.
19. For example, Mesa Verde in southern Colorado is truly spectacular.
20. A visit to this national park makes an interesting trip.

B. Using Comparisons Correctly   All of the following sentences contain errors in comparisons. Find the errors and write each comparison correctly.

21. The Anasazi culture was not the older of all North American cultures.
22. However, it was complexer than most.
23. The most early of the Anasazi people were nomadic hunters.
24. Until they learned to grow crops, it was more hard to get food.

25. The better known of all the skills of the early Anasazi was their basket making.
26. However, cultivating corn and beans was probably importanter.
27. It's hard to say which of those two crops was the most beneficial.
28. Irrigation made it more easier for the Anasazi to farm.
29. Their ability to store food also became more good.
30. The ancienter Anasazi did not have these advantages.
31. Their dwellings, for example, were least comfortable than they would become later.
32. The later Anasazi developed stone masonry, which was much more better than poles and mud for building houses.
33. Also, their pottery became gradually best over a period of time.
34. An even more new development was the growing of cotton.
35. Finally, they began building their great cliff houses—perhaps their splendidest achievement.

C. Using Adjectives Correctly The following sentences contain errors in the use of demonstrative adjectives or the words that accompany them. Rewrite the sentences on your paper, correcting the errors.

36. I've read all sort of historical documents about Anasazi culture.
37. In the 1500s, the Spaniards named these here people the Pueblo.
38. This here group still lives in a few Southwestern states.
39. They honor those kind of customs practiced by their ancestors.
40. Besides farming, the men do weaving and those sort of activities.
41. In fact, that there is one of their oldest crafts.
42. In this here culture, the women help in house construction and make pottery.
43. Those are the sort of skills that are in demand.
44. These here people still practice many of their ancient religious rituals.
45. This kinds of traditions have survived to the present day.

WRITING CONNECTIONS

Elaboration, Revision, and Proofreading

Revise and proofread the following draft of comparison-and-contrast writing. Use the directions that follow the draft. As you proofread the draft, look for errors in grammar, especially in the use of adjectives. Also correct errors in capitalization, punctuation, and spelling.

¹Years ago, people used to say good-bye using the words "See you later, alligator. After a while, crocodile." ²I usually say "So long." ³Ever wonder how to tell alligators and crocodiles apart? ⁴The american alligator and crocodile have similarities and differences. ⁵both of these animals are reptiles they belong to the family Crocodylidae. ⁶Both have long, narrow bodys with powerful tales used for swimming. ⁷Both have short thick legs that are used mainly for walking. ⁸Both animals lay eggs. ⁹and, unlike most reptiles, protect the eggs. ¹⁰There are also definate differences between aligators and crocodiles. ¹¹The alligator is the heaviest of the two. ¹²It's snout is also wider and less pointed. ¹³than the crocodile's. ¹⁴The crocodile is more likelier to attack other animals, however. ¹⁵Both live in marshes, swamps, and rivers.

1. Delete a sentence that doesn't belong.

2. Revise some of the sentences that begin with "both" to avoid repetition. For example, you could say "alligators and crocodiles" or "these reptiles" instead.

3. A crocodile has teeth that show when its mouth is closed, but an alligator does not. Decide where it would be most appropriate to add this fact and insert it in the comparison.

4. Move a sentence so that all the information about the similarities between alligators and crocodiles is together.

5. Divide the passage into two paragraphs and add a closing sentence.

Informative Writing: Explaining What

One way to explain something unfamiliar is to compare and contrast it with something familiar. (See Workshop 5.) When you revise comparison-and-contrast writing, check to be sure that you have given specific examples of similarities and differences. Using precise adjectives can make this type of writing detailed, accurate, and interesting to read.

You're a secret agent man
Who's after the secret plan.
How you act so they don't know you're a spy?
Normally, Normally, Normal L.Y.

Tom Lehrer

"L-Y" from TOO MANY SONGS BY TOM LEHRER

- Begin a detective story by describing a jewel thief approaching a locked vault.

- How did you solve a difficult problem that you faced? Freewrite about the process you went through.

- Write the script for one scene of a TV cooking show. Explain in detail all the steps the chef must follow so that viewers can do the same thing themselves. You may choose to show the chef preparing an actual dish, such as a taco salad, or a humorous dish, such as a mud pie.

Using Adverbs

- **What Is an Adverb?**
- **Adverbs in Comparisons**
- **Adjective or Adverb?**
- **Using Negatives**

Mysteries can be very exciting. Detectives cleverly uncover clues to find out "whodunit." They follow footprints, look for telltale signs of strange behavior, interview people, and then put all the pieces together.

Your writing, however, should not make your readers put on their detective hats. Provide the information they need to know about where, when, or how something happened by using adverbs correctly. In this handbook you will learn that adverbs are not all that mysterious.

WHAT IS AN ADVERB?

> An **adverb** modifies a verb, an adjective, or another adverb.

Suppose you were writing a letter about a graduation ceremony. You might write that the graduates marched *nervously* or *proudly*. You could say that the ceremony was held *outdoors,* or *yesterday,* or that it was *extremely* long. You would be using adverbs to describe what the ceremony was like.

Adverbs modify words by telling *how, when, where,* or *to what extent.* In this handbook you will learn to use adverbs correctly to modify verbs, adjectives, or other adverbs. As you can see from the examples given below, adverbs add specific details to make statements clear and interesting. The adverbs turn flat statements into expressive ones.

The Uses of Adverbs

Adverbs Modify Verbs

The graduates waited.
How? The graduates waited *anxiously.*
Where? The graduates waited *inside.*
When? The graduates waited *today.*

Adverbs Modify Adjectives

One speech was long.
To what extent? One speech was *extremely* long.

The ceremony was over.
To what extent? The ceremony was *nearly* over.

Adverbs Modify Other Adverbs

The audience cheered loudly.
To what extent? The audience cheered *quite* loudly.

The graduates smiled happily.
To what extent? The graduates smiled *very* happily.

Note that when adverbs modify adjectives or other adverbs they usually answer the question *to what extent?*

Practice Your Skills

A. CONCEPT CHECK

Adverbs Write the adverbs from the sentences. Next to each adverb, write the word it modifies. Tell what question the adverb answers about the word it modifies: *How? When? Where?* or *To what extent?* Some sentences may contain more than one adverb.

1. On the Chinese calendar, the celebration of the New Year is extremely important.
2. Everyone carefully prepares for weeks.
3. The festivities finally begin.
4. The faintly smoky aroma of incense greets visitors.
5. Sometimes a guest at the celebration is especially lucky.
6. Her *po pa,* or boiled dumpling, holds a surprise inside.
7. She happily believes the promise of a year of prosperity.
8. Fireworks crackle repeatedly outside.
9. A paper dragon weaves gracefully in front of a procession.
10. Men in costume soon perform the lion dance expertly.

B. APPLICATION IN LITERATURE

Using Adverbs Rewrite this description of a Mojave funeral ceremony by replacing the underlined adverbs with other adverbs. How do your words change the meaning and tone of the passage? Why do you think the author chose these particular adverbs?

[11]Suddenly the flaming mass of the cremation fire broke in the middle. . . . [12]The women began weeping bitterly again. . . . [13]And the wailing of the mourners rose to a sharp, brief crescendo and then rapidly died away. . . . [14]People gathered into little clusters or wandered slowly about, singly or in groups. [15]The great bed of coals in the fire hole still glowed fiercely. [16]Four men stood around it leaning on long-handled shovels, ready to fill the hole and carefully obliterate every evidence of its existence as soon as the coals were ashes.

Charles L. McNichols, *Crazy Weather*

C. APPLICATION IN WRITING

A Description Write a paragraph about a ceremony you have participated in. Use adverbs to make your description precise. Remember that adverbs can modify adjectives, verbs, or adverbs.

FOR MORE PRACTICE
See page 527.

The Position of Adverbs

When an adverb modifies an adjective or another adverb, it usually comes before the word it modifies—for example, *very* sad, *quite* formal, *not* likely. When an adverb modifies a verb, the adverb's position is not usually fixed. The adverb can come after the verb, at the beginning of the sentence, or just before the verb.

After the verb	The ceremony ended *suddenly.*
Beginning of the sentence	*Suddenly,* the ceremony ended.
Before the verb	The ceremony *suddenly* ended.

Sentence Diagraming   For information on diagraming sentences with adverbs, see page 678.

Practice Your Skills

A. CONCEPT CHECK

The Position of Adverbs   Write the adverbs in the following sentences. Then identify the position of each adverb by labeling it *After the verb, Beginning of the sentence,* or *Before the verb.*

1. Interestingly, all cultures have held ceremonies in honor of special occasions.
2. Historically, pioneers in the United States had many noteworthy celebrations.
3. Pioneers, for example, celebrated weddings joyously.
4. People from the surrounding area gladly flocked to a wedding.
5. Sometimes the festivities lasted for several days.
6. Normal tasks were put aside.
7. Pranks often were played on the bride and groom by their friends and relatives.
8. Typically, wedding guests kidnapped the bride or groom.
9. The victims always escaped in plenty of time for the wedding ceremony.
10. The couple enjoyed this attention thoroughly.
11. Normally, the groom's parents organized a wedding feast.
12. These feasts usually lasted the entire night.
13. People danced, sang, and ate their fill heartily.
14. A house-raising frequently was held for the newlyweds.
15. These fun celebrations generally left pioneer communities with a sense of hope for the future.

B. DRAFTING SKILL

Using Adverbs Effectively   Rewrite each sentence, adding an adverb that answers the question. Remember to vary the position of the adverbs in your sentences. Note how your choice of adverb as well as its position can affect the meaning of the sentence.

16. House-raisings were happy occasions. (To what extent?)
17. Pioneers held them for newcomers and newlyweds. (When?)
18. The whole community worked on the new house. (How?)
19. With so many workers, the job went easily. (To what extent?)
20. Some houses were built in a single day. (How?)
21. One group of people went for timber. (Where?)
22. Others built the frame of the house. (How?)
23. Some prepared and served big meals. (Where?)
24. People took breaks for games and dances. (When?)
25. Everyone helped the couple move into their home. (When?)

C H E C K ✔ P O I N T
MIXED REVIEW · PAGES 516–519

Write the adverbs in the following sentences. Next to each adverb, write the word it modifies.

Writing Theme
The Sense of Smell

1. The sense of smell is very important.
2. In fact, scientists think smell is even more important than taste.
3. People recognize certain smells quite readily.
4. For example, the smell of smoke rapidly alerts people to fire.
5. Often the smell of a favorite food can make someone really hungry.
6. The taste of some foods—chocolate, for example—is barely recognizable without its aroma.
7. Many animals rely quite heavily on their sense of smell.
8. A very frightened animal may leave a scent to warn others of danger.
9. A bloodhound's sense of smell is remarkably keen.
10. Trained hounds usually can follow a fairly old trail.

ADVERBS IN COMPARISONS

> Use the **comparative** form of an adverb when you compare two actions. Use the **superlative** form of an adverb when you compare more than two actions.

Suppose you were explaining to a friend how chilly you get during walks in wintertime. You might use sentences like these:

My ears get cold *fast*. In fact, my ears get cold *faster* than my hands. My nose gets cold *fastest* of all, though.

In the sentences above, *fast, faster,* and *fastest* are all adverbs. They are all forms of the adverb *fast*. They compare the different rates at which a person's ears, hands, and nose each get cold. Short adverbs such as *fast* often form the comparative by adding *-er*. They form the superlative by adding *-est*.

Adverb	Comparative	Superlative
close	closer	closest
fast	faster	fastest

Many adverbs end in *-ly*. Most of these adverbs form the comparative with the word *more* and the superlative with the word *most*. Remember that adverbs, like adjectives, use only one form of a comparison at a time. So you should not add both *more* and *-er* to form a comparative. Likewise, do not add both *most* and *-est* to form the superlative.

Adverb	Comparative	Superlative
slowly	more slowly	most slowly
smoothly	more smoothly	most smoothly

Some adverbs change completely to form the comparative and superlative.

Adverb	Comparative	Superlative
well	better	best
much	more	most
little	less	least

Practice Your Skills

A. CONCEPT CHECK

Comparisons with Adverbs   Write the correct modifiers given in parentheses in the following sentences.

Writing Theme
Face Facts

1. Each year, many women search for the product that will color their lips (more better, better) than before.
2. Cosmetics manufacturers have used some of the (more surprisingly, most surprisingly) strange ingredients imaginable.
3. The lipstick that women wear today colors lips (more safely, most safely) than the lipstick of the 1920s.
4. In fact, dangerous ingredients in lipstick made it one of the (more alarmingly, most alarmingly) unhealthy beauty aids of that time.
5. For one thing, lipstick spoiled (faster, fastest) than the products made today.
6. The olive oil in it became rancid (more quickly, more quicker) than the castor oil in today's lipsticks.
7. Also, the coloring agent used (more commonly, most commonly) then was made from dried and crushed insects.
8. Insects were (less, least) harmful than rancid olive oil, however.
9. Today, acids are the agents (more frequently, most frequently) used for color intensity.
10. In addition, fish scales make modern lipsticks glisten (more brightly, most brightly) than ever before.

B. DRAFTING SKILL

Using Adverbs Correctly   Complete the following sentences with the correct form of the adverb given in parentheses.

11. Toothpaste contains ingredients that are even (incredibly) strange than those in lipstick.
12. Bleach whitens teeth (well) than chalk, so bleach is added to toothpaste (often) than chalk.
13. Toothpaste that contains paraffin oil probably flows (smoothly) of all.
14. Also, toothpaste with detergent will foam (quickly) than toothpaste without detergent.
15. The ingredients you probably recognize (well) of all, however, are peppermint oil and other flavorings.

FOR MORE PRACTICE
See pages 527–528.

ADJECTIVE OR ADVERB?

> An **adjective** modifies a noun or pronoun. An **adverb** modifies a verb, an adjective, or another adverb.

Sometimes an adjective or adverb is misused because the speaker or writer did not recognize which part of speech was needed. You must learn to analyze carefully how a word is being used. Try the method described in the examples below:

1. Chen sings (good, well).

   Problem   Is the needed word an adjective or an adverb?

   Question Would the word answer the question *how, when, where,* or *to what extent?*

   Answer   It tells *how* Chen sings.

   Solution The word *well,* an adverb, should be used to modify the verb *sings.*

2. That song is (real, really) great.

   Problem   Is the needed word an adjective or an adverb?

   Question What would the word do?

   Answer   It would modify *great.* It would tell to what extent the song is great.

   Question What is *great?*

   Answer   The word *great* is a predicate adjective.

   Solution The word *really,* an adverb, should be used to modify the adjective *great.*

Using Adjectives and Adverbs

Since adjectives and adverbs are used in similar situations, writers sometimes confuse them. Words that follow linking verbs are the most commonly misused modifiers.

To avoid making mistakes when you use an adjective or an adverb, check to see what kind of word you want to modify. Choose an adjective to modify a noun or a pronoun. Choose an adverb to modify a verb, an adjective, or another adverb. Check to see what is being said about the word being modified. If the word tells *when, where, how,* or *to what extent,* it is an adverb. If it tells *which one, what kind,* or *how many,* it is an adjective.

Notice the reasons for the type of modifier chosen in each of the following sentences.

The child's voice sounds (*sweet,* sweetly).
    (*Sweet* is a predicate adjective modifying the noun *voice.*)
Melba plays (beautiful, *beautifully*).
    (The word *beautifully* is an adverb modifying the verb *plays.*)
The piano was (terrible, *terribly*) off-key.
    (*Terribly,* an adverb, modifies *off-key,* a predicate adjective.)
Tonight's performance seems (*bad,* badly).
    (*Bad* is a predicate adjective modifying the noun *performance.*)

Practice Your Skills

A. CONCEPT CHECK

Adjective or Adverb?   For each sentence, choose the correct modifier from those in parentheses.

1. Miles Davis (1926–1991) was a (great, greatly) jazz trumpeter and band leader.
2. He played the trumpet (powerful, powerfully) and with tremendous emotion.
3. He led many jazz bands (brilliant, brilliantly).
4. Throughout his life, Davis (enthusiastic, enthusiastically) pioneered new directions in jazz.
5. For example, during the 1940s, he was an (important, importantly) force in the development of "cool jazz."
6. He (constant, constantly) explored new kinds of harmony and musical arrangements.
7. Other famous jazz musicians imitated his style (frequent, frequently).
8. Toward the end of his life, Davis experimented with a (new, newly) type of music called fusion.
9. Fusion mixes the use of electronic instruments and the (steady, steadily) beat of rock music with improvisation and other elements of more traditional jazz.
10. Miles Davis was (sure, surely) one of the giants of jazz.

B. PROOFREADING SKILL

Using Modifiers Correctly   Proofread the following paragraph. Then rewrite it correctly. Watch for adjectives or adverbs that are used incorrectly. Also look for other errors in grammar, as well as errors in capitalization, punctuation, and spelling. (12 errors)

The voice of Ella Fitzgerald is one of the true remarkible jazz instruments of all time. She sang good even as a child, and year's of experience have made her voice an incredibly versatile instrument. One evening in 1960, a German audience learned about her remarkable talent. She was part through the song "Mack the Knife" when, all of a sudden, she forget the words of the familiar song For most singers. This would have been a disastor. Fitzgerald, though, knew that English lyrics were not real important to her German listeners. She simply made up words as she went along, letting the sounds of her amazing beautiful voice carry the meaning. It was one of the greater moments in jazz.

FOR MORE PRACTICE
See page 528.

CHECK ✔ POINT
MIXED REVIEW • PAGES 520–524

Write the following sentences correctly. If a sentence has no error, write *Correct*.

1. Marianne Moore (1887–1972), winner of the Pulitzer Prize and other distinguished awards, is regarded more high than many other poets of the twentieth century.
2. As a child, she was extremely shy.
3. She lived quiet with her mother for most of her life.
4. However, her friends were some of the most famous writers and artists in the United States.
5. Her poems sometimes look quite simply.
6. The ideas she expressed were often daring, however.
7. She wrote more profounder about the meaning of beauty, nature, and human feelings than many other poets.
8. Late in life, Moore was near as famous for her unique personality as she was for her poetry.
9. She most oftener wore an old, three-cornered hat.
10. Perhaps she was known most wide, though, for her love of the Brooklyn Dodgers baseball team.

USING NEGATIVES

Never use a **double negative** when you write or speak.

A negative is a word that has the meaning "no." The most common negative words are *no, none, not, nothing,* and *never.*

If two of these words are used in a sentence when only one is needed, the result is a **double negative.**

Mistakes in using double negatives occur most often when one of the negatives is a contraction. *Can't, don't, doesn't, won't, wouldn't, isn't,* and *aren't* are negatives. These words contain the shortened form of *not: n't.* When this kind of contraction is used in a sentence, there is no need for another "no."

Incorrect	Engineers won't never build a longer bridge.
Correct	Engineers won't ever build a longer bridge.
Incorrect	Workers couldn't find nothing to support the bridge.
Correct	Workers couldn't find anything to support the bridge.

Practice Your Skills

CONCEPT CHECK

Negatives   Write the word in parentheses that correctly completes each sentence.

Writing Theme
Unique Bridges

1. Scientists have never found (a, no) bridge older than one across the Kizilcullu River in Izmir, Turkey.
2. This ancient bridge can't be (any, no) less than 2,800 years old.
3. Nobody has built (a, no) taller bridge than the Royal Gorge.
4. This Colorado bridge (has, hasn't) ever been equaled in height.
5. For years, there wasn't (any, no) bridge that rivaled the Humber, in England, for length.
6. During that time, its 4,600-foot span wasn't exceeded by (any other, no other) bridge.
7. Bridgemakers, though, can't (ever, never) seem to rest.
8. No one expected (anything, nothing) like the Akashi-Kaikyo bridge in Japan.
9. Its main span has (a, no) break for almost a mile.
10. We may not create (something, nothing) this long again.

FOR MORE PRACTICE
See page 528.

A. Rewrite each sentence that contains a double negative. If a sentence has no error, write *Correct*.

1. For centuries, there wasn't no bird more abundant in North America than the passenger pigeon.
2. This attractive, dovelike bird didn't make no cooing noises like other pigeons.
3. No, it clucked and crowed, something like a rooster.
4. Once there wasn't no more common sight in the sky than flocks of passenger pigeons flying by.
5. It never took less than two days for all the birds in one particular flock to fly by.
6. In flight, that flock wasn't no less than 250 miles long.
7. Another flock didn't have no fewer than 2 billion birds!
8. For pioneers, the birds weren't nothing less than a miracle.
9. When there were no crops or supplies, there always was pigeon to eat.
10. For years, the birds weren't never far from dinner tables in the United States.

B. Correct the errors in the modifiers in these sentences. If a sentence has no errors, write *Correct*.

11. The passenger pigeon met an amazing fate.
12. It disappeared from earth more quick than most other creatures.
13. In the 1800s, it was the most common of all birds on the North American continent.
14. In less than a century, however, none were left nowhere.
15. With so many birds in the wild, the pigeons were caught quick by hunters.
16. The birds did not fear people, so they did not fly away from hunters and could be killed easy.
17. Millions of the lovely birds were cruel massacred, and the forests where the birds lived were cut down and used for firewood.
18. The giant flocks dwindled gradual to nothing.
19. By the 1880s, there weren't no more large flocks left in the United States.
20. By 1907 there wasn't no passenger pigeon left in the wild.

GRAMMAR
H A N D B O O K
42

Writing Theme
Unusual Creatures

A. Identifying Adverbs Write the adverbs from the following sentences. Next to each adverb write the word it modifies.

1. Flying fish are truly remarkable.
2. These amazing creatures certainly defy gravity.
3. Flying fish live mainly in the warm waters near the equator.
4. These astonishingly agile fish take to the air fairly regularly.
5. You can recognize them quite easily by their outstretched fins.
6. These fins are widely spaced along the fish's body and keep the fish up in the air.
7. Actually, the fish's flights serve as a form of self-defense.
8. This technique has worked quite efficiently for thousands of years.
9. At a sign of danger, a fish beats its tail fin very rapidly.
10. Quickly the fish builds its speed.
11. Then the fish launches itself from the water.
12. With its fins fully extended, the fish turns into an airborne glider.
13. With these "wings" some fish can fly aloft for a quarter of a mile.
14. Some fish leap extremely high.
15. Gradually, they lose speed and return gracefully to the sea.

B. Adverbs in Comparisons For the following sentences, write the correct modifiers from those given in parentheses.

16. Sea horses are (extreme, extremely) interesting marine animals.
17. Many people enjoy raising sea horses (more, most) than any other fish.
18. Sea horses are shaped (more unusually, most unusually) than any other fish.
19. Their snouts extend (farther, farthest) than the snouts of many other fish.
20. However, their snouts resemble those of real horses (closer, more closely) than they resemble the snouts of other fish.
21. Sea horses can fit in your hand (more easily, most easily) than a tennis ball can.
22. The pointy knobs on their bodies protect sea horses (more effectively, most effectively) than smooth skin.
23. A stab from these knobs can sting (more painfully, most painfully) than a paper cut.

24. Sea horses live (more comfortably, most comfortably) at depths of less than 150 feet.

25. They swim (quickest, more quickly) than many other small fish.

C. Choosing the Correct Modifier   Write the correct modifiers from those given in parentheses.

26. Sharks are generally taken (serious, seriously) everywhere.

27. Only (occasional, occasionally), though, have sharks been known to attack people.

28. Still, people should be (careful, carefully) around sharks.

29. The shark's strength alone makes it (true, truly) remarkable.

30. Most sharks also are (huge, hugely) compared with other fish.

31. Despite their size, they are extremely (graceful, gracefully).

32. Few creatures look as (dangerous, dangerously) as sharks.

33. As you might expect, a shark (rare, rarely) meets an enemy.

34. Their only (natural, naturally) enemies are other sharks.

35. A shark's sharp teeth are arranged (tight, tightly) together.

36. Another set of teeth lies (convenient, conveniently) behind them.

37. If a tooth from the first row breaks, a tooth from the other set (eventual, eventually) moves into its place.

38. Sharks have (extraordinarily, extraordinary) keen senses.

39. They can smell things (extreme, extremely) far away.

40. They also can hear the sound of a fish moving (rapid, rapidly) or a swimmer splashing at a distance of one thousand yards.

D. Using Negatives   Rewrite the following sentences, correcting the errors in the use of negatives.

41. Nobody has seen nothing else like the archerfish.

42. An archerfish's prey isn't never safe, even on land.

43. This fish doesn't make no leaps from the water for its prey.

44. Instead, it sneaks up underwater not making no sound at all.

45. Then it shoots a stream of water that no insect can't dodge.

46. The insect can't do nothing but fall into the water.

47. The archerfish doesn't waste no time eating its meal.

48. Amazingly, the archerfish doesn't miss none of its "shots."

49. It doesn't do this without no practice, though.

50. It isn't until an archerfish is older and experienced that it doesn't miss no shots.

GRAMMAR
H A N D B O O K
42

Writing Theme
Early Movies

A. Adverbs in Comparisons Write the form of the word in parentheses that correctly completes each sentence.

1. For many people, the (fantastically) creative movie star of all time was Charlie Chaplin.
2. Chaplin realized the possibilities of film (soon) than many other actors did.
3. He created and acted in some of the (touchingly) funny movies ever.
4. Fans waited (impatiently) for a new Chaplin film than for a film with any other star.
5. His career lasted (long) than almost any other in the movies.
6. Chaplin had to work (hard) for his success than other actors.
7. He was born in England, in 1889, in one of the (desperately) poor sections of London.
8. Through acting, however, he was able to escape the terrible living conditions (easily) than other neighborhood children.
9. By age sixteen, he was performing on the stage (successfully) than actors twice as old.
10. Chaplin came to the United States and became (good) than anyone else at film comedy.
11. He created a character called the Tramp, who became recognized (widely) than any other film character in the world.
12. In his tattered coat and baggy pants, the Tramp dressed (shabbily) than anyone else in the movies.
13. With his cane and hat, though, this character walked (confidently) than a king.
14. Problems and misunderstandings were thrown at him (often) than could be imagined.
15. Still, Charlie's Tramp worked his way into the hearts of moviegoers (thoroughly) than any other film character.

B. Using Modifiers Correctly Write the modifiers that correctly complete the following sentences. Label each modifier *Adverb* or *Adjective*. Write the word each one modifies.

16. The movie industry did not have a (complete, completely) honorable beginning.
17. The first movies were not shown in (real, really) theaters.
18. Early movies (actual, actually) were shown in arcades, similar to today's video game arcades.

Using Adverbs   **529**

19. Audiences were (most, mostly) rough and noisy, and often disreputable too.
20. The films themselves (usual, usually) were not respectable either.
21. Censors often (careful, carefully) inked out portions of the films.
22. Worst of all, films did not (true, truly) tell a story.
23. They (simple, simply) showed a series of individual scenes.
24. For these reasons, early movies did not have a (good, well) reputation.
25. By 1900, movies (final, finally) were being projected onto a large screen.
26. Still, they (general, generally) were shown only as part of variety shows on the vaudeville stage.
27. This situation changed (quick, quickly) when movies began to tell stories.
28. In 1903, people in the United States were amazed by the (sudden, suddenly) appearance of the movie *Life of an American Fireman*.
29. Audiences (immediate, immediately) responded to the story told by this short film.
30. That was the beginning of the (rapid, rapidly) rise of modern motion pictures.

C. Using Negatives Correctly   Rewrite the following sentences, correcting any errors in the use of negatives. If a sentence has no errors, write *Correct*.

31. Haven't you ever seen none of the earliest movies?
32. In those silent films, the actors couldn't say nothing at all.
33. Filmmakers couldn't use any sounds at all to tell the story.
34. Audiences couldn't do nothing but read the actors' lips or the captions.
35. The action usually wasn't hard to understand, though.
36. Therefore, people didn't have no trouble figuring out what was happening even when captions were very short.
37. Some moviegoers, in fact, didn't like no other type of entertainment.
38. These people wouldn't have nothing to do with the newfangled "talking pictures" of the late 1920s.
39. For most people, though, there wasn't nothing like the "talkies."
40. Movies wouldn't never be the same again.

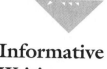

Revise the following draft of part of a report, using the directions given on this page. Then proofread for errors in grammar, capitalization, punctuation, and spelling. Pay particular attention to the use of adverbs.

¹Before the worlds largest ocean liner ever sailed. ²It was advertised as unsinkable. ³People celebrated as it triumphant pulled away from it's port in Southampton, England on April 10, 1912 it was the first and last voyage of the <u>Titanic.</u> ⁴less than three hours after hitting the iceberg, fifteen hundred passengers and crew members found themselves in the icy northern Atlantic ocean. ⁵The water in the south Pacific Ocean is usually much warmer. ⁶On the night of April 14, disaster struck. ⁷The Ship hit an iceburg and sank more quicker than anyone would have believed. ⁸The <u>titanic</u> did have lifeboats, but not near enough for everyone. ⁹A ship that was nearby did not respond to the <u>Titanic</u>'s call for help. ¹⁰Following this accident, an International convention was held in london, England. ¹¹The convention acted quick to set up new rules for sea travel. ¹²All ships would be required to maintain radio operatons continuously. ¹³Each ship would be equipped with enough lifeboats to hold everyone on board. ¹⁴And lifeboat drills would be conducted regular. ¹⁵A special patrol was also organized too warn ships of icebergs.

1. In sentence 2, add an adverb to emphasize how unsinkable the ship was.

2. Delete the sentence that doesn't belong.

3. Move sentence 4 to a more logical position.

4. Add the following clause to sentence 9 to explain why the ship did not respond: "because its radio operator was off duty."

5. Divide the passage into two paragraphs.

Informative Writing: Reports

Writing a report involves gathering information and presenting it in a clear and organized way. (See Workshop 8.) When you revise a report, make sure you have included all the facts your readers need to know in order to understand your topic. Look for ways you can use adverbs to add precision to your writing.

Skills

Directions   One or more of the underlined sections in the following sentences may contain an error in grammar, usage, punctuation, spelling, or capitalization. Write the letter of each incorrect section; then rewrite the item correctly. If there is no error in an item, write *E*.

Example   Most matter expands as it gets <u>hotter</u> and contracts as it
                                                        A
gets <u>colder, however,</u> when water is <u>froze,</u> it grows <u>larger.</u>   <u>No error</u>
           B   **C**   **D**   **E**

Answer   B—colder; however C—frozen

---

1. Because a letter of the alphabet that is <u>spoke</u> over a shortwave <u>radio</u> may be hard
                                                      A   **B**
   to hear <u>correctly,</u> a word is often used to stand for <u>it.</u> "Charlie" stands for the
              C   **D**
   letter "C."   <u>No error</u>
                      E

2. <u>These kind</u> of mushrooms <u>aren't never</u> safe to eat. <u>They're</u> <u>poisonous!</u>   <u>No error</u>
      A   **B**   **C**   **D**   **E**

3. The next time <u>your</u> <u>setting</u> in the gym watching basketball, remember that <u>it's</u>
                    A   **B**   **C**
   the only international game that was invented in the <u>United States.</u>   <u>No error</u>
                                                              D   **E**

4. When Gulliver landed on the <u>island, he</u> <u>met</u> some <u>real</u> small people called
                                    A   **B**   **C**
   <u>Lilliputians.</u>   <u>No error</u>
        D   **E**

5. Though the stegosaurus was one of the <u>larger</u> dinosaurs of its time—more than
                                              A
   $6\frac{1}{2}$ tons—this great <u>creature's</u> brain <u>weighed</u> only $2\frac{1}{2}$ <u>ounces.</u>   <u>No error</u>
                       B   **C**   **D**   **E**

6. A palindrome is a group of <u>words</u> that reads the same whether <u>it's</u> <u>wrote</u> back-
                                  A   **B** **C**
   wards or <u>forwards. One</u> example is "Madam, I'm Adam."   <u>No error</u>
               D   **E**

7. Both Spain and California get hot. If <u>you're</u> looking for record heat, <u>your</u>
                                            A   **B**
   chances are <u>best</u> in California, where the thermometer once <u>risen</u> to 136 degrees
                   C   **D**
   Fahrenheit.   <u>No error</u>
                     E

8. Without doubt <u>bananas</u> are <u>more tastier</u> when <u>they</u> <u>get</u> ripe after being picked.
                A   B   C D
<u>No error</u>
   E

9. In 1630 Native Americans <u>brung</u> the <u>English</u> <u>colonists</u> a <u>dearskin</u> bag filled with
                       A   B   C   D
popped popcorn.   <u>No error</u>
                E

10. The bite of the Gila monster <u>is</u> dangerous, the <u>rattlesnake's</u> bite is <u>worst,</u> and
                           A   B   C
the coral <u>snake's</u> bite is the most dangerous of all.   <u>No error</u>
        D   E

11. Charlotte <u>Brontë's</u> name is now famous all over the world, but <u>she</u> and her <u>sister</u>
         A   B   C
Emily first published <u>their</u> books under the pen names Currer and Ellis Bell.
                    D
<u>No error</u>
   E

12. Once <u>their</u> <u>past</u> the larva stage, moths don't eat <u>wool. An</u> adult moth could
        A   B   C
<u>lay</u> around in your sweaters all day without ever getting an urge to snack.
 D
<u>No error</u>
   E

13. Alice didn't feel <u>badly</u> after she <u>drank</u> the potion; <u>she</u> just <u>growed</u> smaller and
                A   B   C   D
smaller.   <u>No error</u>
        E

14. People swim much <u>slower</u> than <u>they</u> run. The <u>fastest</u> runners do one hundred
                  A   B   C
meters in about ten seconds, and <u>swimmers</u> complete that distance in about a
                                D
minute.   <u>No error</u>
       E

15. Always approach a horse from <u>its</u> left and speak to <u>it</u> as you <u>approach, if</u> you
                        A   B   C
startle the <u>horse, it</u> may kick you.   <u>No error</u>
         D   E

HOW ELECTRICITY WORKS

At the electrical company, fuel oil is burned to set fire to a generator, which gives off electrical energy in the form of sparks, which are put into wires and sent to your home, where the electricity waits in the wall until you turn on your toaster, at which point it rushes through the wire and into the English muffin and from there into your stomach, where it remains until a cold, dry day when you are walking down a hall scuffing your feet on a carpet and you go to open a door, causing the electricity to leap into the doorknob, where it remains forever. . . .

Dave Barry

DAVE BARRY'S HOMES AND OTHER BLACK HOLES

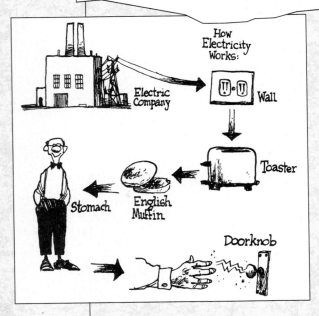

- What do you do particularly well? Swim underwater? Build model airplanes? Sew? Write a short passage explaining how you perform this skill.

- When in history would you like to have been alive? Freewrite about an experience you might have had during that time.

- Imagine that you are an inanimate object—your living-room sofa, a pair of gym shoes, or a basketball, for example. Jot down some ideas for a story told by that object.

Using Prepositions, Conjunctions, and Interjections

- **Prepositions**

- **Prepositional Phrases**

- **Pronouns as Objects of Prepositions**

- **Using Prepositional Phrases**

- **Conjunctions and Interjections**

You can't describe how anything happens or how one thing is connected to another without using prepositions and conjunctions. Like the power lines that link communications and the arrows in the cartoon shown, these words link one thought to another until the light bulb goes on—you get the joke or understand the idea.

In this handbook you will learn how to use prepositions, conjunctions, and interjections effectively in your writing.

PREPOSITIONS

> A **preposition** is a word that relates its object to some other word in the sentence. The noun or pronoun following the preposition is called the **object of the preposition.**

When you write or speak, you use certain words to show relationships between ideas. These words are called **prepositions** and **conjunctions.**

> The truck raced *down* the street. It reached the burning store *and* stopped. Firefighters leapt *from* the truck *and* rushed *to* the building.

In the paragraph above, the prepositions *down, from,* and *to* show the relationship between *raced* and *street,* between *leapt* and *truck,* and between *rushed* and *building.* The conjunction *and* also shows relationships. You will study conjunctions later in this handbook.

The word *preposition* has two parts: *pre,* meaning "before," and *position.* A **preposition** is a word that is positioned before its object and shows the relationship between that object and another word in the sentence. The noun or pronoun following a preposition is the **object of the preposition.**

> *up* the ladder (*up* is the preposition; *ladder* is its object)
> *from* the hoses (*from* is the preposition; *hoses* is its object)

Remember that the job of a preposition is to tie its object to another word in the sentence. Usually this other word appears just before the preposition.

> Firefighters scrambled *up* the ladder.
> Water *from* the hoses put the fire out.

In the first example above, *ladder* is connected with *scrambled* by the preposition *up.* In the second example, *hoses* is connected to *Water* by the preposition *from.* Choose prepositions that express relationships between words as precisely as possible.

Here are some words that are often used as prepositions.

Words Often Used as Prepositions

about	below	from	past
above	beneath	in	through
across	beside	inside	to
after	between	into	toward
against	beyond	near	under
along	but (except)	of	underneath
among	by	off	until
around	down	on	up
as	during	out	with
before	except	outside	within
behind	for	over	without

Preposition or Adverb?

You have seen that you often cannot tell what part of speech a word is until you see how the word is used in a sentence. A number of words in the list above can be used not only as prepositions but also as adverbs. When these words are used as adverbs, however, they do not have objects.

Two firefighters climbed
down. (adverb)
Two firefighters climbed
down the ladder.
(preposition)

When you have a question about whether a word is an adverb or a preposition, think about how the word is used. If it has an object and shows the relationship of one word to another in the sentence, it is probably a preposition. If it is used alone, it is probably an adverb.

Using Prepositions,
Conjunctions, and
Interjections   **537**

Practice Your Skills

A. CONCEPT CHECK

Prepositions   On your paper, write the prepositions in each of the following sentences.

1. The first fire departments were started in ancient Rome.
2. The Emperor Augustus formed fire patrols for Rome about two thousand years ago.
3. Many centuries later, colonists established similar patrols in the United States.
4. During the 1650s, citizens organized a fire watch for New Amsterdam (later renamed New York).
5. Fire patrols walked the city's streets at night.
6. Loud wooden rattles warned citizens about a fire.
7. Volunteers quickly raced to the scene with buckets of water.
8. They threw bucketload after bucketload onto the blaze.
9. New Amsterdam's fire patrols saved many people and buildings from destruction.
10. Other communities soon followed New Amsterdam's example with fire companies of their own.

B. CONCEPT CHECK

Recognizing Prepositions   On your paper, label the italicized words in the following sentences as *Preposition* or *Adverb*.

11. A vehicle pulls *out* and the driver turns the siren and flashing lights *on*.
12. Teams of Emergency Medical Technician (EMT) paramedics are a familiar sight *in* many communities.
13. Countless accident and heart attack victims owe their lives *to* these dedicated people.
14. EMT paramedics get their training *in* colleges and hospitals.
15. Treatment *of* trauma and shock becomes instantaneous.
16. Today's ambulances have a wealth of high-tech gear *inside*.
17. For example, computerized equipment *inside* the ambulance gives the paramedics a head start in treating people.
18. Information about a patient is radioed *ahead* to a hospital.
19. Such information helps the medical staff at the hospital when they take *over* later.
20. All this makes EMT paramedics a community's first line of defense *against* accidents and emergencies.

FOR MORE PRACTICE
See page 549.

PREPOSITIONAL PHRASES

> A **prepositional phrase** is a group of words that begins with a preposition and ends with its object.

The group of words that includes a preposition and its object is called a **prepositional phrase.** Words that modify the object are also part of the phrase. Prepositional phrases can add precision, clarity, and details to an idea.

> Julia is typing her report *on her computer.*
> She also creates artwork *with a graphics program.*

The prepositional phrases in the sentences above are *on her computer* and *with a graphics program.* In the first sentence, the preposition is *on,* the object is *computer,* and the modifier is the pronoun *her* used as an adjective. The preposition in the second sentence is *with,* the object is *program,* and the modifiers are *a* and *graphics.*

Compound Objects

When a preposition has more than one object, the construction is called a **compound object.** Both objects are part of the prepositional phrase. These sentences contain compound objects.

> Computers have many uses *in business and industry.*
> Computers help *with daily tasks and creative activities.*

Practice Your Skills

A. CONCEPT CHECK

Prepositional Phrases   On your paper, write the prepositional phrases in each of the following sentences. Underline the objects of the prepositions.

1. At one time, auto racers had little need for computers.
2. Racers simply sped past each other toward the finish.
3. Now, however, computers play many roles in this sport.
4. Computers are used extensively during a car's design phase.

Writing
── **TIP** ──

In "Abuelo," pages 50–51, Rudolfo Anaya uses prepositional phrases to enrich his writing with important details.

Writing Theme
Computers

Using Prepositions, Conjunctions, and Interjections   **539**

5. Within seconds, car builders can determine the potential of a certain design or feature.
6. Designers can easily customize a feature for a particular kind of race.
7. Computer equipment goes to the track as well.
8. Computers provide information about speed and endurance.
9. Engine performance and handling are instantly changed in response to new conditions on the track.
10. For some drivers, it is like having a "computer co-pilot" beside them in the car.

B. REVISION SKILL

Combining Sentences with Prepositional Phrases   Rewrite the paragraph below. Use prepositional phrases to combine at least four pairs of sentences.

EXAMPLE   Jess designs dresses. She designs dresses with a CAD (Computer-Assisted Design) program.
Jess designs dresses *with a CAD (Computer-Assisted Design) program.*

11 For years Jess designed clothing the "old-fashioned" way. **12** She designed with paper and pencils. **13** Now her job has been transformed. **14** It has been transformed by a computer. **15** She can see an image of each dress taking form. **16** She can see this image on a computer screen. **17** Sleeves get longer or shorter, plain snaps turn into brass buttons, black fabric turns green. **18** All this happens through changes in data. **19** The data are inside the computer. **20** Jess's job has never been so exciting—or so much fun!

FOR MORE PRACTICE
See page 549.

PRONOUNS AS OBJECTS
OF PREPOSITIONS

> When a pronoun is used as the object of a preposition, its **object** form must be used.

The object of a preposition is often a noun, but sometimes it is a pronoun. In that instance, the object form of the pronoun is used. The object forms are *me, us, you, her, him, it, them,* and *whom.*

> The trip was a thrill for *me.*   They called to *her.*

When a preposition has only one pronoun as its object, there is seldom a problem. When a preposition has a compound object, however, it may be difficult to tell which form of the pronoun to use.

Simple Object   Sam rode near *me.*
Compound Object   Josh rode near *Karen and me.*

To make sure you use the correct pronoun in a compound object, first say the pronoun alone after the preposition.

> The guide waited for Josh and (I, me).
> The guide waited for *me.*
> The guide waited for Josh and *me.*

Who and Whom

Remember that the word *whom* is the object form of the interrogative pronoun. *Who* is the subject form.

> *Who* has the camera?   To *whom* did you give the film?

Between and Among

People often use *between* and *among* incorrectly. You usually use *between* when the object of the preposition refers to two people or things. Use *among* when speaking of three or more.

> Chores were divided *between* Sam and me. (two people)
> We divided the packs *among* the five of us. (more than two)

Using Prepositions,
Conjunctions, and
Interjections   **541**

A. CONCEPT CHECK

Prepositions and Pronouns   For each sentence, write the correct word from the pair given in parentheses.

1. Yellowstone Park was unbelievable for Karen and (I, me).
2. Josh's dad had reserved a campsite for Josh and (we, us).
3. We divided the camping supplies (between, among) all of us.
4. Soon our horseback tour with Josh and (they, them) began.
5. Karen and Josh rode ahead with Sam and (I, me) behind.
6. Just beyond Sam and (she, her) was Yellowstone Lake.
7. Josh stood on the shore near Karen and (we, us).
8. Beyond Sam and (he, him) was an island dotted with beautiful trumpeter swans.
9. With the mountains, the lake, and creatures like (they, them) in the distance, it was a magnificent sight.
10. "(Who, Whom) do I write to about coming back next year?" asked Josh.

B. PROOFREADING SKILL

Using the Correct Pronoun Forms   Proofread the following paragraph. Then rewrite the paragraph, correcting all errors in grammar, capitalization, punctuation, and spelling. Pay special attention to the correct use of pronoun forms. (15 errors)

A horseback trip thru Yellowstone National Park can be an amazing experience. For my friend Karen and I, it was a chance to see some remarkable animals in thier own surroundings. It was also a chance for healthy exercise. Among Karen and me, we must have seen a hundred bison and several elk. Caught glimpses of moose, brown bears, coyotes, and bighorn sheep to. Our visits to the parks famous thermal pools and geysers were a special thrill the most spectaculer of these, of course, was Old Faithful. Theres no one for who that giant Geyser is not a memorable sight. The trip was the first of it's kind for Karen and I. We hope it won't be the last

C. APPLICATION IN WRITING

Look at the pictures in the margin. Write a brief paragraph of at least five sentences to describe what is happening in the pictures. Include at least three prepositional phrases in your paragraph.

FOR MORE PRACTICE
See page 550.

USING PREPOSITIONAL PHRASES

> A prepositional phrase, like an adjective or an adverb, modifies a word in the sentence.

Prepositional phrases do the same kind of work in sentences that adjectives and adverbs do. A prepositional phrase that modifies a noun or pronoun is an **adjective phrase.**

The squirrel needed a nest *of its own.*

A prepositional phrase that modifies a verb is an **adverb phrase.**

The squirrel climbed *from the branch.*

Beginning Sentences with Prepositional Phrases

Sometimes, for the sake of emphasis or variety, you may want to begin a sentence with a prepositional phrase.

The squirrel climbed the tree *in a flash.*
In a flash, the squirrel climbed the tree.

For example, if many of your sentences start with the subject, you may want to change some of them to add interest.

Placing Prepositional Phrases Correctly

Some prepositional phrases can be moved without changing the meaning of a sentence. Sometimes, however, the position of a prepositional phrase makes a great deal of difference.

Unclear   The baby watched the squirrel with a quizzical look.
Clear   With a quizzical look, the baby watched the squirrel.

The first example sentence above is unclear because the adjective phrase "with a quizzical look" seems to modify *squirrel.* The second sentence brings the phrase closer to *baby,* the word it modifies.

Sentence Diagraming   For information on diagraming sentences with prepositional phrases, see page 679.

Writing TIP

Use prepositional phrases to add detail and precision to your writing.

Practice Your Skills

A. APPLICATION IN LITERATURE

Adjective Phrases and Adverb Phrases Notice how the prepositional phrases add detail and precision to the following descriptive passage from literature. On your paper, write the prepositional phrases from this passage. Write the word modified beside each phrase. Then label each prepositional phrase *Adjective Phrase* or *Adverb Phrase*. If a sentence has no prepositional phrase, write *None*.

¹ It was the time of day when all furried things come to life.
² A big swamp rabbit hopped . . . on the trail, sat on his haunches, stared at me, and then scampered away. ³ A mother gray squirrel ran out on the limb of a burr oak tree. ⁴ She barked a warning to the four furry balls behind her. ⁵ They melted from sight in the thick green. ⁶ A silent gray shadow drifted down from the top of a tall sycamore. ⁷ There was a squeal and a beating of wings. ⁸ I heard the tinkle of a bell in the distance ahead. ⁹ I knew it was Daisy, our milk cow. . . .

Wilson Rawls, *Where the Red Fern Grows*

B. PROOFREADING SKILL

Using Prepositional Phrases Proofread the following paragraph. Then rewrite the paragraph, correcting all errors in grammar, capitalization, punctuation, and spelling. Make sure that prepositional phrases are positioned close to the words they modify. (10 errors)

The hummingbird is among the smallest birds in the world. One species is no larger than a Bumblebee. The hummingbird is not like other birds. its wings attach to its body only at the shoulders This tiny creature can fly up and down and backwards. Like a helicopter. With rapidly beating wings watch as it hovers above a flower. It sucks the nectar from the flower with it's pointed bill. Like all birds, the hummingbird burns many calories and must eat a tremendous amount. The hungry bird flys from flower to flower and eats rapidly in a straight path. It doesn't slow down as it approaches the flower instead, it just slams on the breaks like a car at a stop sign. This tiny creature is truly amazing to watch.

FOR MORE PRACTICE
See page 550.

CHECK ✔ POINT
MIXED REVIEW · PAGES 536–544

Some of the following sentences contain one or more errors, such as misplaced prepositional phrases, errors in the use of *between* and *among* and *who* and *whom,* and errors in pronoun case. Write the sentences correctly. If a sentence does not contain an error, write *Correct.*

1. The sight of animals in flight always amazes people.
2. However, anyone in the small mammals section of a zoo can observe several such creatures.
3. One flying mammal of Southeast Asia is the flying lemur.
4. A lemur put on quite a show for my friend and I in the primate section of the zoo.
5. A baby all during a "flight" hung from its mother's stomach.
6. Then they divided some fruit among the two of them.
7. The father lemur then "flew" over to chatter at the baby ~~and she.~~
8. Is there anyone for who such a show is not a delight?
9. Surprisingly, the "flying fox" of the Far East is not a fox at all.
10. Just among you and I, it really is a bat.

Writing Theme
Flying Squirrels

CONJUNCTIONS AND INTERJECTIONS

> A **conjunction** is a word that connects words or groups of words.
>
> An **interjection** is a word or short group of words used to express feeling.

Conjunctions and interjections are useful parts of speech. Conjunctions move a sentence along and can be used to combine sentences or sentence parts. Interjections add excitement, realism, emphasis, and a sharp, quick rhythm to your writing.

Coordinating Conjunctions

What is missing in these sentences?

People have enjoyed winter _____ skiing for many years.
Skiing is not easy, _____ most people can master it.
Today, a ski slope can have natural _____ artificial snow.

The missing words—*and, but,* and *or*—are coordinating conjunctions. **Coordinating conjunctions** join words or groups of words that are of equal importance. Most words or groups of words joined this way are called **compound constructions.** The sentences below use coordinating conjunctions.

Patience and humor help beginners through the first lessons.
   (*And* connects *patience* and *humor,* creating a compound subject of the verb *help.*)
Beginners expect a fall or two during their first runs.
   (*Or* connects *fall* and *two,* making them a compound object of the verb *expect.*)

Conjunctions also connect other parts of the sentence, including phrases. Conjunctions can even connect sentences.

Ski jumpers speed down a steep slope, *and* then they make a breathtaking leap into space.
   (*And* connects two sentences.)

Interjections

Read the two sentences below. Each uses an interjection.

Ouch! I fell!   Oh, I'm not afraid.

The expressions *ouch* and *oh* are interjections. An interjection is a word or group of words that expresses feeling. If an interjection expresses strong emotion, it is punctuated with an exclamation mark. An interjection that expresses only mild emotion is punctuated with a comma.

Practice Your Skills

A. CONCEPT CHECK

Conjunctions and Interjections   Write the conjunctions and interjections in the following sentences. Underline each interjection.

Writing Theme
Skiing

1. Most people do not know it, but there are several kinds of snow.
2. People who ski prefer "powder snow" and "corn snow."
3. Powder snow occurs in cold and dry conditions.
4. It runs through your fingers like sand or soap powder.
5. Most skiers cry "Hooray!" at the sight of fresh powder.
6. Corn snow, or "spring snow," is, well, challenging.
7. Granules of corn snow are lumpy and icy but ski-able.
8. "Porridge" or "mashed potato" snow is the worst for skiing.
9. Such wet snow is great for snowballs but not for skiing!
10. Oh, how snow clinging to boots and skis slows down a skier.

B. DRAFTING SKILL

Sentence Combining   Rewrite the following paragraph. Use coordinating conjunctions to make the writing smoother and more polished. Combine sentences 11 and 12, 15 and 16, and 18 and 19.

¹¹ Skiing began in ancient times. ¹² It was not until the twentieth century that it became a popular activity. ¹³ The first skis were made of animal bone. ¹⁴ Wood replaced bone twenty-five hundred to five thousand years ago. ¹⁵ In Scandinavia, skis were used mainly for everyday transportation. ¹⁶ They were also used in warfare. ¹⁷ During the 1800s, bindings were invented. ¹⁸ These hold a ski firmly to a boot. ¹⁹ These permit turns and downhill travel. ²⁰ Once people developed efficient turning maneuvers, skiing grew in popularity.

FOR MORE PRACTICE
See page 550.

Using Prepositions,
Conjunctions, and
Interjections

CHECK ✔ POINT

MIXED REVIEW • PAGES 546–547

A. Use coordinating conjunctions to combine each pair of sentences. Some words may be deleted.

1. The sport of diving can be fun. The sport of diving can be challenging.
2. Competition diving might seem easy. It requires skill.
3. Competition divers leap from a platform. They can also use a springboard.
4. A diver's skill is measured by the number of twists in a dive. The number of somersaults is another measure of a diver's skill.
5. In competition each dive has a set sequence of actions. Divers must follow the sequence exactly.
6. The straight position is one of the three basic positions for competitive dives. The pike is another position. The tuck is the third position.
7. In the pike position, divers bend their bodies at the hips. They keep their legs straight.
8. In the tuck position, divers draw their legs up toward their chests. They sometimes draw their legs up toward their chins.
9. Dives with twists and turns are very exciting. Such dives with twists and turns can be dangerous.
10. These difficult dives are not easy to perform. They can be learned with a great deal of practice.

B. In the following sentences, write and label each *Conjunction, Interjection,* and *Prepositional Phrase.*

11. Gymnastics is one of the oldest sports in the world.
12. Yes, it existed in ancient Egypt and China.
13. Drawings and paintings show leaps, jumps, and even somersaults over dangerous animals.
14. These activities were often part of elaborate entertainments.
15. Oh, how the Greeks changed these activities.
16. For the Greeks, gymnastics was, well, not a sport.
17. It helped soldiers build strength and fighting ability.
18. Athletes used gymnastics for personal fitness and in preparation for other sports.
19. Gymnastics never became part of the Greek Olympics.
20. The Romans used gymnastics in much the same way.

A. Identifying Prepositions
Write and identify each *Preposition* and *Adverb* in the following sentences.

1. Radio has changed and improved our lives in many ways.
2. Radio developed through the efforts of numerous people.
3. The basics of radio were discovered during the 1800s.
4. In 1895 Italian inventor Guglielmo Marconi went further.
5. Without using wires, he transmitted a signal to a point a mile away.
6. After a few years and much work, Marconi's radio could send signals across the Atlantic Ocean.
7. In a short time, scientists perfected other advances for radio technology.
8. America's Lee DeForest, for example, patented a vacuum tube.
9. This tube amplified the signals sent out by radio.
10. With this improvement, possibilities for radio were opened up; voice messages could be transmitted between distant places.
11. Edwin Armstrong, of New York, was another radio pioneer.
12. His work on radio circuits helped make radio broadcasting a reality.
13. At times, feuds erupted among the various inventors.
14. Years after, lawsuits settled most of the important cases.
15. As a result, the radio industry grew up and became an entertainment giant.

B. Identifying Prepositional Phrases
Write the prepositional phrases from the following sentences. Underline the object of each preposition.

16. The Golden Age of Radio began around 1925.
17. Soon, shows of all kinds were broadcast by dozens of radio stations around the country.
18. Millions of people gathered around their radios each day.
19. In particular, young people especially loved certain serial programs.
20. *The Lone Ranger* carried them back to the Old West.
21. *Superman* and *The Green Hornet* brought superheroes into their living rooms.
22. Science fiction also was popular among young people.
23. *Buck Rogers in the 25th Century* was a longtime favorite.
24. Teenagers enjoyed tales of tough-talking detectives too.
25. *Gangbusters* remained a top-ranked show for many years.

Using Prepositions,
Conjunctions, and
Interjections

C. Using Pronouns as Objects of Prepositions   Write the correct form of the pronouns in parentheses.

26. Restoring the antique radio was a project for Kim and (he, him).
27. Soon, though, other people were working with (they, them).
28. We did not know (who, whom) first owned this radio.
29. Work on the speaker was split among Kim, Ryan, and (I, me).
30. Between Sam and (I, me), we found ten old vacuum tubes.
31. To (who, whom) could we turn for help with the circuits?
32. Alexa brought in new wires for Sarah and (she, her).
33. With the help of Erica and (he, him), we made an antenna.
34. Alexa turned the radio on for Kim and (I, me).
35. Our newly restored radio sounded great to Kim and (we, us).

D. Using Prepositional Phrases   Write the prepositional phrases from these sentences. Label them *Adjective* or *Adverb Phrase.*

36. In 1938 an unusual program demonstrated the power of radio.
37. A regular show, *Mercury Theater of the Air,* was broadcast.
38. Suddenly, people heard news reports of terrifying events.
39. Martians had landed in a field in New Jersey.
40. News of the Martian invasion unfolded in great detail.
41. Thousands of listeners panicked and fled their homes.
42. The "invasion," though, was a dramatization by actors.
43. Announcers had explained this before the start of the show.
44. The realism of the broadcast fooled many people.
45. That broadcast, "The War of the Worlds," made radio history.

E. Finding Conjunctions and Interjections   Find and label each *Conjunction* and *Interjection* in the following sentences.

46. Many people own radios, but few people actually broadcast.
47. Amateur, or ham, radio lets people broadcast on their own.
48. Ham operators run their own transmitters and stations.
49. They can talk back and forth with people all over the world.
50. Wow! It is exciting to talk to people in faraway places.
51. Imagine, the whole world is open to you as a ham operator.
52. Ham operators need licenses, but anyone can use a CB radio.
53. No, you do not need to pass a test or have a great deal of equipment to use a CB.
54. CB radios use the citizens' band but have limited power.
55. They are handy for travelers, businesses, and even hobbyists.

A. Identifying Prepositional Phrases   Write the prepositional phrases from the following sentences. Underline each preposition once and each object of a preposition twice.

1. The first undersea divers searched for clams and fish.
2. In time, divers wanted other treasures from the sea.
3. In ancient Bismaya, divers collected mother-of-pearl for wall decorations.
4. The Greeks found many uses for divers during ancient times.
5. One of the most famous dives was made by Scyllias and his daughter.
6. Scyllias and his daughter, Cyana, cut the anchor lines of invading Persian ships.
7. Within hours the Persian fleet was adrift and lost.
8. Later, Alexander the Great included divers among his forces.
9. Divers helped Alexander conquer the island of Tyre.
10. Alexander himself witnessed their work under the water from the safety of a glass barrel.

B. Using Pronouns as Objects of Prepositions   Write the correct form of the pronouns in parentheses.

11. Akiko, an experienced diver, arranged a diving trip for Cara and (I, me).
12. Into a bag I stuffed gear for Akiko and (we, us).
13. I sat in the back of the boat with Akiko and (she, her).
14. Cara asked Mike, our instructor, to hand a snorkel to (she, her).
15. Mike is a diver about (who, whom) you may have heard.
16. When we reached the diving area, Mike gave diving masks to Akiko and (we, us).
17. From (who, whom) can I get help with my mask?
18. After we divided diving weights among Cara, Akiko, and (I, me), my friends slid over the side and into the water.
19. With caution and some concern, I slipped into the water with Mike and (they, them).
20. Cara swam toward (he, him) and some large grouper fish.
21. Akiko swam comfortably among Mike and (they, them).
22. Among Mike and (we, us), we found five sponges.
23. To (who, whom) shall we report our discoveries?
24. I got out of the water with help from Mike and (they, them).
25. On the way home, Mike traded stories with Akiko and (we, us).

Using Prepositions,
Conjunctions, and
Interjections   **551**

C. Prepositional Phrases as Modifiers   Write the prepositional phrases from the following sentences. Beside each phrase write the word it modifies. Then label each phrase *Adjective Phrase* or *Adverb Phrase*.

26. Many kinds of divers go into the sea.
27. "Free divers" use little equipment in their dives.
28. Their equipment consists of a mask, fins, and a snorkel.
29. The most famous free divers are the well-known ama divers of Japan.
30. In current times, ama divers are primarily women.
31. With no special equipment, these women make spectacularly deep dives into the sea.
32. These divers have practiced this feat for fifteen hundred years.
33. The women dive without the benefit of compressed-air tanks or goggles.
34. They dive throughout the year and in all kinds of weather.
35. The ama of long ago probably were pearl divers.
36. Today, the quest for food is their main motive.
37. At the age of eleven, the ama learn this trade.
38. They build their strength and endurance with dozens of practice dives.
39. As a result, they can stay beneath the sea for incredibly long periods of time.
40. Many ama continue their diving careers for several decades.

WRITING CONNECTIONS
Elaboration, Revision, and Proofreading

On your paper, revise this draft of a personal experience, using the directions at the bottom of the page. Proofread your revision for errors in grammar, capitalization, punctuation, and spelling. Make sure that each prepositional phrase is close to the word it modifies.

¹Although Aunt Katie is not known for her cooking ability she helped me bake Moms birthday cake. ²Unlike my Aunt, my uncle is a natural in the kitchen. ³What a mess we had on our hands! ⁴The kitchen looked like a mad scientist's experiment had blew up in it! ⁵Bowls, spoons, ingredients, and batter were everywhere. ⁶Then the real disaster struck. ⁷The cake broke when we took it out of the pan into chunks. ⁸In spite of everything, Aunt katie seemed unconcerned. ⁹She said, "we'll have birthday fondue for your mom's celebration. ¹⁰I wasn't sure this was a good idea, but we cut the chunks of cake into bite-sized pieces anyway. ¹¹We arranged the pieces. ¹²With strawberies and banana slices on a tray. ¹³We put candles on top, and then we served our creation to our guests with chocolate fondue sauce. ¹⁴Mom said, that was the most incredible desert I ever had! ¹⁵Aunt Katie had turned a disaster into a brilliant success.

1. In sentence 5, replace the word *everywhere* with several prepositional phrases describing where the mess was.

2. After sentence 7, add a sentence telling about the writer's reaction to the cake falling apart.

3. Replace the vague, overused adjective in sentence 14 with one that describes the dessert more precisely.

4. Delete the sentence that does not belong.

5. Decide if the passage can be broken into more than one paragraph and divide it if necessary.

Personal and Expressive Writing

Writing about a personal experience is one way to understand the experience better and to share it with others. (See Workshop 1.) When revising this type of writing, look for ways to include details that re-create the experience and make it interesting for your readers. Using prepositional phrases is one way to add such details.

Using Prepositions, Conjunctions, and Interjections   **553**

Sketch Book

Saturday was come, and all the summer world was bright and fresh and brimming with life. There was a song in every heart; and if the heart was young, the music issued at the lips. There was a cheer in every face and a spring in every step. The locust trees were in bloom, and the fragrance of blossoms filled the air. Cardiff Hill, beyond the village and above it, was green with vegetation; and it lay just far enough away to seem a Delectable Land, dreamy, reposeful, and inviting.

Mark Twain
from TOM SAWYER

- What special "first" do you remember? Learning how to read? Seeing a rainbow? Eating ice cream? Freewrite several sentences about the many aspects of that experience. Try combining some of your sentences to make your description flow better.

- Think up a new Saturday morning TV program. Describe how the parts of the show—characters, plot, and setting—will work together.

- Freewrite about a dream you hope to achieve. Can you combine some of the ideas to form more powerful sentences?

Using Compound and Complex Sentences

- **What Are Compound Sentences?**
- **Writing and Punctuating Compound Sentences**
- **Writing Good Compound Sentences**
- **What Are Complex Sentences?**

One person parachuting to earth is a thrilling sight. But how much more spectacular it is when jumpers join together to create a precise pattern in midair.

You can link sentences and phrases in your writing to create patterns that move and delight your readers just as a circle dance in midair delights spectators. This handbook can help you use compound and complex sentences to create those links.

> A **compound sentence** consists of two or more simple sentences joined together.

You now know that *compound* means "having two or more parts." You have worked with compound subjects, verbs, and objects.

So far, however, you have been dealing with simple sentences. A **simple sentence** is a sentence with only one subject and one predicate. Such a sentence is called simple even though both the subject and the predicate may be compound. Note the following examples of simple sentences that contain compound constructions:

Compound subject	The *emperor* and his *advisors* discussed the treaty.
Compound verb	The leader *sat* and *listened* to the members of his council.
Compound object	The people wanted better *land* and more *water*.

Now we come to a different kind of sentence, a sentence that has more than one subject and more than one predicate—the **compound sentence.** The parts of a compound sentence are joined by either a comma and a coordinating conjunction or by a semicolon (;).

> Inca emperors had absolute power, **and** no one dared displease them.
> In the Inca empire the common people were given many benefits, **but** they were treated as slaves.
> Commoners cultivated the land, **or** they worked on vast state projects.
> Some worked in the mines; others served in the army.

The main parts of each compound sentence can be written as separate sentences, as in the examples on page 557.

Writing
TIP

One good way to show a close relationship between two ideas is to put them into a compound sentence.

Inca emperors had absolute power. No one dared displease them.

In the Inca empire the common people were given many benefits. They were treated as slaves.

Commoners cultivated the land. They worked on vast state projects.

Some worked in the mines. Others served in the army.

Compound Sentence or Compound Verb?

The first sentence below is a simple sentence with a compound verb. The second sentence is a compound sentence. Notice the difference in punctuation.

A volcano erupted and destroyed the ancient civilization. (This is a simple sentence. It has only one subject. The conjunction *and* joins the two parts of the compound verb.)

A volcano erupted, and it destroyed the ancient civilization. (This is a compound sentence. It contains two simple sentences, each with a subject—*volcano, it*—and verb—*erupted, destroyed*. The two simple sentences are joined by a comma and *and* to form the compound sentence.)

Sentence Diagraming   For information on diagraming compound sentences, see page 679.

Practice Your Skills

A. CONCEPT CHECK

Simple and Compound Sentences   Write *S* for each simple sentence and *C* for each compound sentence. For each sentence, write every subject and verb.

Writing Theme
Ancient Civilizations

1. The Incas were a South American Indian people; they ruled vast stretches of South America.
2. Their empire was called the *Four Quarters of the Earth*.
3. Much Incan history has been lost, but archaeologists have found many Incan artifacts.
4. Incan workers built enormous stone buildings, and Incan artisans made beautiful gold works of art.

5. Some of these beautiful objects were discovered in tombs.
6. The Incas' stone buildings have survived earthquakes.
7. The Spaniards conquered the *Four Quarters of the Earth,* and they seized the Incas' gold.
8. In 1532, the Spaniards captured the last Incan emperor; then they demanded a huge ransom.
9. The emperor filled a seventeen-foot by twenty-two-foot room with gold.
10. The Spaniards killed the emperor and melted the gold.

B. CONCEPT CHECK

Compound Subjects or Verbs   Write *S* for each simple sentence and *C* for each compound sentence. For each sentence, write every subject and verb, and label any compound subject *(CS)* or any compound verb *(CV).*

11. Great Zimbabwe served as the capital for two South African empires, but only the ruins of the city remain.
12. *Zimbabwe* is a Bantu word; it means "stone dwelling."
13. A tower perches on a hill with more ruins in the valley.
14. Protection and observation were probably the reasons for its location.
15. The only two approaches to the fortress are narrow and were easily defended.
16. Passages through the ruins begin and end for no reason.
17. The tower and other structures were built about A.D. 1000.
18. The structures were made of great stone slabs and were assembled without any mortar.
19. Great Zimbabwe may have been built as a town, or it may have been a trading site.
20. Little is known about Great Zimbabwe; people can only guess its history.

FOR MORE PRACTICE
See page 570.

> When the parts of a compound sentence are joined by a coordinating conjunction, a **comma** precedes the conjunction. Otherwise, the parts are separated by a **semicolon.**

To make a compound sentence easier to read, you must separate its main clauses. Do this by putting either a comma and a coordinating conjunction or a semicolon between the parts of the sentence. Remember that the coordinating conjunctions are *and, but,* and *or.* (See page 546 for a review of conjunctions.)

The fire raged on, **and** the flames reached into the forest.
Fire leapt from tree to tree; it was now out of control.

If the comma had not been used in the first example above, a reader might become confused. The comma helps make it clear that the fire did one thing, and the flames did something else. If the semicolon were not used in the second example, the reader would think two sentences had been carelessly run together.

A compound sentence requires a comma to separate its parts. However, you do not need a comma to separate the two parts of a compound subject, a compound verb, or a compound object.

Writing TIP

Never join simple sentences with a comma alone. A comma is not powerful enough to hold two sentences together.

Incorrect	The scouts from Maine, and those from Iowa were camping nearby.
Correct	The scouts from Maine and those from Iowa were camping nearby. (compound subject)
Incorrect	The ranger climbed the fire tower, and looked for signs of the fire.
Correct	The ranger climbed the fire tower and looked for signs of the fire. (compound verb)

Finally, a comma is not needed in short compound sentences.

Wood smoked and leaves smoldered.
Rain fell but the fire blazed on.

Practice Your Skills

A. CONCEPT CHECK

Punctuation of Compound Sentences   Write each compound sentence, adding a comma or a semicolon where needed.

1. The earliest people did not use fire in fact, it may have even frightened them.
2. These people ate their food raw and they lived without heat.
3. Early human beings did encounter wild fires these were started by lightning or volcanoes.
4. Fire provided warmth but it was also dangerous.
5. Finally, prehistoric people took the first step toward the control of fire they probably snatched a burning branch from a forest fire.
6. Prehistoric people began regularly using fire about 750,000 years ago and it was a great breakthrough for them.
7. Fire changed their lives they depended on it for cooking, warmth, and protection from dangerous animals.
8. A dead fire was a disaster people could not start their own fires.
9. They had to find another wild fire or they would remain cold.
10. Eventually, someone observed a spark from the collision of two stones humankind had stumbled on a great discovery.

B. REVISION SKILL

Sentence Combining   Combine each pair of sentences. Follow the directions in parentheses to create either a simple sentence with a compound subject or verb or a compound sentence using a comma with *and, but,* or *or.*

11. Forest fires can be devastating. They can be useful too. (Compound, *but*)
12. Native Americans witnessed many natural forest fires. They saw the effects. (Simple)
13. Game animals were more plentiful after a fire. Edible plants were more plentiful after a fire. (Simple)
14. Native Americans sometimes hunted in dense, unburned forest. They found little game in those places. (Compound, *but*)
15. Forest fires cleared out trees and brush. Forest fires made the soil richer. (Simple)
16. Burned forest was more open. It produced more grass for animals. (Compound, *and*)

17. Nuts and berries were more plentiful in a burned area. The Native Americans collected these for food. (Compound, *and*)

18. The Native Americans learned from the wild forest fires. Each spring and fall they set their own fires. (Compound, *and*)

19. They had to burn the forest. Food would be scarce. (Compound, *or*)

20. Forest fires can be frightening. For the Native Americans forest fires were part of a natural process. (Compound, *but*)

Writing TIP

Combining simple sentences can be a good way of streamlining the way you express your ideas.

C. PROOFREADING SKILL

Correcting Punctuation Errors in Compound Sentences

Copy the following paragraph and correct errors in grammar, capitalization, punctuation, and spelling. Pay particular attention to the punctuation of compound sentences. (16 errors)

Fires can be beneficial, and should sometimes be allowed to burn they help maintain healthy forests. Controlled burning plays an important roll in the natural forest environment. Fire's affect trees and other plants; but they also influence the numbers and kinds of animals. Some plants, and animals have adapted to places burned by fire. Species forced to live without the right habitat have trouble surviving and they may become extinct. Fires also controll tree diseases, and release the nutrients locked up in trees. These nutrients stimulate plant growth. That is why grasses and other plants quickly recover after a fire, and become abundant. Animals, respond to the additional food source and they often increase in number as a result. National Parks provide an ideal setting for controled burning people and personal property are not indangered.

FOR MORE PRACTICE
See page 570.

WRITING GOOD COMPOUND SENTENCES

> The parts of a compound sentence must be related in thought.

You have learned that the parts of a compound sentence are of equal importance because each part is a simple sentence. This means that the parts balance one another grammatically. They must also balance in thought. That is, the parts of a compound sentence must express thoughts that are related to each other.

Forming Compound Sentences

Not all pairs of sentences make good compound sentences.

1. The doctor saw several of her patients. They all had some symptoms of flu. (Will these simple sentences make a good compound sentence? Yes. Use *and*.)
2. Taro wants to be a doctor. Doctors specialize in many fields of medicine. (The ideas are not closely related enough to make a compound sentence.)
3. Dr. Sanchez examined the X-ray. She had been seeing this patient for many years. (These ideas are not closely related enough to make a compound sentence.)
4. Medical knowledge has advanced very far. There is still much more for doctors to learn. (These two may be made into a compound sentence. Use *but*.)

Practice Your Skills

A. CONCEPT CHECK

Compound Sentences   Write each pair as a compound sentence.

1. To us medieval medical practices are upsetting. We are fascinated by the early procedures.
2. In medieval times doctors worried about patients with too much blood. They started the practice of "bleeding."
3. Doctors in those days removed the extra blood. Patients could then get well.

4. Today physicians do not believe in bleeding. Back then a doctor would cut a patient's vein and catch the blood in a basin.
5. Diseases were associated with different veins. Doctors took blood from various parts of the body.
6. For example, a patient with tuberculosis would be bled from the ankle. A patient with a liver disease would be bled from the arm.
7. The effect of bleeding supposedly was affected by the season. Spring was considered an especially good time.
8. Bloodletting was risky. At least the physicians were ready with remedies in case of any complications.
9. A big risk was uncontrollable bleeding. Another was accidental cutting of tendons.
10. Doctors believed in bleeding. The patient would not have a chance to get well.

B. REVISION SKILL

Evaluating Compound Sentences   Imagine that you are evaluating the writing of another student. For each pair of sentences, suggest a conjunction that might be used to make a compound sentence. If sentence pairs cannot be joined, write *No Compound*.

[11]Modern medical education is thorough and exacting. It was not always that way. [12]In seventeenth-century England, you might be a "physician" trained in a medical school. You might be some other kind of medical person with no formal education at all. [13]"Surgeons" were apprentices at hospitals. They learned on the job. [14]They watched and assisted experienced surgeons. Another kind of medical practitioner was the barber. [15]Barbers and surgeons did many of the same things. Barbers also cut hair. [16]They also pulled teeth. Apothecaries were the seventeenth century's pharmacists. [17]They made, prescribed, and sold drugs. They also gave medical advice. [18]Apothecaries got their education as apprentices. Medical education slowly rose above this primitive system.

C. APPLICATION IN WRITING

An Analysis   Would you like to be a physician? Why or why not? Write a brief paragraph giving your reasons. Use both simple and compound sentences.

FOR MORE PRACTICE
See page 571.

A. Identify each of the following sentences as *Simple* or *Compound.*

1. What could be hiding behind a famous painting?
2. You might be surprised; sometimes it's another famous painting.
3. For example, a picture by nineteenth-century artist Jean Francois Millet was strongly criticized, and it disappeared.
4. The location of the painting was a mystery, but in 1983 it was discovered.
5. Researchers X-rayed a later picture, *The Young Shepherdess,* and found the earlier painting beneath it.
6. Millet and other painters often painted over old pictures.
7. Millet may have disliked this one, or he may have needed the canvas for a new idea.
8. Paintings can be studied with X-rays and infrared photography.
9. Researchers sometimes find earlier paintings or original charcoal outlines and learn more about the artist's methods.
10. True masterpieces are rarely discovered below the surface.

B. Write each compound sentence, adding a comma or semicolon where needed. For each simple sentence, write *S.*

11. Imagine your room in five hundred years it would have gathered dirt and scars.
12. Many paintings receive that kind of punishment and this is especially true for murals, or wall paintings.
13. For example, Leonardo da Vinci's *The Last Supper* was painted on a dining room wall in the 1490s and it has been damaged in many ways.
14. Within twenty years, flakes of paint began falling off.
15. In 1652, a door in the room was enlarged and part of the painting was cut away.
16. The painting has been restored from time to time but in the past these efforts often added to the damage.
17. Only recent technology has provided successful techniques.
18. Dr. P. Brambilla began the latest restoration in 1977.
19. A slow pace was necessary or she might add to the damage.
20. One tiny area the size of a postage stamp was restored at a time in six years only one-quarter of the painting was clean.

WHAT ARE COMPLEX SENTENCES?

A **complex sentence** is a sentence that contains one *main clause* and one or more *subordinate clauses.*

Clauses are the building blocks we use to make complex sentences. Like any builder, you must understand your materials. A **clause** is a group of words that contains a subject and a verb. There are two types of clauses: main clauses and subordinate clauses.

Main Clauses

A clause that can stand by itself as a sentence is a **main clause.** A simple sentence has one main clause. A compound sentence has two or more main clauses.

The monster lived in a cave; it came out at night.

In the example above, *the monster lived in a cave* and *it came out at night* are both main clauses and can stand alone. All clauses in compound sentences are main clauses. Main clauses are sometimes called *independent clauses.*

Subordinate Clauses

A clause that cannot stand by itself as a sentence is called a **subordinate clause.** Read these examples:

When night falls (*what happens?*)

If the monster is hungry (*what will happen?*)

Each of these clauses is a sentence fragment that leaves you wondering, *then what?* Now, cover up the first word in each clause. Note that each clause now expresses a complete thought.

Words such as *if* and *when* **subordinate.** That is, they make it necessary for the clauses they introduce to be linked to a main clause in order to form a complete sentence. Such words are called **subordinating conjunctions,** and they introduce **subordinate clauses.** Common subordinating conjunctions are listed in the box on page 566.

THE FAR SIDE   By GARY LARSON

"I've got it again, Larry . . . an eerie feeling like there's something on top of the bed."

Subordinating Conjunctions

after	because	so	until
although	before	so that	whatever
as	if	than	when
as if	in order that	though	where
as long as	provided	till	wherever
as though	since	unless	while

You now have the building blocks to make complex sentences. A **complex sentence** is a sentence that contains one main clause and one or more subordinate clauses.

> When the dragon coughs, fire shoots from its mouth.
> (SC) (MC)

> The dragon spread its wings as it leaped from the cliff.
> (MC) (SC)

Avoiding Sentence Fragments

When you are writing, remember that a subordinate clause does not express a complete thought. A subordinate clause all by itself is a sentence fragment.

Fragment   When the Loch Ness monster emerged

Complex Sentence When the Loch Ness monster emerged,
        a dozen cameras clicked.

Practice Your Skills

A. CONCEPT CHECK

Main Clauses and Subordinate Clauses Write each sentence and underline each main clause once and each subordinate clause twice.

1. Although dreadful beasts often appear in today's movies, such scary monsters are nothing new.
2. The idea of alien creatures may be older than you think.
3. As long as human beings have been on the earth, they have told stories about strange or terrible creatures.
4. As one looks into those old stories, one finds many different kinds of monsters.

5. Most commonly, however, when people have been afraid of some kind of horrible creature, it was a dragon.
6. Some people actually searched for fiery dragons, while others believed in zombies or vampires.
7. Folklore often presents monsters as horrible animals, although the creatures often possessed human qualities as well.
8. If any people had remarkable myths, it was the ancient Greeks.
9. Perhaps the Greeks spun tales about these imaginary creatures because such stories helped them deal with the mysteries and dangers of life.
10. In Greek mythology, Argus was a monster with a hundred eyes so that he could see everywhere at once.
11. Hydra, the many-headed serpent, would grow a new head whenever one was cut off.
12. The Harpy, half bird and half woman, would steal food from her victims before they could begin their meals.
13. While the Minotaur had the body of a man, his head was definitely that of a bull.
14. Because Medusa had sharp fangs, scary eyes, and snakes instead of hair on her head, she was considered rather ugly.
15. People would turn to stone if they took one look at her.
16. Cerberus seemed like a nice dog until his three heads all barked at once.
17. The fire-breathing Chimera certainly qualified as a monster since she had a lion's head, a goat's body, and a serpent's tail.
18. As long as the world is thought of as a dangerous place, people will probably believe in monsters.
19. No doubt they will dream up even more stories about dreadful creatures as time goes on.
20. Meanwhile, anyone can find out more about the old monster legends if good books on mythology are available.

B. CONCEPT CHECK

Main Clauses and Subordinate Clauses Write each sentence and underline each main clause once and each subordinate clause twice. Identify each sentence as *Simple, Compound,* or *Complex.*

21. A Komodo dragon looks like a real-life monster.
22. Although it's no monster, it is the world's largest lizard.

Using Compound and
Complex Sentences **567**

23. This flesh eater lives on Komodo Island in Indonesia, and the creature was not discovered until 1912.
24. Before it was actually seen, rumors told of giant dragons.
25. Dragon tales continued until scientists visited the island.
26. They found lizards up to twelve feet long.
27. Some weigh three hundred pounds and run ten miles per hour.
28. Komodo dragons have strong claws and sharp, sawlike teeth.
29. They eat carrion, or dead animals, or they catch live animals.
30. The "dragons" hunt small deer or wild pigs; they have even killed human beings.
31. These giant lizards dig burrows deep in the earth, and they usually spend their nights in these caves.
32. The females lay about twenty-eight eggs at a time, and their newly hatched young live in trees for several months.
33. Because hunters and collectors have nearly caused the extinction of the Komodo dragon, it is now protected.
34. Imagine finding one in your back yard!
35. If it is near the creature's supper time, you might be in trouble.

C. REVISION SKILL

Sentence Combining   Revise this paragraph to read more smoothly. Combine the sentence pairs into compound or complex sentences. You may add, delete, or rearrange words as necessary. Items 39 and 45 require no change.

[36]One of the world's most popular monster stories was created in June 1816. This happened when the poets Percy Bysshe Shelley and Lord Byron were visiting with friends. [37]It was a boring, rainy evening. They decided to have a storytelling contest. [38]Shelley and Byron were talented poets. Neither of them created this story. [39]It was invented by Shelley's wife Mary. [40]She was only 18 years old. She had a creative imagination. [41]She heard her husband and Byron talking about electricity. Then she got an idea. [42]They wondered about something. Could electricity bring a dead person back to life? [43]She thought about it all night. This was the reason she couldn't sleep. [44]The next day she had her story. She jotted down the idea. [45]Her contribution to the storytelling contest became a novel about a scientist using electricity to make a monster come alive. [46]You may not know about Mary as the author. You probably know the main character, Dr. Frankenstein's monster.

FOR MORE PRACTICE
See page 571.

CHECK ✓ POINT

A. Write the following sentences. Underline each main clause once and each subordinate clause twice.

Writing Theme
Florence Nightingale

1. Florence Nightingale came from a wealthy English family, and she was known for her wit and beauty.
2. She could speak and read many languages before she turned sixteen.
3. In her twenties, she decided on her true mission in life; she would care for sick people.
4. Since her family did not approve of her plans, she secretly read books on health and nursing.
5. She studied and she waited.
6. Florence became an expert on hospitals and public health.
7. After Florence trained as a nurse in Germany, she became the head of a hospital in London.
8. During the Crimean War in 1854, she cared for wounded soldiers in Turkey and reorganized the military hospitals.
9. The soldiers called Nightingale "The Lady with the Lamp."
10. She is remembered for her compassion; she also represents the freedom of women to choose their own work.

Colored engraving of Florence Nightingale (1820-1910).

B. Application in Literature Identify each sentence as *Simple,* *Compound,* or *Complex.*

^11^The daughters of Mr. and Mrs. Nightingale were born to riches. ^12^Their father, as country squire, was a learned man, and he taught his daughters himself. ^13^Their mother was a society leader. ^14^Florence had been named for the city of Florence, Italy, where she was born in 1820 during a year of travel for the Nightingales. . . .

May McNeer and Lynd Ward,
"Florence Nightingale: Lady with the Lamp"

Using Compound and
Complex Sentences   **569**

GRAMMAR
HANDBOOK
44

Writing Theme
Communication

A. Recognizing Compound Sentences   Write *S* for each simple sentence and *C* for each compound sentence.

1. Long-distance communication is not new; it is ancient technology.
2. Ancient people didn't have telephones, but they had drums, whistles, reed pipes, smoke, and fire.
3. People often communicated in code by sound patterns or signals.
4. Codes had to be elaborate, or people could not communicate with each other.
5. Drums and reed pipes sent sound messages across great distances.
6. Smoke signals could be seen at even greater distances.
7. Native Americans communicated with smoke signals, and ancient Greeks, Chinese, and Egyptians did the same.
8. However, smoke signals were not effective in the dark.
9. At night, fires were built on hilltops, and these signals could be seen far away.
10. A series of fires could communicate effectively over several hundred miles.

B. Punctuating Compound Constructions   Write each compound sentence, adding a comma or a semicolon in the appropriate place. If a sentence does not need punctuation, write *Correct.*

11. At first, prehistoric people could not speak they did not have words.
12. They invented language eventually but we don't know their process.
13. We have theories but they are just educated guesses.
14. People may have imitated animal calls or other natural sounds.
15. This is called the bow-wow theory and it accounts for words such as *thunder, splash, moan,* and *bow-wow.*
16. Another theory is the yo-he-ho theory and it might partly explain language.
17. People work and they grunt.
18. These grunts might develop into words and stand for kinds of work.
19. Other theories exist but there is no proof for any of them.
20. All these theories may be correct or none may be correct.

C. Making Compound Sentences   Write each of the following pairs of sentences as a compound sentence. Be sure to use the correct punctuation.

21. The Sumerians may have invented writing. We're not certain.
22. The Sumerians lived in the Middle East. The area is now in the country of Iraq.
23. Writing was developed in the Sumerian temples. The temples were the center of Sumerian life.
24. Priests kept records of business deals and astronomical observations. They probably created the first writing.
25. The first writing was primitive. It served a useful purpose.
26. For example, a farmer paid his taxes with two oxen. The priest would draw a picture of an ox.
27. Then the priest would make two dots on the picture. The two dots would stand for the two oxen.
28. The first word was a noun. The second was an adjective.
29. The picture is called a pictogram. It communicates the idea of "two oxen."
30. This primitive writing probably was created about 3100 B.C. It may have been developed as early as 3500 B.C.

D. Recognizing Complex Sentences   Identify each of the following sentences as *Simple, Compound,* or *Complex.*

31. When the ancient Egyptians were at the height of their power, they used hieroglyphics, a kind of picture writing.
32. Few Egyptians wrote in hieroglyphics after A.D. 394.
33. It was forgotten after a few centuries because no one used it.
34. Later, people studied the ancient Egyptian civilization, and they wanted to read the hieroglyphics.
35. They tried to interpret it, but no one knew how.
36. Then in 1799, a French soldier found the clue to hieroglyphics.
37. While the French army was building a fort near the town of Rosetta in Egypt, the soldier found a black stone.
38. A message was carved on the Rosetta stone in hieroglyphics, in another ancient Egyptian language, and in ancient Greek.
39. People could read Greek, and they compared it to hieroglyphics.
40. It took twenty-three years before scholars would finally translate hieroglyphics.

Writing Theme
Flight

A. Recognizing Compound Sentences   Write the following sentences. Underline each subject once and each verb twice. Then label each sentence *Simple* or *Compound.*

1. People have always been fascinated by flight, and birds have inspired us with awe.
2. Many inventors have designed wings, strapped them on, and flapped madly.
3. Often, these flying machines never got off the ground, but some had real possibilities.
4. In about 1600, Leonardo da Vinci drew plans for mechanical wings; they used complicated pulleys and levers.
5. Humans did finally become airborne, in a balloon in 1783 and in a glider in 1853.

B. Punctuating Compound Sentences   Write each compound sentence, adding a comma or semicolon in the correct place. For each simple sentence, write *Correct.*

6. Tales of human flight date back thousands of years and many myths record these stories.
7. An ancient Greek myth tells of one early adventure.
8. Daedalus was a renowned inventor and his creativity was put to the test in this myth.
9. The Labyrinth, one of his most famous inventions, was a maze he built it for King Minos of Crete.
10. People could not find their way out of the Labyrinth.
11. Minos later imprisoned a Greek hero in the Labyrinth but Daedalus helped the hero escape.
12. Minos was very angry and imprisoned Daedalus and his son Icarus in the Labyrinth.
13. Even Daedalus could not find his way out of the Labyrinth without a map they probably could fly out, though.
14. He built wings for himself and his son.
15. The father and son leaped up and flew out of the maze.
16. However, they could not fly too near the sun or the wings would melt.
17. Icarus knew about the danger but he was enjoying flying.
18. He soared up and up and he flew too high and close to the sun.
19. His wings melted and he fell into the sea and drowned.
20. Daedalus was sad but he flew on and landed safely in Greece.

C. Complex Sentences   Write each subordinate clause, underlining the subject once and the verb twice.

21. No one had ever flown a plane around the world without refueling until Dick Rutan and Jeana Yeager's *Voyager* accomplished this feat in 1986.
22. Until their plane was designed, aircraft were too heavy and couldn't carry enough fuel for the 25,000-mile flight.
23. When *Voyager* was built, the weight of every piece of equipment was kept to the minimum.
24. The plane weighed less than two thousand pounds before the fuel was added.
25. After *Voyager* was airborne, the nine-day flight was underway.
26. The flight was uneventful until it was almost over.
27. Dick and Jeana had flown three-quarters of the way around the world when they ran into a severe storm.
28. Since *Voyager* was not built for extreme weather, this storm posed a major threat.
29. As the plane was blown sideways, Dick fought for control.
30. After they survived that trial, the jubilant pilots cruised home.

D. Identifying Sentence Structure   Identify each of the following sentences as *Simple, Compound,* or *Complex.*

31. In Greek mythology, when Daedalus sought escape from Crete, he made wings out of feathers and flew to the island Santorini.
32. A plane, the *Daedalus,* made that same journey in 1988; it was also powered solely by human muscle.
33. Human-powered flight could not become a reality until strong, lightweight materials were invented in the 1970s.
34. The *Daedalus* was made of such a material.
35. Its wingspan was 112 feet, but it weighed only 68.5 pounds.
36. Although the craft had huge wings and weighed very little, the pilot required great strength.
37. The craft had a bicycle mechanism, and it was pedaled by an Olympic cyclist from Greece.
38. The athlete trained hard for the flight; it was a test of endurance.
39. The flight was seventy-four miles long and took three hours and fifty-four minutes.
40. Even more advances must be made before ordinary people can power aircraft.

WRITING CONNECTIONS

Elaboration, Revision, and Proofreading

Informative Writing: Explaining *How*

Sometimes writing about a problem allows you to explore solutions to the problem. (See Workshop 4.) Be sure you state the problem clearly and explain why your solution would work. You can help make your writing clear by using complex sentences, which help show the relationships between ideas. Varying your sentences can also make your writing more interesting.

On your paper, revise the following problem-solution statement. Use the directions given and proofread for errors in grammar, capitalization, punctuation, and spelling.

¹My best friend Jaime and I cannot go to the recreation center after school or get together in the homes of our friends. ²Because we have no way of getting there. ³Our parents work, so they cannot drive us where we want to go, and the center is too far away for us to ride our bikes. ⁴We talked to some of our friends. ⁵We learned that they have the same problem.

⁶We think we have a solution to the problem, but we need the schools help the school could provide a few rooms for after-school activities. ⁷Students could use one room for doing homework. ⁸They could watch TV or play games in an other room. ⁹The gym could remain open. ¹⁰Of course, supervisors would be needed. ¹¹The supervisors could park their cars in the school parking lot. ¹²Perhaps parents, interested community members, or teacher would volunteer to supervise the activities. ¹³Our parents wouldn't worry about us. ¹⁴Because we would be in a safe, supervised place. ¹⁵The cost for the school would not be great, because it allready has the rooms, and the supervisors would be volunteers.

1. Add a topic sentence to the first paragraph that clearly states the problem.

2. Combine sentences 4 and 5. Make sentence 4 a subordinate clause introduced by the conjunction *when.* Remember to use correct punctuation.

3. Delete the sentence that doesn't belong.

4. Show that the ideas in sentences 7 and 8 are of equal importance by using the conjunction *and* to form a compound sentence. Remember to use correct punctuation.

5. Add the following clause to sentence 9 to explain why the gym should remain open: "so that students could play sports."

574 Grammar Handbook

Call in the Expert

Once again we are pleased to present Mister Language Person, the internationally recognized expert and author of the authoritative *Oxford Cambridge Big Book o' Grammar*.

Q. What is the correct way to spell words?

A. English spelling is unusual because our language is a rich verbal tapestry woven together from the tongues of the Greeks, the Latins, the Angles, the Klaxtons, the Celtics, the 76ers, and many other ancient peoples, all of whom had severe drinking problems. Look at the spelling they came up with for "colonel" (which is actually pronounced "lieutenant"); or "hors d'oeuvres" or "Cyndi Lauper."

Q. Please explain punctuation?

A. It would be "my pleasure." The main punctuation marks are the period, the coma, the colonel, the semi-colonel, the

probation mark, the catastrophe, the eclipse, the Happy Face, and the box where the person checks "yes" to receive more information. You should place these marks in your sentences at regular intervals to indicate to your reader that some kind of punctuation is occurring. Consider these examples:

WRONG: O Romeo, Romeo, wherefore art thou Romeo?

RIGHT: O Romeo! Yo! *Romeo!!* Where . . . fore ART thou? Huh??

ROMEO: I art down here! Throw me the car keys!

Dave Barry

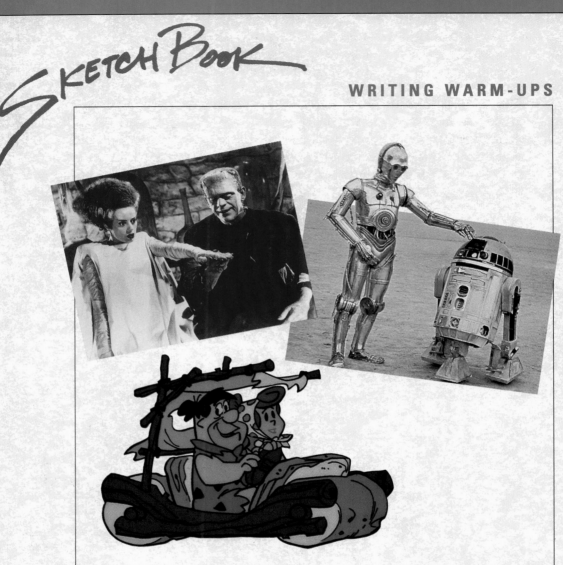

Sketch Book

- Imagine the figures in the pictures above attending a party. Write an eyewitness account. Tell what everyone is doing and what's happening.

- Which were your favorite fairy tales or fables when you were a child? Rewrite one of those stories in your own words.

- Write a review of an interesting book you read or of a television show or movie you saw recently.

Understanding Subject and Verb Agreement

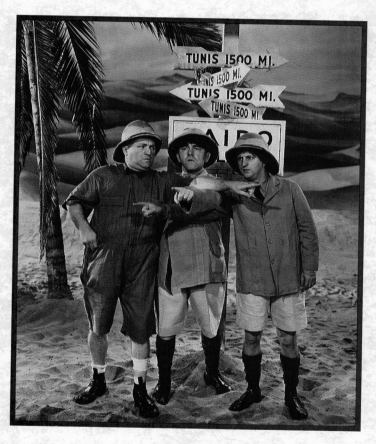

- Agreement of Subject and Verb

- Verbs with Compound Subjects

- Agreement in Inverted Sentences

- Agreement with Indefinite Pronouns

Bringing together characters who don't get along can lead to some hilarious situations. In your writing, however, mixing parts of a sentence that don't get along just creates confusion.

In this handbook you will learn how to make sure that the most important parts of your sentences—the subjects and verbs—work together well.

AGREEMENT OF SUBJECT AND VERB

> A verb must agree with its subject in **number.**

The **number** of a word refers to the difference between singular (one thing or action) and plural (more than one thing or action). When we say that one word agrees with another, we mean that the words are the same in number.

Singular A Shaker *is* a member of a certain religious community.

Plural Shakers *practice* a simple way of life.

Singular and Plural Forms

A noun that stands for one person, place, thing, or idea is **singular.** A noun that stands for more than one is **plural.**

Verbs, too, have singular and plural forms. In a sentence, the verb must agree in number with its subject. A subject and verb agree in number when they are both singular or both plural.

Singular The farmer *plows* the field.
Plural The farmers *plow* the field.

Notice that in the present tense, the third person singular form of most verbs ends in s. Otherwise, the plural form of most verbs does not end in *s.*

Shaker chairs, circa 1840–50.

Special Forms of Certain Verbs

The verbs *be, have,* and *do* have special forms for singular and plural, as you can see in the chart that follows.

Verb	Singular	Plural
be	am, is	are
	was	were
have	has	have
do	does	do

Singular   Shaker style *is* simple.
               The shirt *has* no decoration.
               The seamstress *does* fine work.
Plural   Shaker rocking chairs *are* sturdy.
               The seats *have* no cushions.
               The carpenters *do* their work carefully.

Notice that when a form of *be, do,* or *have* is used as a helping verb in a verb phrase, the helping verb changes to the plural form to agree with the subject. The main part of the verb does not change.

Singular   The child *is reading.*
Plural   The children *are reading.*

The Pronoun *I*

Although the pronoun *I* stands for a single person, it does not usually take a singular verb. The only singular verb forms used with *I* are *am* and *was.*

    I *am* a tour guide.   I *was* a cook last year.

In all other cases, the pronoun *I* takes a plural verb.

    I *give* tours of the Shaker farm.   I *enjoy* showing it.

The Pronoun *You*

The pronoun *you* has the same form for singular and plural. Also, it takes a plural verb even when it refers to a single person.

Singular   Louis, you *gather* information on inventions of the Shakers.
Plural   Girls, you *research* the Shakers' use of medicinal herbs.

Writing Theme
Shaker Life

Interrupting Words and Phrases

Sometimes words and phrases come between, or interrupt, a subject and its verb. The simple subject is never part of these interrupting words.

Singular   The *house* with many windows *was* white.
Plural   *Apples* in the cellar *are* ripe.

The nouns *windows* and *cellar* cannot be subjects because the subject never appears in a prepositional phrase.

Other phrases that might separate the subject and the verb include those beginning with the words *together with, including, as well as, along with,* and *in addition to.*

The *guide,* as well as the tourists, *enjoys* the exhibit.

Practice Your Skills

A. CONCEPT CHECK

Agreement of Subject and Verb   Write the subject and verb from each sentence and write whether each is *Singular* or *Plural*.

1. The history of the Shakers in America begins around 1774.
2. A typical Shaker farm was neat and prosperous.
3. A census of Shaker communities shows a decline after the late 1800s.
4. Museums today provide an accurate picture of Shaker life.
5. Shakers are famous for their simple but well-made crafts.
6. Now only a few artisans do work of this quality.
7. Shaker architecture has a plain and simple style.
8. Objects, regardless of purpose, are useful, not frivolous.
9. You often see pegboards on the walls of many rooms.
10. Clothes, as well as utensils, hang from the pegs.

B. REVISION SKILL

Correcting Subject and Verb Agreement   If a sentence has an error in agreement, write the sentence correctly. If there is no error, write *Correct.*

11. I live in a Shaker community. The year is 1760.
12. The sound of bells wake me daily at 4:30 A.M.
13. I, together with the others, are always quick to wake up.

14. The Shakers in the village has morning chores.
15. I, along with some of the other girls, cleans the sleeping rooms before breakfast.
16. Susan, with three other women, mend clothes.
17. Members of the community comes together for all meals.
18. Work in the shops, fields, and dwellings occupy our day.
19. Even the children in the village does many chores.
20. My friend Edward, like the adult men, do woodworking.
21. Edward, as well as some other boys, makes wooden boxes.
22. I, for the most part, works in the kitchen.
23. Our kitchen provide meals for the Shakers and for visitors to our village.
24. Sister Sarah, along with two helpers, bake pies for us and the visitors.
25. You often have a choice of over 150 of her pies in a week's time.
26. My favorite place on summer afternoons is the flower garden.
27. However, Shakers, by principle, is against gardens just for beauty.
28. All things, even the rose bed, serves a purpose.
29. Rose petals have a use too.
30. Rose water, from the petals, are an ingredient in our apple pies.

CHECK ✔ POINT

MIXED REVIEW · PAGES 578–581

For each of the following sentences, write the form of the verb in parentheses that agrees in number with the subject.

1. I (has, have) a fascination with jewelry, especially rings.
2. You perhaps (knows, know) that rings have three parts.
3. The parts of a ring (is, are) the circle, the shoulders, and the bezel.
4. The bezel, on top of the shoulders, (holds, hold) the stone.
5. Rings occasionally (does, do) more than adorn fingers.
6. For example, some rings during the Renaissance (was, were) made with special bezels.
7. You (opens, open) the bezel.
8. A small compartment within the bezel (holds, hold) tiny keepsakes.
9. A legend about one of these rings (has, have) endured.
10. Its bezel, instead of keepsakes, (hides, hide) poison!

FOR MORE PRACTICE
See page 590.

Writing Theme
Rings

> A **compound subject** consists of two or more subjects that share the verb.

Compound Subjects Joined by *and*

A **compound subject** has two or more parts that share one verb. Compound subjects joined by *and* take a plural verb regardless of the number of each part.

> Ivy and Mel *are* balloonists. (*Ivy* and *Mel* form the compound subject. The verb *are* is plural.)

Compound Subjects Joined by *or* or *nor*

When the parts of a compound subject are joined by *or* or *nor*, the verb agrees with the part of the subject nearer the verb.

> The twins or Tom *trains* the crew. (*Tom* is the subject nearer the verb, so the verb is singular.)
> Neither Carl nor his sisters *have* any experience. (*Sisters* is the subject nearer the verb, so the verb is plural.)

Practice Your Skills

A. CONCEPT CHECK

Compound Subjects   Write the correct form of the verb given in parentheses.

1. Ellen and I (am, are) going hot-air ballooning.
2. Neither Ellen nor I (has, have) been ballooning before.
3. Either a mixture of gases or hot air (causes, cause) balloons to rise.
4. Ascent and descent (is, are) controlled by heating the gas.
5. Morning or evening (is, are) the best time to fly.
6. Crew members or the pilot (prepares, prepare) new ballooners.
7. Neither wind nor obstacles (affects, affect) our ascent.
8. The fields and streams (seems, seem) very far away.
9. Pilot and passengers (bends, bend) their knees for landing.
10. A great flight and a perfect morning (ends, end) too soon.

Writing
═ TIP ═

Forming compound subjects by combining sentences is one way to reduce wordiness in your writing.

Writing Theme
Hot-Air Balloons

B. REVISION SKILL

Sentence Combining   Combine each pair of sentences by using a compound subject. Delete words as necessary.

> EXAMPLES   Balloonists love competitions. Spectators do too.
> Balloonists and spectators love competitions.
>
> Riders do not like storms. Neither does the pilot.
> Neither riders nor the pilot likes storms.

11. Michigan hosts balloon competitions. New Mexico does too.
12. Elbow is the name of an event. Hare and Hound is the name of another event.
13. Early morning is a good time for hot-air balloon races. On the other hand, late afternoon is good too.
14. Wind patterns influence the pilot's plan. The landscape influences the plan as well.
15. Updrafts affect balloon flights. Downdrafts also affect them.
16. The pilots do not want any problems. Neither does the race observer.
17. Skill plays a part in every event. Luck also plays a part.
18. In some races, the landing place of the balloon is judged. In other races, the navigation path is judged.
19. Precision landings are tested in competition. Target drops are also tested.
20. A pilot does not know the winner until the last event. Neither do the spectators.

Hot-air balloons come in all shapes and sizes.

C. APPLICATION IN WRITING

Advertisement   Use at least five of the following compound subjects to write an advertisement for a company that offers hot-air balloon rides. Make sure that subjects and verbs agree.

21. Either crisp morning air or soft afternoon breezes . . .
22. Licensed pilots and excellent equipment . . .
23. Excitement and anticipation . . .
24. Gentle ascents and whisper-soft landings . . .
25. Neither your imagination nor your expectations . . .
26. Customer satisfaction or a full refund . . .
27. Fields and hills . . .
28. Beauty and magic . . .
29. Half-hour rides or one-hour rides . . .
30. Brightly colored balloons and peaceful landscapes . . .

FOR MORE PRACTICE
See page 590.

Word order does not affect subject-verb agreement.

Usually the subject comes before the verb. A person is likely to say, for example, "Beautiful shells lie beyond that reef." To call attention to detail, however, a person may say, "Beyond that reef lie beautiful shells." The second sentence is called an **inverted sentence.** In each sentence, however, the subject is *shells* and the verb is *lie.* In both sentences, the subject and verb must agree.

Toward the reef *swim* the *divers.* (divers, swim)
Around the divers *circles* a playful *dolphin.* (dolphin, circles)
Does Joy or *Ted have* the camera? (Joy or Ted, does have)

Notice the last example above. For questions, inverted order is the ordinary order.

Practice Your Skills

A. CONCEPT CHECK

Agreement in Inverted Sentences   For each of the following sentences, write the correct form of the verb given in parentheses.

1. It is 1939. At the bottom of the ocean (sits, sit) a stranded submarine.
2. Inside the forward compartment (huddles, huddle) the frightened sailors.
3. (Does, Do) the shore commander know they are stranded?
4. Back on shore (waits, wait) an anxious commander.
5. Quickly over the sister ship's radio (comes, come) many messages.
6. (Does, Do) the operator understand the distress signals? Yes!
7. Finally! To the rescue (churns, churn) the *Falcon!*
8. Into the sea (drops, drop) the diving bell and rescuers.
9. Over the submarine's hatch (slips, slip) the diving bell, the lifeline to the crew.
10. Through the hatch (echoes, echo) the welcome words "Hello, fellows! Here we are!"

B. REVISION SKILL

Sentence Variety   Inverted sentences add variety to your writing. In the following exercise, write sentences 11, 14, 17, and 18 as inverted sentences. For all sentences, choose the form of the verb in parentheses that agrees in number with the subject.

11. Hundreds of hammerhead sharks (swims, swim) through the water.
12. (Is, Are) the scuba divers afraid?
13. Of course not! The bubbles from their scuba gear (scares, scare) the sharks away.
14. The sharks (retreats, retreat) far from the strange intruders.
15. Manta rays, though, sometimes (appears, appear) friendly.
16. A friendly ray (approaches, approach) some divers.
17. A diver with protective gloves (rides, ride) on the manta ray's back.
18. The ray, with its rider, (glides, glide) along the ocean floor.
19. Very few people (enters, enter) into this magical world of the Gulf of California.
20. (Does, Do) most divers appreciate this special privilege?

C. PROOFREADING SKILL

Subject-Verb Agreement   Write this paragraph, correcting all errors in grammar, capitalization, punctuation, and spelling. Pay attention to errors in subject-verb agreement. (15 errors)

Into the swimming pool plunges the instructer and her students. I, as always, am the last in the pool. Does the other students or the instructor know how scared i am? Inside my brain scream a voice. "You are not reddy for the exam!" it shouts. Nevertheless, I wet my face mask. Adjust my mouthpeace, and relax. I try all the tests. Neither the equipment nor the tests gives me a problem. Underwater, my instructor smiles at me threw her face mask does her expression mean I passed the exam? Later my instructor, along with my classmates, congratulate me. Now I am realy a Scuba Diver!

FOR MORE PRACTICE
See page 591.

Understanding Subject and Verb Agreement   **585**

Verbs with *There, Where,* and *Here*

The words *there, where,* and *here* often begin sentences. Their job is to get the sentence moving. When *there, where,* or *here* begins a sentence, look for the subject later in the sentence.

Here is a *book* on cacao trees.   There are no *beans* left.
  (*Book* is the subject.)   (*Beans* is the subject.)
Where are my *samples* of cacao?
  (*Samples* is the subject.)

As in any other sentence, the subject and verb must agree. The singular subject *book* takes the singular verb *is.* The plural subjects *beans* and *samples* take the plural verb form *are.* When *there, where,* or *here* begins a sentence, be careful to make the verb agree in number with the subject of the sentence.

When *there* is used near the beginning of an inverted sentence, the sentence is usually a question. Look for the subject later in these sentences as well.

Was there a good *speaker?*   Were there any good *slides?*
  (*Speaker* is the subject.)   (*Slides* is the subject.)

Practice Your Skills

A. CONCEPT CHECK

Verbs with *There, Where,* and *Here*   Write the correct form of the verb given in parentheses.

Writing Theme
Cacao

Cacao fruit pod showing beans.

1. (Is, Are) there a chocolate lover present?
2. Here (is, are) some information for you on cacao.
3. In wet, tropical areas there (grows, grow) cacao trees.
4. Where (has, have) the trees been cultivated?
5. There (is, are) cacao farms in Mexico and South America.
6. Here (sits, sit) some freshly picked cacao pods.
7. Inside each pod there (grows, grow) twenty to forty beans.
8. (Is, Are) there cacao beans you can eat?
9. No. There (is, are) processing plants for making chocolate from the beans.
10. Well! Where (is, are) some chocolate samples we can taste?

B. PROOFREADING SKILL

Correct Agreement in Inverted Sentences   Proofread the following paragraphs correcting all errors in grammar, capitalization, punctuation, and spelling. (16 errors)

Legend of the Cacao Trees

There once were a grove of cacao trees. Here stand the tallest cacao tree of all. It produces eighty cacao pods a year there is many farmers who will give a grate deal to get this tree. What can help. Is there no Magic spells?

Inside his castle pace the prince. He shouts continuously. Who owns that cacao tree? Where is this farmer. Are there any person who knows?

Meanwhile, here beneath the tree sits it's lovely owner. In her dreams, there is a princes beutiful castle and many riches.

FOR MORE PRACTICE
See page 591.

C H E C K P O I N T
MIXED REVIEW · PAGES 582–587

Writing Theme
Chariot Races

Write the form of the verb that agrees with the subject.

1. Here (stands, stand) the Circus Maximus in mighty Rome.
2. There (has, have) never been such a magnificent arena.
3. My father and I (am, are) especially proud this day.
4. My father and grandfather (builds, build) the best chariots.
5. Where (is, are) there any better chariot makers?
6. (Does, Do) any person doubt my word?
7. Into the stands (throngs, throng) 250,000 spectators.
8. Either the earth or I (is, am) shaking with excitement.
9. In my heart (lies, lie) a wish that no one dies today.
10. There (is, are) only the lightest materials on the chariot.
11. A light body and spoked wheels (promotes, promote) speed.
12. Along the center of the arena (is, are) a strong wall.
13. There (has, have) been many crashes against that wall.
14. Today the green team and the blue team (is, are) racing.
15. There (has, have) always been a fierce rivalry between them.
16. Here (is, are) four chariots ready to race.
17. (Is, Are) there any chance our chariot will win?
18. Around the track (speeds, speed) the racers for seven laps.
19. Neither my father nor I (believes, believe) our eyes now.
20. Around the arena (races, race) our chariot to victory!

AGREEMENT WITH INDEFINITE PRONOUNS

> Singular indefinite pronouns are used with singular verbs. Plural indefinite pronouns are used with plural verbs. Some indefinite pronouns may be either singular or plural.

This chart lists singular and plural indefinite pronouns.

Indefinite Pronouns

Singular			Plural
another	either	nobody	both
anybody	everybody	no one	few
anyone	everyone	one	many
anything	everything	somebody	several
each	neither	someone	

Singular Neither of the outfits *fits* well.
Plural Both *are* too long.

The following indefinite pronouns are either singular or plural, depending on their meaning in a sentence: *all, any, most, none, some,* and *much.*

Singular Some of the cloth *is* blue.
Plural Some of the buttons *are* brass.

Practice Your Skills

A. CONCEPT CHECK

Agreement with Indefinite Pronouns   Write the correct form of the verb given in parentheses.

1. One of the most interesting stories in the world of fashion (is, are) the history of blue jeans.
2. Almost everyone (consider, considers) jeans an American garment.
3. Yet almost everything about jeans (has, have) a tie to other cultures.

4. For example, nobody (seem, seems) surprised at the names of French designers on today's jeans.
5. Furthermore, one of Italy's cities, Genoa, (claim, claims) fame for the name *jeans*.
6. Another, the French city of Nîmes, (lend, lends) its name to denim.
7. Of course, all of us (have, has) heard of Levis.
8. However, few (realize, realizes) that Levi Strauss was a German immigrant.
9. Much of the credit for jeans' strength (go, goes) to a Latvian immigrant, the inventor of riveted clothing.
10. Everybody (expect, expects) jeans to be functional and comfortable.
11. No one (want, wants) seams to break or pockets to rip.
12. Considering this fact, some of the current manufacturing processes (seem, seems) a little strange.
13. Many (involve, involves) prewashing and prefading.
14. Either (weaken, weakens) the fabric.
15. Each (are, is) certainly nothing the originators of jeans would approve of.

B. PROOFREADING SKILL

Making Subjects and Verbs Agree Proofread the following passage. Rewrite the paragraphs, correcting all errors in grammar, capitalization, punctuation, and spelling. Check especially for errors of agreement with indefinite pronouns. (10 errors)

The year is 1853, and Levi Strauss have arrived in San Francisco from bavaria. Having brought canvas to make prospectors tents and wagon covers, Strauss hears a casual comment that causes him to make jeans instead.

Someone say, "You should have brought pants to sell. Anyone knows that pants don't last long in the gold mining camps."

Twenty years later another man enters the scene Jacob Davis needs money to apply for a patent for his riveted clothing. He beleives anything in this land of opportunities are possible. Jacob writes to Strauss, offering half the patent rights. To riveted pants in return for financial backing. The two join forces. Both contribute to making jeans a reality. Each become part of American History.

FOR MORE PRACTICE
See page 591.

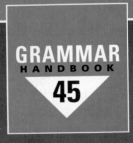

GRAMMAR
HANDBOOK
45

Writing Theme
The Caribbean
Islands

A. Making the Subject and Verb Agree in Number Write the subject of each sentence. Then write the verb in parentheses that agrees in number with the subject.

1. Ever since our class studied the tropics, I (has, have) wanted to go to the Caribbean islands.
2. You probably (knows, know) the islands by their other name, the West Indies.
3. However, I (am, are) having difficulty deciding which islands to visit.
4. Aruba, along with Bonaire and Curaçao, (is, are) part of the kingdom of the Netherlands.
5. Dutch, as well as Spanish and English, (is, are) spoken on these islands.
6. The sunken shipwrecks along the coastlines (attracts, attract) many scuba divers.
7. On the other hand, Jamaica (does, do) offer white sandy beaches and beautiful mountains.
8. You (has, have) no doubt heard of reggae, the music of Jamaica.
9. The sounds of music from a steel band often (greets, greet) arriving planes.
10. Jamaicans (does, do) everything possible to welcome visitors.

B. Using Verbs with Compound Subjects Choose the correct form of the verb from the two given in parentheses.

11. Grenada and the Isle of Spice (is, are) two names for one island.
12. The hills, beaches, and forests (seems, seem) exotic.
13. Today, agriculture and tourism (is, are) important.
14. Fragrant nutmeg or clove (greets, greet) the tourists' senses.
15. Tourists and residents (jogs, jog) along the beaches.
16. Bottles of nutmeg oil or fresh crayfish (tempts, tempt) shoppers in Market Square.
17. Either the market in St. George's or the market in Grenville (merits, merit) a visit on Saturdays.
18. In Grand Etang National Park, mona monkeys and Burmese mongooses (romps, romp) freely.
19. Neither visitors nor residents (wants, want) the island to change.
20. However, the economy and employment (benefits, benefit) from tourism.

C. Using Verbs in Inverted Sentences   Choose the correct form of the verb from the two given in parentheses.

21. Across the ocean (sails, sail) a slave ship in 1794.
22. (Does, Do) the slaves, chained below deck, know their destination?
23. On West Indian sugar plantations (works, work) thousands of slaves.
24. (Does, Do) any person deserve such a fate?
25. (Is, Are) the plantation owners to blame?
26. To the owners (goes, go) riches from the sugar cane.
27. However, in Europe (lies, lie) another source of the trouble.
28. Throughout Europe (rings, ring) the cries for sugar.
29. (Has, Have) any person considered the cost in human lives?
30. From the toil of slaves (comes, come) that sugar.

D. Using Verbs with *There, Where,* and *Here*   Choose the correct form of the verb from the two given in parentheses.

31. In Old San Juan there (was, were) once Spanish soldiers.
32. In recent years, there (has, have) been a steady stream of tourists instead.
33. Here, on this island, (is, are) a wonderful tropical forest.
34. There (seems, seem) no end to the miles of winding paths in El Yunque.
35. Where (is, are) an island lovelier than Puerto Rico?

E. Using Verbs with Indefinite Pronouns   Correct all errors in subject-verb agreement. Write *Correct* if there is no error.

36One of the most distinctive musical forms are calypso. **37**Many of the songs tells of current events. **38**Some of us know calypso through the songs of Harry Belafonte. **39**On the island of Trinidad, much of the news are told in calypso songs. **40**Today, several of the calypso tunes are called "soca." **41**Everyone in Trinidad know that this stands for "soul calypso." **42**Each of the bands on the islands gather to perform for the yearly carnival before Lent. **43**Many of the spectators do "jump dances" to the rhythms. **44**All of the singers competes to be Calypso Monarch of the Year. **45**Everybody wants this respected title.

GRAMMAR
H A N D B O O K
45

Writing Theme
Gems

A. Subject and Verb Agreement   Make two columns labeled *Simple Subjects* and *Verbs.* Write the simple subject of each sentence in the first column. Write the correct form of the verb in parentheses in the second column.

1. You (has, have) undoubtedly heard stories about gems.
2. I (does, do) not believe in such superstitions.
3. However, all major cultures (has, have) some beliefs about gems.
4. In some stories, gems (possesses, possess) power and magic.
5. One of the most powerful gems (is, are) the diamond.
6. Warriors, in more than one ancient culture, (has, have) been known to wear diamonds.
7. The hardness of the diamonds (was, were) supposedly responsible for the warriors' strength in battle.
8. However, diamonds, in addition to turquoise, (loses, lose) their powers if they are purchased.
9. The ancient word for garnet (is, are) carbuncle.
10. Carbuncles, as well as diamonds, reportedly (makes, make) a person invisible.
11. Frankly, this power (does, do) not seem believable.
12. Three of my aunts (wears, wear) diamonds.
13. I (am, are) always able to see the dear ladies.
14. Still, the lore of gems (holds, hold) a fascination for me.
15. You sometimes (finds, find) superstitions entertaining.

B. Agreement of Compound Subjects and Verbs   Write the form of the verb in parentheses that agrees in number with the subject.

16. Iowa and pearls (does, do) not seem connected in any way.
17. The Philippines or Tahiti (is, are) better known for pearls.
18. However, in this year of 1900, my neighbors and I (am, are) beginning to see the connection.
19. John Boepple and his helpers (is, are) making pearl buttons in Muscatine, Iowa.
20. The Mississippi and other rivers (provides, provide) the materials.
21. Freshwater mussels and some other shellfish (has, have) been dredged from the river bottoms.
22. Either their pearls or the pearly lining of the shells (makes, make) beautiful decorations.

23. Mr. Boepple or his assistant (cuts, cut) buttons out of the shells.
24. Neither metal buttons nor glass buttons (lasts, last) as long as Iowa pearl buttons do.
25. Fame and good luck (has, have) come to Muscatine.
26. The citizens and Mr. Boepple (is, are) proud to live in the "Pearl Button Capital of the World."
27. Unfortunately, fishermen and shell hunters (collects, collect) too many mussels.
28. Also, silt and pollution (destroys, destroy) the mussels.
29. Neither the river nor the mussels (is, are) doing well.
30. Pearl buttons and prosperity (does, do) not seem permanent.

C. Agreement in Inverted Sentences   Write the simple subject from each of the following sentences. Then write the form of the verb in parentheses that agrees in number with the subject.

31. Into the dark burial place (slips, slip) the archaeologists.
32. Where (is, are) the scientists going?
33. Through the dark and twisted passages (creeps, creep) the curious procession.
34. Before their eyes (appears, appear) an ancient tomb.
35. Inside the tomb (lies, lie) the mummy of a young woman.
36. Around her neck (hangs, hang) three remarkable necklaces.
37. Here (is, are) fine examples of precious jewels.
38. Some of the jewels (is, are) pendants with sacred symbols.
39. (Has, Have) the carnelians lost their brilliance?
40. Look! (Does, Do) anyone see that beautiful ring?
41. Everyone (notices, notice) the scarab on the ring.
42. Around the mummy's waist (hangs, hang) a belt of gems and gold.
43. In a bracelet (gleams, gleam) semiprecious stones.
44. (Is, Are) there gems in those earrings as well?
45. Near the mummy (rests, rest) three alabaster vases.
46. Some of the balm (remains, remain) inside one vase.
47. Another vase (contains, contain) galena, a cosmetic for the eyes.
48. Here (is, are) a golden-yellow bronze mirror.
49. There (is, are) no name on this tomb.
50. Many (thinks, think) she must have belonged to a noble Egyptian family.

Informative Writing: Reports

A feature article provides interesting facts about people, places, or things. (See Workshop 8.) When revising an article, make sure that your facts are accurate and that you have included details that will hold your readers' interest. Correct subject-verb agreement prevents confusion and helps your readers follow the *who, what,* and *when* of your article.

Revise the following draft of a feature article using the directions at the bottom of the page. Then proofread the article, paying particular attention to errors in subject-verb agreement. Correct any other errors in grammar, and in capitalization, punctuation, and spelling.

¹You probably wouldn't expect that someone who is a Grandmother of eleven would be a popular rock guitarist, but that is exactly what she is. ²She also runs a small record company out of her home in Memphis Tennessee and help promote the work of other musicians. ³Jackson's guitar-playing skills was highlighted in a music video and TV comercial. ⁴These performances soon led to appearances on TV shows. ⁵And has made Jackson a overnight sucess. ⁶However, Jackson say, if this is overnight success, it was a forty-three-year night." ⁷As a teenager, she often appeared on stage with her father who was a band leader. ⁸Jackson were twelve years old when she learned to play the guitar. ⁹She began writing songs. ¹⁰When she was in her twenties and later returned to the stage. ¹¹A performance at the Lone star cafe resulted in her video appearance. ¹²Opportunities to make commercials came along shortly after the video appeared. ¹³Jackson have shown that it's never too late to make your mark.

1. In sentence 1 tell whom the article is about by replacing the vague pronoun *she* with "Cordell Jackson."

2. Add details to sentence 4 by inserting the following phrase: "such as the *Arsenio Hall Show* and *Late Night with David Letterman.*" Add a comma before the word *such.*

3. Move sentence 7 so that it is in correct chronological order.

4. In sentence 11, add the appositive, "a club in New York City," to explain what the cafe is. Add commas before and after the appositive phrase.

5. Divide the passage into three paragraphs.

Fumblerules

English has plenty of rules—some more helpful than others. What happens when you break one of these rules in the very process of stating it? Then you have what William Safire calls a fumblerule, a mistake that calls attention to the rule. Here are some examples.

- Verbs has to agree with their subjects.
- No sentence fragments.
- Avoid run-on sentences they are hard to read.
- A writer must not shift your point of view.
- Do not put statements in the negative form.
- Don't use contractions in formal writing.
- Make an all out effort to hyphenate when necessary but not when un-necessary.
- Don't use capital letters without good REASON.
- Write all adverbial forms correct.
- In their writing everyone should make sure that their pronouns agree with its antecedent.
- Use the semicolon properly, use it between complete and related thoughts; and not between an independent clause and a mere phrase.
- If any word is improper at the end of a sentence, a linking verb is.
- Avoid commas, that are not necessary.
- And don't start a sentence with a conjunction.
- The passive voice should never be used.
- Unless you are quoting other people's exclamations, kill all exclamation points!!!
- Proofread carefully to see if you any words out.

William Safire

Directions   One or more of the underlined sections in the following sentences may contain an error in grammar, usage, punctuation, spelling, or capitalization. Write the letter of each incorrect section; then rewrite the item correctly. If there is no error in an item, write *E*.

> **Example**   Werner Hirzel could play <u>forty-nine</u> <u>instruments</u> at the
> AB
> same <u>time, and</u> carry <u>them</u> on his back too.   <u>No error</u>
> CDE
>
> **Answer**   C—time and

1. The <u>Louisiana Purchase</u> and the <u>Lewis and Clark Expedition</u> <u>was</u> two important
   ABC
   historical <u>events</u> that took place during the presidency of Thomas Jefferson.
   D
   <u>No error</u>
   E

2. Coast <u>redwoods,</u> which grow in California and <u>southern</u> Oregon, <u>is</u> the <u>tallest</u>
   ABCD
   species of tree in the world.   <u>No error</u>
   E

3. English Channel swimmer Gertrude Ederle <u>damaged</u> her <u>hearring</u> during a swim
   AB
   across <u>the Channel, and</u> <u>spent</u> the rest of her life working with deaf children.
   CD
   <u>No error</u>
   E

4. "A fool and <u>his money,</u>" says an old <u>proverb,</u> "are soon parted." A great many
   AB
   people these days would say that <u>them</u> and the fool have a lot in common,
   C
   <u>especially</u> when bills come due.   <u>No error</u>
   DE

5. Malaria sufferers know quinine as <u>good</u> <u>medicine, and</u> it happens to taste pretty
   AB
   <u>well</u> in a soft drink called tonic <u>water.</u>   <u>No error</u>
   CDE

6. Cork is <u>light, and</u> can <u>easily</u> spring back into shape, because nearly <u>five-eighths</u>
   ABC
   of the <u>volume</u> of cork is air.   <u>No error</u>
   DE

7. <u>Absolutely</u> pure gold is very <u>rare, and</u> <u>is</u> <u>softer</u> than some kinds of clay.
   A   B   C   D
<u>No error</u>
E

8. The Panama Canal is only one-twentieth the length of the Grand Canal in

<u>China, and</u> the <u>Chinese</u> <u>canal</u> was built 1,300 years <u>ago!</u>   <u>No error</u>
   A   B   C   D   E

9. The Seven Wonders of the World <u>includes</u> temples, <u>statues, and</u> hanging
                                          A   B

<u>gardens, but</u> the <u>Egyptian</u> pyramids are the only one of the seven structures to
   C   D

survive.   <u>No error</u>
              E

10. Japan's Midori Ito was expected to win the <u>women's</u> figure skating competition
                                                       A

in the <u>1992 Olympics. The</u> battle for the gold medal was between <u>she</u> and
         B   C

<u>Americas'</u> Kristi Yamaguchi.   <u>No error</u>
   D   E

11. <u>Wow.</u> The <u>English</u> language <u>contains</u> nearly a half million <u>words!</u>   <u>No error</u>
   A   B   C   D   E

12. Bermuda, which includes about three hundred separate islands, <u>were</u> uninhabit-
                                                                        A

ed until <u>1609. It</u> <u>lies</u> some distance <u>east</u> of the United States.   <u>No error</u>
            B   C   D   E

13. <u>There's</u> six of the fifty largest <u>cities</u> in the United States in Texas and four in
   A   B

<u>Ohio. California</u> has <u>the most</u> with eight.   <u>No error</u>
   C   D   E

14. "<u>Home, Sweet Home</u>" is hardly an unusual <u>song but</u> it was <u>wrote</u> by a man
         A   B   C

who spent much of his life both homeless and <u>penniless.</u>   <u>No error</u>
                                                 D   E

15. <u>Us</u> drivers in the United States may have our share of traffic <u>problems, but</u> in
   A   B

Amsterdam the police <u>have</u> a special branch of officers <u>who's</u> only job is to deal
                         C   D

with drivers who end up in the city's canals.   <u>No error</u>
                                                   E

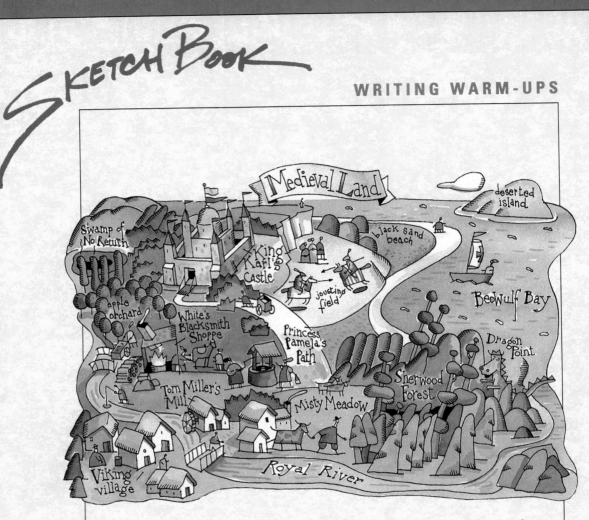

Sketch Book

- Writers often create fictional settings for their stories. Think of a setting for a story. Draw a map of your setting and label several interesting landmarks.

- What is your favorite video game? Write directions that tell how to play it. Be sure to include the names of all the places and characters in the game.

- Ask your parents and other relatives to help you sketch out a family tree. Include the name, date of birth, and a short description of each person.

Capitalization

- **Proper Nouns and Proper Adjectives**

- **Geographical Names**

- **Organizations, History, and Time**

- **Languages, Peoples, Transportation, and Abbreviations**

- **First Words**

Beautifully decorated capital letters, such as this one, were often used in early books to signal the beginning of an important passage. Although modern capital letters are usually not as fancy, they still carry important information. Like the capital letters in the Medieval Land map, they call attention to specific people, places, and things, and they also signal the beginning of a sentence.

This handbook includes the information you need to know about using capital letters correctly.

PROPER NOUNS AND PROPER ADJECTIVES

> Capitalize proper nouns and adjectives.

The use of capital letters is called **capitalization**. When you use a capital letter at the beginning of a word, you have capitalized the word.

A **common noun** is the name of a whole class of persons, places, things, or ideas. It is not capitalized.

man   woman   city   building   freedom

A **proper noun** is the name of a particular person, place, thing, or idea. It is capitalized.

James   Victoria   China   Europe   Islam

A **proper adjective** is an adjective formed from a proper noun:

Victorian   Chinese   European   Islamic

The following rules, along with examples, will help you solve problems in capitalizing proper nouns and proper adjectives.

Names and Titles of Persons

Capitalize the names of persons and also the initials or abbreviations that stand for those names.

Harriet Tubman   **T. S. E**liot   John **F. K**ennedy, **Jr.**

Capitalize titles used with names of persons and abbreviations standing for those titles.

Dr. Goldstein   **M**s. Anderson   **C**aptain Gonzalez

Do not capitalize titles that are used as common nouns.

One of the **d**octors in our town is Dr. Goldstein.
Ms. Anderson was elected **m**ayor of our city.
Captain Gonzalez is the youngest of the police **c**aptains.

Capitalize titles of people and groups whose rank is very important.

Capitalize the following titles even when they are used alone if the titles refer to the current holders of the positions: the President and Vice-President of the United States, the Queen of England, and the Pope.

The **P**resident appointed a member to the **S**upreme **C**ourt.

Family Relationships

Capitalize words such as *mother, father, aunt,* and *uncle* when these words are used as names.

When is **M**other arriving, **D**ad?
We visited **U**ncle Bob in Boston.

These words are not used as names when they are preceded by a possessive or by such words as *a* or *the.*

Our **u**ncle took us to the movies.
The **m**other wrapped the baby in a blanket.

The Pronoun *I*

Capitalize the pronoun *I.*

Does anyone have a pencil **I** could borrow?

Religious Names and Terms

Capitalize all words referring to the Deity, to the Holy Family, and to religious scriptures.

God   the **B**ible   the **T**orah   **J**esus   the **G**ospel   **A**llah

Practice Your Skills

A. CONCEPT CHECK

Proper Nouns and Proper Adjectives   Write the words that should be capitalized in each sentence.

1. My aunt has traveled in europe, asia, and africa.
2. Aunt sophie knows about famous buildings such as the parthenon.

3. The parthenon is an ancient greek temple in athens.
4. notre dame cathedral, in france, is a monument to god.
5. The emperor justinian built the hagia sophia, a christian church.
6. This building later served as an islamic mosque.
7. The first pyramid, or tomb, in egypt was built for king zoser.
8. The indian ruler shah jahan built the taj mahal.
9. The shah wanted a memorial for his wife mumtaz mahal.
10. When i listen to aunt sophie, i realize how fascinating architecture is.

B. PROOFREADING SKILL

Using Proper Nouns and Adjectives   On your paper, write the following paragraph, correcting errors in capitalization. (30 errors)

Hearst Castle architect Julia Morgan's watercolor of a chateau in the French countryside. She was a student at the School of Fine Arts, Paris.

As a child in oakland, california, julia morgan loved to draw. Her Mother encouraged her to go to College. Julia studied architecture at the university of california. She also attended the School of Fine Arts in paris, france. In 1902 she set up an office in san francisco, where she redesigned the fairmont hotel after the 1906 earthquake. Later, William Randolph Hearst hired julia to design a Mansion of spanish design for him near san simeon, California. A famous publisher who had served in the house of representatives, Mr. Hearst traveled extensively and collected art and Antiques. His collection included european choir stalls, Italian windows, and french paintings. Julia had to keep adjusting the mansion's design to make room for w. r. hearst's treasures. Finally, it became a 144-room wonder known as hearst castle. It remains the best-known building ms. Morgan designed.

C. PROOFREADING SKILL

Correct Capitalization   Write the paragraph, correcting all errors in capitalization, spelling, punctuation, and grammar. (15 errors)

Angkor was the capitol of an ancient Empire in cambodia. The city was larger than european capital's of the time. Acording to a Chinese traveler. Angkor was one of the gratest cities in asia. King suryavarman II built a tempel called Angkor Wat. An example of Hindu architecture outside india, the temple is the world's largest relijious structure. Angkor Wat also served as an observatory and a Royal tomb. After the empire declined, angkor was abandoned to the jungle.

FOR MORE PRACTICE
See page 615.

GEOGRAPHICAL NAMES

> Capitalize major words in geographical names. Also capitalize names of sections of the country but not compass directions.

The following are examples of geographical names:

Continents	**S**outh **A**merica, **A**ustralia, **A**ntarctica
Bodies of Water	the **P**acific **O**cean, **L**ake **H**uron, the **R**ed **R**iver
Landforms	the **S**ierra **N**evada, the **G**obi **D**esert
Political Units	**C**alifornia, **St**. Louis, the **P**rovince of **Q**uebec
Public Areas	**Y**ellowstone **N**ational **P**ark, **F**ort **T**iconderoga
Roads and Highways	**R**idge **R**oad, **M**ichigan **A**venue, **I**nterstate 10, **R**oute 12, **M**ain **S**treet

Directions and Sections

Capitalize names of sections of the United States but not directions of the compass.

Population is declining in the **N**ortheast.
He lives **s**outh of the river; I live **w**est of the airport.

Capitalize proper adjectives derived from names of sections of the country or the world. Do not capitalize adjectives derived from words indicating directions.

a **W**estern saddle   an **e**astern flight

Practice Your Skills

A. CONCEPT CHECK

Geographical Names   Write the words that should be capitalized in each sentence.

1. Can you answer these questions about united states geography?
2. Is mt. mckinley the highest mountain in alaska?
3. Yes, and it is also the highest mountain in north america.
4. But in the continental united states, mt. whitney is the highest.

5. What state borders utah on the south? What state borders it on the west?
6. Arizona borders utah on the south; nevada borders utah on the west.
7. Which of these states are in the midwest: ohio, rhode island, illinois, vermont, new jersey, iowa?
8. Ohio, illinois, and iowa are in the midwest; rhode island, vermont, and new jersey are in the northeast.
9. What are the locations of sequoia national park and fort sumter national monument?
10. The national park is located in the sierra nevada in california.
11. Fort sumter is on an island near charleston, south carolina.
12. What river flows from minnesota to the gulf of mexico?
13. The mississippi river flows from lake itasca, minnesota, to the louisiana coast.
14. If you drive north on interstate 65 from birmingham, alabama, what state will you enter next?
15. Tennessee is north of alabama.

B. PROOFREADING SKILL

Focus on Capitalization   On your paper, write the following paragraph, correcting all errors in capitalization, spelling, punctuation, and grammar. (25 errors)

Many people consider san francisco, California, the most beautiful city in the United States and one of the most beautiful citys in the world. It is located on a hilly green penensula between the Pacific ocean and San Francisco Bay. Fog rolls in from the ocean. Over the Golden Gate Bridge, which connects the city to marin county on the north. The bridge is one of San Franciscos' famous landmarks. The city is also known for its cabel cars, which are a National Historic Landmark. People cling to the cars chugging up the citys' steap hills. One line of cars runs East and West on california street down to the area known as the Embarcadero, two other lines run north toward fisherman's Wharf, with its fishing boats, seafood restrants, and spectacular views of the bay. Nearby is ghirardelli Square, once the site of a chocolate factory. Now a group of shops and restaurants. More good food can be found in the numrous restaurants in chinatown, home to the largest chinese community outside of asia.

FOR MORE PRACTICE
See page 615.

C. APPLICATION IN WRITING

A Travelogue   Imagine you are going on a trip. Write a description of your trip, telling about real or imaginary places along the way. Be sure to capitalize the names of all locations correctly.

CHECK✔POINT
MIXED REVIEW · PAGES 600–605

Write the following sentences, adding capital letters where necessary. If a sentence needs no added capitalization, write *Correct.*

1. Books can take you many places, real and imaginary.
2. Willa cather based several novels on her experiences growing up in nebraska among immigrant farmers.
3. She admired the european settlers who tamed the great Plains.
4. Laura ingalls Wilder also wrote about growing up on the prairies of the midwest.
5. Her family homesteaded in minnesota and the dakota Territory.
6. For several of his books, Mark Twain drew upon memories of his childhood in hannibal, missouri.
7. Twain also wrote about his life as a riverboat pilot on the mississippi river.
8. pearl Buck set several of her novels in the far east.
9. Buck grew up in China, where her parents were missionaries.
10. charles dickens described London slums in several novels.
11. As a child he was forced to toil in a squalid factory.
12. The writer William Faulkner created an imaginary county named yoknapatawpha.
13. jefferson, the county seat, was based on oxford, Mississippi, faulkner's real-life hometown.
14. j.r.r. tolkien created Middle-earth, an imaginary world.
15. Tolkien's knowledge of old english, scandinavian, and german stories helped him create his world of hobbits, elves, and goblins.

"Bilbo Comes to the Huts of the Raftelves," illustration from *The Hobbit,* written and illustrated by J. R. R. Tolkien.

Capitalization   **605**

ORGANIZATIONS, HISTORY, AND TIME

Capitalize the names of
- organizations
- institutions
- historical events
- documents
- periods of time
- months
- days
- holidays

Organizations and Institutions

Capitalize all the important words in the names of organizations and institutions.

Children's **M**emorial **H**ospital	**P**an-**A**merican **C**ongress
League of **W**omen **V**oters	**F**irst **B**ank of **D**eerfield
Rogers and **M**ark **C**orporation	**E**lm **P**lace **S**chool

Do not capitalize such words as *school, college, church,* and *hospital* when they are not used as parts of names.

Please come to the open house at our **s**chool.
My brother will start **c**ollege this year.
Go one block past the **c**hurch and turn right.
Manuel does volunteer work at the **h**ospital.

Events, Documents, and Periods of Time

Capitalize the names of historical events, documents, and periods of time.

Louisiana **P**urchase	**V**ietnam **W**ar
Bill of **R**ights	**B**ronze **A**ge
Emancipation **P**roclamation	**P**rohibition

Months, Days, and Holidays

Capitalize the names of months, days, and holidays but not the names of seasons.

January	**T**uesday	**E**arth **D**ay	**w**inter
August	**P**residents' **D**ay	**s**ummer	**f**all

Practice Your Skills

A. CONCEPT CHECK

Organizations, History, and Time   Write the words that should be capitalized in each sentence.

Writing Theme
Civil Rights

1. The oldest political organization in South Africa is the african national congress (ANC), a civil rights group.
2. Black South Africans founded the ANC in january 1912.
3. After world war II, ANC membership greatly increased.
4. The ANC objected to laws like the native land act that denied blacks the right to vote and to live where they wanted.
5. The ANC wrote the freedom charter, a document that demanded equal rights for blacks.
6. The pan-african congress, an offshoot of the ANC, led protests.
7. On friday, april 8, 1960, the South African government outlawed both groups.
8. The government sentenced ANC leader Nelson Mandela to life imprisonment in june 1964.
9. However, the African national congress continued its fight.
10. Finally, on february 11, 1990, Mandela was set free.

Nelson Mandela greets Soweto (South African township) children after his release from prison.

B. REVISION SKILL

Correcting Capitalization Errors   Write the following sentences correcting all errors in capitalization.

11. Throughout his career, Thurgood Marshall worked to protect rights granted by the United States constitution.
12. After graduating from howard university, he became a lawyer.
13. Marshall then worked for the national association for the advancement of colored people (NAACP).
14. The NAACP, a civil rights Organization, was founded in 1909.
15. In 1950 Marshall won a case that upheld the right of African Americans to attend the university of texas and other Colleges.
16. In another case, he argued successfully that Laws allowing segregated housing were against the fourteenth amendment.
17. On may 17, 1954, Marshall won an important case that outlawed separate public schools for African Americans.
18. As a result, several Schools became integrated.
19. On monday, october 2, 1967, Thurgood Marshall became the first African American named to the United States Supreme Court.
20. He served on the supreme court for more than twenty years.

FOR MORE PRACTICE
See page 615.

Capitalization   **607**

Capitalize the names of
- languages
- races
- nationalities
- religions
- transportation

Abbreviations:
- B.C.
- A.D.
- A.M.
- P.M.

Languages, Races, Nationalities, and Religions

Capitalize the names of languages, ethnic groups, nationalities, and religions, and also the adjectives derived from them.

Spanish   **A**rabian horse   **C**hinese opera

African folk tales   **A**ustralian movie   **P**olish customs

Native **A**merican   **C**hristian church   **H**indu beliefs

Ships, Trains, Aircraft, and Automobiles

Capitalize the names of ships, trains, and aircraft. Capitalize brand names of automobiles.

Clermont (steamboat)   *Concorde* (supersonic jet)

Denver Zephyr (train)   *Spirit of St. Louis* (airplane)

Discovery (spacecraft)   Model T (automobile)

Abbreviations

Capitalize the abbreviations *B.C.* and *A.D.*

In **A.D.** 1990, archaeologists discovered the remains of the ancient city of Ubar.
Objects from Ubar, in Arabia, date back to 2000 **B.C.**

Capitalize the abbreviations *A.M.* and *P.M.*

We arrived at the site at 7:30 **A.M.**
We uncovered a piece of pottery at 1:10 **P.M.**

Writing
TIP

Remember to place A.D. before the year and B.C. after the year.

Practice Your Skills

A. CONCEPT CHECK

Languages, Peoples, Transportation, and Abbreviations

Write the words that should be capitalized in each sentence.

1. Howard Carter made an important contribution to the study of a civilization that existed before the greek and roman empires.
2. He uncovered the tomb of Tutankhamen, an egyptian pharaoh.
3. Tutankhamen reigned from about 1348 to 1339 b.c.
4. His tomb lay sealed from the 1300s b.c. until a.d. 1922.
5. Carter, a british archaeologist, found the entrance to the tomb on November 5, 1922.
6. The antechamber of the tomb housed magnificent treasures of egyptian art.
7. Carter asked an american to photograph these treasures.
8. On February 17, 1923, at about 2:00 p.m., Carter entered the burial chamber itself.
9. americans seemed especially fascinated by Carter's discovery.
10. As a result, Carter came to the United States aboard the S.S. *berengaria* for a speaking tour.

B. PROOFREADING SKILL

Capitalization   Write the following paragraph. Correct all errors in capitalization, punctuation, grammar, and spelling. (20 errors)

FOR MORE PRACTICE
See page 616.

On october 30, 1839, John Lloyd Stephens arived in Central America. Aboard the british ship the *mary ann.* Stephens, an american, was interested in archaeology. He hoped to find ancient indian ruins. He saled up the Copán River with a british artist he had hired to draw pictures of the trip. To their great joy, they found the ruins of a Maya city hidden in the thick jungles of Honduras? The mayas were Native americans whose civilezation dated from about 2500 b.c. By a.d. 950, their cities were abbandoned and left to the jungle. Stephens had found the city of Copán, a trade senter of the Mayas. The artist drew pictures of the temples and the karved statues of the great Maya city in the honduran jungle.

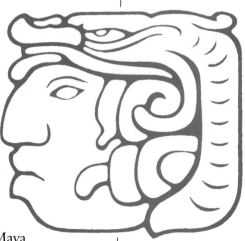

A. Rewrite each sentence, correcting all capitalization errors.

1. Born on tuesday, october 6, 1914, Thor Heyerdahl grew up to become a well-known adventurer.
2. He led the famous *kon-Tiki* expedition.
3. The *kon-tiki* was a large wooden raft with a square sail.
4. It resembled the rafts stone age peruvians used.
5. Heyerdahl thought these peruvians had used these rafts to cross the Pacific.
6. He believed they settled on Pacific islands about a.d. 500.
7. Heyerdahl planned the *kon-tiki* voyage to prove people could sail thousands of miles on a raft.
8. In april 1947 the tugboat *guardian rios* pulled the *kon-tiki* out to sea.
9. A pet parrot that screamed spanish words accompanied the crew.
10. Heyerdahl wondered whether he would live to raise the norwegian flag on a Pacific island.

B. APPLICATION IN LITERATURE

Capitalization   Write the following passage, correcting all errors in capitalization.

[11]The Raft was left alone. [12]The date was april 29, 1947. [13]The leader of the men on the raft was named Thor heyerdahl. [14]He was norwegian, thirty-two years old, a lean, hard-muscled man with blond hair, blue eyes, and a nose like the beak of a hawk. [15]The raft, its name *kon-tiki,* and the incredible Journey ahead were all his ideas. [16]He had gathered together the five Men with him, and now he felt responsible for their lives. [17]As he watched the Tug sail away, he knew there was a good chance that neither he nor any of the men with him would live to see another human being. [18]Even so, thor heyerdahl had spent many Months and all his money fighting for the chance to be there, adrift on a raft of balsa. [19]To him it was far more than simple Adventure. [20]He wanted to test a scientific Theory: Heyerdahl believed that the first men to settle the Polynesian islands of the South Seas had come from the coast of South america.

Wyatt Blassingame, *Thor Heyerdahl Viking Scientist*

FIRST WORDS

Capitalize the first words in
- sentences
- most lines of poetry
- quotations
- outline entries
- greetings and closings of letters
- important words in titles

Sentences

Capitalize the first word of every sentence.

My brother helps coach my soccer team.

Poetry

Capitalize the first word in most lines of poetry.

The biggest
Surprise
On the library shelf
Is when you suddenly
Find yourself
Inside a book—
(**T**he *hidden* you)
　　　You wonder how
　　　The author knew.

Sometimes in modern poetry, the lines of a poem do not begin with a capital letter.

Quotations

Capitalize the first word of a direct quotation.

Talia asked, "**D**o you want to go skating or see a movie?"

When a quotation is interrupted, it is called a **divided quotation.** Do not capitalize the first word of the second part of a divided quotation unless it starts a new sentence.

"**W**ithout a doubt," Jessie replied, "**w**e want to go skating."
"**W**ear your mittens," said Talia. "**I**t is cold outside."

Outlines

When you write an outline, capitalize only the first word in each line.

    I. **M**odern poetry
       A. **E**lements of poetry
          1. **R**hythm and meter
          2. **S**ound devices
          3. **I**magery
       B. **F**orms of poetry
          1. **F**ree verse
          2. **S**ong lyrics

Letters

In the greeting of a letter, capitalize all the important words.

    Dear **E**ditor: **D**ear **M**s. **C**rotty: **S**ir or **M**adam:

In the closing of a letter, capitalize only the first word.

    Very truly yours,   **S**incerely yours,

Titles

Capitalize the first word, the last word, and all important words in titles.

Book	*The **S**ign of the **B**eaver*
Poem	"**M**other to **S**on"
Newspaper	*The **N**ew **Y**ork **T**imes*
Play	*Romeo and Juliet*
Painting	*Mother of the Artist*
Musical Composition	*Rhapsody in Blue*
Short Story	"**T**he **C**ircuit"
Movie	*Star Wars*
Article	"**P**oetry **I**s **A**live and **W**ell"

Writing
TIP

The titles of books, newspapers, plays, paintings, long musical compositions, and movies are underlined when typed or written. The titles of poems, short stories, and articles are placed in quotation marks.

Practice Your Skills

A. CONCEPT CHECK

First Words   Write the words that should be capitalized.

1. An outline on children's poetry might begin like this:
    I. children's poetry
        A. classical children's poetry
2. The poem "mary had a little lamb" is a familiar nursery rhyme.
3. Robert Louis Stevenson's poem "the swing" is widely read.
4. It begins this way: how do you like to go up in a swing,
        up in the air so blue?
5. Many young children prefer modern poems like those in Shel Silverstein's book *where the sidewalk ends.*
6. children also delight in the poems of Jack Prelutsky.
7. Writing about Prelutsky, a critic said, "mr. Prelutsky writes clever, funny poems with definite child appeal."
8. children sometimes write to publishers requesting information about poets.
9. Their letters begin with a greeting such as "dear publisher."
10. The closing contains a phrase such as "sincerely yours."

B. REVISION SKILL

Correcting First Words and Titles   Write the words that should be capitalized in each sentence.

11. Carl Sandburg, a famous poet, storyteller, and biographer, once wrote for the *Chicago daily news.*
12. "poetry," Carl Sandburg said, "is a spot halfway between where you listen and where you wonder what you heard."
13. Have you read any of his great works, such as the poem "fog"?
14. Sandburg's first book of poems, *chicago poems,* appeared in 1916.
15. he called Chicago the "City of the Big shoulders."
16. This is not the Chicago described in the song "my kind of town."
17. *abraham lincoln: The prairie Years* was Sandburg's first book in the series about Abraham Lincoln.
18. the last book in the series, *Abraham lincoln: The war years,* won a Pulitzer Prize in 1940.
19. Sandburg's books for children include *rootabaga Stories.*
20. One of his children's books includes a story with the whimsical title "The two skyscrapers decided To have a child."

PLEASE DO NOT MAKE F UN OF ME AN D PLEAS E DON'T LAUGH IT ISN'T EASY T O WRIT E A PO EM ON THE NE CK OF A RUN NING GIRA FFE.

Shel Silverstein

C. PROOFREADING SKILL

Correcting Errors in Capitalization   Write the following paragraph, correcting all errors in capitalization, grammar, punctuation, and spelling. (20 errors)

In 1926 Langston Hughes published *the weary blues,* his first Book of poetry. "the dream keeper," the title poem of a later collection, begins, "bring me all your dreems." it was just one of his poems about dreams. During his career, Hughes wrote several books of poetry, he also wrote a collumn for the *new york post* and plays, including *black nativity.* Hughes told his life story in his autobiography, *the big sea.*

FOR MORE PRACTICE
See page 616.

C H E C K  P O I N T
MIXED REVIEW · PAGES 611–614

Write each sentence, correcting all errors in capitalization.

1. Several women Writers have won Pulitzer Prizes for their Work.
2. The first african american poet to win one was gwendolyn Brooks.
3. *A street in Bronzeville* was her first book of poetry.
4. It was named for the area in chicago where she grew up.
5. Gwendolyn Brooks once said, "poetry is life distilled."
6. Brooks has encouraged several young Writers to get their work published in newspapers such as the *chicago tribune.*
7. The movie *To kill a Mockingbird* was based on Harper lee's novel.
8. In the Movie, gregory peck played the Father of the main character and narrator, a girl named scout.
9. The story takes place in a small southern town.
10. The action unfolds in maycomb, Alabama, in the 1930s.
11. Playwright lorraine hansberry dealt with problems in the city.
12. She chose a modern setting instead of a historical setting for her play *a raisin in the sun.*
13. "never before, in the entire history of the american theater," said writer James Baldwin, "Has so much of the truth of black people's lives been seen on the stage."
14. Barbara w. tuchman won Pulitzer Prizes for two of her works.
15. About writing History barbara w. tuchman said, "there should be a beginning, a middle, and an end."

A. Capitalizing Proper Nouns and Proper Adjectives Write the sentences, using correct capitalization.

1. My uncle bill is writing a book about american explorers.
2. He asked me if i knew about lewis and clark.
3. After purchasing the louisiana territory, president thomas jefferson wanted to send an expedition there.
4. meriwether lewis and william clark led the expedition.
5. They thought they would be serving god and the united states.
6. Lewis and clark left st. louis and headed up the missouri river.
7. sacagawea, a shoshone indian, and her french-canadian husband joined the expedition as guides and interpreters.
8. The expedition crossed montana, idaho, and washington.
9. After reaching the pacific ocean, Lewis and clark headed back to missouri.
10. Only sergeant charles floyd died during the journey.

B. Capitalizing Geographical Names Write the words that should be capitalized in each sentence.

11. Ferdinand Magellan wanted to reach the spice islands by sailing west from Europe.
12. He believed he could find a passage through the americas.
13. Five ships set sail from sanlúcar de barrameda, spain, in 1519.
14. The ships stopped at the canary islands, off the coast of africa.
15. The ships then crossed the atlantic ocean to brazil.
16. Sailing down the south american coast, Magellan finally found the passage now named the strait of magellan.
17. Magellan then sailed across the *mar pacifico,* or pacific ocean.
18. On the philippine island of mactan, Magellan was killed.
19. Two of magellan's ships reached the spice islands, now called the moluccas.
20. Only one ship returned to spain; it traveled across the indian ocean, around the cape of good hope, and up the coast of africa.

C. Capitalizing Names Related to Organizations, History, and Time Correct errors in capitalization.

21. Before world war I, Norwegian explorers reached the South Pole.
22. In january 1911, Roald Amundsen landed in Antarctica.
23. The royal greenland trading company had provided sled dogs.
24. Amundsen's group spent a mild Winter at the base camp.

GRAMMAR
HANDBOOK
46

Writing Theme
Exploring the
Unknown

25. At the first hint of Spring, Amundsen set out toward the South Pole but soon returned to his base camp.
26. Amundsen's group tried again in october 1911.
27. On december 14, 1911, they reached the South Pole.
28. The night before achieving his goal, Amundsen said he felt like a little boy "on the night before christmas eve."
29. Amundsen's group stayed at the South Pole until december 17.
30. The group returned to the base camp on january 25, 1912.

D. Capitalizing Languages, Peoples, Transportation, and Abbreviations Write the words that should be capitalized in each sentence.

31. Even before the ancient greeks, people explored the unknown.
32. In 814 b.c., the Phoenicians founded a colony at Carthage.
33. In the third century b.c., a greek explorer described Britain.
34. In a.d. 43, the romans traveled to and conquered Britain.
35. Leif Ericson explored the American coast in a.d. 1000.
36. By 1270 the portuguese had begun exploring the African coast.
37. At 2:00 a.m. on October 12, 1492, the *pinta* made history.
38. Columbus's spanish expedition had reached America.
39. In 1957 the soviets launched the satellite *sputnik.*
40. In the 1980s, the *voyager* spacecraft explored the solar system.

E. Capitalizing First Words and Titles Write the words that should be capitalized in each sentence.

41. edgar Allan Poe mentioned the moon in several of his poems.
42. One begins like this: at midnight in the month of June,
                              i stand beneath the mystic moon.
43. Poe's story "The Unparalleled adventures of one hans pfall" tells about traveling to the moon.
44. Movies such as *destination Moon* also told of moon exploration.
45. A script outline for *Destination moon* might look like this:
    I. preparing for travel to the moon
    II. conditions on board the craft
46. the movie gave a fictional account of moon exploration.
47. until 1969 traveling to the moon was just science fiction.
48. In 1969 Neil Armstrong exclaimed, "the *Eagle* has landed!"
49. he was announcing the moon landing of U.S. astronauts.
50. "that's one small step for man," Armstrong said, "one giant leap for mankind."

A. Rewrite the following letter, correcting the words that should be capitalized.

dear maria,

dad said, "it's best to get an early start," and so we all piled into the car at 5:00 a.m. Before long, we were on interstate 80. javier, mom, and i slept for the first few hours of the trip. By 9:00 a.m., we were all awake and hungry. dad said that we would stop for breakfast at the amana colonies in iowa. The amana colonies are made up of seven villages. They were founded by a german religious group called the amanites. The amanites believe in living simple lives devoted to god.

Late that afternoon, we stopped in des moines, which is the capital of iowa. mom and dad decided to take us to see a play at the summer theater. That night we saw *man of la mancha,* a musical based on the book *don quixote* by cervantes, a famous spanish writer. i liked all the songs, but my favorites were "dulcinea" and "the impossible dream."

We spent one day in omaha, nebraska, which is just across the missouri river from council bluffs, iowa. There we visited the joslyn art museum and saw its collection of american western art. Javier liked a painting by seth eastman called sioux indians. Afterward, we went to boys town, which is just west of omaha. A priest named father flanagan founded the community to provide homes for orphans and other needy children.

On saturday we arrived in cheyenne, wyoming. We got there in time for a festival called frontier days. This celebration is held every year in july. A few days later, we were finally at yellowstone park. did you know it is our oldest national park? On march 1, 1872, the united states congress passed a law making yellowstone the first national park. We have a camping permit from the national park service and are sleeping in a tent. tomorrow we are going to see old faithful. Javier and i cannot wait to see that geyser spew water high into the air.

your friend,
francesca

B. Write the words that should be capitalized in each sentence.

1. In april my class went to washington, d.c., for three days.
2. On monday we lined up at 8:00 a.m. to tour the white house.
3. It was designed by an irish architect, James Hoban.

4. Every president since john adams has lived in this historic building.
5. The house george washington lived in was burned by the british.
6. Then we visited the washington monument.
7. We also visited the memorials to president thomas jefferson and President abraham lincoln.
8. The words of lincoln's gettysburg address and second inaugural address are inscribed on his memorial.
9. In the afternoon we kayaked on the potomac river.
10. On tuesday we went to the national air and space museum.
11. We saw charles lindbergh's airplane, *spirit of st. louis.*
12. lindbergh made the first nonstop solo flight across the atlantic ocean.
13. The space capsule john glenn rode in as he orbited the earth was right next to lindbergh's plane.
14. Space capsules back then are certainly primitive by comparison to shuttles such as the *atlantis.*
15. We really enjoyed an IMAX film called *to fly.*
16. This film made us feel as if we were soaring over phoenix and the grand canyon.
17. At the national museum of american history, we saw the flag that flew over fort mcHenry during the war of 1812.
18. That flag inspired francis scott key to write the "star-spangled banner," now our national anthem.
19. The museum has a little of everything, including dorothy's red shoes from the *wizard of oz* and archie bunker's armchair.
20. The national archives has two important documents: the declaration of independence and the constitution of the united states.
21. The constitution begins with the words "we the people."
22. This document identifies the rights of all united states citizens.
23. On wednesday we visited ford's theatre, which is now a theater and museum.
24. president lincoln was shot at the theater on april 14, 1865.
25. Lincoln died at william petersen's house across the street.
26. We were very quiet at arlington national cemetery.
27. In this cemetery is a memorial to general robert e. lee.
28. Many who served in the U. S. armed forces are buried at arlington.
29. Two presidents, william howard taft and john f. kennedy, are also buried there.
30. The tomb of the unknowns, a memorial to those killed in world wars I and II, the korean war, and the vietnam war, is located in this cemetery.

WRITING CONNECTIONS

Elaboration, Revision, and Proofreading

On your paper, revise the following first draft of an interpretation, using the directions at the bottom of this page. Also proofread the paragraph, correcting errors in grammar, capitalization, punctuation, and spelling. You can assume that lines of the poem are copied correctly.

¹The poem "the road not taken" seems short and simple. **²**however, when I read the lines carefully. **³**I realize that they have a deep meaning i see the two roads in the wood as different ways of life. **⁴**It is about a traveler who choses to journey down one road rather than another. **⁵**I'm not sure yet what my life will be like. **⁶**I think the road chosen stands for the way of life the poems traveler decides to lead! **⁷**the traveler says, ". . . long I stood / And looked down one as far as I could." **⁸**To me, these lines mean that although people try to see into the future, they cannot tell what life will be like. **⁹**have to choose a road and follow where it leads. **¹⁰**I think robert frost is saying that the choices people make can have many different outcomes. **¹¹**When I think about the roads standing for life, the poems last line makes me think about how important choices can be.

1. In sentence 1, identify the poet by adding the phrase "by Robert Frost" to the first sentence.

2. Move the sentence that tells what the poem is about so it directly follows the sentence giving the title and the author of the poem.

3. Delete the sentence that doesn't belong in the draft.

4. Give details about the types of choices people make. Add the words "about friends, activities, and careers" or other details of your own to sentence 10.

5. Insert the last line of the poem, "And that has made all the difference," in sentence 11.

Responding to Literature

Writing an interpretation is one way to explore your understanding of a poem. (See Workshop 7.) When you are revising an interpretation, check to be sure that you have named the poem and its author. Also check that you have supported your ideas with examples or lines from the poem. Remember to capitalize and punctuate lines from the poem exactly as they appear in the original.

Sketch Book

- A checkered flag is to auto racing what a period is to a sentence. Sketch a flag or other symbol that would signal a short pause (like a comma) or excitement (like an exclamation point). Write a sentence or two explaining your symbol.

- When have you felt lost, afraid, very happy, or very angry? Write a short skit about one of those experiences. Be sure to set the scene and include dialogue between the characters.

- Freewrite for ten minutes about anything that comes into your head. Don't use any punctuation as you write. Then go back and punctuate the passage to make the flow of your ideas clear.

Punctuation

- End Marks
- Commas That Separate Ideas
- Commas That Set Off Special Elements
- Other Uses of the Comma
- The Semicolon and the Colon
- The Hyphen
- The Apostrophe
- Quotation Marks

"The white flag. One more lap. After almost three hours of speed, strategy, courage, danger . . . one more lap. And there it is! The car flashes past! Time balks at the sight—the checkered flag!"

Tom Carnegie, from *The Indy 500*

An auto race may look like just a blur of speeding images. However, the race is actually punctuated by colored flags that pace the drivers and tell them how far they have to go. In the same way, you can use punctuation to pace your writing and make sure your message is absolutely clear.

END MARKS

> Use a **period,** a **question mark,** or an **exclamation point** to end a sentence.

In speaking, your tone of voice helps you to communicate when you are excited, when you are asking a question, or when you have completed a thought. In writing, you must use punctuation marks to give your reader such messages. Three punctuation marks show where a complete expression ends. These **end marks** are the **period,** the **question mark,** and the **exclamation point.**

The Period

Use a period at the end of a declarative sentence.

A **declarative sentence** makes a statement. Use a declarative sentence when you want to tell somebody something.

My aunt is studying an unusual flower from Malaysia.
It is called a monster flower.

Use a period at the end of an imperative sentence.

An **imperative sentence** makes a request or tells someone to do something. Use a period at the end of an imperative sentence unless you wish to express excitement or emotion at the same time. In that case, use an exclamation point.

Come with me to find a monster flower.
Please don't touch the petals. Be careful!

Use a period at the end of an indirect question.

An **indirect question** reports what someone asked, without using the speaker's exact words. Use a period at the end of an indirect question. A **direct question** is written exactly as it was originally asked. Use a question mark at the end of a direct question.

Indirect Question	Jen asked if this flower is the largest on earth.
Direct Question	Jen asked, "Is this flower the largest on earth?"

The Question Mark

Use a question mark at the end of an interrogative sentence.

An **interrogative sentence** is a sentence that asks a question.

Does a single flower really weigh twenty-four pounds**?**
Can the blossoms measure thirty-six inches across**?**

The Exclamation Point

Use an exclamation point at the end of an exclamatory sentence.

An **exclamatory sentence** expresses strong feeling.

This flower is huge**!**
It smells awful**!**

Use an exclamation point at the end of an imperative sentence expressing emotional excitement. Other imperative sentences should be followed by a period.

Stop**!**
Listen to it hiss as it opens**.**

Use an exclamation point after an interjection or any other exclamatory expression.

An **interjection** is a word or group of words used to express strong feeling.

Oh**!** How strange**!**
Look**!** What an unusual plant**!**
Yuck**!**

Rick Moranis with the carnivorous plant in the movie *Little Shop of Horrors.*

Use an exclamation point after a declarative sentence that you want to emphasize.

Declarative sentences generally end with a period. However, you may want to add extra feeling to the sentence by using an exclamation point instead of a period.

The name, *monster flower,* fits it well**.** (declarative sentence)
The flower deserves the name *monster***!** (exclamation)

Writing
TIP

Use exclamations sparingly in your writing. Overuse of exclamations lessens their importance.

Practice Your Skills

A. CONCEPT CHECK

End Marks   Write the following sentences, adding the proper end marks.

1. Do you know what the oldest living things on earth are
2. Surprise They are trees called bristlecone pines
3. Some bristlecone pines are more than two thousand years old
4. Look at this Here is one older than four thousand years
5. Bristlecone pines grow in California, Nevada, and Utah
6. You might wonder how tall such old trees become
7. Would you expect them to tower above all other trees
8. Actually, you are not likely to see one taller than sixty feet
9. Some bristlecone pines may look dead at first sight
10. Look again Leaves on the branches prove that the trees are still alive

B. APPLICATION IN LITERATURE

End Marks   Write the following passage. Add the appropriate end marks to each sentence.

[11]Who do you think invented flypaper [12]If you say it was man, you are wrong [13]Long before people even existed on earth, certain plants were already producing mucilage-covered insect traps [14]These plants can certainly be classed as trappers because they capture insects and use them for food [15]They are called by various names

Philip Goldstein, *Animals and Plants That Trap*

C. PROOFREADING SKILL

End Marks   Write the following paragraph. Correct all errors in capitalization, punctuation, grammar, and spelling. (15 errors)

Have you ever seen a Venus' flytrap It is a strange-looking Plant that actually eats insects You may have asked yourself how the plant catches its prey each leaf of the flytrap has three sensative hairs. When anything touchs these hairs. The leaves of the plant close up like a jaw. Snap. Can you beleive that the leafs close in only half of a second. The leaves then secrete a sap that digests the insect It takes ten days for the flytrap to finish digesting. It's amazing? Think about it. the Flytrap is a fascinating plant.

FOR MORE PRACTICE
See page 653.

Other Uses of the Period

Use a period after most abbreviations and after initials.

A period is used in other places besides the end of a sentence. Periods are also used after most abbreviations and after initials.

An **abbreviation** is a shortened, or an abbreviated, form of a word or phrase. Notice how periods are used in the following:

U.S. (United States)   Dr. (Doctor)
Aug. (August)   Fri. (Friday)
P.M. (post meridiem, after noon)   B.A. (Bachelor of Arts)

Some abbreviations do not need a period. When in doubt about whether to use a period after an abbreviation, look up the abbreviation in the dictionary. Dictionaries, newspapers, and magazines vary in the use of periods after an abbreviation. See what your teacher prefers.

TV (television)   mph (miles per hour)
mm (millimeter)   NATO (North Atlantic Treaty Organization)

Abbreviations are helpful when taking notes and doing other kinds of informal writing. However, these abbreviations are not acceptable in formal writing: names of cities, states, and countries, and names of months and days of the week.

Put a period after initials in a name. An initial is the first letter of a name. It is used alone to stand for the name. Also put a period after an abbreviation of a person's title.

John F. Kennedy
Mrs. P. T. Hernandez
Dr. Maureen H. O'Hara

Use a period after the letters or numbers in an outline or list.

Outline	List
I. President	1. George Washington
A. Domestic policy	2. John Adams
1. Economy	3. Thomas Jefferson
2. Housing	4. James Madison
B. Foreign policy	5. James Monroe
II. Congress	6. John Quincy Adams

A. CONCEPT CHECK

Periods   The following sentences are notes that were taken for a report. Write the sentences, adding or removing periods and end marks where necessary. If a sentence does not require additional punctuation, write *Correct*.

1. On Oct 13, 1925, a future prime minister of Great Britain, Margaret H Thatcher, was born.
2. She was the second daughter of Mr and Mrs Alfred Roberts.
3. Did you know she graduated from Oxford U
4. She earned three academic degrees: a BA, a BS, and an MA.
5. Mrs Thatcher first ran for Parliament in 1950.
6. She was not elected as a Member of Parliament, or MP, then.
7. However, she did win a seat as an M.P. in 1959.
8. Mrs Thatcher was elected prime minister in 1979.
9. She was the first woman in Eur. history to hold that office.
10. As prime minister, Mrs. Thatcher strongly supported N.A.T.O.
11. She sent Brit troops to the Falkland Islands in 1982
12. These islands, controlled by Great Britain, lie about 500 km off the coast of S America.
13. In Apr of 1982, Argentina had invaded the Falklands.
14. In June, after ten wks of fighting, G B won the war.
15. The next year, Mrs Thatcher began a second term as prime minister, and she served until her resignation in 1990.

B. PROOFREADING SKILL

Punctuating Correctly   Imagine that a friend has asked you to read and correct the following class report. Write the report, correcting all errors in grammar, capitalization, punctuation, and spelling. Remember to spell out words that should not be abbreviated in formal writing. (20 errors)

Anwar el-Sadat was the thirteenth child of poor egyptian villagers Few people would have expected the young Sadat to grow up to become pres. of Egypt. However, following the death of President Gamal A Nasser in Sept 1970, Mr Sadat was elected president of egypt. As president, Mr. Sadat worked to end hostilities between Egypt and Israel on Nov. 20, 1977, he made a historic speach before the Israeli parliament, saying he

Writing Theme
World Leaders

had come in peace. He, the Israeli prime minister, and the President of the US negotiated together. They met at Camp David, in MD, to arrange for a peace agreement. They finally signed the aggreement on Mar. 26, 1979, in Washington, DC. Important dates for Mr. Sadat are the following:

1 Born on December 25, 1918
2 Awarded the Nobel Peace Prize on December 10, 1978
3 Assassinated on Oct. 6, 1981

C. APPLICATION IN WRITING

Paragraph Outline   Think about a world leader you admire. Create an outline for a paragraph about the leader. Remember to place periods after the letters and numbers in the outline. If you wish, write a paragraph based on your outline.

FOR MORE PRACTICE
See page 653.

C H E C K ✔ P O I N T
MIXED REVIEW · PAGES 622–627

The following sentences are notes for a report on the Berlin Wall. Write the sentences, adding periods, question marks, and exclamation points where needed.

Writing Theme
Great Moments in History

1. Have you heard a song that has the words "and the walls came tumbling down" as part of the chorus
2. A historic wall tumbled down in 1989 between East and West Berlin
3. On Aug 13, 1961, E Germany began building the Berlin Wall to shut the E Germans off from W Germans
4. The E German government issued orders to shoot anyone trying to escape over or under the wall into W Berlin
5. Can you believe a government would do such a thing
6. What a frightening idea
7. You might wonder how long Berlin was divided
8. For almost thirty years, the wall divided the city
9. Then, in 1989, government reform led to the opening of the wall   The celebration began
10. Dates involved in this great period in history include these:
    1 1961—wall constructed
    2 1989—wall torn down

After twenty-eight years of dividing a country, the Berlin Wall comes down.

Use a **comma** before the conjunction in a compound sentence and to separate items in a series.

In speaking, you put words into groups and pause between the groups to help your listeners understand which words go together. In writing, commas are like pauses. They help your reader understand which words go together and make your meaning clear.

Commas in Compound Sentences

A **compound sentence** is a sentence in which independent sentences are joined with a conjunction.

Use a comma before the conjunction that joins two sentences in a compound sentence.

It took a long time, but women won suffrage.

Short sentences joined with *and* do not require a comma. However, sometimes using a comma in sentences joined with *but* or *or* improves clarity.

The judge may rule now, or she may not.

In a sentence with a two-part compound predicate, do not use a comma between the parts. In a three-part compound predicate, use a comma after each of the first two parts.

Two-Part Compound Predicate   Judy Garland sang and danced.
Three-Part Compound Predicate   Jeannette Rankin did social work, served in Congress, and worked for women's rights.

1920. Young girls show their support for the suffrage movement.

Practice Your Skills

A. CONCEPT CHECK

Commas in Compound Sentences   Write the following sentences, adding commas where necessary.

1. Elizabeth Cady Stanton was a reformer and she was a leader.
2. Stanton went to a meeting but women had no rights there.

3. The women could not vote speak or even sit with the men.
4. The women protested but the men would not change the rules.
5. Stanton decided women should take some action to demand their rights or nothing would change.
6. She met with other reformers discussed the issue and helped organize the Women's Rights Convention of 1848.
7. This meeting marked the beginning of her women's rights work and Stanton continued this work until she was eighty-seven.
8. She planned meetings joined protests and addressed gatherings.
9. Stanton worked for over fifty years but women still did not have the right to vote by the time she died in 1902.
10. Women in the United States obtained the right to vote in 1920 but the broader issue of women's rights still exists today.

B. DRAFTING SKILL

Sentence Combining   Combine each of the following pairs of sentences to form a compound sentence. Add a comma and the conjunction *and, but,* or *or* where appropriate.

11. Harriet Tubman was born into slavery. She escaped to freedom.
12. She helped other slaves to escape. She spoke against slavery.
13. The Fugitive Slave Act was passed in 1850. It said escaped slaves found in the North had to be returned to their owners.
14. People had to return escapees. Otherwise they would be breaking the law.
15. Tubman and others knew about the act. They chose to risk their own freedom to help slaves become free.
16. Escaping slaves headed for Free States in the North. In some cases, they went all the way to Canada.
17. Tubman successfully led more than three hundred slaves to freedom. As a result, she was called "the Moses of her people."
18. At one point, rewards of as much as forty thousand dollars were offered for Tubman's capture. She was never caught.
19. During the Civil War, Tubman cooked and did laundry for Union soldiers. Sometimes she served as a guide and a spy.
20. The war ended in 1865. Then Tubman went to live in Auburn, New York.
21. She helped set up schools for ex-slaves. She died in Auburn in 1913.
22. Harriet Tubman began life humbly. She achieved status and success by helping others.

FOR MORE PRACTICE
See pages 653–654.

Commas in a Series

Use a comma after each item in a series except the last one.

A **series** consists of three or more items of the same kind written one after the other in a sentence.

> I can sing, dance, and play the guitar. (verbs in a series)
> Karl, Yomika, and Tanya play the violin. (nouns in a series)
> The conductor waved the baton in and out, up and down, and back and forth. (groups of adverbs in a series)
> Will you play at the concert hall, at the theater, or in the park? (prepositional phrases in a series)
> It was getting late, the musicians were tired, and the star had still not arrived. (independent sentences in a series)

When two or more adjectives precede and modify the same noun but do not express a closely related thought, use a comma after each adjective except the last one.

If you can use *and* between the adjectives in a series and can reverse the order of the adjectives without changing the meaning, use a comma after each adjective except the last one.

> The young *and* talented pianist performed last night. (The *and* sounds natural, and reversing the adjectives does not change the meaning, so use a comma between the adjectives.)
> The young, talented pianist performed last night.

If two adjectives preceding the noun work together to express a single idea, do not use a comma between the adjectives.

> *Large marching* bands played on the football field.

Practice Your Skills

A. CONCEPT CHECK

Commas in a Series   Write the following sentences, adding commas where needed. If the sentence is correct, write *Correct.*

1. Mozart was a musician composer and conductor.
2. Mozart learned music quickly easily and eagerly.
3. He played the harpsichord, wrote musical pieces, and performed before royalty when he was just six years old.

Writing Theme
Music

4. Mozart his sister and his father toured Europe together in 1762.
5. They played music in Austria in Hungary and in Germany.
6. Audiences considered the young Mozart a gifted child musician.
7. He played in concerts studied his lessons and wrote music.
8. Mozart composed operas symphonies sonatas and serenades.
9. He wrote *The Magic Flute Don Giovanni* and *Requiem*.
10. His beautiful masterful works are still played today.

B. DRAFTING SKILL

Sentence Combining   Make each pair of sentences into a single sentence by combining the underlined items into a series and by adding correct punctuation.

11. During her career African-American performer Marian Anderson exhibited <u>musical</u> abilities. The abilities were <u>remarkable</u>.
12. She sang <u>alto</u> parts. She also sang <u>soprano and tenor</u> parts.
13. She sang <u>gospel music</u>. She sang <u>opera and show songs</u>.
14. Her voice had a <u>strong</u> quality. It had a <u>pure</u> quality.
15. She earned <u>scholarships</u>. She <u>studied voice and sang on stage</u>.
16. Anderson sang <u>in Britain</u>. She sang <u>in Austria and in Norway</u>.
17. Because of discrimination, Anderson was not allowed to sing in some concert halls in the United States, so she sang at <u>colleges</u>. She sang <u>in town halls and at the Lincoln Memorial</u>.
18. Audiences gave her <u>standing</u> ovations. The ovations were <u>long</u>.
19. On tour in 1957, she <u>traveled thirty-five thousand miles</u>. She <u>visited twelve nations and sang for countless audiences</u>.
20. She received many awards, such as <u>the Spingarn Medal</u>. She also received <u>the Bok Award and the Presidential Medal of Freedom</u>.

C. PROOFREADING SKILL

Commas in a Series   Write the paragraph, correcting all errors in spelling, capitalization, punctuation, and grammar. (15 errors)

  Louis Armstrong, the tallented Jazz musician, was a cornet player trumpet player and singer. Louis grew up. In New Orleans. in 1922 he moved to chicago to play cornet with the Creole Jazz Band and soon he was famous throughout the World. Armstrong was amung the first jazz soloists. He was known for his outstanding ability on the trumpet his jolly personality and his gravelly voice. He apeared in movies performed in concerts and made records.

Marian Anderson

FOR MORE PRACTICE
See pages 653–654.

COMMAS THAT SET OFF SPECIAL ELEMENTS

> Use a **comma** to set off introductory elements, interrupters, nouns of direct address, and appositives.

In speaking, you pause to set off special elements in a sentence. In writing, you use commas for the same purpose. Special elements include introductory words or phrases, interrupters, nouns used in addressing a person or persons directly, and appositives. These elements add extra information to a sentence but could be left out without changing the meaning of the sentence.

Commas After Introductory Elements

Use a comma after an introductory word or phrase to separate it from the rest of the sentence.

An **introductory word or phrase** introduces a sentence. Put a comma after the introductory element. This is where you would pause if you were saying the sentence aloud.

> Yes, rain is forecast again.
> Carrying my umbrella, I am prepared for rain.
> When the thunderstorm hits, we will be safe at home.

If the pause is only a short one, you may omit the comma.

> In town there was no fog.

Commas with Interrupters

Use commas before and after interrupters.

Interrupters are words or phrases that interrupt, or break, the flow of thought in a sentence. The commas used with interrupters mark pauses before and after the interruption.

> It could, however, clear up tomorrow.
> Clear skies, instead of clouds, will be a welcome sight.
> My aunt, who is never wrong about weather, says it will rain.

Writing
TIP

Varying the position of interrupting elements is one way to achieve sentence variety.

Practice Your Skills

A. CONCEPT CHECK

Commas with Introductory Elements and Interrupters   Write the following sentences, adding commas where necessary. If a sentence is correct, write *Correct.*

Writing Theme
Predictions and Nature

1. Many geologists especially in the past few decades have tried to find the cause of earthquakes.
2. From their research geologists know that most earthquakes are caused by the movement of flat plates in the earth's crust.
3. Actually these movements are too slow for people to detect.
4. Using instruments scientists can measure these movements.
5. As the plates slide past each other their edges grind together.
6. The grinding action which is quite powerful puts pressure on the rocks that lie along the edges of the plates.
7. Often nothing happens on the surface as a result of this grinding.
8. If pressure on those rocks becomes too great however the rocks break and shift.
9. When that happens the earth begins to shake.
10. Geologists despite all their efforts cannot predict when an earthquake will occur.

B. DRAFTING SKILL

Sentence Composing   Rewrite each sentence to include the word or phrase in parentheses as an introductory or interrupting element. Vary the placement of the elements, and use commas to punctuate your new sentences correctly.

11. A huge earthquake destroyed a Chinese town. (in February 1975)
12. Very few people died in that destructive earthquake. (however)
13. The town had been evacuated. (before the quake hit)
14. Authorities had predicted the earthquake. (fortunately)
15. People had been noticing strange happenings. (for months)
16. Hibernating snakes woke up and left their holes. (for example)
17. The snakes froze to death. (because of the cold winter weather)
18. Some people believed that the snakes were predicting an earthquake by their odd behavior. (rightly or wrongly)
19. People began feeling tremors. (just days before the earthquake)
20. Officials evacuated the town and saved the people. (thinking an earthquake was imminent)

FOR MORE PRACTICE
See page 654.

Commas with Nouns of Direct Address

Use commas to set off nouns used in direct address.

A **noun used in direct address** is the name or title of the person to whom you are speaking. Look at the following examples.

Incorrect   We will leave Matthew and be in Beijing Sunday.
Correct   We will leave, Matthew, and be in Beijing Sunday.

Incorrect   Call me Susan if you want information about flights.
Correct   Call me, Susan, if you want information about flights.

The incorrect sentences are confusing because the names *Matthew* and *Susan* have not been set off with commas.

Commas with Appositives

Use commas to set off most appositives.

An **appositive** is a noun or phrase that identifies the person or thing preceding it. When an appositive adds extra information about the word preceding it, the appositive should be set off with commas. Notice the examples in italics below.

> Confucius, *a Chinese philosopher,* lived about 500 B.C.
> Confucius said people must respect their elders, *older people.*

When an appositive is not just adding extra information but is needed to make the meaning clear, it is not set off with commas.

> The Asian country China has over one billion citizens.

Practice Your Skills

A. CONCEPT CHECK

Using Commas Write the conversation below, adding commas where they are necessary. If a sentence is correct, write *Correct.*

1. Sara: Dad today my teacher Ms. Luan said that the magnetic compass a direction-finding tool is a Chinese invention.
2. Dad: That is true Sara.
3. Elisa: Dad when did your parents Grandpa and Grandma Li come to America from China?
4. Dad: Well Elisa they made that trip in 1949. They are now proud to be Chinese Americans.

5. Dad: Girls do you know any other contributions we Chinese have made throughout history?
6. Sara: Sure. Chinese cooks prepare my favorite food egg rolls.
7. Elisa: A Chinese writer created "Lon Po Po" a fairy tale.
8. Dad: The Chinese people Sara and Elisa are noted for their writing.
9. Dad: Did you know that the Chinese historian Tu Yu wrote the first historical encyclopedia in about A.D. 800?
10. Sara: Do you mean Dad that encyclopedias are that old?
11. Dad: Yes, and they were written on paper a Chinese invention.
12. Elisa: What are some other Chinese inventions Dad?
13. Dad: See if you can guess Elisa.
14. Dad: What do we watch on the Fourth of July Independence Day?
15. Elisa: I know Dad. We watch fireworks.
16. Dad: Right Elisa! Chinese inventors developed gunpowder which is used in fireworks.
17. Dad: Our ancestors also invented porcelain the material that is often called china.
18. Sara: Grandma Li's favorite rice bowl the blue and white one is made of porcelain.
19. Dad: Yes Sara she brought that bowl with her from China.
20. Sara: Someday I would like to visit China the home of our ancestors.

Chinese porcelain bowls from the Qing Dynasty, Kangxi Period (1662–1722).

B. DRAFTING SKILL

Sentence Combining   Rewrite the following choppy paragraph. Make the style smoother by combining sentences and using the italicized words as appositives. Remember to punctuate all appositives correctly.

²¹Marco Polo was *a famous Venetian explorer.* ²²He traveled to China when he was seventeen. ²³Marco's father and uncle were *Venetian merchants.* ²⁴They had journeyed to China two years before their trip with Marco. ²⁵Marco, his father, and his uncle traveled over land from Hormuz to Beijing. ²⁶Hormuz is *a city on the Persian Gulf.* ²⁷This journey lasted for three years. ²⁸In China the Polos worked for Kublai Khan. ²⁹Kublai Khan was *the ruler of China.* ³⁰The Polos remained in China for seventeen years. ³¹When Marco returned to Venice, he wrote a book about his journey. ³²This book is titled *The Travels of Marco Polo.*

FOR MORE PRACTICE
See pages 654–655.

Rewrite the sentences. Add commas where they are needed, and delete any unnecessary commas.

1. The scarecrow is on fire Dorothy throws water and the wicked witch is hit by the water, and melts.
2. How did the filmmakers of *The Wizard of Oz* make the witch become smaller smaller and smaller and then disappear?
3. Using dry ice an elevator and clothes on the floor the clever, filmmakers caused the witch to "melt."
4. Margaret Hamilton who played the witch was actually lowered beneath the stage by an elevator.
5. At the same time dry ice was used to create a cloudy haze.
6. Dry ice solid carbon dioxide gives off a misty gas as it melts.
7. When *The Wizard of Oz* was made in 1938 it was one of the first movies to use special effects illusions created by technology.
8. Special effects as you know are an important part of movies and the effects are much more sophisticated now than in 1938.
9. Readers have you seen the movies *E.T. Raiders of the Lost Ark* and *Jaws?*
10. If so, you have seen movies with spectacular, special effects.
11. Do you know how technicians made E.T. Elliot and the other boys in the movie *E.T.* appear to fly on bicycles?
12. Pictures were taken of the scenery the actors were filmed pedaling stationary bicycles and the films were combined.
13. Using a special screen the filmmakers were able to block out part of the scenery in the first film.
14. In the blocked-out part the pictures of the actors on bicycles were inserted.
15. The result gave the illusion of story characters flying on bicycles above police cars over hills and across the full moon.
16. Movie makers use many other amazing clever special effects.
17. Movie fans have you seen trains crash cars explode or buildings burn in the movies?
18. They were probably tiny lifelike scale models.
19. Robots computers and other technological tools are used to create special effects today.
20. Thanks to special effects the movies can take you to a world of fantasy adventure or just everyday surroundings.

OTHER USES OF THE COMMA

> Use a **comma** to set off quotations, dates, addresses, and parts of a letter. Also use a comma to prevent misreading.

There are specific elements in your writing that will always require commas. In this section, you will learn about these elements.

Commas in Quotations

Use commas to set off explanatory words that come before or after a direct quotation.

A **direct quotation** is a restatement of someone's exact words. These exact words are enclosed in quotation marks.

A direct quotation may be introduced by or followed by an explanatory phrase. Use a comma after an explanatory phrase that precedes a direct quotation and after a direct quotation that is followed by an explanatory phrase.

> My dad used to say, "Things always look better after a good night's sleep."
> "You shouldn't go swimming right after you've eaten a meal," said Joanna.

A direct quotation may be separated into two parts, with an explanatory phrase between the parts. Such a form is called a **divided quotation.** In a divided quotation, a comma is used after the last word of the first part of the quotation. Another comma is used after the last word in the explanatory phrase.

> "If you take an umbrella with you," said Mother, "then it probably won't rain."

An **indirect quotation** is a restatement in different words of something that was said. An indirect quotation is usually introduced by the word *that* and does not require a comma.

> David said that he drinks eight glasses of water every day.
> My uncle says that eating yogurt every day keeps him healthy.

Practice Your Skills

CONCEPT CHECK

Commas in Quotations   Write the sentences, adding commas if necessary. If a sentence does not need commas, write *Correct*.

1. Mrs. Ortiz said "A stitch in time saves nine."
2. Dan asked "What does that mean?"
3. "It means" said Amy "that a little work now saves more later."
4. Dan said that he still didn't understand.
5. "Make a little tear in a piece of paper" suggested Mrs. Ortiz.
6. "Now" she said "put a piece of tape over the tear."
7. Amy asked "Why doesn't the paper tear some more?"
8. Dan exclaimed "The tape keeps the tear from getting bigger!"
9. Mrs. Ortiz said that a little tape now saves more tape later.
10. "I think" said Dan "that is good advice."

Commas in Dates, Addresses, and Parts of Letters

Use commas to separate the parts of dates, addresses, and letters.

Use a comma between the day of the month and the year. If a date is part of a sentence, use a comma after the year too. Do not use a comma if only the month and the year are given.

> February 29, 1964
> On May 22, 1989, my dad got a new job in Georgia.
> Kim has lived in California since October 1985.

When writing an address in a sentence, use a comma after the names of the addressee, the street, and the city. Do not use a comma between the state and the ZIP code. Use a comma after the ZIP code if the sentence continues. When only a city and a state or country are given, use a comma after each part.

> The address is 84 Cedar Lane, Rome, Georgia 30161.
> I wonder if Rome, Georgia, is named after Rome, Italy.

In friendly letters, use a comma after the greeting. In both friendly and business letters, use a comma after the closing.

> Dear Aunt Sue,   Yours truly,

Practice Your Skills

A. CONCEPT CHECK

Commas in Dates and Addresses   Write the following sentences, adding commas where necessary.

Writing Theme
Letters and Visits

1. My cousin John came to visit us in Chicago in May 1987.
2. He has lived in many places, from Juneau Alaska to Bangor Maine.
3. He was born in Oak Ridge Tennessee on April 28 1964.
4. When he was growing up, his family lived in Missoula Montana and Reno Nevada.
5. I have always lived at 27 Mango Street Chicago Illinois 60646.
6. My family moved here on August 15 1978 before I was born.
7. John moved to Stockton California on January 1 1989.
8. He got a new job in Lahaina Hawaii in June 1991.
9. He invited me to go with him to Honolulu Hawaii this August.
10. I now write to him at 274 Surf Lane Lahaina HI 96761.

B. REVISION SKILL

Using Commas Correctly   Write the following letter, adding commas as necessary.

March 28 1994

Dear Lucy

You asked if I had heard anything about Trey Nylund's "Sound Off" tour. I wrote to his fan club on December 4 1993 when we first heard about the tour. I finally received a newsletter from his club in Denver Colorado and it says that his tour will include concerts in Lincoln Nebraska and Kansas City Kansas. Would you like to go to one of the concerts in Lincoln? The dates are July 14 and July 15. If we can't get tickets to a concert in Lincoln, I'm going to ask Dad if I can visit my aunt in Prairie Village Kansas; it's near Kansas City. Can you come with me? The concert dates in Kansas City are July 20 and July 21. Please write and let me know what you think. Did I tell you that we are moving? My new address will be 7194 Sixth Street Seward Nebraska 68434 as of next Monday.

Love
Allison

P.S. You really should join Trey's fan club. Write to Trey's Troops 828 Washington Street Denver Colorado 80203.

FOR MORE PRACTICE
See pages 654–655.

Writing
TIP

Although commas can add clarity, take care not to overuse structures that require commas. Too many pauses can confuse your reader and make your sentences difficult to read.

Writing Theme
Confusing Situation

FOR MORE PRACTICE
See pages 654–655.

Commas to Prevent Misreading

Use a comma to separate any sentence parts that might be improperly joined or misunderstood without the comma.

When speaking, you sometimes pause to prevent your listeners from becoming confused. In writing, commas prevent such misunderstanding. Notice how inserting a comma in the following sentence eliminates the possibility of misunderstanding.

Confusing   After searching my brother found a recipe for brownies.

Clear   After searching, my brother found a recipe for brownies.

Practice Your Skills

CONCEPT CHECK

Commas for Clarity   Write the following sentences, adding commas to prevent misreading.

1. The night before my brother asked me to help him bake brownies.
2. I found the nine- by twelve-inch pan and the flour was in a canister on the counter.
3. Before greasing the pan had to be clean and dry.
4. No matter what you should not grease the pan too heavily.
5. I measured the sugar and the eggs were already in the bowl.
6. After stirring my brother carefully added the flour.
7. By the time he finished the batter was thick and smooth.
8. As I stirred the chocolate made the batter brown.
9. Carefully pouring my brother filled the pan to the top.
10. After the brownies baked my brother put them on a wire rack to cool.

> Use a **semicolon** to separate the parts of a compound sentence.
>
> Use a **colon** to introduce a list of items, to set off the greeting in a business letter, and to separate hours from minutes in time expressions.

The Semicolon

An end mark indicates the end of an expression. A comma indicates a pause in a sentence. A **semicolon (;)** indicates a longer pause and more definite break than a comma does.

Use a semicolon to separate the parts of a compound sentence when you do not use a coordinating conjunction.

Tom files the new orders; it is part of his job.
Anne wants to be a veterinarian; she likes helping animals.

Use a semicolon to separate items in a series that are already punctuated with commas.

The company opened offices in Akron and Toledo, Ohio;
Flint and Detroit, Michigan; and Pella, Iowa.

Use a semicolon between the parts of a compound sentence when these clauses are long or complicated, or when they contain commas.

For the basketball team, Mario chose James, Tina, and Inez;
and I chose David and Jim.
Cassie collects wildflowers; and she dries them thoroughly,
arranges them, and gives the arrangements as gifts.

In the first sentence, commas separate the parts of the direct object *James, Tina, and Inez.* In the second sentence, commas separate the parts of the compound predicate: *dries, arranges,* and *gives.* In both cases, a semicolon is used to separate the parts of the compound sentence even though the sentence has a coordinating conjunction. The semicolon breaks the sentence into clearly visible separate parts.

Writing
TIP

Remember that the parts of a compound sentence must express thoughts that are closely related to each other. Do not join unrelated ideas with a semicolon.

The Colon

Use a colon (:) to introduce or draw attention to information that follows.

Use a colon to introduce a list of things, or use it after the greeting in a business letter to introduce the body of the letter.

List   The office needs the following supplies: pencils, black pens, printer ribbons, and large rubber bands.

Greetings   Dear Mrs. Olivos: Dear Sir: Dear Park Director:

In introducing a list, a colon always follows a complete sentence; it never comes directly after the verb.

Incorrect   I need: a glove, a bat, and a ball.

Correct   I need the following things: a glove, a bat, and a ball.

Use a colon between numbers that represent hours and minutes in time expressions and between chapter and verse in biblical references.

before 10:30 P.M.   at 3:15 A.M.   Genesis 2: 4–7

Practice Your Skills

A. CONCEPT CHECK

Semicolons and Colons   Add semicolons and colons to these sentences where necessary.

1. Fishing is a sport it can also be a job.
2. People who fish for sport are called anglers they enjoy hooking fish.
3. Many anglers start fishing before 500 A.M.
4. They might bring the following equipment on a fishing trip rods, hats, food for themselves, and bait for the fish.
5. For bait, fishing enthusiasts use artificial lures made of plastic, metal, feathers, and other materials, worms or insects.
6. Fishing is fun for some it is a serious business for others.
7. Commercial fishing provides food for people, animal feed, and jobs and it has been a major food industry for centuries.
8. Even the Bible mentions commercial fishing, in Mark 1 16-20.
9. Commercial boats use these kinds of nets seines, trawls, or gill nets.
10. Some fishing boats bring in a fresh catch daily and others stay out for weeks and freeze, can, or dry their daily catch.

B. PROOFREADING SKILL

Using Semicolons and Colons Correctly   Proofread and then write the following paragraphs. Correct all errors in capitalization, punctuation, spelling, and grammar. (15 errors)

Photography is an interesting hobby and it can be a challenging career in such feilds as advertising, journalism, medicine, and engineering. Photographers need these things a camera, film, light, and a subject. Follow these steps for taking a picture find an interesting subject, make sure their is enough light, and hold the camera still. To avoid blurry pictures.

The best way to learn photography is to take photos as offen as you can. Don't try to take pictures on sunny days from 1200 P.M. to 300 P.M., too much light is as bad as too little.

Would you like to be a Professional photographer. Write to Professional Photographers of america, 1090 Executive Way, Des Plaines Illinois 60018 for information.

FOR MORE PRACTICE
See page 655.

CHECK ✔ POINT
MIXED REVIEW · PAGES 637–643

Write the following letter, adding any commas, semicolons, and colons that have been left out.

Writing Theme
Drama

June 18 19_ _

Dear Mr. Holmes

As soon as I heard you, the great Sherlock Holmes, say "Watson, the game's afoot" I knew I was going to enjoy this play. I have seen your plays in New York City Paris, France and Dallas; but I expected this performance to be special.

The play was wonderful I had a great time. I will always remember two moments the lights going down at 700 P.M. and the applause and bows at 900 P.M. For those two hours I felt like I was in your sitting room in Victorian London it was a real place to me. By the time I left my knees were so stiff that I could hardly walk!

Now I am writing a mystery story and I would appreciate any advice you could give me. Please write to me at Bayard Lodge Route 112 Worthington Massachusetts 01098.

Sincerely
Michael Weitz

THE HYPHEN

Use a **hyphen** to mark the division of a word at the end of a line. Use a **hyphen** in compound adjectives, some compound nouns, compound numbers, and fractions.

Use a hyphen to divide a word at the end of a line.

Only words of two or more syllables may be divided at the end of a line. Words should be divided between syllables only.

> The local Sierra Club voted to send two members to the con-ference on recycling.

Do not divide words so as to leave a single letter at the end or the beginning of a line.

| *Incorrect* | c-hapter | meetin-g |
| *Correct* | chap-ter | meet-ing |

Use a hyphen in compound adjectives when they precede the word they modify and with certain compound nouns.

Hyphen	Caroline reviewed her well-received report.
No Hyphen	Caroline's report was well received.
Compound Nouns	president-elect ex-secretary

Use a hyphen in compound numbers from twenty-one through ninety-nine and in fractions.

> seventy-five chapters   a two-thirds majority

Practice Your Skills

CONCEPT CHECK

Hyphens   Write the sentences, adding hyphens where necessary.

[1]This was the twenty third meeting of Pineview's Sierra Club. [2]Two thirds of the forty five regular members attended. [3]The new vice president asked that all still active members be contacted. [4]He noted that the all important regional meeting would be coming up in two weeks. [5]He asked the member ship committee to provide an up to date membership list.

Writing
TIP

Consult a dictionary if you are unsure about hyphenating a compound.

Writing Theme
Minutes of a Meeting

FOR MORE PRACTICE
See pages 655–656.

THE APOSTROPHE

Use an **apostrophe** to show possession, to show where letters are omitted in a contraction, and to form the plurals of letters and words used as words.

The apostrophe is most commonly used in forming possessive nouns and contractions. It is also used in special plural forms.

Apostrophes with Possessives

The **possessive form** of a noun indicates that the person named owns or possesses something.

To form the possessive of a singular noun, add 's.

woman + **'s** = woman's   boy + **'s** = boy's
worker + **'s** = worker's   James + **'s** = James's

To form the possessive of a plural noun that ends in s, add only an apostrophe.

girls + **'** = girls'   birds + **'** = birds'
boys + **'** = boys'   animals + **'** = animals'

To form the possessive of a plural noun that does not end in s, add 's.

men + **'s** = men's   children + **'s** = children's

Writing Theme
Animal Senses

Practice Your Skills

CONCEPT CHECK

Apostrophes with Possessives   Some words in the following sentences have errors in the use of apostrophes. Write each word correctly.

1. Animals senses are quite different from humans senses'.
2. For example, a cats' sense of hearing is very well developed.
3. Cat's ears can be aimed in different direction's to collect sound waves and improve the creatures hearing.
4. Cats' can even hear a mouses very high-pitched squeaking; neither adults nor childrens ears can pick up such sounds.

5. A humans' sense of smell is not nearly as sensitive as a dogs.
6. The sense of smell is a dogs most highly developed sense.
7. The moisture on dogs noses' helps these animals detect odors.
8. The bloodhounds ability to recognize and follow one persons scent is remarkable.
9. Beagles sensory abilities help them track wild animal's.
10. In addition, a dogs whiskers help the dog identify the winds direction, so that the dog can locate the source of an odor.

FOR MORE PRACTICE
See pages 655–656.

Apostrophes with Contractions

Use an apostrophe to show where letters are omitted in a contraction.

A **contraction** is a shortened word formed from two words. An apostrophe is used in a contraction to show where one or more letters have been omitted. Some commonly used contractions are shown in the following chart.

Commonly Used Contractions

we are ⟶ we're	where is ⟶ where's
she is ⟶ she's	they are ⟶ they're
there is ⟶ there's	cannot ⟶ can't
I would ⟶ I'd	could not ⟶ couldn't
we will ⟶ we'll	will not ⟶ won't
they will ⟶ they'll	was not ⟶ wasn't
they have ⟶ they've	would not ⟶ wouldn't
it is ⟶ it's	who is ⟶ who's

Be careful not to confuse a contraction with a possessive pronoun. Remember that apostrophes are not used in possessive pronouns: *your, yours, its, his, hers, ours, their, theirs, whose.*

Contraction	Possessive
it's (*it is* or *it has*)	its
who's (*who is* or *who has*)	whose
you're (*you are*)	your
they're (*they are*)	their

To form the plurals of letters and words used as words, add 's.

I can't tell the difference between the *e*'**s** and the *i*'**s**.
How many *and*'**s** are there in this paragraph?

Note that plurals of numbers and years do not use an apostrophe.

Your *5***s** and *6***s** look the same. She was born in the *1940***s**.

Practice Your Skills

Writing Theme
Reviewing Writing

A. CONCEPT CHECK

Apostrophes in Contractions   Write the correct word given in parentheses.

1. (Isn't, Isnt) that (you're, your) poem in the school paper?
2. I think (it's, its) very funny.
3. It reminds me of Ogden (Nashes', Nash's) poems.
4. His poems always make me laugh, as (yours, your's) do.
5. I also liked (Carlos', Carlos's) and (Tina's, Tinas') poetry.
6. Did you hear (they're, their) poems in class yesterday?
7. (Here's, Heres) an announcement of a poetry contest.
8. (Its, It's) open to amateur poets; (their, they're) invited to send in as many poems as they wish.
9. I think (your, you're) the one (who's, whose) going to win.
10. (We'll, Well) just wait for the (judge's, judges') opinions.

B. REVISION SKILL

Using Apostrophes Correctly   Rewrite the paragraph, adding and deleting apostrophes as necessary.

11In Dads old trunk, I found an autograph book from the 1860s that belonged to Great-Grandma Pollys great-grandmother. **12**Thats our grandmother with three *greats'* in front. **13**Most people just wrote they're name and hometown and the date. **14**There are a few *Your's Trulys* here and there. **15**I could'nt believe how beautiful the handwriting was! **16**The letters have loops and strokes we dont use today. **17**For example, the capital *Ms'* are pointy with a big loop at the end. **18**I was confused by the double *s*'es in Massachusetts, because the two *s*'s don't look alike. **19**Some of the numbers' are unusual too. **20**The 7's are huge and extend way below the base line.

FOR MORE PRACTICE
See pages 655–656.

QUOTATION MARKS

> Use **quotation marks** at the beginning and the end of direct quotations and to set off titles of short works.

Direct Quotations

Use quotation marks to enclose direct quotations.

A **direct quotation** is a restatement of someone's exact words. Use quotation marks to show where the exact words of a speaker or writer begin and end. Quotation marks are not used with indirect quotations.

> Anita said, "Someday I want to be an astronaut."
> Anita said that someday she wants to be an astronaut.

When a direct quotation is interrupted by explanatory words, enclose each part of the quotation in quotation marks.

> "Someday," Anita said, "I want to be an astronaut."

Use either a period or a comma after the explanatory words in a divided quotation. If the first part completes a sentence, use a period. If the sentence continues, use a comma.

Do not capitalize the first word of the second part of a divided quotation unless it begins a new sentence, is a proper noun, or is the pronoun *I*.

> "Traveling to the stars," said Anita, "would be exciting."
> "I can see the stars now," said Thomas. "I use my telescope."

Quotation Marks with Other Punctuation

Sentences that contain direct quotations will contain other types of punctuation as well as quotation marks.

Place quotation marks outside commas and end marks following direct quotations.

> Jill said, "The nearest star is 4.3 light-years away."
> "The nearest star is 4.3 light-years away," Jill said.
> "Find the Big Dipper," said Tom, "and you see Ursa Major."

Use quotation marks outside question marks and exclamation points if those marks are part of the quotation itself. Place quotation marks inside question marks and exclamation points if they are not part of the quotation.

Jill asked, "Did you see the Pleiades last night**?**"
"They were so bright**!**" exclaimed Anita.
Did Thomas say, "Bring the star map"**?**
How exciting to hear Anita say, "I can see it"**!**

Practice Your Skills

A. CONCEPT CHECK

Quotation Marks   Write the following sentences, adding all needed punctuation marks.

1. Did I just hear Ms. García, our tour guide, say The Hubble Space Telescope (HST) will still work
2. Greg answered That's what she said. Weren't you listening
3. You see explained our guide even with a flawed mirror it can still observe objects more clearly than telescopes on Earth can
4. Wow Greg exclaimed How can it do that
5. Oh no I thought to myself he interrupted Ms. García
6. What a relief to hear Ms. García say That's a good question
7. She pointed to a model of the solar system and answered As you know, the HST is traveling outside of Earth's atmosphere
8. Out in space she continued gases and particles in the atmosphere will not interfere with the telescope's view
9. After it is repaired, it will be able to observe objects fifty times fainter than any other telescope can Ms. García said
10. So the HST will help us learn more after all she concluded

B. APPLICATION IN LITERATURE

Using Quotation Marks   Write the following passage, adding quotation marks and other punctuation as needed.

[11] . . . Why, he said to Wagnall, is this star so important?
[12] Wagnall looked incredulous then pained then understanding.
[13] Well, he began, I guess stars are like people. [14] The well-behaved ones never attract much attention. [15] They teach us something of course but we can learn a lot more from the ones that go off the rails

Writing Theme
The Stars

16And do stars do that sort of thing very often?

17Every year about a hundred blow up in our galaxy alone, but those are only ordinary novae.

18. . . There was a knock at the door and Jamieson entered, carrying some still-damp photographic plates.

19Those last exposures did it! he said jubilantly. **20**They show the shell expanding round the nova. **21**And the speed agrees with your Doppler shifts.

22So I should hope, growled Moulton. **23**Lets look at them.

Arthur C. Clarke, *Earthlight*

Quotation Marks in Dialogue

A **dialogue** is a conversation between two or more people. When you are writing a dialogue, begin a new paragraph every time the speaker changes, and use quotation marks as you do for all direct quotations.

"Congratulations, Amelia," Railey said. "Are you excited?"

She replied, "Excited? No. All I did was lie on my stomach and take pictures of the clouds. Bill did all the fly-ing—had to. I was just baggage, like a sack of potatoes."

"What of it? You're still the first woman to fly the Atlantic, and what's more, the first woman pilot."

"Oh, well," Amelia said, "someday I'll try it alone."

Practice Your Skills

REVISION SKILL

Punctuating Dialogue   Write the following conversation. Use the correct punctuation, and create a new paragraph for each new speaker.

1What are you reading, Kim asked Carmen **2**I'm reading a really good book about Beryl Markham answered Kim **3**Who asked Carmen **4**I've never heard of her **5**Oh, you should read this book **6**Beryl Markham was a fascinating woman Kim exclaimed **7**She was the first person to fly alone over the Atlantic from Europe to the Americas **8**She was also the first professional female pilot to fly in the African wilderness **9**She sounds interesting Carmen agreed **10**Did she know Amelia Earhart?

FOR MORE PRACTICE
See page 656.

Writing
TIP

Use dialogue in your writing to help your reader see your characters more vividly. For an example of dialogue used in characterization, see Writer's Workshop 2, pages 50–51.

Writing Theme
Famous Pilots

Titles of Short Works

Use quotation marks to set off the titles of short works: book chapters, stories, reports, articles, songs, and poems.

Chapter 4, "The Early Years"   "Realism in Poe's Poetry"
"The Pit and the Pendulum"   "Annabel Lee"

Titles of Longer Works

Underline the titles of longer works: books, plays, newspapers, magazines, motion pictures, television series, epic poems, musical compositions, and paintings. Also underline the names of ships, airplanes (but not the type of plane), spacecraft, and trains.

Collected Stories of Edgar Allan Poe   Mystery Theater
The Saturday Evening Post   The Black Crypt

Terms that are underlined in writing will appear in italics in print.

Practice Your Skills

CONCEPT CHECK

Punctuation of Titles   Write the following sentences, punctuating the titles as required.

1. Edgar Allan Poe was an American author who is best known for his scary stories, such as The Tell-Tale Heart.
2. His famous poem The Raven first appeared in 1845 in a newspaper called the Evening Mirror.
3. Poe also wrote The Poetic Principle and other literary essays.
4. He even wrote a play, titled Politian.
5. Poe became the father of detective fiction when he wrote the story The Murders in the Rue Morgue.
6. The story was first published in Graham's Lady's and Gentleman's Magazine in April 1841.
7. Many of Poe's stories were collected in the book Tales of the Grotesque and Arabesque, published in 1840.
8. Plays, musical compositions, and movies have been made from Poe's stories, including the terrifying film House of Usher.
9. Rachmaninoff based his symphony The Bells on a Poe poem.
10. Do you suppose there is an airplane named The Raven?

Writing
━━TIP━━
Capitalized letters draw attention to the most important words in a title. To review the guidelines for capitalizing words in titles, see page 612.

Writing Theme
Edgar Allan Poe

FOR MORE PRACTICE
See page 656.

CHECK ✔ POINT

A. Write the following sentences, adding hyphens and apostrophes where necessary.

1. Mount Vesuviuss eruption in A.D. 79 buried the city of Pompeii.
2. One writers eyewitness report described how the citys buildings disappeared under hot ashes, cinders, and stones.
3. The citys well preserved ruins were discovered in the 1700s.
4. Archaeologists didnt begin excavating the ruins systematically until after 1860.
5. By now, theyve uncovered about three fourths of the city.
6. The ruins provide a time capsule view of first century Roman life.
7. The once thriving city looks much as it did nineteen hundred years ago.
8. Ordinary citizens two story houses line the streets.
9. Pompeiis central square is surrounded by a theater, an amphitheater, temples, and public baths.
10. Beautiful floor mosaics, furniture, and glass objects show the Pompeiians well developed artistic skills.

B. Write the following sentences, using quotation marks, commas, underlining, and end marks correctly.

11. Jennifer said Let's make a time capsule to put in the wall of the new school building
12. Mr. Chung said he thought that was a good idea
13. We could put in things that tell about our lives now suggested Jennifer or things that are important to us
14. Mark exclaimed I'd put in the movie The Rivers Run
15. I'd put in my favorite book, Sarah's Journey said Angela
16. Michelle asked Could we contribute music we like
17. She said she wanted to include the Beatles' song Michelle
18. Bradley asked if he could put in a design he had made for a spaceship he called Star Explorer
19. We could make a video Ron said and show people in the future what we did during a day at school
20. Does everyone like that idea Mr. Chung asked How many want to work on a class video

Writing Theme
Memoirs and
Autobiographies

A. Using End Marks   Write the following notes, adding periods, question marks, and exclamation points where needed.

1. Anne Frank was a thirteen-year-old girl when she and her family and four other people went into hiding in Holland

2. Why did they go into hiding

3. During World War II, Nazis in Europe imprisoned Jews and other groups of people in concentration camps

4. Because they were Jewish, Mr and Mrs Frank decided that they had to hide from the Nazis to protect their family

5. With the help of non-Jewish friends, they were able to hide in the top floors of a business building

6. For two years, seven or eight people lived together in just a few small rooms

7. They lived in constant fear of being discovered

8. Imagine All that time they never got to go outside

9. They had to whisper and keep fairly still whenever other people were in the rest of the building

10. Anne often wondered how she could keep so quiet for such long stretches of time

11. Did all these precautions help save the family

12. No

13. In Aug 1944, the Nazis found the hiding place

14. Anne and the others were sent to prison camps, and all but Mr Frank died in the camps

15. We know their story because Anne Frank kept a diary that was published after her death

B. Using Commas to Separate Ideas   Write the following sentences, adding commas where necessary.

16. Ernesto Galarza was born in Mexico in 1905 but he came to the United States with his family in 1911.

17. He became an educator a labor leader and a writer.

18. Galarza was an able determined and outspoken supporter of farm workers' rights.

19. He tried to organize a union of farm workers in 1947 but his efforts were opposed by big business farmers.

20. Galarza wrote a report in 1956 that described the low wages filthy living conditions and poor treatment of farm workers in the United States.

21. Galarza said that big business farmers earned huge profits by unfairly controlling the water supply the farm workers and the markets for farm products.
22. Galarza went on to say that the farm workers deserved to make a decent living and he worked hard to help them make better lives.
23. In the late 1960s, Galarza left the union he began teaching school and he spent more time writing.
24. He wrote his autobiography, *Barrio Boy* and he published it.
25. The book tells about how his family emigrated from Mexico to the United States settled in a California city and began a new life.

C. Using Commas to Set Off Special Elements Write the sentences, adding commas where they are needed.

26. Have you read *Millie's Book* the memoirs of Mildred Kerr Bush?
27. The book tells about living in the President's home the White House.
28. Readers do you know who Mildred is?
29. Mildred is Millie the pet dog of George and Barbara Bush.
30. Of course Millie could not have written the book herself.
31. Dogs you know cannot write.
32. Actually Mrs. Bush wrote *Millie's Book.*
33. The book which was written from Millie's point of view includes many photographs of Millie with movie stars and world leaders.
34. Near the end there is even a picture of one of Millie's puppies with Queen Elizabeth II of Great Britain.
35. Proceeds from the book were given to the Barbara Bush Foundation for Family Literacy an organization that promotes learning to read and write.

D. Using Commas with Dates, Direct Quotations, and Addresses and to Prevent Misreading Write the following sentences, adding commas where necessary.

36. Helen Keller was born on June 27 1880 in the town of Tuscumbia Alabama.
37. In February 1882 an illness took her sight and hearing.
38. On March 3 1887 Anne Sullivan came to the Kellers' house to be Helen's teacher.
39. Anne, who was partially blind, had studied at the Perkins Institution in Boston Massachusetts since October 7 1880.

40. Helen later said "The most important day I remember in all my life is the one on which my teacher came to me."

41. Before teaching Helen Anne had to break through the silence and darkness that surrounded the girl.

42. Anne had patience and the desire to learn was strong in Helen.

43. Six weeks after her arrival, Anne said "Helen knows the meaning of more than a hundred words now."

44. By the time they finished few subjects were unknown to Helen.

45. After Helen entered Radcliffe College in Cambridge Massachusetts in 1900, she wrote her autobiography.

E. Using Semicolons and Colons   Write the following letter, adding semicolons and colons where necessary.

46Dear Ms. Gillespie

47Thank you for your letter I am glad you enjoy my books.

48You asked me for the following information the reason I came to Yorkshire, England whether I still work as a vet what my favorite Yorkshire dale village is and what advice I would give on writing memoirs. **49**In the 1930s, during the Depression, a position as a vet was hard to come by and I was lucky enough to find a job in Yorkshire. **50**Today, even with 200 A.M. calls, I still enjoy working with animals it beats sitting at a desk all day! **51**As for my favorite village, I hate to choose one over the others they are all special.

52My advice on writing memoirs is to begin by reading others' writings their memoirs, letters, diaries, journals. **53**Plan a beginning, a middle, and an end to your story and you should try to get your reader to see things as you do. **54**When you begin to write, all you really need are these things a pen, some paper, and your memories.

55Sincerely,
James Herriot

F. Using Hyphens and Apostrophes   Write the following paragraph, adding hyphens and apostrophes where necessary.

56Im interested in finding out about writers childhoods. **57**Thats why I read writers autobiographies. **58**There are two Id especially recommend. **59**Right now Im reading Beverly Clearys book *A Girl from Yamhill.* **60**Cleary is a well known childrens author. **61**Shes written at least thirty nine books in her forty year career. **62**When did she make the all important decision to become a writer? **63**A much loved teacher praised twelve year old Beverlys writing. **64**The teachers encouragement made her think about being a writer. **65**Recently Ive also read Milton Meltzers memoir, *Starting from Home.* **66**The number of books hes written is at least in the 70s and includes both histories and biographies. **67**Meltzer began writing professionally in the late 1930s. **68**The Great Depression affected both Meltzers youth in Massachusetts and Clearys childhood in Oregon. **69**Also, both writers were influenced by their close knit, hard working families. **70**Both these writers autobiographies earn As from me.

G. Using Quotation Marks with Other Punctuation   Write the following sentences, adding punctuation where necessary.

71. Good morning television audience cried Johnny B., the show's host. Welcome to Book Talk, your favorite daytime series

72. Here's our first guest Johnny said Anna, what did you read

73. Anna said I read a book called The Memoirs of Chief Red Fox

74. He was a Sioux Indian born in 1870, six years before the Battle of the Little Big Horn she explained

75. Later Anna said he was sent to government boarding schools

76. Wow said Johnny B. Didn't he resent having to leave his family

77. He was sad but resigned to learning a new way of life Anna answered

78. She said In 1893 he became part of Buffalo Bill's traveling Wild West Show

79. Didn't he think that was embarrassing the host asked

80. No, he felt the show actually improved the popular image of Native Americans Anna answered

81. Anna continued Red Fox traveled all across America and Europe

82. He met many famous people she said like Theodore Roosevelt, Thomas Edison, Alexander Graham Bell, and Jack London

83. Red Fox, however, never forgot that he was a member of the Sioux she said

84. He said that he adapted to his environment, but he was still a native of the wilderness Anna concluded

85. Audience Johnny B. asked do you agree with his statement

A. Using Commas and End Marks   Write the sentences, adding commas and end marks where they are needed. If a sentence is correctly punctuated, write *Correct.*

1. Do you collect sports cards or do you have a friend who does
2. If you do collect sports cards you are one among millions.
3. Card collecting has become a popular hobby but it has also become a business
4. Today collectors can buy and sell baseball football hockey and basketball cards at card stores auctions or conventions.
5. The condition of a card affects its worth.
6. A creased wrinkled torn or frayed card is not worth much.
7. Even a card in perfect condition however may have little value if few people want to buy it.
8. What do you suppose is the most valuable card
9. It is a rare 1910 card of Honus Wagner who was a shortstop for the Pittsburgh Pirates
10. In 1991 his card sold for over $450,000

B. Using Commas and Semicolons   Write the sentences, adding commas and semicolons where necessary.

11. On October 2 1982 Ken Hakuta's two sons Justin and Kenzo received a package from their grandparents in Japan.
12. It contained books and an eight-legged toy a rubbery octopus.
13. Hakuta told Kenzo his older son to throw the toy at the wall.
14. Hakuta said "Throw Kenzo and it will climb down the wall!"
15. The toy slithered stopped slithered and stopped.
16. Hakuta knew a good thing when he saw it he acquired rights to distribute the toy in the United States.
17. The toy became popular and stores sold it a cereal company gave it away and a fast-food chain made it a prize in a meal.
18. American children loved the toy everyone wanted one.
19. Hakuta heavily promoted this small rubbery toy the wallwalker.
20. It became a craze Hakuta became a millionaire.

C. Using Apostrophes and Quotation Marks   Write the following sentences, adding apostrophes, quotation marks, and commas in quotation marks where necessary.

21. Youre no doubt familiar with the fairy tale Rapunzel.
22. According to the story, Rapunzels hair was so long it could reach to the ground from the high window of a witchs tower.

GRAMMAR
H A N D B O O K
47

Writing Theme
Fads and Fashions

23. Rapunzel, Rapunzel cried the handsome prince let down your long hair!
24. Whats in style, whether long hair, short hair, or outrageous fashions, has interested people for ages.
25. Youd be surprised at some of the styles that have been popular through history.
26. In ancient Egypt, for example, mens and womens heads were often shaved to keep them cool and clean.
27. If we want hair, we can wear a wig the people said.
28. During the 1700s, ladies in one French kings court wore their hair piled up to three feet high on their heads.
29. Some of the ladies hairdos were decorated with feathers, jewels, or even a bird cage with live birds inside!
30. Most of todays hairstyles are much simpler than those French ones, but not quite as simple as the Egyptians shaved heads.

D. Application in Literature Write the following passage and restore any missing punctuation.

[31]Pa was washing his hands and Ma was putting supper on the table when Laura came in, breathless [32]Quietly Ma asked Where have you been Laura

[33]Im sorry Ma. [34]I only meant to take a minute" Laura apologized [35]She told them about name cards. [36]Of course she did not say that she wanted some [37]Pa remarked that Jake was up-and-coming, bringing out such novelties.

[38]How much do they cost he asked and Laura answered that the cheapest cost twenty five cents a dozen.

[39]It was almost bedtime, and Laura was staring at the wall thinking about the War of 1812, when Pa folded his paper laid it down and said Laura.

[40]Yes Pa?

[41]You want some of these new fangled name cards dont you Pa asked

[42]I was just thinking the same thing Charles said Ma

[43]Well yes I do want them Laura admitted [44]But I dont *need* them

[45]Pas eyes smiled twinkling at her as he took from his pocket some coins and counted out two dimes and a nickel

Laura Ingalls Wilder, *Little Town on the Prairie*

Revise and proofread the following advertisement for a new computer game. Follow the suggestions shown on this page. When proofreading, look for errors in punctuation as well as errors in grammar, capitalization, and spelling. Be sure that the punctuation correctly conveys the message of each sentence.

[1]Will you help save the Earth from certain doom. [2]The Mighty Mandrake must be stopped. [3]Before his magnetic field send our planet spinning out of orbet. [4]Don't delay. [5]Play today.

[6]This fast-paced challenging Game is not for everybody. [7]You need a cool head; a good memory and quick refleckses Does this describe you. [8]Some people might not like this game, but that's their problem. [9]Be the first person on your street to play. [10]and the first too win. [11]This game is great. [12]You'll never want to play an other computer game again.

1. In sentence 5, identify the product that is being advertised by adding the words "the new computer game, Mandrake's Match" after the word *Play*. Place a comma after the words *Mandrake's Match*.

2. Delete the sentence that doesn't belong in the ad.

3. In the second paragraph, add a sentence that describes the game: "You must locate the hidden demagnetizer and divert Moja from his path of destruction."

4. Replace the vague adjective in sentence 11 with a more descriptive one.

5. In sentence 12, make the ad more persuasive by telling why readers won't want to play other computer games. Do this by adding the clause "because Mandrake's Match is so much more challenging than all the rest."

Persuasion

When you write an advertisement, you use many of the techniques used in writing persuasion. (See Workshop 6.) As you revise an ad, check to be sure that the product and its benefits are presented clearly. The language should be simple and direct, and the arguments for buying the product should be convincing. Correct punctuation will help convey an ad's message quickly and effectively.

Skills

Directions   One or more of the underlined sections in the following sentences may contain an error in grammar, usage, punctuation, spelling, or capitalization. Write the letter of each incorrect section; then rewrite the item correctly. If there is no error in an item, write *E*.

Example   The <u>well-known</u> poet James Weldon Johnson was <u>also:</u> a
                       A   **B**

lawyer, a vaudeville comedian, U.S. Consul to Venezuela and Nicaragua,

a <u>college</u> <u>professor, and</u> national secretary of the NAACP.   <u>No error</u>
   C   **D**   **E**

Answer   B—also

---

1. In 1950 the <u>Nobel Peace Prize</u> was awarded to <u>dr. Ralph Bunche</u>, who was the
                 A   **B**
first <u>African</u> American to win that <u>Prize.</u>   <u>No error</u>
    C   **D**   **E**

2. "Win without <u>boasting,"</u> said Albert <u>P.</u> <u>Terhune. Lose</u> without <u>excuse"</u>.
             A   **B**   **C**   **D**
<u>No error</u>
  E

3. The Sioux, <u>the Mohawk, and</u> the Hopi <u>are</u> among the Native American tribes
           A   **B**
for <u>who</u> reservations <u>were</u> established.   <u>No error</u>
   C   **D**   **E**

4. In his autobiography Thomas Edison, explaining his success, <u>wrote</u> <u>"Genius</u> is
                                               A   **B**
one percent inspiration and <u>ninety-nine</u> percent <u>perspiration."</u>   <u>No error</u>
                       C   **D**   **E**

5. Science <u>fiction</u> writer <u>Isaac Asimov</u> was once asked what he would do if he had
       A   **B**
only six <u>months</u> to live. "Type <u>faster,"</u> he said.   <u>No error</u>
        C   **D**   **E**

6. The period from about <u>A.D. 400 to 900</u> <u>is</u> often called the <u>dark ages.</u> That
                    A   **B**   **C**
name refers to a lack of <u>learning,</u> not of sunlight.   <u>No error</u>
                 D   **E**

7. Almost one-third of the books in the Library of <u>congress</u> are too brittle to be
 <u>**A**</u>
<u>handled, their</u> ideas will last much <u>longer</u> than their <u>paper.</u> <u>No error</u>
 **B** **C** **D** **E**

8. <u>"You</u> can tell the ideals of a nation," said <u>writer</u> Norman Douglas, <u>"By</u> <u>its</u> adver-
 **A** **B** **C** **D**
tisements." <u>No error</u>
 **E**

9. By <u>knitting Mrs.</u> Janice Marwick got into the <u>*Guinness Book of World Records*</u>
 **A** **B**
in <u>1971. Her</u> <u>needles</u> did not stop clicking for ninety hours. <u>No error</u>
 **C** **D** **E**

10. The <u>Caspian sea</u> is <u>actualy</u> a lake—the <u>largest</u> lake in the <u>world!</u> <u>No error</u>
 **A** **B** **C** **D** **E**

11. From a jail in <u>Birmingham, Alabama</u> Martin Luther King, Jr., <u>wrote,</u> <u>"Injustice</u>
 **A** **B** **C**
anywhere is a threat to justice <u>everywhere".</u> <u>No error</u>
 **D** **E**

12. The African-American leader <u>W E B</u> Du Bois <u>spoke</u> of Pan-Africanism, an atti-
 **A** **B**
tude which <u>emphasises</u> the common interest of all people of <u>African</u> descent.
 **C** **D**
<u>No error</u>
 **E**

13. Six of the seven dwarfs in <u>Disney's</u> <u>Snow White and the Seven Dwarfs</u> <u>has</u>
 **A** **B** **C**
<u>beards, Dopey</u> does not. <u>No error</u>
 **D** **E**

14. The names of many <u>states</u> <u>comes</u> from Native American <u>words;</u> these names
 **A** **B** **C**
include Minnesota, Missouri, Tennessee, <u>Utah and</u> Wisconsin. <u>No error</u>
 **D** **E**

15. Many <u>kings</u> of several <u>countries</u> have been named <u>Ferdinand. Some</u> of the kings
 **A** **B** **C**
<u>were</u> related, but many were not. <u>No error</u>
 **D** **E**

Directions   One or more of the underlined sections in the following sentences may contain an error in grammar, usage, punctuation, spelling, or capitalization. Write the letter of each incorrect section; then rewrite the item correctly. If there is no error in an item, write *E*.

Example   One of the <u>earlyest</u> <u>American</u> paintings shows a group of
                        A   **B**

<u>men</u> watching a <u>Boxing</u> match.   <u>No error</u>
C   **D**   **E**

Answer   A—earliest D—boxing

---

1. In 1970 David White <u>catched</u> a rainbow trout that <u>weighed</u> more than forty-
                                A   **B**
   two pounds. <u>That's</u> one big <u>fish!</u>   <u>No error</u>
                        C   **D**   **E**

2. Getting to the island of <u>Bouvet</u> is not <u>easy.</u> <u>It</u> <u>lays</u> about one thousand miles
                                    A   **B** **C**
   from any other <u>land.</u>   <u>No error</u>
                        D   **E**

3. <u>Susan B. Anthony</u> <u>made</u> her mark on history. Elizabeth Cady Stanton and <u>her</u>
      A   **B**   **C**
   founded the first <u>American</u> organization that worked to secure women's rights.
                            D
   <u>No error</u>
   E

4. Florida and <u>South Dakota</u> have something in common; both <u>calls</u> <u>itself</u> the
                    A   **B**   **C**
   <u>Sunshine State.</u>   <u>No error</u>
      D   **E**

5. Usually, each <u>ruler</u> of England is the son or daughter of the ruler who came
                    A
   before. However, <u>Queen</u> Elizabeth I <u>taken</u> the throne immediately after her sis-
                        B   **C**
   ter, not her <u>Father.</u>   <u>No error</u>
                    D   **E**

6. Two of the largest cakes ever baked <u>were</u> created for the <u>Seattle World's Fair</u> and
                                            A   **B**
   the <u>British Columbia Centennial.</u> Each of the cakes <u>were</u> about twenty-five
            C   **D**
   thousand pounds in weight.   <u>No error</u>
                                        E

7. President William Henry Harrison was the <u>Grandfather</u> of another president,
   A
   Benjamin Harrison. There <u>is</u> other relatives <u>among</u> <u>U.S.</u> presidents.   <u>No error</u>
   B   **C**   **D**   **E**

8. The <u>English</u> must be the <u>most cleanest</u> people in the <u>world. At</u> least, they use
   A   **B**   **C**
   the most soap, about $2\frac{1}{2}$ <u>pounds</u> per person per year.   <u>No error</u>
   D   **E**

9. With enough <u>patience, you</u> can write a <u>hole</u> book with one <u>pencil, the</u> average
   A   **B**   **C**
   pencil will write two hundred <u>pages.</u>   <u>No error</u>
   D   **E**

10. Spiders are not <u>insects;</u> insects <u>have</u> six legs <u>and spiders</u> <u>have</u> eight.   <u>No error</u>
   A   **B**   **C**   **D**   **E**

11. Sarah Bernhardt, a great <u>French</u> <u>actress,</u> continued to act even after having one
   A   **B**
   leg amputated. She <u>took</u> only parts she could perform while <u>setting.</u>   <u>No error</u>
   C   **D**   **E**

12. Elizabeth Blackwell, first woman in the United States to graduate from <u>Medical</u>
   A
   <u>School,</u> did <u>good</u> in <u>classes but</u> was insulted and rejected by many <u>classmates.</u>
   A   **B**   **C**   **D**
   <u>No error</u>
   E

13. In a great many <u>ancient societies</u> cattle served as a form of <u>money; even</u> today
   A   **B**
   coins are <u>said</u> to have heads and <u>tails.</u>   <u>No error</u>
   C   **D**   **E**

14. In her poem <u>"Your World,"</u> Georgia Douglas Johnson said <u>that your</u> world is as
   A   **B**
   big as you make <u>it.</u> <u>That's</u> a good thing to remember.   <u>No error</u>
   C   **D**   **E**

15. <u>Its</u> a coincidence that Thomas Jefferson and John Adams, <u>writer's</u> of the
   A   **B**
   <u>declaration of independence,</u> both died on the <u>Fourth of July</u> in 1826, fifty
   C   **D**
   years after the signing of the famous document.   <u>No error</u>
   E

Detail from Wandering Raven totem pole in Totem Bight State Park, near Ketchikan, Alaska. Shown here is the bottom of the pole, which serves as the entrance to a traditional Tlingit-style house. The Tlingit are a Native American people. The figure pictured is, in Tlingit legend, the wife of the chief who owned the Sun.

Appendix

Sharing your writing with peer readers is a good way to celebrate what you have accomplished. It is also a way to find out what specific things in your writing your readers like and what ideas may not be clear. Here are some techniques to help you get responses that are most useful to you.

Sharing

How to Use   Read your writing aloud to some friends. Your purpose is to share your words and to hear how they sound. You may simply wish to enjoy your finished piece by sharing it, or you may want to discover new meanings as you hear the words spoken.

At this stage, your peer readers offer no response beyond listening carefully.

When to Use   You may do this when you are exploring and trying out ideas. Do this also when your writing is finished and you want to show what you have done.

Pointing

How to Use   Ask readers to tell you what they like best in your writing. Tell them to avoid simply saying, "I liked it."

Have readers point to specific words and phrases and ideas that they liked and ask them to tell why those words are especially memorable to them.

When to Use   Use this technique when you want to find out what is actually getting through to readers and when you want some encouragement and support.

Summarizing

How to Use Ask readers to tell you what they understand to be the main idea in your writing. If a reader begins to focus on specific words or details, get him or her back on track by saying, "For now I'd like you to keep focusing on what you heard as my main idea."

Remind readers that at this stage you are not asking for specific criticism of your writing.

When to Use Use this technique when you want to see whether the main ideas or goals of your writing are clear to readers.

Telling

How to Use Ask readers to tell you a bit about what happened to them as they read your words. For example, did they laugh when reading the beginning of your story? Did they have questions about certain aspects of volcanoes as they read your report?

Ask your readers to connect their reactions to specific places in the writing.

When to Use Use this strategy when you want to see whether your words are having the effect you intended. This strategy is useful at any stage.

Identifying

How to Use Ask for feedback on specific features of the writing, such as the organization, the development of ideas, or the choice of words.

Ask readers to respond to specific questions, such as these: Do any ideas need more examples to be clear? Where do the ideas flow smoothly? Is the organization clear enough so you could follow the ideas easily?

When to Use Use this technique when you want to focus on specific strengths and weaknesses of your piece.

An outline is a way of organizing information. It can help you arrange main points and supporting details in logical order. It can be a blueprint, or plan for your writing, or it can help you organize notes. In a **sentence outline,** headings and subpoints are stated as complete sentences. A **topic outline** uses words or phrases, as in this model.

Volcanoes

Thesis Statement: The pressure from melted rock in the earth's interior causes volcanoes to form and erupt.

I. The origin of volcanoes (Main point)
  A. How magma forms (First subpoint)
    1. Heat at the earth's interior (Details for A)
    2. Production of gas
  B. How magma rises (Second subpoint)
    1. Magma lighter than solid rock (Details for B)
    2. Gaps melted in surrounding rock
    3. Formation of reservoirs, or magma chambers
II. The eruption of volcanoes (Main point)
  A. Pressure of surrounding rock on reservoirs (First subpoint)
  B. Conduits in fractured parts of rock (Second subpoint)
    1. Central vent in crater (Details for B)
    2. Side vents

Correct Outline Form

1. Write the title at the top of the outline.
2. Arrange numerals and letters as in the model above.
3. Indent each division of the outline.
4. Do not use a single subheading. A heading should not be broken down if it cannot be divided into at least two points. For example, if there is a *1* under *A,* there must also be a *2.*
5. In a topic outline, use the same form for items of the same rank. For example, if a noun is used for subpoint A, then nouns should be used for subpoints B and C.
6. Capitalize the first word in each line. In a topic outline, use no end punctuation.

Business Letter

Heading 1104 Balsana Avenue
Boulder, Colorado 80302
April 27, 19——

Sports Extras Company   Inside Address
2134 Peachtree Avenue
Atlanta, Georgia 30308

Dear Sir or Madam: Salutation

Body In the March issue of <u>Runner's World</u> I saw
your advertisement for visor headbands. Please
send the item indicated as soon as possible.

I am enclosing a money order for the amount
of $5.00. Thank you for your prompt response.

Sincerely,   Closing

Pat Williams   Signature

Pat Williams

Friendly Letter

Heading 603 Pine Street
Alton, Pennsylvania 18406
August 7, 19——

Dear Beth,   Salutation

Body I enjoyed your last letter so much that I had
to hurry and answer it. How did you learn to ride
a horse so quickly? In the photo you sent me,
you look very impressive up there in the saddle.
Do you ride in shows or just for fun? Wish me
luck when I learn to ride!

Write and tell me more about your wilderness
rides. Say "hi" to your family for me.

Your friend,   Closing

José   Signature

Heading   These lines contain your street address, your town or city, state and ZIP code, and the date of the letter.

Inside Address   This is used only in business letters. Include the name of an individual if you know it and the name and address of the organization.

Salutation   In a business letter, follow the person's name with a colon. In a friendly letter, follow the person's name with a comma.

Body   Business letters should be brief and clear. Friendly letters can be as informal as a conversation.

Closing   In a business letter, the closing is always formal. "Sincerely" and "Yours truly" are examples. In both business and friendly letters, capitalize only the first word of the closing and use a comma at the end.

Signature   For a business letter, skip four spaces below the closing, print or type your name, and write your signature in the space. In a friendly letter you usually write only your first name.

Good spelling is important in all writing, from personal letters to research reports. You can improve your spelling by practicing a few good habits. Read and write as frequently as you can. Keep a list of words you are not sure how to spell and review this list regularly. The following tips may also be helpful.

Ways to Improve Your Spelling

1. **Identify your spelling demons and conquer them.** Keep a list of the words you have misspelled in written assignments.

2. **Pronounce words carefully.** Pronouncing words correctly will help you spell them correctly. For example, if you pronounce the word *probably* correctly, you will not misspell it as *probly*.

3. **Get into the habit of seeing the letters in a word.** Look carefully at new or difficult words. For example, look at a word like *picnic,* close your eyes and picture the word in your mind, and spell it to yourself: *p-i-c-n-i-c*.

4. **Create a memory device for a tricky word.** Notice the following examples of memory devices.

bus**i**ness (i)	**I** was involved in big business.
princi**pal**(pal)	The princi**pal** is my **pal**.
princi**ple** (ple)	Follow this princi**ple, ple**ase.
station**er**y (er)	Station**er**y is fine pap**er**.

How to Master the Spelling of Difficult Words

1. Look at the word and say it one syllable at a time.

2. Look at the letters and say each one.

3. Write the word without looking at it.

4. Check to see whether you spelled the word correctly. If you made a mistake, repeat steps 1–3.

One of the best ways to improve your spelling is to learn the following rules.

Words Ending in a Silent *e*

When a suffix beginning with a vowel is added to a word ending in a silent *e*, the *e* is usually dropped.

relate + -ion = relation   create + -ive = creative
amaze + -ing = amazing   fame + -ous = famous

When a suffix beginning with a consonant is added to a word ending in a silent *e*, the *e* usually is retained.

hope + -ful = hopeful   noise + -less = noiseless
state + -ment = statement   wide + -ly = widely

The following words are exceptions: *truly, argument, ninth, wholly.*

Words Ending in *y*

When a suffix is added to a word ending in *y* preceded by a consonant, the *y* usually is changed to *i*.

easy + -ly = easily   sixty + -eth = sixtieth

When *-ing* is added, however, the *y* does not change.

hurry + -ed = hurried *but* hurry + -ing = hurrying
study + -ed = studied *but* study + -ing = studying

When a suffix is added to a word ending in *y* preceded by a vowel, the *y* usually does not change.

employ + -er = employer   play + -ing = playing

Words Ending in a Consonant

In words of *one* syllable that end in *one* consonant preceded by *one* vowel, double the final consonant before adding an ending that begins with a vowel, such as *-ing, -ed,* or *-er.* These are sometimes called **1+1+1 words.**

bat + -ed = batted   bed + -ing = bedding
run + -er = runner   grab + -ed = grabbed

The rule does not apply to words of one syllable that end in one consonant preceded by two vowels.

treat + -ing = treating   loot + -ed = looted
near + -er = nearer   feel + -ing = feeling

The Suffixes *-ness* and *-ly*

When the suffix *-ly* is added to a word ending in *l,* both *l*'s are retained. When *-ness* is added to a word ending in *n,* retain both of the *n*'s.

actual + -ly = actually   thin + -ness = thinness

Prefixes

When a prefix is added to a word, do not drop a letter from either the prefix or the base word.

mis- + spell = misspell   re- + place = replace
il- + legal = illegal   im- + perfect = imperfect
un- + even = uneven   dis- + approve = disapprove
pre- + view = preview   ir- + regular = irregular

Words with the *Seed* Sound

Only one English word ends in *-sede: supersede.* Three words end in *-ceed: exceed, proceed,* and *succeed.* All other verbs ending in the sound *seed* are spelled with *-cede.*

concede   precede   recede   secede

Words with *ie* and *ei*

When the sound is long *e* (ē), the word is spelled *ie* except after *c.*

i **before** *e*			**except after** *c*		
believe	shield	yield	receive	ceiling	deceive
niece	brief	field	conceive	conceit	receipt

The following words are exceptions: *either, weird, species, neither, seize, leisure.*

Like good musicians or good athletes, good writers do the little things well. One of these "little things" is the correct use of words. It is actually one of the keys to good writing. As you look at the following groups of words, notice how the words' meanings differ. Try to create memory devices to help you associate words and meanings.

accept, except   *Accept* means "to agree to something" or "to receive something." *Except* usually means "not including."

> Kay did *accept* the invitation to go camping.
> Everyone *except* the reporters dashed onto the field.

all ready, already   *All ready* means "all are ready" or "completely prepared." *Already* means "previously."

> The astronauts were *all ready* for the landing.
> The other team has *already* started practicing.

all right   *All right* is the correct spelling. *Alright* is nonstandard English and should not be used.

a lot   *A lot* is informal. It should not be used in formal writing. *Alot* is always incorrect.

borrow, lend   *Borrow* means "to receive something on loan." *Lend* means "to give out temporarily."

> Some students *borrow* money to pay for a college education.
> Please *lend* me a pencil.

capital, capitol, the Capitol   *Capital* means "excellent," "most serious," or "most important"; it also means "seat of government." *Capitol* is a "building in which a state legislature meets." *The Capitol* is "the building in Washington, D.C., in which the U.S. Congress meets."

> Murder is a *capital* crime.
> The state senate held hearings at the *capitol*.
> In 1814 British soldiers burned the White House and
>   *the Capitol*.

desert, dessert *Des'ert* means "a wilderness" or "a dry, sandy, barren region." *Desert'* means "to abandon." *Dessert* is a sweet food, such as cake or pie, served at the end of a meal.

> The Gobi *Desert* is in eastern Asia.
> The soldiers *deserted* their dangerous position.
> Strawberry pie is a delicious *dessert*.

good, well *Good* is always an adjective. *Well* is usually an adverb. *Well* can be an adjective meaning "in good health."

> Juan felt *good* about finishing the marathon.
> Julio plays the drums *well*.
> Marco did not feel *well* enough to play soccer.

hear, here *Hear* means "to listen to." *Here* means "in this place."

> Because of the noisy crowd, we couldn't *hear* the candidate.
> After leaving Italy, my grandparents settled *here* in Chicago.

its, it's *Its* is a possessive pronoun. *It's* is a contraction for *it is* or *it has*.

> The city lost *its* electricity during the storm.
> *It's* almost time for summer vacation.

lay, lie *Lay* is a verb that means "to place." It takes a direct object. *Lie* is a verb that means "to be in a certain place" or "to be in a horizontal position." *Lie* never takes a direct object.

> *Lay* the books on the desk.   Our land *lies* near the river.

lead, led *Lead* can be a noun that means "a heavy metal" or a verb that means "to show the way." *Led* is the verb's past tense form.

> A plumb is a weight made of *lead*.
> Maria *leads* the league in home runs.
> She *led* a discussion on ways to help the homeless.

learn, teach *Learn* means "to gain knowledge." *Teach* means "to instruct."

> Raul is *learning* how to play chess.
> Alicia is *teaching* Spanish to preschool children.

like, as, as if   Use *as* or *as if*, not *like*, to introduce a clause.

> He walks *as if* his ankle were sore.

loose, lose   *Loose* means "free" or "not fastened." *Lose* means "to mislay or suffer the loss of something."

> The door hinges are *loose*.   The plane began to *lose* altitude.

of   Use *have*, not *of*, in phrases such as *could have*, *should have*, and *must have*.

> We could *have* won if our leading scorer had not fouled out.

passed, past   *Passed* is the past tense of *pass* and means "went by." *Past* is an adjective that means "of a former time." *Past* is also a noun that means "the time gone by."

> We *passed* through the Grand Tetons during our vacation.
> Our *past* experiences have taught us we can win.
> Ebenezer Scrooge is a character who relives his *past*.

peace, piece   *Peace* means "calm or quiet." *Piece* means a "section or part of something."

> Music can bring a sense of *peace*.   We cut the pizza into *pieces*.

principal, principle   *Principal* means "of chief or central importance" or "the head of a school." *Principle* is a "basic truth," "standard," or "rule of behavior."

> The *principal* cities of France include Paris and Marseilles.
> The *principal* of our school presented the awards.
> In social studies we discussed the *principles* of government.

raise, rise   *Raise* means "to lift" or "to make something go up." It takes a direct object. *Rise* means "to go upward." It does not take a direct object.

> Dr. King's speeches *raised* hopes for a more just society.
> The sun *rises* in the east.

set, sit   *Set* means "to place." It takes a direct object. *Sit* means "to occupy a seat or a place." It does not take a direct object.

> He *set* the papers on the desk.   Let's *sit* here.

stationary, stationery   *Stationary* means "fixed or unmoving." *Stationery* means "fine paper for writing letters."

> A *stationary* clock glowed at the far end of the gym.
> I received a letter written on White House *stationery*.

than, then   *Than* is used to introduce the second part of a comparison. *Then* means "next in order."

> The pen is mightier *than* the sword.
> The air grew still, and *then* raindrops pattered on the roof.

their, there, they're   *Their* means "belonging to them." *There* means "in that place." *They're* is the contraction for *they are*.

> In 1804, Lewis and Clark led *their* expedition from St. Louis.
> The explorers built a fort in what is now North Dakota, and they spent the winter *there*.
> Lewis and Clark collected valuable information about the geography of the Pacific Northwest; *they're* remembered for *their* wilderness travels.

to, too, two   *To* means "toward" or "in the direction of." *Too* means "also" or "very." *Two* is the number 2.

> We went *to* the Library of Congress in Washington, D. C.
> It was *too* cold to play baseball.
> *Two* newspapers sent critics to review the new play.

weather, whether   *Weather* refers to "conditions such as temperature or cloudiness." *Whether* expresses a choice.

> Meteorologists use computers to forecast the *weather*.
> We must decide *whether* to speak out or remain silent.

whose, who's   *Whose* is the possessive form of *who. Who's* is a contraction for *who is* or *who has*.

> *Whose* arguments seem more convincing?
> *Who's* going to volunteer to work at the hospital?

your, you're   *Your* is the possessive form of *you. You're* is a contraction for *you are*.

> Please take *your* places at the starting line.
> *You're* going to the library after school, aren't you?

A sentence diagram is a drawing that shows the parts of a sentence and their relationships. Use the following models as guides.

Subjects and Verbs

To diagram a subject and a verb, draw a horizontal line. Write the subject on the left side of the line and the verb on the right. Then draw a vertical line between the subject and the verb. Capitalize words capitalized in the sentence. Do not use punctuation except for abbreviations.

Dogs bark.

Dogs	bark

Questions, Exclamations, and Commands

In a sentence that asks a question, the subject often comes after the verb. In diagraming, place the subject before the verb.

Can astronauts exercise?

astronauts	Can exercise

In a command or an exclamation, the subject is usually understood to be *you*. In diagraming, place the understood subject *you* to the left of the vertical line. Enclose *you* in parentheses.

Listen.

(you)	Listen

Hurry!

(you)	Hurry

Compound Subjects and Compound Verbs

To diagram a compound subject, split the subject line. Write the conjunction on a dotted line. Diagram compound verbs similarly.

Louise and Mary disagreed.
(*Compound subject*)

Bigfoot snarled and growled.
(*Compound verb*)

Direct Objects and Indirect Objects

Write a direct object after the verb. Draw a short vertical line between the verb and the direct object. Write the indirect object on a horizontal line below the verb.

Placido Domingo gave him lessons.

Predicate Words

Write a predicate word after the verb. Separate the predicate word from the verb by a line slanting toward the subject.

Mr. Williams looks angry.

Adjectives

Write an adjective on a slanted line connected to the word it modifies. Treat possessive nouns and pronouns as adjectives.

A tall tree shades the old cabin.

Adverbs

Write an adverb on a slanted line connected to the word it modifies.

Fairly young students can play the piano well.

Prepositional Phrases

Since a prepositional phrase does the work of an adjective or an adverb, diagram it in a similar way. Write the preposition on a line slanting down from the word modified. On a horizontal line attached to the preposition line, write the object. Write any words modifying the object on lines that slant down from it.

The Minutemen rushed to the river.

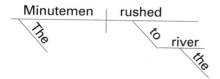

Compound Sentences

It is not difficult to diagram compound sentences if you already know how to diagram simple sentences. A compound sentence is really two or more simple sentences joined together. Therefore, you diagram the first half of the sentence, draw a dotted-line "step" between the verbs for the conjunction, and then draw the diagram for the second half.

Mario slept soundly, but the other boys did not close their eyes.

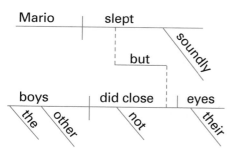

ADJECTIVE a word that modifies a noun or pronoun: *red* car.

ADVERB a word that modifies a verb, an adjective, or another adverb; in "He ran fast," *fast* is an adverb modifying *ran*.

AUDIENCE your readers or listeners.

BRAINSTORMING a way of generating ideas that involves listing them without stopping to judge them.

CHRONOLOGICAL arranged in order of occurrence.

CLICHÉ an overused expression, such as "white as snow."

CLUSTER a kind of map made up of clusters—circled groupings of related details.

COHERENCE a quality of connectedness; a paragraph has coherence when its sentences are arranged logically; a composition has coherence when its paragraphs are connected logically.

COMPLEX SENTENCE a sentence that contains one independent clause and one or more subordinate clauses.

CONJUNCTION a word or pair of words that connect other words or groups of words: Joel *and* David went out.

CONNOTATION the ideas and feelings associated with a word as opposed to the dictionary definition of the word.

DENOTATION the dictionary definition of a word.

DIALECT a form of a language that is characterized by a particular pronunciation, vocabulary, and word order.

DIALOGUE spoken conversation; the representation of spoken conversation in novels, stories, plays, poems, or essays.

ELABORATION the support or development of a main idea with facts, statistics, sensory details, incidents, examples, or quotations.

FIGURATIVE LANGUAGE the imaginative and poetic use of words; writing that contains such figures of speech as similes, metaphors, or personification.

FREEWRITING   a way of exploring ideas, thoughts, or feelings that involves writing freely—without stopping or otherwise limiting the flow of ideas—for a specific length of time.

GLEANING   a way of finding ideas for writing that involves observing, listening, talking to others, and scanning newspapers, books, and magazines and then noting anything of interest.

GRAPHIC DEVICE   a visual presentation of details. Graphic devices include charts, graphs, outlines, clusters, and idea trees.

IDEA TREE   a graphic device in which main ideas are written on "branches" and details related to them are noted on "twigs."

INTERJECTION   a word or phrase used to express strong feeling.

JOURNAL   a personal notebook in which you can freewrite, collect ideas, and record thoughts, feelings, and experiences.

LEARNING LOG   a kind of journal specifically for recording and reflecting on what you have learned and for noting problems and questions to which you want to find answers.

METAPHOR   a figure of speech that makes a comparison without using the word *like* or *as;* "he is a rock" is a metaphor.

NONSEXIST LANGUAGE   language that includes both men and women when making reference to a role or group in which people of either sex could belong; "a doctor may speak plainly if he or she wishes" and "doctors may speak plainly if they wish" are two nonsexist ways of expressing the same idea.

NOUN   a word that names a person, a place, a thing, or an idea.

PARAGRAPH   a group of related sentences that develop a single main idea or accomplish a single purpose.

PARAPHRASE   a restatement in your own words that retains the ideas, tone, and general length of the original passage.

PEER RESPONSE   suggestions and comments on a piece of writing provided by peers, or classmates.

PERSONIFICATION   a figure of speech that gives human qualities to nonhuman things.

PLAGIARISM   the dishonest act of presenting someone else's words or ideas as if they were your own.

POINT OF VIEW   the angle, or perspective, from which a story is told, such as first-, third-, or second-person point of view.

PORTFOLIO   a container (usually a folder) for notes on work in progress, drafts and revisions, finished pieces, and peer responses.

PREPOSITION   a word that relates its object to some other word in the sentence; in "Bill hit the ball to Sue," *to* is the preposition.

PRONOUN   a word that is used to take the place of a noun or another pronoun; in "He hit it to Sue," *He* and *it* are pronouns.

SIMILE   a figure of speech that uses the word *like* or *as* to make a comparison; "smelled *like* an old dictionary" is a simile.

SPATIAL ORDER   organization in which details are arranged in the order that they appear in space, such as from left to right.

SUMMARY   a brief restatement in your own words of the main idea of a passage; supporting details are not included in a summary.

THESIS STATEMENT   a one- to two-sentence statement of the main idea or purpose of a piece of writing.

TIME LINE   a graphic device that presents events in chronological order.

TOPIC SENTENCE   a sentence that expresses the main idea of a paragraph.

TRANSITION   a connecting word or phrase that clarifies relation-ships between details, sentences, or paragraphs.

UNITY   a quality of oneness; a paragraph has unity if all its sen-tences support the same main idea or purpose; a composition has unity if all its paragraphs help to achieve the same overall goal.

VERB   a word that expresses an action, a condition, or a state of being; in "Haley ran down the block," *ran* is a verb.

WRITING VOICE   the personality of the writer conveyed indirectly by word choices and sentence structure.

Dialogue, 320–22, 680
  guidelines for, 322
  in personal and expressive writing, 34, 36
  quotation marks with, 650
Dictionary, 310
Direct address, 634
Direct objects, 466
  diagraming, 678
  nouns as, 412
  pronouns as, 412, 437
Direct quotations, 637
  quotation marks with, 648
Discovery workshop, 11–21
Discussion, for writing ideas, 79, 101, 144, 221
Divided quotations, 611, 637
Double negatives, 525
Drafting, 6–7, 15–18, 235–53
  adventuresome, 235
  advertisement, 155
  autobiographical incident, 34–35
  careful, 235
  character sketch, 56–58
  conclusions, 278–80
  elaboration and, 249–50, 254–60
  form and, 17, 237
  goals and, 17
  informing and defining, 124–25
  interpreting poetry, 172–73
  introductions, 275–77
  oral history, 65
  organization and, 17, 238–42
  paragraphs and, 243–53
  problem and solution essay, 102–103
  questions for peer readers, 35, 57, 81, 103, 125, 147, 173, 201
  questions for yourself, 35, 57, 81, 103, 125, 147, 173, 201
  reports, 199–201
  revision and, 236
  short story, 80–81
  supporting opinions, 146–48
Drama, 321
Drawing, for writing ideas, 223

E

-ed, adding to words, 303
Editing. See Proofreading
Either/Or argument, 333
Elaboration, 254–60, 680
  anecdotes, 56, 57, 58, 102
  dialogue, 34, 36, 58, 80
  examples, 146, 172, 249, 256–57

  exploring and, 258
  facts, 249, 254
  graphic devices and, 259
  incidents, 146, 249, 256
  paragraphs, 249–50
  questioning and, 258
  quotations, 172, 174, 257
  research and, 259
  sensory details, 34, 82, 255
  showing, not telling, 262–65
  sources of, 258–59
  statistics, 146, 254
  types of, 249
Emotional appeals, 333–34
Empty sentences, 297
Encyclopedias, 353
  crediting, 199
  source cards for, 197
English
  formal/informal, 311
  standard/nonstandard, 311
Essay questions, 362–63
Evaluation, standards for
  character sketch, 60
  definition, 128
  interpretation of poetry, 176
  multimedia report, 204
  narrative writing, 84
  personal narrative, 38
  persuasive writing, 150
  problem and solution writing, 106
Examples, for elaboration, 102, 116, 146, 172, 186, 249, 256–57
except, accept, 673
Exclamation points, 623
  in dialogue, 322
  with exclamatory sentences, 387
  quotation marks with, 649
Exclamations, 390
Exclamatory sentences, 386, 390
  diagraming, 677
  exclamation points with, 623
Expository writing. See Informative writing entries

F

Fact and opinion, 146
Facts
  to correct emotional appeals, 334
  for correcting empty sentences, 297
  for elaboration, 102, 186, 249, 254
  for introductions, 275
  for reports, 186

O

Object of the preposition, 536, 539, 541
  compound, 539
  pronouns as, 437
Object pronouns, 432, 433, 437
Objects
  compound, 437, 556
  see also Direct objects; Indirect objects;
    Object of the preposition
Observation and description, 48–69
  see also Character sketch; Oral history
Observation charts, 227
of, 675
Onomatopoeia, 316
or, compound subjects joined by, 582
Oral discussion, 79, 101, 110–11, 134, 144,
  170
  see also Speaking and listening
Oral history, 62–66, 67
  drafting, 65
  interviewing for, 64–65
  proofreading, 66
  publishing and presenting, 66
  revising, 66
Oral presentations, 358–59
Order of importance, 239, 272
Organization, 228–30, 234, 238–42
  cause and effect, 240, 245, 273
  for character sketch, 56–57
  chronological order, 200, 209, 239,
    271–72
  classification, 241
  coherence and, 270–74
  comparison and contrast, 133–34, 242,
    273
  graphic devices and, 228–30, 234
  for interpreting poetry, 172
  for magazine article, 209
  main idea and supporting details, 238
  order of familiarity, 200
  order of importance, 200, 209, 239, 272
  for reports, 198, 200
  spatial order, 209, 241, 272
  for supporting opinions, 147
  test taking and, 159
  unity and, 266–68
Outlines, 668
  capitalization in, 612
  essay questions and, 159, 363
  note-taking and, 336
  periods with, 625
  for reports, 198
Overgeneralization, 332
Oxymorons, 183

P

Padded sentences, 298–99
Paintings
  capitalization in titles of, 612
  underlining/italics for titles of, 651
Paragraphs, 243–53, 266–69, 681
  coherence in, 244–45, 251, 270–74
  constructing, 247–50
  defined, 243
  developing, 249–50, 251
  in dialogue, 322
  elaboration in, 249–50
  goals and, 247
  guidelines for, 251
  in informative writing, 126
  in narrative writing, 82
  in persuasive writing, 148
  in poetry interpretation, 174
  in problem-solution essay, 105
  in reports, 202
  single focus in, 59
  topic sentences, 247–48, 251, 267
  transitions, 271–73
  unity in, 244, 266–68
Paraphrasing, 198, 341–42
Parts of speech. *See* Adjectives; Adverbs;
  Conjunctions; Interjections; Nouns;
  Prepositions; Pronouns; Verbs
passed, past, 675
Past form of verbs, 477
Past participle, 477
Past perfect tense, 475
Past tense, 474, 475
peace, piece, 675
Peer response, 4, 7, 18, 81, 281–84,
  666–67, 681
  character sketch, 57–58
  questions for, 35, 57, 81, 103, 125, 147,
    173, 201
Periodical indexes, 347, 354–55
Periodicals, 347, 354
Periods, 622, 625
  with declarative sentences, 387
  in dialogue, 322
  with imperative sentences, 387
  quotation marks with, 648
Personal and expressive writing, 26–47
  see also Autobiographical incident; Collage
Personal pronouns, 432
Personal voice, 312–13
Personification, 315–16, 681
Persuasive writing, 138–63
  see also Advertisement; Supporting opinions
Phrases

plagiarism and, 343
from poems, 176
in reports, 204

R

raise, rise, 675
Readers' Guide to Periodical Literature,
  354–55
Reading-comprehension questions, 364
Reading rate, 339
Reading skills, 338–39
  understanding graphic aids, 346
Recalling, 218
  for elaboration, 258
Recordings, source cards for, 197
Reference section, in library, 347
Reference works, 349, 353–55
  source cards for, 197
Reflecting on your writing, 8, 21
  autobiographical incident, 39
  character sketch, 61
  informing and defining, 129
  interpreting poetry, 177
  problem and solution essay, 107
  report, 205
  short story, 85
  supporting opinions, 151
Reflexive pronouns, 443
Regular verbs, 477
Reports, 194–205
  crediting sources for, 199, 202
  conclusions for, 200
  drafting, 199–201
  introductions for, 200
  prewriting, 194–96
  proofreading, 204
  publishing and presenting, 205
  quotation marks with titles of, 651
  reflecting on, 205
  research for, 196–99
  revising, 202–203
Research
  for elaboration, 259
  for writing ideas, 145
Research paper. *See* Reports
Research skills
  avoiding plagiarism, 343
  paraphrasing, 341–42
  for reports, 196–99
  summarizing, 342–43
  understanding graphic aids, 344–46
  using the library, 347–56
Responding to literature, 164–85

  see also Poetry, interpreting
Restatement context clues, 327
Reviewing
  note-taking and, 336
  reading and, 339
Revising, 7, 19, 285–87
  advertisement, 156
  autobiographical incident, 36–37
  character sketch, 58–59
  form and language, 286
  ideas, 285
  informing and defining, 126–27
  interpreting poetry, 174–75
  oral history, 66
  paragraphs, 251–52
  paraphrasing and, 341
  problem and solution essay, 104–105
  purpose and, 231
  reports, 202–203
  short story, 82–83
  supporting opinions, 148–49
  see also Elaboration; Showing
Run-on sentences, 295, 394–96, 404

S

Schedule, of assignments, 335
Second-person point of view, 319
-self, 443
-selves, 443
Semicolons, 641
  in compound sentences, 559
Sensory details
  for elaboration, 70, 255
  in personal and expressive writing, 34
Sentence(s), 294–309, 373–405
  appositives in, 307
  beginning with prepositional phrases, 543
  beginning with *there,* 392
  beginning with *there, where,* and *here,*
    586
  capitalization in, 611
  closing clauses, 184–85
  closing phrases, 162–63
  combining, 60, 300–309
  complex, 565–66
  compound, 556–64, 628, 641
  compound subjects, 384
  compound verbs, 384
  correcting problem, 294–99
  declarative, 386, 622, 623
  diagraming, 677–79
  empty, 297
  exclamatory, 386, 390, 623

TV
source cards for, 197
underlining/italics for titles of series on,
651

U
Underlining, for titles, 651
Unity, 682
in paragraphs, 244, 266–68
organization and, 266–68
us, we, 442
Usage, proofreading for, 288

V
Venn diagrams, 230
Verb, the (simple predicate), 376
Verb phrases, 380, 472, 579
Verb suffix, 331
Verbs, 463–493, 682
action, 378, 464
adverbs modifying, 516
agreement with subjects, 577–95
choosing the right, 482–84
compound, 384, 556, 557
confusing pairs of, 482–84
diagraming, 677
direct objects and, 466
helping, 380, 472, 475, 579
intransitive, 468
irregular, 477–78
linking, 378, 435, 464–65, 470, 499
main, 380, 472
predicate words and, 470
principal parts of, 477–78
regular, 477
separated parts of, 382
state of being, 378
tenses of, 474–75
transitive, 468
verb phrases, 380, 472
Vertical files, 354
very, overuse of, 516
Visual aids, for oral presentations, 359
Vocabulary, 326–31
comparison and contrast context clues,
328
context clues, 327–28
definition context clues, 327
example context clues, 327
inferring meaning, 328

restatement context clues, 327
word parts, 330–31
Vocabulary questions, 365

W
we, us, 442
weather, whether, 676
well, good, 674
where, sentences beginning with, 586
which
for combining sentences, 306–307
correct use of, 306
which is, eliminating, 299
who, for combining sentences, 306
who is, eliminating, 299
who, whom, 442, 541
whose, who's, 676
Word choice, 310–11
using specific words, 38
verbs, 464
Word order
adverbs, 518
in exclamatory sentences, 390
in interrogative sentences, 390
prepositional phrases, 543
in sentences, 388
subject-verb agreement and, 584
Works cited, 197, 202
in student paper, 193
Writing as discovery, 11–21
Writing ideas. *See* Ideas for writing
Writing portfolios. *See* Portfolios
Writing process. *See* Process of writing
Writing prompts, in essay questions, 158,
362
Writing voice, 682

Y
-y, adding to words, 303
Yearbooks, 353
you
and subject-verb agreement, 579
as understood subject, 390
your, you're, 440, 646, 676

Z
ZIP codes, 638

ACKNOWLEDGMENTS

Sources of Quoted Materials

50: Rudolfo Anaya: For an excerpt from "A Celebration of Grandfathers" ("Abuelo") by Rudolfo Anaya, first published in *New Mexico Magazine*. **52**: The Gifted Child Today, Inc.: For excerpts from "The End of Innocence," an essay by Eric Gould, age 15, which first appeared in *Creative Kids,* Feb. 1992. Reprinted by permission of GCT, Inc., Mobile, Alabama. **62**: John A. Ware Literary Agency: For excerpts from pages 171-173 of *American Mosaic: The Immigrant Experience in the Words of Those Who Lived It;* copyright © 1980 by Joan Morrison and Charlotte Fox Zabusky. Editions: Dutton, 1980; NAL/Meridian, 1982; U. of Pittsburgh Press, 1992. **72**: Macmillan Publishing Company: For "Papa's Parrot," from *Every Living Thing* by Cynthia Rylant; copyright ©1985 by Cynthia Rylant. Reprinted by permission of Bradbury Press, an Affiliate of Macmillan, Inc. **76**: Merlyn's Pen: For "Mind's Flight" by Adam Baughman, first appeared in *Merlyn's Pen: The National Magazine of Student Writing,* April/May 1989 issue. **86**: Landmark Editions, Inc.: For text and illustrations of pages 6 and 7 from *Oliver and the Oil Spill,* written and illustrated by Aruna Chandrasekhar; copyright © 1991 by Aruna Chandrasekhar. Reprinted by permission of Landmark Editions, Inc., Kansas City, Missouri. **96**: Random House, Inc.: For excerpts from *Iron and Silk* by Mark Salzman; copyright © 1986 by Mark Salzman. **108**: Scholastic, Inc.: For "The Homeless: Should Cities Evict Street People from Public Places?" by Katie Monagle, from *Scholastic Update,* January 10, 1992; copyright © 1992 by Scholastic Magazines, Inc. Reprinted by permission. **118**: Marjorie Jackson: For excerpts from "Shadow Puppets of Indonesia" by Marjorie Jackson from *Cricket,* January 1992. **166**: Larry Rubin: For "Outdistanced," first published in *The New Mexico Quarterly*. Reprinted by permission of the author. **167**: Naomi Long Madgett: For "Woman with Flower," from *Star by Star* by Naomi Long Madgett, Lotus Press, Detroit, © 1965, 1970. Reprinted by permission of the author. **167**: Reprinted by permission of Random House, Inc.: For "The Dream Keeper," from *The Dream Keeper and Other Poems* by Langston Hughes; copyright 1932 & renewed © 1960 by Langston Hughes. Reprinted by permission of Alfred A. Knopf, Inc. **206**: YSB Magazine: For excerpts from pages 52 and 66 of "Harlem Boys Choir Voices Rise High as the Listening Skies" by James Earl Hardy, from YSB, Dec./Jan. 1992 issue. **611**: Beverly McLoughland: For "Surprise" by Beverly McLoughland, originally appeared in *Cricket,* 1985. Reprinted by permission of the author, who controls all rights.

The authors and editors have made every effort to trace the ownership of all copyrighted selections in this book and to make full acknowledgment for their use.

Illustration and Photography Credits

Commissioned Illustrations: Meg Birnbaum: **72/73, 74/75**; Allan Brunettin: **62/63**; Ruta Daugavietis: **45**, *handcoloring* 211, 293, 314, 317, 349, 351, 352, 355, 356, 366, 498, 500, 623, 627; Joe Fournier: **154, 292, 638**; Qigu Jiang: **96/97**; Mary Jones: **384**; Linda Kelen: **363**; Carl Kock: **386**; Armen Kojoyian: **50/51**; Robin Lareaux: **598**; Jared D. Lee: **4, 6, 7, 8, 91, 113, 183, 225, 261, 323, 405, 429, 459, 494, 575, 595**; Rich Lo: *background* **86/87, 514**; Eric Masi: **99, 309, 640**; Ruben Ramos: **26**; Pamela Rossi: **166/167**; Richard Shanks: **514**; Slug Signorino: **145, 406**; Russell Thurston: **130/131**, *handcoloring and background* **140/141**; Amy L. Wasserman: **40/41**; Matthew Wawiorka: **324**; **Assignment Photography**: Ralph J. Brunke: **33, 39, 160, 248**; Jack DeMuth: **195, 196, 199, 201, 205**; John Morrison: **12/13, 22/23, 28/29, 30/31, 37, 52/53, 76/77, 98/99, 120/121, 142/143, 152/153, 168/169, 188/189, 190/191, 192/193**; Art Wise: **ii**.
Art and Photography: xxii: Private Collection; **22/23**: tickets courtesy The Chicago White Sox and Major League Baseball Properties; **24**: Photography courtesy The Asia Society Galleries, New York; **28/29**: photo of Nadja Salerno-Sonnenberg and her mother used by permission of the *Cherry Hill Courier-Post,* NJ; **36**: © J.H. Robinson/Photo Researchers, Inc.; **45**: Steve Dininno; **45**: Lake County (IL) Museum, Curt Teich Postcard Archives; **48**: Bill Plympton; **52**: © 1992 Bob Sacha; **54**: *t* © Norma Morrison/Hillstrom Stock Photo; *b* © David Barnes; **56, 59, 61**: © David Barnes; **62**: Courtesy Rev. James White; **63**: Arnold Kramer, Photographer/Collection of the U.S. Holocaust Memorial Museum; **67**: *tl* The Granger Collection, New York; *tr* Ket Tom; *b* David Hockney, "Gregory Walking Towards Me, Venice, CA. Feb. 1983" © David Hockney; **70**: from *The Mysteries of Harris Burdick* by Chris Van Allsburg. © 1984 by Chris Van Allsburg. Reprinted by permission of Houghton Mifflin Company. All rights reserved; **77**: © Jordan Coonrad 1992; **79**: John Batchelor; **81**: Peter Stackpole, LIFE Magazine © 1942 Time Warner Inc.; **82**: Air Portraits Colour Library; **84**: Courtesy of DuPont Company; **85**: © Farrell Grehan/Photo Researchers, Inc.; **86/87**: From the published book, *Oliver and the Oil Spill,* written and illustrated by Aruna Chandrasekhar, © 1991. Reprinted by permission of Landmark Editions, Inc., Kansas City, MO; **89**: *t* From *A Million Fish...More or Less* by Patricia C. McKissack, illustrated by Dena Schutzer ©1992. Reprinted by permission of Random House, Inc.; *b* From the published book, *Strong and Free,* written and illustrated by Amy Hagstrom, ©1987. Reprinted by permission of Landmark Editions, Inc., Kansas City, MO; **90**: *t* © Travelpix/FPG; *b* David Milgrim; **100**: © Tom Rider/ Index Stock; **104**: © 1991 Paul Barton/The Stock Market; **107**: Rob Day; **112**: Photofest; **116**: Arnie Ten; **118/119**: *inset* © Ann Saxon; © Michael Clark; **120**: © Oxford Scientific Films/Animals, Animals; book cover courtesy of Gareth Stevens Publishing, Milwaukee; **122**: Philip K. Sharpe © Oxford Scientific Films/ Animals, Animals; **123**: © Barrie Watts/ Eagle Books Ltd.; **124**: © Zig Leszczynski/ Animals, Animals; **125**: © Denys Ovenden/ Eagle Books Ltd.; **129**: © Michael Fogden/ Animals, Animals; **130/131**: Technical drawings from Salamander Books, London; **133**: © Eric Meola/The Image Bank; **135**: *t* Culver Pictures; *b* Collection Dr. & Mrs. Arthur E. Kahn/Photography by Jim Strong, Inc.; **138**: © Robert Holcepl; **140/141**: photograph (Neg. #20665) courtesy National Museum of the American Indian/Smithsonian Institution; **142/143**: THE NEW MUTANTS is a trademark of Marvel Entertainment Group, Inc., and is used with permission. © 1992 Marvel Entertainment Group, Inc. All rights reserved; **145**: THE UNCANNY X-MEN and CAPTAIN AMERICA are trademarks of Marvel Entertainment Group, Inc., and are used with permission. © 1992 Marvel Entertainment Group, Inc. All rights reserved; **149**: KITTY is a trademark of Marvel Entertainment Group, Inc., and is used with permission. © 1992 Marvel Entertainment Group, Inc. All rights reserved; **151**: SPIDER-MAN: TM & © 1992 Marvel Entertainment Group, Inc. All Rights Reserved; **153**: Courtesy of Woolworth's; **156**: Reprinted by permission: Tribune Media Services; **161**: *t* © 1991 by Consumers Union of United States, Inc., Yonkers, NY 10703. Reprinted by permission from ZILLIONS, April/May 1991; *bl* © Jon Riley/TSW; *br* Courtesy Arnold Chase Collection, Photofest; **164**: Mead Art Museum, Amherst College, Gift of Charles and Janet Morgan. EL 1984.51; **171**: Reproduced with permission of Landkreis Osterholz,

Germany; **174**: Eric Sanford/Tom Stack & Associates; **175**: George Steinmetz; **176**: Greg Gillis; **177**: © 1992, Chicago Tribune Company, all rights reserved, used with permission. Photo by Charles Cherney; **178**: *top* Mary Kate Denny/Photo Edit; *t/bl* David Linn; *br* J.C. Stevenson/Animals, Animals; **179**: © Robert Daemmrich/TSW; **182**: *t* Focus on Sports; *b* Daniel Craig; *c* Photofest; **186**: © 1912 by the New York Times Company. Reprinted by permission; **188**: *l* © Peter Gridley/FPG; *r* © Roger Malloch/Magnum Photos, Inc.; **190**: *t* © R. Pleasant/FPG; *c* © R. Moller/FPG; *b* © Frank Gordon/FPG; **193**: *l* © G. Lemmo/ FPG; *r* CD photo by Philip Gould, CD used by permission of Swallow Records; **206**: The Boys Choir of Harlem; **207**: Peter Cunningham; **209**: The Boys Choir of Harlem; **211**: Laurence Danbom/FPG; **214**: Courtesy The May Weber Museum of Cultural Arts, Chicago; **216**: Illustration used with permission from Minolta Corporation Business Equipment Division/Jerry Lofaro illustrator; **217**: © Joe Viesti/Viesti Associates, Inc.; **219**: © Photoworld/FPG; **221**: © Scott Markewitz/FPG; **233**: © Larry Ross/The Image Bank; **235**: Barbara Gladstone Gallery, NYC; **237**: © 1992 Earth Care Paper Inc.; **240**: © Anchorage Daily News/ Gamma-Liaison; **246**: © Tom McHugh/ Photo Researchers, Inc.; **248**: Mr. & Mrs. Potato Head are registered trademarks of Playskool, Inc. All rights reserved ©1992 Playskool; **253**: © 1992, Chicago Tribune Company, all rights reserved, used with permission. Photo by Charles Cherney; **255**: The Granger Collection, New York; **258**: Randy Lyhus; **265**: Kang Yi; **269**: © Gerard Vandystadt/Photo Researchers, Inc.; **270**: © Ronald H. Cohn/The Gorilla Foundation; **274**: Courtesy Sheila McGraw from *Papier-Mâché Today*. Reprinted by permission from Firefly Books Ltd.; **276**: © Joel Meyerowitz, 1976. Hartwig House, Truro. Courtesy of James Danziger Gallery, New York; **281**: Courtesy of The Museum of Contemporary Art, Chicago, and Tony D'Orio; **284**: © Leonard Von Matt/Photo Researchers, Inc.; **287**: © James Sugar/Black Star; **295**: Photography courtesy of the New York State Museum; **296**: © George Trabant; **300**: David Wilcox; **302**: Superstock; **305**: Reprinted with permission by Campbell-Thiebaud Gallery, San Francisco/Photography courtesy of Allport Editions, Portland, OR; **313**: © Jeff Leedy/The Image Bank; **317**: Photofest; **325**: © Terry O'Neill/Globe Photos; **326**: © Thomas Lochray/The Image Bank; **331**: Courtesy of Books Americana Inc.; **333**: Anthony Russo; **339**: © Peter A. Simon/Phototake, NYC; **343**: © Scott Markewitz/FPG; **353**: National Museum of American Art, Washington, DC, 1969.47.24; **354**: Michelle Barnes; **358**:

The Granger Collection, New York; **368**: Photograph courtesy of the Thos. K. Woodard American Antiques & Quilts, NYC; **372**: Archive Photos; **373**: Courtesy Open Software Foundation/Paul Schulenberg illustrator; **374**: © John Feingersh/The Stock Market; **378**: © Jim Pickerell/FPG; **383**: Photofest; **388**: Photofest; **391**: © Weinberg, Clark/The Image Bank; **393**: Courtesy Greater Orlando Aviation Authority; **407**: © Roger Tully/TSW; **408**: The Library of Congress; **413**: © Philippe Plailly/Science Photo Library/Photo Researchers, Inc.; **416**: public domain; **421**: © Jean Kugler/FPG; **430**: © J. Gajda/FPG; **431**: The Granger Collection, New York; **434**: © Ramon Gonzales Teja/The Image Bank; **437**: © Travelpix/ FPG; **439**: © Laurie Rubin/Chicago; **444**: The Granger Collection, New York; **446**: © 1991, Chicago Tribune Company, all rights reserved, used with permission. Photo by John Irvine; **462**: Reprinted by permission: Tribune Media Services; **463**: © Richard Hutchings/INFOEDIT; **464**: Brown Brothers; **470**: Giraudon/Art Resource, New York; **473**: The Granger Collection, New York; **479**: The Granger Collection, New York; **483**: American Stock Photography; **485**: Focus on Sports; **495**: © Keith Kent/Science Photo Library, Photo Researchers, Inc.; **498**: Brian Calanan; **500**: © Stan Osolinski/Earth Scenes; **503**: Susan Greenstein; **505**: Permission granted by the Missouri Division of Tourism; **507**: © D. Cox/Allstock; **508**: Mary Kay Baumann; **515**: The Museum of Modern Art/Film Stills Archive; **516**: Comstock; **519**: © Rocky Weldon/FPG; **523**: © Guy Le Querrec/ Magnum Photos, Inc.; **526**: © Stouffer Productions/Animals, Animals; **534**: Reprinted by permission: Tribune Media Services, illustration © Jeff MacNelly from *Homes and Other Black Holes* by Dave Barry; **535**: TSW; **537**: Archive Photos; **540**: © 1991, ModaCAD Inc., Los Angeles; **542**: *t* © Perry Conway/The Stock Broker; *b* © Johnny Johnson/Alaska Stock Images; **545**: © Nick Bergkessel, The National Audubon Society Collection/Photo Researchers, Inc.; **554**: © Gabriel M. Covian/The Image Bank; **555**: © G. Sauvage, Vandtstadt/Photo Researchers, Inc.; **558**: © Thomas Nebbia; **561**: © David Austen/TSW; **565**: The Far Side cartoon by Gary Larson is reprinted by permission of Chronicle Features, San Francisco, CA; **567**: Mike Radencich; **569**: The Granger Collection, New York; **576**: *t* © Photoworld/FPG; *bl* © Hanna-Barbera/ Shooting Star; *br* Archive Photos; **577**: Photofest; **578**: Private Collection/ Photography by Jim Strong Inc.; **579**: Courtesy of The Shaker Museum and Library, Old Chatham, NY; **583**: © Travelpix/FPG; **585**: Comstock; **586**: © Anthony Mercieca/Photo Researchers, Inc.; **599**: Stift Kremsmunster (Benedictine Abbey) Austria/SSI; **600**: Gretchen Geser;

602: Special Collections, California Polytechnic State University, San Luis Obispo; **605**: © George Allen & Unwin Ltd., an imprint of HarperCollins Publishers Ltd. UK; **607**: © Louise Gubb/JB Pictures; **609**: Design by Nancy Woodard, The Albuquerque (NM) Museum; **613**: Poem, by Shel Silverstein, from the book *Where the Sidewalk Ends*, © 1974 by Evil Eye Music, Inc.; **620**: © Dick Luria/FPG; **621**: © Jon Eisberg/FPG; **623**: © Murray Close/Sygma Photo News; **627**: © Erich Hartmann/Magnum Photos, Inc.; **628**: The Granger Collection, New York; **631**: The Granger Collection, New York; **635**: From *Blue and White China* © 1987 by John Esten, Olaf Wahlund and Rosalind Fischell. By permission of Little, Brown and Co.; **645**: *t* © A. Giampiccolo/FPG; *b* © The Telegraph Colour Library/FPG; **648**: © Jerry Schad/Photo Researchers, Inc.; **664**: © Wim Swaan/FPG.

McDougal, Littell & Company has made every effort to locate the copyright holders for the images used in this book and to make full acknowledgment for their use.

Cover
Ryan Roessler